WILLIAM SHAKESPEARE

The Century Studies in Literature

JAMES F. HOSIC, Editor

A STUDY

OF THE

TYPES OF LITERATURE

BY

MABEL IRENE RICH

Head of the English Department
Missoula County High School
Missoula, Montana

ILLUSTRATED 43005

NEW YORK

THE CENTURY CO.

PRINTED IN U. S. A.

TO
MY MOTHER
WHO FIRST INTERESTED ME
IN BOOKS AND
READING

PREFACE

This course in the types of literature has been worked out with senior classes in high school during the past five years, but there are also included here the results of practical class-room experience covering a much longer period of time. For this reason it is impossible to make a separate acknowledgment of indebtedness to each of the large number of authorities and experts in each type that have been consulted at various times, and to whom I owe much by way of information and inspiration. I am, however, deeply grateful to them.

In the arrangement of the material of this book, the aim has been to make it clear, compact, and interesting to high school pupils; to stimulate the students' own thoughts; to give breadth of view; to make books and reading as attractive as possible; to arouse love for the best things that have been written, not only in the past but in the present time, and to focus the attention on the literature itself rather than on its history. Even though, in this book, the group plan of study is used, an effort is made to lead the pupils to see that literature is a living, growing thing and cannot be bound down by absolute, exact rules; that, instead, it is constantly showing modifications, resulting from the influence of race, time, environment, and individuality of the authors. Since there are, however, so many pieces of literature that naturally fall into more or less distinct groups, the classification and definition of them as embodied here is justified.

The chronological method of arrangement has been followed. Each type has been traced from its earliest appearance to the present time, and those that have come to be regarded as the best examples of each form have been especially noted, and, wherever possible, studied. Some of these, however, have been omitted here because they are usually emphasized in earlier years of the high school course, and others, because they are not suitable for high school study. The chronological tables given in the back of the book will be of value in keeping before the pupil the time sequence so that the types will not become detached in his mind from their literary periods.

It has been deemed wise to include everything essential to the course in this one volume, with the exception of the material for outside readings, and the text of "The Tale of Two Cities," full notes of which, however, are given. It is hoped that this wide choice of material, as well as the very full lists for outside readings in connection with each type, will make the book very adaptable and useful for the needs of experienced teachers even though they may, perhaps, wish to make some additions or substitutions for the selections used. It is also hoped that it will prove of especial value to inexperienced teachers, to those who have small library facilities, and to students who must economize in the cost of a course. Should there not be time to read in class all of the selections given here, some of this work could be assigned for outside readings.

In the selection of illustrative material *wholes* have been emphasized. Only in the case of less than a dozen selections have extracts been used and these have been organized into smaller wholes by means of explanatory paragraphs. For instance, a pupil would get a comprehensive idea of "Beowulf," "The Canterbury Tales," "Sir Gawain and the Green Knight," and the first book of "The Faerie Queene," from what has been given here. The other extracts from "Adonaïs," "In Memoriam," "Slumber Songs of the Madonna," "Drake," and the scenes from "Doctor Faustus" and "Edward the Second" are self-explanatory.

This study of the types of literature in the fourth year of high school, presupposes courses given in the second and third years in which the most important American and English authors are studied. Such courses are admirably provided for in other numbers of this series of anthologies. A teacher could arrange such preliminary courses, using the various inexpensive classics for the readings, and referring the students to the literary histories for the biographical and background material. Emphasis, however, should, in high school, always be placed on the study of the literature itself rather than the history of literature. With such courses as a basis, this study of types would have a firm foundation. Moreover, the different point of view shown here is likely to attract the average high school senior, open up a new field of interest to him, and inspire a deeper love for books and reading than would be possible in the chronological study of authors and works alone. In reality, it will be found that this viewpoint is the pupil's own, for, in his unguided reading, he has always thought of books in terms of types. He has consciously selected novels, stories, plays, or poems as such, seldom thinking who wrote them, or when. The plan of study presented here, therefore, comes close to the student's life and experience and will have its appeal for him. He will recognize his favorite types and will want to know more about them, as well as of those that are new to him. Thus his attention and interest will be held, and the purpose for which any course in literature is given will be most effectively served. Such a course of study as this will, moreover, teach him how to distinguish one type from another as he meets it in his general reading; it will show him what to look for in each, and how to go about it; in fact, it will broaden his outlook, give him a keener sense of values, and help him to become an intelligent, self-dependent *reader*. A pupil pursuing such a course should also be unusually well fitted either to meet the college entrance requirements, or to guide his own reading if a college education be denied him. The reading list placed at the end of each chapter, giving for each type a large number of examples drawn from different periods of time, will aid him greatly in choosing what is worth while. Although this list is not exhaustive, it is very comprehensive and varied, and will serve as a valuable guide, while allowing the student a great deal of freedom in making his own selections.

Inasmuch as this book enters a field which in many ways differs from that usually covered by a high school course, it will not be amiss to give a few directions as to its use. Experienced teachers will probably wish to handle the material in their own way, but the young teacher will, no doubt, find suggestions helpful. It is intended that, after the pupil has been given a bird's-eye view of the whole course, such as is found in the *Introduction*, the different types will be taken up in the order presented. Just before proceeding to the characteristics of each type, the teacher should, by means of a few informal questions, lead the pupil to make the connection between what he already knows and the unfamiliar, inspiring him to have toward the new type the attitude of an explorer of unknown territory who is anxious to discover how the new differs from the old. As he proceeds, the pupil will be alert to note the signs of change, as well as the things familiar to him. After the characteristics of a type have been presented and some knowledge has been gained regarding its importance and historical development, examples are studied, the student being encouraged to notice how the sub-divisions of a general class of poetry, or prose, are related, and at the same time are different from each other, and how even two examples of the same type will shcw marked differences as well as similarities. He must not lose sight of the fact, though, that he is to discover why the classification is justified in each case. Thus not only will the interpretation of the particular piece of literature be of interest to him, but also its relation to other literature. In connection with the class work, the student will read as many examples of the particular type outside of class as the time will allow, reporting either orally or in writing of the things which have interested him in the reading. Sometimes, when the opportunity offers, he may even try to produce something similar himself in connection with his regular theme work. If the teacher will encourage the student to make constant use of the letter addressed to him, to be found at the end of this preface, it will do much toward bringing the desired results.

Though this method of studying literature in high school may seem to be a departure in many ways from the beaten track, it will in practice be found to be stimulating, practical, adaptable to both large and small schools, useful in fitting the student for college or for life, and workable. It has been thoroughly tested in actual class exercises during a period of five years and has proved unusually successful, both in securing the aims of literature study and in developing power in composition through the distinct benefit derived from the oral and written reports called for in the studies.

Aside from the acknowledgment of indebtedness given above, I wish to express my grateful appreciation to Professor James Fleming Hosic for his unfailing kindness and valuable criticisms; to Principal G. A. Ketcham, of the Missoula county high school, for encouraging me at first to undertake the work and for his wise and helpful counsel; and to Mr. Lyle Lane for material aid in arranging the index.

M. I. R., Missoula, Montana.

THE AUTHOR TO THE STUDENT

My dear Student,

This letter is placed here with the hope that it will help you to get the most that is possible out of a book which has been written expressly for you. It is also hoped that the material presented here may become a working factor in your life—not only while you are in school, but after you leave it, for the great types of literature discussed here will last through the ages, and you will constantly be meeting examples of them as you go onward through the years.

You who are nearing the end of your high school course should have gained a considerable knowledge of literature from your English work in other years, and from your general reading. To this new course, then, you will have something of your own to contribute, and, at the same time, it is hoped, you will be able to get a deeper view of literature than you have had before. If you will approach this study in the spirit of the man who wants to know his tools so he can use them intelligently; to know things so that he can make use of them in his own daily life, you will get more from the work than otherwise.

In order to make a real success of this study of literary types, you should constantly keep in mind the little outline given in the *Introduction* in order to see just what types are closely related. This will help you to organize more clearly in your own mind the things that you are learning. The following suggestions will help you to get and keep the investigating attitude toward your work. You will also find that this will add to your enjoyment of what you read.

1. Before taking up a new chapter, always try to sum up all you think you know about the type to be discussed, and its relationship to other types.

2. Read carefully the *characteristics* of the particular type as given in this book, noting just what *distinguishes* it from others. See, too, how many things you find that you really did know before as well as those that throw new light on the subject. Study this material not merely to repeat again in a class recitation, but *to know* these things so that they will form a working basis for your own investigations.

3. Note what writers are considered by the most competent critics to have been the greatest masters of the type. This bit of information will be valuable to have.

4. Now apply what you have learned to the examples given. Read these first to get the thought, story, or feeling expressed and then study them, both to see how many of the characteristics pointed out are embodied in these particular selections, and also to see wherein they show any divergence from the usual form. You will be sure to find some differences, for every writer is free to use his own individuality.

5. Next, in your outside readings, apply what you know and write a brief report of your discoveries.

6. Perhaps there may be some types that you will like to try to write yourself. If so, do it in lieu of your regular theme work.

There will be other suggestions found scattered through the chapters, but always, as you study a type, keep what has been said here in mind. This sort of work will bring good results.

With best wishes for a happy and profitable year, I am

Sincerely your friend,

MABEL I. RICH.

INTRODUCTION

BY

JAMES FLEMING HOSIC, PH.D., GENERAL EDITOR

The newer conception of the aims of literature study in high schools demands reorganization of the subject matter and redirection of the activities of the pupils. The older conception, though not denying the possibility of other values, was inclined to lay stress on mental discipline, academic information, and rhetorical analysis. By contrast the modern tendency is to regard literature as primarily a means to the enlargement of experience, the formation of ideals, and the unselfish enjoyment of leisure. It would treat discipline, general information, and critical technique not as ends but as means and attainment in them as inevitable by-products of sincere efforts to master literary works approached as human documents rather than as forms for dissection.

The shift in method is no less marked. Ceasing to be a "recitation" of verbal facts committed to memory from notes or a handbook, the class exercise in literature partakes more of the nature of a literary club, where willing readers compare and correct the impressions gained from their studies, spur each other on to new endeavors, and consciously develop effective ways of approaching and mastering typical pieces of prose and verse. Theme, organization, pictures, and associations receive more attention and linguistic oddities and erudite references less. The teacher's questions are more far-reaching and less meticulous and the pupils do more thinking, reading aloud, and acting and far less of explaining minutiæ and of labeling with grammatical and rhetorical terms. In a word, the newer ideal of method in high school literature appears to be to train the ordinary citizen in the use of books and the enjoyment of the theatre through their actual use and enjoyment in school days. Editorial and critical specialists will find their opportunity later on.

From such a point of view the reading for young people is selected somewhat differently from what it once was. Variety of experience reasonably within the range of the pupils' comprehension becomes the chief criterion. Value as a means of training in method of approach also ranks high. Excellence is thought necessary for the cultivation of taste and judgment, but it must be seen to be excellence by contrast with that less worthy. And since the object of the work is in large part to establish well-regulated habits of reading magazines and books in ordinary life, the contemporary must be included side by side with the classical. Contemporary art must, however, not be thought of as necessarily youthful because it is new nor the classics mature because they are old. It is the author's attitudes, his way of thinking and feeling about his subject, that must determine.

Several numbers will compose the present series, at least one for each school grade. The pupils will first be introduced to the systematic study of literature by means of typical experiences in reading a variety of pieces in verse and prose, selected not only because they are worth-while in themselves and suited in theme and treatment to early high-school years but because they are *representative* of the problems which pieces of their class present. The pupils will be *made to realize that they are learning how to read.*

Succeeding numbers will stress American and British ideas and ideals brought into comparison with those of other countries, and while carrying forward, enforcing, and enlarging the training in methods of reading and study developed in the first part of the course, will show the pupil how he may find in the writings of representative authors forceful expression of interests and points of view which he can begin to recognize as more or less characteristic of the people of the country as a whole. In a word, he is started on the way to finding in literature a reflection not only of the life of individuals but also of the life common to groups, communities, and nations.

The present volume, though the first of the series to appear, is planned as part of a progressive scheme, and while well-adapted to the upper years of any secondary school course will prove most effective in classes which have had the advantage of using the earlier volumes in the series.

In her *Study of the Types of Literature* Miss Rich has at last provided a way of escape from the over-mature and formal history of English literature, on the one hand, and the over-minute and pedantic study of three or four examinable masterpieces on the other. Recognizing the need of organizing one's knowledge of literature, she has provided for the closing years of high-school work a comparatively simple and objective view of literature as a whole and thus has enabled the young man or young woman about to go out into life or on into college to bring all of his reading into perspective and so to generalize his experiences with various types of writing that he has a good working basis for further adventures. It is remarkable that she should have been able in so small a space to compass so much and with such admirable restraint. The temptation to indulge in critical estimates, to trace literary influences, and to purvey details of authors' lives must have been considerable.

The necessary apparatus for gaining a really useful knowledge of books and authors she has, however, painstakingly supplied. The pupil need go no farther to find the essential facts as to who wrote what and when—such facts at least as a young person can probably find use for. And other facts may wait till needed. In reality they usually do, courses of study and textbook makers to the contrary notwithstanding.

CONTENTS

BOOK ONE

PART ONE.—NARRATIVE POETRY

CONTENTS

PART TWO.—LYRIC POETRY

CHARACTERISTICS OF LYRIC POETRY.—CLASSES OF LYRIC POETRY

PART THREE.—DRAMATIC POETRY

BOOK TWO

TYPES OF PROSE

LIST OF ILLUSTRATIONS

A STUDY OF THE TYPES OF LITERATURE

INTRODUCTION

Reasons for the Study of Literature.—If we wish to understand a people fully, we shall find the historical account alone inadequate for our purpose. History, it is true, will show us what place these people have won among the nations and what part they have had in the progress of the world; but regarding their innermost thoughts and feelings—their real life—it will have little to say. This information can be obtained only from the literature which they themselves have brought forth. The historical records, valuable as they are, will often be misleading if we do not see "the other side of the shield"; if we do not understand the thoughts and emotions that lie back of the deeds. Furthermore, literature is the treasure-house of ideals. The man who is not guided by an ideal is worthless, and even dangerous, to society. Literature not only stores up the noblest ideals that the world has known, but it inspires and fosters these in men.

Therefore, since literature reveals the deepest thoughts and feelings of the human race, cherishes the ideals that lie at the basis of all that we hold to be most precious in our world to-day, and helps us to understand more fully this complex life that we have to live, it is one of the most valuable and really practical subjects that a student can pursue.

The Aim of True Literature.—Literature in its wider meaning includes everything that has been expressed through the written or printed page. In its narrow or restricted sense, however, it has a special object to serve. That object is not only to give pleasure to the reader through the expression of true and beautiful thoughts in fitting language, but also to fire the imagination and arouse noble, unselfish emotions. True literature is thus concerned with the needs of our higher natures.

Divisions of Literature.—True literature is divided into two great classes: poetry and prose.

Outline of Literary Types.

Narrative poetry	Great epic Metrical romance Ballad Metrical tale
Lyric poetry	Ode Sonnet Elegy Song—sacred and secular Simple lyric
Dramatic poetry	Comedy Dramatic history Tragedy Mask The dramatic monologue
Minor forms of poetry	Descriptive poetry { Pastoral / Idyl Didactic poetry Satiric poetry

Prose drama

Essay

Prose fiction	Prose allegory Prose romance Tale of adventure or experience Novel Novelette Short-story

Oration

Miscellaneous prose

Importance of Poetry.—Of the two great classes of literature, poetry was the first to be developed. The very best literary works, moreover, have been done in this form. The greatest names in the literature of the world are those of poets. This may seem strange to us of the twentieth century, who have seen in our own day the great popularity of prose literature, as is shown by the floods of novels, short-stories, prose plays, essays, magazine articles and other forms of prose that have streamed forth from the printing presses of all lands. Important as these works are to us, however, we shall have to admit that no prose writers have ever equaled David, Homer, Æschylus, Sophocles, Euripides, Virgil, Dante, Shakespeare or Milton.

Since poetry is the first of the great classes of literature, both in order of time and rank, we shall begin our present study of literary types with this class.

The Great Classes of Poetry.—Poetry is usually divided into three great classes, according to whether it tells a story, voices the author's own thoughts and feelings, or portrays life and character through action. These classes are narrative, lyric, and dramatic poetry.

Minor Forms of Poetry.—There are also three minor forms that are sometimes distinguished. These are descriptive, didactic, and satiric poetry. As regards the first of these classes, however, description enters so largely into the composition of all of the other forms of poetry, that it is scarcely worth while to try to make a separate classification. Although the names *idyl* and *pastoral* are applied where there is a "little picture" or a description of country or shepherd life, yet such descriptions usually form only a part of some narrative, lyric, or even dramatic poem. For instance, Milton's "Lycidas" is not only the finest *pastoral* in English literature, but it is also an *elegy*, one of the types of lyric poetry; and Tennyson's "Dora" is both an *idyl* and a *metrical tale*, a type of narrative poetry.

As regards the other minor forms, didactic and satiric poetry, still less may be said. These are not, strictly speaking, true poetry, even though they are in the poetic form. Their purpose is not to serve the needs of our higher natures, but to give instruction, or to criticize and ridicule. The best known examples of didactic poetry, Pope's "Essay on Man" and "Essay on Criticism," would probably have been better if they had been in prose; and such satiric poems as Pope's "Dunciad" and Byron's "English Bards and Scotch Reviewers," though given in rhyme, do not possess truly poetic qualities.

In this study of literary types, therefore, we shall consider only the three great classes of poetry and their sub-divisions.

BOOK ONE

PART ONE—NARRATIVE POETRY

Narrative or story-telling poetry, which relates events in an order of time, is divided into four types. These are (1) the great epic,[1] (2) the metrical romance, (3) the ballad, and (4) the metrical tale.

---

[1] The term "epic" is sometimes applied to any narrative poem, but throughout this book it is used only with reference to the *great epic* as a type of narrative poetry.

1

CHAPTER I

THE GREAT EPIC

Characteristics of the Great Epic.—The great epic is the most majestic type of poetry. It is a long narrative poem, the theme of which is so mighty in its scope that it reaches far beyond the affairs of mere individuals to things concerning an entire people, nation, or even the world as a whole. Its subject-matter is taken from history, religion, legend, or mythology. The supernatural element is usually very pronounced, events being often under its control. The action is, therefore, always on a huge scale, and the characters are mighty heroes, demigods, demons, or celestial beings. Events center in a prodigious effort or struggle to carry out some great and just purpose against powerful opposing forces, which are destined to be overcome in the end. In the great epic deep elemental passions are set forth, such as hate, revenge, jealousy, ambition, and love of power or glory. It is not a love story, though love may be present. Although there may be a moral, it is never summed up, but is embedded deep in the story itself. One of the most important characteristics of the great epic is that in it may be found practically all that has been given to civilization by a great religion, or by a whole race, nation, or people at a particular stage or period of development.

A character in a great epic is interesting to us for the part he has in furthering, or hindering, the accomplishment of the great struggle in which he is engaged, rather than because of his own individuality or personality. We think of him more in connection with the whole group than alone. The action, therefore, is much more prominent than the individual.

The great epic, as a story, is made up of many distinct parts or episodes. These are formed into books, or cantos, each practically complete in itself, and yet so bound together by a common relationship to some great hero, action, and time, that the result

3

is a single poem of exceeding dignity and power. The large number of legends and stories out of which a great epic is made probably at first circulated orally, as tradition, being sung by many minstrels. At last some greater poet's eye saw the significance which lay in and around them, as parts of a larger action, and made them the expression of a whole heroic age. The author of a great epic never obtrudes himself upon the reader; in fact, the story seems almost to be telling itself.

As has been said, several of the great world epics appear to have grown up, as it were, among a people and to have been put in their final form by the last of a line of bards. The name *folk-epic* is applied to such poems, since they have come straight from the hearts of the people. They are more simple than the *literary epic*, which is the conscious, more labored work of some literary man who deliberately chooses to use the epic form for a work of his own composition. "The Iliad," "The Odyssey," "Beowulf," and "The Nibelungenlied" are examples of the folk-epic, while "The Æneid," "The Divine Comedy," "Paradise Lost," "Paradise Regained," and "Drake" are literary epics.

The Great Epics of the World.—The most important of the great epics of the world's literature are "The Iliad" and "The Odyssey," by Homer; "The Æneid," by Virgil; "The Shah Namah," by Firdausi; "The Divine Comedy," by Dante; "Jerusalem Delivered," by Tasso; "The Lusiad," by Camoëns; "The Cid," author unknown; "The Nibelungenlied," author unknown; "The Song of Roland," attributed to Théroulde; "Kalevala," by Lönnrot; "Beowulf," author unknown; "Paradise Lost" and "Paradise Regained," by Milton; and perhaps may be included with these "Drake," by Alfred Noyes.[1]

(1) "The Iliad" and (2) "The Odyssey" are the great epics of ancient Greece. Although they have always been attributed to Homer, it is now believed that he was only the last of a number of poets who made contributions to the work. They bear his name because he was the one who gave them their final shape. They are, therefore, to be classed among the folk-epics. "The Iliad" and "The Odyssey" are considered to be the greatest examples of epic poetry in the literature of the entire world. They are of course largely products of the imagination, and, no doubt, idealize to a considerable extent the life depicted, yet in them may be

---

[1] Besides these there are two great epics, "The Ramayana" and "The Mahabharata," produced by the Hindus, the events dating back to about 2000 B. C.

seen the essentials of Greek life in the Homeric age—its customs, manners, and ideals. Here we find their religious ceremonies, their methods of warfare, government, laws, household arrangements, industries, domestic relations, their buildings, ships, armor, weapons, dress, utensils, ornaments and fabrics.

(3) "The Æneid" is the great epic of Rome. It is the conscious work of one writer, Virgil, who follows the struggles of Æneas, the great ancestor of the Roman people, and his band of Trojans until they finally succeed in establishing themselves in the promised land of Italy. Through a revelation made to Æneas by the shade of his father, Anchises, we also learn the subsequent history and glory of Rome down to Virgil's own time. Thus are summed up the important elements which contributed to the splendor and greatness of "Immortal Rome."

(4) "The Shah Namah" is the great epic of Persia and shows what she gave to civilization down to the tenth century B. C. This poem is the work of one man, Firdausi,[1] the "Persian Homer," who deliberately put in this form the history and traditions of his native land. An episode from this great epic has been written in English verse by Matthew Arnold under the title, "Sohrab and Rustum."

(5) "The Divine Comedy," by Dante, is the great epic of Italy and of mediæval Christianity. As has been said, "All of mediæval history, science, philosophy, scholarship, poetry, religion may be reconstructed from a right reading and entire understanding of this single monumental poem."[2] Dante divides his poem into three great parts. The first, called "The Inferno," consists of thirty-four cantos; the second, "Purgatory," has thirty-three cantos, and the third, "Paradise," also has thirty-three cantos. The great purpose to be accomplished in this epic is the salvation of the soul. This poem is one of the most difficult to follow and understand of all the great epics.

(6) "Jerusalem Delivered," by Tasso, is also a great epic of Christianity, but it deals with the time of the Crusades, which was two centuries earlier than that covered in "The Divine Comedy." The struggle set forth is to rescue the Holy Sepulchre from the Saracens.

(7) "The Lusiad," by Camoëns, is the great epic of Portugal at

[1] Also spelled Firdusi. "Firdausi," meaning "Singer of Paradise," was the name applied to the author (whose real name was Abul Kasim Mansur) by the Shah of Persia for whom the poem was written.

[2] Clayton Hamilton in *Materials and Methods of Fiction*.

the time of her greatest development, explorations, and conquests. The story centers around the adventures and achievements of Vasco da Gama, who in 1497 sailed his ships through unknown waters and discovered the new route to India.

(8) "The Cid" is the great folk-epic of Spain, written about 1200. The story has, as its center, the deeds of the great "Cid," or "lord," Rodrigo, in his wars with the Moors.

(9) "The Nibelungenlied" is the great folk-epic of Germany, dating as far back as the sixth or seventh century.

(10) "The Song of Roland," which is thought to be the work of Théroulde, is the great epic of France in the time of Charlemagne and his paladins, Roland and Oliver.

(11) "The Kalevala," the great epic of Finland, was put in its present form by Lönnrot in the early part of the nineteenth century. Some of the episodes of which it is composed date back over three thousand years.

(12) "Beowulf" gives the civilization of the early Anglo-Saxons.

(13) "Paradise Lost" and (14) "Paradise Regained" sum up Christianity in the days of Puritan England.

(15) "Drake" gives almost a complete view of Elizabethan England.

Of these great epics, those easiest to understand are: "The Iliad," "The Odyssey," "The Æneid," "The Nibelungenlied," "The Song of Roland," "Beowulf" and "Drake."

SUGGESTIONS TO STUDENTS[1]

1. Choose a particular portion of "The Iliad," "The Odyssey," "The Æneid," "The Song of Roland," or "The Nibelungenlied," and, either orally or in the form of a theme, report as fully as possible all that you are able to discover regarding the civilization of the ancient Greeks, Romans, French, or Germans. Try to imagine that all other books on the subject have been lost and you are seeking to find out all you can about this particular civilization. Some of the best references for this work are Books I, VI, XXII, XXIII, and XXIV of "The Iliad" in any of the poetical or prose translations; Books I, VI, VII, VIII, XIII, and XVII of "The Odyssey"; Books II, V, VI, and VII of "The Æneid"; Part II of "The Song of Roland"; and the first eighteen "Adventures" of "The Nibelungenlied." Remember that, although the translations read may be in prose, the originals are all in the poetic form.

2. Point out some of the most striking episodes. 3. What partic-

[1] These student-helps, given at intervals throughout this book, are, of course, not exhaustive, but suggest possibilities that may make the study more valuable.

ular great action, time, and hero are binding these together? 4. Can you determine the cause of the struggle that is depicted? 5. Who are the opposing forces? 6. Did you find the story interesting? Which interested you more—the story of the adventures experienced, or what was revealed regarding the life and ideals of the people?

The Great Epics of England.—Of the great epics named, those that belong especially to English literature will need a little fuller treatment.

Beowulf.—This poem is the oldest and one of the greatest of the English epics. It was probably composed, in large part, before the Anglo-Saxons left their continental home in Scandinavia, but it was not until about the eighth or ninth century that some Christian monk of Anglo-Saxon descent put it in its present form. Although there are Christian touches, the poem is pagan in warp and woof. Some scholars still maintain that the events related took place after the coming of the Anglo-Saxons to England in 449 A.D. In any case, the poem deals with the life of our Anglo-Saxon forefathers, and is of especial value to us because it reveals the kind of people they really were.

The poem itself is divided into three parts.[1] The first deals with the story of Scyld, the king of the Spear Danes, the ancestor of Hrothgar, for whom the hero, Beowulf, does his mighty deeds. Thus the first and second parts of the story are but slightly connected. The second part deals with the main deeds of Beowulf, who leaves his home in the land of the Geats (southern Sweden) to go to the rescue of his father's friends, the Spear Danes. The Danes have for twelve years suffered because of the terrible raids of the monster, Grendel, whom no weapon could harm. After many of King Hrothgar's best warriors have been devoured, Beowulf finally arrives upon the scene and succeeds, after a terrible fight, in killing Grendel, and, later, his mother, the monster mere-wife.

[1] This outline of the story of "Beowulf" is purposely made short, because good detailed accounts may be found in almost all of the histories of English literature. Some of the best of these references in reach of high school students are Long's *English Literature*, pp. 10-18; Halleck's *History of English Literature*, pp. 23-26; Moody and Lovett's *History of English Literature*, pp. 5-9; Newcomer's *English Literature*, pp. 18-21; Pancoast's *Introduction to English Literature*, pp. 37-43; Saintsbury's *A Short History of English Literature*, p 5; Scudder's *English Literature*, pp. 31-33; Simond's *A Student's History of English Literature*, pp. 10-14; Taine's *History of English Literature*, pp. 62-67; Guerber's *Legends of the Middle Ages*, pp. 9-21; Long's *English and American Literature*, pp. 9-13.

FACSIMILE OF THE FIRST PAGE OF "BEOWULF"
(Manuscript in the British Museum)

The third part of the poem takes up the story of Beowulf's last fight. The scene here is laid fifty years after the events related in part two. Beowulf is successful in overcoming a frightful fire-drake, but the monster's fiery breath enters his lungs. He dies, but not before he has obtained for his people the vast treasures found in the fire-drake's cave.

SUGGESTIONS TO STUDENTS

1. From the following extracts from "Beowulf" what information may be gained concerning the civilization of the Anglo-Saxons? See how much even these few lines reveal as to their attitude towards women; the virtues they most admired; what they *had, did, knew,* or *believed.* 2. What is the great struggle depicted? What are the most interesting episodes? 3. What points of comparison can you make between the life found here and that which you discovered in "The Iliad," "Odyssey," "Æneid," "Song of Roland," or "Nibelungenlied"? How far apart in time were they? 4. Which story interested you more? Why? 5. What familiar story are you reminded of in that of Scyld? Which is the older story?

1. THE DEATH OF SCYLD

Then Scyld departed at the hour of fate,
The warlike to go into his Lord's keeping:
They him then bore to the ocean's wave,
His trusty comrades, as he himself bade,
Whilst with words ruled the friend of the Scyldings,   5
Beloved land-prince; long wielded he power.
There stood at haven with curved prow,
Shining and ready, the prince's ship:
The people laid their dear war-lord,
Giver of rings, on the deck of the ship.   10
The mighty by th' mast. Many treasures were there,
From distant lands, ornaments brought;
Ne'er heard I of keel more comelily filled
With warlike weapons and weeds of battle,
With bills and byrnies! On his bosom lay   15
A heap of jewels which with him should
Into the flood's keeping afar depart:

.   .   .   .

Then placed they yet a golden standard
High over his head, let the waves bear
Their gift to the sea; sad was their soul,   20
Mourning their mood.[1]

[1] Garnett's translation of "Beowulf," lines 26–42: 47–50. All these extracts used by special permission of Mrs. James Mercer Garnett, owner of the copyright.

2. Hrothgar's Mead-hall

It came into his mind
That he a great hall would then command,
A greater mead-hall his men to build
Than children of men ever had heard of,
And there within would he all deal out   5
To young and to old, as God him gave,
Except the folk-land and lives of men.
Then far and wide heard I the work was ordered
To many a tribe throughout this mid-earth
The folk-hall to deck. Him in time it befell   10
Quickly with men, that it was all ready,
The greatest of halls: Heorot as name gave he it,
He who with his word power far and wide had.
He belied not his promise, bracelets he dealt,
Treasure at banquet. The halls arose   15
Lofty and pinnacled.[1]

3. Grendel's First Raid

Thus were the warriors living in joys
Happily then, until one began
Great woes to work, a fiend of hell:
The wrathful spirit was Grendel named,
The mighty mark-stepper who the moors held,   5
Fen and fastness: the sea-fiend's abode.

.   .   .   .

Then went he to seek out, after night came,
The high-built house, how the Ring-Danes,
After their beer-feast, it had arranged.
He found then therein a band of nobles   10
Asleep after feasting; sorrows they knew not,
Misfortunes of men. The demon of death,
Grim and greedy, soon was ready,
Fierce and furious, and in rest took
Thirty of thanes: thence back he departed,   15
Exulting in booty, homeward to go.
With his fill of slaughter to seek out his dwelling.

.   .   .   .

That was great sorrow of the friend of the Scyldings,
Misery of mind! Many oft sat
Mighty in council; plans they devised,   20
What with bold mind then would be best
'Gainst the sudden attacks for them to do.

[1] Lines 67–82.

Sometimes they vowed at their temples of idols
To their gods worship, with words they prayed
The destroyer of spirits would render them help   25
Against their folk-sorrows.   Such was their custom.[1]

4. Scenes in Hrothgar's Hall After the Arrival of Beowulf

Then was in joy the giver of treasure,
Gray-haired and war-fierce; help he expected,
The ruler of Bright-Danes; in Beowulf heard
The people's shepherd the firm-set purpose.
There was laughter of heroes, the harp merry sounded,   5
Winsome were words.   Went Wealhtheow forth,
The queen of Hrothgar, mindful of courtesies,
Gold-adorned greeted the men in the halls,
And the high-born woman then gave the cup
First to the East-Danes' home-protector;   10
Bade him be blithe at the beer-drinking,
Him dear to his people.   In joy he received
The food and the hall-cup, victorious king.
Then around went the Helmings' lady
To every division of old and of young.   15
Costly gifts gave, until the time came
That she to Beowulf, the ring-adorned queen,
Noble in mind, the mead-cup bore.[2]

5. Beowulf's Fight with Grendel

Then came from the moor 'neath the misty slopes
Grendel going, God's anger he bore.
The wicked foe thought of the race of man
Some one to entrap in that high hall:
He went 'neath the clouds whither he the wine-hall,   5
The gold-hall of men, most thoroughly knew,
Shining with gold-plates: that was not the first time
That he of Hrothgar the home had sought.
Ne'er in his life-time before nor after
Bolder warriors, hall-thanes, did he find!   10
Then came to the hall the being approaching,
Of joys deprived.   The door soon sprang open
Fast in its fire-bands, when he with hands touched it.
Then burst the bale-bringer, since he was enraged,
The door of the hall.   Soon after that   15
On the many-colored floor the fiendish one trod.

[1] Lines 99–104; 115–125; 170–178.
[2] Lines 607–624.

Mad in mind he went: from his eyes stood
A loathsome light likest to flame.
He saw in the hall many of warriors,
A band in peace sleeping all together,   20
A heap of kin-warriors. Then laughed his mood:
He thought that he would, ere day came, divide,
The terrible monster, of every one
The life from the body, since to him was fallen
A hope of much food. That no longer was fated,   25
That he might more of the race of man
Devour by night.

.   .   .   .

Remembered he then, good kinsman of Hygelac,
His evening-speech; upright he stood
And him fast seized: his fingers cracked   30
The eoten would outwards: the earl further stepped;
The mighty one thought, whereso he might,
Afar to escape, and away thence
Flee to the marshes: he knew that his fingers
Were in his foe's grip: That was a bad journey   35
That the harm-bringing foe had taken to Heorot.

.   .   .   .

For earls the ale spilt. Angry were both
Furious contestants: the hall cracked aloud:
Then was it great wonder that the wine-hall
Withstood the fierce fighters, that it to ground fell not,   40
The fair folk-hall: but it was too fast
Within and without in its iron bands
By cunning skill forged. There from the sill fell
Many a mead-bench, as I have heard say
Adorned with gold, where the foes fought.   45

.   .   .   .

                      Pain of body endured
The terrible monster: there was on his shoulder
An evident wound; apart sprang the sinews,
The bone-frame burst. To Beowulf was
Battle-fame given.[1]

6. The Death of Beowulf. (Fifty years after his fight with Grendel.)

"Now I for the hoard of jewels have paid
Mine own aged life; do ye now supply
The needs of my people; I may not longer be here.

[1] Garnett's translation, lines 710–736; 758–766; 769–777; 815–819

Courtesy of G. P. Putnam's Sons.

THE DEATH OF BEOWULF

Bid ye the war-famed a mound to make
Bright after the pyre at the sea's point.   5
Which shall for remembrance to mine own people
Raise itself high on the Whale's ness,
That it the sea-farers hereafter may call
Beowulf's mound, who shall their high ships
O'er the sea's mists from afar drive."   10
He put from his neck the golden ring,
The bold-minded prince, gave to the thane,
The young spear-warrior, his gold-adorned helm,
Collar and byrnie, bade him use them well:
"Thou art the last left of our own kindred   15
Of the Waegmundings. Weird carried away all
Of mine own kinsmen at the time appointed,
Earls in their strength: I shall go after them."
That was to the aged the very last word
In his breast-thoughts.[1]   20

Different explanations have been given for the events of the
poem. Some people believe that the story is based on fact, there
having been, at some time, a real Northern hero
who delivered the people from great dangers.
Different Explanations of the Poem[2] The superhuman powers that are attributed to this
hero would hence be due to the imagination of the
scops who handed down the stories. They lived
in the "childhood of the race," when all things were deemed
possible.

It may be, as other students of the subject suggest, that the
fights that Beowulf had with the three monsters are to be taken
allegorically. Thus the fight with Grendel is really to represent
the overcoming of the dangers from malaria through the drain-
ing of the stagnant pools and marshes. The fight with the sea-
wife is the conquering of the power of the ocean when man discovered how to make it serve his needs, or, perhaps, how to hold
it back by means of dykes. The fight with the fire-drake is to
represent the struggle to control other forces of nature that en-
dangered man's existence—possibly to fight, successfully, forest-
fires.

The poem consists of over 3180 lines. The Anglo-Saxons had
no knowledge of rhyme, but their poetry had rhythm, produced
by a certain arrangement of accents, and by consonantal alliteration, or the use of the same consonant to begin two or more

[1] Lines 2799–2818.
[2] Note other interpretations of "Beowulf," pages 29–30, Miller's *English
Literature.*

words in a line. Each line of Anglo-Saxon poetry had four
strong accents and was divided into two parts by
The Poetic a pause in the middle. In the first half the two
Form of most important words usually began with the same
Beowulf consonant. That same letter was also used to begin an important word in the second half of the
line.

> "Misery of mind! Many oft sat."
> "Grendel going, God's anger bore."
> "Bucklers bright; on the bench were there."
> "Beds and bolsters.—One beer-carouser
> In danger of doom lay down in the hall."
> "A warrior watching and waiting the fray."
> "Sea-dragons strange that sounded the deep."

Although alliteration is not always observed in translations of
"Beowulf," it characterized the original poem.

The Anglo-Saxons.[1]—If it is desired, further work may be
done on the Anglo-Saxons as a people,—their racial characteristics; their reasons for coming to Britain; their effect on the later
language and literature of England. Material for this work may be
found in any good history of England, or in the chapters dealing
with the Anglo-Saxon period in any of the literary histories.

Paradise Lost.—The second great epic of England was the deliberate work of one writer, Milton. "Paradise Lost" is, therefore, a literary epic. It is based on the first three chapters of
Genesis and sets forth the circumstances and motives which led
Satan to go to the Garden of Eden, the temptation and fall of
Adam and Eve, their expulsion from Paradise, and the plan of re-
demption through Christ. The setting is stupendous. Milton has
taken as a background for his mighty scenes all of Heaven, Chaos,
the planetary Universe, and Hell. "Paradise Lost" has been
called the greatest single poem in the English language. It is wonderful for the magnificent word-pictures presented.

Paradise Regained.—This poem is the natural sequel of "Paradise Lost." As Paradise is lost when Adam and Eve yield to the
temptation of Satan, so Paradise is regained when Christ, although
tempted in all points the same as man, resists the tempter. "Paradise Regained" is founded on the first eleven verses of the fourth
chapter of *St. Matthew*. Although Milton regarded this work as
his masterpiece, it is ranked below "Paradise Lost" in the judgment of the rest of the world.

[1] See especially "The Saxons" in Miller's *English Literature.*

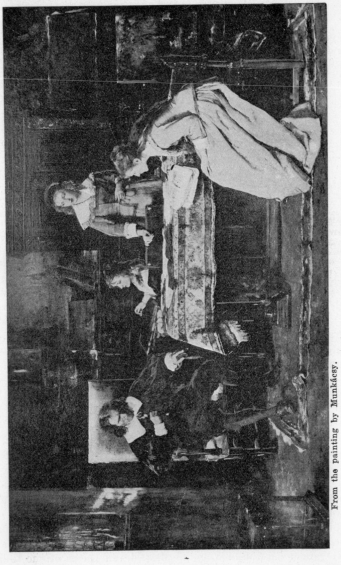

From the painting by Munkácsy.

MILTON DICTATING "PARADISE LOST"

Drake.—The last English great epic, "Drake," written in 1906, is the only successful completed [1] representative, in modern times, of this type of literature. The author, Alfred Noyes, was but twenty-six years of age when he wrote it. The central figure is the great English Admiral, Sir Francis Drake, but the poem sums up Elizabethan civilization as a whole. The poem lacks, however, the supernatural element usually found in great epics. It may not be possible to study this epic in class, but it will prove very interesting and profitable outside reading. A few lines, taken from the *Exordium*,[2] will serve to show something of the spirit with which the poem is written:

When on the highest ridge of that strange land,
Under the cloudless, blinding tropic blue,
Drake and his band of swarthy seamen stood
With dazed eyes gazing round them, emerald fans
Of palm that fell like fountains over cliffs   5
Of gorgeous red anana bloom obscured
Their sight on every side. Illustrious gleams
Of rose and green and gold streamed from the plumes
That flashed like living rainbows through the glades.
Piratic glints of musketoon and sword,   10
The scarlet scarves around the tawny throats,
The bright brass ear-rings in the sun-black ears,
And the calm faces of the negro guides
Opposed their barbarous bravery to the noon:
Yet a deep silence dreadfully beseiged   15
Even those mighty hearts upon the verge
Of the undiscovered world. Behind them lay
The old earth they knew. In front they could not see
What lay beyond the ridge. Only they heard
Cries of the painted birds troubling the heat   20
And shivering through the woods; till Francis Drake
Plunged through the hush, took hold upon a tree,
The tallest near them, and clomb upward, branch by branch,
And lo! as he swung clear above
The steep-down forest, on his wondering eyes   25
Mile upon mile of rugged shimmering gold
Burst through the unknown immeasurable sea.
Then he descended; and with a new voice
Vowed that, God helping, he would one day plough
Those virgin waters with an English keel.   30

[1] See note on the new American great epic, by John Neihardt, at end of this section.

[2] Used by permission of, and by special arrangement with, the Frederick A. Stokes Company, owners of the copyright.

So here before the unattempted task,
Above the Golden Ocean of my dream
I clomb and saw in splendid pageant pass
The wild adventures and heroic deeds
Of England's epic age—a vision lit   35
With mighty prophecies, fraught with a doom
Worthy the great Homeric roll of song,
Yet all unsung and unrecorded quite
By those who might have touched with Raphael's hand
The large imperial legend of our race.   40

. . . .

Mother and love, fair England, hear my prayer;
Help me that I may tell the enduring tale
Of that great seaman, good at need, who first
Sailed round this globe and made one little isle,
One little isle against that huge Empire   45
Of Spain, whose might was paramount on earth,
O'ertopping Babylon, Nineveh, Greece and Rome,
Carthage and all huge Empires of the past—
He made this little isle, against the world,
Queen of the earth and sea.   Nor this alone   50
The theme; for, in a mightier strife engaged
Even than he knew, he fought for the new faiths,
Championing our manhood as it rose
And cast its feudal chains before the seat
Of kings;—nay, in a mightier battle yet   55
He fought for the soul's freedom, fought the fight
Which, though it still rings in our wondering ears,
Was won then and for ever.

. . . .

                                    If my poor song
Now spread too wide a sail, forgive thy son
And lover, for thy love was ever wont   60
To lift men up in pride above themselves.
To do great deeds which of themselves alone
They could not, thou hast led the unfaltering feet
Of even thy meanest heroes down to death,
Lifted poor knights to many a great emprise,   65
Taught them high thoughts, and though they kept their souls
Lowly as little children, bidden them lift
Eyes unappalled by all the myriad stars
That wheel around the great white throne of God.

.

SUGGESTIONS TO STUDENTS

1. See if you can discover from these lines of the *Exordium* of "Drake" what the great epic struggle is and how it ends. Can you also see what will tend to unify the series of adventures or episodes that will be treated in the longer poem? 2. You will be interested in reading the whole epic, for the movement is rapid and the adventures thrilling. It will have an added interest for you if you have studied the Elizabethan period in your history class. 3. In what marked respects does this epic, written in the twentieth century, differ from those of an earlier time? Can you explain why? 4. What material for a great epic can you find in the World War of the twentieth century? In what respects is this another heroic age? What is the great epic cause or struggle? What are the powerful opposing forces? How and why are they overcome? 5. Show that the theme is of epic magnitude. What are the deep, elemental passions involved? 6. Show that the moral lies deeply embedded in the events. 7. What elements of twentieth century civilization are shown? 8. Who are the great characters that further or hinder the accomplishment of the struggle in which they are engaged? What especially causes our interest in them? 9. Name some of the distinct episodes. What binds them together? 10. What other epic characteristics can you find? 11. Why is it not possible for such a poem to be adequately treated before a lapse of years?

Note.—The first true American great epic seems to be in the process of realization in the cycle of poems which Mr. John Neihardt is now weaving about the region between the British possessions and Mexico, and westward from the Missouri river to the Pacific coast. He has chosen as the general time of his epic the days of the Ashley-Henry fur-trading expeditions of the first part of the nineteenth century. Two poems of the cycle that have already been evolved, "The Song of Three Friends" [1] and "The Song of Hugh Glass," [1] show what may be anticipated from the finished work. These have been published separately, but will later, it seems, become parts of the larger whole. They are exceedingly fascinating, and well worth reading.

Some Other Works Closely Allied to the Great Epic.—

There are several other works that come near the great epic in general spirit and yet are not, truly speaking, great epics. Tennyson's "Idylls of the King" are "a series of epical episodes" rather than a closely welded, unified epic. This material might have been treated so that it would have become a great epic of Arthurian or Celtic England. Tennyson, however, deliberately gave up this idea, for he says:

[1] Published by the Macmillan Company.

A truth
Looks freshest in the fashion of the day.

.   .   .   .

Why take the style of those heroic times?
For nature brings not back the Mastodon,
Nor we those times; and why should any man
Remodel models? These twelve books of mine
Were faint Homeric echoes, nothing worth.[1]

Longfellow's "Hiawatha" is almost a great epic of early American Indian life.

"The Robin Hood Ballads" are also not closely enough woven together and unified to become a true epic, although here again is material that might have been made into an epic of Norman England. There are some thirty-five or forty of these short poems that grew up among the people, and they are mentioned in this connection because the material in them is the kind out of which folk-epics have been made. Indeed here we may really see a great epic in the process of development, although, unfortunately, it was never fully completed. Some poet, it is true, saw the larger significance behind the many stories and attempted to unite them into one.[2] Although he told an interesting story for the most part, he failed, however, to set forth a great epic purpose toward which the action tended, and the poem falls away into confusion at the end. Today we think of the Robin Hood poems more as separate ballads, a type which will be understood more fully through the study of the chapter on ballads.

Pope, in his "Rape of the Lock," wrote a mock-epic purely for the sake of ridicule. In this poem he imitated the style and movement of the great epic, but made the theme, characters, and cause utterly trivial. De Quincey said of it, " 'The Rape of the Lock' is the most exquisite monument of playful fancy that universal literature offers."

SUGGESTIONS TO STUDENTS

1. Since you, no doubt, have some knowledge of "The Idylls of the King" and "Hiawatha" from the work of other years of your course, try to see for yourselves why these are not truly great epics. Although Arthur is the central figure of "The Idylls of the King," for instance, and the scenes are laid at his court, among the Knights of the Round Table,

[1] "The Epic" by Tennyson.
[2] "The Geste of Robin Hood."

do you find that there is a great, unifying action or struggle which dominates everything else? Do you not, instead, find that, though there might have been abundant reasons for such a struggle, the author has been content to focus our attention only on the experiences of individual knights and ladies instead of making the big, heroic national story the main thing? Can you see now just what prevents the different *Hiawatha* poems from becoming a great epic? Are we interested in Hiawatha for himself, or because he is furthering a great national struggle?

2. It may prove interesting for you to read "The Rape of the Lock," or parts of it, outside of class, in order to see how Pope imitates the characteristics of a great epic, but makes everything ridiculous because so petty. Here the struggle is over a lock of hair which a young noble of Queen Anne's court cuts off, at a ball, from a young lady's head. The weapons used in the struggle are "killing glances," frowns, and piercing words. The supernatural beings who control the situation are not gods and goddesses, but tiny creatures—the sprites, nymphs, salamanders, and gnomes.

REVIEW

1. Before going on to the next chapter, review what you have learned about the great epic as a type. Do you think you will be able to recognize the type and to prove why a poem is, or is not, a great epic? 2. What general information regarding the epics of the world have you gained? 3. Have you enjoyed this work? If you have, you have made good progress, because, aside from Shakespeare, King David, and the three great writers of Greek tragedy, the greatest writers of world literature are to be found among the epic poets.

By John Pettie, R. A.

THE VIGIL

A step in the Preparation for Knighthood

CHAPTER II

THE METRICAL ROMANCE

Characteristics of the Metrical Romance.—The metrical romance is a long, rambling love story in verse. It is the type of
literature most characteristic of the Middle Ages, "when knighthood was in flower," and hence it is filled with the ideals of that
time. Chivalry, romantic love, and religion predominate. Wonderful and impossible adventures are set forth. Everywhere is
there much more of fancy than reality. The characters are always
high born. In the older romances, in that magic "Once upon a
time," the mailed knight sallies forth to do mighty deeds. He
has taken upon himself the sacred vows of knighthood—to right
wrongs, "uphold the Christ," do courteous, brave deeds, and, so
far as lies in his power, to further the cause of truth, honor, and
freedom. He is also anxious to increase his fame as a knight, and
to win the favor of the beautiful lady of his choice. The love
element is especially strong in the romance. Many of the adventures related are undertaken in the interests of some beautiful distressed maiden, and the happy marriage of the knight and lady is
usually the culmination of the story. The metrical romance pictures beautiful scenes, personages, or events. There is much of
color and pageantry. There are spectacular and gorgeous court
scenes, tourneys, and gay processions of knights and ladies who,
dressed in suits of forest green, go a-maying or follow the hunt.
The hideous element is also to be found in the form of some wicked
magician or ugly monster that must be overcome by knightly valor.
The theme of the metrical romance is not so noble and stately as
that of the great epic. Although the supernatural element is
prominent in all the older metrical romances, it disappears in the
more modern ones. The latter are true to the type, nevertheless,
since they are long, rambling love stories in verse, in which the
imagination is given such play that we feel the events depicted are
removed from the life we see about us. An effort is usually made
to give these events the appearance of truth, but their improbability
is none the less apparent.

23

The Earlier Romances in England.—About the time of the Norman Conquest of England, the metrical romance was the most popular form of literature on the continent of Europe. Consequently, the Normans carried this type with them to England. The chief romances of the time were grouped into five great collections or circles of stories, centering around (1) King Arthur and the Knights of the Round Table, (2) Charlemagne and his Paladins, (3) Robin Hood and his Merrymen, (4) Alexander the Great, and (5) the old heroes of the Trojan war. Of these groups the first has the greatest interest for us since the Arthur stories have been told and retold by so many of our later writers.

One of the most interesting of the earlier metrical romances is "Sir Gawain and the Green Knight," which dates from about the middle of the fourteenth century. Students who have read Tennyson's "Idylls of the King" will be interested in the story of this old romance since it tells the adventures of a knight of the Round Table. The story is briefly told in prose in Moody and Lovett's *A History of English Literature,* pp. 26–28; Long's *English Literature,* pp. 57–58; *The Cambridge History of English Literature,* Vol. I, pp. 364–365; Ten Brink's *English Literature,* Vol. I, pp. 337–347.

After taking up the story as outlined in one of the above references, read the following passages from "Sir Gawain and the Green Knight"[1] as put into modern verse by Miss Jessie L. Weston:

DESCRIPTION OF THE GREEN KNIGHT

All green bedight that knight, and green his garments fair;
A narrow coat that clung straight to his side he ware,
A mantle plain above, lined on the inner side
With costly fur and fair, set on good cloth and wide,
So sleek, and bright in hue therewith his hood was gay   5
Which from his head was doffed, and on his shoulders lay.
Full tightly drawn his hose, all of the self-same green,
Well clasped about his calf—there-under spurs full keen
Of gold on silken lace, all striped in fashion bright,
That dangled beneath his legs—so rode that gallant knight.   10
His vesture, verily, was green as grass doth grow,
The barring of his belt, the blithe stones set a-row,
That decked in richest wise his raiment fine and fair,
Himself, his saddle-bow, in silken broideries rare,

---

[1] Used by special arrangement with the publishers, Houghton Mifflin Company. From Miss Weston's *Chief Middle English Poets.*

'Twere hard to tell the half, so cunning was the wise 15
In which 'twas broidered all with birds, and eke with flies!
Decked was the horse's neck, and decked the crupper bold,
With gauds so gay of green, the center set with gold.
And every harness boss was all enamelled green,
The stirrups where he stood were of the self-same sheen, 20
The saddle-bow behind, the girths so long and fair,
They gleamed and glittered all with green stones rich and rare.
The very steed beneath the self-same semblance ware.

                         he rides
       A green horse great and tall;
       A steed full stiff to guide, 25
       In broidered bridle all
       He worthily bestrides.

The Challenge

"Nay, here I crave no fight, in sooth I say to thee
The knights about thy board but beardless bairns they be:
An I were fitly armed, upon this steed so tall,
For lack of strength no man might match me in this hall!
Therefore within thy court I crave a Christmas jest. 5
'Tis Yuletide, and New Year, and here be many a guest.
If any in this hall himself so hardy hold,
So valiant of his hand, of blood and brain so bold,
That stroke for counter-stroke with me exchange He dare,
I give him of free gift this gisarm rich and fair, 10
This axe of goodly weight, to wield as he see fit,
And I will bide a blow, as bare as here I sit.
If one will list my words, and be of valiant mood,
Then let him swiftly come, and take this weapon good,—
Here I renounce my claim, the axe shall be his own. 15
And I will stand his stroke, here, on this floor of stone,
And I in turn a blow may deal, that boon alone
                         I pray,
       Yet respite shall he have
       A twelvemonth, and a day.
       Now quickly I thee crave— 20
       Who now hath aught to say?"

The Encounter

The Green Knight on the ground made ready speedily.
He bent his head a-down, that so his neck was free,
His long and lovely locks, across the crown they fell,
His bare neck to the nape all men might see right well.

Gawain, he gripped the axe, and swung it up on high,　　　　5
The left foot on the ground he setteth steadily;
Upon the neck so bare he let the blade alight,
The sharp edge of the axe the bones asunder smite—
Sheer thro' the flesh it smote, the neck was cleft in two,
The brown steel on the ground it hit, so strong the blow,　　　　10
The fair head from the neck fell even to the ground,
Spurned by the horse's hoof, e'en as it rolled around,
The red blood spurted forth, and stained the green so bright,
But ne'er for that he failed, nor fell, that stranger knight.
Swiftly he started up, on stiff and steady limb,
And stretching forth his hand, as all men gaped at him,　　　　15
Grasped at his goodly head, and lift it up again,
Then turned him to his steed, and caught the bridle rein,
Set foot in stirrup-iron, bestrode the saddle fair,
The while he gripped his head e'en by the flowing hair.
He set himself as firm in saddle, so I ween,　　　　20
As naught had ailed him there, though headless he was seen
　　　　　　　　　　　　　　　　　　In hall;
　　　　　He turned his steed about,
　　　　　That corpse, that bled withal.
　　　　　Full many there had doubt
　　　　　Of how the pledge might fall!　　　　25

The Departure of the Green Knight

The head, within his hand he held it up a space;
Toward the royal dais, forsooth, he turned the face,
The eyelids straight were raised, and looked with glance so clear,
Aloud it spake, the mouth, e'en as ye now may hear:
"Look, Gawain, thou be swift to speed as thou hast said,　　　　5
And seek, in all good faith, until thy search be sped,
E'en as thou here didst swear, in hearing of these knights—
To the Green Chapel come, I charge thee now aright.
The blow thou hast deserved, such as was dealt to-day,
E'en on the New Year's morn I pledge me to repay.　　　　10
Full many know my name, 'Knight of the Chapel Green,'
To find me, should'st thou seek, thou wilt not fail, I ween,
Therefore thou need'st must come, or be for recreant found."
With fierce pull at the rein he turned his steed around,
His head within his hand, forth from the hall he rode,　　　　15
Beneath his horse's hoofs the sparks they flew abroad,
No man in all the hall wist where he took his way,
Nor whence that knight had come durst any of them say,
　　　　　　　　　　　　　　　　　　When then?

The King and Gawain there 20
They gazed, and laughed again.
Proven it was full fair
A marvel unto men!

SUGGESTIONS TO STUDENTS

1. Make a comparison between Sir Gawain, the hero of this metrical romance, who does valorous deeds with a desire for knightly fame, and the hero of the great epic, "Beowulf," who, prompted by the great desire to save a people, undertakes his perilous enterprises. 2. There are other interesting points of comparison which will bring out the differences between the great epic and the metrical romance. For instance, which poem shows a greater love for beauty and the refinements of life? Which one shows the more imagination? Which one represents the deeper human emotions? The nobler ideals? Which one deals with life on the larger scale? In which one is the moral of the story most evident? What is this moral? Is there a moral to be found in the other? If so, what is it? Which poem shows the love element to the greater degree? Which one has the grander theme? How many people are vitally interested in the deeds of Sir Gawain? In those of Beowulf? Which shows the greater love for color and pageantry? Notice the methods of warfare used in each poem. How did Beowulf's adversary compare with that of Sir Gawain?

The Faerie Queene.—The greatest English metrical romance, as well as poetic allegory, is Spenser's [1] "Faerie Queene," which was written in the time of Queen Elizabeth and dedicated to her. According to the original plan, the author intended to write twenty-four books: the first twelve to portray the twelve moral virtues shown in Prince Arthur; and the other twelve books to set forth the twelve political virtues which Arthur possessed after he became king. Of this plan only six books were completed, and yet, abbreviated as the poem is, it is the longest one in our language. Each book of the "Faerie Queene" is complete in itself, since, for the most part, it tells the story of a set of characters not found in the other books. These books are bound into an organic whole, however, by the fact that the hero of each sets out on his mission from the same court, that of Gloriana, the Faerie Queene; and, furthermore, each knight is rescued from his worst peril by Prince Arthur, who, on his way to find his foreordained bride, the Faerie Queene, rides up at the most critical moment when the knight is unable to

[1] Edmund Spenser, 1552–1599.

EDMUND SPENSER
Author of England's Greatest Metrical Romance

help himself. Thus Prince Arthur and Gloriana are the unifying characters of the poem.

The first book of the "Faerie Queene" is considered to be the best one. It tells the story of the Red Cross Knight, or Holiness, who, accompanied by the lady Una, or Truth, goes to rescue Una's parents, who have been imprisoned by a terrible dragon. On the way they meet with many perilous adventures. **The First Book** They first are overtaken by a fearful storm, and, **of The** seeking refuge in a shady grove near by, they lose **Faerie Queene** their way in a labyrinth, and encounter the dragon, Error, in her den in the thickest woods. The knight, by means of his spiritual armor and weapons, is able to kill the monster, and he and the lady at last regain the highway. Not long afterward they encounter Archimago, or Hypocrisy, who, in the guise of a venerable hermit, beguiles them to his cell with the promise of rest and food. The old man is a wicked magician, who succeeds in weaving such a spell about the young knight, that he thinks his lady Truth, is false, and he therefore forsakes her. He goes on alone for some time, but finally falls in with a Saracen, who is accompanied by a seemingly beautiful lady. The Red Cross Knight overcomes the Saracen, whereupon the lady throws herself upon his protection. Her story is so plausible that the knight is deceived. She is, in reality, a very wicked witch, Duessa, or False-hood, and she is the cause of all of his subsequent misfortunes. She leads him to the House of Pride, and, later, persuades him to remove his heavenly armor and to drink of an enchanted fountain. He at once loses his strength, and falls an easy prey to a terrible giant, who takes him captive.

In the meanwhile the lady Una, who is seeking everywhere for the Red Cross Knight, has various experiences. She is followed by a lion, which becomes her protector for a time; she encounters many perils, but escapes; and, at last, meets the dwarf, her own servant, who had become separated from her at the house of Archimago. From him she learns of the imprisonment of the Red Cross Knight. She despairs at first of being able to help him, but finally comes upon Prince Arthur, who, when he has heard her story, goes at once with her to the giant's stronghold, and rescues the knight. The Red Cross Knight is, at first, very despondent because of his failures and sinfulness in the past; but Una leads him to the House of Religion, where he is ministered to by the three daughters of the house, Faith, Hope. and Charity, until he recovers his strength.

He then is able to attack the fearful dragon, and, after a three days' fight, succeeds in rescuing Una's parents. The book properly ends with the marriage of the knight and his faithful Una.

In the "Faerie Queene" we are interested not only in the story, but in the historical and, especially, the spiritual allegories that the poet has woven into this poem. In the story of the Red Cross Knight and his battles, Spenser has given us the allegory of the human soul, which struggles against the temptations and sins of the world, until, through God's grace, at last it triumphs gloriously because it is able to maintain the fight to the end.

SUGGESTIONS TO STUDENTS

1. Read some of the pictures which Spenser has given and note the beauty and melody of the lines. The following are especially good: the description of the Red Cross Knight and Una, Canto I, stanzas 1–5; the house of Morpheus, stanzas 39–44; Una and the lion, Canto III, stanzas 4–6, 9; the house of Pride, Canto IV, stanzas 4–8. Also make a brief study of the life of Spenser, the man who wrote the "Faerie Queen."

2. Try to work out a little of Spenser's allegory. For instance, in the first few stanzas of Canto I (1–14), what is meant by the "mightie armes and silver shield" that the young knight has on? (See Ephesians VI. 13–17.) Why does the young knight have on an old armor? Why does the armor show many "dints of deep wounds"? What is meant by the steed's disdaining to yield to the curb? Why the cross on the knight's breast and shield? What is the dragon that he has started out to overcome? Who is the lady? Notice her attributes: humility, innocence, purity;—how shown? Why is she veiled? Why does she mourn? What does the dwarf stand for? What is meant by the storm? The labyrinth? Why is one path so much broader and easier to follow than the rest? Why is the monster's cave in the thickest part of the woods? What is the significance of the lady's warning the knight of danger? Account for the spirit of the knight here. Why does the monster hide in the darkest part of the cave? How is the knight able to see the monster? What is signified by the thousand young ones? Why of different shapes, yet all ill favored? This, perhaps, will be sufficient to give you an idea as to how the allegory is carried out.

Later Metrical Romances.—The best metrical romances of later English literature are Scott's "Lady of the Lake," "Marmion," and "Lay of the Last Minstrel"; Moore's "Lalla Rookh"; and Tennyson's "The Princess." [1] Tennyson's "Idylls of the King" are on the border-land between the metrical romance and the great

---

[1] Chaucer's "Knight's Tale" is really a metrical romance, although classed by him as a tale.

epic, being neither one nor the other wholly. They are romantic in spirit, but more like the great epic in general treatment.

SUGGESTIONS TO STUDENTS AND QUESTIONS FOR REVIEW

1. Read, if there is time, one of the above mentioned metrical romances that you have not read before, or apply what you have learned here about the metrical romance to those with which you are already familiar. 2. What is the force of the word "metrical"? Have you ever read a romance to which this term did not apply? 3. What differences did you note between an earlier metrical romance like "Sir Gawain and the Green Knight," or "The Faerie Queene," and one of the more modern metrical romances? How do you account for these differences? 4. Which of these romances interested you more? 5. Prove that the modern romances belong to the general type. 6. Can you point out any distinctions as regards the hero of a romance and the hero of a great epic? In which case are you especially impressed by the man himself as an individual? 7. How do the women characters of a romance differ in importance in the story from those of a great epic? 8. In what other particulars do you find a marked difference between a metrical romance and a great epic? 9. Do you think you can recognize a metrical romance when you see one? How?

CHAPTER III

THE BALLAD

The Origin of the Ballad.—The true ballads are distinguished
from all other narrative poems because they are the songs of the
unlettered folk instead of the work of educated writers. Inasmuch
as the people could neither read nor write, the ballads were told,
or sung; and, as there was no fixed form, each teller changed or
modified the details to suit himself. Thus there are many varia-
tions of the same story. For instance, there are twenty-seven different versions in English of the ballad of the "Twa Sisters," and
it is still sung by peasants in the British Isles, who have received
it from past generations by word of mouth.

Let us see if we can imagine the circumstances under which a
ballad was first produced. Story-telling itself is as old as mankind because it arises from a social instinct lying deep in the human
heart. The uneducated folk would have plenty of material out of
which ballads could be made, since the whole community would
know and have a common interest in events of their own lives,
stories of war, love, human wrongs, or adventures. It was customary in those old days for the people to gather together and
dance upon the village green after the day's work was done.
Moved by the rhythm of the dance, some leader among them, with
keener imagination than the rest of the throng, might, on the
spur of the moment, composing as he went along, put into verse
some story known to them all. The people might join in a sort
of refrain or chorus, or some other singer be inspired to make additions to the verses. Thus the song would be started. It would
then become popular and be handed down by word of mouth from
one generation to another. Women, especially, would sing these
ballads to their children and their children's children.

Although the ballad form dates back to about the eleventh century,[1] it is only since the seventeenth century that ballad collecting
has been done to any extent. Educated people have gone among
the peasants and taken down, word for word, the ballads as they

[1] They are probably older than that, but none have been preserved of
those of earlier date.

were being sung by them. There is now a large and interesting collection.[1]

Characteristics of the Ballad.—The ballad belonged to the people and not to the educated class; it was not written down, at first, but recited or sung; it was listened to and not read; it was therefore flexible in form and the wording was easily changed. It was very short, as a usual thing, and told with great rapidity, there being much more omitted, or suggested, than told. There were no explanations given. It told a simple, serious story which usually had a tragic ending; love, tragedy, and the supernatural predominated. It was full of superstition .because it voiced the actual beliefs of the singers. The passions depicted were strong ones such as jealousy, love, hate, anger, and revenge. There was also shown an admiration for courage, loyalty, kindness, constancy, and self-sacrifice. There was a constant mixture of fact and fiction. The ballad was told impersonally; dialogue was prominent. There was much repetition and similarity of wording, one stanza frequently being simply a repetition of the one preceding it, excepting that a new line, or thought, was added. The ballad singers loved to lead up to a climax through a series of three statements. They loved to sing of lords and ladies, kings and courts, and had much to say about gold, jewels, and beautiful clothing. It must be remembered, however, that these things were viewed not from the standpoint of reality, but through the imagination of peasants.

Classification of Ballads.—There is such variety shown in the subject matter of the ballads that a true classification is impossible. The following forms, however, are some that have been recognized: The ballad of tragedy in family life, the supernatural ballad, the outlaw ballad, the love ballad, the lyrical ballad, the ballad of mourning, and the historical ballad.

The Ballad Meter.—The ballad is usually, although not always, arranged in four-line stanzas with the second and last lines rhyming. The first and third lines usually contain four feet, and the second and fourth lines, three feet. The meter, however, is not exact.

SUGGESTIONS TO STUDENTS

1. In reading the following ballads, try to think of them as being sung by some aged peasant woman as she sits before the peat fire in the evening, crooning to the grandchild on her lap the songs she learned in childhood from the lips of her own mother or grandmother. 2. These ballads should

[1] See *The English and Scottish Popular Ballads,* by Professor F. J. Child.

be read rapidly to get their best effect.[1] 3. We must not think of them as silly, though the wording is very different from what we would find in other narrative poems. We must remember that the peculiarities are there because of the circumstances under which they were composed and handed down. The peasants sang them with simple dignity. Let us try to get their point of view, and find out, as nearly as possible, what they thought and felt.

4. After reading a ballad, see how many of the characteristics pointed out above you can find illustrated. You will probably not find them all in any one. What passion seemed to be most prominent? If there is a tragedy, what seemed to be its cause? Were there any superstitions embodied? What were they? Would the ballad be included in any of the classes mentioned above? Did you enjoy it? Why?

THE TWA SISTERS

1. There was twa sisters in a bowr,
     Edinburgh, Edinburgh,
   There was twa sisters in a bowr,
     Stirling for ay,
   There was twa sisters in a bowr,
   There came a knight to be their
     wooer   6
   Bonny Saint Johnston stands
     upon Tay.

2. He courted the eldest wi' glove
     and ring,
   But he lovd the youngest above
     a' thing.

3. He courted the eldest wi brotch [2]
     and knife,   10
   But lovd the youngest as his life.

4. The eldest she was vexed sair,
   An much envi'd her sister fair.

5. Upon a morning fair and clear,
   She cried upon her sister dear:

6. "O sister, come to yon sea
     stran,   16
   An see our father's ships come
     to lan."

7. She's taen her by the milk-white
     han,
   An led her down to yon sea
     stran.

8. The youngest stood upon a
     stane,   20
   The eldest came and threw her
     in.

9. She took her by the middle sma,
   And dashed her bonnie back to
     the jaw.

10. "O sister, sister, tak my han,
    An Ise mack you heir to a' my
      lan.   25

11. "O sister, sister, tak my middle,
    An yes get my goud and my
      gouden girdle.

12. "O sister, sister, save my life,
    An I swear Ise never be nae
      man's wife."

13. "Foul fa the han that I should
      take

[1] Perhaps the teacher will read aloud to the class so that pronunciation of the words may be caught and the effect of the whole be properly felt.
[2] brooch.

It twind me an my warldes
   make.[1]

14. "Your cherry cheeks an yellow
      hair
   Gars [2] me gae maiden for ever-
      mair."

15. Sometimes she sank, an some-
      times she swam,
   Till she came down yon bonny
      mill-dam.   35

16. O out it came the miller's son
   And saw the fair maid swimmin
      in.

17. "O father, father, draw your
      dam,
   Here's either a mermaid or a
      swan."

18. The miller quickly drew the
      dam,   40
   And there he found a drownd
      woman.

19. You couldna see her yellow hair
   For gold and pearle that were
      so rare.

20. You could not see her middle
      sma
   For gouden girdle that was so
      braw.[3]   45

21. You could not see her fingers
      white
   For gouden rings that was sae
      gryte.[4]

22. An by there came a harper fine,
   That harped to the king at
      dine.

23. When he did look that lady
      upon,   50
   He sighd and made a heavy
      moan.

24. He's taen three locks o her yel-
      low hair,
   An wi them strung his harp sae
      fair.

25. The first tune he did play and
      sing
   Was, "Farewell to my father
      the king."   55

26. The next in tune that he playd
      syne
   Was, "Farewell to my mother
      the queen."

27. The lasten tune that he playd
      then
   Was, "Wae to my sister, fair
      Ellen."

[1] It parted me and my world's mate.   [2] causes, makes.
[3] handsome.   [4] great.

Note.—Another variation of this ballad sums up the story in the
following words:

> Then bespake the treble string,
> "O yonder is my father the king,"
> Then bespake the second string,
> "O yonder sits my mother the queen."
> And then bespake the strings all three,   5
> "O yonder is my sister that drowned me."

Here we have one of the common superstitions of the *folk*, which appeared often in their ballads, that of the speaking harp. According to primitive beliefs, the dead girl's hair, which the harper used as strings for his harp, had the power to tell the story of her murder. Wicked elder sisters, or step-mothers, or mothers-in-law were frequent characters of the ballads.

THE CRUEL BROTHER

1. There was three ladies playd at the ba,
   With a hey ho and a lillie gay,
   There came a knight and played oer them a',
   As the primrose spreads so sweetly.

2. One o them was clad in red: 5
   He asked if she wad be his bride.

3. One o them was clad in green:
   He asked if she wad be his queen.

4. The last o them was clad in white:
   He asked if she wad be his heart's delight. 10

5. "Ye may ga ask my father, the king:
   Sae maun ye ask my mither, the queen.

6. "Sae maun ye ask my sister Anne:
   And dinna forget my brither John."

7. He has asked her father, the king: 15
   And sae did he her mither, the queen.

8. And he has asked her sister Anne:

But he has forgot her brither John.

9. Now, when the wedding day was come,
   The knight would take his bonny bride home. 20

10. And many a lord and many a knight
    Came to behold that ladie bright.

11. And there was nae man that did her see,
    But wished himself bridegroom to be.

12. Her father dear led her down the stair, 25
    And her sisters twain they kissed her there.

13. Her mother dear led her thro the closs,
    And her brother John set her on her horse.

14. She leand her o'er the saddle-bow,
    To give him a kiss ere she did go. 30

15. He has taen a knife, baith lang and sharp,
    And stabbd that bonny bride to the heart.

16. She hadno ridden half thro the
    town,
    Until her heart's blude staind
    her gown.

17. "Ride up, ride up," said the
    foremost man;   35
    "I think our bride comes hooly
    on."

18. "Ride up, ride up," said the
    second man;
    "I think our bride looks pale
    and wan."

19. "O lead me gently up yon hill,
    And I 'll there sit down, and
    make my will."   40

20. "O what will you leave to your
    father dear?"
    "The silver-shod steed that
    brought me here."

21. "What will you leave to your
    mother dear?"
    "My velvet pall and my silken
    gear."

22. "What will you leave to your
    sister Anne?"   45
    "My silken scarf and my gow-
    den fan."

23. "What will you leave to your
    sister Grace?"
    "My bloody cloaths to wash and
    dress."

24. "What will you leave to your
    brother John?"
    "The gallows-tree to hang him
    on."   50

25. "What will you leave to your
    brother John's wife?"
    "The wilderness to end her
    life."

Note.—In this ballad we have two old *folk* themes:—one, where
the last will and testament leaves ill luck to the murderer or murderers; and the other, the necessity of asking a brother's consent to
the marriage of his sister.

BABYLON: OR THE BONNIE BANKS OF FORDIE

1. There were three ladies lived in
   a bower,
   Eh vow bonnie,
   And they went out to pull a
   flower
   On the bonnie banks o Fordie.

2. They hadna pu'ed a flower but
   ane,   5
   When up started to them a
   banisht man.

3. He 's taen the first sister by the
   hand,

And he 's turned her round and
   made her stand.

4. "It 's whether will ye be a rank
   robber's wife,
   Or will ye die by my wee pen-
   knife?"   10

5. "It 's I 'll not be a rank robber's
   wife,
   But I 'll rather die by your wee
   pen-knife."

6. He 's killed this may, and he 's
   laid her by,

For to bear the red rose company.

7. He's taken the second ane by
the hand,　　　　　15
And he's turned her round and
made her stand.

8. "It's whether will ye be a rank
robber's wife,
Or will ye die by my wee pen-
knife?"

9. "I'll not be a rank robber's
wife,
But I'll rather die by your wee
pen-knife."　　　20

10. He's killed this may, and he's
laid her by,
For to bear the red rose company.

11. He's taken the youngest ane by
the hand,
And he's turned her round and
made her stand.

12. Says, "Will ye be a rank robber's wife,　　　.25

Or will ye die by my wee pen-
knife?"

13. "I'll not be a rank robber's
wife,
Nor will I die by your wee pen-
knife.

14. "For I hae a brother in this
wood,
And gin ye kill me, it's he'll
kill thee."　　　30

15. "What's thy brother's name?
Come tell to me."
"My brother's name is Baby
Lon."

16. "O sister, sister, what have I
done!
O have I done this ill to thee!

17. "O since I've done this evil
deed,　　　35
Good sall never be seen o me."

18. He's taken out his wee pen-
knife,
And he's twyned himsel o his
ain sweet life.

Note.—According to the old beliefs, the green-wood,—leaves,
flowers, branches were regarded as dangerous. If one picked anything in the green-wood, evil was sure to befall. In those lawless
times, death hid in every forest glade or bend of the unfrequented
roads.

THE WIFE OF USHER'S WELL

1. There lived a wife at Usher's
Well,
And a wealthy wife was she;
She had three stout and stal-
wart sons,
And sent them o'er the sea.

2. They hadna been a week from
her,　　　5
A week but barely ane,
When word came to the carline
wife
That her three sons were gane.

3. They hadna been a week from
   her,
   A week but barely three,   10
   When word came to the carline [1]
   wife
   That her sons she'd never see.

4. "I wish the wind may never
   cease,
   Nor fashes [2] in the flood,
   Till my three sons come hame
   to me,   15
   In earthly flesh and blood."

5. It fell about the Martin-mass, [3]
   When nights are lang and mirk,
   The carline wife's three sons
   came hame,
   And their hats were o the birk. [4]

6. It neither grew in syke [5] nor
   ditch,   21
   Nor yet in any sheugh; [6]
   But at the gates o Paradise,
   That birk grew fair enough.

   .   .   .   .   .

7. "Blow up the fire, my maidens!
   Bring water from the well!   26
   For a' my house shall feast this
   night,
   Since my three sons are well."

8. And she has made to them a
   bed,
   She's made it large and wide, 30
   And she's ta'en her mantle her
   about,
   Sat down at the bed-side.

   .   .   .   .   .

9. Up then crew the red, red cock,
   And up and crew the grey;
   The eldest to the youngest said,
   "'Tis time we were away."   36

10. The cock he hadna craw'd but
    once,
    And clappd his wings at a',
    When the youngest to the eldest
    said,
    "Brother, we must awa.   40

11. "The cock doth craw, the day
    doth daw,
    The channerin [7] worm doth
    chide;
    Gin we be mist out o our place,
    A sair pain we maun bide.

12. "Fare ye weel, my mother dear!
    Farewell to barn and byre! [8] 46
    And fare ye weel, the bonny lass
    That kindles my mother's fire!"

[1] old woman. [2] troubles, disturbances, storms. [3] The feast of St. Martin, the 11th of November. [4] birch. [5] marsh. [6] furrow. [7] fretting. [8] stable.

Note.—Again we find that we must understand the beliefs of the folk if we would understand their ballads. Two popular superstitions are here set forth. The first is the power of the wish. So great is thought to be the power of a wish, that the person wished for must come even though he has to come back from the grave. The other is the belief that spirits must vanish at the crowing of the cock.

HIND HORN

1. In Scotland there was a babie
   born,
     Lill lal, etc.
   And his name it was called
   young Hind Horn.
     With a fal lal, etc.

2. He sent a letter to our king
   That he was in love with his
   daughter Jean.

3. The king an angry man was he;
   He sent young Hind Horn to
   the sea.

4. He's gien to her a silver wand,
   With seven living lavrock's [1] sitting thereon.

5. She's gien to him a diamond
   ring,
   With seven bright diamonds set
   therein.

6. "When this ring grows pale and
   wan,
   You may know by it my love is
   gane." [2]

7. One day as he looked his ring
   upon,
   He saw the diamonds pale and
   wan.

8. He left the sea and came to
   land,
   And the first that he met was an
   old beggar man.

9. "What news, what news?" said
   young Hind Horn;
   "No news, no news," said the
   old beggar man.

10. "No news," said the beggar, "no
    news at a',

But there is a wedding in the
king's ha."

11. "Will ye lend me your begging
    coat?
    And I'll lend you my scarlet
    cloak.

12. "Will you lend me your beg-
    gar's rung? [3]
    And I'll gie you my steed to
    ride upon.

13. "Will you lend me your wig o
    hair,
    To cover mine, because it is
    fair?"

14. The auld beggar man was
    bound for the mill,
    But Young Hind Horn for the
    king's hall.

15. The auld beggar man was bound
    for to ride,
    But young Hind Horn was
    bound for the bride.

16. When he came to the king's
    gate,
    He sought a drink for Hind
    Horn's sake.

17. The bride came down with a
    glass of wine,
    When he drank out the glass,
    and dropt in the ring.

18. "O got ye this be sea or land?
    Or got ye it off a dead man's
    hand?"

19. "I got not it by sea, I got it by
    land,
    And I got it, madam, out of
    your own hand."

20. "O I 'll cast off my gowns of
brown,
And beg wi you frae town to
town.

21. "O I 'll cast off my gowns of
red,
And I'll beg wi you to win my
bread."

22. "Ye needna cast off your gowns
of brown,   45
For I 'll make you lady o many
a town.

23. "Ye needna cast off your gowns
of red,
It 's only a sham, the begging o
my bread."

1 larks.   2 in danger.   3 staff.

Note.—In this ballad the superstition shown is that of the sympathetic jewel which warns its owner of danger through changing color.

SIR PATRICK SPENS

1. The king sits in Dumferling
toune,
Drinking the blude-reid wine:
"O whar will I get guid sailor,
To sail this schip of mine?"

2. Up and spak an eldern knicht, 5
Sat at the kings richt kne:
"Sir Patrick Spence is the best
sailor,
That sails upon the se."

3. The king has written a braid
letter,
And signd it wi his hand,   10
And sent it to Sir Patrick
Spence,
Was walking on the sand.

4. The first line that Sir Patrick
red,
A loud lauch lauched he;
The next line that Sir Patrick
red,   15
The teir blinded his ee.

5. "O wha is this has don this
deid,
This ill deid don to me,

To send me out this time o the
yeir,
To sail upon the se!   20

6. "Mak hast, mak hast, my mirry
men all,
Our guid schip sails the morne";
"O say na sae, my master deir,
For I feir a deadlie storme.

7. "Late late yestreen I saw the
new moone,   25
Wi the auld moone in hir arms,
And I feir, I feir, my deir master,
That we will come to harme."

8. O our Scots nobles wer richt
laith
To weet their cork-heild schoone;
Bot lang owre a' the play wer
played,   31
Their hats they swam aboone.

9. O lang, lang may their ladies
sit,
Wi thair fans into their hand,
Or eir they se Sir Patrick
Spence   35
Cum sailing to the land.

10. O lang, lang may the ladies stand,
Wi thair gold kems in their hair,
Waiting for thair ain deir lords,
For they'll se thame na mair. 40

11. Haf owre, haf owre to Aberdour,
It's fiftie fadom deip,
And thair lies guid Sir Patrick Spence,
Wi the Scots lords at his feit.

Note.—This is called one of the finest of the ballads.

SOME BALLADS FOR OPTIONAL READING [1]

Note.—Report in writing on at least five or six ballads from this list, giving for each, so far as you are able to determine, its classification, the chief passion depicted, superstitions shown, or any other interesting things about them that you may find. Which ballad did you like best? Why?

"Edward"
"Lord Randal"
"Lord Thomas and Fair Annet"
"Kemp Owyne"
"Barbara Allen's Cruelty"
"The Two Corbies"
"The Douglas Tragedy"
"The Twa Brothers"
"The Wee, Wee Man"
"Clerk Colvin"
"Young Beichan"
"The Gay Goshawk"
"Young Waters"
"The Bonny Earl of Murray"
"The Bailiff's Daughter of Islington"

"Thomas Rymer"
"Robin Hood and Allen-a-Dale"
"Robin Hood Rescues the Widow's Three Sons"
"Robin Hood and Guy of Gisborne"
"The Death of Robin Hood"
"Edom o'Gordon"
"Katharine Jeffray"
"Willie Drowned in Yarrow"
"Helen of Kirkonnell"
"The Battle of Otterbourne"
"Chevy Chase"
"Kinmont Willie"
"The Nutbrown Mayde"

Imitation Ballads.—From the foregoing discussion of the ballad, it will be seen that the so-called modern ballads are not really such, but only imitations, written by literary men. These are not struck out of the hearts of the uneducated peasants. They do not give the genuine beliefs and interpretation of the life of these people, but are composed by educated men, who strive to give them the ballad sound. Although these imitation ballads are fine, spirited poems, they really bear a closer relation to the metrical tale than they do to the true folk-ballad. Compare the following modern ballads with

[1] These may be found in collections of ballads, or, often, in the general collections of English poetry.

those that have been handed down by word of mouth, from a distant
past. What do they lack which the genuine ballad possessed?

THE BALLAD OF THE OYSTERMAN [1]

Oliver Wendell Holmes [2]

It was a tall young oysterman lived by the river-side,
His ship was just upon the bank, his boat was on the tide;
The daughter of a fisherman, that was so straight and slim,
Lived over on the other bank, right opposite to him.

It was the pensive oysterman that saw a lovely maid,   5
Upon a moonlight evening, a-sitting in the shade;
He saw her wave her handkerchief, as much as if to say,
"I'm wide awake, young oysterman, and all the folks away."

Then up arose the oysterman, and to himself said he,
"I guess I'll leave the skiff at home, for fear that folks should see;   10
I read it in the story-book, that, for to kiss his dear,
Leander swam the Hellespont,—and I will swim this here."

And he has leaped into the waves, and crossed the shining stream,
And he has clambered up the bank, all in the moonlight gleam;
O there were kisses sweet as dew, and words as soft as rain,—   15
But they have heard her father's step, and in he leaps again!

Out spoke the ancient fisherman,—"O what was that, my daughter?"
"'Twas nothing but a pebble, sir, I threw into the water."
"And what is that, pray tell me, love, that paddles off so fast?"
"It's nothing but a porpoise, sir, that's been a-swimming past."   20

Out spoke the ancient fisherman, "Now bring me my harpoon!
I'll get into my fishing-boat, and fix the fellow soon."
Down fell that pretty innocent, as falls a snow-white lamb,
Her hair drooped round her pallid cheeks like seaweed on a clam.

Alas for those two loving ones! she waked not from her swound,   25
And he was taken with the cramp, and in the waves was drowned;
But Fate has metamorphosed them, in pity of their woe,
And now they keep an oyster shop for mermaids down below.

---

[1] Used by permission of Houghton Mifflin Company.
[2] Oliver Wendell Holmes, 1809–1894.

ROSABELLE [1]

Sir Walter Scott

O listen, listen, ladies gay!
　No haughty feat of arms I tell;
Soft is the note, and sad the lay,
　That mourns the lovely Rosabelle.

"Moor, moor the barge, ye gallant
　　crew!　　　　　　　　　　5
And, gentle ladye, deign to stay,
Rest thee in Castle Ravensheuch,
　Nor tempt the stormy firth to-
　　day.

"The blackening wave is edged with
　white;
To inch [2] and rock the sea-mews
　fly;　　　　　　　　　　　10
The fishers have heard the Water-
　Sprite,
Whose screams forbode that
　wreck is nigh.

"Last night the gifted Seer did
　view
A wet shroud swathed round
　ladye gay;
Then stay thee, Fair, in Ravens-
　heuch:　　　　　　　　　15
Why cross the gloomy firth to-
　day?"—

" 'Tis not because Lord Lindesay's
　heir
　To-night at Roslin leads the
　　ball,
But that my ladye-mother there
　Sits lonely in her castle-hall.　20

" 'Tis not because the ring they ride,
　And Lindesay at the ring rides
　　well,
But that my sire the wine will chide,
　If 'tis not fill'd by Rosabelle."—

O'er Roslin all that dreary night　25
　A wondrous blaze was seen to
　　gleam;
'Twas broader than the watch-fire's
　light,
　And redder than the bright moon-
　　beam.

It glared on Roslin's castled rock,
　It ruddied all the copse-wood
　　glen;　　　　　　　　　　30
'Twas seen from Dryden's groves
　of oak;
　And seen from cavern'd Haw-
　　thornden.

Seem'd all on fire that chapel proud,
　Where Roslin's chiefs uncoffin'd
　　lie,
Each Baron, for a sable shroud,　35
　Sheathed in his iron panoply.

Seem'd all on fire, within, around,
　Deep sacristy [3] and altar's pale,[4]
Shone every pillar foliage-bound,
　And glimmer'd all the dead men's
　　mail,　　　　　　　　　40

Blazed battlement and pinnet [5] high,
　Blazed every rose-carved buttress
　　fair—
So still they blaze, when fate is
　nigh
　The lordly line of high St. Clair.

There are twenty of Roslin's barons
　　bold　　　　　　　　　　45
　Lie buried within that proud
　　chapelle;
Each one the holy vault doth hold—
　But the sea holds lovely Rosa-
　　belle.

And each St. Clair was buried there,
  With candle, with book, and with
      knell;   50

But the sea-caves rung, and the wild
      winds sung,
  The dirge of lovely Rosabelle.

[1] From "The Lay of the Last Minstrel." [2] island. [3] vestry. [4] inclosure.
[5] pinnacle.

THE WELL OF ST. KEYNE

Robert Southey

A well there is in the West country,
  And a clearer one never was seen;
There is not a wife in the West
    country
But has heard of the Well of St.
    Keyne.

An oak and an elm tree stand be-
    side,   5
And behind does an ash-tree grow,
And a willow from the bank above
  Droops to the water below.

A traveller came to the Well of St.
    Keyne;
  Joyfully he drew nigh,   10
For from cock-crow he had been
    travelling,
  And there was not a cloud in the
    sky.

He drank of the water so cool and
    clear,
  For thirsty and hot was he,
And he sat down upon the bank, 15
  Under the willow-tree.

There came a man from the house
    hard by
  At the well to fill his pail;
On the well-side he rested it,
  And he bade the stranger hail. 20

"Now art thou a bachelor,
    stranger?" quoth he,
  "For an if thou hast a wife,

The happiest draught thou hast
    drank this day
  That ever thou didst in thy life.

"Or has thy good woman, if one
    thou hast   25
  Ever here in Cornwall been?
For an if she have, I'll venture my
    life
  She has drunk of the Well of St.
    Keyne."

"I have left a good woman who
    never was here,"
  The stranger he made reply; 30
"But that my draught should be the
    better for that,
  I pray you answer me why."

"St. Keyne," quoth the Cornish-
    man, "many a time
  Drank of this crystal well,
And before the Angel summoned
    her   35
  She laid on the water a spell.

"If the Husband of this gifted well
  Shall drink before his Wife,
A happy man thenceforth is he,
  For he shall be Master for life. 40

"But if the Wife should drink of it
    first,
  God help the Husband then!"
The stranger stooped to the Well of
    St. Keyne,
  And drank of the waters again.

"You drank of the well, I warrant,
　　betimes?"　　　　　　　　45
He to the Cornish-man said.
But the Cornish-man smiled as the
　　stranger spake,
And sheepishly shook his head.

"I hastened, as soon as the wedding
　　was done,
And left my wife in the porch. 50
But i' faith, she had been wiser than
　　me,
For she took a bottle to Church."

LA BELLE DAME SANS MERCI

John Keats

O what can ail thee, knight-at-arms,
　　Alone and palely loitering?
The sedge has wither'd from the
　　lake,
　　And no birds sing,

O what can ail thee, knight-at-
　　arms,　　　　　　　　　5
　　So haggard and so woe-begone?
The squirrel's granary is full,
　　And the harvest's done.

I see a lily on thy brow
　　With anguish moist and fever
　　dew,　　　　　　　　　10
And on thy cheeks a fading rose
　　Fast withereth too.

"I met a lady in the meads,
　　Full beautiful—a faery's child;
Her hair was long, her foot was
　　light,　　　　　　　　　15
　　And her eyes were wild.

"I made a garland for her head,
　　And bracelets too, and fragrant
　　zone;
She look'd at me as she did love,
　　And made sweet moan.　　20

"I set her on my pacing steed,
　　And nothing else saw all day long,
For sideways would she lean, and
　　sing
　　A faery's song.

"She found me roots of relish
　　sweet,　　　　　　　　　25
And honey wild, and manna-dew,
And sure in language strange she
　　said—
　　'I love thee true.'

"She took me to her elfin grot,
　　And there she wept and sigh'd full
　　sore,　　　　　　　　　30
And there I shut her wild, wild eyes,
　　With kisses four.

"And there she lullèd me asleep,
　　And there I dream'd—ah! woe
　　betide!—
The latest dream I ever dream'd 35
　　On the cold hill's side.

"I saw pale kings and princes too,
　　Pale warriors, death-pale were
　　they all;
They cried—'La Belle Dame sans
　　Merci
　　Hath thee in thrall!'　　40

"I saw their starved lips in the
　　gloam
　　With horrid warning gapèd wide,
And I awoke and found me here
　　On the cold hill's side.

"And this is why I sojourn here 45
　　Alone and palely loitering,
Though the sedge is wither'd from
　　the lake,
　　And no birds sing."

IMITATION BALLADS FOR OPTIONAL READING [1]

Note.—Report on at least seven imitation ballads. Give author and central thought of each. With what degree of success did the author catch the genuine ballad spirit and subject-matter? In what particulars did he fail? Which of these ballads read seemed to you to be the best imitation?

"The Battle of Agincourt"	Michael Drayton
"John Gilpin's Ride"	Cowper
"The True Ballad of Charitie," from "The Rowley Papers"	Chatterton
"The Bristowe Tragedie," from "The Rowley Papers"	Chatterton
"The De'il's Awa' wi' the Exciseman"	Burns
"The Battle of Blenheim"	Southey
"The Inchcape Rock"	Southey
"The Rime of the Ancient Mariner"	Coleridge
"Jock o' Hazeldean"	Scott
"Lochinvar"	Scott
"The Outlaw"	Scott
"Border Ballad"	Scott
"Alice Brand" (from "Lady of the Lake")	Scott
"The Maid of Neidpath"	Scott
"The Eve of St. John"	Scott
"The Rover"	Scott
"Madge Wildfire's Song"	Scott
"Casabianca"	Mrs. Hemans
"Hale in the Bush, 1776"	Anon.
"The Battle of the Kegs"	Francis Hopkinson
"Horatius at the Bridge"	Macaulay
"The Ballad of Nathan Hale"	Anon.
"Lord Ullin's Daughter"	Thomas Campbell
"The Sands of Dee"	Kingsley
"The Three Fishers"	Kingsley
"Driving Home the Cows"	Osgood
"Hervè Riel"	Browning
"How They Brought the Good News"	Browning
"A Musical Instrument"	Mrs. Browning
"The Revenge"	Tennyson
"The Forsaken Merman"	Matthew Arnold
"The Captain's Daughter"	Fields
"Jock Johnstone the Tinkler"	James Hogg
"The Wreck of the Hesperus"	Longfellow
"The Skeleton in Armor"	Longfellow

[1] These ballads may be found in general collections of English and American poetry or in connection with the author's works.

"The Singing Leaves"...........................Lowell
"Skipper Ireson's Ride".........................Whittier
"Maud Muller"...................................Whittier
"The Pipes of Lucknow"..........................Whittier
"The Exiles"....................................Whittier
"The Courtin'"..................................Lowell
"The Night Before Christmas"....................C. C. Moore
"The Ballad of Trees and the Master"............Lanier
"The Miller of the Dee".........................Mackay
"Fuzzy-Wuzzy" ....Kipling
"The Ballad of East and West"...................Kipling
"Mandalay" ....Kipling
"The Last Suttee"...............................Kipling
"The Gift of the Sea"...........................Kipling
"Soldier, Soldier"..............................Kipling
"Tommy" ....Kipling
"The Ballad of Father Gilligan".................Wm. Butler Yeats
"The Fiddler of Dooney".........................Wm. Butler Yeats
"Burial Party" (from "Salt Water Ballads").......Masefield
"Bill" (from "Salt Water Ballads")..............Masefield
"Harbour Bar" (from "Salt Water Ballads").......Masefield
"The Turn of the Tide" (from "Salt Water
    Ballads") ....Masefield
"Cape Horn Gospel I" (from "Salt Water
    Ballads") ....Masefield
"The Cremation of Sam McGee"....................Service
"Ballad of Manila Bay"..........................C. G. D. Roberts
"Soldier, Soldier" ....Maurice Hewlett
"Ballad of Lieutenant Miles"....................Clinton Scollard
"Langemarck at Ypres"...........................Wilfred Campbell

REVIEW

1. Sum up what you have learned regarding the ballad. 2. What special interest have you found in ballads? Have you caught something of their charm? Can you make yourselves look sympathetically at life through the eyes of the ballad singers? 3. Do you see why it is hard to write successful imitation ballads? What authors, have you found, wrote them with the nearest approach to success?

CHAPTER IV

THE METRICAL TALE

Characteristics of the Metrical Tale.—The metrical tale is a narrative poem, usually so short that it can be read easily at one sitting. It leaves a single impression with the reader. It is not so long as the metrical romance, and not so fanciful, and it deals with any emotion or phase of life. It makes no attempt to handle extraordinary situations, but to tell a simple, straightforward story in as realistic a manner as possible. The characters are common every-day people and not those of a special class. The metrical tale is to poetry what the short-story is to prose. Many of the modern or imitation ballads may really be classified as metrical tales. The only reason for placing them with the ballads is because of the swing, spirit, and rapidity of the story.

Chaucer.—The first great writer of the metrical tale in England, as regards both order of time and rank, was Chaucer.

Note.—Since the metrical tale is to be emphasized here as a literary type, it seems wise to omit the thorough study of the *Prologue* to the "Canterbury Tales," inasmuch as it forms only the introduction, and is not a tale in itself. A brief account of the "Canterbury Tales" as a whole is given here, however, so that the student may get an idea of the general plan and spirit of the work. If it is desired, of course, the *Prologue* may be taken up at this point, using one of the texts found in any of the regular series of classics.

The Canterbury Tales.—Chaucer's masterpiece, "The Canterbury Tales," is a large collection of otherwise isolated stories, which are welded into one unified work by means of the prologue and the interludes, or links between the tales. In this *Prologue* the author introduces twenty-nine pilgrims who are going on a pilgrimage to the shrine of the martyred Archbishop, Thomas à Becket, at Canterbury. They meet by chance at the Tabard Inn in Southwark, and, as they discover that they are all bound on the same errand, they decide to travel together. Chaucer represents himself as one of the number, and takes occasion to give us vivid pictures of the other members of the party before they set out upon

CHAUCER, ENGLAND'S GREATEST WRITER OF
METRICAL TALES

their journey. He not only gives us an idea of their rank and position in life, but their characteristics, personal appearance, and dress, as well. Nowhere else in literature is there to be found such a set of full-length portraits as here. In this art gallery we see all ranks and conditions found in fourteenth century English society.

First we are shown the dignified, earnest Christian knight who loves "chivalry, truth, honor, freedom and courtesy"; his son, the gay young squire, and his one servant, the yeoman, clad in coat and hood of green. Next we see the dainty, tender-hearted prioress, Madame Eglentyne, and her companions, the second nun and the three priests; besides these there are the worldly monk; the selfish, corrupt, begging friar; the shrewd, careful merchant; the earnest student of Oxford; the lawyer, who knew all the cases and their decisions which had come down from the time of King William; the pleasure-loving, hospitable frankelyn, or country squire; the guildmen; the cook; the shipman; the doctor of medicine, who cured his patients by his natural magic; the wife of Bath, who had had five husbands; the gentle parish priest, a true example to his flock; the plowman, who loved his neighbor as himself; the miller who stole corn and took toll three times; the maunciple or steward of a law school; the reve, a tricky overseer of a gentleman's estate; and the two corrupt ecclesiasts,—the summoner to the ecclesiastical courts, and the seller of indulgences. These are the people whose pictures Chaucer has painted for us, and who become the tellers of the "Canterbury Tales."

After describing the party of pilgrims, Chaucer gives the circumstances under which they tell the stories. The genial host of the Tabard, Harry Bailey, in order to make the journey to Canterbury more pleasant for his guests, proposes that they each tell four stories,—two on the way to the shrine, and two more on their return journey. He volunteers to go with them to Canterbury and to act as judge of the stories told. He suggests that the one who tells the best tale shall be given a dinner at the expense of the rest of the party, on the return from their pilgrimage. The *Prologue* ends with the drawing of cuts to determine which one shall tell the first story. Since the cut falls to the Knight, the "Knight's Tale" [1] is the first of the series given.

By means of the interludes, or links between the tales, the reader is kept in touch with the pilgrims as they ride; he hears their com-

[1] As has been said before, "The Knight's Tale" is really a metrical romance rather than a tale.

After a painting by Thomas Stothard.

THE CANTERBURY PILGRIMS

ments on the stories told; sees how the coarser characters thrust themselves upon the notice of the others; notes the skillful manner in which the host arranges the story-telling so that there will be the right proportion of merry as well as moral tales; hears the querulous retorts of the miller and reve, and the summoner and friar, who delight in saying disparaging things about each other;— while, over all, he finds the humor of Chaucer, enlivening what is dull, and pointing out with kindly satire the follies and failings of men.

Although Chaucer's original plan was to have each of the twenty-nine pilgrims tell four stories, this is not carried out, there being but twenty-four told in all, and some of these are left unfinished. Chaucer has adroitly covered up this defect, for the most part, by having the stories, which for some reason he does not care to finish, interrupted, in the telling, by different pilgrims, and thus the lack of completion seems wholly fitting and natural.

Of the twenty-four stories told, the following are generally regarded as the best:

(1) The Knight's tale about Palamon and Arcite and their loved lady, the fair Emelye.

(2) The Nun's tale about little Hugh of Lincoln, who sang the hymn of praise even after his throat had been cut by the Jews.

(3) The Nun's Priest's tale about a cock, a hen, and a fox that exhibit human characteristics. The hen, Pertelote, is intended to represent the practical woman who combats the theories of her husband, Chanticleer. This is the most humorous of the tales.

(4) The Physician's tale of Virginius and Virginia. (Macaulay has treated the same story in his "Lays of Ancient Rome.")

(5) The Clerk's tale about patient Griseida.

(6) The Second Nun's tale of St. Cecilia and her martyrdom.

Chaucer did not tell us which one of the story tellers was awarded the supper upon their return to the Tabard Inn, but the "Knight's Tale" has usually been given the highest place by modern critics.[1]

Some Other Groups of Metrical Tales.—In each of the following groups of tales, the author had a plan not unlike that of Chaucer, since he bound a large number of single tales into a larger unit:—

(1) "The Tales of a Wayside Inn," by Henry W. Longfellow.

(2) "The Tent on the Beach," by J. G. Whittier.

(3) "Tales of the Mermaid Tavern," by Alfred Noyes.

---

[1] Chaucer's life may be studied at this point if it is desired. Material may be found in any good history of English literature. It will be interesting to note the various experiences which brought him in contact with people, thus fitting him for the particular work that he did.

[2] See Miller's *English Literature*, pages 68–76, for good outlines of the various tales told by Canterbury pilgrims.

SUGGESTIONS TO STUDENTS

An interesting exercise might be based on the different prologues, interludes, and finales of these three modern groups of metrical tales. The following things are suggested:

1. Try to find the means used by each author to bind the stories together into a complete whole. How does Alfred Noyes's plan differ from that of Longfellow, or Whittier? Which one is the easiest to follow? The most interesting? 2. How do these plans compare with Chaucer's as regards naturalness? What particular information is given in each case? Who are the story-tellers in each? Who are the listeners? Are these persons real or fictitious? Does the author himself seem to be one of the party? 3. In which one of the groups do the people represent the most varied interests or occupations in life? How do they compare, in this particular, with Chaucer's group of pilgrims? 4. Which of the story-tellers mentioned have you ever heard of outside of these particular poems? Which one did you think had the most interesting personality?

5. Write a report on a tale chosen from each of these groups. Which author do you think told the most interesting tale, judging from those you read? Give in a sentence or two the main point of each story.

Examples of Single Metrical Tales.—Because we have, thus far, been dealing with *groups* of tales, the student must not lose sight of the fact that each tale is a unit in itself and could be cut loose from the others with which it is bound. The two tales which follow are single tales:

THE HIGHWAYMAN [1]

Alfred Noyes (1906)

Part One

I

The wind was a torrent of darkness among the gusty trees,
The moon was a ghostly galleon tossed upon cloudy seas,
The road was a ribbon of moonlight over the purple moor,
And the highwayman came riding—
    Riding—riding—   5
The highwayman came riding, up to the old inn door.

[1] From *Poems* by Alfred Noyes. Used here by special arrangement with the Frederick A. Stokes Company.

II

He 'd a French cocked hat on his forehead, a bunch of lace at his chin,
A coat of the claret velvet, and breeches of brown doeskin;
They fitted with never a wrinkle: his boots were up to the thigh!
And he rode with a jeweled twinkle,   10
    His pistol butts a-twinkle,
His rapier hilt a-twinkle, under the jeweled sky.

III

Over the cobbles he clattered and clashed in the dark innyard,
And he tapped with his whip on the shutters, but all was locked and barred;
He whistled a tune to the window, and who should be waiting there   15
But the landlord's blackeyed daughter,
    Bess, the landlord's daughter,
Plaiting a dark red love-knot into her long black hair.

IV

And dark in the dark old innyard a stable-wicket creaked
Where Tim the ostler listened; his face was white and peaked;   20
His eyes were hollows of madness, his hair like moldy hay,
But he loved the landlord's daughter,
    The landlord's red-lipped daughter;
Dumb as a dog he listened, and he heard the robber say—

V

"One kiss, my bonny sweetheart, I 'm after a prize tonight,   25
But I shall be back with the yellow gold before the morning light;
Yet, if they press me sharply, and harry me through the day,
Then look for me by moonlight,
    Watch for me by moonlight,
I 'll come to thee by moonlight, though hell should bar the way."   30

VI

He rose upright in the stirrups; he scarce could reach her hand.
But she loosened her hair i' the casement! His face burned like a brand
As the black cascade of perfume came tumbling over his breast;
And he kissed its waves in the moonlight,
    (Oh, sweet black waves in the moonlight!)   35
Then he tugged at his rein in the moonlight and galloped away to the west.

Part Two

I

He did not come in the dawning; he did not come at noon;
And out o' the tawny sunset, before the rise o' the moon,
When the road was a gypsy's ribbon, looping the purple moor,
A redcoat troop came marching—   40
    Marching—marching—
King George's men came marching, up to the old inn door.

II

They said no word to the landlord, they drank his ale instead,
But they gagged his daughter and bound her to the foot of her narrow bed;
Two of them knelt at her casement, with muskets at their side!   45
There was death at every window;
    And hell at one dark window;
For Bess could see, through her casement, the road that *he* would ride.

III

They had tied her up to attention, with many a sniggering jest;
They had bound a musket beside her, with the barrel beneath her breast! 50
"Now keep good watch!" and they kissed her.
She heard the dead man say
Look for me by moonlight;
    Watch for me by moonlight;
I'll come to thee by moonlight, though hell should bar the way!   55

IV

She twisted her hands behind her, but all the knots held good!
She writhed her hands till her fingers were wet with sweat or blood!
They stretched and strained in the darkness, and the hours crawled by
    like years,
Till, now on the stroke of midnight,
    Cold on the stroke of midnight,   60
The tip of one finger touched it! The trigger at least was hers!

V

The tip of one finger touched it; she strove no more for the rest!
Up, she stood up to attention, with the barrel beneath her breast,
She would not risk their hearing; she would not strive again;
For the road lay bare in the moonlight;   65
    Blank and bare in the moonlight;
And the blood of her veins in the moonlight throbbed to her love's refrain.

VI

Tlot-tlot; tlot-tlot! Had they heard it? The horse-hoofs ringing clear;
Tlot-tlot; tlot-tlot, in the distance! Were they deaf that they did not hear?
Down the ribbon of moonlight, over the brow of the hill,   70
The highwayman came riding—
    Riding—riding!
The redcoats looked to their priming! She stood up straight and still.

VII

Tlot-tlot, in the frosty silence! *Tlot-tlot,* in the echoing night!
Nearer he came and nearer! Her face was like a light!   75
Her eyes grew wide for a moment; she drew one last deep breath,
Then her finger moved in the moonlight,
    Her musket shattered the moonlight,
Shattered her breast in the moonlight, and warned him—with her death.

VIII

He turned; he spurred to the Westward; he did not know who stood   80
Bowed, with her head o'er the musket, drenched with her own red blood!
Not till the dawn he heard it, and slowly blanched to hear
How Bess, the landlord's daughter,
    The landlord's black-eyed daughter,
Had watched for her love in the moonlight, and died in the darkness
       there.   85

IX

Back he spurred like a madman, shrieking a curse to the sky,
With the white road smoking behind him, and his rapier brandished high!
Blood-red were his spurs i' the golden noon; wine-red was his velvet coat;
When they shot him down on the highway,
    Down like a dog on the highway,   90
And he lay in his blood on the highway, with the bunch of lace at his throat.

X

And still of a winter's night, they say, when the wind is in the trees,
When the moon is a ghostly galleon tossed upon cloudy seas,
When the road is a ribbon of moonlight over the purple moor,
A highwayman comes riding—   95
    Riding—riding—
A highwayman comes riding, up to the old inn door.

XI

Over the cobbles he clatters and clangs in the dark innyard;
And he taps with his whip on the shutters, but all is locked and barred;
He whistles a tune to the window, and who should be waiting there   100
But the landlord's black-eyed daughter,
     Bess, the landlord's daughter,
Plaiting a dark red love-knot into her long black hair.

THE BROTHERS [1]

From "Fires," by Wilfrid Wilson Gibson, 1912

All morning they had quarrelled, as they worked,
A little off their fellows, in the pit;
Dick growled at Robert; Robert said Dick shirked;
And when the roof dropt more than they had reckoned,
Began to crack and split,   5
Though both rushed like a shot to set
The pit-props in their places,
Each said the other was to blame,
When, all secure, with flushed and grimy faces,
They faced each other for a second.   10
All morning they had quarrelled: yet,
Neither had breathed her name.

Again they turned to work:
And in the dusty murk
Of that black gallery   15
Which ran out three miles underneath the sea,
There was no sound at all,
Save whispering creak of roof and wall,
The crack of coal, and tap of pick,
And now and then a rattling fall: 20
While Robert worked on steadily, but Dick
In fits and starts, with teeth clenched tight,
And dark eyes flashing in his lamp's dull light.
And when he paused, nigh spent, to wipe the sweat
From off his dripping brow: and Robert turned   25
To fling some idle gibe at him, the spark
Of anger, smouldering in him, flared and burned—
Though all his body quivered, wringing wet—
Till that black hole
To him blazed red,   30

[1] Used by permission of, and special arrangement with, the Macmillan Company.

As if the very coal
Had kindled underfoot and overhead:
Then, gripping tight his pick,
He rushed upon his brother:
But Robert, turning quick,   35
Leapt up, and now they faced each other.

They faced each other; Dick with arm up-raised,
In act to strike, and murder in his eyes . . .
When, suddenly, with noise of thunder,
The earth shook round them, rumbling o'er and under;   40
And Dick saw Robert, lying at his feet:
As, close behind, the gallery crashed in:
And almost at his heel, earth gaped asunder.
By black disaster dazed,
His wrath died; and he dropped the pick;   45
And staggered, dizzily and terror-sick.
But, when the dust and din
Had settled to a stillness, dread as death,
And he once more could draw his breath,
He gave a little joyful shout   50
To find the lamps had not gone out.

And on his knees he fell
Beside his brother, buried in black dust:
And, full of tense misgiving,
He lifted him, and thrust   55
A knee beneath his head; and cleared
The dust from mouth and nose: but could not tell
Awhile if he were dead or living.
Too fearful to know what he feared,
He fumbled at the open shirt   60
And felt till he could feel the heart,—
Still beating with a feeble beat:
And then he saw the closed lids part,
And saw the nostrils quiver;
And knew his brother lived, though sorely hurt.   65

Again he staggered to his feet,
And fetched his water-can, and wet
The ashy lips, and bathed the brow,
Until his brother sat up with a shiver,
And gazed before him with a senseless stare   70
And dull eyes strangely set.
Too well Dick knew that now

They must not linger there,
Cut off from all their mates, to be o'ertaken
In less than no time by the deadly damp,   75
So, picking up his lamp,
He made his brother rise:
Then took him by the arm,
And shook him, till he'd shaken
An inkling of the danger and alarm   80
Into those dull, still eyes:
Then dragged him, and half-carried him in haste,
To reach the airway, where 't would still be sweet
When all the gallery was foul with gas:
But, soon as they had reached it, they were faced   85
By a big fall of roof they could not pass:
And found themselves cut off from all retreat,
On every hand, by that black shining wall;
With naught to do but sit and wait
Till rescue came, if rescue came at all,   90
And did not come too late.

And in the fresher airway, light came back
To Robert's eyes, although he never spoke:
And not a sound the deathly quiet broke,
As they sat staring at that wall of black—   95
As, in the glimmer of the dusky lamp,
They sat and wondered, wondered if the damp—
The stealthy after-damp that creeping, creeping,
Takes strong lads by the throat, and drops them sleeping,
To wake no more for any woman's weeping—   100
Would steal upon them, ere the rescue came . . .
And if the rescuers would find them sitting,
Would find them' sitting cold. . . .
Then, as they sat and wondered, like a flame
One thought burned up both hearts: 105
Still neither breathed her name.

And now their thoughts dropped back into the pit,
And through the league-long gallery went flitting
With speed no fall could ɴɔſɑ:
They wondered how their mates had fared: 110
If they 'd been struck stone-dead,
Or if they shared
Like fate with them, or reached the shaft,
Unhurt, and only scared,
Before disaster overtook them: 115

And then, although their courage ne'er forsook them,
They wondered once again if they must sit
Awaiting death . . . but knowing well
That even for a while to dwell
On such like thoughts will drive a strong man daft: 120

They shook themselves until their thoughts ran free
Along the drift, and clambered in the cage,
And in a trice were shooting up the shaft:
But when their thoughts had come to the pit-head,
And found the fearful people gathered there,   125
Beneath the noonday sun,
Bright-eyed with terror, blinded by despair,
Dick rose, and with his chalk wrote on the wall
This message for their folk:
"We can't get any further, 12, noonday"—   130
And signed both names; and, when he'd done,
Though neither of them spoke,
They both seemed easier in a way.
Now that they'd left a word,
Though nothing but a scrawl.   135

And silent still they sat,
And never stirred:
And Dick's thoughts dwelt on this and that:
How, far above their heads, upon the sea
The sun was shining merrily,   140
And in its golden glancing
The windy waves were dancing:
And how he'd slipt that morning on his way:
And how on Friday, when he drew his pay,
He'd buy a blanket for his whippet,[1] Nell: 145
He felt dead certain she would win the race,
On Saturday . . . though you could never tell,
There were such odds against her . . . but his face
Lit up as though, even now, he saw her run,
A little slip of lightning, in the sun: 150
While Robert's thoughts were ever on the match
His team was booked to play on Saturday;
He placed the field, and settled who should play
The centre-forward; for he had a doubt
Will Bum was scarcely up to form although . . .   155

[1] A racing dog (see dictionary).

Just then, the lamp went slowly out.
Still neither stirred,
Nor spoke a word;
Though either's breath came quickly, with a catch,
And now again one thought   160
Set both their hearts afire
In one fierce flame
Of quick desire:
Though neither breathed her name.

Then Dick stretched out his hand; and caught   165
His brother's arm; and whispered in his ear:
"Bob, lad, there 's naught to fear . . .
And, when we 're out, lad, you and she shall wed."

Bob gripped Dick's hand; and then no more was said,
As, slowly, all about them rose   170
The deadly after-damp; but close
They sat together, hand in hand.
Then their minds wandered; and Dick seemed to stand
And shout till he was hoarse
To speed his winning whippet[1] down the course . . .   175
And Robert, with the ball
Secure within his oxter,[2] charged ahead
Straight for the goal, and none could hold,
Though many tried a fall.
Then, dreaming they were lucky boys in bed,   180
Once more, and lying snugly by each other:
Dick, with his arms clasped tight about his brother,
Whispered with failing breath
Into the ear of death:
"Come, Robert, cuddle closer, lad, it 's cold." | 185

[1] A racing dog (see dictionary).   [2] Under the arm.

SOME SINGLE METRICAL TALES FOR OPTIONAL READING

Note.—In the following list of single metrical tales, you will find many
old friends. You should, however, read several of these tales that you
have not read before. Although they are very similar, what real distinction
can you see between a metrical tale and an imitation ballad? Write a
report similar to the one you made for the tales which you chose from
the three groups.

Fourteenth Century

"The Knight's Tale" from "Canterbury Tales"....Chaucer

Eighteenth Century

"Tam o' Shanter"..............................Burns

Nineteenth Century

"Michael" ....Wordsworth
"Mazeppa" ....Byron
"The Prisoner of Chillon"......................Byron
"The Glove and the Lion"......................Leigh Hunt
"The Eve of St. Agnes"........................Keats
"Enoch Arden" ....Tennyson
"The Victim" ....Tennyson
"Dora" ....Tennyson
"The Gardener's Daughter"....................Tennyson
"The Defence of Lucknow"....................Tennyson
"The Lord of Burleigh"......................Tennyson
"Rizpah" ....Tennyson
"Lady Clare" ....Tennyson
"The May Queen" ....Tennyson
"In the Children's Hospital"...................Tennyson
"An Incident of the French Camp".............Browning
"The Pied Piper of Hamelin"..................Browning
"Evangeline" ....Longfellow
Any of the tales from "Tales of a Wayside
    Inn" ....Longfellow
"The Courtship of Miles Standish"............Longfellow
"The Birds of Killingworth"..................Longfellow
"Sella" ....Bryant
"How the Old Horse Won the Bet".............Holmes
"Grandmother's Story of Bunker Hill Battle"... Holmes
"The One Hoss Shay" ....Holmes
Any of the tales from "Tent on the Beach"... Whittier
"Barbara Frietchie"..........................Whittier
"Mabel Martin" ....Whittier
"The Vision of Sir Launfal"...................Lowell
"Fitz Adam's Story"..........................Lowell
"Sheridan's Ride"...........................Thos. B. Read
"The Power of Prayer: Or the First Steam-
    boat up the Alabama"....................Sidney Lanier
"How He Saved St. Michael's".................Mrs. Stansbury
"The Raven" ....Poe.
"The Fool's Prayer"..........................Edward Rowland Sill
"Darius Green and His Flying Machine".......Trowbridge

Twentieth Century

"Dauber," a sea-tale (given extra credit because long).............................Masefield
"Spanish Waters"............................Masefield
"The Vain King"...............................Henry Van Dyke
"The Legend of Service".........................Henry Van Dyke
"The Lighthouse," from "Fires".................Wilfrid W. Gibson
"The Blind Rower," from "Fires"..............Wilfrid W. Gibson
"The Money," from "Fires"....................Wilfrid W. Gibson
"The Snow," from "Fires".....................Wilfrid W. Gibson
"Between the Lines," from "Fires".............Wilfrid W. Gibson
Any of the tales from "Tales of the Mermaid Tavern" ....Alfred Noyes
"Vive La France!"............................Charlotte H. Crawford
Any Metrical Tale in "One Hundred Narrative Poems" ....Ed. by George E. Teter

REVIEW

1. Before turning to the very different kind of poetry given in Part II of this book, you should take a backward look at the four types of narrative poetry discussed in Part I. Why are all these classed as *narrative* poetry? 2. Do you think you will be able to *distinguish* a metrical tale from a great epic, a metrical romance, and a ballad? What is the bond of relationship which classes them together? 3. Which one of these types were you most interested in? Why? 4. Which is the greatest of these types? 5. How did the central character of a tale differ, for the most part, from that of a metrical romance? A great epic?

PART II—LYRIC POETRY

PART TWO—LYRIC POETRY

Characteristics of Lyric Poetry.—Lyric poetry is the utterance of the human heart in poetic form. It usually expresses the author's own experiences, moods, reflections, and emotions in musical language. The prose form most nearly like a lyric poem is the essay. In both we are conscious of the standpoint of the author himself and are looking at life through his eyes. In dramatic and narrative poetry, on the other hand, we forget all about the author and are interested more in the action, story, or thing portrayed than in anything else. Sometimes we find both narrative and lyric elements in the same poem, as for instance in "The Cotter's Saturday Night." They are usually separated, however. In the lyric the author seems to be singing to himself. We hear notes of love, hope, grief, despair, joy, patriotism, aspiration, devotion, fear, lamentation, exultation,—indeed all the feelings of the soul. As some one has expressed it, "Though we hear an oration, we seem to *overhear* a lyric poem." The lyric derives its name from the musical instrument, the lyre, and was primarily intended to be sung. Not all lyrics are singable, although they are all melodious. A great lyric must be sincere, spontaneous, and express strong emotion. It is usually very short, although not necessarily so. The *Psalms* of King David are the greatest lyrics in the literature of the world. Those beginning "The Lord is my Shepherd," [1] and "I will lift up mine eyes unto the hills," [2] are especially fine.

Classes of Lyric Poetry.—Lyric poetry is divided into five types: the ode, the sonnet, the elegy, the song—sacred and secular, and the simple lyric.

[1] Psalm XXIII. [2] Psalm CXXI.

CHAPTER I

THE ODE

Characteristics of the Ode.—The ode is the most exalted form of lyric poetry. The theme is always a noble one and the emotion is high and of great dignity. It may express enthusiasm, lofty praise of some person or thing, deep reflection, or restrained feeling. The ode has been used especially by the poets laureate of England in commemorating great public events. Because of its majestic qualities, the ode is difficult to write and is thus less frequently found than the other lyric types. In structure the ode is usually very irregular, although there are exceptions. The verse length often varies from one to eight feet, and the stanzas are long or short according to the nature of the thought expressed.

Some Examples of the Ode.—Although the ode is an old form of poetry, dating back to the time of Pindar in ancient Greece, it was produced in England in greater numbers during the nineteenth century than in any other period. Probably the finest ode in our language is Milton's "On the Morning of Christ's Nativity," written in 1629. Next to this, Wordsworth's "Intimations of Immortality from Recollections of Early Childhood" (1807) is usually given the highest place. The other great writers of this lyric form are Dryden, Collins, Gray, Shelley, and Keats.

ALEXANDER'S FEAST: OR THE POWER OF MUSIC

A Song in Honor of St. Cecilia's Day

John Dryden, 1697

1

'Twas at the royal feast for Persia won
 By Philip's warlike son.
 Aloft in awful state
 The godlike hero sate
  On his imperial throne;   5
His valiant peers were placed around,
Their brows with roses and with myrtles bound;

(So should desert in arms be crown'd.)
The lovely Thais, by his side,
Sate like a blooming Eastern bride,   10
In flow'r of youth and beauty's pride.
    Happy, happy, happy pair!
        None but the brave,
        None but the brave,
None but the brave deserves the fair.   15

2

Timotheus, plac'd on high
    Amid the tuneful quire,
With flying fingers touch'd the lyre:
    The trembling notes ascend the sky,
        And heav'nly joys inspire.   20
    The song began from Jove,
    Who left his blissful seats above,
        (Such is the pow'r of mighty love.)
    A dragon's fiery form bely'd the god;
    Sublime on radiant spires he rode.   25

.   .   .   .

The listening crowd admire the lofty sound,
A present deity, they shout around;
A present deity, the vaulted roofs rebound.
    With ravished ears
    The monarch hears,   30
    Assumes the god,
    Affects to nod,
And seems to shake the spheres.

3

The praise of Bacchus then the sweet musician sung,
    Of Bacchus ever fair, and ever young: 35
The jolly god in triumph comes;
Sound the trumpets, beat the drums;
    Flushed with a purple grace
    He shows his honest face;
Now give the hautboys breath; he comes, he comes.   40
    Bacchus, ever fair and young,
        Drinking joys did first ordain;
        Bacchus' blessings are a treasure.
        Drinking is the soldier's pleasure.
            Rich the treasure,   45
            Sweet the pleasure,
        Sweet is pleasure after pain.

4

Sooth'd with the sound the king grew vain;
    Fought all his battles o'er again;
And thrice he routed all his foes, and thrice he slew the slain.   50
    The master saw the madness rise,
    His glowing cheeks, his ardent eyes:
And while he heaven and earth defy'd,
Changed his hand, and check'd his pride.
        He chose a mournful Muse,   55
        Soft pity to infuse;
He sung Darius great and good,
    By too severe a fate
Fallen, fallen, fallen, fallen,
    Fallen from his high estate,   60
And welt'ring in his blood,
Deserted at his utmost need
By those his former bounty fed;
On the bare earth expos'd he lies,
With not a friend to close his eyes.   65
With downcast looks the joyless victor sate,
    Revolving in his alter'd soul
        The various turns of chance below:
And, now and then, a sigh he stole,
        And tears began to flow.   70

5

    The mighty master smil'd to see
    That love was in the next degree:
    'Twas but a kindred sound to move,
    For pity melts the mind to love.
        Softly sweet, in Lydian measures,   75
        Soon he soothed his soul to pleasures.
War, he sung, is toil and trouble;
Honor but an empty bubble;
    Never ending, still beginning,
Fighting still, and still destroying;   80
    If the world be worth thy winning,
Think, O think it worth enjoying:
Lovely Thais sits beside thee,
Take the good the gods provide thee.
The many rend the skies with loud applause;   85
So Love was crown'd, but Music won the cause.
    The prince, unable to conceal his pain,
        Gaz'd on the fair
        Who caused his care.

And sigh'd and look'd, sigh'd and look'd.   90
Sigh'd and look'd, and sigh'd again.

.   .   .   .

6

Now strike the golden lyre again;
A louder yet, and yet a louder strain.
Break his bonds of sleep asunder,
And rouse him, like a rattling peal of thunder.   95
 Hark, hark, the horrid sound
  Has rais'd up his head,
  As awak'd from the dead,
 And amaz'd he stares around.
Revenge, revenge, Timotheus cries;   100
 See the Furies arise;
  See the snakes that they rear,
  How they hiss in their hair,
 And the sparkles that flash from their eyes!
  Behold a ghastly band,   105
  Each a torch in his hand!
Those are Grecian Ghosts, that in battle were slain,
  And unburied remain
  Inglorious on the plain:
  Give the vengeance due   110
  To the valiant crew.
Behold how they toss their torches on high,
 How they point to the Persian abodes,
And glittering temples of their hostile gods.
The princes applaud with a furious joy;   115
And the king seized a flambeau with zeal to destroy;
  Thais led the way,
  To light him to his prey,
And, like another Helen, fired another Troy.

7

 Thus long ago,   120
Ere heaving bellows learn'd to blow,
 While organs yet were mute,
 Timotheus, to his breathing flute
  And sounding lyre,
Could swell the soul to rage, or kindle soft desire.   125
  At last divine Cecilia came,
  Inventress of the vocal frame;
The sweet enthusiast, from her sacred store,

Enlarged the former narrow bounds,
And added length to solemn sounds, 130
With Nature's mother-wit, and arts unknown before.
Let old Timotheus yield the prize,
Or both divide the crown;
He raised a mortal to the skies;
She drew an angel down. 135

Note.—The author wrote this ode at one sitting in response to a request from a musical society for a poem to be given at the Feast of St. Cecilia. Dryden himself boasted that a finer ode had never been written and never would be.

SUGGESTIONS TO STUDENTS

1. The lofty praise that the poet expresses in this poem is given to music, which has the power to sway the moods and wills of men. In order to get others to share his own feeling, Dryden introduces an historical background and makes his reader feel the power of music by watching its effect upon the great Macedonian, Alexander, who is moved from one mood to another until he is influenced to do the very thing which the musician wanted him to do, but which Alexander had previously determined not to do.

2. In order to fully appreciate this poem, you should know the historical setting. Find out from a good Ancient History why the Athenians (represented in the poem by Timotheus and Thais) should be especially anxious for the destruction of Persepolis. 3. What was the occasion for Alexander's feast? What was he planning to do with the Persian capital he had won? What had become of Darius III, the former owner of the "imperial throne" on which Alexander was sitting? 4. What was Alexander's pet vanity which caused him to visit the oracle of Zeus in the Libyan desert in Egypt just before he took up his march toward Persepolis? How does Timotheus play upon this vanity? 5. Why did the music in stanza 2 have the effect that it did upon Alexander? 6. What was the cause of the death of Darius? 7. What reference to the Furies in stanza 6? For what did they stand in Greek mythology? 8. What was the Greek idea regarding the dead that remained unburied? 9. Explain the last line of stanza 6. 10. How many different moods did Timotheus arouse in Alexander? Name the emotion in each. 11. What is the reason for the abrupt change in stanze 7? 12. For what purpose was the poem written? 13. Look up the story of St. Cecelia and find out (1) for what she was famed, and (2) what is meant by "She drew an angel down." What did Dryden mean by "He raised a mortal to the skies"?

Although there is the atmosphere of a story in this ode, the author's mood and thought are the things especially emphasized.

ODE ON INTIMATIONS OF IMMORTALITY FROM RECOLLECTIONS OF EARLY CHILDHOOD

Wordsworth, 1807

There was a time when meadow, grove, and stream,
The earth, and every common sight
   To me did seem
  Apparell'd in celestial light,
The glory and the freshness of a dream.   5
It is not now as it hath been of yore;—
   Turn wheresoe'er I may,
    By night or day,
The things which I have seen I now can see no more.

   The rainbow comes and goes,   10
   And lovely is the rose;
   The moon doth with delight
  Look round her when the heavens are bare;
   Waters on a starry night
   Are beautiful and fair;   15
  The sunshine is a glorious birth;
  But yet I know, where'er I go,
That there hath passed away a glory from the earth.

Now, while the birds thus sing a joyous song,
  And while the young lambs bound   20
   As to the tabor's sound,
To me alone there came a thought of grief;
A timely utterance gave that thought relief,
  And I again am strong.
The cataracts blow their trumpets from the steep;— 25
No more shall grief of mine the season wrong:
I hear the echoes through the mountains throng,
The winds come to me from the fields of sleep,
   And all the earth is gay;
    Land and sea   30
  Give themselves up to jollity,
   And with the heart of May
  Doth every beast keep holiday;—
    Thou child of joy
Shout round me, let me hear thy shouts, thou happy shepherd-boy! 35

Ye blessèd Creatures, I have heard the call
  Ye to each other make; I see

The heavens laugh with you in your jubilee;
    My heart is at your festival,
    My head hath its coronal,
The fulness of your bliss, I feel—I feel it all.
    Oh evil day! if I were sullen
    While Earth herself is adorning
      This sweet May-morning;
    And the children are culling
      On every side
    In a thousand valleys far and wide,
  Fresh flowers; while the sun shines warm
And the babe leaps up on his mother's arm:—
    I hear, I hear, with joy I hear!
    —But there's a tree, of many, one,
A single field which I have look'd upon,
Both of them speak of something that is gone:
      The pansy at my feet
      Doth the same tale repeat:
Whither is fled the visionary gleam?
Where is it now, the glory and the dream?

Our birth is but a sleep and a forgetting;
The Soul that rises with us, our life's Star,
    Hath had elsewhere its setting
      And cometh from afar;
    Not in entire forgetfulness,
    And not in utter nakedness,
But trailing clouds of glory we do come
      From God, who is our home:
Heaven lies about us in our infancy!
Shades of the prison-house begin to close
      Upon the growing Boy,
But he beholds the light, and whence it flows,
      He sees it in his joy;
The Youth, who daily farther from the east
    Must travel, still is Nature's priest,
      And by the vision splendid
      Is on his way attended;
At length the Man perceives it die away,
And fade into the light of common day.

Earth fills her lap with pleasures of her own;
Yearnings she hath in her own natural kind,
And, even with something of a mother's mind
      And no unworthy aim,
    The homely nurse doth all she can

To make her foster-child, her inmate, Man,
   Forget the glories he hath known,
And that imperial palace whence he came.

Behold the Child among his new-born blisses,
A six years' darling of a pigmy size!
See, where 'mid work of his own hand he lies,   85
Fretted by sallies of his mother's kisses,
With light upon him from his father's eyes!
See, at his feet, some little plan or chart,
Some fragment from his dream of human life,   90
Shaped by himself with newly-learnèd art;
  A wedding or a festival,
  A mourning or a funeral;
  And this hath now his heart,
  And unto this he frames his song: 95
  Then will he fit his tongue
To dialogues of business, love, or strife;
  But it will not be long
  Ere this be thrown aside,
  And with new joy and pride   100
The little actor cons another part;
Filling from time to time his 'humorous stage'
With all the Persons, down to palsied Age,
That life brings with her in her equipage;
  As if his whole vocation   105
  Were endless imitation.

Thou, whose exterior semblance doth belie
  Thy soul's immensity;
Thou best philosopher, who yet dost keep
Thy heritage, thou eye among the blind,   110
That, deaf and silent, read'st the eternal deep,
Haunted for ever by the eternal Mind,—
  Mighty Prophet! Seer blest!
  On whom those truths do rest
Which we are toiling all our lives to find,   115
In darkness lost, the darkness of the grave;
Thou, over whom thy Immortality
Broods like the day, a master o'er a slave,
A Presence which is not to be put by;
Thou little child, yet glorious in the might   120
Of heaven-born freedom on thy being's height,
Why with such earnest pains dost thou provoke
The years to bring the inevitable yoke,

Thus blindly with thy blessedness at strife?
Full soon thy soul shall have her earthly freight,
And custom lie upon thee with a weight
Heavy as frost, and deep almost as life! 125

O joy! that in our embers
Is something that doth live,
That Nature yet remembers 130
What was so fugitive!
The thought of our past years in me doth breed
Perpetual benediction: not indeed
For that which is most worthy to be blest, 135
Delight and liberty, the simple creed
Of Childhood, whether busy or at rest,
With new-fledged hope still fluttering in his breast:—
—Not for these I raise
The song of thanks and praise;
But for those obstinate questionings 140
Of sense and outward things,
Fallings from us, vanishings;
Blank misgivings of a creature
Moving about in worlds not realized, 145
High instincts, before which our mortal nature
Did tremble like a guilty thing surprised:
But for those first affections,
Those shadowy recollections,
Which, be they what they may, 150
Are yet the fountain-light of all our day,
Are yet a master-light of all our seeing;
Uphold us, cherish, and have power to make
Our noisy years seem moments in the being
Of the eternal Silence: truths that wake, 155
To perish never;
Which neither listlessness, nor mad endeavour,
Nor man nor boy
Nor all that is at enmity with joy,
Can utterly abolish or destroy! 160
Hence, in a season of calm weather
Though inland far we be,
Our souls have sight of that immortal sea
Which brought us hither;
Can in a moment travel thither— 165
And see the children sport upon the shore,
And hear the mighty waters rolling evermore.

Then, sing ye birds, sing, sing a joyous song!
      And let the young lambs bound
      As to the tabor's sound!
   We, in thought, will join your throng   170
      Ye that pipe and ye that play,
      Ye that through your hearts to-day
      Feel the gladness of the May!
What though the radiance which was once so bright
Be now for ever taken from my sight,   175
   Though nothing can bring back the hour
Of splendour in the grass, of glory in the flower;
      We will grieve not, rather find
      Strength in what remains behind;
      In the primal sympathy   180
      Which having been must ever be;
      In the soothing thoughts that spring
      Out of human suffering;
      In the faith that looks through death,
In years that bring the philosophic mind.   185

And O, ye Fountains, Meadows, Hills, and Groves,
Forbode not any severing of our loves!
Yet in my heart of hearts I feel your might;
I only have relinquish'd one delight
To live beneath your more habitual sway: 190
I love the brooks which down their channels fret
Even more than when I tripp'd lightly as they;
The innocent brightness of a new-born day
         Is lovely yet;
The clouds that gather round the setting sun
Do take a sober colouring from an eye   195
That hath kept watch o'er man's mortality;
Another race hath been, and other palms are won.
Thanks to the human heart by which we live,
Thanks to its tenderness, its joys, and fears,
To me the meanest flower that blows can give   200
Thoughts that do often lie too deep for tears.

SUGGESTIONS TO STUDENTS

   This ode, "Intimations of Immortality from Recollections of Early Childhood," is a difficult one to understand fully. It grows upon us, yielding more and more of its meaning as we become better acquainted with it. A complete comprehension of the poem will not be reached now, yet there is so much in it that the average high school senior will enjoy that it will repay his study. The title, expanded, is as follows:

Hints, or indirect suggestions that would tend to prove that the soul lives forever, obtained from recollections of the poet's own early childhood and his observations of other children. First, read the poem as a whole; then, with the following explanation in mind, study it carefully. Someone has said of Wordsworth that "he stirs our memories deeply so that in reading him we live once more in the vague, beautiful wonderland of our own childhood." See if this is true here.

In the opening stanzas of the poem, Wordsworth gives expression to the feeling that has taken possession of him that life, as it appeared to him in childhood, has, in some way, lost its light and freshness and splendor. Although he still sees beauty in Nature and the things about him, "there has passed away a glory from the earth." He begins to study this problem that has presented itself, "Why is this true?"

As he ponders over the question, he sees the happiness of young life around him, and decides that

> To me alone there came a thought of grief.

He thinks that this is only his own mood and would not be true of other people, and so he tries to shake off the feeling and to enter into the spirit and joy of the "blessed creatures" around him. So long as he allows himself only a general view of Nature in her varied forms and the happy young life everywhere, he succeeds in persuading himself that it was really his own mood that had brought the thought of grief. Then his eye rests on some particular thing—a tree, a single field, a pansy, and, as he studies the effect of each upon himself, he discovers that he has a different feeling regarding each of them than he used to have; that he has not been mistaken, and that a glory has really passed away from life. He, at this time, is not able to give an explanation for this change, and, as a result, he leaves the poem at this point and does not take it up again until more than two years later.

In stanza 5 he resumes the subject and gives a solution for the problem. He believes that if the soul has an existence after death, it must have had an existence before its little life on this earth, and that, when a child is born, its soul comes straight from that beautiful world,

> But trailing clouds of glory we do come
> From God, who is our home.

Thus in his babyhood he is so near the glory-world that its light and splendor are all around him. As time goes on and the baby grows into boyhood, and then into youth, the world begins to get hold of him, and he loses, little by little, the glories he has known until,

> At length the Man perceives it die away,
> And fade into the light of common day.

In stanzas 6–8 the author sets forth the ways by which Earth wins her foster-child to herself, so that he will forget "that imperial palace whence he came." The things that in manhood and womanhood will be the serious business of life, the child uses as play and eagerly anticipates those things that later will lie upon him with a weight

Heavy as frost, and deep almost as life!

Thus he gradually gets farther and farther from the glory-world and more and more under the sway of Earth and her customs.

But even though the glamour and freshness of life pass away as we grow older, yet we can still remember "what was so fugitive" and can appreciate and feel the joyousness of happy childhood because we have known and experienced it ourselves. Because of this fact, and also the knowledge that, as we get nearer the end of life, we become aware of newer and greater beauties to be found than we had known in the past, we are made to understand that "our noisy years" of life are only like moments in the greater life of the soul, which lived before our earthly existence, and will go on living after our earthly existence.

Thus these recollections of early childhood are hints, suggestions, links in the chain of evidence, which would tend to prove the deathlessness of the soul.

1. Be sure to master the word "immortality" (im+mortal+ity) so that you will never confuse it with a word of a similar sound. 2. Prove that this poem is an ode. 3. Are any memories of your own childhood called to mind by lines 84–106? What are they?

ODE TO THE WEST WIND

Shelley, 1819

I

O Wild West Wind, thou breath of Autumn's being,
Thou, from whose unseen presence the leaves dead
Are driven, like ghosts from an enchanter fleeing,
Yellow, and black, and pale, and hectic red,
Pestilence-stricken multitudes: O thou   5
Who chariotest to their dark wintry bed
The wingèd seeds, where they lie cold and low,
Each like a corpse within its grave, until
Thine azure sister of the Spring shall blow
Her clarion o'er the dreaming earth, and fill   10
(Driving sweet buds like flocks to feed in air)
With living hues and odours plain and hill:
Wild Spirit, which art moving everywhere,
Destroyer and preserver; hear, oh, hear!

II

Thou on whose stream, 'mid the steep sky's commotion, 15
Loose clouds like earth's decaying leaves are shed,
Shook from the tangled boughs of Heaven and Ocean,
Angels of rain and lightning: there are spread
On the blue surface of thine airy surge,
Like the bright hair uplifted from the head 20
Of some fierce Mænad, even from the dim verge
Of the horizon to the zenith's height,
The locks of the approaching storm. Thou dirge
Of the dying year, to which this closing night
Will be the dome of a vast sepulchre, 25
Vaulted with all thy congregated might
Of vapours, from whose solid atmosphere
Black rain, and fire, and hail will burst: oh, hear!

III

Thou who didst waken from his summer dreams
The blue Mediterranean, where he lay, 30
Lulled by the coil of his crystalline streams,
Beside a pumice isle in Baiæ's bay,
And saw in sleep old palaces and towers
Quivering within the wave's intenser day,
All overgrown with azure moss, and flowers 35
So sweet the sense faints picturing them! Thou
For whose path the Atlantic's level powers
Cleave themselves into chasms, while far below
The sea-blooms and the oozy woods, which wear
The sapless foliage of the ocean, know 40
Thy voice, and suddenly grow gray with fear,
And tremble and despoil themselves: oh, hear!

IV

If I were a dead leaf thou mightest bear;
If I were a swift cloud to fly with thee;
A wave to pant beneath thy power, and share 45
The impulse of thy strength, only less free
Than thou, O uncontrollable! If even
I were as in my boyhood, and could be
The comrade of thy wanderings over heaven,
As then, when to outstrip thy skyey speed 50
Scarce seemed a vision; I would ne'er have striven
As thus with thee in prayer in my sore need.
Oh, lift me as a wave, a leaf, a cloud!

I fall upon the thorns of life! I bleed!
A heavy weight of hours has chained and bowed   55
One too like thee: tameless, and swift, and proud.

V

Make me thy lyre, even as the forest is:
What if my leaves are falling like its own!
The tumult of thy mighty harmonies
Will take from both a deep autumnal tone,   60
Sweet though in sadness. Be thou, Spirit fierce,
My spirit! Be thou me, impetuous one!
Drive my dead thoughts over the universe
Like withered leaves to quicken a new birth!
And, by the incantation of this verse,   65
Scatter, as from an unextinguished hearth,
Ashes and sparks, my words among mankind!
Be through my lips to unawakened earth
The trumpet of a prophecy! O wind,
If Winter comes, can Spring be far behind?   70

SUGGESTIONS TO STUDENTS

The odes are usually much harder to understand than other lyrical poems because of the lofty thoughts set forth. It is therefore necessary to study them in greater detail to get their full meaning. We should especially try to feel the author's emotions. Has Shelley made you feel his mood in this poem? How does the West Wind, in an unusual degree, typify Shelley's spirit?

Stanza I. How is the West Wind both a destroyer and a preserver? What pictures are called up by lines 3–5; 5–8? What comparison is made between the wind, "the breath of Autumn," and its "azure sister of the Spring" as regards their power?

Stanza II. To what does the poet liken the wind in this stanza? To what does he liken the clouds in lines 2–3; 6–9? What was a Mænad? What is likened to it? For what is the *sepulchre* in line 11 being prepared?

Stanza III. How did the wind "waken the blue Mediterranean" "from his summer dreams"? What were those dreams, lines 5–8? Can you catch the author's thought here? Do you see the quivering reflections before the placid sea is aroused? How do the "sea-blooms" of the Atlantic "know thy voice"?

Stanza IV. Upon what was the wind represented as exerting its strength in Stanza I? Stanza II? Stanza III? How are these three ideas brought together in Stanza IV? What glimpses of Shelley's personality do you find here?

Stanza V. What is Shelley's passionate desire set forth in this stanza?

How is the thought of lines 7–8 connected with what he said in Stanza I? Of what value are the dead leaves? What is the poet's feeling expressed in the last line?

Can you prove that this is an ode? Did you enjoy it?

LINCOLN, THE MAN OF THE PEOPLE [1]

Edwin Markham, 1919

When the Norn Mother saw the Whirlwind Hour
Greatening and darkening as it hurried on,
She left the Heaven of Heroes and came down
To make a man to meet the mortal need.
She took the tried clay of the common road—   5
Clay warm yet with the genial heat of Earth,
Dashed through it all a strain of prophecy;
Tempered the heap with thrill of human tears;
Then mixed a laughter with the serious stuff.
Into the shape she breathed a flame to light   10
That tender, tragic, ever-changing face;
And laid on him a sense of the Mystic Powers,
Moving—all hushed—behind the mortal veil.
Here was a man to hold against the world,   15
A man to match the mountains and the sea.

The color of the ground was in him, the red earth;
The smack and tang of elemental things:
The rectitude and patience of the cliff;
The good-will of the rain that loves all leaves;
The friendly welcome of the wayside well;   20
The courage of the bird that dares the sea;
The gladness of the wind that shakes the corn;
The pity of the snow that hides all scars;
The secrecy of streams that make their way
Under the mountain to the rifted rock;   25
The tolerance and equity of light
That gives as freely to the shrinking flower
As to the great oak flaring to the wind—
To the grave's low hill as to the Matterhorn
That shoulders out the sky. Sprung from the West,   30
He drank the valorous youth of a new world.
The strength of virgin forests braced his mind,
The hush of spacious prairies stilled his soul.
His words were oaks in acorns; and his thoughts
Were roots that firmly gripped the granite truth.   35

[1] Copyright by Edwin Markham, 1919. Used by permission of the author.

Up from log cabin to the Capitol,
One fire was on his spirit, one resolve—
To send the keen ax to the root of wrong,
Clearing a free way for the feet of God,
The eyes of conscience testing every stroke,　　　　40
To make his deed the measure of a man.
He built the rail-pile as he built the State,
Pouring his splendid strength through every blow:
The grip that swung the ax in Illinois
Was on the pen that set a people free.　　　　45

So came the Captain with the mighty heart;
And when the judgment thunders split the house,
Wrenching the rafters from their ancient rest,
He held the ridgepole up, and spiked again
The rafters of the Home. He held his place—　　　　50
Held the long purpose like a growing tree—
Held on through blame and faltered not at praise.
And when he fell in whirlwind, he went down
As when a lordly cedar, green with boughs,
Goes down with a great shout upon the hills,　　　　55
And leaves a lonesome place against the sky.

SUGGESTIONS TO STUDENTS

1. What is meant by the "Norn Mother"? (See dictionary). 2. What is meant by "the Whirlwind Hour"? 3. Sum up the characteristics of Lincoln set forth. 4. Explain stanza 4. What is the "house"? 5. How did Lincoln "spike again the rafters of the Home"? 6. Memorize at least stanza 3. (It is all worth learning.) 7. What points of similarity and contrast can you find between this ode and the others you have read?

A SONG OF VICTORY [1]

A Carol at the End of the World War

Edwin Markham, 1919

I

O bugles, ripple and shine,
Calling the heroes home from the battle line.
Praise, praise, praise,
For the last of the desperate days!

[1]From *The Gates of Paradise*, copyright by Edwin Markham. Used by permission of the author.

Shake out the lyrical notes **5**
From the silvery deep of your throats.
Burst into joy-mad carols: tell again
The story and glory of heroic men.

Glad are the love-birds in the leafy tree,
But none so glad as we. **10**
High leap the rock-flung billows to the sky,
But none leaps up so gladly and wildly high
As leap our jubilant hearts.
The Fear that croucht upon the world departs,
And Joy comes back pavilioned by the sun: **15**
Let all the mountains clap their hands and run:
Let all the oceans from their throats of thunder
Shout to the streams and storms and stars the wonder!

II

O bugles, circle on from sky to sky,
Travel the roads of the world with joyous cry. **20**
Blow, bugles, turn dead air to thrilling breath:
Cry, cry eternal victory over death—
Cry into the ear of time the shining word—
Cry solemnly yet elate—
That man is ever greater than his fate, **25**
That—at some touch of God—his soul is stirred
By swift translunar gleams
Which give him power to perish for his dreams.

Praise, praise, praise,
For the new beginning of days! **30**
Praise for the living, honor for the dead—
Praise for the wreathèd and the wreathless head.
Praise and victorious peace
On hearts that beat and on the hearts that cease—
Peace on the mortal and the immortal way— **35**
Peace on the heroes vanisht from our day,
Called back from out these bounds of fleeting breath
To join the old democracy of death.

III

Sing and be glad, O nations, in these hours:
Blow clarions from all towers! **40**
Let bright horns revel and the joy-bells rave;
Yet there are lips whose smile is ever vain
And wild wet eyes behind the window pane,

For whom the whole world dwindles to one grave,
A lone grave at the mercy of the rain.   45
The victor's laurel wears a wintry leaf:
Sing softly, then, as tho the mouth of Grief,
Remembering all the agony and wrong,
Should stir with mighty song.
Not all the glad averment of the guns,   50
Not all our odes, nor all our orisons,
Can sweeten these intolerable tears,
These silences that fall between the cheers.

And yet our hearts must sing,
Carol and clamor like the tides of Spring.   55
For the great work is ended, and again
The world is safe for men;
The world is safe for high heroic themes;
The world is safe for dreams.

IV

But now above the thunder of the drums—   60
Where, brightening on, the face of Victory comes—
Hark to a mighty sound,
A cry out of the ground:
Let there be no more battles: field and flood
Are weary of battle blood.   65
Even the patient stones
Are weary of shrieking shells and dying groans.
Lay the sad swords asleep:
They have their fearful memories to keep.
And fold the flags; they weary of battle days,   70
Weary of wild flights up the windy ways.
Quiet the restless flags,
Grown strangely old upon the smoking crags.
Look where they startle and leap—
Look where they hollow and heap—   75
Now greatening into glory and now thinned,
Living and dying momently on the wind.
And bugles that have cried on sea and land
The silver blazon of their high command—
Bugles that held long parley with the sky—   80
Bugles that shattered the nights on battle walls,
Lay them to rest in dim memorial halls;
For they are weary of that curdling cry
That tells men how to die.
And cannons worn out with their work of hell—   85

The brief abrupt persuasion of the shell—
Let the shrewd spider lock them, one by one,
With filmy cables glancing in the sun;
And let the bluebird in their iron throats
Build his safe nest and spill his rippling notes.   90
Let there be no more battles, men of earth:
The new age rises singing into birth!

SOME GREAT ODES FOR OPTIONAL READING

1. Read at least four odes outside of class. What in each case is the object of the poet's high praise? 2. Has he made you feel his mood? What kind of a mood was it? 3. Was the verse and stanza structure regular or irregular? 4. Which ode did you like best? Why?

"On the Morning of Christ's Nativity" (One
 of the greatest odes in the language).... Milton
"Ode on St. Cecilia's Day"...................Dryden
"Ode on a Distant Prospect of Eton College".. Gray
"The Bard" ....Gray
"Ode to Spring"...........................Gray
"Ode to Evening"..........................Collins
"The Passions: An Ode to Music"...........Collins
"The American Flag".......................Joseph Rodman Drake
"Ode to Duty"............................Wordsworth
"Apostrophe to the Ocean" (from "Childe Har-
 old's Pilgrimage," Canto IV)............Byron
"Ode: Oh Venice! Venice!"...............Byron
"Ye Mariners of England"..................Campbell
"Battle of the Baltic"......................Campbell
"Ode to Liberty"...........................Shelley
"Ode to a Cloud"...........................Shelley
"Ode to a Skylark".........................Shelley
"Ode to Night".............................Shelley
"Ode to a Nightingale".....................Keats
"Ode on a Grecian Urn".....................Keats
"Ode: Bards of Passion and of Mirth"......Keats
"Ode on the Death of the Duke of Welling-
 ton" ....Tennyson
"What Constitutes a State".................Sir William Jones
"Commemoration Ode".......................Lowell
"The Flood of Years".......................Bryant
"The Antiquity of Freedom"................Bryant
"God of the Open Air".....................Henry Van Dyke
"Victor Hugo".............................Henry Van Dyke
"Summer" ....Alfred Noyes

[1] This is both an ode and an elegy.

CHAPTER II

THE SONNET

Characteristics of the Sonnet.—The sonnet is a lyric poem exactly fourteen lines in length. It produces only one emotional effect, but the lines are arranged in two sets, because two waves of thought are expressed. The first, consisting of eight lines, is called the octave. This gives the main thought or rising emotion. The second set, consisting of six lines, is called the sestet. This gives the falling emotion. There is usually this upward and downward movement in a sonnet. In the octave the emotion, question, problem, hope, desire, or whatever it may be, rises to its climax; and in the sestet it goes down to its conclusion. There is scarcely any variation allowed in the arrangement of the rhymes in the octave. Here there should be but two different rhyming words and these should be arranged *a b b a a b b a.* In the sestet, however, greater liberty is given. There are usually three rhyming words, but they must be different from those used in the octave. Any combination of these rhymes may be made, excepting that the last two lines of a perfect sonnet, according to the original models, do not rhyme. Many writers of sonnets, however, have modified the rhyming plan to suit themselves:[1] The regular meter of the sonnet is iambic pentameter.

Early Sonnets in England.—The sonnet form was first used in Italy, and was introduced into English literature by Sir Thomas Wyatt and the Earl of Surrey in the first part of the sixteenth century. This type, although quite difficult to write because of its exact rules, at once became popular. It was taken up by Shakespeare, Spenser, Sidney, and others of the Elizabethans. Shakespeare liked the sonnet so well that he wrote one hundred and fifty-four of them. In structure his sonnets, however, differ in many particulars from those usually seen, although they show the two waves of feeling.[2]

[1] The student should constantly be reminded that authors are not slaves to custom, and modifications are to be found everywhere, although, in general, a work shows the chief characteristics of the type with which it is classed.

[2] The sonnets of Shakespeare differ so generally from those introduced into England from Italy, that they are commonly recognized as a distinct type of sonnet under the name of Shakespearian Sonnet.

Later Sonnet Writers.—Wordsworth is generally regarded as our greatest sonneteer. He wrote over four hundred of these poems, some of which have never been excelled. Other writers who have been especially successful with this form are Milton, Keats, Elizabeth Barrett Browning, and Dante Rossetti.

Study of the Sonnet.—In each of the following sonnets notice the two waves of thought, and the rhyming-scheme in octave and sestet. See in what particulars the sonnets of Shakespeare differ from the others.

SONNET XXIX

Shakespeare

Paraphrase
Ink

When in disgrace with Fortune and men's eyes
I all alone beweep my outcast state,
And trouble deaf Heaven with my bootless cries,
And look upon my-self, and curse my fate,
Wishing me like to one more rich in hope,   5
Featur'd like him, like him with friends possest,
Desiring this man's art, and that man's scope
With what I most enjoy contented least;
Yet in these thoughts myself almost despising
Happily I think on thee,—and then my state   10
(Like to the lark at break of day arising
From sullen earth) sings hymns at heaven's gate;
    For thy sweet love rememb'red, such wealth brings,
    That then I scorn to change my state with Kings.

SONNET XXX

Shakespeare

When to the sessions of sweet silent thought
I summon up remembrance of things past,
I sigh the lack of many a thing I sought,
And with old woes now wail my dear time's waste;
Then can I drown an eye unus'd to flow,   5
For precious friends hid in death's dateless night,
And weep afresh love's long-since cancel'd woe,
And moan the expense of many a vanisht sight.
Then can I grieve at grievances foregone,
And heavily from woe to woe tell o'er   10
The sad account of fore-bemoanèd moan,
Which I now pay as if not paid before.
    But if the while I think on thee, dear friend,
    All losses are restored, and sorrows end.

MILTON'S SONNET ON HIS BLINDNESS

When I consider how my light is spent
Ere half my days, in this dark world and wide,
And that one talent, which is death to hide,
Lodged with me useless, though my soul more bent
To serve therewith my Maker, and present   5
My true account, lest he, returning, chide;
Doth God exact day labor, light denied?
I fondly ask. But Patience, to prevent
That murmur, soon replies, God doth not need,
Either man's work or his own gifts. Who best   10
Bear his mild yoke, they serve him best. His state
Is kingly; thousands at his bidding speed,
And post o'er land and ocean without rest;
They also serve who only stand and wait.

COMPOSED UPON WESTMINSTER BRIDGE, 1802

Wordsworth

Earth has not anything to show more fair:
Dull would he be of soul who could pass by
A sight so touching in its majesty:
This City now doth like a garment wear
The beauty of the morning; silent, bare,   5
Ships, towers, domes, theatres and temples lie
Open unto the fields, and to the sky;
All bright and glittering in the smokeless air.
Never did sun more beautifully steep
In his first splendour valley, rock, or hill;   10
Ne'er saw I, never felt, a calm so deep!
The river glideth at his own sweet will;
Dear God! the very houses seem asleep
And all that mighty heart is lying still!

LONDON, 1802 (TO MILTON)

Wordsworth

Milton! thou should'st be living at this hour:
England hath need of thee: she is a fen
Of stagnant waters: altar, sword, and pen,
Fireside, the heroic wealth of hall and bower,
Have forfeited their ancient English dower   5

Of inward happiness. We are selfish men;
Oh! raise us up, return to us again;
And give us manners, virtue, freedom, power.
Thy soul was like a Star, and dwelt apart:
Thou hadst a voice whose sound was like the sea:　10
Pure as the naked heavens, majestic, free,
So didst thou travel on life's common way,
In cheerful godliness; and yet thy heart
The lowliest duties on herself did lay.

ON FIRST LOOKING INTO CHAPMAN'S HOMER

Keats

Much have I travell'd in the realms of gold,
And many goodly states and kingdoms seen:
Round many western islands have I been
Which bards in fealty to Apollo hold.
Oft of one wide expanse had I been told　5
That deep-brow'd Homer ruled as his demesne:
Yet did I never breathe its pure serene
Till I heard Chapman speak out loud and bold:
Then felt I like some watcher of the skies
When a new planet swims into his ken,　10
Or like stout Cortez [1] when with eagle eyes
He stared at the Pacific—and all his men
Looked at each other with a wild surmise—
Silent, upon the peak in Darien.

SONNET XLIII

From "Sonnets from the Portuguese"

Elizabeth Barrett Browning

How do I love thee? Let me count the ways.
I love thee to the depth and breadth and height
My soul can reach, when feeling out of sight
For the ends of Being and ideal Grace.
I love thee to the level of every day's　5
Most quiet need, by sun and candlelight.
I love thee freely, as men strive for Right;
I love thee purely, as they turn from Praise;
I love thee with the passion put to use
In my old griefs, and with my childhood's faith;　10

[1] Balboa, not Cortez, discovered the Pacific Ocean.

I love thee with a love I seemed to lose
With my lost saints,—I love thee with the breath,
Smiles, tears, of all my life,—and, if God choose,
I shall but love thee better after death.

NATURE [1]

Longfellow

As a fond mother, when the day is o'er
Leads by the hand her little child to bed,
Half willing, half reluctant to be led,
And leave his broken playthings on the floor;
Still gazing at them through the open door,   5
Nor wholly reassured and comforted
By promises of others in their stead,
Which, though more splendid, may not please him more;
So Nature deals with us, and takes away
Our playthings one by one, and by the hand   10
Leads us to rest so gently, that we go
Scarce knowing if we wish to go or stay,
Being too full of sleep to understand
How far the unknown transcends the what we know.

WORK [2]

Henry Van Dyke

Let me but do my work from day to day,
    In field or forest, at the desk or loom,
    In roaring market-place or tranquil room;
Let me but find it in my heart to say,
When flagrant wishes beckon me astray,   5
    "This is my work; my blessing, not my doom;
    Of all who live, I am the one by whom
This work can best be done in the right way."

Then shall I see it not too great, nor small,
    To suit my spirit and to prove my powers;   10
    Then shall I cheerful greet the labouring hours,
And cheerful turn, when the long shadows fall
At eventide, to play and love and rest,
Because I know for me my work is best.

[1] Used by permission of the Houghton Mifflin Company.
[2] From *Music and Other Poems* by Henry Van Dyke, Copyright, 1904, Charles Scribner's Sons. Used by special arrangement with the publishers.

VOICES[1]

Louis Untermeyer

All day with anxious heart and wondering ear
  I listened to the city; heard the ground
  Echo with human thunder, and the sound
Go reeling down the streets and disappear.
The headlong hours, in their wild career,   5
    Shouted and sang until the world was drowned
    With babel-voices, each one more profound. . . .
All day it surged—but nothing could I hear.

That night the country never seemed so still;
    The trees and grasses spoke without a word   10
      To stars that brushed them with their silver wings.
Together with the moon I climbed the hill,
    And, in the very heart of Silence, heard
      The speech and music of immortal things.

SUGGESTIONS TO STUDENTS

The following sonnets, written by high school seniors, are placed here with the hope that they may inspire other students to try the sonnet form.

OUR STAR OF GOLD

A golden star upon the field of white,
Surrounded all with stars of deeper hue,
With crosses red, and living stars of blue.
A hero-boy upon the field of fight,
His life has gone protecting honor, right.   5
His soul was large; his heart beat strong and true;
He gave his all in just defence of you.
What means it all—these golden stars tonight?
That in the dawn of life, again, and love,
Which sees no more the battle, death, and tears,   10
We all must on our way; our life enhance;
Must do our best, with help of God above,
To add to ours their hopes and aims and cares;
To give their best, the lads who sleep in France.

                          (V. C. '20.)

[1] Used by special arrangement with the publishers, The Century Co.

TO OUR SERVICE FLAG

You youthful flag with stars of deepest blue,   4
You seem to breathe of youthful heroes' deeds
In France—there where the poppy blows its seeds.
You seem to tell us of devotion true.
Oh see that star of shining golden hue!   5
It speaks of death—death for all nations' needs.
It shows a soul of fearless youth which leads
And cries, "I leave my half-done task to you!"
Oh flag, tell them who in the years will come,
That they whose names are represented here   10
Went forth to war with willing hearts and hands,
E'en though they knew of those, the fated some,
Who, having not a single trace of fear,
Soon after were as dust in foreign lands!

(C. K. '20.)

SOME SONNETS FOR OPTIONAL READING

Note.—Read at least eight sonnets. For each give the two waves of thought and the rhyming scheme. Is it a perfect sonnet? If not, why? Which ones did you like best?

CHAPTER III

THE ELEGY

Characteristics of the Elegy.—The elegy is a lyric poem which expresses grief for a personal or public loss, or gives reflections on death in general. Although it is a poem of lamentation, there usually are suggestions of hope and faith which tend to allay and soothe the sorrow.

The Great English Elegies.—The greatest elegies in the English language are Milton's "Lycidas," in memory of his college friend, Edward King; Shelley's "Adonaïs," a tribute to Keats; Matthew Arnold's "Thyrsis," a lament on the death of his friend Clough; and "In Memoriam," Tennyson's expression of grief for his dearest friend, Arthur Hallam. Gray's "Elegy Written in a Country Churchyard" is also one of the great English elegies, although here there is no expression of personal grief, but solemn reflections called forth by the turf-covered graves in the lonely churchyard. The "Ode on the Death of the Duke of Wellington" is both an elegy and an ode. Milton's "Lycidas," and "Uriel," by Percy MacKaye, may also be classed as odes.

LYCIDAS

John Milton

Yet once more, O ye laurels, and once more,
Ye myrtles brown, with ivy never sere,
I come to pluck your berries harsh and crude,
And with forced fingers rude
Shatter your leaves before the mellowing year.　　　5
Bitter constraint, and sad occasion dear,
Compel me to disturb your season due;
For Lycidas is dead, dead ere his prime,
Young Lycidas, and hath not left his peer.
Who would not sing for Lycidas? He knew　　　10
Himself to sing, and build the lofty rhyme.
He must not float upon his watery bier
Unwept, and welter to the parching wind,

Without the meed of some melodious tear.
    Begin, then, Sisters of the sacred well   15
That from beneath the seat of Jove doth spring;
Begin, and somewhat loudly sweep the string.
Hence with denial vain, and coy excuse!
    So may some gentle Muse
With lucky words favour my destined urn,   20
    And, as he passes, turn,
And bid fair peace be to my sable shroud!
    For we were nursed upon the self-same hill,
Fed the same flock, by fountains, shade, and rill;
Together both, ere the high lawns appeared   25
Under the opening eyelids of the Morn,
We drove a-field, and both together heard
What time the grey-fly winds her sultry horn,
Battening our flocks with the fresh dews of night,
Oft till the star that rose, at evening bright   30
Toward heaven's descent had sloped his westering wheel.
Meanwhile the rural ditties were not mute;
    Tempered to the oaten flute,
Rough Satyrs danced, and Fauns with cloven heel
From the glad sound would not be absent long;   35
And old Damætas loved to hear our song.
    But, oh! the heavy change, now thou art gone,
Now thou art gone, and never must return!
Thee, Shepherd, thee the woods and desert caves,
With wild thyme and the gadding vine o'ergrown,   40
And all their echoes, mourn.
The willows, and the hazel copses green,
Shall now no more be seen
Fanning their joyous leaves to thy soft lays.
As killing as the canker to the rose,   45
Or taint-worm to the weanling herds that graze,
Or frost to flowers, that their gay wardrobe wear
When first the white-thorn blows;
Such, Lycidas, thy loss to shepherd's ear.
    Where were ye, Nymphs, when the remorseless deep   50
Closed o'er the head of your loved Lycidas?
For neither were ye playing on the steep,
Where your old bards, the famous Druids, lie,
Nor on the shaggy top of Mona high,
Nor yet where Deva spreads her wizard stream.   55
Ay me! I fondly dream
"Had ye been there,"—for what could that have done?
What could the Muse herself that Orpheus bore,

The Muse herself, for her enchanting son,
Whom universal nature did lament, 60
When, by the rout that made the hideous roar,
His gory visage down the stream was sent,
Down the swift Hebrus to the Lesbian shore?
　　Alas! what boots it with uncessant care
To tend the homely, slighted shepherd's trade, 65
And strictly meditate the thankless Muse?
Were it not better done, as others use,
　　To sport with Amaryllis in the shade,
Or with the tangles of Neæra's hair?
Fame is the spur that the clear spirit doth raise 70
(That last infirmity of noble mind)
To scorn delights, and live laborious days;
But the fair guerdon when we hope to find,
And think to burst out into sudden blaze,
Comes the blind Fury with the abhorrèd shears, 75
And slits the thin-spun life. "But not the praise,"
Phœbus replied, and touched my trembling ears:
"Fame is no plant that grows on mortal soil,
Nor in the glistering foil
Set off to the world, nor in broad rumour lies; 80
But lives and spreads aloft by those pure eyes
And perfect witness of all-judging Jove;
As he pronounces lastly on each deed,
Of so much fame in Heaven expect thy meed."
　　O fountain Arethuse, and thou honour'd flood, 85
Smooth-sliding Mincius, crowned with vocal reeds,
That strain I heard was of a higher mood.
But now my oat proceeds,
And listens to the Herald of the Sea
That came in Neptune's plea; 90
He asked the waves, and asked the felon winds,
What hard mishap hath doomed this gentle swain?
And questioned every gust of rugged wings
That blows from off each beakèd promontory.
They knew not of his story; 95
And sage Hippotades their answer brings
That not a blast was from his dungeon strayed:
The air was calm, and on the level brine
Sleek Panope with all her sisters played.
It was that fatal and perfidious bark, 100
Built in the eclipse, and rigged with curses dark,
That sunk so low that sacred head of thine.
　　Next, Camus, reverend sire, went footing slow,

His mantle hairy, and his bonnet sedge,
Inwrought with figures dim, and on the edge   105
Like to that sanguine flower inscribed with woe.
"Ah! Who hath reft," quoth he, "my dearest pledge?"
Last came, and last did go,
The Pilot of the Galilean lake;
Two massy keys he bore of metals twain   110
(The golden opes, the iron shuts amain).
He shook his mitred locks, and stern bespake:
"How well could I have spared for thee, young swain,
Enow of such as, for their bellies' sake,
Creep, and intrude, and climb into the fold!   115
Of other care they little reckoning make,
Than how to scramble at the shearers' feast,
And shove away the worthy bidden guest;
Blind mouths! that scarce themselves know how to hold
A sheep-hook, or have learnt aught else the least   120
That to the faithful herdman's art belongs!
What recks it them? What need they? They are sped;
And when they list, their lean and flashy songs
Grate on their scrannel pipes of wretched straw;
The hungry sheep look up, and are not fed,   125
But, swoln with wind and the rank mist they draw,
Rot inwardly, and foul contagion spread;
Besides what the grim wolf with privy paw
Daily devours apace, and nothing said.
But that two-handed engine at the door   130
Stands ready to smite once, and smite no more."

    Return, Alpheus, the dread voice is past
That shrunk thy streams; return, Sicilian Muse,
And call the vales, and bid them hither cast
Their bells and flowerets of a thousand hues.   135
Ye valleys low, where the mild whispers use
Of shades, and wanton winds, and gushing brooks,
On whose fresh lap the swart star sparely looks,
Throw hither all your quaint enamelled eyes,
That on the green turf suck the honeyed showers,   140
And purple all the ground with vernal flowers.
Bring the rathe primrose that forsaken dies,
The tufted crow-toe, and pale jessamine,
The white pink, and the pansy freaked with jet,
The glowing violet,   145
The musk-rose, and the well-attired woodbine,
With cowslips wan that hang the pensive head,
And every flower that sad embroidery wears;

Bid amaranthus all his beauty shed,
And daffodillies fill their cups with tears, 150
To strew the laureate hearse where Lycid lies.
For so, to interpose a little ease,
Let our frail thoughts dally with false surmise.
Ay me! Whilst thee the shores and sounding seas
Wash far away, where'er thy bones are hurl'd; 155
Whether beyond the stormy Hebrides,
Where thou perhaps under the whelming tide
Visit'st the bottom of the monstrous world;
Or whether thou, to our moist vows denied,
Sleep'st by the fable of Bellerus old, 160
Where the great vision of the guarded mount
Looks toward Namancos and Bayona's hold.
Look homeward, Angel, now, and melt with ruth;
And, O ye dolphins, waft the hapless youth.
　　Weep no more, woeful shepherds, weep no more; 165
For Lycidas, your sorrow, is not dead,
Sunk though he be beneath the watery floor.
So sinks the day-star in the ocean bed,
And yet anon repairs his drooping head,
And tricks his beams, and with new spangled ore 170
Flames in the forehead of the morning sky:
So Lycidas sunk low, but mounted high,
Through the dear might of Him that walked the waves,
Where, other groves and other streams along,
With nectar pure his oozy locks he laves, 175
And hears the unexpressive nuptial song,
In the blest kingdoms meek of joy and love.
There entertain him all the saints above,
In solemn troops, and sweet societies,
That sing, and singing in their glory move, 180
And wipe the tears for ever from his eyes.
Now, Lycidas, the shepherds weep no more;
Henceforth thou art the Genius of the shore,
In thy large recompense, and shalt be good
To all that wander in that perilous flood. 185
　　Thus sang the uncouth swain to the oaks and rills,
While the still morn went out with sandals grey;
He touched the tender stops of various quills,
With eager thought warbling his Doric lay.
And now the sun had stretched out all the hills, 190
And now was dropt into the western bay.
At last he rose, and twitched his mantle blue:
To-morrow to fresh woods, and pastures new.

Notes on "Lycidas."—This poem is not only the greatest of our elegies, but it is also our greatest pastoral poem. Representing himself as a shepherd mourning for his comrade, Lycidas, Milton expresses his grief for the death of his friend, Edward King.

General Plan of the Poem.—

(1) Milton's reason for writing the poem, lines 1–14.
(2) Appeal to the Muses for inspiration, lines 15–22.
(3) The companionship of Milton and King given under the semblance of shepherd life, lines 23–36.
(4) Expression of sorrow over the greatness of the loss, lines 37–49.
(5) Reproof given to the nymphs for not saving Lycidas. (This thought is a natural one at such a time)—"Why couldn't something have been done to prevent it!" Lines 50–63.
(6) A feeling of despondency which often comes—"What good does it do to deny one's self pleasures and spend long laborious hours in preparation for work that can never be accomplished!" Lines 64–76.
(7) The gloom dispelled by the thought that the highest fame is not of earth, but of immortal growth;—that all is not done in vain, lines 76–84.
(8) Return to the pastoral mood, which had been lost for a moment while taking up the two ideas of fame, lines 85–88.
(9) Inquiry made as to the cause of the accident, lines 89–102. (Not caused by a storm.)
(10) Mourners for Lycidas:
    (a) Camus-Cambridge. A loss to the University, lines 103–107.
    (b) St. Peter. A loss to the Church, lines 108–112.
(11) Charges brought against the false clergy.—The reasons why the Church needs men like Lycidas, lines 113–131.
(12) Return to pastoral mood after this digression. Apostrophe to Alpheus to call the vales to bring flowers for the "laureate hearse" of Lycidas, lines 132–153.
(13) Lament over the fact that the body of Lycidas was not recovered, lines 154–164.
(14) Apostrophe to the shepherds to "weep no more," for, although the body has sunk low, the soul of Lycidas has "mounted high," lines 165–185.
(15) Conclusion, lines 186–193.

SUGGESTIONS TO STUDENTS

1. What were the circumstances of King's death?[1] 2. Of Milton's writing this poem? What does Milton mean by the opening lines, "Yet once more"? Why is he reluctant to write this poem? What does he mean by plucking "with forced fingers" the "berries harsh and crude" "before the mellowing year"? What spirit does he show here? 3. What bits of information do you gather from the poem regarding the life, aspirations, and accomplishments of Edward King? 4. What is the meaning of line 14? Why the appeal to the muses? 5. Follow out the allegory of the poem, especially lines 23–36; 64–69. 6. What allusions show Milton to be a lover of classical stories? 7. What are the two kinds of fame that Milton points out? What does he think will be the true poet's reward? 8. Explain lines 73–76. Notice that the sun-god, Phœbus, who is in a position to see and know everything regarding the affairs of men, is made the speaker in lines 76–84. 9. What is meant by lines 87–88? Why should Neptune and the Herald of the Sea be concerned because of the death of Lycidas? 10. What caused the accident? 11. Why is Camus represented as being so old? So slow of movement? Why his "mantle hairy and bonnet sedge"? What two ideas is Milton consolidating in Camus? 12. What is the reason for St. Peter's interest in Lycidas? 13. What types of corrupt clergy does Milton portray? 14. Look up Ruskin's "Sesame and Lilies," 20–22, for his famous explanation of lines 109–131 of "Lycidas." Why, especially, are the false clergy "blind mouths"? 15. What fact is referred to in lines 151–164? 16. What contrast does Milton bring out between the body and the soul of Lycidas in lines 154–185? 17. Why does Milton in his conclusion, lines 186–193, change the person of the mourner from the first to the third person? 18. The last line refers to what circumstance in Milton's own life?

Most elegies are so easy to understand that, for the others given here, notes will be unnecessary. The author's emotion is the main thing. *Feel* as you read. Is the loss public or private, or are these reflections simply on death in general?

FROM CYMBELINE

Shakespeare

Fear no more the heat o' th' sun,
  Nor the furious winter's rages;

[1] The student will have an added interest in "Lycidas" when he remembers that the *Tuscania* went down only a little over a hundred miles from where Edward King was drowned, and also that the death of Lord Kitchener, near the Orkney Islands, had many similar circumstances. See the elegy, "Kitchener," by John Helston in *A Treasury of War Poetry* (Clarke).

Thou thy worldly task hast done,
　Home art gone, and ta'en thy wages:
Golden lads and girls all must,　　　　　5
As chimney-sweepers, come to dust.

Fear no more the frown o' th' great;
　Thou art past the tyrant's stroke;
Care no more to clothe and eat;
　To thee the reed is as the oak:　　　　10
The Sceptre, Learning, Physic, must
All follow this, and come to dust.

Fear no more the lightning-flash,
　Nor th' all-dreaded thunder-stone;
Fear not slander, censure rash;　　　　15
　Thou hast finished joy and moan:
All lovers young, all lovers must
Consign [1] to thee, and come to dust.

No exorciser harm thee;
　Nor no witchcraft charm thee!　　　　20
Ghost unlaid forbear thee!
　Nothing ill come near thee!
Quiet consummation have;
And renownèd be thy grave!

Note.—When Tennyson lay dying, he had a volume of Shakespeare beside him open at this poem.

LAMENT FOR CULLODEN

Robert Burns

The lovely lass o' Inverness.
Nae joy nor pleasure can she see;
For e'en and morn she cries, Alas!
And aye the saut tear blins her ee:
Drumossie moor—Drumossie clay—　　　5
A woefu' day it was to me!
For there I lost my father dear,
My father dear, and brethren three.

Their winding-sheet the bluidy clay,
Their graves are growing green to see　10
And by them lies the dearest lad

[1] Resign themselves.

That ever blest a woman's ee!
Now wae to thee, thou cruel lord,
A bluidy man I trow thou be:
For mony a heart thou hast made sair   15
That ne'er did wrang to thine or thee.

Note.—The battle of Culloden was fought during the Jacobite
Rebellion of 1745. The Young Pretender, Prince Charles Edward,
landed in Scotland and drew to his support a few of the High-
land clans. His small army was completely defeated by the
English at Culloden and the prince forced to flee to France. The
Highlanders called this battle field Drumossie.

A BARD'S EPITAPH

Robert Burns

Is there a whim-inspirèd fool,
Owre [1] fast for thought, owre hot for rule,
Owre blate [2] to seek, owre proud to snool [3]?
        Let him draw near;
And owre this grassy heap sing dool. [4]   5
        And drap a tear.

Is there a bard of rustic song
Who, noteless, steals the crowds among,
That weekly this area [5] throng?—
        Oh, pass not by!   10
But with a frater-feeling strong
        Here heave a sigh.

Is there a man whose judgment clear
Can others teach the course to steer,
Yet runs himself life's mad career   15
        Wild as the wave?
Here pause—and thro' the starting tear
        Survey this grave.

The poor inhabitant below
Was quick to learn and wise to know,   20
And keenly felt the friendly glow
        And softer flame;
But thoughtless follies laid him low,
        And stained his name!

[1] over.   [2] bashful.   [3] fawn.   [4] dole, lamentation.   [5] Refers to the churchyard. **Pronounced here** *are'a.*

Reader, attend! Whether thy soul   25
Soars fancy's flights beyond the pole,
Or darkling grubs this earthly hole
    In low pursuit;
Know, prudent, cautious, self-control
    Is wisdom's root.   30

Those who have read Carlyle's *Essay on Burns* will understand the references to Burns's own life.

SHE DWELT AMONG THE UNTRODDEN WAYS

William Wordsworth

She dwelt among the untrodden ways
  Beside the springs of Dove;
A maid whom there were none to praise,
  And very few to love.

A violet by a mossy stone   5
  Half-hidden from the eye!
Fair as a star, when only one
  Is shining in the sky.

She lived unknown, and few could know
  When Lucy ceased to be;   10
But she is in her grave, and, oh!
  The difference to me!

CORONACH

Sir Walter Scott

He is gone on the mountain,
  He is lost to the forest,
Like a summer-dried fountain,
  When our need was the sorest.
The font reappearing   5
  From the raindrops shall borrow,
But to us comes no cheering,
  To Duncan no morrow!

The hand of the reaper
  Takes the ears that are hoary,   10
But the voice of the weeper
  Wails manhood in glory;

The autumn winds rushing

 Waft the leaves that are searest,
But our flower was in flushing　　　　15
 When blighting was nearest.

Fleet foot on the correi,[1]
 Sage counsel in cumber,[2]
Red hand in the foray,[3]
 How sound is thy slumber!　　　　20
Like the dew on the mountain,
 Like the foam on the river,
Like the bubble on the fountain,
 Thou art gone, and for ever!

"The Coronach of the Highlanders was a wild expression of lamentation poured forth by the mourners over the body of a departed friend. When the words of it were articulate, they expressed the praises of the deceased, and the loss the clan would sustain by his death."—Scott.

ELEGY

Byron

Oh snatch'd away in beauty's bloom!
On thee shall press no ponderous tomb;
But on thy turf shall roses rear
Their leaves, the earliest of the year,
And the wild cypress wave in tender gloom:　　　　5

And oft by yon blue gushing stream
Shall Sorrow lean her drooping head,
And feed deep thought with many a dream,
And lingering pause and lightly tread;
Fond wretch! as if her step disturbed the dead!　　　　10

Away! we know that tears are vain,
That Death nor heeds nor hears distress.
Will this unteach us to complain?
Or make one mourner weep the less?
And thou, who tell'st me to forget,　　　　15
Thy looks are wan, thine eyes are wet.

1 hiding-place of game.　2 trouble.　3 a raid.

Extracts from ADONAÏS[1] ✓

Percy Bysshe Shelley

I weep for Adonaïs—he is dead!
O, weep for Adonaïs! though our tears
Thaw not the frost which binds so dear a head!
And thou, sad Hour, selected from all years
To mourn our loss, rouse thy obscure compeers,   5
And teach them thine own sorrow, say: "With me
Died Adonaïs; till the Future dares
Forget the Past, his fate and fame shall be
An echo and a light unto eternity."

    .   .   .   .

To that high Capital, where kingly Death   10
Keeps his pale court in beauty and decay,
He came; and bought, with price of purest breath,
A grave among the eternal.—Come away!
Haste, while the vault of blue Italian day
Is yet his fitting charnel-roof! While still   15
He lies, as if in dewy sleep he lay;
Awake him not! Surely he takes his fill
Of deep and liquid rest, forgetful of all ill.

    .   .   .   .

All he had loved, and moulded into thought,
From shape, and hue, and odour, and sweet sound,   20
Lamented Adonaïs. Morning sought
Her eastern watch-tower and her hair unbound,
Wet with the tears which should adorn the ground,
Dimmed the aërial eyes that kindle day;
Afar the melancholy thunder moaned,   25
Pale Ocean in unquiet slumber lay,
And the wild winds flew round, sobbing in their dismay.

    .   .   .   .

He has outsoared the shadow of our night;
Envy and calumny and hate and pain,
And that unrest which men miscall delight,   30
Can touch him not and torture not again;
From the contagion of the world's slow stain
He is secure, and now can never mourn
A heart grown cold, a head grown grey in vain;
Nor, when the spirit's self has ceased to burn,   35
With sparkless ashes load an unlamented urn.

[1] This elegy is in memory of John Keats.

Extracts from IN MEMORIAM [1]

Tennyson

I

I held it truth, with him who sings
  To one clear harp in divers tones,
  That men may rise on stepping-
    stones
Of their dead selves to higher things.

But who shall so forecast the years 5
  And find in loss a gain to match?
  Or reach a hand thro' time to
    catch
The far-off interest of tears?

LIV

Oh yet we trust that somehow good
  Will be the final goal of ill,   10
  To pangs of nature, sins of will,
Defects of doubt, and taints of
    blood;

That nothing walks with aimless
    feet;
  That not one life shall be de-
    stroy'd,
  Or cast as rubbish to the void, 15
When God hath made the pile com-
    plete;

That not a worm is cloven in vain;
  That not a moth with vain desire
  Is shrivell'd in a fruitless fire,
Or but subserves another's gain. 20

Behold, we know not anything:
  I can but trust that good shall
    fall

At last—far off—at last, to all,
And every winter change to spring.

So runs my dream; but what am
    I?   25
  An infant crying in the night:
  An infant crying for the light:
And with no language but a cry.

LVII

Peace; come away: the song of
    woe
  Is after all an earthly song: 30
  Peace; come away: we do him
    wrong
To sing so wildly; let us go.

Come; let us go; your cheeks are
    pale;
  But half my life I leave behind:
  Methinks my friend is richly
    shrined;   35
But I shall pass; my work will fail.

Yet in these ears, till hearing
    dies,
  One set slow bell will seem to
    toll
  The passing of the sweetest soul
That ever looked with human
    eyes.   40

I hear it now, and o'er and o'er,
  Eternal greetings to the dead;
  And "Ave, Ave, Ave," said.
"Adieu, adieu" for evermore.

[1] This elegy is in memory of Tennyson's dearest friend, Arthur Hallam. Used by permission of the Macmillan Company.

ALFRED TENNYSON

BREAK, BREAK, BREAK[1] V

Tennyson

Break, break, break,
　On thy cold grey stones, O Sea!
And I would that my tongue could utter
　The thoughts that arise in me.

O well for the fisherman's boy,　　　　　　　　　5
　That he shouts with his sister at play!
O well for the sailor lad,
　That he sings in his boat on the bay!

And the stately ships go on
　To their haven under the hill;　　　　　　　　10
But O for the touch of a vanish'd hand,
　And the sound of a voice that is still!

Break, break, break,
　At the foot of thy crags, O Sea!
But the tender grace of a day that is dead　　　15
　Will never come back to me

SUSPIRIA[2]

Henry W. Longfellow

Take them, O Death! and bear away
　Whatever thou canst call thine own!
Thine image, stamped upon this clay,
　Doth give thee that, but that alone!

Take them, O Grave! and let them lie　　　　　5
　Folded upon thy narrow shelves,
As garments by the soul laid by,
　And precious only to ourselves!

Take them, O great Eternity!
　Our little life is but a gust　　　　　　　　10
That bends the branches of thy tree,
　And trails its blossoms in the dust!

[1] Used by permission of the Macmillan Company.
[2] Used by permission of the Houghton Mifflin Company.

THE DEAD [1]
Rupert Brooke

I

Blow out, you bugles, over the rich Dead!
  There's none of these so lonely and poor of old,
  But, dying, has made us rarer gifts than gold.
These laid the world away; poured out the red
Sweet wine of youth; gave up the years to be   5
  Of work and joy, and that unhoped serene
  That men call age; and those who would have been
Their sons they gave, their immortality.

  Blow, bugles, blow! They brought us, for our dearth,
    Holiness, lacked so long, and Love, and Pain.   10
  Honour has come back, as a king, to earth,
     And paid his subjects with a royal wage;
     And Nobleness walks in our ways again;
     And we have come into our heritage.

II

  These hearts were woven of human joys and cares   15
Washed marvellously with sorrow, swift to mirth.
  The years had given them kindness. Dawn was theirs,
And sunset, and the colours of the earth.
  These had seen movement and heard music; known
Slumber and waking; loved; gone proudly friended;   20
    Felt the quick stir of wonder; sat alone;
Touched flowers and furs and cheeks. All this is ended.

  There are waters blown by changing winds to laughter
    And lit by the rich skies, all day. And after,
Frost, with a gesture, stays the waves that dance   25
    And wandering loveliness. He leaves a white
Unbroken glory, a gathered radiance,
    A width, a shining peace, under the night.

[1] Used by special arrangement with the John Lane Company. From *Collected Poems of Rupert Brooke.*

TO THE FIRE-BRINGER [1]

(In Memory of William Vaughn Moody)

Percy MacKaye

Bringer of fire
Down from the star
Quivering far
In quiet eternal:
Bringer of fire!—   5
Ashes we are
If to thy pyre
Out of our hearts
Ashes we bring.

Vernal, vernal,   10
Divine and burning—
A wreath of worlds
And wings—was thy vision:
Fadeless now,
That fiery wreath   15
Wrought of thy yearning
We lay in death
Bright on thy brow.

Singer and lover,
Brother and friend,   20
Ashes can end
Only the dross of thee:
Quick, Promethéan,
Out of the dirge
And the dark loss of thee   25
Leaps thy star-wrestling
Spirit in pæan!

Fire, fire,
Fire was thy bringing,
An urn elemental   30
Of burning song:
So on thy pyre
We leave it flaming—
Where Death cannot follow—
Toward thee, who camest singing:
"Apollo, Apollo!"   36

SUGGESTIONS TO STUDENTS

1. Who was William Vaughn Moody? 2. How was he a "bringer of fire down from the star"? 3. What is meant by "A wreath of worlds and wings"? 4. What is the force of the word "Promethean" in the next to the last stanza? Who was Prometheus in Greek mythology? 5. What is the "fire" brought by the "fire-bringer" of this poem? 6. What is meant by "star-wrestling spirit"? 7. Why cannot Death follow? (See last stanza.) 8. What work by William Vaughn Moody suggested this title?

ELEGIES FOR OPTIONAL READINGS

Note.--Read at least seven elegies. Which did you like the best? Who is mourned in each case?

"Elegy Written in a Country Churchyard"......Gray
"The Loss of the Royal George"...............Cowper
"Highland Mary"..........................Burns

[1] From *Uriel and Other Poems*, by Percy MacKaye, Copyright, 1912, by Percy MacKaye. Used by special permission of the author.

CHAPTER IV

THE SONG: SACRED AND SECULAR

The song is a short lyric poem which differs from the other forms in that it is intended, primarily, to be sung. It has that particular melodious quality required by the singing voice. Songs are either sacred or secular. The sacred songs include hymns, anthems, and oratorios. The secular songs may have any theme or emotion. Burns is called the greatest song-writer of the world because of the number, variety, and quality of his songs. Some of the finest songs that we have are strewn through Shakespeare's plays. Thomas Moore, Tennyson, Longfellow, and Eugene Field are also noted song-writers. Although our song-writers are not, as a general thing, poets, yet many of our poets have written songs.[1] The best songs were *composed* to music instead of adapted to it.

SOME SONGS FROM SHAKESPEARE'S PLAYS

From A MIDSUMMER NIGHT'S DREAM (Puck's Song)

> Over hill, over dale,
> Thorough bush, thorough brier,
> Over park, over pale,
> Thorough flood, thorough fire,
> I do wander everywhere,   5
> Swifter than the moonës sphere;
> And I serve the Fairy Queen,
> To dew her orbs upon the green.
> The cowslips tall her pensioners be;
> In their gold coats spots you see: 10
> Those be rubies, fairy favours,
> In those freckles live their savours.
> I must go seek some dewdrop here,
> And hang a pearl in every cowslip's ear.

[1] Since there are few school buildings now that do not include at least one phonograph in their equipment, it is suggested that a musical program be given in place of the regular English lesson. Songs should be *felt*, not studied.

From CYMBELINE

Hark, hark! the lark at heaven's gate sings
  And Phœbus 'gins arise,
His steeds to water at those springs
  On chaliced flowers that lies:
And winking Mary-buds begin   5
  To ope their golden eyes:
With every thing that pretty is,
  My lady sweet, arise!
    Arise, arise!

From TWO GENTLEMEN OF VERONA

Who is Silvia? What is she,
  That all our swains commend her?
Holy, fair, and wise is she;
  The heaven such grace did lend her,
That she might admired be.   5

Is she kind as she is fair?
  For beauty lives with kindness.
Love doth to her eyes repair
  To help him of his blindness,
And being helped, inhabits there.   10

Then to Silvia let us sing,
  That Silvia is excelling;
She excels each mortal thing,
  Upon the dull earth dwelling:
To her let us garlands bring.   15

From LOVE'S LABOUR'S LOST

When icicles hang by the wall,
  And Dick the shepherd blows his nail,
And Tom bears logs into the hall,
  And milk comes frozen home in pail,
When blood is nipped and ways be foul,   5
Then nightly sings the staring owl,
  Tu-whit, tu-who! a merry note,
While greasy Joan doth keel [1] the pot.

When all aloud the wind doth blow,
  And coughing drowns the parson's saw,   10

[1] stir.

And birds sit brooding in the snow,
   And Marian's nose looks red and raw,
When roasted crabs hiss in the bowl,
Then nightly sings the staring owl,
   Tu-whit! tu-who! a merry note,   15
While greasy Joan doth keel the pot.

From As You Like It

Blow, blow, thou winter wind!
Thou art not so unkind
As man's ingratitude;
Thy tooth is not so keen,
Because thou art not seen,   5
   Although thy breath be rude.

Heigh ho! sing, heigh ho! unto the green holly:
Most friendship is feigning, most loving mere folly:
   Then, heigh ho, the holly!
   This life is most jolly.   10

Freeze, freeze, thou bitter sky!
That dost not bite so nigh
As benefits forgot;
Though thou the waters warp,
Thy sting is not so sharp   15
   As friend remembered not.

Heigh ho! sing, heigh ho! unto the green holly: 4
Most friendship is feigning, most loving mere folly:
   Then, heigh ho, the holly!
   This life is most jolly.   20

From As You Like It

Under the greenwood tree
Who loves to lie with me,
And tune his merry note
Unto the sweet bird's throat,
Come hither! come hither! come hither!   5
   Here shall he see
   No enemy
But winter and rough weather.

Who doth ambition shun
And loves to live i' the sun,   10
Seeking the food he eats
And pleased with what he gets,
Come hither! come hither! come hither!
Here shall he see
No enemy   15
But winter and rough weather.

SONG TO CELIA

Ben Jonson

Drink to me only with thine eyes,
  And I will pledge with mine;
Or leave a kiss but in the cup
  And I'll not look for wine.

The thirst that from the soul doth rise   5
  Doth ask a drink divine;
But might I of Jove's nectar sup,
  I would not change for thine.

I sent thee late a rosy wreath,
  Not so much honoring thee   10
As giving it a hope, that there
  It could not wither'd be.

But thou thereon didst only breathe,
  And sent'st it back to me;
Since when it grows, and smells, I swear,   15
  Not of itself, but thee.

SCOTS WHA HAE

Robert Burns

Scots, wha hae wi' Wallace bled,
Scots, wham Bruce has aften led;
Welcome to your gory bed,
    Or to victory!
Now's the day, and now's the hour;   5
See the front o' battle lour;
See approach proud Edward's power—
    Chains and slavery!

Wha will be a traitor knave?
Wha can fill a coward's grave?   10
Wha sae base as be a slave?
    Let him turn and flee!
Wha for Scotland's king and law
Freedom's sword will strongly draw,
Freeman stand, or Freeman fa',   15
    Let him follow me!

By oppression's woes and pains,
By your sons in servile chains!
We will drain our dearest veins,
    But they shall be free!   20
Lay the proud usurpers low!
Tyrants fall in every foe!
Liberty's in every blow!—
    Let us do or die!

JOHN ANDERSON

Robert Burns

John Anderson, my jo, John,
When we were first acquent
Your locks were like the raven,
Your bonnie brow was brent;
But now your brow is bald, John,   5
Your locks are like the snow;
But blessings on your frosty pow,
John Anderson, my jo.

John Anderson, my jo, John,
We clamb the hill thegither,   10
And mony a cantie day, John,
We've had wi' ane anither:
Now we maun totter down, John,
But hand in hand we'll go,
And sleep thegither at the foot,   15
John Anderson, my jo.

AE FOND KISS

Robert Burns

Ae fond kiss, and then we sever;
Ae fareweel, and then forever!
Deep in heart-wrung tears I 'll pledge thee,
Warring sighs and groans I 'll wage thee.
Who shall say that Fortune grieves him,   5
While the star of hope she leaves him?
Me, nae cheerfu' twinkle lights me;
Dark despair around benights me.

I 'll never blame my partial fancy,
Naething could resist my Nancy;   10
But to see her was to love her;
Love but her, and love forever.
Had we never lov'd sae kindly,
Had we never lov'd sae blindly,
Never met—or never parted—   15
We had ne'er been broken-hearted.

Fare thee weel, thou first and fairest!
Fare thee weel, thou best and dearest!
Thine be ilka joy and treasure,
Peace, enjoyment, love, and pleasure!   20
Ae fond kiss, and then we sever;
Ae fareweel, alas, forever!
Deep in heart-wrung tears I 'll pledge thee,
Warring sighs and groans I 'll wage thee!

THE HARP THAT ONCE THROUGH TARA'S HALLS [1]

Thomas Moore

The harp that once through Tara's halls
    The soul of music shed,
Now hangs as mute on Tara's walls
    As if that soul were fled.
So sleeps the pride of former days,   5
    So glory's thrill is o'er,
And hearts that once beat high for praise
    Now feel that pulse no more!

[1] The palace of the kings of Ireland.

No more to chiefs and ladies bright
　　The harp of Tara swells:
The chord alone that breaks at night
　　Its tale of ruin tells.
Thus Freedom now so seldom wakes,
　　The only throb she gives
Is when some heart indignant breaks
　　To show that still she lives.

10

15

THE BUGLE SONG [1]

(*From* "The Princess")

Tennyson

The splendor falls on castle walls
And snowy summits old in story;
The long light shakes across the lakes,
And the wild cataract leaps in glory.
Blow, bugle, blow, set the wild echoes flying,
Blow, bugle; answer, echoes, dying, dying, dying.

5

O hark! O hear! how thin and clear,
And thinner, clearer, farther going,
O sweet and far, from cliff and scar,
The horns of Elfland faintly blowing.
Blow, let us hear the purple glens replying,
Blow, bugle; answer, echoes, dying, dying, dying.

10

O love, they die in yon rich sky,
They faint on hill, or field, or river;
Our echoes roll from soul to soul,
And grow forever, and forever.
Blow, bugle, blow, set the wild echoes flying,
And answer, echoes, answer, dying, dying, dying.

15

THE ARROW AND THE SONG [2]

Longfellow

I shot an arrow into the air,
It fell to earth, I knew not where;
For, so swiftly it flew, the sight
Could not follow it in its flight.

[1] By permission of the Macmillan Company.
[2] By permission of the Houghton Mifflin Company.

I breathed a song into the air,   5
It fell to earth, I knew not where;
For who has sight so keen and strong,
   That it can follow the flight of song?

Long, long afterward, in an oak
I found the arrow, still unbroke;   10
And the song, from beginning to end,
I found again in the heart of a friend.

LITTLE BLUE PIGEON [1]

(JAPANESE LULLABY)

Eugene Field

Sleep, little pigeon, and fold your wings—
   Little blue pigeon with velvet eyes;
Sleep to the singing of mother-bird swinging—
   Swinging the nest where her little one lies.

Away out yonder I see a star—
   Silvery star with a tinkling song:
To the soft dew falling I hear it calling—
   Calling and tinkling the night along.

In through the window a moonbeam comes—
   Little gold moonbeam with misty wings: 10
All silently creeping, it asks: "Is he sleeping—
   Sleeping and dreaming while mother sings?"

Up from the sea there floats the sob
   Of the waves that are breaking upon the shore,
As though they were groaning in anguish, and moaning—   15
   Bemoaning the ship that shall come no more.

But sleep, little pigeon, and fold your wings—
   Little blue pigeon with mournful eyes;
Am I not singing?—see, I am swinging—
   Swinging the nest where my darling lies.   20

[1] Used by special arrangement with Charles Scribner's Sons.

From SLUMBER SONGS OF THE MADONNA [1]

Alfred Noyes

Sleep, little baby, I love thee,
Sleep, little king, I am bending above thee,
    How should I know what to sing?

Here in my arms as I swing thee to sleep,
    Hushaby low,   5
    Rockaby so.

Kings may have wonderful jewels to bring,
Mother has only a kiss for her king!
Why should my singing so make me to weep?
    Only I know that I love thee, I love thee,   10
    Love thee, my little one, sleep.

SUGGESTIONS TO STUDENTS

Read or recite each song until it can be spoken with easy familiarity. Try always to catch and to express through the voice the author's spirit and the lights and shadows of his changing mood.

SOME OTHER WELL-KNOWN SONGS [1]

"My Love Is Like a Red, Red Rose"..........Burns
"Duncan Gray" ....Burns
"Auld Lang Syne"..........................Burns
"Sweet Afton" ....Burns
"Bonnie Doon" ....Burns
"Comin' thru the Rye"......................Burns
"Blue Bells of Scotland"....................Burns
"Highland Mary"...........................Burns
"Hail to the Chief" from "Lady of the Lake"....Scott
"Ave Maria" from "Lady of the Lake".........Scott
"Believe Me If All Those Endearing Young
    Charms" ....Thomas Moore
"Oft' in the Stilly Night"....................Thomas Moore
"The Last Rose of Summer"..................Thomas Moore
"Annie Laurie".............................Lady John Scott
"The Land o' the Leal"......................Lady Catherine Nairne

[1] From *Collected Poems*, Vol. I. Copyright, 1913, Frederick A. Stokes Company. Used by special permission.

"Come into the Garden, Maud"............... Tennyson
"Sweet and Low" from "The Princess"........ Tennyson
"Tears, Idle Tears" from "The Princess"........ Tennyson
"Ring Out, Wild Bells" from "In Memoriam"... Tennyson
The Song from "Pippa Passes"............... Browning
"Cavalier Tunes"........................... Browning
"The Ivy Green"............................ Dickens
"Home, Sweet Home"........................ John Howard Payne
"The Old Oaken Bucket".................... Samuel Woodworth
"The Bridge".............................. Longfellow
"The Day is Done"......................... Longfellow
"The Curfew".............................. Longfellow
"Knee Deep in June"....................... James Whitcomb Riley
"Little Boy Blue".......................... Eugene Field
"Hushabye, Sweet, My Own"................ Eugene Field
"Wynken, Blynken, and Nod" (Dutch Lullaby).. Eugene Field
"Old Folks at Home"....................... Stephen C. Foster
"My Old Kentucky Home".................... Stephen C. Foster
"On the Road to Mandalay"................. Kipling
Songs from "Drake"........................ Alfred Noyes
"Men Who March Away" (September, 1914)... Thomas Hardy

A GROUP OF PATRIOTIC SONGS

American:

"The Star-Spangled Banner"............. Francis Scott Key, 1814
"Hail, Columbia" .... J. Hopkinson, 1798; (O. W.
                                        Holmes added three stan-
                                        zas, 1887)
"America" .... Samuel F. Smith, 1832
"The Red, White, and Blue"............. David T. Shaw
"Battle Hymn of the Republic".......... Julia Ward Howe

English:

"Rule, Britannia"
"God Save the King"

SOME OF THE BEST-KNOWN SACRED SONGS

"The Spacious Firmament on High"........Joseph Addison
"While Shepherds Watched Their Flocks by
    Night" ....Nahum Tate, 1702

1 For published airs for songs in *The Golden Treasury*, see list by Miss
Jeanette F. Abrams, *The English Journal*, p. 387, June, 1915.

"Praise God, from Whom All Blessings
Flow" .... Thomas Ken
"Hark, the Herald Angels Sing 'Glory to Our
New-Born King'" .... Charles Wesley, 1739
"Jesus, Lover of My Soul"................. Charles Wesley, 1740
"O for a Closer Walk with God"............ William Cowper, 1772
"Rock of Ages, Cleft for Me".............. Augustus M. Toplady, 1776
"Lead, Kindly Light"...................... Cardinal Newman, 1833
"The Lost Chord".......................... Adelaide Proctor
"Nearer, My God, to Thee"................. Sarah E. Adams, 1841
"Abide with Me"........................... Henry F. Lyte, 1847
"Now the Day is Over"..................... S. Baring Gould, 1865
"Day is Dying in the West"............... Mary A. Lathbury, 1877
"The Recessional" .... Rudyard Kipling, 1897

CHAPTER V

THE SIMPLE LYRIC

Under the heading, simple lyric, are placed all of those lyrical poems that do not properly belong under any of the other types of lyrics. With the possible exception of the song, more poems are included in this class than in any other in the whole field of literature. The simple lyric touches every mood and emotion of the human heart. These poems are found in every period of English literature, from that of the Anglo-Saxons to the present day, but only a few of them can be given here.

THE COMPLAINT TO HIS EMPTY PURSE
Chaucer, 1399

To you, my purs, and to non other wight [1]
Campleyne I, for ye be my lady dere!
I am so sory, now that ye be light;
For certes, but [2] ye make me hevy chere,[3]
Me were as leef be leyd upon my bere; [4]   5
For whiche unto your mercy thus I crye:
Beth [5] hevy ageyn, or elles mot I dye!

Now vouchethsauf [6] this day, or [7] hit be night,
That I of you the blisful soun may here,
Or see your colour lyk the sonne bright,   10
That of yelownesse hadde never pere.[8]
Ye be my lyf, ye be myn hertes stere,[9]
Quene of comfort and of good companye,
Beth hevy ageyn, or elles mot I dye!

Now purs, that be to me my lyves light,   15
And saveour, as down in this worlde here,
Out of this toune help me through your might,
Sin that ye wole nat ben my tresorere:
For I am shave as nye as any frere.

[1] creature, thing.   [2] unless.   [3] cheer.   [4] bier.   [5] be.   [6] vouchsafe, grant.
[7] ere.   [8] an equal.   [9] guide.

But yit I pray unto your curtesye: 20
Beth hevy ageyn, or elles mot I dye!

SUGGESTIONS TO STUDENTS

What does Chaucer mean by being "Shaven as close as any friar"?
What is the mood of this poem? See story of Chaucer's life for the causes
and results of this poem. Try putting this into modern English prose.
Does it gain or lose anything by the change?

L'ALLEGRO

John Milton

Hence, loathed Melancholy,
  Of Cerberus and blackest Midnight born,
In Stygian cave forlorn,
  'Mongst horrid shapes, and shrieks, and sights unholy,
Find out some uncouth cell, 5
  Where brooding darkness spreads his jealous wings,
And the night-raven sings;
There under ebon shades, and low-browed rocks,
As ragged as thy locks,
In dark Cimmerian desert ever dwell. 10
But come, thou Goddess fair and free,
In heaven yclept Euphrosyne,
And by men, heart-easing Mirth,
Whom lovely Venus at a birth
With two sister Graces more 15
To ivy-crownèd Bacchus bore;
Or whether (as some sager sing)
The frolic wind that breathes the spring,
Zephyr, with Aurora playing,
As he met her once a-Maying, 20
There on beds of violets blue,
And fresh-blown roses washed in dew,
Filled her with thee a daughter fair,
So buxom, blithe, and debonair.
Haste thee, Nymph, and bring with thee 25
Jest, and youthful Jollity,
Quips and cranks and wanton wiles,
Nods and becks and wreathèd smiles,
Such as hang on Hebe's cheek,
And love to live in dimple sleek; 30
Sport that wrinkled Care derides,
And Laughter holding both his sides.
Come, and trip it, as ye go,
On the light fantastic toe;

And in thy right hand lead with thee   35
The mountain-nymph, sweet Liberty;
And if I give thee honor due,
Mirth, admit me of thy crew,
To live with her, and live with thee,
In unreprovèd pleasures free;   40
To hear the lark begin his flight,
And, singing, startle the dull night,
From his watch-tower in the skies,
Till the dappled dawn doth rise;
Then to come, in spite of sorrow,   45
And at my window bid good-morrow,
Through the sweetbrier, or the vine,
Or the twisted eglantine;
While the cock, with lively din,
Scatters the rear of darkness thin,   50
And to the stack, or the barn door,
Stoutly struts his dames before:
Oft listening how the hounds and horn
Cheerly rouse the slumbering morn,
From the side of some hoar hill,   55
Through the high wood echoing shrill:
Sometime walking, not unseen,
By hedgerow elms, on hillocks green,
Right against the eastern gate,
Where the great Sun begins his state,   60
Robed in flames and amber light,
The clouds in thousand liveries dight;
While the plowman, near at hand,
Whistles o'er the furrowed land,
And the milkmaid singeth blithe,   65
And the mower whets his scythe,
And every shepherd tells his tale
Under the hawthorn in the dale.
Straight mine eye hath caught new pleasures,
Whilst the landskip round it measures: 70
Russet lawns, and fallows gray,
Where the nibbling flocks do stray;
Mountains on whose barren breast
The laboring clouds do often rest:
Meadows trim, with daisies pied;   75
Shallow brooks, and rivers wide;
Towers and battlements it sees
Bosomed high in tufted trees,
Where perhaps some beauty lies,

The cynosure of neighbouring eyes.　　　　　　　80
Hard by, a cottage chimney smokes
From betwixt two aged oaks,
Where Corydon and Thyrsis met,
Are at their savoury dinner set
Of herbs and other country messes,　　　　　　　85
Which the neat-handed Phillis dresses;
And then in haste her bower she leaves,
With Thestylis to bind the sheaves;
Or, if the earlier season lead,
To the tanned haycock in the mead.　　　　　　　90
Sometimes with secure delight
The upland hamlets will invite,
When the merry bells ring round,
And the jocund rebecks sound
To many a youth, and many a maid,　　　　　　　95
Dancing in the chequered shade;
And young and old come forth to play
On a sunshine holyday,
Till the livelong daylight fail:
Then to the spicy nut-brown ale,　　　　　　　100
With stories told of many a feat,
How Faery Mab the junkets eat.
She was pinched and pulled, she said;
And he, by Friars' lantern led,
Tells how the drudging goblin sweat,　　　　　　105
To earn his cream-bowl duly set,
When in one night, ere glimpse of morn,
His shadowy flail hath threshed the corn
That ten day-labourers could not end;
Then lies him down, the lubber-fiend,　　　　　　110
And, stretched out all the chimney's length,
Basks at the fire his hairy strength;
And crop-full out of doors he flings,
Ere the first cock his matin rings.
Thus done the tales, to bed they creep,　　　　　　115
By whispering winds soon lulled asleep.
Towered cities please us then,
And the busy hum of men,
Where throngs of knights and barons bold
In weeds of peace high triumphs hold,　　　　　　120
With store of ladies, whose bright eyes
Rain influence, and judge the prize
Of wit or arms, while both contend
To win her grace whom all commend.

There let Hymen oft appear   125
In saffron robe, with taper clear,
And pomp, and feast, and revelry,
With mask, and antique pageantry;
Such sights as youthful poets dream
On summer eves by haunted stream.   130
Then to the well-trod stage anon,
If Jonson's learnèd sock be on,
Or sweetest Shakespeare, Fancy's child,
Warble his native wood-notes wild.
And ever against eating cares,   135
Lap me in soft Lydian airs,
Married to immortal verse,
Such as the meeting soul may pierce,
In notes with many a winding bout
Of linkèd sweetness long drawn out,   140
With wanton heed and giddy cunning,
The melting voice through mazes running;
Untwisting all the chains that tie
The hidden soul of harmony;
That Orpheus self may heave his head   145
From golden slumber on a bed
Of heaped Elysian flowers, and hear
Such strains as would have won the ear
Of Pluto to have quite set free
His half-regained Eurydice.   150
These delights, if thou canst give,
Mirth, with thee I mean to live.

SUGGESTIONS TO STUDENTS

The title means—*the joyous or merry man.* This poem is a companion to "Il Penseroso," *the pensive or thoughtful man.* In these two poems Milton has represented not necessarily two different types of men, but two different moods that the same man might have. In order to enjoy this poem, enter into its spirit and try to feel the pleasures that the merry man would have.

Notice throughout the poem how expressive Milton's adjective modifiers are: e.g., "heart-easing Mirth"; "wrinkled Care"; Laughter *"holding both his sides,"* etc.

Since the poem is so full of allusions to classical mythology and English folk-lore, the glossary will be found helpful in understanding Milton's meaning. Were there any allusions that particularly interested you? If so, what were they?

THE GENERAL PLAN OF THE POEM

I. The banishment of Melancholy to the place where she belongs. (Why is she banished? Where is she sent?)

II. The calling forth of Mirth and her companions. (Who are they?)

III. Pleasures of a merry man:
- A. In the open country,
  - 1. In early morning,
    - (a) Pleasing sounds:
      - (1) ....
      - (2) .... (Enumerate those given,—lines 41–68.)
      - (3) .... etc.
    - (b) Pleasing sights:
      - (1) Beauties of sunrise.
      - (2) .... (Enumerate those given,—lines 69–80.)
      - (3) .... etc.
  - 2. At noon, in and around a farm cottage.
    - (a) The farm life, showing thrift and contentment. (What are some of the things that would especially give pleasure?)
- B. In the country hamlet,
  - 1. On a holiday afternoon,
    - (a) ....
    - (b) .... (Enumerate those pleasures,—lines 93–98.)
    - (c) ....
  - 2. In the evening,
    - (a) ....
    - (b) .... (Enumerate,—lines 100–116.)
- C. In the towered city,
  - (a) .... (Enumerate pleasures,—lines 117–150.)
  - (b) ....

IV. Conclusion.

Complete the above outline, noting carefully the viewpoint at every step.

GLOSSARY

Aurora, goddess of the dawn.

Bacchus, god of wine.

Cerberus, the three-headed watch dog of Hades.

Cimmerian, pertaining to the Cimmerians. These people are represented as living in a land of perpetual darkness.

Corydon, name of shepherd used in pastoral poetry.

Cranks, twists or turns of speech.

Cynosure, center of attraction.

Dight, decked, dressed.

Drudging goblin, Robin Goodfellow, or Puck. He, Mab, and Friar Rush, or the will-o'-the-wisp, were the three most mischievous sprites in English folk-tales.

Elysian, pertaining to Elysium, the dwelling place of happy souls after death. This was usually located by the ancients on the western margin of the world.

Eurydice, the wife of Orpheus, the famous mythical musician. According to the classical story,[1] when Eurydice died, Orpheus sought her in the lower world. There he so charmed Pluto with his music, that Eurydice was allowed to follow her husband back to earth on condition that Orpheus did not look back until they reached the upper air. He was so fearful that Eurydice was not coming, however, that he looked back, and lost her forever.

Friar's lantern, Friar Rush, or the will-o'-the-wisp, was popularly supposed to mislead travelers by the light of his lantern.

Hamlet, a small village.

Hebe, goddess of youth, and cup-bearer to the gods.

Hymen, god of marriage.

Jonson's learned sock, comedies of Ben Jonson. The *sock* was the name given to the low-heeled shoe worn by comedians. Tragedians wore the buskin, or high-heeled shoe.

Mab, a fairy queen. See note under *drudging goblin.*

Orpheus, see note on *Eurydice.*

Phillis, name of shepherdess in old pastoral poetry.

Pied, of two or more colors.

Pluto, god of Hades, or the lower world.

Quips, jests.

Rebeck, a stringed instrument, akin to the viol.

Stygian, pertaining to the Styx, a river in Hades.

Tale, number. "Tells his tale" = counts his sheep.

Thestylis }
Thyrsis } names given to shepherds in pastoral poetry.

Uncouth, unknown, strange.

Venus, goddess of love and beauty.

Wiles, tricks.

Yclep'd, called, named.

Zephyr, the West Wind.

SUGGESTIONS TO STUDENTS

1. Which do you think is the main purpose of this poem—to interest the reader in mythology and folk-lore, or to present the mood which the author wants him to feel? 2. Are there any personal glimpses of Milton to be

---

[1] Notice how Milton has referred to this same story in "Lycidas" and in "Il Penseroso."

found in the poem? If so, what are they? 3. What is there remarkable in the fact that a *Puritan* should write lines 32–34? 4. What was Milton's opinion of Shakespeare? 5. Can you name some of the plays he evidently had in mind when he wrote "uttered his native wood notes wild"? 6. In this connection what type of plays would a *merry* man enjoy? 7. What is meant by "Jonson's learned *sock*"? 8. Do you remember how Washington Irving made use of lines 139–140 of this poem in his description of Ichabod Crane in "The Legend of Sleepy Hollow"? If not, look up the passage.

IL PENSEROSO

John Milton

Hence, vain deluding joys,
The brood of folly without father bred!
How little you bested,
Or fill the fixèd mind with all your toys;
Dwell in some idle brain,   5
And fancies fond with gaudy shapes possess,
As thick and numberless
As the gay motes that people the sunbeams,
Or likest hovering dreams,
The fickle pensioners of Morpheus' train.   10
But hail! thou Goddess sage and holy,
Hail, divinest Melancholy!
Whose saintly visage is too bright
To hit the sense of human sight,
And therefore to our weaker view,   15
O'erlaid with black, staid Wisdom's hue.
Black, but such as in esteem
Prince Memnon's sister might beseem,
Or that starred Ethiop queen that strove
To set her beauty's praise above   20
The Sea-Nymphs, and their powers offended.
Yet thou art higher far descended:
Thee bright-haired Vesta, long of yore,
To solitary Saturn bore;
His daughter she (in Saturn's reign,   25
Such mixture was not held a stain);
Oft in glimmering bowers and glades
He met her, and in secret shades
Of woody Ida's inmost grove,
While yet there was no fear of Jove.   30
Come, pensive Nun, devout and pure,
Sober, steadfast, and demure,

All in a robe of darkest grain,
Flowing with majestic train,
And sable stole of cypress lawn   35
Over thy decent shoulders drawn.
Come, but keep thy wonted state,
With even step, and musing gait,
And looks commercing with the skies,
Thy rapt soul sitting in thine eyes: 40
There, held in holy passion still,
Forget thyself to marble, till
With a sad leaden downward cast,
Thou fix them on the earth as fast.
And join with thee calm Peace and Quiet,   45
Spare Fast, that oft with gods doth diet,
And hears the Muses in a ring,
Aye round about Jove's altar sing.
And add to these retired Leisure,
That in trim gardens takes his pleasure;   50
But, first and chiefest, with thee bring
Him that yon soars on golden wing,
Guiding the fiery-wheelèd throne,
The Cherub Contemplation;
And the mute Silence hist along,   55
'Less Philomel will deign a song,
In her sweetest, saddest plight,
Smoothing the rugged brow of Night,
While Cynthia checks her dragon yoke,
Gently o'er th' accustomed oak.   60
Sweet bird that shunn'st the noise of folly,
Most musical, most melancholy!
Thee, chauntress, oft the woods among
I woo to hear thy even-song;
And, missing thee, I walk unseen   65
On the dry smooth-shaven green,
To behold the wandering moon,
Riding near her highest noon,
Like one that had been led astray
Through the heaven's wide pathless way;   70
And oft, as if her head she bowed,
Stooping through a fleecy cloud.
Oft, on a plat of rising ground,
I hear the far-off curfew sound
Over some wide-watered shore,   75
Swinging low with sullen roar;
Or if the air will not permit,

Some still removèd place will fit,
Where glowing embers through the room
Teach light to counterfeit a gloom;   80
Far from all resort of mirth,
Save the cricket on the hearth,
Or the bellman's drowsy charm,
To bless the doors from nightly harm.
Or let my lamp, at midnight hour,   85
Be seen in some high lonely tower,
Where I may oft outwatch the Bear,
With thrice-great Hermes, or unsphere
The spirit of Plato, to unfold
What worlds, or what vast regions hold   90
The immortal mind, that hath forsook
Her mansion in this fleshly nook;
And of those demons that are found
In fire, air, flood, or underground,
Whose power hath a true consent   95
With planet or with element.
Sometimes let gorgeous Tragedy
In sceptred pall come sweeping by,
Presenting Thebes, or Pelops' line,
Or the tale of Troy divine.   100
Or what (though rare) of later age
Ennobled hath the buskined stage.
But, O sad Virgin! that thy power
Might raise Musæus from his bower;
Or bid the soul of Orpheus sing   105
Such notes as, warbled to the string,
Drew iron tears down Pluto's cheek,
And made Hell grant what love did seek.
Or call up him that left half told
The story of Cambuscan bold,   110
Of Camball, and of Algarsife,
And who had Canace to wife,
That own'd the virtuous ring and glass,
And of the wondrous horse of brass,
On which the Tartar king did ride;   115
And if aught else great bards beside,
In sage and solemn tunes have sung,
Of tourneys, and of trophies hung;
Of forests, and enchantments drear,
Where more is meant than meets the ear.   120
Thus, Night, oft see me in thy pale career,
Till civil-suited Morn appear,

Not tricked and frounced, as she was wont
With the Attick boy to hunt,
But kerchieft in a comely cloud,   135
While rocking winds are piping loud,
Or ushered with a shower still,
When the gust hath blown his fill,
Ending on the rustling leaves,
With minute-drops from off the eaves.   130
And, when the sun begins to fling
His flaring beams, me, Goddess, bring
To archèd walks of twilight groves,
And shadows brown, that Sylvan loves,
Of pine, or monumental oak,   135
Where the rude ax with heavèd stroke
Was never heard the nymphs to daunt,
Or fright them from their hallowed haunt.
There in close covert, by some brook,
Where no profaner eye may look,   140
Hide me from day's garish eye,
While the bee with honeyed thigh,
That at her flowery work doth sing,
And the waters murmuring,
With such consort as they keep,   145
Entice the dewy-feathered sleep.
And let some strange mysterious dream
Wave at his wings, in airy stream
Of lively portraiture displayed,
Softly on my eyelids laid.   150
And, as I wake, sweet music breathe
Above, about, or underneath,
Sent by some spirit to mortals good,
Or the unseen Genius of the wood.
But let my due feet never fail   155
To walk the studious cloister's pale,
And love the high embowèd roof,
With antique pillars massy-proof,
And storied windows richly dight,
Casting a dim religious light.   160
There let the pealing organ blow,
To the full-voiced quire below,
In service high and anthems clear,
As may with sweetness, through mine ear,
Dissolve me into ecstasies   165
And bring all Heaven before mine eyes.
And may at last my weary age

Find out the peaceful hermitage,
The hairy gown and mossy cell,
Where I may sit and rightly spell,   170
Of every star that heaven doth shew,
And every herb that sips the dew;
Till old experience do attain
To something like prophetic strain.
These pleasures, Melancholy, give,   175
And I with thee will choose to live.

1. What is indicated by the fact that "Il Penseroso" is so much longer than "L'Allegro"? 2. What new element does Milton introduce that was lacking in the other poem? 3. What times and places are emphasized here? How do they compare with those made prominent in "L'Allegro"? Do you think these are well chosen? 4. How do the pleasures of *evening* differ for the two types of men, or the two different moods? How do their pleasures in the *daytime* differ? 5. What type of plays would a thoughtful man enjoy? 6. What is meant by "the buskined stage"? 7. Can you name a poem which Milton evidently had in mind in lines 116–120? 8. What particular intellectual pleasure does the thoughtful man find in the fire-lighted room? The tower? The woods in the afternoon? The dim cathedral?

THE GENERAL PLAN OF THE POEM

I.   The banishment of Mirth
II. The calling forth of Melancholy and her companions.
III. Description of Melancholy.
IV. Pleasures of a pensive, or thoughtful man:
    A. In earlier part of life.
      1. At night:
       (a) Out of doors.
         (1) In the woods.
           (a') .... (Pleasures?)
         (2) On a dry smooth-shaven green.
           (a') .... (Pleasures?)
         (3) On a hillside.
           (a') .... (Pleasures?)
       (b) Indoors:
         (1) In a quiet fire-lighted room, earlier in evening.
           (a') ....
           (b') ....
           (c') .... (Pleasures?)
           (d') .... etc.

(2) In a lonely tower at midnight.
    (a′) ....
        (1′) ....   (Pleasures?)
        (2′) ....
(3) In places of amusement, or of recreation:
    (a′) ....
        (1′) ....   (Pleasures?)
        (2′) ....
        (3′) ....
    (b′) ....
    (c′) ....
        (1′) ....
        (2′) ....
        (3′) ....

2. In the daytime:
  (a) In the house on a dark, rainy morning.
    (1) ....
    (2) ....   (Pleasures?)
  (b) Out of doors in the middle of day.
    (1) ....
        (a′) ....
        (b′) ....
        (c′) ....   (Pleasures?)
        (d′) ....
  (c) In dim cathedrals.
    (1) ....
    (2) ....
    (3) ....
    (4) ....   (Pleasures?)
    (5) ....
    (6) ....
B. In old age:
  1. ....
    (a) ....
    (b) ....   (Pleasures?)
    (c) ....
V. Conclusion.
Complete the above outline, noting the point of view at every step.

GLOSSARY

Algarsife, See note on *Cambuscan.*
Attick boy, Cephalus of Attica, Greece. According to Ovid, the goddess
  of the dawn, Aurora, loved Cephalus and went hunting with him.

Bear, The constellation of the Bear. "To outwatch the Bear" would be to stay up all night.

bested, assist, avail.

buskin'd stage, The buskins were high-heeled shoes worn by tragic actors. Lines 102–103 mean the best examples of tragedy.

Camball, See note on *Cambuscan.*

Cambuscan, Cambus Khan. In lines 109–115, Milton refers to the unfinished story that Chaucer puts into the mouth of the Squire in the "Canterbury Tales."

Canace, See note on *Cambuscan.*

Cynthia, another name for Artemis or Diana; hence the moon personified.

Cypress lawn, black crêpe.

decent, comely.

Ethiop queen, Cassiopeia, afterwards made a constellation.

grain, Milton here means Tyrian purple.

Hermes, The Greek god identified with the Roman Mercury was also identified with the Egyptian Thoth. He may be "thrice great" on this account; or it may refer to Thoth, who was great as philosopher, priest, and king.

hist, bring along silently.

Ida, Mount Ida.

Jove, identified with Zeus, or Jupiter, the king of gods and men.

Memnon, an Ethiopian prince celebrated for his beauty.

Morpheus, god of Sleep.

Musæus, a half mythological Greek poet.

Orpheus, See note on *Eurydice* in Glossary for "L'Allegro."

Pelops, Thebes, Pelops' line, and Troy were the great subjects of the tragedies of Æschylus, Sophocles, and Euripides, the tragic trio of Greece. The unhappy descendants of Pelops ruled the Peloponnesus.

Philomel, nightingale.

Plato, Greek philosopher.

Pluto, god of Hades, or the under-world. See note under *Eurydice* in Glossary for "L'Allegro."

Saturn, father of Jove. His son usurped his power and became king of the gods.

Starr'd Ethiop queen, Cassiopeia.

Sylvan, Silvanus, a rural deity, guardian of woods, fields, flocks, and herdsmen's homes.

Thebes, a city-state of ancient Greece.

Vesta, goddess of the hearth.

Of these companion poems which one seems to be Milton's favorite? Which is yours?

ETUDE REALISTE [1]

Swinburne

I

A baby's feet, like sea-shells pink,
  Might tempt, should heaven see
      meet,
An angel's lips to kiss, we think,
  A baby's feet.

Like rose-hued sea-flowers toward
      the heat   5
They stretch and spread and wink
Their ten soft buds that part and
      meet.

No flower-bells that expand and
      shrink
  Gleam half so heavenly sweet
As shine on life's untrodden brink 10
  A baby's feet.

II

A baby's hands, like rosebuds furled
  Whence yet no leaf expands,
Ope if you touch, though close up-
      curled,
  A baby's hands.   15

Then, fast as warriors grip their
      brands

[1] Study from life.

When battle's bolt is hurled,
They close, clenched hard like tight-
      ening bands.

No rosebuds yet by dawn impearled
  Match, even in loveliest lands, 20
The sweetest flowers in all the
      world—
  A baby's hands.

III

A baby's eyes, ere speech begin,
  Ere lip learn words or sighs,
Bless all things bright enough to
      win   25
  A baby's eyes.

Love, while the sweet thing laughs
      and lies,
  And sleep flows out and in,
Sees perfect in them Paradise.

Their glance might cast out pain
      and sin,   30
  Their speech make dumb the wise,
By mute glad god-head felt within
  A baby's eyes.

LOST YOUTH [1]

Robert Louis Stevenson

Sing me a song of a lad that is gone,
  Say, could that lad be I?
Merry of soul he sailed on a day
  Over the sea to Skye.[2]

Mull [2] was astern, Egg [2] on the port,
  Rum [2] on the starboard bow; 6
Glory of youth glowed in his soul:
  Where is that glory now?

[1] Used by permission of Charles Scribner's Sons.
[2] Names of islands northwest of Scotland.

Fradelle & Young.

ROBERT LOUIS STEVENSON
Aged 14 (1865)

138

Sing me a song of a lad that is gone,
  Say, could that lad be I?   10
Merry of soul he sailed on a day
  Over the sea to Skye.

Give me again all that was there,
  Give me the sun that shone!
Give me the eyes, give me the soul, 15
  Give me the lad that 's gone!

Sing me a song of a lad that is gone,
  Say, could that lad be I?
Merry of soul he sailed on a day
  Over the sea to Skye.   20

Billows and breeze, islands and seas,
  Mountains of rain and sun,
All that was good, all that was fair,
  All that was me is gone.

THE CELESTIAL SURGEON [1]

Robert Louis Stevenson

If I have faltered more or less
In my great task of happiness;
If I have moved among my race
And shown no glorious morning face;
If beams from happy human eyes   5
Have moved me not; if morning skies,
Books, and my food, and summer rain
Knocked on my sullen heart in vain;—
Lord, thy most pointed pleasure take
And stab my spirit broad awake;   10
Or, Lord, if too obdurate I,
Choose Thou, before that spirit die,
A piercing pain, a killing sin,
And to my dead heart run them in!

VICTORY IN DEFEAT [2]

Edwin Markham

Defeat may serve as well as victory
To shake the soul and let the glory out.
When the great oak is straining in the wind,
The boughs drink in new beauty, and the trunk
Sends down a deeper root on the windward side   5
Only the soul that knows the mighty grief
Can know the mighty rapture. Sorrows come
To stretch out spaces in the heart for joy.

---

[1] Used by special arrangement with Charles Scribner's Sons.
[2] Used by special permission of the author.

A MILE WITH ME [1]

Henry Van Dyke

O who will walk a mile with me
  Along life's merry way?
A comrade blithe and full of glee,
Who dares to laugh out loud and free,
And let his frolic fancy play,   5
Like a happy child, through the flowers gay
That fill the field and fringe the way
  Where he walks a mile with me.

And who will walk a mile with me
  Along life's weary way?   10
A friend whose heart has eyes to see
The stars shine out o'er the darkening lea,
And the quiet rest at the end o' the day,—
A friend who knows, and dares to say,
The brave, sweet words that cheer the way   15
  Where he walks a mile with me.

With such a comrade, such a friend,
I fain would walk till journeys end,
Through summer sunshine, winter rain,
And then?—Farewell, we shall meet again!   20

A BELL [2]

Clinton Scollard

Had I the power
To cast a bell that should, from some grand tower,
At the first Christmas hour,
Out-ring,
And fling   5
A jubilant message wide,
The forgèd metals should be thus allied;—
No iron Pride,
But soft Humility and rich-veined Hope
Cleft from a sunny slope,   10
And there should be

---

[1] From *Music and Other Poems* by Henry Van Dyke, Copyright 1904, Charles Scribner's Sons. Used by special arrangement with the publishers.
[2] Used by permission of Houghton Mifflin Co.

White Charity,
And silvery Love, that knows not Doubt nor Fear,
To make the peal more clear;
And then, to firmly fix the fine alloy,   15
There should be Joy!

THE HERITAGE [1]

Abbie Farwell Brown

No matter what my birth may be,
  No matter where my lot is cast,
I am the heir in equity
  Of all the precious Past.

The art, the science, and the lore 5
  Of all the ages long since dust,
The wisdom of the world in store,
  Are mine, all mine in trust.

The beauty of the living earth,
  The power of the golden sun,   10
The Present, whatsoe'er my birth,
  I share with everyone.

As much as any man am I
  The owner of the working day;
Mine are the minutes as they fly 15
  To save or throw away.

And mine the Future to bequeath
  Unto the generations new;
I help to shape it with my breath,
  Mine as I think or do.   20

Present and Past my heritage,
  The Future laid in my control;—
No matter what my name or age,
  I am a Master-soul!

THE SOLDIER [2]

Rupert Brooke

If I should die, think only this of me:
That there's some corner of a foreign field
That is forever England. There shall be
In that rich earth a richer dust concealed;
A dust whom England bore, shaped, made aware,   5
Gave, once, her flowers to love, her ways to roam;
A body of England's, breathing English air,
Washed by the rivers, blest by suns of home.

And think, this heart, all evil shed away,
A pulse in the eternal mind, no less,   10
Gives somewhere back the thoughts by England given;

[1] From *Songs of Sixpence.* Used by special arrangement with the Houghton Mifflin Company.
[2] Used by special arrangement with the John Lane Company. From *Collected Poems of Rupert Brooke.*

Her sights and sounds; dreams happy as her day;
And laughter, learnt of friends; and gentleness,
In hearts at peace, under an English heaven.

IN FLANDERS FIELDS [1]

John McCrae [2]

In Flanders fields the poppies blow
Between the crosses, row on row,
That mark our place, and in the sky
The larks, still bravely singing, fly,
Scarce heard amid the guns below.　　　　　5

We are the dead; short days ago
We lived, felt dawn, saw sunset glow,
Loved and were loved, and now we lie
　In Flanders fields.
Take up our quarrel with the foe!　　　　　10
To you from failing hands we throw
The torch; be yours to hold it high!
If you break faith with us who die
We shall not sleep, though poppies grow
　In Flanders fields.　　　　　15

THE BEST

Nelson Robins

Did you fail in the race?
Did you faint in the spurt
Where the hot dust choked and burned?
Did you breast the tape 'midst the flying dirt
That the leader's spikes had spurned?　　　　　5
Did you do your best—
Oh, I know you lost. I know that your time was bad.
The best of it since the beginning, lad,
Is in taking your licking and grinning, lad,
If you gave them the best you had.　　　　　10

Did your tackle fall short?
Did the runner flash by

[1] Used by courtesy of G. P. Putnam's Sons.
[2] Both Lieutenant Brooke and Colonel John McCrae gave their lives during the World War. The former lies on the Island of Skyros, and the latter in "Flanders fields."

With the score that won the game?
Did it break your heart when you missed the try?
Did you choke with the hurt and shame?   15
If you did your best—
Oh, I know the score; I followed you all the way through.
And that is why I am saying, lad,
That the best of the fight is the staying, lad,
And the best of all games is the playing, lad,   20
If you give them the best in you.

SUGGESTIONS TO STUDENTS

The simple lyric, for the most part, needs little comment. It is to be read, talked over informally, and *enjoyed*. What can you infer in each case regarding the personality of the author? Do you think you would like to have him as a friend?

The following simple lyrics written by high school seniors are given here with the hope that other students will also try to write something in this type.

JUST A FRIEND

Dost thou know what it is that binds thee
With the strength of a thousand chains
Through the brightest of joyful sunshine,
Through the hardest of darkest rains?
Dost thou know what it is that binds thee   5
To the heart of your dearest friend?
Hast thou learned the age-old lesson
From the primal beginning to end?

If thou hast not, dear fellow human,
Then list and I'll tell you the charm;   10
I have found that the keynote is service—
Observations have sounded alarm;
I have come to this final conclusion:
'Tis toiling for dear ones that brings
To your heart all the joys of true friendship,   15
And robs it of achings and stings.

It is service allayed with your blessing,
Which is not of the body alone,
But your heart must be deep in your toiling,
Otherwise laugh will turn to a moan.   20
Then, 'tis silent and deep understanding

Which, along with your smiles and your aid,
Makes warmer the heart e'en in breaking,
And you're glad of the price you have paid.

(V. C. '20.)

WAVES

Waves, sparkling waves upon the sea
That come splashing in to me;
Dainty little water crests,
Laughing little water jests,
That come smiling in to me,   5
On this joyous, joyous sea.

Waves, playing in the sun's first rays,
Sprightly little water fays,
That are holding fairy court
In the garden of their sport,   10
Playing in the sun's first rays,
Joyous little water fays.

Wavelets, slumbering in the sun's hot noon,
Have you gone so very soon
From upon the waxèd ocean,   15
Without thought or gentle motion?
Slumbering in the sun's hot noon,
Wavelets, have you gone so soon?

Silver moon, with thoughts of thee,
Riding on the jet-black sea,   20
Ocean moves in harmony;
Waves come dancing in to me
As I stand upon the sand,
Looking down the darkened strand.

Wavelets, if you wash upon the shore,   25
I shall stand forever more,
Watching your fantastic dance,
Glorying, wondering, all entranced—
Wavelets, if you break upon the shore,
I shall stand here evermore.   30

(N. F. M. '20.)

A FEW FAMOUS LYRICAL POEMS FOR OPTIONAL READING

(Read those not read before)

Note.—Read as many as you have time for. Give in each case the author's mood and central thought. Which poems did you like best?

"On Receipt of My Mother's Picture"	Cowper
'To Mary"	Cowper
"A Man's a Man"	Burns
"To a Mountain Daisy"	Burns
"To a Mouse"	Burns
"To an Evening Star"	Blake
"To the Muses"	Blake
"Ruth"	Thomas Hood
"The Song of the Shirt"	Thomas Hood
"Past and Present"	Thomas Hood
"The Journey Onwards"	Thomas Moore
"The Soldier's Dream"	Thomas Campbell
"To the Daisy"	Wordsworth
"We Are Seven"	Wordsworth
"The Daffodils"	Wordsworth
"The Reverie of Poor Susan"	Wordsworth
"She Was a Phantom of Delight"	Wordsworth
"She Walks in Beauty"	Byron
"When We Two Parted"	Byron
"The Recollection"	Shelley
"Lines Written Among the Euganean Hills"	Shelley
"Lines on the Mermaid Tavern"	Keats
"The Cry of the Children"	Mrs. Browning
"Home Thoughts from Abroad"	Browning
"Home Thoughts from the Sea"	Browning
"Merlin and the Gleam"	Tennyson
"The Salt of the Earth"	Swinburne
"To a Waterfowl"	Bryant
"Robert o' Lincoln"	Bryant
"The Psalm of Life"	Longfellow
"The Builders"	Longfellow
"The Hanging of the Crane"	Longfellow
"The Eternal Goodness"	Whittier
"The Barefoot Boy"	Whittier
"The Chambered Nautilus"	Holmes
"The Rhodora"	Emerson
"Each and All"	Emerson
"Tampa Robins"	Sidney Lanier
"The Marshes of Glynn"	Sidney Lanier

Grouped together in this picture are some of the principal poets of America with three visitors from England. The photograph was made at a poet's dinner at the Hotel Astor with John Masefield as guest of honor. In the group *standing, from left to right*: Lawrence Housman, Witter Bynner, Percy MacKaye, Edwin Markham, Cale Young Rice, Louis Untermeyer, Vachel Lindsay. *Sitting, from left to right*: Amy Lowell, Josephine Daskam Bacon, John Masefield, Alfred Noyes.

Selections from the poems of Alice Meynell, Richard Le Gallienne, Sara Teasdale, Edith Wyatt, Vachel Lindsay, Amelia J. Burr, Willard Wattles, Margaret Widdemer, Jessie B. Rittenhouse, Hermann Hagedorn, William Rose Benét.

Any selection from *The Little Book of Modern Verse,* ed. by Jessie B. Rittenhouse.

Any selection from *Poems of the Great War,* ed. by J. W. Cunliffe.

Any selection from *A Treasury of War Poetry,* ed. by George Herbert Clarke.

Any selection from *High Tide,* ed. by Mrs. Waldo Richards.

Any selection from the collections of American and British poems ed. by Louis Untermeyer.

REVIEW

1. Compare the five types of lyric poetry that you have just studied, pointing out their *similarities* and *differences*. 2. Can you recognize an ode, sonnet, elegy, song, and simple lyric when you see them? What do you look for in order to determine in each case? Is the main distinction in thought or form, or in both? 3. What is the great distinction between lyric and narrative poetry? What is the position of the author in a narrative poem? In a lyric poem? 4. Which of these two great divisions of poetry did you like the better? Why? 5. Memorize beautiful passages in the lyric poems that you read.

PART THREE—DRAMATIC POETRY

PART THREE—DRAMATIC POETRY

In dramatic poetry there is an effort made to set forth life and character by means of speech and action. In its highest form, this type is written in a flexible blank verse, but occasionally both rhyme and prose are mingled with it. There are three important subdivisions of the regular poetic drama. They are comedy, dramatic history, and tragedy. Besides these, two lesser forms, the farce and the melodrama, may be named. The mask and the dramatic monologue, though not classed as dramas, are also important dramatic types.

The Beginning of the Drama in England.[1]—Although the drama as a literary type is very old, dating back, in ancient Greece, to the sixth century B. C., it did not have its beginning in England until shortly after the Norman Conquest, in the eleventh century A. D. At this time the priests, in their efforts to make some of the Bible lessons clearer to their uneducated parishioners, began introducing into the church service certain tableaux, or scenes, drawn from Bible stories. At Christmas they found it easy to represent the manger, the babe, the shepherds and the wise men, and to have the song of the angels given by the full-voiced choir. These scenes were simple to arrange and exceedingly impressive, and they carried home the Christmas story more effectively than would have been possible in any other way. On Good Friday it was easy to represent the burial of Christ's body. A crucifix, wrapped in long strips of cloth, was solemnly placed in a tomb erected for the purpose near the altar. Three days later, on Easter Sunday, the empty tomb was shown with an angel sitting beside it. As the women, bearing sweet spices, approached him, he announced that Christ had come forth from the tomb, and again the choir represented the angels singing in heaven their praise of the Risen Lord.[2]

---

[1] Before taking up the story of the evolution of the drama, read the *Suggestions to Students* to be found on pages 158–159.

[2] For interesting accounts of these ceremonies and their stage directions, see Pollard's *English Miracle Plays*, pp. xvi and xvii of the Introduction; Chambers's *Mediaeval Stage*, Vol. II, or Gayley's *Plays of Our Forefathers*, pp. 14 ff.

The Miracle and Mystery Plays.[1]—Other Biblical scenes, as well as those drawn from the lives of the saints, were from time to time presented.[2] Thus were developed the Miracle and Mystery plays. As there were not priests enough to take all of the parts, certain of the laymen were called in to help in the productions. At first all of the scenes were given in the church itself. Later, as these plays became more popular, they were performed on a platform erected in the church-yard. Gradually the laymen became more and more important in the presentations until, at last, they practically took things into their own hands and introduced material not found in the Biblical account. This the priests would not sanction, and accordingly they refused to have the plays performed any longer under the auspices of the church.

When the Miracle plays were in this way driven from the church-yards, they were taken up by the trade guilds. By this time whole cycles, or circles, of plays had been evolved, which covered all of Biblical history from the Creation to the Day of **The Cycles of Plays** Judgment. Each town developed its own cycle[3] and so the number of plays differed in different towns. Each guild was responsible for the performance of a single play. For instance, the masons' guild played the Creation, the shipwrights the building of the ark, the horseshoers the flight into Egypt, the bakers the Last Supper, the butchers the Crucifixion—and thus, as far as possible, they divided up the plays in accordance with their various occupations.

Although the Biblical story was followed quite rigidly, there were a few places where, aside from the comic scenes produced by the ranting of Herod, or the antics of the devil, other comic material was introduced, which was not to be found in the **Comic Material** Scriptures. In the play "Noah's Flood," for example, the wife of Noah is very stubborn and will not enter the ark. A quarrel results and blows are freely exchanged. The wife at last has her way and remains outside until the angry waters force her to rush on board the ship. Here the quarrel is resumed and continues until Noah begs for mercy, because, as he says, his back "is nere in two."

[1] These terms were used interchangeably in England, although a distinction was made between them on the Continent.

[2] The earliest known Miracle play in England was *The Ludus de Sancta Katharina*, first played about 1110.

[3] The manuscripts of only four of these cycles have come down to the present time. They are those of the cities of York, Coventry, and Chester; and the Towneley plays, so named from the family owning the manuscripts.

The finest bit of comedy to be found in the early Miracle plays is that given in connection with the ''Second Shepherds' Play.'' This shows real originality on the part of those who planned the play, since there is not the slightest suggestion for it in the Bible. On the first Christmas Eve, as the shepherds are watching their flocks, a man named Mak, known for his dishonesty, asks to join them. They hesitate at first, but at last consent, placing him in the center of the circle. When they have fallen asleep, Mak gets out without awaking them, seizes a sheep and carries it home. Then he and his wife, Gyll, devise a scheme whereby they will escape detection. If the shepherds decide to search their house, they will hide the sheep in the cradle and make believe it is a young child. Mak, in the meantime, hastens back to where the shepherds are still sleeping and lies down again in their midst. Later in the night, when the shepherds awake and count the sheep, they miss one, and, since Mak is at once under suspicion, they go to his house to hunt for it. Mak and his wife urge them to look thoroughly but to be careful not to awaken the baby. After a fruitless search the shepherds are about to leave, when one of them, sorry for their unjust suspicions, returns and asks permission to kiss the child and give it a coin. Before Mak can prevent him, he turns back the cover and finds the sheep. After tossing Mak in a sheet to show their resentment, the shepherds lie down again to sleep, but are prevented by the appearance of the Angel of the Lord, who announces the birth of Christ.

Thus in the Miracle plays are to be found the early beginnings of comedy, and of tragedy as well; for such plays as ''The Crucifixion,'' the ''Slaughter of the Innocents,'' and the ''Sacrifice of Isaac'' are filled with tragic elements. The pathos of this last play is especially touching. There is set forth the **Tragic Elements** terrible anguish of Abraham when, to test his faith, he is commanded to take the life of his beloved son Isaac; and the bravery of the noble boy, who, out of pity for his father's grief, overcomes his fear and urges his father to hasten.

> And let me hense be gone.''
> "O dere father, doe awaye, do awaye
> Your makeinge so moche mone!
> Nowe, trewlye, father, this talkinge
> Doth but make longe taryeinge
> I praye you, come and make endinge,

When the Miracle plays were taken over by the guilds, they were presented on movable platforms, or carts, which the apprentices drew from one street corner to another where the crowds were waiting for them. There was a special cart for each play, and when the performance was over in one part of the city, the cart would move on, its place being taken by the one presenting the next play. In this regular order the plays would be given until the cycle was complete. As a usual thing the plays began each year on Corpus Christi day [1] and it took several days to finish the series.[2]

The Presentation of the Miracle Plays

In England these movable stages consisted of two stories, the upper, on which the main action was given, and the lower story, which was used for the dressing room. In some of the plays this lower stage also represented hell, the entrance to it being a huge dragon's head which ejected smoke and fire. From this opening the devils, dressed in appropriate costumes, would come, perform their antics among the crowd, and, when the play was over, return, bearing lost souls with groans and shrieks to their place of punishment.

On the Continent the carts frequently had a third story, which represented heaven, in which case the middle platform would be earth, and the lower one hell.

"The Passion Play," [3] which has been given at Ober-Ammergau, Bavaria, every ten years since the beginning of the seventeenth century, is the best known modern example of the Miracle play that we have.

The Moralities.—Beginning a little later in time, but, for the most part, growing up side by side with the Miracle plays, were the Moralities, which dealt with abstractions and aimed to teach moral lessons. In one particular these were superior to the Miracle plays; for they showed inventive skill, while the Miracle plays were confined quite closely to the Scriptural story. In every other way, however, the Moralities were inferior, for they were heavy and uninteresting. When characters are known to represent, not real people, but abstract virtues such as Good Deeds, Charity, Wisdom, Pity, Perseverance, Discretion, and vices like

[1] Usually in the first week in June.
[2] An interesting description of the performance of one of these plays is given in Moody and Lovett's *A History of English Literature*, pp. 89–90.
[3] See Stoddard's *Lectures*, Vol IV, for an interesting illustrated account of this play.

Jealousy, Slander, Hypocrisy and the like, the human interest is lost. However, in time the Moralities became more humanized and therefore more interesting, since, being used to suggest greatly needed reforms, they represented living persons under the guise of a virtue or a vice. The most important character in the Morality plays was known as the Vice.[1] He, with the devil, which was brought over from the Miracle plays, made fun for the audience, and the play usually ended with the Vice's beating the devil over the head with a stick or bladder as he was being carried off on the devil's shoulders into hell-mouth.

"Everyman" is the best known of the early Morality plays. To-day modern audiences have an opportunity to see in "Everywoman" a play that not only gives them a better idea of the old Moralities, but is very interesting as well, because of a real human appeal which it has.

The Interludes.—Closely connected with the Moralities and growing out of them,[2] were the Interludes, which consisted of amusing scenes played in gentlemen's halls between the courses of a dinner, or to brighten the uninteresting parts of a Miracle or Morality play. The most famous writer of Interludes was John Heywood, a jester at the court of Queen Mary. "The Four P's" was his best production. The interest of the Interludes centered in the humorous dialogues. In the "Four P's," a Palmer, a Pardoner, a Peddler, and a Potycary are engaged in conversation when a dispute arises as to which can tell the bigger lie, the Palmer or the Pardoner. They at once decide to have a regular contest to settle the point. As a result the Palmer wins when he makes the declaration that he has seen five hundred thousand women—

> "Yet in all places where I have been
> Of all the women that I have seen,
> I never saw or knew in my conscience
> *Any one woman out of patience.*"

The First Real Comedies in England.—Although, as has been said, there were elements of comedy to be found in the native drama, the first genuine comedy produced in England did not appear until about the middle of the sixteenth century, and this was under classical influence. Ever since the beginning of the

[1] The Vice was the direct forerunner of the fool of Shakespeare's plays.
[2] Both the Moralities and the Interludes were presented by professional actors who strolled about giving their performances in the halls of rich men or in the open city squares.

Renaissance, there had been much interest in the plays of the Latin playwrights, Terence and Plautus. Finally Nicholas Udall, the headmaster of Eton, made a translation of a comedy by Plautus, introduced some English elements, and had his boys act the play. This was "Ralph Royster Doyster," the first real comedy given in England. Although almost wholly of Latin origin, this play was important since it gave suggestions in construction to English playwrights, which they were not long in making use of. The next comedy to appear, "Gammer Gurton's Needle," [1] was wholly of English origin, and, although the humor is much coarser than that of "Ralph Royster Doyster," the play marks an important stage in the history of the drama in England. Here there is a following of the classical model as regards construction, but the life set forth is wholly English.

The Rise of Tragedy.—The first tragedy, "Gorboduc," was written about 1561 by Sackville and Norton. The latter wrote the first three acts, but, for some reason or other, Sackville completed the work. Tragedy did not appear until more than ten years after the production of the first comedy, because it was harder to write, harder to act, and harder to make interesting to an uneducated audience than comedy. Unfortunately, tragedy in England got a poor start, since the first ones were modeled after those of the Latin writer, Seneca, and were absolutely lacking in action. Although there was plenty of war and bloodshed off the stage, the audience heard only reports of what was going on. Thus in "Gorboduc" four old men occupied the center of the stage and received the messengers who brought the news, and the play ended with their long, moralized summary of events.

Although this was not interesting to the people as a whole, since they had had their taste for action on the stage formed by the earlier plays, yet the University men held to the methods used by the classical writers and tried to guide the drama along the lines laid down by the Greeks and Romans. In the clas-

The Lead Taken by the Popular Drama Over the Classical

sical plays the unities of time, place, and action were rigidly adhered to. This meant that the time should not extend over more than twenty-four hours, that there should be no change of scene, and that the action should be simple and unified. Then, too, comedy and tragedy were so completely separated that

[1] Quite an interesting account of this play may be found in Long's *English Literature*, pp. 124–125.

Reproduced by permission of "The Quarterly Review" from the article on
"The Elizabethan Stage," by William Archer.

INTERIOR OF THE FORTUNE THEATER, LONDON,
BUILT IN 1599

The drawing is from Mr. Walter H. Godfrey's reconstruction from
the builder's contract. Dimensions: Width of main stage, 43 ft.;
depth of main stage to rear stage opening, 27 ft. 6 in.; depth of
rear stage, 7 ft.; width of rear stage opening, 17 ft.; height of
rear stage, 12 ft.

no suggestion of the one was ever found in the other. The popular
dramatists, on the other hand, studied the people and found out
what they liked. They, therefore, refused to abide by all of the
classical traditions, and yet they learned from the classical plays
certain lessons in construction which made their own work more
consistent and true to life. They soon saw the absurdity, for in-

stance, of representing a child in the first act, and his great-grand-child in the last act of the same play, or of crowding into a scene a multitude of details. And so they learned to hold their imaginations within bounds, and, step by step, built up the foundation on which Shakespeare's wonderful work was to rest.

During the early years of the regular drama, the performances were given in inn-yards by strolling bands of players. In 1576, however, the first permanent playhouse, "The Theater," was built in Finsbury Fields, just outside the city limits of London, and by the end of that century there were eleven theaters in all, presided over by licensed companies of players.[1]

What Shakespeare Owed to Others.—Shakespeare so far out-distanced all other dramatic writers that he had no second, and yet what he would have been without the inspiration and suggestions and methods which he received from the works of a large number of immediate predecessors and contemporaries, it is impossible to tell. It is certain that he owed them much. To the greatest of these, Marlowe, was Shakespeare indebted for many things, but especially for the particular form of blank verse which he used and without which even he would have been seriously hampered in giving dramatic expression to the beauty and greatness of his thought. Symonds has said regarding the importance of Marlowe's work for the drama: "It was he who irrevocably decided the destinies of the romantic drama; and the whole subsequent evolution of that species, including Shakespeare's work, can be regarded as the expansion, rectification, and artistic ennoblement of the type fixed by Marlowe's epoch-making tragedies."

SUGGESTIONS TO STUDENTS

1. In order more fully to understand and appreciate dramatic poetry, as well as the prose plays, you will want to know something as to how the present forms have been evolved. The story is an interesting and profitable one. Read carefully what has been given above, trying to imagine yourselves as interested spectators of the different kinds of plays so that they will seem real to you. 2. Look up the references given in the footnotes to interesting accounts of performances of some of these

[1] For good descriptions of these early theaters, their equipment and the presentation of plays, see Symond's *A Student's History of English Literature*, pp. 119–121; Halleck's *New English Literature*, pp. 158–166; Long's *English Literature*, pp. 128–130; Moody and Lovett's *A History of English Literature*, pp. 99–100; Gettemy's *Outline Studies in the Shakespearean Drama*, pp. 40–44.

plays. Notice the chief changes in the plays at each step—the Miracle and Mystery plays, the Moralities, the Interludes, Early Comedies and Tragedies, bringing the story down to Shakespeare's time. 3. Work out, from what has been said, the evolution of the *stage* and *actors* through the different periods. 4. Write a theme, choosing some such title as "What I Saw in Coventry on Corpus Christi Day, 1350," or "My Visit to 'The Theater' in Finsbury Fields"—here describing an imaginary experience on the day this theater was first opened to the public.

5. The following scenes from Marlowe's plays are given here so that you may see something of what it must have meant, by way of inspiration, to Shakespeare to have had a predecessor who could write such powerful scenes as these. If all parts of Marlowe's plays had been as strong as these scenes, he would have been a dangerous rival to Shakespeare himself. As it is, the best of Marlowe's dramatic work is to be found right here. There is not a single play that he wrote strong enough throughout to make it actable on the stage to-day.

You will not need to make a detailed study of these scenes, but read them outside of class, and feel the power in them.

Following are some of the great scenes from Marlowe's [1] plays :—

From DOCTOR FAUSTUS [2]

In this play Marlowe represents a medieval German scholar who sells his soul to the devil in return for twenty-four years of absolute world-knowledge, which he passionately desires.

A part of SCENE V

(*Re-enter Mephistophilis with Devils, who give crowns and rich apparel to Faustus, dance and depart.*

    Faust. Speak, Mephistophilis, what means this show?
    Meph. Nothing, Faustus, but to delight thy mind withall,
      And to show thee what magic can perform.
    Faust. But may I raise up spirits when I please?
    Meph. Ay, Faustus, and do greater things than these.   5
    Faust. Then there's enough for a thousand souls.
      Here, Mephistophilis, receive this scroll,
      A deed of gift of body and of soul:

[1] Look up in any good history of English literature the life and work of Marlowe. If possible, read the play "Marlowe," by Josephine Preston Peabody, a modern writer.

[2] Although this play, as a whole, is weak in its general structure, it has one or two powerful scenes which are not unworthy to be compared with some from Shakespeare's plays. Goethe's "Faust" is based on the same story.

But yet conditionally that thou perform
All articles prescribed between us both.   10

Meph. Faustus, I swear by hell and Lucifer
To effect all promises between us made.

Faust. Then hear me read them: *On these conditions following. First, that Faustus may be a spirit in form and substance. Secondly, that Mephistophilis shall be his servant, and at his command. Thirdly, shall do for and bring him whatsoever he desires. Fourthly, that he shall be in his chamber or house invisible. Lastly, that he shall appear to the said John Faustus, at all times and in what form or shape soever he pleases. I, John Faustus, of Wertenberg, Doctor, by these presents do give both body and soul to Lucifer, Prince of the East, and his minister, Mephistophilis: and furthermore grant unto them, that twenty-four years being expired, the articles above written inviolate, full power to fetch or carry the said John Faustus, body and soul, flesh, blood, or goods, into their habitation wheresoever. By me, John Faustus.*

Meph. Speak, Faustus, do you deliver this as your deed?

Faust. Ay, take it, and the Devil give thee good on 't.

Meph. Now, Faustus, ask what thou wilt.

Faust. First will I question thee about hell.
Tell me where is the place that men call hell?

SCENE XVI

(Twenty-four years later)

Enter Faustus with Scholars

Faust. Ah, gentlemen!

1st Schol. What ails Faustus?

Faust. Ah, my sweet chamber-fellow, had I lived with thee, then had I lived still! but now I die eternally. Look, comes he not, comes he not?

2nd Schol. What means Faustus?

3rd Schol. Belike he is grown into some sickness by being over solitary.

1st Schol. If it be so, we 'll have physicians to care him. 'Tis but a surfeit. Never fear, man.

Faust. A surfeit of deadly sin that hath damned both body and soul.

2nd Schol. Yet, Faustus, look up to heaven: remember God's mercies are infinite.

Faust. But Faustus' offences can never be pardoned: the serpent that tempted Eve may be saved, but not Faustus. Ah, gentlemen, hear me with patience, and tremble not at my speeches! Though my heart pants and quivers to remember that I have been a student here these thirty years, oh, would I had never seen Wertenberg, never read book! And what wonders I have done, all Germany can witness, yea, all the world. For which Faustus hath lost both Germany and the world, yea Heaven itself, Heaven, the seat of God, the throne of the blessed, the kingdom of joy; and must remain in hell forever, hell, oh, hell, forever! Sweet friends! What shall become of Faustus being in hell forever?

3rd Schol. Yet, Faustus, call on God.

Faust. On God, whom Faustus hath abjured! On God, whom Faustus hath blasphemed! Ah, my God, I would weep, but the Devil draws in my tears. Gush forth blood instead of tears! Yea, life and soul! Oh, he stays my tongue! I would lift up my hands, but see, they hold them, they hold them!

All. Who, Faustus?

Faust. Lucifer and Mephistophilis. Ah, gentlemen, I gave them my soul for my cunning!

All. God forbid!

Faust. God forbade it indeed; but Faustus hath done it: for vain pleasure of twenty-four years hath Faustus lost eternal joy and felicity. I writ them a bill with mine own blood, the date is expired; the time will come, and he will fetch me.

1st Schol. Why did not Faustus tell us of this before, that divines might have prayed for thee?

Faust. Oft have I thought to have done so: but the Devil threatened to tear me in pieces if I named God; to fetch both body and soul if I once gave ear to divinity: and now 'tis too late. Gentlemen, away! Lest you perish with me.

2nd Schol. Oh, what shall we do to save Faustus?

Faust. Talk not of me, but save yourselves, and depart.

3rd Schol. God will strengthen me: I will stay with Faustus.

1st Schol. Tempt not God, sweet friend; but let us into the next room, and there pray for him.

Faust. Ay, pray for me, pray for me! and what noise soever ye hear, come not unto me, for nothing can rescue me.

2nd Schol. Pray thou, and we will pray that God may have mercy upon thee.

Faust. Gentlemen, farewell: if I live till morning I'll visit you: if not—Faustus is gone to hell.

All. Faustus, farewell.

(*Exeunt Scholars. The clock strikes eleven.*)

Faust. Ah, Faustus,
Now hast thou but one bare hour to live,
And then thou must be damned perpetually!
Stand still, you ever-moving spheres of Heaven,
That time may cease, and midnight never come;
Fair Nature's eye, rise, rise again and make

Perpetual day; or let this hour be but
A year, a month, a week, a natural day,
That Faustus may repent and save his soul!

.   .   .   .

The stars move still, time runs, the clock will strike,
The Devil will come, and Faustus must be damned.
O, I'll leap up to my God! Who pulls me down?
See, see where Christ's blood streams in the firmament!
One drop would save my soul—half a drop: ah, my Christ!
Ah, rend not my heart for naming of my Christ!—
Yet will I call on him: O spare me, Lucifer!—
Where is it now, 'tis gone; and see where God
Stretcheth out his arm, and bends his ireful brows!
Mountain and hills come, come and fall on me,
And hide me from the heavy wrath of God!
No! no!
Then will I headlong run into the earth;
Earth gape! O no it will not harbour me!
You stars that reigned at my nativity,
Whose influence hath allotted death and hell,
Now draw up Faustus like a foggy mist
Into the entrails of yon labouring clouds,
That when they vomit forth into the air,
My limbs may issue from their smoky mouths,
So that my soul may but ascend to Heaven.

            (*The clock strikes the half hour.*)

Ah, half the hour is past! 't will all·be past anon!
O God!
If thou wilt not have mercy on my soul,
Yet for Christ's sake whose blood hath ransomed me,
Impose some end to my incessant pain;
Let Faustus live in hell a thousand years—
A hundred thousand, and—at last—be saved!
O, no end is limited to damnèd souls!
Why wert thou not a creature wanting soul?
Or why is this immortal that thou hast?
Ah, Pythagoras' metempsychosis! were that true,
This soul should fly from me, and I be changed,
Unto some brutish beast: all beasts are happy,
For when they die,
Their souls are soon dissolved in elements;
But mine must live, still to be plagued in hell.
Curst be the parents that engendered me!
No, Faustus, curse thyself: curse Lucifer
That hath deprived thee of the joys of Heaven.

(The clock strikes twelve.)
O, it strikes, it strikes! now body, turn to air
Or Lucifer will bear thee quick to hell.
(Thunder and lightning.)
O soul, be changed into little water-drops,
And fall into the ocean—ne'er to be found.
(Enter Devils.)
My God! my God! look not so fierce on me!
Adders and serpents, let me breathe awhile!
Ugly hell, gape not   Come not, Lucifer;
I 'll burn my books!—Ah Mephistophilis!
(Exeunt Devils with Faustus.)

From EDWARD THE SECOND

In this play Marlowe has taken up the story of one of England's
weakest kings.   Because of the weakness and misrule of the king
and because he had lavished great honors and wealth upon certain
favorites of low rank, his barons rose against him, imprisoned him
in Killingworth Castle, and demanded his abdication.   His Queen,
Isabella of France, also turned against him and, together with her
lover, Roger Mortimer, plotted the King's death.   He was secretly
murdered at their instigation.   In the following scene the nobles
are demanding the crown in the interest of the young prince, afterward Edward III.

ACT THE FIFTH

Scene I [1]

Enter King Edward, Leicester, the Bishop of Winchester, and Trussel.

Leices.   Be patient, good my lord, cease to lament,
   Imagine Killingworth Castle were your court,
   And that you lay for pleasure here a space,
   Not of compulsion or necessity.
K. Edw.   Leicester, if gentle words might comfort me,   5
   Thy speeches long ago had eased my sorrows;
   For kind and loving hast thou always been.
   The griefs of private men are soon allayed,
   But not of kings.   The forest deer, being struck,
   Runs to an herb that closeth up the wounds;   10
   But, when the imperial lion's flesh is gored,

[1] The scene is an apartment in Killingworth Castle.

He rends and tears it with his wrathful paw,
And highly scorning that the lowly earth
Should drink his blood, mounts up to the air.
And so it fares with me, whose dauntless mind   15
The ambitious Mortimer would seek to curb,
And that unnatural queen, false Isabel,
That thus hath pent and mewed me in a prison;
For such outrageous passions cloy my soul,
As with the wings of rancour and disdain,   20
Full often am I soaring up to Heaven,
To plain me to the gods against them both.
But when I call to mind I am a king,
Methinks I should revenge me of my wrongs,
That Mortimer and Isabel have done.   25
But what are kings, when regiment [1] is gone,
But perfect shadows in a sunshine day?
My nobles rule, I bear the name of king;
I wear the crown, but am controlled by them,
By Mortimer and my unconstant queen,   30

.   .   .   .

Whilst I am lodged within this cave of care,
Where sorrow at my elbow still attends,
To company my heart with sad laments,
That bleeds within me for this strange exchange.
But tell me, must I now resign my crown,   35
To make usurping Mortimer a king?
B. of Win. Your grace mistakes; it is for England's good,
And princely Edward's right we crave the crown.
K. Edw. No, 'tis for Mortimer, not Edward's head;
For he 's a lamb, encompassèd by wolves,   40
Which in a moment will abridge his life.
But if proud Mortimer do wear this crown,
Heavens turn it to a blaze of quenchless fire!
Or like the snaky wreath of Tisiphon,
Engirt the temples of his hateful head;   45
So shall not England's vine be perishèd,
But Edward's name survives, though Edward dies.
Leices. My lord, why waste you thus the time away?
They stay your answer; will you yield the crown?
K. Edw. Ah, Leicester, weigh how hardly I can brook   50
To lose my crown and kingdom without cause;
To give ambitious Mortimer my right,
That like a mountain overwhelms my bliss,
In which extreme my mind here murdered is.

[1] Right to rule.

But what the heavens appoint, I must obey!   55
Here, take my crown; the life of Edward too;
       (Taking off the crown.)
Two kings in England cannot reign at once.
But stay awhile, let me be king till night,
That I may gaze upon this glittering crown;
So shall my eyes receive their last content,   60
My head, the latest honour due to it,
And jointly both yield up their wishèd right.
Continue ever, thou celestial sun;
Let never silent night possess this clime:
Stand still, you watches of the elements;   65
All times and seasons, rest you at a stay,
That Edward may be still fair England's king!
But day's bright beams doth vanish fast away,
And needs I must resign my wishèd crown.
Inhuman creatures! nursed with tiger's milk!   70
Why gape you for your sovereign's overthrow!
My diadem I mean, and guiltless life.
See, monsters, see, I 'll wear my crown again!
       (He puts on the crown.)
What, fear you not the fury of your king?
But, hapless Edward, thou art fondly [1] led;   75
They care not for thy frowns as late they did,
But seek to make a new-elected king,
Which fills my mind with strange despairing thoughts,
Which thoughts are martyrèd with endless torments,
And in this torment comfort find I none,   80
But that I feel the crown upon my head;
And therefore let me wear it yet awhile.
Trus. My lord, the parliament must have present news.
And therefore say, will you resign or no?
      (The King rageth.)
K. Edw. I 'll not resign; but whilst I live be king.   85
Traitors, be gone! and join you with Mortimer!
Elect, conspire, install, do what you will:—
Their blood and yours shall seal these treacheries!
B. of Win. This answer we 'll return, and so farewell.
      (Going with Trussel.)
Leices. Call them again, my lord, and speak them fair;   90
For if they go, the prince shall lose his right.
K. Edw. Call thou them back, I have no power to speak.
Leices. My lord, the king is willing to resign.
B. of Win. If he be not, let him choose.
K. Edw. O would I might! but heavens and earth conspire   95

[1] Foolishly.

To make me miserable! Here, reecive my crown;
Receive it? No, these innocent hands of mine
Shall not be guilty of so foul a crime.
He of you all that most desires my blood,
And will be called the murderer of a king,   100
Take it. What, are you moved? Pity you me?
Then send for unrelenting Mortimer,
And Isabel, whose eyes, being turned to steel,
Will sooner sparkle fire than shed a tear.
Yet stay, for rather than I'll look on them,   105
Here, here!   (*Gives the crown.*)
      Now, sweet God of Heaven,
Make me despise this transitory pomp,
And sit for aye enthronizèd in Heaven!
Come, death, and with thy fingers close my eyes,
Or if I live, let me forget myself.   110

B. of Win. My lord—

K. Edw. Call me not lord; away—out of my sight:
Ah, pardon me: grief makes me lunatic!
Let not that Mortimer protect my son;
More safety there is in a tiger's jaws,   115
Than his embracements. Bear this to the queen
Wet with my tears, and dried again with sighs;
        (*Gives a handkerchief.*)
If with the sight thereof she be not moved,
Return it back and dip it in my blood.
Commend me to my son, and bid him rule   120
Better than I. Yet how have I transgressed,
Unless it be with too much clemency?

Trus. And thus most humbly do we take our leave.

K. Edw. Farewell;
   (*Exeunt the Bishop of Winchester and Trussel.*)
I know the next news that they bring
Will be my death; and welcome it shall be;   125
To wretched men, death is felicity.[1]

---

[1] Scenes IV, V, and VI of Act. V are also interesting. Charles Lamb said,
"The death-scene of Marlowe's King moves pity and terror beyond any scene,
ancient or modern, with which I am acquainted." For further readings see
The Mermaid Series of the Best Plays of the Old Dramatists, the volume on
Marlowe.

Shakespeare.—

SHAKESPEARE—THE PLAYER [1]

Percy MacKaye

His wardrobe is the world, and day and night
His many-mirror'd dressing-room: At dawn
He apes the elfish faun,
Or, garbed in saffron hose and scarlet shoon,
Mimics the madcap sprite   5
Of ever-altering youth: at chime of noon
He wears the azure mail and blazoned casque
Of warring knighthood; till, at starry stroke
Of dark, all pale he dons his "inky cloak"
And meditates—the waning moon his tragic mask.   10

His theater is the soul, and man and woman
His infinite repertory: Age on age,
Treading his fancy's stage,
Ephemeral shadows of his master mind,
We act our parts—the human   15
Players of scenes long since by him designed;
And stars, that blaze in tinsel on our boards,
Shine with a moment's immortality
Because they are his understudies, free
For one aspiring hour to sound his magic chords.   20

For not with scholars and their brain-worn scripts,
Nor there behind the footlights' fading glow
Shakespeare survives: ah, no!
Deep in the passionate reality
Of raging life above the darkling crypts   25
Of death, he meditates the awed "To be
Or not to be" of millions, yet to whom
His name is nothing, there, on countless quests
Unlettered *Touchstones* quibble with his jests,
Unlaureled *Hamlets* yearn, and anguished *Lears* uploom. 30

Leave, then, to Avon's spire and silver stream
Their memory of ashes sung and sighed:
Our Shakespeare never died,
Nor e'er was born, save as the god is born
From every soul that dares to doubt and dream.   35

[1] Used by permission of the author. From *Collected Poems* by Percy MacKaye, published by the Macmillan Company.

He dreams—but is not mortal: eve and morn,
Dirge and delight, float from his brow like **prayer.**
Beside him, charmed Apollo lifts his lyre;
Below, the heart of man smolders in fire;
Between the two he stands, timeless—the poet—player.   40

SUGGESTIONS TO STUDENTS

1. How would you classify the above poem? Why? 2. How many of the references made do you recognize from your own reading of Shakespeare?

There is so much good material available on Shakespeare's life, place, and influence that the student is referred to the literary histories for this information. The following references are good ones: Halleck's *History of English Literature*, pp. 148–166; Halleck's *New English Literature*, pp. 174–198; Long's *English Literature*, pp. 137–154; Gettemy's *Outline Studies in the Shakespearean Drama*, pp. 48–64; Simonds's *A Student's History of English Literature*, pp. 129–147; Dowden's *Shakespeare Primer;* Sidney Lee's *A Life of William Shakespeare;* Hamilton Wright Mabie's *Shakespeare: Poet, Dramatist and Man;* or any good history of English literature.

Some of the Chief Characteristics of the Older Drama.[1]—Plays were written primarily to be played in the theater, and they stand or fall, as plays, according to the degree of success attained there. Thus it is not essential for a play to have literary qualities. There are, however, many great plays that are also great pieces of literature. As Professor Brander Matthews has said, they are "lifted into literature by skill of structure, by veracity of character, by felicity of dialogue." Such plays, then, may be enjoyed and interpreted through reading or study. We must not forget, though, that the action is the main thing. We should keep it constantly in mind, for the story is told and character and life are revealed wholly by means of dialogue and action. The word "drama" means to *do* or *act*.

Importance of Action

The writer of a play, according to the old ideals, has to attract all classes of people or fail in his endeavors. He is thus obliged to find some point of interest common to all, and this, it has been thought, lies in some kind of a conflict or struggle either comic or tragic. The emotion which gives rise to the struggle may be of any

The Conflict

[1] The characteristics of the modern dramas will be found to differ materially from those of the Elizabethan age.

kind, and the conflict may arouse in the audience, or reader, laughter, thought, horror, or tears. The removal of the obstacle which is causing the trouble will, then, be the main object to be attained in the course of the play. In the end of one of these great dramas, however, we are always left with the feeling that we have seen a bit of life and that life is still going on although these particular incidents have been finished and the curtain has been rung down.

Since everything must be revealed through the play itself, it must be closely unified and self-explanatory. **Need for Unity in the Drama** Nothing should be introduced that does not contribute in some way to the advancement of the plot or the accomplishment of the author's purpose.

One of the first things that a good playwright of the old school does, is to arouse expectancy that a certain event will come to pass. He foreshadows, thus letting his audience, or reader, anticipate things which are hidden from the characters themselves. **The Author's Method of Procedure** He, however, keeps people in suspense, making them await his own time, but he never disappoints them with reference to what he has led them to expect. It does not cause an audience to lose interest because an end is expected, since the real interest is not so much in the event itself as in the way it will affect the people of the drama when it does come. The author also has opportunities for the use of surprise in the particular way in which an end, though expected, is accomplished.

Every one of these plays naturally falls into three great divisions: first, the introduction, in which the atmosphere, background situations, and the leading characters are presented; second, the middle part, which takes the action or **The Three Great Divisions of a Play** conflict from its starting point to the climax; and, third, the conclusion, in which the threads are untangled and the obstacles removed. This ending, it will be noted, differs from that found in many modern plays, where the particular situation is completed but the real problem is left open to be solved by the audience itself.

The older plays are divided into five acts with intervals of time between them. This is not a necessary arrangement but a convenience. In a five-act play the following plan is usually followed:

Act One gives the introduction, necessary explanations, and the starting point of the action.

Act Two gives the development of the conflict, the entangling of the threads. Here the author hastens the action in one place, holds it back in another, keeps the audience in suspense, brings in a series of situations each with its own crisis, but he always advances the plot toward a definite end.

Act Three usually shows the full entanglement of the threads and the tying of the "great knot," which is the climax. The scene

Usual Plan for a Five-Act Play
containing the climax is the most important one because it is the turning point of the play, but it is not necessarily the scene which arouses the greatest interest. Although the climax of a play of five acts is usually found in the third act, this is not always true.

Act Four shows the fall of the action. Here the threads are one by one disentangled, and the complications unraveled. The author in this part of the play again has to retard and delay the action so that the end will not be reached too soon.

Act Five gives the final solution of difficulties and conformity of the characters to the new conditions in which they are placed. The end is the logical result of what has happened throughout the play. It should satisfy by being in keeping with what has gone before.

Although the modern plays usually have fewer than five acts, there frequently being four, three, or even one, yet in many of them the same general arrangement of material is followed excepting that it is crowded more closely together.

In every older drama there are three points which stand out with special distinctness and are essential in the action. These are: first, the *incitement* or starting point of the conflict; second, the *climax* or turning point, which is the highest place of entanglement; and third, the *catastrophe,* or conclusion. Besides

The Five Important Points
these essential points, there are two others of particular dramatic interest which are usually found in tragedy, though not always in comedy. These are the *concluding crisis,*[1] which is an event of surprising nature coming very soon after the climax, and giving a sudden downward turn to the action of the play; and the *retarding point,* which is a pause in the middle of the downward action, in which there is a suggestion of a different ending than the one which follows. Here there seems to be a choice of two paths, one leading

[1] Although the action really turns at the climax, this is not evident to all at first. This becomes apparent to all concerned at the concluding crisis. Thus it takes both these points to make the full turn.

to life, and the other to death.   The following diagram will illustrate these points:

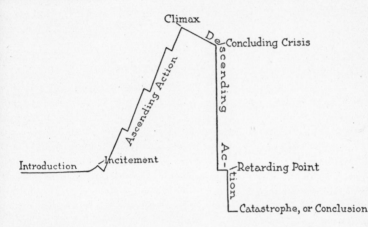

These illustrations from well known plays will help to make the
points clearer.

In "The Merchant of Venice" the *incitement* is where Antonio
agrees to sign the bond;—this makes possible the conflict.   The
climax is where Shylock gets Antonio in prison, because that is as
far as he can go unchecked.   It is the worst thing that he is
able to accomplish.   The *concluding crisis* is where Portia tells
Shylock he may have the pound of flesh, but—if he sheds one drop
of blood, or takes one particle more or less than an exact pound,
his life is forfeited.   This changes suddenly the course of the play
and gives the full control of the situation into the hands of Portia.
The *retarding point* is where Shylock is given the choice between
making a deed of gift of all of which he dies possessed to Lorenzo
and Jessica, or forfeiting his life.   The *catastrophe* [1] in this play
is where Shylock conforms to the demands and says, "I am content."

In "Julius Cæsar" the *incitement* is where Brutus drops out of
the procession on its way to the course.   This gives Cassius an
opportunity to work upon him and win him to the conspiracy.
The *climax* is the death of Cæsar.   The *concluding crisis* is Mark
Antony's funeral oration when he turns the Roman mob against
the conspirators.   The *retarding point* is where the decision is made
by Brutus to meet the enemy at Philippi instead of having the

[1] Better called *conclusion* here.

enemy come to them. This was a fatal decision. The *catastrophe* is the death of Brutus and Cassius.

In "Macbeth" the *incitement* is where Duncan makes his son Malcolm Prince of Cumberland. The *climax* is the death of Banquo and escape of Fleance. The *concluding crisis* is the self-revelation of Macbeth in the Banquet Scene. The *retarding point* is where Macbeth refuses to fight and Macduff tells him,

> Then yield thee, coward,
> And live to be the show and gaze of the time.

The *catastrophe* is the death of Macbeth.

The drama—without making that end its deliberate aim—may entertain, instruct, or have a molding effect upon character, for it presents life itself. No drama, however, should aim to preach sermons as such. A true play must always be moral, though the moral is to be found not in the words, but in deeds. It may deal with crime, vice, and other terrible things, yet the results of a great play always make us hate more fully the evils of life.

The Classes of Plays Handled by Shakespeare.—There are, in reality, five distinct types of plays represented among the Shakespearian dramas. They are the farce, melodrama, comedy, dramatic history, and tragedy. Besides these there are some plays where one form seems to blend with another. The farce and the melodrama are not nearly so high as the others, and yet Shakespeare deigned to use them.

In both the farce and the melodrama, the plot situations and incidents are more important than anything else. The characters are mere puppets who exist only for the plot and are wholly at its

The Farce
and
Melodrama

mercy. They are free to do only what the situation will allow. Thus their movements are seen to be controlled not by themselves but by others. The farce has very swift movement, has ridiculous situations, and does not stimulate thought. Shakespeare's "Comedy of Errors," "The Merry Wives of Windsor," and "The Taming of the Shrew" are more like farces than anything else. In melodrama, the events follow each other with rapidity but seem always to be governed by chance. The characters are victims in the hands of a merciless fate. Shakespeare made use of this type in plays like "Titus Andronicus" and "Cymbeline."

Comedy is a very important type. It is to-day, and always has been, the most truly popular of the dramatic forms. True comedy is really serious and full of deep meaning, and yet it is infused with

Comedy

wit, sparkle, delicate satire, and new ideas. Comedy thus arouses thought even with the laughter. There are not usually many incidents in a comedy, and these are there because it seems as though it could not be otherwise. In no case does the plot seem to be governing the actions of the characters. On the contrary, the plot is caused by what the characters are and do, and is, therefore, made by them. The characters are never puppets but seem to be real living men and women. In comedy our attention is fixed on the things which need correcting, although no sermon is preached. We are not only made to see, but to think over the follies, peculiarities, vanities, insincerities, and other imperfections of human life. As Austin Dobson has said of comedy:

> It lashes the vicious, it laughs at the fool,
> And it brings all the prigs and pretenders to school.
>
> .   .   .   .
>
> Its thrust, like a rapier's, though cutting, is clean,
> And it pricks affectation all over the scene.
>
> .   .   .   .
>
> Its mission is neither to praise nor to blame;
> Its weapon is ridicule; folly, its game.[1]

In Shakespeare's comedies, especially, the individual may do bad things, make serious mistakes, but, if his deed is of such a nature that harmony can be restored by his repenting and conforming to the good, the play ends happily, because the thing producing the discord is removed. Repentance is therefore one of the central ideas of this type of play.

Dramatic history is based on historical facts. The playwright chooses a stirring period of history, or some national hero, and builds up a drama around this as a center. The historical drama

Dramatic History

is not so perfectly welded together as the other types, and yet the dramatist, by addition of things not found in the pages of history, succeeds in giving it the play form. To concentrate the action and make it more interesting, he usually crowds events more closely

[1] "*La Bonne Comédie.*"

together than they really were in history. Besides this he creates new characters and associates them with the historical personages, and he gives experiences and events that, in reality, never happened. In this way he builds up a play that may be either tragic or comic in its general treatment, and yet is a form distinct in itself.

Tragedy, in the Elizabethan sense,[1] is a play in which a human will is engaged in a terrible struggle with some unyielding, indestructible force, and death is the necessary result. The hero of such a play must die by the law of his own sin, whether it is of commission or of omission. The thing he does, or neglects to do, is of such a nature that there can be no other solution of the difficulties but death. In all of Shakespeare's tragedies, the hero is a man of high rank, of especial value to his country, and his terrible fall is caused by some defect in his character. This defect may take the form of ambition for power which leads to crime, of pride, wilfulness, inability to judge the true from the false and to grasp a vital situation, or of irresolution and neglect of a great duty. In any case, the consequences for which the tragic character is responsible are so serious that his own life is forfeited. Other people in a tragedy besides the tragic characters may die, but they are regarded as victims and not deserving of their death. In tragedy the catastrophe is always foreshadowed, and when it comes seems to be a necessary thing.

Tragedy

REVIEW

Think back over what you have learned about (1) the development of the drama to Shakespeare's time, and (2) the chief characteristics of the older drama.

---

[1] The modern idea of tragedy is quite different from that of the Elizabethan. It will be treated in connection with the work on the modern drama.

THE TRAGEDY OF HAMLET, PRINCE OF DENMARK

Shakespeare

[SCENE: Elsinore, the ancient capital of Denmark, and adjoining country.]

NAMES OF THE CHARACTERS

CLAUDIUS, king of Denmark.
HAMLET, son to the late, and nephew to the present king.
POLONIUS, lord chamberlain.
HORATIO, friend to Hamlet.
LAERTES, son to Polonius.
VOLTIMAND,
CORNELIUS,
ROSENCRANTZ, } courtiers.
GUILDENSTERN,
OSRIC,
A Priest.

MARCELLUS,
BERNARDO, } officers.
FRANCISCO,
REYNALDO, servant to Polonius.
Players.
Two Clowns, grave-diggers.
FORTINBRAS, prince of Norway.
A Captain under Fortinbras.
English Ambassador.
GERTRUDE, queen of Denmark, and mother to Hamlet.
OPHELIA, daughter to Polonius.
Lords, Ladies, Officers, Soldiers, Sailors, Messengers, and other Attendants.
Ghost of Hamlet's Father.

ACT FIRST

SCENE I.—[*Elsinore. A platform before the castle.*]

[*Francisco at his post. Enter to him Bernardo.*]

Ber. Who's there?
Fran. Nay, answer me: stand, and unfold yourself.
Ber. Long live the king!
Fran. Bernardo?
Ber. He.   5
Fran. You come most carefully upon your hour.
Ber. 'Tis now struck twelve; get thee to bed, Francisco.
Fran. For this relief much thanks: 't is bitter cold,
      And I am sick at heart.
Ber. Have you had quiet guard?
Fran.   Not a mouse stirring.   10
Ber. Well, good night.
      If you do meet Horatio and Marcellus,
      The rivals of my watch, bid them make haste.
Fran. I think I hear them. Stand, ho! Who's there?

Enter Horatio and Marcellus.

Hor. Friends to this ground.
Mar.   And liegemen to the Dane.   15

Fran. Give you good night.

Mar. O, farewell, honest soldier:
Who hath reliev'd you?

Fran. Bernardo has my place.
Give you good night. [*Exit Fran.*]

Mar. Holla! Bernardo!

Ber. Say,
What, is Horatio there?

Hor. A piece of him.

Ber. Welcome, Horatio: welcome, good Marcellus. 20

Mar. What, has this thing appear'd again tonight?

Ber. I have seen nothing.

Mar. Horatio says 't is but our fantasy,
And will not let belief take hold of him
Touching this dreaded sight, twice seen of us: 25
Therefore I have entreated him along
With us to watch the minutes of this night;
That if again this apparition come,
He may approve our eyes and speak to it.

Hor. Tush, tush, 'twill not appear.

Ber. Sit down awhile; 30
And let us once again assail your ears,
That are so fortified against our story,
What we have two nights seen.

Hor. Well, sit we down,
And let us hear Bernardo speak of this.

Ber. Last night of all, 35
When yond same star that 's westward from the pole
Had made his course t' illume that part of heaven
Where now it burns, Marcellus and myself,
The bell then beating one,—

Enter the Ghost.

Mar. Peace, break thee off. Look, where it comes again! 40

Ber. In the same figure, like the king that 's dead.

Mar. Thou art a scholar; speak to it, Horatio.

Ber. Looks it not like the king? mark it, Horatio.

Hor. Most like: it harrows me with fear and wonder.

Ber. It would be spoke to.

Mar. Question it, Horatio. 45

Hor. What art thou that usurp'st this time of night,
Together with that fair and warlike form
In which the majesty of buried Denmark
Did sometimes march? by heaven I charge thee, speak!

Mar. It is offended.

Ber.   See, it stalks away!   50
Hor.   Stay! speak, speak! I charge thee, speak!   [*Exit the Ghost.*]
Mar.   'Tis gone, and will not answer.
Ber.   How now, Horatio! you tremble and look pale:
   Is not this something more than fantasy?
   What think you on't?   55
Hor.   Before my God, I might not this believe
   Without the sensible and true avouch
   Of mine own eyes.
Mar.   Is it not like the king?
Hor.   As thou art to thyself:
   Such was the very armour he had on   60
   When he th' ambitious Norway cómbated;
   So frown'd he once, when, in an angry parle,
   He smote the sledded Polacks on the ice.
   'Tis strange.
Mar.   Thus twice before, and jump at this dead hour,   65
   With martial stalk hath he gone by our watch.
Hor.   In what particular thought to work I know not;
   But in the gross and scope of my opinion,
   This bodes some strange eruption to our state.
Mar.   Good now, sit down, and tell me, he that knows,   70
   Why this same strict and most observant watch
   So nightly toils the subject of the land,
   And why such daily cast of brazen cannon,
   And foreign mart for implements of war;
   Why such impress of shipwrights, whose sore task 75
   Does not divide the Sunday from the week;
   What might be toward, that this sweaty haste
   Doth make the night joint labourer with the day:
   Who is 't that can inform me?
Hor.   That can I;
   At least, the whisper goes so. Our last king,   80
   Whose image even but now appear'd to us,
   Was, as you know, by Fortinbras of Norway,
   Thereto prick'd on by a most emulate pride,
   Dar'd to the combat; in which our valiant Hamlet—
   For so this side of our known world esteem'd him— 85
   Did slay this Fortinbras; who, by a seal'd compact,
   Well ratified by law and heraldry,
   Did forfeit, with his life, all those his lands
   Which he stood seiz'd of, to the conqueror:
   Against the which, a moiety competent   90
   Was gaged by our king; which had return'd
   To the inheritance of Fortinbras,

Had he been vanquisher; as, by the same covenant,
And carriage of the article design'd,
His fell to Hamlet. Now, sir, young Fortinbras,   95
Of unimproved mettle hot and full,
Hath in the skirts of Norway here and there
Shark'd up a list of lawless resolutes,
For food and diet, to some enterprise
That hath a stomach in 't; which is no other—   100
As it doth well appear unto our state—
But to recover of us, by strong hand
And terms compulsative, those foresaid lands
So by his father lost: and this, I take it,
Is the main motive of our preparations,   105
The source of this our watch and the chief head
Of this post-haste and romage in the land.
Ber. I think it be no other but e'en so:
Well may it sort that this portentous figure
Comes armed through our watch; so like the king   110
That was and is the question of these wars.
Hor. A mote it is to trouble the mind's eye.
In the most high and palmy state of Rome,
A little ere the mightiest Julius fell,
The graves stood tenantless and the sheeted dead   115
Did squeak and gibber in the Roman streets:
As stars with trains of fire and dews of blood,
Disasters in the sun; and the moist star
Upon whose influence Neptune's empire stands
Was sick almost to doomsday with eclipse: 120
And even the like precurse of fierce events,
As harbingers preceding still the fates
And prologue to the omen coming on,
Have heaven and earth together demonstrated
Unto our climatures and countrymen.—   125

Enter Ghost again.

But soft, behold ! lo, where it comes again!
I 'll cross it, though it blast me. Stay, illusion!
If thou hast any sound, or use of voice,
Speak to me:
If there be any good thing to be done,   130
That may to thee do ease and grace to me,
Speak to me:
If thou art privy to thy country's fate,
Which, happily, foreknowing may avoid,
O, speak!   135

Or if thou hast uphoarded in thy life
Extorted treasure in the womb of earth,
For which, they say, you spirits oft walk in death,
Speak of it.   *[The cock crows.]*
      Stay, and speak! Stop it, Marcellus.

Mar. Shall I strike at it with my partisan?   140
Hor. Do, if it will not stand.
Ber.   'T is here!
Hor.   'T is here!
Mar. 'T is gone!   *[Exit Ghost.]*
We do it wrong, being so majestical,
To offer it the show of violence;
For it is, as the air, invulnerable,   145
And our vain blows malicious mockery.
Ber. It was about to speak, when the cock crew.
Hor. And then it started like a guilty thing
Upon a fearful summons. I have heard,
The cock, that is the trumpet to the morn,   150
Doth with his lofty and shrill-sounding throat
Awake the god of day; and, at his warning,
Whether in sea or fire, in earth or air,
Th' extravagant and erring spirit hies
To his confine: and of the truth herein   155
This present object made probation.
Mar. It faded on the crowing of the cock.
Some say that ever 'gainst that season comes
Wherein our Saviour's birth is celebrated,
The bird of dawning singeth all night long: 160
And then, they say, no spirit dare stir abroad;
The nights are wholesome; then no planets strike,
No fairy takes, nor witch hath power to charm,
So hallow'd and so gracious is the time.
Hor. So have I heard and do in part believe it.   165
But, look, the morn, in russet mantle clad,
Walks o'er the dew of yon high eastern hill:
Break we our watch up; and by my advice,
Let us impart what we have seen to-night
Unto young Hamlet; for, upon my life,   170
This spirit, dumb to us, will speak to him.
Do you consent we shall acquaint him with it,
As needful in our loves, fitting our duty?
Mar. Let's do 't, I pray; and I this morning know
Where we shall find him most conveniently.   *[Exeunt.]*

SCENE II.—[*Interior of the castle.*]

Enter Claudius King of Denmark, Gertrude the Queen, Hamlet, Polonius, Laertes, and his sister Ophelia, Voltimand and Cornelius, and Lords Attendant.

King. Though yet of Hamlet our dear brother's death
The memory be green, and that it us befitted
To bear our hearts in grief and our whole kingdom
To be contracted in one brow of woe,
Yet so far hath discretion fought with nature   5
That we with wisest sorrow think on him,
Together with remembrance of ourselves.
Therefore our sometime sister, now our queen,
Th' imperial jointress of this warlike state,
Have we, as 'twere with a defeated joy,—   10
With one auspicious and one dropping eye,
With mirth in funeral and with dirge in marriage,
In equal scale weighing delight and dole,—
Taken to wife: nor have we herein barr'd
Your better wisdoms, which have freely gone   15
With this affair along. For all, our thanks.
Now follows, that you know, young Fortinbras,
Holding a weak supposal of our worth,
Or thinking by our late dear brother's death
Our state to be disjoint and out of frame,   20
Colleagued with the dream of his advantage,
He hath not fail'd to pester us with message,
Importing the surrender of those lands
Lost by his father, with all bonds of law,
To our most valiant brother. So much for him.   25
Now for ourself and for this time of meeting:
Thus much the business is: we have here writ
To Norway, uncle of young Fortinbras,—
Who, impotent and bed-rid, scarcely hears
Of this his nephew's purpose,—to suppress   30
His further gait herein; in that the levies,
The lists and full proportions, are all made
Out of his subject: and we here despatch
You, good Cornelius, and you, Voltimand,
For bearers of this greeting to old Norway;   35
Giving to you no further personal power
To business with the king, more than the scope
Of these dilated articles allow.
Farewell, and let your haste commend your duty.

Vol. In that and all things will we show our duty.   40
King. We doubt it nothing: heartily farewell.
                          [*Exeunt Voltimand and Cornelius.*]
    And now, Laertes, what 's the news with you?
    You told us of some suit; what is 't, Laertes?
    You cannot speak of reason to the Dane,
    And lose your voice: what wouldst thou beg, Laertes,   45
    That shall not be my offer, not thy asking?
    The head is not more native to the heart,
    The hand more instrumental to the mouth,
    Than is the throne of Denmark to thy father.
    What wouldst thou have, Laertes?
Laer.   Dread my lord,   50
    Your leave and favour to return to France;
    From whence though willingly I came to Denmark,
    To show my duty in your coronation,
    Yet now, I must confess, that duty done,
    My thoughts and wishes bend again towards France   55
    And bow them to your gracious leave and pardon.
King. Have you your father's leave? What says Polonius?
Pol. He hath, my lord, wrung from me my slow leave
    By laboursome petition, and at last
    Upon his will I seal'd my hard consent: 60
    I do beseech you, give him leave to go.
King. Take thy fair hour, Laertes; time be thine,
    And thy best graces spend it at thy will!
    But now, my cousin Hamlet, and my son,—
Ham. [*Aside*] A little more than kin, and less than kind.   65
King. How is it that the clouds still hang on you?
Ham. Not so, my lord; I am too much i' the sun.
Queen. Good Hamlet, cast thy nighted colour off,
    And let thine eye look like a friend on Denmark.
    Do not for ever with thy vailed lids   70
    Seek for thy noble father in the dust:
    Thou know'st 'tis common; all that lives must die,
    Passing through nature to eternity.
Ham. Ay, madam, it is common.
Queen.   If it be,
    Why seems it so particular with thee?   75
Ham. Seems, madam! nay, it is; I know not 'seems.'
    'Tis not alone my inky cloak, good mother,
    Nor customary suits of solemn black,
    Nor windy suspiration of forc'd breath,
    No, nor the fruitful river in the eye,   80
    Nor the dejected haviour of the visage,

Together with all forms, moods, shapes of grief,
That can denote me truly: these indeed seem,
For they are actions that a man might play:
But I have that within which passeth show;   85
These but the trappings and the suits of woe.
King. 'Tis sweet and commendable in your nature, Hamlet,
To give these mourning duties to your father:
But, you must know, your father lost a father;
That father lost, lost his, and the survivor bound   90
In filial obligation for some term
To do obsequious sorrow: but to persevere
In obstinate condolement is a course
Of impious stubborness; 'tis unmanly grief;
It shows a will most incorrect to heaven,   95
A heart unfortified, a mind impatient,
An understanding simple and unschool'd:
For what we know must be and is as common
As any the most vulgar thing to sense,
Why should we in our peevish opposition   100
Take it to heart? Fie! 'tis a fault to heaven,
A fault against the dead, a fault to nature,
To reason most absurd; whose common theme
Is death of fathers, and who still hath cried,
From the first corse till he that died to-day,   105
"This must be so." We pray you, throw to earth
This unprevailing woe, and think of us
As of a father: for let the world take note,
You are the most immediate to our throne;
And with no less nobility of love   110
Than that which dearest father bears his son,
Do I impart towards you. For your intent
In going back to school in Wittenberg,
It is most retrograde to our desire:
And we beseech you, bend you to remain   115
Here, in the cheer and comfort of our eye,
Our chiefest courtier, cousin, and our son.
Queen. Let not thy mother lose her prayers, Hamlet:
I pray thee, stay with us; go not to Wittenberg.
Ham. I shall in all my best obey you, madam.   120
King. Why, 'tis a loving and a fair reply:
Be as ourself in Denmark. Madam, come;
This gentle and unforc'd accord of Hamlet
Sits smiling to my heart: in grace whereof,
No jocund health that Denmark drinks to-day,   125
But the great cannon to the clouds shall tell,

And the king's rouse the heavens shall bruit again,
Re-speaking earthly thunder. Come away.

                  [Flourish. Exeunt all but Hamlet.]

Ham. O, that this too too solid flesh would melt,
Thaw, and resolve itself into a dew!   130
Or that the Everlasting had not fix'd
His canon 'gainst self-slaughter! O God! O God!
How weary, stale, flat, and unprofitable,
Seem to me all the uses of this world!
Fie on 't! O fie! 'tis an unweeded garden,   135
That grows to seed; things rank and gross in nature
Possess it merely. That it should come to this!
But two months dead: nay, not so much, not two:
So excellent a king; that was, to this,
Hyperion to a satyr; so loving to my mother   140
That he might not beteem the winds of heaven
Visit her face too roughly. Heaven and earth!
Must I remember? why, she would hang on him,
As if increase of appetite had grown
By what it fed on: and yet, within a month—   145
Let me not think on 't—Frailty, thy name is woman!—
A little month, or ere those shoes were old
With which she follow'd my poor father's body,
Like Niobe, all tears:—why she, even she —
O God! a beast, that wants discourse of reason,   150
Would have mourn'd longer—married with my uncle,
My father's brother, but no more like my father
Than I to Hercules: within a month:
Ere yet the salt of most unrighteous tears
Had left the flushing in her galled eyes,   155
She married. O, most wicked speed, to post
With such dexterity to incestuous sheets!
It is not nor it cannot come to good:
But break, my heart; for I must hold my tongue.

        Enter Horatio, Bernardo, and Marcellus.

Hor. Hail to your lordship!
Ham.   I am glad to see you well.   160
  Horatio,—or I do forget myself.
Hor. The same, my lord, and your poor servant ever.
Ham. Sir, my good friend; I'll change that name with you:
  And what make you from Wittenberg, Horatio?
  Marcellus?   165
Mar. My good lord—

Ham. I am very glad to see you. [*To Bernardo*] Good even
    sir.
But what, in faith, make you from Wittenberg?
Hor. A truant disposition, good my lord.
Ham. I would not have your enemy say so,   170
Nor shall you do mine ear that violence,
To make it truster of your own report
Against yourself: I know you are no truant.
But what is your affair in Elsinore?
We'll teach you to drink deep ere you depart.   175
Hor. My lord, I came to see your father's funeral.
Ham. I pray thee, do not mock me, fellow-student;
I think it was to see my mother's wedding.
Hor. Indeed, my lord, it follow'd hard upon.
Ham. Thrift, thrift, Horatio! the funeral bak'd meats 180
Did coldly furnish forth the marriage tables.
Would I had met my dearest foe in heaven
Or ever I had seen that day, Horatio!
My father!—methinks I see my father.
Hor. O where, my lord?
Ham.   In my mind's eye, Horatio.   185
Hor. I saw him once; he was a goodly king.
Ham. He was a man, take him for all in all,
I shall not look upon his like again.
Hor. My lord, I think I saw him yesternight.
Ham. Saw? who?   190
Hor. My lord, the king your father.
Ham.   The king my father!
Hor. Season your admiration for a while
With an attent ear, till I may deliver,
Upon the witness of these gentlemen,
This marvel to you.
Ham.   For God's love, let me hear. 195
Hor. Two nights together had these gentlemen,
Marcellus and Bernardo, on their watch,
In the dead waste and middle of the night,
Been thus encounter'd. A figure like your father,
Armed at point exactly, cap-a-pie,   200
Appears before them, and with solemn march
Goes slow and stately by them: thrice he walk'd
By their oppress'd and fear-surprised eyes,
Within his truncheon's length; whilst they, distill'd
Almost to jelly with the act of fear,   205
Stand dumb and speak not to him. This to me
In dreadful secrecy impart they did;

And I with them the third night kept the watch:
Where, as they had deliver'd, both in time,
Form of the thing, each word made true and good,   210
The apparition comes: I knew your father;
These hands are not more like.

Ham.   But where was this?

Mar. My lord, upon the platform where we watch'd.

Ham. Did you not speak to it?

Hor.   My lord, I did;
But answer made it none: yet once methought   215
It lifted up its head and did address
Itself to motion, like as it would speak;
But even then the morning cock crew loud,
And at the sound it shrunk in haste away,
And vanish'd from our sight.

Ham.   'Tis very strange.   220

Hor. As I do live, my honour'd lord, 'tis true;
And we did think it writ down in our duty
To let you know of it.

Ham. Indeed, indeed, sirs, but this troubles me.
Hold you the watch to-night?

Mar.   We do, my lord.   225
Ber.

Ham. Arm'd, say you?

Mar. }
Ber. } Arm'd, my lord.

Ham. From top to toe?

Mar. }
Ber. }   My lord, from head to foot.

Ham. Then saw you not this face?

Hor. O, yes, my lord; he wore his beaver up.   230

Ham. What, look'd he frowningly?

Hor. A countenance more in sorrow than in anger.

Ham. Pale or red?

Hor. Nay, very pale.

Ham.   And fix'd his eyes upon you?

Hor. Most constantly.

Ham.   I would I had been there.   231

Hor. It would have much amaz'd you.

Ham. Very like, very like. Stay'd it long?

Hor. While one with moderate haste might tell a hundred.

Mar. }
Ber. } Longer, longer.

Hor. Not when I saw 't.

Ham.   His beard was grizzled,—no?   240

Hor. It was, as I have seen it in his life,
   A sable silver'd.
Ham.   I 'll watch to-night;
   Perchance 'twill walk again.
Hor.   I warrant it will.
Ham. If it assume my noble father's person,
   I 'll speak to it, though hell itself should gape   245
   And bid me hold my peace. I pray you all,
   If you have hitherto conceal'd this sight,
   Let it be tenable in your silence still;
   And whatsoever else shall hap to-night,
   Give it an understanding, but no tongue: 250
   I will requite your loves. So, fare you well:
   Upon the platform, 'twixt eleven and twelve,
   I 'll visit you.
All.   Our duty to your honour.
Ham. Your love, as mine to you: farewell.

                              [*Exeunt all but Hamlet.*]
   My father's spirit in arms! all is not well;   255
   I doubt some foul play: would the night were come!
   Till then sit still, my soul: foul deeds will rise,
   Though all the earth o'erwhelm them, to men's eyes.   *Exit.*

            Scene III.—[*The house of Polonius.*]

                Enter Laertes and Ophelia.

Laer. My necessaries are embark'd: farewell:
   And, sister, as the winds give benefit
   And convoy is assistant, do not sleep,
   But let me hear from you.
Oph.   Do you doubt that?
Laer. For Hamlet and the trifling of his favours,   5
   Hold it a fashion and a toy in blood,
   A violet in the youth of primy nature,
   Forward, not permanent, sweet, not lasting,
   The perfume and suppliance of a minute;
   No more.
Oph. No more but so?
Laer.   Think it no more: 10
   For nature crescent does not grow alone
   In thews and bulk, but, as his temple waxes,
   The inward service of the mind and soul
   Grows wide withal. Perhaps he loves you now,
   And now no soil nor cautel doth besmirch   15

The virtue of his will: but you must fear,
His greatness weigh'd, his will is not his own;
For he himself is subject to his birth:
He may not, as unvalued persons do,
Carve for himself; for on his choice depends   20
The sanctity and health of the whole state;
And therefore must his choice be circumscrib'd
Unto the voice and yielding of that body
Whereof he is the head. Then if he says he loves you,
It fits your wisdom so far to believe it   25
As he in his peculiar sect and force
May give his saying deed; which is no further
Than the main voice of Denmark goes withal.
Then weigh what loss your honour may sustain,
If with too credent ear you list his songs,   30
Or lose your heart . . . . .
To his unmaster'd importunity.
Fear it, Ophelia, fear it, my dear sister,
And keep you in the rear of your affection,
Out of the shot and danger of desire.   35
The chariest maid is prodigal enough,
If she unmask her beauty to the moon:
Virtue itself scapes not calumnious strokes:
The canker galls the infants of the spring,
Too oft before their buttons be disclos'd,   40
And in the morn and liquid dew of youth
Contagious blastments are most imminent.
Be wary then; best safety lies in fear:
Youth to itself rebels, though none else near.
Oph. I shall th' effect of this good lesson keep,   45
As watchman to my heart. But, good my brother,
Do not, as some ungracious pastors do,
Show me the steep and thorny way to heaven;
Whilst, like a puff'd and reckless libertine,
Himself the primrose path of dalliance treads,   50
And recks not his own rede.
Laer.   O, fear me not.

Enter Polonius.

I stay too long: but here my father comes.
A double blessing is a double grace;
Occasion smiles upon a second leave.
Pol. Yet here, Laertes! aboard, aboard, for shame!   55
The wind sits in the shoulder of your sail,
And you are stay'd for. There; my blessing with you!

And these few precepts in thy memory
See thou cháracter. Give thy thoughts no tongue,
Nor any unproportion'd thought his act.   60
Be thou familiar, but by no means vulgar.
The friends thou hast, and their adoption tried,
Grapple them to thy soul with hoops of steel;
But do not dull thy palm with entertainment
Of each new-hatch'd, unfledg'd comrade. Beware   65
Of entrance to a quarrel, but being in,
Bear't that the opposed may beware of thee.
Give every man thy ear, but few thy voice;
Take each man's censure, but reserve thy judgment.
Costly thy habit as thy purse can buy,   70
But not express'd in fancy; rich, not gaudy;
For the apparel oft proclaims the man,
And they in France of the best rank and station
Are of a most select and generous chief in that.
Neither a borrower nor a lender be;   75
For loan oft loses both itself and friend,
And borrowing dulls the edge of husbandry.
This above all: to thine own self be true,
And it must follow, as the night the day,
Thou canst not then be false to any man.   80
Farewell: my blessing season this in thee!
Laer. Most humbly do I take my leave, my lord.
Pol. The time invites you; go; your servants tend.
Laer. Farewell, Ophelia; and remember well
    What I have said to you.
Oph.   'Tis in my memory lock'd,   85
    And you yourself shall keep the key of it.
Laer. Farewell.   *Exit Laertes.*
Pol. What is 't, Ophelia, he hath said to you?
Oph. So please you, something touching the Lord Hamlet.
Pol. Marry, well bethought: 90
    'T is told me, he hath very oft of late
    Given private time to you; and you yourself
    Have of your audience been most free and bounteous:
    If it be so, as so 't is put on me,
    And that in way of caution, I must tell you,   95
    You do not understand yourself so clearly
    As it behoves my daughter and your honour.
    What is between you? give me up the truth.
Oph. He hath, my lord, of late made many tenders
    Of his affection to me.   100
Pol. Affection! pooh! you speak like a green girl,

Unsifted in such perilous circumstance.
Do you believe his tenders, as you call them?

Oph. I do not know, my lord, what I should think.

Pol. Marry, I 'll teach you: think yourself a baby; 105
That you have ta'en his tenders for true pay,
Which are not sterling. Tender yourself more dearly;
Or—not to crack the wind of the poor phrase,
Running it thus—you 'll tender me a fool.

Oph. My lord, he hath impórtun'd me with love 110
In honourable fashion.

Pol. Ay, fashion you may call it; go to, go to.

Oph. And hath given countenance to his speech, my lord,
With almost all the holy vows of heaven.

Pol. Ay, springes to catch woodcocks. I do know, 115
When the blood burns, how prodigal the soul
Lends the tongue vows: these blazes, daughter,
Giving more light than heat, extinct in both,
Even in their promise, as it is a-making,
You must not take for fire. From this time, daughter, 120
Be somewhat scanter of your maiden presence;
Set your entreatments at a higher rate
Than a command to parley. For Lord Hamlet,
Believe so much in him, that he is young,
And with a larger tether may he walk 125
Than may be given you: in few, Ophelia,
Do not believe his vows; for they are brokers,
Not of that dye which their investments show,
But mere implorators of unholy suits,
Breathing like sanctified and pious bawds, 130
The better to beguile. This is for all:
I would not, in plain terms, from this time forth,
Have you so slander any moment leisure,
As to give words or talk with the Lord Hamlet.
Look to 't, I charge you: come your ways. 135

Oph. I shall obey, my lord. [*Exeunt.*]

SCENE IV.—[*The platform.*]

Enter Hamlet, Horatio, and Marcellus.

Ham. The air bites shrewdly; is it very cold?

Hor. It is a nipping and an eager air.

Ham. What hour now?

Hor.   I think it lacks of twelve.

Mar. No, it is struck.

Hor. Indeed? I heard it not: then it draws near the season 5
Wherein the spirit held his wont to walk.
        [*A flourish of trumpets, and two pieces go off within.*]
What does this mean, my lord?
Ham. The king doth wake to-night and takes his rouse,
Keeps wassail, and the swaggering up-spring reels;
And, as he drains his draughts of Rhenish down, 10
The kettle-drum and trumpet thus bray out
The triumph of his pledge.
Hor.   Is it a custom?
Ham. Ay, marry, is 't:
But to my mind, though I am native here
And to the manner born, it is a custom 15
More honour'd in the breach than the observance.
This heavy-headed revel east and west
Makes us traduc'd and tax'd of other nations:
They clepe us drunkards, and with swinish phrase
Soil our addition; and indeed it takes 20
From our achievements, though perform'd at height,
The pith and marrow of our attribute.
So, oft it chances in particular men,
That for some vicious mole of nature in them,
As, in their birth—wherein they are not guilty, 25
Since nature cannot choose his origin—
By the o'ergrowth of some complexion,
Oft breaking down the pales and forts of reason,
Or by some habit that too much o'er-leavens,
The form of plausive manners, that these men, 30
Carrying, I say, the stamp of one defect,
Being nature's livery, or fortune's star,—
Their virtues else—be they as pure as grace,
As infinite as man may undergo—
Shall in the general censure take corruption 35
From that particular fault: the dram of eale
Doth all the noble substance of a doubt
To his own scandal.

Enter Ghost.

Hor.   Look, my lord, it comes!
Ham. Angels and ministers of grace defend us!
Be thou a spirit of health or goblin damn'd, 40
Bring with thee airs from heaven or blasts from hell,
Be thy intents wicked or charitable,
Thou com'st in such a questionable shape
That I will speak to thee: I 'll call thee Hamlet,

King, father, royal Dane: O, answer me! 45
Let me not burst in ignorance; but tell
Why thy canóniz'd bones, hearsed in death,
Have burst their cerements; why the sepulchre,
Wherein we saw thee quietly inurn'd,
Hath op'd his ponderous and marble jaws, 50
To cast thee up again. What may this mean,
That thou, dead corse, again in complete steel
Revisit'st thus the glimpses of the moon,
Making night hideous; and we fools of nature
So horridly to shake our disposition 55
With thoughts beyond the reaches of our souls?
Say, why is this? wherefore? what should we do?

[Ghost beckons Hamlet.]

Hor. It beckons you to go away with it,
As if it some impartment did desire
To you alone.

Mar.   Look, with what courteous action 60
It waves you to a more removed ground:
But do not go with it.

Hor.   No, by no means.

Ham. It will not speak; then will I follow it.

Hor. Do not, my lord.

Ham.   Why, what should be the fear?
I do not set my life at a pin's fee; 65
And for my soul, what can it do to that,
Being a thing immortal as itself?
It waves me forth again: I 'll follow it.

Hor. What if it tempt you toward the flood, my lord,
Or to the dreadful summit of the cliff 70
That beetles o'er his base into the sea,
And there assume some other horrible form,
Which might deprive your sovereignty of reason
And draw you into madness? think of it:
The very place puts toys of desperation, 75
Without more motive, into every brain
That looks so many fathoms to the sea
And hears it roar beneath.

Ham.   It waves me still.
Go on; I 'll follow thee.

Mar. You shall not go, my lord.

Ham.   Hold off your hand. 80

Hor. Be rul'd; you shall not go.

Ham.   My fate cries out,
And makes each petty artery in this body

As hardy as the Nemean lion's nerve.
Still am I call'd? Unhand me, gentlemen.
By heaven, I'll make a ghost of him that lets me! 85
I say, away! Go on; I'll follow thee.

[Exeunt Ghost and Hamlet.]

Hor. He waxes desperate with imagination.
Mar. Let's follow; 't is not fit thus to obey him.
Hor. Have after. To what issue will this come?
Mar. Something is rotten in the state of Denmark. 90
Hor. Heaven will direct it.
Mar. Nay, let's follow him. *[Exeunt.]*

Scene V.—*[Another part of the platform.]*

Enter Ghost and Hamlet.

Ham. Where wilt thou lead me? speak; I'll go no further.
Ghost. Mark me.
Ham. I will.
Ghost. My hour is almost come,
When I to sulphurous and tormenting flames
Must render up myself.
Ham. Alas, poor ghost!
Ghost. Pity me not, but lend thy serious hearing 5
To what I shall unfold.
Ham. Speak; I am bound to hear.
Ghost. So art thou to revenge, when thou shalt hear.
Ham. What?
Ghost. I am thy father's spirit,
Doom'd for a certain term to walk the night, 10
And for the day confin'd to fast in fires,
Till the foul crimes done in my days of nature
Are burnt and purg'd away. But that I am forbid
To tell the secrets of my prison-house,
I could a tale unfold whose lightest word 15
Would harrow up thy soul, freeze thy young blood,
Make thy two eyes, like stars, start from their spheres,
Thy knotted and combined locks to part
And each particular hair to stand on end,
Like quills upon the fretful porpentine: 20
But this eternal blazon must not be
To ears of flesh and blood. List, list, O, list!
If thou didst ever thy dear father love—
Ham. O God!
Ghost. Revenge his foul and most unnatural murther. 25
Ham. Murther!

Ghost. Murther most foul, as in the best it is;
But this most foul, strange, and unnatural.
Ham. Haste me to know 't, that I, with wings as swift
As meditation or the thoughts of love,   30
May sweep to my revenge.
Ghost.   I find thee apt;
And duller shouldst thou be than the fat weed
That rots itself in ease on Lethe wharf,
Wouldst thou not stir in this. Now, Hamlet, hear:
'T is given out that, sleeping in mine orchard,   35
A serpent stung me; so the whole ear of Denmark
Is by a forged process of my death
Rankly abus'd: but know, thou noble youth,
The serpent that did sting thy father's life
Now wears his crown.
Ham.   O my prophetic soul!   40
Mine uncle!
Ghost. Ay, that incestuous, that adulterate beast,
With witchcraft of his wit, with traitorous gifts,—
O wicked wit and gifts, that have the power
So to seduce!—won to his shameful lust   45
The will of my most seeming-virtuous queen:
O Hamlet, what a falling-off was there!
From me, whose love was of that dignity
That it went hand in hand even with the vow
I made to her in marriage, and to decline   50
Upon a wretch whose natural gifts were poor
To those of mine!
But virtue, as it never will be moved,
Though lewdness court it in a shape of heaven,
So lust, though to a radiant angel link'd,   55
Will sate itself in a celestial bed,
And prey on garbage.
But, soft! methinks I scent the morning air;
Brief let me be. Sleeping within mine orchard,
My custom always in the afternoon,   60
Upon my secure hour thy uncle stole,
With juice of cursed hebenon in a vial,
And in the porches of mine ears did pour
The leperous distilment; whose effect
Holds such an enmity with blood of man   65
That swift as quicksilver it courses through
The natural gates and alleys of the body,
And with a sudden vigour it doth posset
And curd, like eager droppings into milk,

The thin and wholesome blood: so did it mine;   70
And a most instant tetter bark'd about,
Most lazar-like, with vile and loathsome crust,
All my smooth body.
Thus was I, sleeping, by a brother's hand
Of life, of crown, and queen, at once despatch'd: 75
Cut off even in the blossoms of my sin,
Unhousel'd, disappointed, unanel'd,
No reckoning made, but sent to my account
With all my imperfections on my head:
O, horrible! O, horrible! most horrible!   80
If thou hast nature in thee, bear it not;
Let not the royal bed of Denmark be
A couch for luxury and damned incest.
But, howsoever thou pursuest this act,
Taint not thy mind, nor let thy soul contrive   85
Against thy mother aught: leave her to heaven
And to those thorns that in her bosom lodge,
To prick and sting her.   Fare thee well at once!
The glow-worm shows the matin to be near,
And 'gins to pale his uneffectual fire: 90
Adieu, adieu!   Hamlet, remember me.   [*Exit.*]
Ham.   O all you host of heaven!   O earth! what else?
And shall I couple hell?   O, fie!   Hold, hold, my heart;
And you, my sinews, grow not instant old,
But bear me stiffly up.   Remember thee!   95
Ay, thou poor ghost, while memory holds a seat
In this distracted globe.   Remember thee!
Yea, from the table of my memory
I 'll wipe away all trivial fond records,
All saws of books, all forms, all pressures past,   100
That youth and observation copied there;
And thy commandment all alone shall live
Within the book and volume of my brain,
Unmix'd with baser matter: yes, yes, by heaven!
O most pernicious woman!   105
O villain, villain, smiling, damned villain!
My tables,—meet it is I set it down,
That one may smile, and smile, and be a villain;
At least I 'm sure it may be so in Denmark:
                                                               [*Writing.*]
So, uncle, there you 'are.   Now to my word;   110
It is "Adieu, adieu! remember me."
I have sworn 't.
Hor. & Mar. [*Within*]   My lord, my lord,—

Mar.   [*Within*] Lord Hamlet,—
Hor.   [*Within*] Heaven secure him!
Ham. So be it!
Hor. [*Within*] Hillo, ho, ho, my lord!   115
Ham. Hillo, ho, ho, boy! come, bird, come.

Enter Horatio and Marcellus.

Mar. How is 't, my noble lord?
Hor.   What news, my lord?
Ham. O, wonderful!
Hor.   Good my lord, tell it.
Ham. No; you 'll reveal it.
Hor. Not I, my lord, by heaven.
Mar.   Nor I, my lord.   120
Ham. How say you, then; would heart of man once think it?
  But you 'll be secret?
Both.   Ay, by heaven, my lord.
Ham. There 's ne'er a villain dwelling in all Denmark
  But he 's an arrant knave.
Hor. There needs no ghost, my lord, come from the grave   125
  To tell us this.
Ham.   Why, right; you are i' the right;
  And so, without more circumstance at all,
  I hold it fit that we shake hands and part:
  You, as your business and desires shall point you;
  For every man has business and desire,   130
  Such as it is; and for mine own poor part,
  Look you, I 'll go pray.
Hor. These are but wild and whirling words, my lord.
Ham. I 'm sorry they offend you, heartily;
  Yes, 'faith, heartily.
Hor.   There 's no offence, my lord.   135
Ham. Yes, by Saint Patrick, but there is, Horatio,
  And much offence too, touching this vision here.
  It is an honest ghost, that let me tell you:
  For your desire to know what is between us,
  O'ermaster 't as you may. And now, good friends,   140
  As you are friends, scholars, and soldiers,
  Give me one poor request.
Hor. What is 't, my lord? we will.
Ham. Never make known what you have seen tonight.
Both. My lord, we will not.
Ham.   Nay, but swear 't.
Hor.   In faith,   145
  My lord, not I.

Mar.   Nor I, my lord, in faith.

Ham.   Upon my sword.

Mar.   We have sworn, my lord, already.

Ham.   Indeed, upon my sword, indeed.

Ghost.   Swear.   [*Beneath.*]

Ham.   Ah, ha, boy! say'st thou so? art thou there, truepenny?   150
Come on—you hear this fellow in the cellarage—
Consent to swear.

Hor.   Propose the oath, my lord.

Ham.   Never to speak of this that you have seen.
Swear by my sword.

Ghost.   [*Beneath*] Swear.   155

Ham. Hic et ubique? then we 'll shift our ground.
Come hither, gentlemen,
And lay your hands again upon my sword:
Never to speak of this that you have heard,
Swear by my sword.   160

Ghost.   [*Beneath*] Swear.

Ham.   Well said, old mole! canst work i' the ground so fast?
A worthy pioner! Once more remove, good friends.

Hor.   O day and night, but this is wondrous strange!

Ham.   And therefore as a stranger give it welcome.   165
There are more things in heaven and earth, Horatio,
Than are dreamt of in your philosophy.
But come;
Here, as before, never, so help you mercy,
How strange or odd soe'er I bear myself,   170
As I perchance hereafter shall think meet
To put an antic disposition on,
That you, at such times seeing me, never shall,
With arms encumber'd thus, or thus, head shake,
Or by pronouncing of some doubtful phrase,   175
As "Well, well, we know," or "We could, and if we would,"
Or "If we list to speak," or "There be, and if they might,"
Or such ambiguous giving out, to note
That you know aught of me: this not to do,
So grace and mercy at your most need help you,   180
Swear.

Ghost.   [*Beneath*] Swear.

Ham.   Rest, rest, perturbed spirit! So, gentlemen,
With all my love I do commend me to you:
And what so poor a man as Hamlet is   185
May do, to express his love and friending to you,
God willing, shall not lack. Let us go in together;
And still your fingers on your lips, I pray.

The time is out of joint: O cursed spite,
That ever I was born to set it right!   190
Nay, come, let's go together.   [*Exeunt.*]

ACT SECOND

Scene I.—[*House of Polonius.*]

Enter Polonius and Reynaldo.

Pol. Give him this money and these notes, Reynaldo.
Rey. I will, my lord.
Pol. You shall do marvellous wisely, good Reynaldo,
  Before you visit him, to make inquire
  Of his behaviour.
Rey.   My lord, I did intend it.   5
Pol. Marry, well said; very well said. Look you, sir.
  Inquire me first what Danskers are in Paris;
  And how, and who, what means, and where they keep,
  What company, at what expense; and finding
  By this encompassment and drift of question   10
  That they do know my son, come you more nearer
  Than your particular demands will touch it:
  Take you, as 't were, some distant knowledge of him;
  As thus, "I know his father and his friends,
  And in part him:" do you mark this, Reynaldo?   15
Rey. Ay, very well, my lord.
Pol. "And in part him; but" you may say "not well:
  But, if 't be he I mean, he's very wild;
  Addicted so and so:" and there put on him
  What forgeries you please; marry, none so rank   20
  As may dishonour him; take heed of that;
  But, sir, such wanton, wild, and usual slips
  As are companions noted and most known
  To youth and liberty.
Rey.   As gaming, my lord.
Pol. Ay, or drinking, fencing, swearing, quarrelling,   25
  Drabbing: you may go so far.
Rey. My lord, that would dishonour him.
Pol. 'Faith, no; as you may season it in the charge.
  You must not put another scandal on him,
  That he is open to incontinency;   30
  That's not my meaning: but breathe his faults so quaintly
  That they may seem the taints of liberty,
  The flash and outbreak of a fiery mind,
  A savageness in unreclaimed blood.

      Of general assault.

Rey.   But, my good lord,—   35

Pol.   Wherefore should you do this?

Rey.   Ay, my lord,

      I would know that.

Pol.   Marry, sir, here's my drift;

      And, I believe, it is a fetch of warrant:

      You laying these slight sullies on my son,

      As 't were a thing a little soil'd i' the working,   40

      Mark you,

      Your party in converse, him you would sound,

      Having ever seen in the prenominate crimes

      The youth you breathe of guilty, be assur'd

      He closes with you in this consequence: 45

      "Good sir," or so, or "friend," or "gentleman,"

      According to the phrase and the addition

      Of man and country.

Rey.   Very good, my lord.

Pol.   And then, sir, does he this—he does—what was I about to say?

      By the mass, I was about to say something: where did I leave?   50

Rey.   At "closes in the consequence," at "friend or so," and "gentleman."

Pol.   At "closes in the consequence," ay, marry;

      He closes with you thus: "I know the gentleman;

      I saw him yesterday, or t'other day,

      Or then, or then; with such, and such; and, as you say,   55

      There was he gaming; there o'ertook in 's rouse;

      There falling out at tennis:" or perchance,

      "I saw him enter such a house of sale,"

      Videlicet, a brothel, or so forth.

      See you now;   60

      Your bait of falsehood takes this carp of truth:

      And thus do we of wisdom and of reach,

      With windlasses and with assays of bias,

      By indirections find directions out:

      So by my former lecture and advice,   65

      Shall you my son. You have me, have you not?

Rey.   My lord, I have.

Pol.   God be wi' you; fare you well.

Rey.   Good my lord!

Pol.   Observe his inclination in yourself.

Rey.   I shall, my lord.   70

Pol.   And let him ply his music.

Rey.   Well, my lord.   [*Exit.*]

Pol.   Farewell!

Enter Ophelia.

How now, Ophelia! what's the matter?

Oph. Alas, my lord, I have been so affrighted!

Pol. With what, i' the name of God?

Oph. My lord, as I was sewing in my chamber,   75
Lord Hamlet, with his doublet all unbrac'd;
No hat upon his head; his stockings foul'd,
Ungarter'd, and down-gyved to his ankle;
Pale as his shirt; his knees knocking each other;
And with a look so piteous in purport   80
As if he had been loosed out of hell
To speak of horrors,—he comes before me.

Pol. Mad for thy love?

Oph.   My lord, I do not know:
But truly, I do fear it.

Pol.   What said he?

Oph. He took me by the wrist and held me hard;   85
Then goes he to the length of all his arm;
And, with his other hand thus o'er his brow,
He falls to such perusal of my face
As he would draw it. Long stay'd he so;
At last, a little shaking of mine arm   90
And thrice his head thus waving up and down,
He raised a sigh so piteous and profound
That it did seem to shatter all his bulk
And end his being: that done, he lets me go:
And, with his head over his shoulder turn'd,   95
He seem'd to find his way without his eyes;
For out o' doors he went without their help,
And, to the last, bended their light on me.

Pol. Come, go with me: I will go seek the king.
This is the very ecstasy of love,   100
Whose violent property fordoes itself
And leads the will to desperate undertakings
As oft as any passion under heaven
That does afflict our natures. I am sorry.
What, have you given him any hard words of late?   105

Oph. No, my good lord, but, as you did command,
I did repel his letters and denied
His access to me.

Pol.   That hath made him mad.
I am sorry that with better heed and judgment
I had not quoted him: I fear'd he did but trifle,   110
And meant to wreck thee; but, beshrew my jealousy!
By heaven, it is as proper to our age

To cast beyond ourselves in our opinions
As it is common for the younger sort
To lack discretion. Come, go we to the king: 115
This must be known; which, being kept close, might move
More grief to hide than hate to utter love.

[*Exeunt.*]

SCENE II.—[*A room in the castle.*]

Enter King, Queen, Rosencrantz, Guildenstern, and attendants.

King. Welcome, dear Rosencrantz and Guildenstern!
    Moreover that we much did long to see you,
    The need we have to use you did provoke
    Our hasty sending. Something have you heard
    Of Hamlet's transformation; so I call it,   5
    Since not th' exterior nor the inward man
    Resembles that it was. What it should be,
    More than his father's death, that thus hath put him
    So much from the understanding of himself,
    I cannot deem of. I entreat you both,   10
    That, being of so young days brought up with him,
    And since so neighbour'd to his youth and humour,
    That you vouchsafe your rest here in our court
    Some little time: so by your companies
    To draw him on to pleasures, and to gather,   15
    So much as from occasions you may glean,
    Whether aught, to us unknown, afflicts him thus,
    That, open'd, lies within our remedy.
Queen. Good gentlemen, he hath much talk'd of you;
    And sure I am two men there are not living   20
    To whom he more adheres. If it will please you
    To show us so much gentry and good will
    As to expend your time with us awhile,
    For the supply and profit of our hope,
    Your visitation shall receive such thanks   25
    As fits a king's remembrance.
Ros.   Both your majesties
    Might, by the sovereign power you have of us,
    Put your dread pleasures more into command
    Than to entreaty.
Guil.   But we both obey,
    And here give up ourselves, in the full bent   30
    To lay our services freely at your feet,
    To be commanded.
King. Thanks, Rosencrantz and gentle Guildenstern.

Queen. Thanks, Guildenstern and gentle Rosencrantz:
   And I beseech you instantly to visit   35
   My too much changed son. Go, some of ye,
   And bring the gentlemen where Hamlet is.
Guil. Heavens make our presence and our practices
   Pleasant and helpful to him!
Queen.   Ay, amen!
         [*Exeunt Rosencrantz, Guildenstern, and some Attendants.*]

                   Enter Polonius.

Pol. Th' ambassadors from Norway, my good lord,   40
   Are joyfully return'd.
King. Thou still hast been the father of good news.
Pol. Have I, my lord? Assure you, my good liege,
   I hold my duty, as I hold my soul,
   Both to my God and to my gracious king: 45
   And I do think, or else this brain of mine
   Hunts not the trail of policy so sure
   As it hath us'd to do, that I have found
   The very cause of Hamlet's lunacy.
King. O, speak of that; that do I long to hear.   50
Pol. Give first admittance to th' ambassadors;
   My news shall be the fruit to that great feast.
King. Thyself do grace to them, and bring them in.
                                      [*Exit Polonius.*]
   He tells me, my sweet queen, that he hath found
   The head and source of all your son's distemper.   55
Queen. I doubt it is no other but the main:
   His father's death, and our o'erhasty marriage.
King. Well, we shall sift him.

          Enter Polonius, Voltimand, and Cornelius.

                        Welcome, good friends!
   Say, Voltimand, what from our brother Norway?
Volt. Most fair return of greetings and desires.   60
   Upon our first, he sent out to suppress
   His nephew's levies; which to him appear'd
   To be a preparation 'gainst the Polack;
   But, better look'd into, he truly found
   It was against your highness: whereat grieved,   65
   That so his sickness, age, and impotence
   Was falsely borne in hand, sends out arrests
   On Fortinbras; which he, in brief, obeys;
   Receives rebuke from Norway, and in fine
   Makes vow before his uncle never more   70

To give th' assay of arms against your majesty.
Whereon old Norway, overcome with joy,
Gives him three thousand crowns in annual fee,
And his commission to employ those soldiers,
So levied as before, against the Polack: 75
With an entreaty, herein further shown,

                                    [*Giving a paper.*]

That it might please you to give quiet pass
Through your dominions for his enterprise,
On such regards of safety and allowance
As therein are set down.
King.   It likes us well;   80
And at our more consider'd time we 'll read,
Answer, and think upon this business.
Meantime we thank you for your well-took labour.
Go to your rest; at night we 'll feast together:
Most welcome home!   [*Exeunt Ambassadors.*]
Pol.   This business is well ended.   85
My liege, and madam, to expostulate
What majesty should be, what duty is,
Why day is day, night night, and time is time,
Were nothing but to waste night, day, and time.
Therefore, since brevity is the soul of wit,   90
And tediousness the limbs and outward flourishes,
I will be brief: your noble son is mad.
Mad call I it; for, to define true madness,
What is 't but to be nothing else but mad?
But let that go.
Queen.   More matter, with less art.   95
Pol.   Madam, I swear I use no art at all.
That he is mad, 't is true: 't is true 't is pity;
And pity 't is 't is true: a foolish figure;
But farewell it, for I will use no art.
Mad let us grant him, then: and now remains   100
That we find out the cause of this effect,
Or rather say, the cause of this defect,
For this effect defective comes by cause:
Thus it remains, and the remainder thus.
Perpend.   105
I have a daughter—have whilst she is mine—
Who, in her duty and obedience, mark,
Hath given me this: now gather, and surmise.

                                              [*Reads.*]

"To the celestial and my soul's idol, the most beautified
Ophelia,"—   110

That's an ill phrase, a vile phrase; "beautified" is a vile phrase:
but you shall hear. Thus:

[Reads.]

"In her excellent white bosom, these."
Queen. Came this from Hamlet to her?
Pol. Good madam, stay awhile; I will be faithful.   *[Reads.]* 115
   "Doubt thou the stars are fire;
     Doubt that the sun doth move;
   Doubt truth to be a liar;
     But never doubt I love.
"O dear Ophelia, I am ill at these numbers; I have not art to   120
reckon my groans: but that I love thee best, O most best, believe it.
Adieu.
   "Thine evermore, most dear lady, whilst this machine is to him,
     HAMLET."
This, in obedience, hath my daughter shown me,   125
And, more above, hath his solicitings,
As they fell out by time, by means and place,
All given to mine ear.
King.   But how hath she
Receiv'd his love?
Pol.   What do you think of me?
King. As of a man faithful and honourable.   130
Pol. I would fain prove so. But what might you think,
When I had seen this hot love on the wing—
As I perceived it, I must tell you that,
Before my daughter told me—what might you,
Or my dear majesty your queen here, think,   135
If I had play'd the desk or table-book,
Or given my heart a winking, mute and dumb,
Or look'd upon this love with idle sight;
What might you think? No, I went round to work,
And my young mistress thus I did bespeak: 140
"Lord Hamlet is a prince, out of thy star;
This must not be:" and then I precepts gave her,
That she should lock herself from his resort,
Admit no messengers, receive no tokens.
Which done, she took the fruits of my advice;   145
And he, repulsed—a short tale to make—
Fell into a sadness, then into a fast,
Thence to a watch, thence into a weakness,
Thence to a lightness, and, by this declension,
Into the madness wherein now he raves,   150
And all we mourn for.
King.   Do you think 't is this?

Queen. It may be, very likely.

Pol. Hath there been such a time—I'd fain know that—
That I have positively said " 'T is so,"
When it prov'd otherwise?

King.   Not that I know.   155

Pol. [*Pointing to his head and shoulder*] Take this from this, if this
be otherwise:
If circumstances lead me, I will find
Where truth is hid, though it were hid indeed
Within the centre.

King.   How may we try it further?

Pol. You know, sometimes he walks four hours together   160
Here in the lobby.

Queen.   So he does indeed.

Pol. At such a time I'll loose my daughter to him:
Be you and I behind an arras then;
Mark the encounter: if he love her not
And be not from his reason fall'n thereon,   165
Let me be no assistant for a state,
But keep a farm and carters.

King.   We will try it.

Enter Hamlet, reading on a book.

Queen. But, look, where sadly the poor wretch comes reading.

Pol. Away, I do beseech you, both away:
I'll board him presently.

                              [*Exeunt King and Queen.*]
                    O, give me leave: 170
How does my good Lord Hamlet?

Ham. Well, God-a-mercy.

Pol. Do you know me, my lord?

Ham. Excellent, excellent well; y' are a fish-monger.

Pol. Not I, my lord.   175

Ham. Then I would you were so honest a man.

Pol. Honest, my lord!

Ham. Ay, sir; to be honest, as this world goes, is to be one man
picked out of ten thousand.

Pol. That's very true, my lord.   180

Ham. For if the sun breed maggots in a dead dog, being a god kissing carrion,—Have you a daughter?

Pol. I have, my lord.

Ham. Let her not walk i' the sun: Friend, look to 't.   184

Pol. [*Aside*] How say you by that? Still harping on my daughter:
yet he knew me not at first; he said I was a fish-monger: he is far

gone, far gone: and truly in my youth I suffered much extremity for love; very near this. I 'll speak to him again. [*Aloud.*] What do you read, my lord?

Ham. Words, words, words. 190

Pol. What is the matter, my lord?

Ham. Between who?

Pol. I mean, the matter that you read, my lord.

Ham. Slanders, sir: for the satirical slave says here that old men have grey beards, that their faces are wrinkled, their eyes purging thick amber or plum-tree gum, and that they have a plentiful lack of wit, together with weak hams: all which, sir, though I most powerfully and potently believe, yet I hold it not honesty to have it thus set down, for you yourself, sir, should be old as I am, if like a crab you go backward. 200

Pol. [*Aside*] Though this be madness, yet there is method in 't. Will you walk out of the air, my lord?

Ham. Into my grave.

Pol. Indeed, that is out o' the air. [*Aside*] How pregnant sometimes his replies are! a happiness that often madness hits on, which reason and sanity could not so prosperously be delivered of. I will leave him, and suddenly contrive the means of meeting between him and my daughter.—My honourable lord, I will most humbly take my leave of you. 209

Ham. You cannot, sir, take from me anything that I will more willingly part withal: except my life, except my life, except my life.

Pol. Fare you well, my lord.

Ham. These tedious old fools!

Enter Rosencrantz and Guildenstern.

Pol. You go to seek my Lord Hamlet; there he is. 215

Ros. [*To Polonius*] God save you, sir!

[*Exit Polonius.*]

Guil. Mine honoured lord!

Ros. My most dear lord!

Ham. My excellent good friends! How dost thou, Guildenstern? Ah, Rosencrantz! Good lads, how do ye both? 220

Ros. As the indifferent children of the earth.

Guil. Happy, in that we are not over-happy;
On fortune's cap we are not the very button.

Ham. Nor the soles of her shoe?

Ros. Neither, my lord.

Ham. What's the news? ²³⁰

Ros. None, my lord. but that the world's grown honest.

Ham. Then is doomsday near: but your news is not true. Let me question more in particular: what have you, my good friends, deserved at the hands of fortune, that she sends you to prison, hither? ²³⁵

Guil. Prison, my lord!

Ham. Denmark's a prison.

Ros. Then is the world one.

Ham. A goodly one; in which there are many confines, wards, and dungeons, Denmark being one o' the worst. ²⁴⁰

Ros. We think not so, my lord.

Ham. Why, then, 't is none to you; for there is nothing either good or bad, but thinking makes it so: to me it is a prison.

Ros. Why then, your ambition makes it one; 't is too narrow for your mind. ²⁴⁵

Ham. O God, I could be bounded in a nutshell and count myself a king of infinite space, were it not that I have bad dreams.

Guil. Which dreams indeed are ambition, for the very substance of the ambitious is merely the shadow of a dream.

Ham. A dream itself is but a shadow. ²⁵⁰

Ros. Truly, and I hold ambition of so airy and light a quality that it is but a shadow's shadow.

Ham. Then are our beggars bodies, and our monarchs and outstretched heroes the beggars' shadows. Shall we to the court? for, by my fay, I cannot reason. ²⁵⁵

Both. We'll wait upon you.

Ham. No such matter: I will not sort you with the rest of my servants, for, to speak to you like an honest man, I am most dreadfully attended. But, in the beaten way of friendship, what make you at Elsinore? ²⁶⁰

Ros. To visit you, my lord; no other occasion.

Ham. Beggar that I am, I am even poor in thanks; but I thank you: and sure, dear friends, my thanks are too dear a halfpenny. Were you not sent for? Is it your own inclining? Is it a free visitation? Come, deal justly with me: come, come; nay, speak. ²⁶⁵

Guil. What should we say, my lord?

Ham. Why, any thing, but to the purpose. You were sent for; and there is a kind of confession in your looks which your modesties have not craft enough to colour: I know the good king and queen have sent for you. ²⁷⁰

Ros. To what end, my lord?

Ham. That you must teach me. But let me conjure you, by the rights of our fellowship, by the consonancy of our youth, by the obligation of our ever-preserved love, and by what more dear a better proposer could charge you withal, be even and direct with me; whether you were sent for, or no?

Ros. [*Aside to Guil.*] What say you?

Ham. [*Aside*] Nay, then, I have an eye of you.—If you love me, hold not off.

Guil. My lord, we were sent for. 280

Ham. I will tell you why; so shall my anticipation prevent your discovery, and your secrecy to the king and queen moult no feather. I have of late—but wherefore I know not—lost all my mirth, forgone all custom of exercise; and indeed it goes so heavily with my disposition that this goodly frame, the earth, seems to me a sterile promontory, this most excellent canopy, the air, look you, this brave o'erhanging firmament, this majestical roof fretted with golden fire, why, it appears no other thing to me than a foul and pestilent congregation of vapours. What a piece of work is a man! how noble in reason! how infinite in faculty! in form and moving how express and admirable! in action how like an angel! in apprehension how like a god! the beauty of the world! the paragon of animals! And yet, to me, what is this quintessence of dust? man delights not me: no, nor woman neither, though by your smiling you seem to say so. 295

Ros. My lord, there was no such stuff in my thoughts.

Ham. Why did you laugh then, when I said "man delights not me"?

Ros. To think, my lord, if you delight not in man, what lenten entertainment the players shall receive from you: we coted them on the way; and hither are they coming, to offer you service. 300

Ham. He that plays the king shall be welcome; his majesty shall have tribute of me; the adventurous knight shall use his foil and target; the lover shall not sigh gratis; the humorous man shall end his part in peace; the clown shall make those laugh whose lungs are tickled of the sere; and the lady shall say her mind freely, or the blank verse shall halt for 't. What players are they?

Ros. Even those you were wont to take delight in, the tragedians of the city.

Ham. How chances it they travel? their residence, both in reputation and profit, was better both ways. 310

Ros. I think their inhibition comes by the means of the late innovation.

Ham. Do they hold the same estimation they did when I was in the city? are they so followed?

Ros. No, indeed, they are not.

Ham. How comes it? do they grow rusty? 315

Ros. Nay, their endeavour keeps in the wonted pace: but there is, sir, an aery of children, little eyases, that cry out on the top of question, and are most tyrannically clapped for 't: these are now

the fashion, and so berattle the common stages—so they call them
—that many wearing rapiers are afraid of goose-quills and dare
scarce come thither. 321

Ham. What, are they children? who maintains 'em? how are they
escoted? Will they pursue the quality no longer than they can
sing? will they not say afterwards, if they should grow themselves
to common players—as it is most like, if their means are no better
—their writers do them wrong, to make them exclaim against their
own succession? 327

Ros. 'Faith, there has been much to do on both sides; and the nation
holds it no sin to tarre them to controversy: there was, for a while,
no money bid for argument, unless the poet and the player went
to cuffs in the question.

Ham. Is 't possible? 332

Guil. O, there has been much throwing about of brains.

Ham. Do the boys carry it away?

Ros. Ay, that they do, my lord; Hercules and his load too.

Ham. It is not very strange; for mine uncle is king of Denmark,
and those that would make mows at him while my father lived,
give twenty, forty, fifty, an hundred ducats a-piece for his picture
in little. 'Sblood, there is something in this more than natural, if
philosophy could find it out. 340

[Flourish for the players.]

Guil. There are the players.

Ham. Gentlemen, you are welcome to Elsinore. Your hands, come:
the appurtenance of welcome is fashion and ceremony: let me comply with you in this garb, lest my extent to the players, which, I
tell you, must show fairly outward, should more appear like entertainment than yours. You are welcome: but my uncle-father and
aunt-mother are deceived.

Guil. In what, my dear lord?

Ham. I am but mad north-north-west: when the wind is southerly
I know a hawk from a hand-saw. 350

Enter Polonius.

Pol. Well be with you, gentlemen!

Ham. Hark you, Guildenstern; and you too: at each ear a hearer:
that great baby you see there is not yet out of his swathing-
clouts.

Ros. Happily he 's the second time come to them; for they say an
old man is twice a child.

Ham. I will prophesy he comes to tell me of the players; mark it.
You say right, sir: for a-Monday morning, 't was so indeed.

Pol. My lord, I have news to tell you.

Ham. My lord, I have news to tell you. 360
　　When Roscius was an actor in Rome,—
Pol. The actors are come hither, my lord.
Ham. Buz, buz!
Pol. Upon mine honour,—
Ham. Then came each actor on his ass,— 365
Pol. The best actors in the world, either for tragedy, comedy, history,
　　pastoral, pastoral-comical, historical-pastoral, tragical-historical,
　　tragical-comical-historical-pastoral, scene individable, or poem un-
　　limited: Seneca cannot be too heavy, nor Plautus too light. For the
　　law of writ and the liberty, these are the only men. 370
Ham. O Jephthah, judge of Israel, what a treasure hadst thou!
Pol. What a treasure had he, my lord?
Ham. Why,
　　"One fair daughter, and no more,
　　　　The which he loved passing well." 375
Pol. [*Aside*] Still on my daughter.
Ham. Am I not i' the right, old Jephthah?
Pol. If you call me Jephthah, my lord, I have a daughter that I
　　love passing well.
Ham. Nay, that follows not. 380
Pol. What follows, then, my lord?
Ham. Why?
　　　　"As by lot, God wot,"
　　and then, you know,
　　　　"It came to pass, as most like it was,"— 385
　　the first row of the pious chanson will show you more; for look,
　　where my abridgements come.

Enter four or five Players.

Y' are welcome, masters; welcome, all. I am glad to see thee
well. Welcome, good friends. O, my old friend! thy face is
valanced since I saw thee last: comest thou to beard me in Denmark? What, my young lady and mistress! By'r lady, your
ladyship is nearer heaven than when I saw you last, by the altitude
of a chopine. Pray God, your voice, like a piece of uncurrent
gold, be not cracked within the ring. Masters, you are all welcome. We'll e'en to 't like French falconers, fly at any thing we
see: we'll have a speech straight: come, give us a taste of your
quality; come, a passionate speech. 397
First Play. What speech, my lord?
Ham. I heard thee speak me a speech once, but it was never acted;
　　or, if it was, not above once; for the play, I remember, pleased not
　　the million; 'twas caviare to the general: but it was—as I re-
　　ceived it, and others, whose judgement in such matters cried in

the top of mine—an excellent play, well digested in the scenes, set
down with as much modesty as cunning. I remember, one said
there were no sallets in the lines to make the matter savoury, nor
no matter in the phrase that might indict the author of affectation;
but called it an honest method, as wholesome as sweet, and by very
much more handsome than fine. One speech in it I chiefly loved:
't was Æneas' tale to Dido; and thereabout of it especially, where
he speaks of Priam's slaughter: if it live in your memory, begin
at this line: let me see, let me see— 411

   "The rugged Pyrrhus, like th' Hyrcanian beast,"—
It is not so:—it begins with Pyrrhus:—

   "The rugged Pyrrhus, he whose sable arms,
Black as his purpose, did the night resemble 415
When he lay couched in the ominous horse,
Hath now this dread and black complexion smear'd
With heraldry more dismal; head to foot
Now is he total gules; horridly trick'd
With blood of fathers, mothers, daughters, sons, 420
Baked and impasted with the parching streets,
That lend a tyrannous and damned light
To their lords' murther: roasted in wrath and fire,
And thus o'er-sized with coagulate gore,
With eyes like carbuncles, the hellish Pyrrhus 425
Old grandsire Priam seeks."

So, proceed you.

Pol. 'Fore God, my lord, well spoken, with good accent and good
discretion.

First Play.   "Anon he find him 430
Striking too short at Greeks; his antique sword,
Rebellious to his arm, lies where it falls,
Repugnant to command: unequal match'd,
Pyrrhus at Priam drives; in rage strikes wide;
But with the whiff and wind of his fell sword 435
Th' unnerved father falls. Then senseless Ilium,
Seeming to feel this blow, with flaming top
Stoops to his base, and with a hideous crash
Takes prisoner Pyrrhus' ear: for, lo! his sword,
Which was declining on the milky head 440
Of reverend Priam, seem'd i' th' air to stick:
So, as a painted tyrant, Pyrrhus stood,
And like a neutral to his will and matter,
Did nothing.
But, as we often see, against some storm, 445
A silence in the heavens, the rack stand still,
The bold winds speechless and the orb below

As hush as death, anon the dreadful thunder
Doth rend the region, so, after Pyrrhus' pause,
Aroused vengeance sets him new a-work;   450
And never did the Cyclops' hammers fall
On Mars's armour forg'd for proof eterne
With less remorse than Pyrrhus' bleeding sword
Now falls on Priam.
    Out, out, thou strumpet, Fortune! All you gods,   455
In general synod, take away her power;
Break all the spokes and fellies from her wheel,
And bowl the round nave down the hill of heaven,
As low as to the fiends!"

Pol. This is too long.   460

Ham. It shall to the barber's, with your beard. Prithee, say on:
he's for a jig or a tale of bawdry, or he sleeps: say on: come to
Hecuba.

First Play. "But who, O, who had seen the mobled queen—"

Ham. "The mobled queen?"   465

Pol. That's good; "mobled queen" is good.

First Play. "Run barefoot up and down, threatening the flame
With bisson rheum; a clout upon that head
Where late the diadem stood, and for a robe,
About her lank and all o'er-teemed loins,   470
A blanket, in th' alarm of fear caught up;
Who this had seen, with tongue in venom steep'd,
'Gainst Fortune's state would treason have pronounc'd:
But if the gods themselves did see her then
When she saw Pyrrhus make malicious sport   475
In mincing with his sword her husband's limbs,
The instant burst of clamour that she made,
Unless things mortal move them not at all,
Would have made milch the burning eyes of heaven,
And passion in the gods."   480

Pol. Look, wh'er he has not turned his colour and has tears in's
eyes. Pray you, no more.

Ham. 'T is well; I'll have thee speak out the rest soon. Good my
lord, will you see the players well bestowed? Do ye hear, let them
be well used; for they are the abstracts and brief chronicles of
the time: after your death you were better have a bad epitaph
than their ill report while you live.   487

Pol. My lord, I will use them according to their desert.

Ham. God's bodykins, man, much better: use every man after his
desert, and who should scape whipping? Use them after your own
honour and dignity: the less they deserve, the more merit is in
your bounty. Take them in.   491

Pol. Come, sirs.

Ham. Follow him, friends: we 'll hear a play to-morrow. [*Exit Polonius with all the Players but the First.*] Dost thou hear me, old friend; can you play the Murther of Gonzago? 496

First Play. Ay, my lord.

Ham. We 'll ha 't to-morrow night. You could, for a need, study a speech of some dozen or sixteen lines, which I would set down and insert in 't, could ye not? 500

First Play. Ay, my lord.

Ham. Very well. Follow that lord; and look you mock him not. [*Exit First Player.*] My good friends, I 'll leave you till night: you are welcome to Elsinore.

Ros. Good my lord! 505

[*Exeunt Ros. and Guil.*]

Ham. Ay, so, God be wi' ye. Now I am alone.
O, what a rogue and peasant slave am I!
Is it not monstrous that this player here,
But in a fiction, in a dream of passion,
Could force his soul so to his own conceit 510
That from her working all his visage wann'd,
Tears in his eyes, distraction in 's aspect,
A broken voice, and his whole function suiting
With forms to his conceit? and all for nothing!
For Hecuba! 515
What 's Hecuba to him, or he to Hecuba,
That he should weep for her? What would he do,
Had he the motive and the cue for passion
That I have? He would drown the stage with tears
And cleave the general ear with horrid speech, 520
Make mad the guilty and appal the free,
Confound the ignorant, and amaze indeed
The very faculties of eyes and ears.
Yet I,
A dull and muddy-mettled rascal, peak, 525
Like John-a-dreams, unpregnant of my cause,
And can say nothing; no, not for a king,
Upon whose property and most dear life
A damn'd defeat was made. Am I a coward?
Who calls me villain? breaks my pate across? 530
Plucks off my beard, and blows it in my face?
Tweaks me by the nose? gives me the lie i' the throat,
As deep as to the lungs? who does me this?
Ha!
'Swounds, I should take it: for it cannot be 53
But I am pigeon-liver'd and lack gall

To make oppression bitter, or ere this
I should have fatted all the region kites
With this slave's offal: bloody, bawdy villain!
Remorseless, treacherous, lecherous, kindless villain! 540
O, vengeance!
Why, what an ass am I! This is most brave,
That I, the son of a dear father murther'd,
Prompted to my revenge by heaven and hell,
Must, like a whore, unpack my heart with words, 545
And fall a-cursing, like a very drab,
A scullion!
Fie upon 't! foh! About, my brain! I have heard
That guilty creatures sitting at a play
Have by the very cunning of the scene 550
Been struck so to the soul that presently
They have proclaim'd their malefactions;
For murther, though it have no tongue, will speak
With most miraculous organ. I 'll have these players
Play something like the murder of my father 555
Before mine uncle: I 'll observe his looks;
I 'll tent him to the quick: if he but blench,
I know my course. The spirit that I have seen
May be the devil: and the devil hath power
T' assume a pleasing shape; yea, and perhaps 560
Out of my weakness and my melancholy,
As he is very potent with such spirits,
Abuses me to damn me: I 'll have grounds
More relative than this: the play 's the thing
Wherein I 'll catch the conscience of the king. 565

[*Exit.*]

ACT THIRD

Scene I.—[*A room in the castle.*]

*Enter King, Queen, Polonius, Ophelia, Rosencrantz, Guildenstern,
and Lords.*

King. And can you, by no drift of circumstance,
   Get from him why he puts on this confusion,
   Grating so harshly all his days of quiet
   With turbulent and dangerous lunacy?
Ros. He does confess he feels himself distracted; 5
   But from what cause he will by no means speak.
Guil. Nor do we find him forward to be sounded,
   But, with a crafty madness, keeps aloof,

When we would bring him on to some confession
Of his true state.

Queen.   Did he receive you well?   10
Ros. Most like a gentleman.
Guil. But with much forcing of his disposition.
Ros. Niggard of question; but, of our demands,
Most free in his reply.

Queen.   Did you assay him
To any pastime?   15

Ros. Madam, it so fell out, that certain players
We o'er-raught on the way: of these we told him;
And there did seem in him a kind of joy
To hear of it: they are about the court,
And, as I think, they have already order   20
This night to play before him.

Pol.   'T is most true:
And he beseech'd me to entreat your majesties
To hear and see the matter.

King. With all my heart; and it doth much content me
To hear him so inclined.   25
Good gentlemen, give him a further edge,
And drive his purpose on to these delights.

Ros. We shall, my lord.

                [*Exeunt Rosencrantz and Guildenstern.*]
King.   Sweet Gertrude, leave us too;
For we have closely sent for Hamlet hither,
That he, as 't were by accident, may here   30
Affront Ophelia:
Her father and myself, lawful espials,
Will so bestow ourselves that, seeing, unseen,
We may of their encounter frankly judge,
And gather by him, as he is behav'd,   35
If 't be th' affliction of his love or no
That thus he suffers for.

Queen.   I shall obey you.
And for your part, Ophelia, I do wish
That your good beauties be the happy cause
Of Hamlet's wildness: so shall I hope your virtues   40
Will bring him to his wonted way again,
To both your honours.

Oph.   Madam, I wish it may.   [*Exit Queen.*]
Pol. Ophelia, walk you here. Gracious, so please ye,
We will bestow ourselves. [*To Ophelia*] Read on this book;
That show of such an exercise may colour   45
Your loneliness. We are oft to blame in this,—

'T is too much prov'd—that with devotion's visage
And pious action we do sugar o'er
The devil himself.

King.   [*Aside*] O, 't is too true!
How smart a lash that speech doth give my conscience!   50
The harlot's cheek, beautied with plastering art,
Is not more ugly to the thing that helps it
Than is my deed to my most painted word:
O heavy burthen!

Pol. I hear him coming: let 's withdraw, my lord.   55
                                                    [*Exeunt.*]

Enter Hamlet.

Ham.   To be, or not to be: that is the question:
Whether 't is nobler in the mind to suffer
The slings and arrows of outrageous fortune,
Or to take arms against a sea of troubles,
And by opposing end them?   To die: to sleep;   60
No more; and by a sleep to say we end
The heart-ache and the thousand natural shocks
That flesh is heir to?   'T is a consummation
Devoutly to be wish'd.   To die, to sleep;
To sleep: perchance to dream: ay, there 's the rub;   65
For in that sleep of death what dreams may come,
When we have shuffled off this mortal coil,
Must give us pause: there 's the respect
That makes calamity of so long life;
For who would bear the whips and scorns of time,   70
Th' oppressor's wrong, the proud man's contumely,
The pangs of despis'd love, the law's delay,
The insolence of office, and the spurns
That patient merit of the unworthy takes,
When he himself might his quietus make   75
With a bare bodkin? who would fardels bear,
To grunt and sweat under a weary life,
But that the dread of something after death,
The undiscover'd country from whose bourn
No traveller returns, puzzles the will   80
And makes us rather bear those ills we have
Than fly to others that we know not of?
Thus conscience does make cowards of us all;
And thus the native hue of resolution
Is sicklied o'er with the pale cast of thought,   85
And enterprises of great pith and moment
With this regard their currents turn awry,

And lose the name of action.—Soft you now!
The fair Ophelia! Nymph, in thy orisons
Be all my sins remember'd.

Oph. Good my lord, 90
How does your honour for this many a day?

Ham. I humbly thank you; well, well, well.

Oph. My lord, I have remembrances of yours,
That I have longed long to re-deliver;
I pray you, now receive them.

Ham. No, not I; 95
I never gave you aught.

Oph. My honour'd lord, I know right well you did;
And, with them, words of so sweet breath compos'd
As made the things more rich: their perfume lost,
Take these again; for to the noble mind 100
Rich gifts wax poor when givers prove unkind.
There, my lord.

Ham. Ha, ha! are you honest?

Oph. My lord?

Ham. Are you fair? 105

Oph. What means your lordship?

Ham. That if you be honest and fair, your honesty should admit
no discourse to your beauty.

Oph. Could beauty, my lord, have better commerce than with honesty? 110

Ham. Ay, truly; for the power of beauty will sooner transform honesty from what it is to a bawd than the force of honesty can
translate beauty into his likeness: this was sometime a paradox, but
now the time gives it proof. I did love you once.

Oph. Indeed, my lord, you made me believe so. 115

Ham. You should not have believed me; for virtue cannot so in-
oculate our old stock but we shall relish of it: I loved you not.

Oph. I was the more deceived.

Ham. Get thee to a nunnery: why wouldst thou be a breeder of sin-
ners? I am myself indifferent honest; but yet I could accuse
me of such things that it were better my mother had not borne
me: I am very proud, revengeful, ambitious, with more offences
at my beck than I have thoughts to put them in, imagination to
give them shape, or time to act them in. What should such fellows
as I do crawling between earth and heaven? We are arrant knaves,
all; believe none of us. Go thy ways to a nunnery. Where's
your father? 127

Oph. At home, my lord.

Ham. Let the doors be shut upon him, that he may play the fool no
where but in 's own house. Farewell. 130

Oph. O, help him, you sweet heavens!

Ham. If thou dost marry, I 'll give thee this plague for thy dowry:
be thou as chaste as ice, as pure as snow, thou shalt not escape
calumny. Get thee to a nunnery, go: farewell. Or, if thou wilt
needs marry, marry a fool; for wise men know well enough what
monsters you make of them. To a nunnery, go, and quickly too.
Farewell. ¹³⁷

Oph. O heavenly powers, restore him!

Ham. I have heard of your paintings too, well enough; God has
given you one face, and you make yourself another: you jig, you
amble, and you lisp, and nick-name God's creatures, and make your
wantonness your ignorance. Go to, I 'll no more on 't; it hath made
me mad. I say, we will have no more marriages: those that are
married already, all but one, shall live; the rest shall keep as they
are. To a nunnery, go. [*Exit Hamlet.*] ¹⁴⁵

Oph. O, what a noble mind is here o'erthrown!
The courtier's, soldier's, scholar's, eye, tongue, sword;
The expectancy and rose of the fair state,
The glass of fashion and the mould of form,
The observ'd of all observers, quite, quite down! ¹⁵⁰
And I, of ladies most deject and wretched,
That suck'd the honey of his music vows,
Now see that noble and most sovereign reason
Like sweet bells jangled out of tune and harsh;
That unmatch'd form and feature of blown youth ¹⁵⁵
Blasted with ecstasy: O, woe is me,
To have seen what I have seen, see what I see!

Enter King and Polonius.

King. Love! his affections do not that way tend;
Nor what he spake, though it lack'd form a little,
Was not like madness. There 's something in his soul ¹⁶⁰
O'er which his melancholy sits on brood;
And I do doubt the hatch and the disclose
Will be some danger: which to prevent,
I have in quick determination
Thus set it down: he shall with speed to England, ¹⁶⁵
For the demand of our neglected tribute:
Haply the seas and countries different
With variable objects shall expel
This something-settled matter in his heart,
Whereon his brains still beating puts him thus ¹⁷⁰
From fashion of himself. What think you on 't?

Pol. It shall do well: but yet do I believe
The origin and commencement of his grief

Sprung from neglected love.—How now, Ophelia!
You need not tell us what Lord Hamlet said;   175
We heard it all. My lord, do as you please;
But, if you hold it fit, after the play
Let his queen mother all alone entreat him
To show his griefs: let her be round with him;
And I'll be plac'd, so please you, in the ear   180
Of all their conference. If she find him not,
To England send him, or confine him where
Your wisdom best shall think.
King.   It shall be so:
Madness in great ones must not unwatch'd go.

                                                              [*Exeunt.*]

Scene II.—[*A hall in the castle.*]

Enter Hamlet and two or three of the Players.

Ham. Speak the speech, I pray you, as I pronounced it to you,
trippingly on the tongue: but if you mouth it, as many of your
players do, I had as lief the town-crier spoke my lines. Nor do
not saw the air too much with your hand, thus, but use all gently;
for in the very torrent, tempest, and, as I may say, the whirlwind of
passion, you must acquire and beget a temperance that may give
it smoothness. O, it offends me to the soul to see a robustious
periwig-pated fellow tear a passion to tatters, to very rags, to split
the ears of the groundlings, who for the most part are capable of
nothing but inexplicable dumb-shows and noise: I could have such
a fellow whipped for o'erdoing Termagant; it out-herods Herod:
pray you, avoid it.   12
Player. I warrant your honour.
Ham. Be not too tame neither, but let your own discretion be your
tutor: suit the action to the word, the word to the action; with
this special observance, that you o'erstep not the modesty of nature: for any thing so overdone is from the purpose of playing,
whose end, both at the first and now, was and is, to hold, as 't were,
the mirror up to nature; to show virtue her own feature, scorn
her own image, and the very age and body of the time his form
and pressure. Now this overdone, or come tardy off, though it
make the unskilful laugh, cannot but make the judicious grieve;
the censure of the which one must in your allowance o'erweigh a
whole theatre of others. O, there be players that I have seen
play, and heard others praise, and that highly, not to speak it
profanely, that, neither having the accent of Christians nor the
gait of Christian, pagan, nor man, have so strutted and bellowed
that I have thought some of nature's journeymen had made men,
and not made them well, they imitated humanity so abominably.

Player. I hope we have reformed that indifferently with us, sir. 30
Ham. O, reform it altogether. And let those that play your clowns
speak no more than is set down for them; for there be of them that
will themselves laugh, to set on some quantity of barren spectators
to laugh too; though, in the meantime, some necessary question of
the play be then to be considered: that's villainous, and shows a
most pitiful ambition in the fool that uses it. Go, make you
ready.   [*Exeunt Players.*]

Enter Polonius, Rosencrantz, and Guildenstern.

How now, my lord! will the king hear this piece of work?
Pol. And the queen too, and that presently.
Ham. Bid the players make haste.   [*Exit Polonius.*]
Will you two help to hasten them?   40
Both.   We will, my lord.
               [*Exeunt Rosencrantz and Guildenstern.*]
Ham. What ho! Horatio!

Enter Horatio.

Hor. Here, sweet lord, at your service.
Ham. Horatio, thou art e'en as just a man
As e'er my conversation cop'd withal.   45
Hor. O, my dear lord!
Ham.   Nay, do not think I flatter;
For what advancement may I hope from thee
That no revénue hast but thy good spirits,
To feed and clothe thee? Why should the poor be flatter'd?
No, let the candied tongue lick absurd pomp,   50
And crook the pregnant hinges of the knee
Where thrift may follow fawning. Dost thou hear?
Since my dear soul was mistress of my choice
And could of men distinguish, her election
Hath seal'd thee for herself; for thou hast been   55
As one, in suffering all, that suffers nothing,
A man that fortune's buffets and rewards
Hath ta'en with equal thanks: and blest are those
Whose blood and judgement are so well commingled,
That they are not a pipe for fortune's finger   60
To sound what stop she please. Give me that man
That is not passion's slave, and I will wear him
In my heart's core, ay, in my heart of heart,
As I do thee.—Something too much of this.—
There is a play to-night before the king;   65
One scene of it comes near the circumstance
Which I have told thee of my father's death:

I prithee, when thou seest that act afoot,
Even with the very comment of thy soul
Observe mine uncle; if his occulted guilt   70
Do not itself unkennel in one speech,
It is a damned ghost that we have seen,
And my imaginations are as foul
As Vulcan's stithy. Give him heedful note;
For I mine eyes will rivet to his face,   75
And after we will both our judgements join
In censure of his seeming.
Hor.   Well, my lord:
If he steal aught the whilst this play is playing,
And scape detecting, I will pay the theft.
Ham. They are coming to the play; I must be idle: 80
Get you a place.

*Enter King, Queen, Polonius, Ophelia, Rosencrantz, Guildenstern,
and other Attendants, with guards carrying torches. Danish march.
Sound a flourish.*

King. How fares our cousin Hamlet?
Ham. Excellent, i' faith; of the chameleon's dish: I eat the air,
     promise-crammed: you cannot feed capons so.   84
King. I have nothing with this answer, Hamlet; these words are
     not mine.
Ham. No, nor mine now. [*To Polonius*] My lord, you played once
     i' the university, you say?
Pol. That I did, my lord; and was accounted a good actor.
Ham. And what did you enact?   90
Pol. I did enact Julius Cæsar: I was killed i' the Capitol; Brutus
     killed me.
Ham. It was a brute part of him to kill so capital a calf there.
     Be the players ready?
Ros. Ay, my lord; they stay upon your patience.   95
Queen. Come hither, my dear Hamlet, sit by me.
Ham. No, good mother, here 's metal more attractive.
                              [*Lying down at Ophelia's feet.*]
Pol. [*To the King*] O, ho! do you mark that?

.   .   .   .

Oph. You are merry, my lord.
Ham. Who, I?
Oph. Ay, my lord.   110
Ham. O God, your only jig-maker. What should a man do but
     be merry? for, look you, how cheerfully my mother looks, and
     my father died within 's two hours.
Oph. Nay, 't is twice two months, my lord.   114

Ham. So long? Nay then, let the devil wear black, for I'll have a
suit of sables. O heavens! die two months ago, and not forgotten
yet? Then there's hope a great man's memory may outlive his
life half a year: but, by'r lady, he must build churches, then; or
else shall he suffer not thinking on, with the hobby-horse, whose
epitaph is "For, O, for, O, the hobby horse is forgot."   120

Hautboys play. The dumb-show enters.

Enter a King and Queen very lovingly; the Queen embracing him,
She kneels, and makes show of protestation unto him. He takes
her up, and declines his head upon her neck: lays him down upon
a bank of flowers. She, seeing him asleep, leaves him. Anon
comes in a fellow, takes off his crown, kisses it, and pours poison
in the King's ears, and exit. The Queen returns; finds the King
dead, and makes passionate action. The Poisoner, with some two
or three Mutes, comes in again, seeming to lament with her. The
dead body is carried away. The Poisoner wooes the Queen with
gifts: she seems loath and unwilling awhile, but in the end accepts
his love.   [Exeunt.]

Oph. What means this, my lord?
Ham. Marry, this is miching mallecho; it means mischief.
Oph. Belike this show imports the argument of the play.

Enter Prologue.

Ham. We shall know by this fellow: the players cannot keep
counsel; they'll tell all.   135
Oph. Will he tell us what this show meant?
Ham. Ay, or any show that you'll show him: be not you ashamed
to show, he'll not shame to tell you what it means.
Oph. You are naught, you are naught: I'll mark the play.
Pro. For us, and for our tragedy,   140
  Here stooping to your clemency,
  We beg your hearing patiently.   [Exit.]
Ham. Is this a prologue, or the posy of a ring?
Oph. 'T is brief, my lord.
Ham. As woman's love.   145

Enter two Players, King and Queen.

P. King. Full thirty times hath Phœbus' cart gone round
  Neptune's salt wash and Tellus' orbed ground,
  And thirty dozen moons with borrow'd sheen
  About the world have times twelve thirties been,
  Since love our hearts and Hymen did our hands   150
  Unite commutual in most sacred bands.

P. Queen. So many journeys may the sun and moon
Make us again count o'er ere love be done!
But, woe is me, you are so sick of late,
So far from cheer and from your former state,   155
That I distrust you. Yet, though I distrust,
Discomfort you, my lord, it nothing must:
For women's fear and love holds quantity;
In neither aught, or in extremity.
Now, what my love is, proof hath made you know;   160
And as my love is siz'd, my fear is so:
Where love is great, the littlest doubts are fear;
Where little fears grow great, great love grows there.
P. King. 'Faith, I must leave thee, love, and shortly too;
My operant powers their functions leave to do: 165
And thou shalt live in this fair world behind,
Honour'd, belov'd; and haply one as kind
For husband shalt thou—
P. Queen.   O, confound the rest!
Such love must needs be treason in my breast:
      In second husband let me be accurst!   170
None wed the second but who kill'd the first.
Ham. [*Aside*] Wormwood, wormwood.
P. Queen. The instances that second marriage move
Are base respects of thrift, but none of love:
A second time I kill my husband dead,   175
When second husband kisses me in bed.
P. King. I do believe you think what now you speak;
But what we do determine oft we break.
Purpose is but the slave to memory,
Of violent birth, but poor validity: 180
Which now, like fruit unripe, sticks on the tree;
But falls, unshaken, when it mellow be.
Most necessary 't is that we forget
To pay ourselves what to ourselves is debt:
What to ourselves in passion we propose,   185
The passion ending, doth the purpose lose.
The violence of either grief or joy
Their own enactures with themselves destroy:
Where joy most revels, grief doth most lament;
Grief joys, joy grieves, on slender accident.   190
This world is not for aye, nor 't is not strange
That even our loves should with our fortunes change;
For 't is a question left us yet to prove,
Whether love lead fortune, or else fortune love.
The great man down, you mark his favourite flies;   195

The poor advanc'd makes friends of enemies;
And hitherto doth love on fortune tend;
For who not needs shall never lack a friend,
And who in want a hollow friend doth try,
Directly seasons him his enemy.   200
But, orderly to end where I begun,
Our wills and fates do so contrary run
That our devices still are overthrown;
Our thoughts are ours, their ends none of our own:
So think thou wilt no second husband wed;   205
But die thy thoughts when thy first lord is dead.
P. Queen.   Nor earth to me give food, nor heaven light!
Sport and repose lock from me day and night!
To desperation turn my trust and hope!
An anchor's cheer in prison be my scope!   210
Each opposite that blanks the face of joy
Meet what I would have well and it destroy!
Both here and hence pursue me lasting strife,
If, once a widow, ever I be wife!
Ham.   If she should break it now!   215
P. King.   'T is deeply sworn.   Sweet, leave me here awhile;
My spirits grow dull, and fain I would beguile
The tedious day with sleep.   [*Sleeps.*]
P. Queen.   Sleep rock thy brain;
And never come mischance between us twain!   [*Exit.*]
Ham.   Madam, how like you this play?   220
Queen.   The lady protests too much, methinks.
Ham.   O, but she 'll keep her word.
King.   Have you heard the argument?   Is there no offence in 't?
Ham.   No, no, they do but jest, poison in jest; no offence i' the
world.   225
King.   What do you call the play?
Ham.   The Mouse-trap.   Marry, how?   Tropically.   This play is
the image of a murder done in Vienna: Gonzago is the duke's name;
his wife, Baptista: you shall see anon; 't is a knavish piece of
work: but what o' that? your majesty and we that have free souls,
it touches us not: let the galled jade wince, our withers are un-
wrung.   231

Enter Lucianus.

This is one Lucianus, nephew to the king.
Oph.   You are a good chorus, my lord.
Ham.   I could interpret between you and your love, if I could see
the puppets dallying.   235
Oph.   You are keen, my lord, you are keen.
Ham.   It would cost you a groaning to take off my edge.

Oph. Still better, and worse.

Ham. So you must take your husbands. Begin, ·murderer; pox, leave thy damnable faces, and begin. Come: "The croaking raven doth bellow for revenge." 241

   Luc. Thoughts black, hands apt, drugs fit, and time agreeing;
     Confederate season, else no creature seeing;
     Thou mixture rank, of midnight weeds collected,
     With Hecate's ban thrice blasted, thrice infected, 245
     Thy natural magic and dire property,
     On wholesome life usurp immediately.

                        [*Pours the poison in the sleeper's ears.*]

Ham. He poisons him i' the garden for 's estate. His name 's Gonzago: the story is extant, and writ in choice Italian: you shall see anon how the murderer gets the love of Gonzago's wife.

Oph. The king rises. 251

Ham. What, frighted with false fire!

Queen. How fares my lord?

Pol. Give o'er the play.

King. Give me some light: away! 255

All. Lights, lights, lights!

                     [*Exeunt all but Hamlet and Horatio.*]

Ham. Why, let the stricken deer go weep,
     The hart ungalled play;
   For some must watch, while some must sleep:
     So runs the world away. 260

Would not this, sir, and a forest of feathers—if the rest of my fortunes turn Turk with me—with two Provincial roses on my razed shoes, get me a fellowship in a cry of players, sir?

Hor. Half a share.

Ham. A whole one, I. 265

   For thou does know, O Damon dear,
     This realm dismantled was
   Of Jove himself; and now reigns here
     A very, very—pajock.

Hor. You might have rhymed. 270

Ham. O good Horatio, I 'll take the ghost's word for a thousand pound. Didst perceive?

Hor. Very well, my lord.

Ham. Upon the talk of the poisoning?

Hor. I did very well note him. 275

Enter Rosencrantz and Guildenstern.

Ham. Ah, ha! Come, some music! come, the recorders!
   For if the king like not the comedy,
   Why then, belike, he likes it not, perdy.

Come, some music!

Guil. Good my lord, vouchsafe me a word with you. 280

Ham. Sir, a whole history.

Guil. The king, sir,—

Ham. Ay, sir, what of him?

Guil. Is in his retirement marvellous distempered.

Ham. With drink, sir? 285

Guil. No, my lord, rather with choler.

Ham. Your wisdom should show itself more richer to signify this to his doctor; for, for me to put him to his purgation would perhaps plunge him into far more choler.

Guil. Good my lord, put your discourse into some frame and start not so wildly from my affair. 291

Ham. I am tame, sir: pronounce.

Guil. The queen, your mother, in most great affliction of spirit, hath sent me to you.

Ham. You are welcome. 295

Guil. Nay, good my lord, this courtesy is not of the right breed. If it shall please you to make me a wholesome answer, I will do your mother's commandment: if not, your pardon and my return shall be the end of my business.

Ham. Sir, I cannot. 300

Guil. What, my lord?

Ham. Make you a wholesome answer; my wit's diseased: but, sir, such answers as I can make, you shall command; or, rather, as you say, my mother: therefore no more, but to the matter: my mother, you say,— 305

Ros. Then thus she says; your behaviour hath struck her into amazement and admiration.

Ham. O wonderful son, that can so astonish a mother! But is there no sequel at the heels of this mother's admiration? Impart.

Ros. She desires to speak with you in her closet, ere you go to bed. 311

Ham. We shall obey, were she ten times our mother. Have you any further trade with us?

Ros. My lord, you once did love me.

Ham. So I do still, by these pickers and stealers. 315

Ros. Good my lord, what is your cause of distemper? you do freely bar the door of your own liberty, if you deny your griefs to your friend.

Ham. Sir, I lack advancement.

Ros. How can that be, when you have the voice of the king himself for your succession in Denmark? 321

Ham. Ay, but, "While the grass grows,"—the proverb is something musty.

Enter one with a recorder.

O, the recorder! let me see. To withdraw with you:—why do you go about to recover the wind of me, as if you would drive me into a toil?   326

Guil. O, my lord, if my duty be too bold, my love is too unmannerly.

Ham. I do not well understand that. Will you play upon this pipe?

Guil. My lord, I cannot.

Ham. I pray you.   330

Guil. Believe me, I cannot.

Ham. I do beseech you.

Guil. I know no touch of it, my lord.

Ham. 'T is as easy as lying: govern these ventages with your fingers and thumb, give it breath with your mouth, and it will discourse most excellent music. Look you, there are the stops.   336

Guil. But these cannot I command to any utterance of harmony; I have not the skill.

Ham. Why, look you now, how unworthy a thing you make of me! You would play upon me; you would seem to know my stops; you would pluck out the heart of my mystery; you would sound me from my lowest note to the top of my compass: and there is much music, excellent voice, in this little organ; yet cannot you make it speak. 'Sblood, do you think I am easier to be played on than a pipe? Call me what instrument you will, though you can fret me, you cannot play upon me.   346

Enter Polonius.

God bless you, sir!

Pol. My lord, the queen would speak with you, and presently.

Ham. Do you see that cloud that 's almost in shape like a camel?

Pol. By the mass, and it 's like a camel, indeed.   350

Ham. Methinks it is like a weasel.   350

Pol. It is backed like a weasel.

Ham. Or like a whale?

Pol. Very like a whale.

Ham. Then I will come to my mother by and by. They fool me to the top of my bent. I will come by and by.   356

Pol. I will say so.   [*Exit.*]

Ham. By and by is easily said. Leave me, friends.

[*Exeunt all but Hamlet.*]

'T is now the very witching time of night,
When churchyards yawn and hell itself breathes out   360
Contagion to this world: now could I drink hot blood,   360
And do such bitter business as the day
Would quake to look on. Soft! now to my mother.

O heart, lose not thy nature; let not ever
The soul of Nero enter this firm bosom: 365
Let me be cruel, not unnatural:
I will speak daggers to her, but use none;
My tongue and soul in this be hypocrites;
How in my words soever she be shent,
To give them seals never, my soul, consent!   *[Exit.]*   370

SCENE III.—[*A room in the castle.*]

Enter King, Rosencrantz, and Guildenstern.

King. I like him not, nor stands it safe with us
   To let his madness range.   Therefore prepare you;
   I your commission will forthwith despatch,
   And he to England shall along with you:
   The terms of our estate may not endure   5
   Hazard so dangerous as doth hourly grow
   Out of his lunacies.
Guil.   We will ourselves provide:
   Most holy and religious fear it is
   To keep those many many bodies safe
   That live and feed upon your majesty.   10
Ros.   The single and peculiar life is bound,
   With all the strength and armour of the mind,
   To keep itself from noyance; but much more
   That spirit upon whose weal depends and rests
   The lives of many.   The cease of majesty   15
   Dies not alone; but, like a gulf, doth draw
   What's near it with it: it is a massy wheel,
   Fix'd on the summit of the highest mount,
   To whose huge spokes ten thousand lesser things
   Are mortis'd and adjoin'd; which, when it falls,   20
   Each small annexment, petty consequence,
   Attends the boisterous ruin.   Never alone
   Did the king sigh, but with a general groan.
King.   Arm you, I pray you, to this speedy voyage;
   For we will fetters put upon this fear,   25
   Which now goes too free-footed.
Both.   We will haste us.
        [*Exeunt Rosencrantz and Guildenstern.*]

Enter Polonius.

Pol.   My lord, he's going to his mother's closet:
   Behind the arras I'll convey myself,
   To hear the process; I'll warrant she'll tax him home:

And, as you said, and wisely was it said,   30
'T is meet that some more audience than a mother,
Since nature makes them partial, should o'erhear
The speech, of vantage. Fare you well, my liege:
I 'll call upon you ere you go to bed,
And tell you what I know.

King.   Thanks, dear my lord.   35

                                        [Exit Polonius.]

O, my offence is rank, it smells to heaven;
It hath the primal eldest curse upon't,
A brother's murther. Pray can I not,
Though inclination be as sharp as will:
My stronger guilt defeats my strong intent;   40
And, like a man to double business bound,
I stand in pause where I shall first begin,
And both neglect. What if this cursed hand
Were thicker than itself with brother's blood,
Is there not rain enough in the sweet heavens   45
To wash it white as snow? Whereto serves mercy
But to confront the visage of offence?
And what 's in prayer but this two-fold force,
To be forestalled ere we come to fall,
Or pardon'd being down? Then, I 'll look up;   50
My fault is past. But, O, what form of prayer
Can serve my turn? "Forgive me my foul murther"?
That cannot be; since I am still possess'd
Of those effects for which I did the murther,
My crown, mine own ambition and my queen.   55
May one be pardon'd and retain the offence?
In the corrupted currents of this world
Offence's gilded hand may shove by justice,
And oft 't is seen the wicked prize itself
Buys out the law: but 't is not so above;   60
There is no shuffling, there the action lies
In his true nature; and we ourselves compell'd,
Even to the teeth and forehead of our faults,
To give in evidence. What then? what rests?
Try what repentance can: what can it not?   65
Yet what can it when one can not repent?
O wretched state! O bosom black as death!
O limed soul, that, struggling to be free,
Art more engag'd! Help, angels! Make assay!
Bow, stubborn knees; and, heart with strings of steel,   70
Be soft as sinews of the new-born babe!
All may be well.   *[Kneels.]*

Enter Hamlet.

Ham. Now might I do it pat, now he is praying;
And now I 'll do 't. And so he goes to heaven;
And so am I reveng'd. That would be scann'd: 75
A villain kills my father; and for that,
I, his sole son, do this same villain send
To heaven.
O, this is hire and salary, not revenge.
He took my father grossly, full of bread;   80
With all his crimes broad blown, as flush as May;
And how his audit stands who knows save heaven?
But in our circumstance and course of thought,
'T is heavy with him: and am I then reveng'd,
To take him in the purging of his soul,   85
When he is fit and season'd for his passage?
No!
Up, sword; and know thou a more horrid hent:
When he is drunk asleep, or in his rage,
Or in the incestuous pleasure of his bed;   90
At gaming, swearing, or about some act
That has no relish of salvation in 't;
Then trip him, that his heels may kick at heaven,
And that his soul may be as damn'd and black
As hell, whereto it goes. My mother stays: 95
This physic but prolongs thy sickly days.   [*Exit.*]
King. [*Rising*] My words fly up, my thoughts remain below:
Words without thoughts never to heaven go.   [*Exit.*]

SCENE IV.—[*The Queen's closet.*]

Enter Queen and Polonius.

Pol. He will come straight. Look you lay home to him:
Tell him his pranks have been too broad to bear with,
And that your grace hath screen'd and stood between
Much heat and him. I 'll sconce me even here.
Pray you, be round with him.   5
Ham. [*Within.*] Mother, mother, mother!
Queen.   I 'll warrant you,
Fear me not. Withdraw, I hear him coming.
                        [*Polonius hides behind the arras.*]

Enter Hamlet.

Ham. Now, mother, what 's the matter?
Queen. Hamlet, thou hast thy father much offended.

Ham. Mother, you have my father much offended.   10
Queen. Come, come, you answer with an idle tongue.
Ham. Go, go, you question with a wicked tongue.
Queen. Why, how now, Hamlet!
Ham.   What's the matter now?
Queen. Have you forgot me?
Ham.   No, by the rood, not so:
  You are the queen, your husband's brother's wife;   15
  And—would it were not so!—you are my mother.
Queen. Nay, then, I'll set those to you that can speak.
Ham. Come, come, and sit you down; you shall not budge;
  You go not till I set you up a glass
  Where you may see the inmost part of you.   20
Queen. What wilt thou do? thou wilt not murther me?
  Help, help, ho!
Pol. [*Behind*] What, ho! help, help, help!
Ham. [*Drawing*] How now! a rat? Dead, for a ducat, dead!
                                    [*Kills Polonius.*]

Pol. [*Behind*] O, I am slain!
Queen. O me, what hast thou done?
Ham.   Nay, I know not: 25
  Is it the king?
Queen. O, what a rash and bloody deed is this!
Ham. A bloody deed! almost as bad, good mother,
  As kill a king, and marry with his brother.
Queen. As kill a king?
Ham.   Ay, lady, 't was my word.   30
                [*Lifts up the arras and discovers Polonius.*]
  Thou wretched, rash, intruding fool, farewell!
  I took thee for thy better: take thy fortune;
  Thou find'st to be too busy is some danger.
  Leave wringing of your hands: peace! sit you down,
  And let me wring your heart; for so I shall,   35
  If it be made of penetrable stuff,
  If damned custom have not braz'd it so
  That it is proof and bulwark against sense.
Queen. What have I done, that thou darest wag thy tongue
  In noise so rude against me?
Ham.   Such an act   40
  That blurs the grace and blush of modesty,
  Calls virtue hypocrite, takes off the rose
  From the fair forehead of an innocent love
  And sets a blister there, makes marriage-vows
  As false as dicers' oaths: O, such a deed   45
  As from the body of contraction plucks

The very soul, and sweet religion makes
A rhapsody of words: heaven's face doth glow;
Yea, this solidity and ·compound mass,
With tristful visage, as against the doom,   50
Is thought-sick at the act.
Queen.   Ay me, what act,
That roars so loud, and thunders in the index?
Ham.   Look here, upon this picture, and on this,
The counterfeit presentment of two brothers.
See, what a grace was seated on his brow;   55
Hyperion's curls; the front of Jove himself;
An eye like Mars, to threaten or command;
A station like the herald Mercury
New-lighted on a heaven-kissing hill;
A combination and a form indeed,   60
Where every god did seem to set his seal,
To give the world assurance of a man:
This was your husband. Look you now, what follows:
Here is your husband; like a mildew'd ear,
Blasting his wholesome brother. Have you eyes?   65
Could you on this fair mountain leave to feed,
And batten on this moor? Ha! have you eyes?
You cannot call it love; for at your age
The hey-day in the blood is tame, it's humble,
And waits upon the judgement: and what judgement   70
Would step from this to this? Sense, sure, you have,
Else could you not have motion; but sure, that sense
Is apoplex'd; for madness would not err,
Nor sense to ecstasy was ne'er so thrall'd
But it reserv'd some quantity of choice,   75
To serve in such a difference. What devil was't
That thus hath cozen'd you at hoodman-blind?
Eyes without feeling, feeling without sight,
Ears without hands or eyes, smelling sans all,
Or but a sickly part of one true sense   80
Could not so mope.
O shame! where is thy blush? Rebellious hell,
If thou canst mutine in a matron's bones,
To flaming youth let virtue be as wax,
And melt in her own fire: proclaim no shame   85
When the compulsive ardour gives the charge,
Since frost itself as actively doth burn
And reason panders will.
Queen.   O Hamlet, speak no more:
Thou turn'st mine eyes into my very soul;

And there I see such black and grained spots   90
As will not leave their tinct.

 . . . .

     O, speak to me no more;
These words, like daggers, enter in mine ears;   95
No more, sweet Hamlet!
Ham.   A murderer and a villain;
A slave that is not twentieth part the tithe
Of your precedent lord; a vice of kings;
A cutpurse of the empire and the rule,
That from a shelf the precious diadem stole,   100
And put it in his pocket!
Queen.   No more!
Ham. A king of shreds and patches,—

    Enter Ghost.

Save me, and hover o'er me with your wings,
You heavenly guards! What would you, gracious figure?
Queen. Alas, he's mad!   105
Ham. Do you not come your tardy son to chide,
That, laps'd in time and passion, lets go by
The important acting of your dread command?
O, say!
Ghost. Do not forget: this visitation   110
Is but to whet thy almost blunted purpose.
But, look, amazement on thy mother sits:
O, step between her and her fighting soul:
Conceit in weakest bodies strongest works:
Speak to her, Hamlet.
Ham.   How is it with you, lady?   115
Queen. Alas, how is 't with you,
That you do bend your eye on vacancy
And with th' incorporal air do hold discourse?
Forth at your eyes your spirits wildly peep;
And, as the sleeping soldiers in th' alarm,   120
Your bedded hair, like life in excrements,
Start up, and stand an end. O gentle son,
Upon the heat and flame of thy distemper
Sprinkle cool patience. Whereon do you look?
Ham. On him, on him! Look you, how pale he glares!   125
His form and cause conjoin'd, preaching to stones,
Would make them capable. Do not look upon me;
Lest with this piteous action you convert
My stern effects: then what I have to do
Will want true colour; tears perchance for blood.   130

Queen.   To whom do you speak this?
Ham.   Do you see nothing there?
Queen.   Nothing at all; yet all that is I see.
Ham.   Nor did you nothing hear?
Queen.   No, nothing but ourselves.
Ham.   Why, look you there! look, how it steals away!
  My father, in his habit as he liv'd!   135
  Look, where he goes, even now, out at the portal!   [*Exit Ghost.*]
Queen.   This is the very coinage of your brain:
  This bodiless creation ecstasy
  Is very cunning in.
Ham.   Ecstasy?
  My pulse, as yours, doth temperately keep time,   140
  And makes as healthful music: it is not madness
  That I have utter'd: bring me to the test,
  And I the matter will re-word, which madness
  Would gambol from.   Mother, for love of grace,
  Lay not that flattering unction to your soul,   145
  That not your trespass, but my madness speaks:
  It will but skin and film the ulcerous place,
  Whilst rank corruption, mining all within,
  Infects unseen.   Confess yourself to heaven;
  Repent what's past; avoid what is to come;   150
  And do not spread the compost o'er the weeds,
  To make them rank.   Forgive me this my virtue;
  For in the fatness of these pursy times
  Virtue itself of vice must pardon beg,
  Yea, curb and woo for leave to do him good.   155
Queen.   O Hamlet, thou hast cleft my heart in twain.
Ham.   O, throw away the worser part of it,
  And live the purer with the other half.
  Good night: . . . .
  Assume a virtue, if you have it not.   160
  That monster, custom, who all sense doth eat,
  Of habits devil, is angel yet in this,
  That to the use of actions fair and good
  He likewise gives a frock or livery,
  That aptly is put on.   Refrain to-night,   165
  And that shall lend a kind of easiness
  To the next abstinence: the next more easy;
  For use almost can change the stamp of nature,
  And either . . . the devil, or throw him out
  With wondrous potency.   Once more, good night: 170
  And when you are desirous to be bless'd,
  I'll blessing beg of you.   For this same lord,

[Pointing to Polonius.]

I do repent: but heaven hath pleas'd it so,
To punish me with this and this with me,
That I must be their scourge and minister.　　　175
I will bestow him, and will answer well
The death I gave him. So, again, good night.
I must be cruel, only to be kind:
Thus bad begins and worse remains behind.
One word more, good lady.
Queen.　　　　　　　　　　　What shall I do?　　　180
Ham. Not this, by no means, that I bid you do:
　Let the bloat king . . .
　　　　　　　　　　　. . . call you his mouse;
And let him, for a pair of reechy kisses,
Or paddling in your neck with his damn'd fingers,　　185
Make you to ravel all this matter out,
That I essentially am not in madness,
But mad in craft. 'T were good you let him know;
For who, that's but a queen, fair, sober, wise,
Would from a paddock, from a bat, a gib,　　　190
Such dear concernings hide? who would do so?
No, in despite of sense and secrecy,
Unpeg the basket on the house's top,
Let the birds fly, and, like the famous ape,
To try conclusions, in the basket creep,　　　195
And break your own neck down.
Queen. Be thou assur'd, if words be made of breath,
And breath of life, I have no life to breathe
What thou hast said to me.
Ham. I must to England; you know that?
Queen.　　　　　　　　　　　　　　Alack,　　　200
　I had forgot: 't is so concluded on.
Ham. There's letters seal'd: and my two schoolfellows,
Whom I will trust as I will adders fang'd,
They bear the mandate; they must sweep my way,
And marshal me to knavery. Let it work;　　　205
For 't is the sport to have the engineer
Hoist with his own petar: and 't shall go hard
But I will delve one yard below their mines,
And blow them at the moon: O, 't is most sweet,
When in one line two crafts directly meet.　　　210
This man shall set me packing:
I 'll lug the guts into the neighbour room.
Mother, good night. Indeed this counsellor
Is now most still, most secret, and most grave,

Who was in life a foolish prating knave.   215
Come, sir, to draw toward an end with you.
Good night, mother.

       [Exit Hamlet dragging in Polonius.]

ACT FOURTH

SCENE I.—*[Room in the castle.]*

Enter King and Queen.

King. There's matter in these sighs, these profound heaves:
 You must translate: 't is fit we understand them.
 Where is your son?
Queen. Ah, my good lord, what have I seen to-night!
King. What, Gertrude? How does Hamlet?   5
Queen. Mad as the sea and wind, when both contend
 Which is the mightier: in his lawless fit,
 Behind the arras hearing something stir,
 Whips out his rapier, cries, "A rat, a rat!"
 And, in his brainish apprehension kills   10
 The unseen good old man.
King.   O heavy deed!
 It had been so with us, had we been there:
 His liberty is full of threats to all;
 To you yourself, to us, to every one.
 Alas, how shall this bloody deed be answer'd?   15
 It will be laid to us, whose providence
 Should have kept short, restrain'd, and out of haunt,
 This mad young man: but so much was our love,
 We would not understand what was most fit;
 But, like the owner of a foul disease,   20
 To keep it from divulging, let it feed
 Even on the pith of life. Where is he gone?
Queen. To draw apart the body he hath kill'd;
 O'er whom his very madness, like some ore
 Among a mineral of metals base,   25
 Shows itself pure; he weeps for what is done.
King. O Gertrude, come away!
 The sun no sooner shall the mountains touch,
 But we will ship him hence: and this vile deed
 We must, with all our majesty and skill,   30
 Both countenance and excuse. Ho, Guildenstern!

Enter Rosencrantz and Guildenstern.

Friends both, go join you with some further aid:
Hamlet in madness hath Polonius slain,
And from his mother's closet hath he dragg'd him:
Go seek him out; speak fair, and bring the body   35
Into the chapel. I pray you, haste in this.
                    [*Exeunt Rosencrantz and Guildenstern.*]
Come, Gertrude, we'll call up our wisest friends;
And let them know, both what we mean to do,
And what's untimely done.
Whose whisper o'er the world's diameter,   40
As level as the cannon to his blank,
Transports his poison'd shot, may miss our name,
And hit the woundless air. O, come away!
My soul is full of discord and dismay.   [*Exeunt.*]

SCENE II.—[*Another part of the castle.*]

Enter Hamlet.

Ham. Safely stowed.
Gentlemen. [*Within.*] Hamlet! Lord Hamlet!
Ham. But soft, what noise? who calls on Hamlet? O, here they
    come.

Enter Rosencrantz and Guildenstern.

Ros. What have you done, my lord, with the dead body?   5
Ham. Compounded it with dust, whereto 't is kin.
Ros. Tell us where 't is, that we may take it thence
    And bear it to the chapel.
Ham. Do not believe it.
Ros. Believe what?   10
Ham. That I can keep your counsel and not mine own. Besides,
    to be demanded of a sponge, what replication should be made by
    the son of a king?
Ros. Take you me for a sponge, my lord?   14
Ham. Ay, sir, that soaks up the king's countenance, his rewards,
    his authorities. But such officers do the king best service in the
    end: he keeps them, like an ape, in the corner of his jaw; first
    mouthed, to be last swallowed: when he needs what you have
    gleaned, it is but squeezing you, and, sponge, you shall be dry
    again.   20
Ros. I understand you not, my lord.
Ham. I am glad of it: a knavish speech sleeps in a foolish ear.
Ros. My lord, you must tell us where the body is, and go with us
    to the king.

Ham. The body is with the king, but the king is not with the body.
The king is a thing—   26
Guil. A thing, my lord!
Ham. Of nothing: bring me to him. Hide fox, and all after.
                                                    [*Exeunt.*]

SCENE III.—[*Another room.*]

Enter King, attended.

King. I have sent to seek him, and to find the body.
How dangerous is it that this man goes loose!
Yet must not we put the strong law on him:
He 's lov'd of the distracted multitude,
Who like not in their judgment, but their eyes;   5
And where 't is so, the offender's scourge is weigh'd,
But never the offence. To bear all smooth and even,
This sudden sending him away must seem
Deliberate pause: diseases desperate grown
By desperate appliance are reliev'd,   10
Or not at all.

Enter Rosencrantz.

                How now! what hath befall'n?
Ros. Where the dead body is bestow'd, my lord,
We cannot get from him.
King.   But where is he?
Ros. Without, my lord; guarded, to know your pleasure.
King. Bring him before us.   15
Ros. Ho, Guildenstern! bring in my lord.

Enter Hamlet and Guildenstern.

King. Now, Hamlet, where 's Polonius?
Ham. At supper.
King. At supper! where?   19
Ham. Not where he eats, but where he is eaten: a certain convocation
of politic worms are e'en at him. Your worm is your only emperor
for diet: we fat all creatures else to fat us, and we fat ourselves
for maggots: your fat king and your lean beggar is but variable
service, two dishes, but to one table; that 's the end.
King. Alas, alas!   25
Ham. A man may fish with the worm that hath eat of a king, and
eat of the fish that hath fed of that worm.
King. What dost thou mean by this?
Ham. Nothing but to show you how a king may go a progress
through the guts of a beggar.   30

King. Where is Polonius?

Ham. In heaven; send thither to see: if your messenger find him
not there, seek him i' the other place yourself. But indeed, if you
find him not within this month, you shall nose him as you go up the
stairs into the lobby.   35

King. Go seek him there. [*To Attendants.*]

Ham. He will stay till ye come.   [*Exeunt Attendants.*]

King. Hamlet, this deed, for thine especial safety,—
Which we do tender, as we dearly grieve
For that which thou hast done,—must send thee hence   40
With fiery quickness: therefore prepare thyself;
The bark is ready, and the wind at help,
The associates tend, and every thing is bent
For England.

Ham.   For England!

King.   Ay, Hamlet.

Ham.   Good.

King. So is it, if thou knew'st our purposes.   45

Ham. I see a cherub that sees them. But, come; for England!
Farewell, dear mother.

King. Thy loving father, Hamlet.

Ham. My mother: father and mother is man and wife; man and
wife is one flesh; and so, my mother. Come, for England!   50
                                        [*Exit.*]

King. Follow him at foot; tempt him with speed aboard;
Delay it not; I'll have him hence to-night:
Away! for everything is seal'd and done
That else leans on the affair: pray you, make haste.
                    [*Exeunt Rosencrantz and Guildenstern.*]
And, England, if my love thou hold'st at aught—   55
As my great power thereof may give thee sense,
Since yet thy cicatrice looks raw and red
After the Danish sword, and thy free awe
Pays homage to us—thou mayst not coldly set
Our sovereign process; which imports at full,   60
By letters conjuring to that effect,
The present death of Hamlet. Do it, England;
For like the hectic in my blood he rages,
And thou must cure me: till I know 't is done,
Howe'er my haps, my joys were ne'er begun.   [*Exit.*]   65

Scene IV.—[*Open country near Elsinore.*]

Enter Fortinbras, with a Captain, and an army.

For.   Go, captain, from me greet the Danish king;
   Tell him that, by his license, Fortinbras
   Craves the conveyance of a promis'd march
   Over his kingdom. You know the rendezvous.
   If that his majesty would aught with us,   5
   We shall express our duty in his eye;
   And let him know so.
Cap.   I will do 't, my lord.
For.   Go softly on.   [*Exit.*]

Enter Hamlet, Rosencrantz, &c.

Ham.   Good sir, whose powers are these?
Cap.   They are of Norway, sir.   10
Ham.   How purpos'd, sir, I pray you?
Cap.   Against some part of Poland.
Ham.   Who commands them, sir?
Cap.   The nephew to old Norway, Fortinbras.
Ham.   Goes it against the main of Poland, sir,   15
   Or for some frontier?
Cap.   Truly to speak, and with no addition,
   We go to gain a little patch of ground
   That hath in it no profit but the name.
   To pay five ducats, five, I would not farm it;   20
   Nor will it yield to Norway or the Pole
   A ranker rate, should it be sold in fee.
Ham.   Why, then the Polack never will defend it.
Cap.   Yes, it is already garrison'd.
Ham.   Two thousand souls and twenty thousand ducats   25
   Will not debate the question of this straw:
   This is th' imposthume of much wealth and peace,
   That inward breaks, and shows no cause without
   Why the man dies. I humbly thank you, sir.
Cap.   God be wi' you, sir.   [*Exit.*]
Ros.   Will 't please you go, my lord?   30
Ham.   I 'll be with you straight. Go a little before.
                              [*Exeunt all except Hamlet.*]
   How all occasions do inform against me,
   And spur my dull revenge! What is a man,
   If his chief good and market of his time
   Be but to sleep and feed? a beast, no more.   35
   Sure, he that made us with such large discourse,

Looking before and after, gave us not
That capability and god-like reason
To fust in us unus'd. Now, whether it be
Bestial oblivion, or some craven scruple   40
Of thinking too precisely on the event,
A thought which, quarter'd, hath but one part wisdom
And ever three parts coward, I do not know
Why yet I live to say "This thing's to do;"
Sith I have cause and will and strength and means   45
To do 't. Examples gross as earth exhort me:
Witness this army of such mass and charge
Led by a delicate and tender prince,
Whose spirit with divine ambition puff'd
Makes mouths at the invisible event,   50
Exposing what is mortal and unsure
To all that fortune, death and danger dare,
Even for an egg-shell. Rightly to be great
Is not to stir without great argument,
But greatly to find quarrel in a straw   55
When honour's at the stake. How stand I then,
That have a father kill'd, a mother stain'd,
Excitements of my reason and my blood,
And let all sleep? while, to my shame, I see
The imminent death of twenty thousand men,   60
That, for a fantasy and trick of fame,
Go to their graves like beds, fight for a plot
Whereon the numbers cannot try the cause,
Which is not tomb enough and continent
To hide the slain? O, from this time forth,   65
My thoughts be bloody, or be nothing worth!

Exit.

SCENE V.—[*A room in the castle.*]

Enter Queen and Horatio.

Queen. I will not speak with her.
Hor. She is importunate, indeed distract:
  Her mood will needs be pitied.
Queen.   What would she have?
Hor. She speaks much of her father; says she hears
  There's tricks i' the world; and hems, and beats her heart;   5
  Spurns enviously at straws; speaks things in doubt,
  That carry but half sense: her speech is nothing,
  Yet the unshap'd use of it doth move
  The hearers to collection; they aim at it,
  And botch the words up fit to their own thoughts;   10

Which, as her winks and nods and gestures yield them,
Indeed would make one think there might be thought,
Though nothing sure, yet much unhappily.
Queen. 'T were good she were spoken with; for she may strew
Dangerous conjectures in ill-breeding minds.   15
Let her come in.   *[Exit Horatio.]*
To my sick soul, as sin's true nature is,
Each toy seems prologue to some great amiss:
So full of artless jealousy is guilt,
It spills itself in fearing to be spilt.   20

Enter Horatio, with Ophelia, distracted.

Oph. Where is the beauteous majesty of Denmark?
Queen. How now, Ophelia!
Oph. [*Sings*] How should I your true love know
    From another one?
  By his cockle hat and staff,   25
    And his sandal shoon.
Queen. Alas, sweet lady, what imports this song?
Oph. Say you? nay, pray you, mark.
[*Sings*] He is dead and gone, lady,
    He is dead and gone;   30
  At his head a grass-green turf,
    At his heels a stone.
Queen. Nay, but, Ophelia,—
Oph. Pray you, mark.
[*Sings*] White his shroud as the mountain snow,—   35

Enter King.

Queen. Alas, look here, my lord.
Oph. [*Sings*] Larded with sweet flowers;
  Which bewept to the grave did go
    With true-love showers.
King. How do ye, pretty lady?   40
Oph. Well, God 'ild you! They say the owl was a baker's daughter.
Lord, we know what we are, but know not what we may be. God
be at your table!
King. Conceit upon her father.   44
Oph. Pray you, let's have no words of this; but when they ask you
what it means, say you this:
[*Sings*] To-morrow is Saint Valentine's day,
    All in the morning betime,
  And I a maid at your window,
    To be your Valentine.   50

King. Pretty Ophelia!　　　　　　　　　　　　　　　　　　　55
Oph. Indeed, la, without an oath, I'll make an end on't:

. . . .

King. How long hath she been thus?　　　　　　　　　　　66
Oph. I hope all will be well. We must be patient: but I cannot
　choose but weep, to think they should lay him i' the cold ground.
　My brother shall know of it: and so I thank you for your good
　counsel. Come, my coach! Good night, ladies; good night, sweet
　ladies; good night, good night.　　　　　　　　　　　*[Exit.]*
King. Follow her close; give her good watch, I pray you.
　　　　　　　　　　　　　　　　　　　[Exit Horatio.]

　O, this is the poison of deep grief; it springs
　All from her father's death. O Gertrude, Gertrude,
　When sorrows come, they come not single spies,　　　　75
　But in battalions. First, her father slain:
　Next, your son gone; and he most violent author
　Of his own just remove: the people muddied,
　Thick and unwholesome in their thoughts and whispers,
　For good Polonius' death; and we have done but greenly,　80
　In hugger-mugger to inter him: poor Ophelia
　Divided from herself and her fair judgement,
　Without the which we are pictures, or mere beasts:
　Last, and as much containing as all these,
　Her brother is in secret come from France;　　　　　85
　Feeds on his wonder, keeps himself in clouds,
　And wants not buzzers to infect his ear
　With pestilent speeches of his father's death;
　Wherein necessity, of matter beggar'd,
　Will nothing stick our persons to arraign　　　　　　90
　In ear and ear. O my dear Gertrude, this,
　Like to a murdering-piece, in many places
　Gives me superfluous death.　　　　*[A noise within.]*
Queen.　　　　　　　　Alack, what noise is this?
King. Where are my Switzers? Let them guard the door.

　　　　　　　Enter a Messenger.

　What is the matter?
Mess.　　　　　　　　Save yourself, my lord:　　　　95
　The ocean, overpeering of his list,
　Eats not the flats with more impetuous haste
　Than young Laertes, in a riotous head,
　O'erbears your officers. The rabble call him lord;
　And, as the world were now but to begin,　　　　　100
　Antiquity forgot, custom not known,
　The ratifiers and props of every word,

They cry "Choose we: Laertes shall be king:"
Caps, hands, and tongues, applaud it to the clouds:
"Laertes shall be king, Laertes king!"   105
Queen. How cheerfully on the false trail they cry!
  O, this is counter, you false Danish dogs!
King. The doors are broke.   [*Noise within.*]

Enter Laertes followed by a mob.

Laer. Where is the king? Sirs, stand you all without.
All. No, let's come in.
Laer.   I pray you, give me leave.   110
All. We will, we will.
                    [*They retire without the door.*]
Laer. I thank you: keep the door. O thou vile king,
  Give me my father!
Queen.   Calmly, good Laertes.
Laer. That drop of blood that's calm proclaims me bastard,
  Cries cuckold to my father, brands the harlot   115
  Even here, between the chaste unsmirched brow
  Of my true mother.
King.   What is the cause, Laertes,
  That thy rebellion looks so giant-like?
  Let him go, Gertrude; do not fear our person:
  There's such divinity doth hedge a king,   120
  That treason can but peep to what it would,
  Acts little of his will. Tell me, Laertes,
  Why thou art thus incensed. Let him go, Gertrude.
  Speak, man.
Laer. Where is my father?
King.   Dead.
Queen.   But not by him.   125
King. Let him demand his fill.
Laer. How came he dead? I'll not be juggled with:
  To hell, allegiance! vows, to the blackest devil!
  Conscience and grace, to the profoundest pit!
  I dare damnation. To this point I stand,   130
  That both the worlds I give to negligence,
  Let come what comes; only I'll be reveng'd
  Most throughly for my father.
King.   Who shall stay you?
Laer. My will, not all the world:
  And for my means, I'll husband them so well,   135
  They shall go far with little.
King.   Good Laertes,
  If you desire to know the certainty

Of your dear father's death, is't writ in your revenge,
That, swoopstake, you will draw both friend and foe,
Winner and loser?   140
Laer. None but his enemies.
King.   Will you know them then?
Laer. To his good friends thus wide I'll ope my arms;
And like the kind life-rendering pelican,
Repast them with my blood.
King.   Why, now you speak
Like a good child and a true gentleman.   145
That I am guiltless of your father's death,
And am most sensible in grief for it,
It shall as level to your judgement pierce
As day does to your eye.

                    [*A noise within:* "*Let her come in.*"]
Laer. How now! what noise is that?   150

Enter Ophelia.

O heat, dry up my brains; tears seven times salt,
Burn out the sense and virtue of mine eye!
By heaven, thy madness shall be paid by weight,
Till our scale turns the beam. O rose of May!
Dear maid, kind sister, sweet Ophelia!   155
O heavens! is't possible, a young maid's wits
Should be as mortal as an old man's life?
Nature is fine in love, and where 't is fine,
It sends some precious instance of itself
After the thing it loves.   160
Oph. [*Sings*]
    They bore him barefac'd on the bier;
    Hey non nonny, nonny, hey nonny;
    And on his grave rains many a tear:—
  Fare you well, my dove!
Laer. Hadst thou thy wits, and didst persuade revenge, 165
It could not move thus.
Oph. [*Sings*] You must sing down a-down,
        And you call him a-down-a.

  O, how the wheel becomes it! It is the false steward, that stole his
  master's daughter.   170
Laer. This nothing's more than matter.
Oph. There's rosemary, that's for remembrance; pray, love, re-
  member: and there is pansies, that's for thoughts.
Laer. A document in madness, thoughts and remembrance fitted. 174
Oph. There's fennel for you, and columbines: there's rue for you;
  and here's some for me: we may call it herb-grace o' Sundays: O,

you must wear your rue with a difference. There's a daisy: I would
give you some violets, but they withered all when my father died:
they say he made a good end,—
[*Sings*] For bonny sweet Robin is all my joy.   180
Laer. Thought and affliction, passion, hell itself,
 She turns to favour and to prettiness.
Oph. [*Sings*] And will he not come again?

   And will he not come again?
    No, no, he is dead: 185
    Go to thy death-bed:
   He never will come again.

   His beard was white as snow,
   All flaxen was his poll:
    He is gone, he is gone,   190
    And we cast away moan:
   Gramercy on his soul!

And of all Christian souls, I pray God. God be wi' ye. [*Exit.*]
Laer. Do you see this, you gods?
King. Laertes, I must cómmune with your grief,   195
 Or you deny me right. Go but apart,
 Make choice of whom your wisest friends you will,
 And they shall hear and judge 'twixt you and me:
 If by direct or by collateral hand
 They find us touch'd, we will our kingdom give,   200
 Our crown, our life, and all that we call ours,
 To you in satisfaction; but if not,
 Be you content to lend your patience to us,
 And we shall jointly labour with your soul
 To give it due content.
Laer.   Let this be so;   205
 His means of death, his obscure burial—
 No trophy, sword, nor hatchment o'er his bones,
 No noble rite nor formal ostentation—
 Cry to be heard, as 't were from heaven to earth,
 That I must call 't in question.
King.   So you shall;   210
 And where the offence is let the great axe fall.
 I pray you, go with me.   [*Exeunt.*]

SCENE VI.—[*Horatio's lodging.*]

Enter Horatio with an Attendant.

Hor. What are they that would speak with me?
Serv. Sailors, sir: they say they have letters for you.
Hor. Let them come in. [*Exit Servant.*]
  I do not know from what part of the world
  I should be greeted, if not from lord Hamlet. 5

Enter Sailor.

Sail. God bless you, sir.

Hor. Let him bless thee too.
Sail. He shall, sir, and 't please him. There 's a letter for you, sir;
  it comes from the ambassador that was bound for England; if
  your name be Horatio, as I am let to know it is. 10
Hor. [*Reads the letter.*] "Horatio, when thou shalt have overlooked
  this, give these fellows some means to the king: they have letters
  for him. Ere we were two days old at sea, a pirate of very warlike appointment gave us chase. Finding ourselves too slow of
  sail, we put on a compelled valour. In the grapple I boarded them:
  on the instant they got clear of our ship; so I alone became their
  prisoner. They have dealt with me like thieves of mercy: but they
  knew what they did; I am to do a good turn for them. Let the
  king have the letters I have sent; and repair thou to me with as
  much haste as thou wouldst fly death. I have words to speak in
  thine ear will make thee dumb; yet are they much too light for
  the bore of the matter. These good fellows will bring thee where
  I am. Rosencrantz and Guildenstern hold their course for England: of them I have much to tell thee. Farewell. 24

            "He that thou knowest thine, HAMLET."
  Come, I will give you way for these your letters;
  And do 't the speedier, that you may direct me
  To him from whom you brought them. [*Exit with sailor.*]

SCENE VII.—[*A room in the castle.*]

Enter King and Laertes.

King. Now must your conscience my acquittance seal,
  And you must put me in your heart for friend,
  Sith you have heard, and with a knowing ear,
  That he which hath your noble father slain
  Pursued my life.
Laer.   It well appears: but tell me 5
  Why you proceeded not against these feats,
  So crimeful and so capital in nature,

As by your safety, wisdom, all things else,
You mainly were stirr'd up.

King.   O, for two special reasons;   10
  Which may to you, perhaps, seem much unsinew'd,
  And yet to me they are strong. The queen his mother
  Lives almost by his looks; and for myself—
  My virtue or my plague, be it either which—
  She's so conjunctive to my life and soul,   15
  That, as the star moves not but in his sphere,
  I could not but by her. The other motive,
  Why to a public count I might not go,
  Is the great love the general gender bear him;
  Who, dipping all his faults in their affection,   20
  Would, like the spring that turneth wood to stone,
  Convert his gyves to graces; so that my arrows,
  Too slightly timber'd for so loud a wind,
  Would have reverted to my bow again,
  And not where I had aim'd them.

Laer. And so have I a noble father lost;   25
  A sister driven into desperate terms,
  Whose worth, if praises may go back again,
  Stood challenger on mount of all the age
  For her perfections: but my revenge will come.

King. Break not your sleeps for that: you must not think   30
  That we are made of stuff so flat and dull
  That we can let our beard be shook with danger
  And think it pastime. You shortly shall hear more:
  I lov'd your father, and we love ourself;
  And that, I hope, will teach you to imagine—   35

Enter a Messenger.

How now! what news?

Mess.   Letters, my lord, from Hamlet:
  This to your majesty; this to the queen.

King. From Hamlet? who brought them?

Mess. Sailors, my lord, they say; I saw them not:
  They were given me by Claudio; he received them   40
  Of him that brought them.

King.   Laertes, you shall hear them.
  Leave us.   [*Exit Messenger.*]

[*Reads*] "High and mighty, you shall know I am set naked on your
  kingdom. To-morrow shall I beg leave to see your kingly eyes:
  when I shall, first asking your pardon thereunto, recount the occasions of my sudden and more strange return.

                                          HAMLET." 45

What should this mean? Are all the rest come back?
Or is it some abuse, and no such thing?

Laer. Know you the hand?

King. 'T is Hamlet's character. "Naked!"
And in a postscript here, he says "alone."
Can you advise me? 50

Laer. I 'm lost in it, my lord. But let him come;
It warms the very sickness in my heart,
That I shall live and tell him to his teeth,
"Thus didest thou."

King. If it be so, Laertes—
As how should it be so? how otherwise?— 55
Will you be rul'd by me?

Laer. So you 'll not o'errule me to a peace.

King. To thine own peace. If he be now return'd,
As checking at his voyage, and that he means
No more to undertake it, I will work him 60
To an exploit, now ripe in my device,
Under the which he shall not choose but fall:
And for his death no wind of blame shall breathe,
But even his mother shall uncharge the practice
And call it accident.

Laer. My lord, I will be rul'd; 65
The rather, if you could devise it so
That I might be the organ.

King. It falls right.
You have been talk'd of since your travel much,
And that in Hamlet's hearing, for a quality
Wherein, they say, you shine: your sum of parts 70
Did not together pluck such envy from him
As did that one, and that, in my regard,
Of the unworthiest siege.

Laer. What part is that, my lord?

King. A very riband in the cap of youth,
Yet needful too; for youth no less becomes 75
The light and careless livery that it wears
Than settled age his sables and his weeds,
Importing health and graveness. Two months since,
Here was a gentleman of Normandy:—
I 've seen myself, and serv'd against, the French, 80
And they can well on horseback: but this gallant
Had witchcraft in 't; he grew into his seat;
And to such wondrous doing brought his horse,
As had he been incorps'd and demi-natur'd
With the brave beast: so far he topp'd my thought, 85

That I, in forgery of shapes and tricks,
Come short of what he did.
Laer.   A Norman was 't?
King.   A Norman.
Laer.   Upon my life, Lamond.
King.   The very same.
Laer.   I know him well: he is the brooch indeed   90
And gem of all the nation.
King.   He made confession of you,
And gave you such a masterly report
For art and exercise in your defence
And for your rapier most especial,   9*
That he cried out, 't would be a sight indeed,
If one could match you. The scrimers of their nation,
He swore, had neither motion, guard, nor eye,
If you oppos'd them. Sir, this report of his
Did Hamlet so envenom with his envy   100
That he could nothing do but wish and beg
Your sudden coming o'er, to play with him.
Now, out of this,—
Laer.   What out of this, my lord?
King.   Laertes, was your father dear to you?
Or are you like the painting of a sorrow,   105
A face without a heart?
Laer.   Why ask you this?
King.   Not that I think you did not love your father;
But that I know love is begun by time;
And that I see, in passages of proof,
Time qualifies the spark and fire of it.   110
There lives within the very flame of love
A kind of wick or snuff that will abate it;
And nothing is at a like goodness still;
For goodness, growing to a plurisy,
Dies in his own too much: that we would do,   115
We should do when we would; for this "would" changes
And hath abatements and delays as many
As there are tongues, are hands, are accidents;
And then this "should" is like a spendthrift sigh,
That hurts by easing. But, to the quick o' the ulcer:—   120
Hamlet comes back: what would you undertake,
To show yourself your father's son in deed
More than in words?
Laer.   To cut his throat i' the church.
King.   No place, indeed, should murder sanctuarize;
Revenge should have no bounds. But, good Laertes,   125

Will you do this, keep close within your chamber.
Hamlet return'd shall know you are come home:
We 'll put on those shall praise your excellence
And set a double varnish on the fame
The Frenchman gave you, bring you in fine together   130
And wager on your heads: he, being remiss,
Most generous and free from all contriving,
Will not peruse the foils; so that, with ease,
Or with a little shuffling, you may choose
A sword unbated, and in a pass of practice   135
Requite him for your father.
Laer.   I will do 't:
And, for that purpose, I 'll anoint my sword.
I bought an unction of a mountebank,
So mortal that, but dip a knife in it,
Where it draws blood no cataplasm so rare,   140
Collected from all simples that have virtue
Under the moon, can save the thing from death
That is but scratch'd withal: I 'll touch my point
With this contagion, that, if I gall him slightly,
It may be death.
King.   Let 's further think of this: 145
Weigh what convenience both of time and means
May fit us to our shape: if this should fail,
And that our drift look through our bad performance,
'T were better not assay'd: therefore this project
Should have a back or second, that might hold,   150
If this should blast in proof. Soft! let me see:
We 'll make a solemn wager on your cunnings:
I ha 't:
When in your motion you are hot and dry—
As make your bouts more violent to that end—   155
And that he calls for drink, I 'll have prepar'd him
A chalice for the nonce, whereon but sipping,
If he by chance escape your venom'd stuck,
Our purpose may hold there.

Enter Queen.

                            How now, sweet queen!
Queen.   One woe doth tread upon another's heel,   160
   So fast they follow: your sister's drown'd, Laertes.
Laer.   Drown'd! O, where?
Queen.   There is a willow grows aslant a brook,
   That shows his hoar leaves in the glassy stream;
   There with fantastic garlands did she come   165

Of crow-flowers, nettles, daisies, and long purples
That liberal shepherds give a grosser name,

. . . .

There, on the pendant boughs her coronet weeds
Clambering to hang, an envious sliver broke;   170
When down her weedy trophies and herself
Fell in the weeping brook. Her clothes spread wide;
And, mermaid-like, awhile they bore her up:
Which time she chanted snatches of old tunes;
As one incapable of her own distress,   175
Or like a creature native and indued
Unto that element: but long it could not be
Till that her garments, heavy with their drink,
Pull'd the poor wretch from her melodious lay
To muddy death.
Laer.   Alas, then, is she drown'd?   180
Queen. Drown'd, drown'd.
Laer. Too much of water hast thou, poor Ophelia,
  And therefore I forbid my tears: but yet
  It is our trick; nature her custom holds,
  Let shame say what it will: when these are gone,   185
  The woman will be out. Adieu, my lord:
  I have a speech of fire, that fain would blaze,
  But that this folly douts it.   [*Exit.*]
King.   Let's follow, Gertrude:
  How much I had to do to calm his rage!
  Now fear I this will give it start again;   190
  Therefore let's follow.   [*Exeunt.*]

ACT FIFTH

Scene I.—[*A churchyard.*]

Enter two Clowns.

First Clo. Is she to be buried in Christian burial that wilfully seeks
her own salvation?

Sec. Clo. I tell thee she is; and therefore make her grave straight:
the crowner hath sat on her, and finds it Christian burial.

First Clo. How can that be, unless she drowned herself in her own
defence?   6

Sec. Clo. Why, 't is found so.

First Clo. It must be "se offendendo;" it cannot be else. For here
lies the point: if I drown myself wittingly, it argues an act: and
an act hath three branches; it is, to act, to do, and to perform:
argal, she drowned herself wittingly.   11

Sec. Clo. Nay, but hear yóu, goodman delver,—

First Clo. Give me leave. Here lies the water; good: here stands the man; good: if the man go to this water, and drown himself, it is, will he, nill he, he goes,—mark you that; but if the water come to him and drown him, he drowns not himself: argal, he that is not guilty of his own death shortens not his own life.   17

Sec. Clo. But is this law?

First Clo. Ay, marry, is 't; crowner's quest law.

Sec. Clo. Will you ha' the truth on 't? If this had not been a gentle-woman, she should have been buried out of Christian burial.

First Clo. Why, there thou say'st: and the more pity that great folk should have countenance in this world to drown or hang themselves, more than their even Christian. Come, my spade. There is no ancient gentlemen but gardeners, ditchers, and grave-makers: they hold up Adam's profession.   26

Sec. Clo. Was he a gentleman?

First Clo. He was the first that ever bore arms.

Sec. Clo. Why, he had none.

First Clo. What, art a heathen? How dost thou understand the Scripture? The Scripture says "Adam digged:" could he dig with-out arms? I 'll put another question to thee: if thou answerest me not to the purpose, confess thyself—   33

Sec. Clo. Go to.

First Clo. What is he that builds stronger than either the mason, the shipwright, or the carpenter?

Sec. Clo. The gallows-maker; for that frame outlives a thousand tenants.   38

First Clo. I like thy wit well, in good faith: the gallows does well; but how does it well? it does well to those that do ill: now thou dost ill to say the gallows is built stronger than the church: argal, the gallows may do well to thee. To 't again, come.

Sec. Clo. "Who builds stronger than a mason, a shipwright, or a carpenter?"

First Clo. Ay, tell me that, and unyoke.   45

Sec. Clo. Marry, now I can tell.

First Clo. To 't.

Sec. Clo. Mass, I cannot tell.

Enter Hamlet and Horatio, afar off.

First Clo. Cudgel thy brains no more about it, for your dull ass will not mend his pace with beating; and, when you are asked this question next, say "a grave-maker:" the houses that he makes last till doomsday. Go, get thee to Yaughan: fetch me a stoup of liquor.

[*Exit Sec. Clown.*]

[First Clown digs, and sings.]

In youth, when I did love, did love,
  Methought it was very sweet,
To contract, O, the time, for, ah, my behove,   55
  O, methought, there was nothing meet.

Ham. Has this fellow no feeling of his business, that he sings at grave-making?

Hor. Custom hath made it in him a property of easiness.

Ham. 'T is e'en so: the hand of little employment hath the daintier sense.   61

Clown. *[Sings.]*

But age, with his stealing steps,
  Hath caught me in his clutch,
And hath shipped me intil the land,
  As if I had never been such.   65

[Throws up a skull.]

Ham. That skull had a tongue in it, and could sing once: how the knave jowls it to the ground, as if it were Cain's jaw-bone, that did the first murther! It might be the pate of a politician, which this ass now o'er-reaches; one that would circumvent God, might it not?   70

Hor. It might, my lord.

Ham. Or of a courtier; which could say "Good morrow, sweet lord! How doest thou, good lord?" This might be my lord such-a-one, that praised my lord such-a-one's horse, when he meant to beg it; might it not?   75

Hor. Ay, my lord.

Ham. Why, e'en so: and now my Lady Worm's; chapless, and knocked about the mazzard with a sexton's spade: here's fine revolution, if we had the trick to see 't. Did these bones cost no more the breeding, but to play at loggats with 'em? mine ache to think on 't.   81

Clown. *[Sings.]*

A pick-axe, and a spade, a spade,
  For such a guest is meet.
O, a pit of clay for to be made
  For such a guest is meet.   85

[Throws up another skull.]

Ham. There's another: why might not that be the skull of a lawyer? Where be his quiddities now, his quillets, his cases, his tenures, and his tricks? why does he suffer this rude knave now to knock him about the sconce with a dirty shovel, and will not tell him of his action of battery? Hum! This fellow might be in 's time a great buyer of land, with his statutes, his recognizances, his fines, his double vouchers, his recoveries: is this the fine of his fines, and the recovery of his recoveries, to have his fine pate full of fine dirt? will his vouchers vouch him no more of his purchases, and double ones too, than the length and breath of a pair of indentures? The very conveyances of his lands will hardly lie in this box; and must the inheritor himself have no more, ha? 97

Hor. Not a jot more, my lord.

Ham. Is not parchment made of sheep-skins?

Hor. Ay, my lord, and of calf-skins too. 100

Ham. They are sheep and calves that seek out assurance in that. I will speak to this fellow. Whose grave 's this, sirrah?

Clown. Mine, sir.

[*Sings*] O, a pit of clay for to be made
          For such a guest is meet. 105

Ham. I think it be thine, indeed; for thou liest in 't.

Clo. You lie out on 't, sir, and therefore it is not yours: for my part, I do not lie in 't, and yet it is mine.

Ham. Thou dost lie in 't, to be in 't and say 't is thine: 't is for the dead, not for the quick; therefore thou liest. 110

Clo. 'T is a quick lie, sir; 't will away again, from me to you.

Ham. What man dost thou dig it for?

Clo. For no man, sir.

Ham. What woman, then?

Clo. For none, neither. 115

Ham. Who is to be buried in 't?

Clo. One that was a woman, sir; but, rest her soul, she 's dead.

Ham. How absolute the knave is! we must speak by the card, or equivocation will undo us. By the Lord, Horatio, these three years I have taken note of it; the age is grown so picked that the toe of the peasant comes so near the heel of the courtier, he galls his kibe. How long hast thou been a grave-maker?

Clo. Of all the days i' the year, I came to 't that day that our last king Hamlet overcame Fortinbras.

Ham. How long is that since? 125

Clo. Cannot you tell that? every fool can tell that: it was the very day that young Hamlet was born; he that was mad, and sent into England.

Ham. Ay, marry, why was he sent into England?

Clo. Why, because he was mad: he shall recover his wits there; or, if he do not, it 's no great matter there. 131

Ham. Why?

Clo. 'T will not be seen in him there; there the men are as mad as he.

Ham. How came he mad? 135

Clo. Very strangely, they say.

Ham. How strangely?

Clo. Faith, e'en with losing his wits.

Ham. Upon what ground?

Clo. Why, here in Denmark. I have been sexton here, man and boy, thirty years. [141]

Ham. How long will a man lie i' the earth ere he rot?

Clo. I' faith, if he be not rotten before he die—as we have many pocky corses now-a-days, that will scarce hold the laying in—he will last you some eight year or nine year: a tanner will last you nine year. [146]

Ham. Why he more than another?

Clo. Why, sir, his hide is so tanned with his trade, that he will keep out water a great while; and your water is a sore decayer of your whoreson dead body. Here's a skull now; this skull has lain in the earth three and twenty years. [151]

Ham. Whose was it?

Clo. A whoreson mad fellow's it was: whose do you think it was?

Ham. Nay, I know not.

Clo. A pestilence on him for a mad rogue! a' poured a flagon of Rhenish on my head once. This same skull, sir, was Yorick's skull, the king's jester. [157]

Ham. This?

Clo. E'en that.

Ham. Let me see. [*Takes the skull.*] Alas, poor Yorick! I knew him, Horatio: a fellow of infinite jest, of most excellent fancy: he hath borne me on his back a thousand times; and now, how abhorred in my imagination it is! my gorge rises at it. Here hung those lips that I have kissed I know not how oft. Where be your gibes now? your gambols? your songs? your flashes of merriment, that were wont to set the table on a roar? Not one now, to mock your own grinning? quite chap-fallen? Now get you to my lady's chamber, and tell her, let her paint an inch thick, to this favour she must come; make her laugh at that. Prithee, Horatio, tell me one thing. [170]

Hor. What's that, my lord?

Ham. Dost thou think Alexander looked o' this fashion i' the earth?

Hor. E'en so.

Ham. And smelt so? pah! [*Puts down the skull.*]

Hor. E'en so, my lord. [175]

Ham. To what base uses we may return, Horatio! Why may not imagination trace the noble dust of Alexander, till he find it stopping a bung-hole?

Hor. 'T were to consider too curiously, to consider so.

Ham. No, faith, not a jot; but to follow him thither with modesty enough, and likelihood to lead it: as thus: Alexander died, Alexander was buried, Alexander returneth unto dust; the dust is earth;

of earth we make loam; and why of that loam, whereto he was
converted, might they not stop a beer-barrel?

Imperial Cæsar, dead and turn'd to clay,   185
Might stop a hole to keep the wind away:
O, that that earth, which kept the world in awe,
Should patch a wall t' expel the winter's flaw!
But soft! but soft! aside: here comes the king.

Enter King, Queen, Laertes, the bier of Ophelia, with Priest and Lords
attendant.

The queen, the courtiers: who is that they follow?   190
And with such maimed rites? This doth betoken
The corse they follow did with desperate hand
Fordo its own life: 't was of some estate.
Couch we awhile, and mark.

                     [Retiring with Horatio.]

Laer. What ceremony else?
Ham.   That is Laertes,   195
A very noble youth: .mark.
Laer. What ceremony else?
Priest. Her obsequies have been as far enlarg'd
As we have warrantise: her death was doubtful;
And, but that great command o'ersways the order,   200
She should in ground unsanctified have lodg'd
Till the last trumpet; for charitable prayer,
Shards, flints, and pebbles should be thrown on her:
Yet here she is allow'd her virgin crants,
Her maiden strewments and the bringing home   205
Of bell and burial.
Laer. Must there no more be done?
Priest.   No more be done:
We should profane the service of the dead
To sing a requiem and such rest to her
As to peace-parted souls.
Laer.   Lay her i' the earth: 210
And from her fair and unpolluted flesh
May violets spring! I tell thee, churlish priest,
A ministering angel shall my sister be,
When thou liest howling.
Ham.   What, the fair Ophelia!
Queen. Sweets to the sweet: farewell!   215

                     [Scattering flowers.]

I hop'd thou shouldst have been my Hamlet's wife;
I thought thy bride-bed to have deck'd, sweet maid,
And not t' have strew'd thy grave.

Laer.   O, treble woe
 Fall ten times treble on that cursed head,
 Whose wicked deed thy most ingenious sense   220
 Depriv'd thee of! Hold off the earth awhile,
 Till I have caught her once more in mine arms:
           [Leaps into the grave.]
 Now pile your dust upon the quick and dead,
 Till of this flat a mountain you have made,
 T' o'ertop old Pelion, or the skyish head   225
 Of blue Olympus.
Ham. *[Advancing]* What is he whose grief
 Bears such an emphasis? whose phrase of sorrow
 Conjures the wandering stars, and makes them stand
 Like wonder-wounded hearers? This is I,
 Hamlet the Dane.   *[Leaps into the grave.]*
Laer.   The devil take thy soul!   230
         [Grappling with him.]

Ham. Thou pray'st not well.
 I prithee, take thy fingers from my throat;
 For, though I am not splenitive and rash,
 Yet have I something in me dangerous,
 Which let thy wiseness fear. Away thy hand.   235
King. Pluck them asunder.
Queen.   Hamlet, Hamlet!
Attendants. Gentlemen,—
Hor.   Good my lord, be quiet.
 [The Attendants part them, and they come out of the grave.]
Ham. Why, I will fight with him upon this theme
 Until my eyelids will no longer wag.
Queen. O my son, what theme?   240
Ham. I lov'd Ophelia: forty thousand brothers
 Could not, with all their quantity of love,
 Make up my sum. What wilt thou do for her?
King. O, he is mad, Laertes.
Queen. For love of God, forbear him.   245
Ham. 'Swounds, show me what thou 'lt do:
 Woo 't weep? woo 't fight? woo 't fast? woo 't tear thyself?
 Woo 't drink up eisel? eat a crocodile?
 I 'll do 't. Dost thou come here to whine?
 To outface me with leaping in her grave?   250
 Be buried quick with her, and so will I:
 And if thou prate of mountains, let them throw
 Millions of acres on us, till our ground,
 Singeing his pate against the burning zone,
 Make Ossa like a wart! Nay, and thou 'lt mouth,   255
 I 'll rant as well as thou.

Queen.   This is mere madness:
And thus awhile the fit will work on him;
Anon, as patient as the female dove
When that her golden couplets are disclos'd,
His silence will sit drooping.
Ham.   Hear you, sir;   260
What is the reason that you use me thus?
I lov'd you ever: but it is no matter;
Let Hercules himself do what he may,
The cat will mew, and dog will have his day.   [*Exit.*]
King. I pray you, good Horatio, wait upon him.   265
                                                   [*Exit Horatio.*]
[*To Laertes*] Strengthen your patience in our last night's speech;
We'll put the matter to the present push.
Good Gertrude, set some watch over your son.
This grave shall have a living monument:
An hour of quiet shortly shall we see;   270
Till then, in patience our proceeding be.   [*Exeunt.*]

SCENE II.—[*A hall in the castle.*]

Enter Hamlet and Horatio.

Ham. So much for this, sir: now let me see the other;
You do remember all the circumstance?
Hor. Remember it, my lord!
Ham. Sir, in my heart there was a kind of fighting,
That would not let me sleep: methought I lay   5
Worse than the mutines in the bilboes. Rashly,
And prais'd be rashness for it; let us know,
Our indiscretion sometimes serves us well,
When our deep plots do pall: and that should teach us
There's a divinity that shapes our ends,   10
Rough-hew them how we will,—
Hor.   That is most certain.
Ham. Up from my cabin,
My sea-gown scarf'd about me, in the dark
Grop'd I to find out them; had my desire,
Finger'd their packet, and in fine withdrew   15
To mine own room again; making so bold,
My fears forgetting manners, to unseal
Their grand commission; where I found, Horatio,—
O royal knavery!—an exact command,
Larded with many several sorts of reasons   20
Importing Denmark's health and England's too,
With, ho! such bugs and goblins in my life,

That, on the supervise, no leisure bated,
No, not to stay the grinding of the axe,
My head should be struck off.
Hor.   Is 't possible?   25
Ham. Here 's the commission: read it at more leisure.
But wilt thou hear me how I did proceed?
Hor.   I beseech you.
Ham.   Being thus be-netted round with villainies,—
Ere I could make a prologue to my brains,   30
They had begun the play,—I sate me down,
Devis'd a new commission, wrote it fair:
I once did hold it, as our statists do,
A baseness to write fair, and labour'd much
How to forget that learning, but, sir, now   35
It did me yeoman's service: wilt thou know
The effect of what I wrote?
Hor.   Ay, good my lord.
Ham.   An earnest conjuration from the king,
As England was his faithful tributary,
As love between them as the palm should flourish,   40
As peace should still her wheaten garland wear
And stand a comma 'tween their amities,
And many such-like "As'es" of great charge,
That, on the view and knowing of these contents,
Without debatement further, more or less,   45
He should the bearers put to sudden death,
Not shriving-time allow'd.
Hor.   How was this seal'd?
Ham.   Why, even in that was heaven ordinant.
I had my father's signet in my purse,
Which was the model of that Danish seal;   50
Folded the writ up in form of the other,
Subscrib'd it, gave 't th' impression, plac'd it safely,
The changeling never known. Now, the next day
Was our sea-fight; and what to this was sequent
Thou know'st already.   55
Hor.   So Guildenstern and Rosencrantz go to 't.
Ham.   Why, man, they did make love to this employment;
They are not near my conscience; their defeat
Doth by their own insinuation grow:
'T is dangerous when the baser nature comes   60
Between the pass and fell incensed points
Of mighty opposites.
Hor.   Why, what a king is this!
Ham. Does it not, think'st thee, stand me now upon—

He that hath kill'd my king and stained my mother,
Popp'd in between th' election and my hopes, 65
Thrown out his angle for my proper life,
And with such cozenage—is 't not perfect conscience,
To quit him with this arm? and is 't not to be damn'd,
To let this canker of our nature come
In further evil? 70

Hor. It must be shortly known to him from England
What is the issue of the business there.

Ham. It will be short: the interim is mine ;
And a man's life 's no more than to say "One."
But I am very sorry, good Horatio, 75
That to Laertes I forgot myself;
For, by the image of my cause, I see
The portraiture of his: I 'll court his favours:
But, sure, the bravery of his grief did put me
Into a towering passion.

Hor.   Peace! who comes here? 80

Enter young Osric.

Osr. Your lordship is right welcome back to Denmark.
Ham. I humbly thank you, sir.
   [*To Horatio.*] Dost know this water-fly?
Hor. No, my good lord.
Ham. Thy state is the more gracious; for 't is a vice to know him.
He hath much land, and fertile: let a beast be lord of beasts, and
his crib shall stand at the king's mess: 't is a chough; but, as I say,
spacious in the possession of dirt.
Osr. Sweet lord, if your lordship were at leisure, I should impart
a thing to you from his majesty. 90
Ham. I will receive it, sir, with all diligence of spirit. Put your
bonnet to his right use; 't is for the head.
Osr. I thank your lordship, 't is very hot.
Ham. No, believe me, 't is very cold; the wind is northerly.
Osr. It is indifferent cold, my lord, indeed. 95
Ham. But yet methinks it is very sultry and hot for my complexion.
Osr. Exceedingly, my lord; it is very sultry,—as 't were,—I cannot
tell how. But, my lord, his majesty bade me signify to you that he
has laid a great wager on your head: sir, this is the matter,—
Ham. I beseech you, remember— 100
          [*Hamlet moves him to put on his hat.*]
Osr. Nay, good my lord; for mine ease, in good faith. Sir, here
is newly come to court Laertes; believe me, an absolute gentleman,
full of most excellent differences, of very soft society and great
showing: indeed, to speak feelingly of him, he is the card or

calendar of gentry, for you shall find in him the continent of what part a gentleman would see. 106

Ham. Sir, his definement suffers no perdition in you; though, I know, to divide him inventorially would dizzy the arithmetic of memory, and yet but yaw neither, in respect of his quick sail. But, in the verity of extolment, I take him to be a soul of great article; and his infusion of such dearth and rareness, as, to make true diction of him, his semblable is his mirror; and who else would trace him, his umbrage, nothing more. 113

Osr. Your lordship speaks most infallibly of him.

Ham. The concernancy, sir? why do we wrap the gentleman in our more rawer breath?

Osr. Sir?

Hor. Is 't not possible to understand in another tongue? You will do 't, sir, really.

Ham. What imports the nomination of this gentleman? 120

Osr. Of Laertes?

Hor. His purse is empty already; all 's golden words are spent.

Ham. Of him, sir.

Osr. I know you are not ignorant—

Ham. I would you did, sir; yet, in faith, if you did, it would not much approve me. Well, sir? 126

Osr. You are not ignorant of what excellence Laertes is—

Ham. I dare not confess that, lest I should compare with him in excellence; but, to know a man well, were to know himself.

Osr. I mean, sir, for his weapon; but in the imputation laid on him by them, in his meed he 's unfellowed. 131

Ham. What 's his weapon?

Osr. Rapier and dagger.

Ham. That 's two of his weapons: but, well.

Osr. The king, sir, hath wagered with him six Barbary horses: against the which he imponed, as I take it, six French rapiers and poniards, with their assigns, as girdle, hangers, and so: three of the carriages, in faith, are very dear to fancy, very responsive to the hilts, most delicate carriages, and of very liberal conceit.

Ham. What call you the carriages? 140

Hor. I knew you must be edified by the margent ere you had done.

Osr. The carriages, sir, are the hangers.

Ham. The phrase would be more germane to the matter, if we could carry cannon by our sides: I would it might be hangers till then. But, on: six Barbary horses against six French swords, their assigns, and three liberal-conceited carriages; that 's the French bet against the Danish. Why is this "imponed," as you call it? 149

Osr. The king, sir, hath laid, that in a dozen passes between you and him, he shall not exceed you three hits: he hath laid on twelve for nine; and that would come to immediate trial, if your lordship would vouchsafe the answer.

Ham. How if I answer "no"?

Osr. I mean, my lord, the opposition of your person in trial.　　155

Ham. Sir, I will walk here in the hall: if it please his majesty, 't is the breathing time of day with me; let the foils be brought, the gentleman willing, and the king hold his purpose, I will win for him if I can; if not, I will gain nothing but my shame and the odd hits.　　160

Osr. Shall I re-deliver you e'en so?

Ham. To this effect, sir; after what flourish your nature will.

Osr. I commend my duty to your lordship.

Ham. Yours, yours. [*Exit Osric.*] He does well to commend it himself; there are no tongues else for 's turn.　　165

Hor. This lapwing runs away with the shell on his head.

Ham. He did comply with his dug, before he sucked it. Thus has he—and many more of the same breed that I know the drossy age dotes on—only got the tune of the time and outward habit of encounter; a kind of yesty collection, which carries them through and through the most fond and winnowed opinions; and do but blow them to their trial, the bubbles are out.

Enter a Lord.

Lord. My lord, his majesty commended him to you by young Osric, who brings back to him, that you attend him in the hall: he sends to know if your pleasure hold to play with Laertes, or that you will take longer time.

Ham. I am constant to my purposes; they follow the king's pleasure: if his fitness speaks, mine is ready; now or whensoever, provided I be so able as now.

Lord. The king and queen and all are coming down.　　180

Ham. In happy time.

Lord. The queen desires you to use some gentle entertainment to Laertes before you fall to play.

Ham. She well instructs me.　　[*Exit Lord.*]

Hor. You will lose this wager, my lord.　　185

Ham. I do not think so; since he went into France, I have been in continual practice; I shall win at the odds. But thou wouldst not think how ill all 's here about my heart: but it is no matter.

Hor. Nay, good my lord,—

Ham. It is but foolery; but it is such a kind of gain-giving as would perhaps trouble a woman.　　191

Hor. If your mind dislike any thing, obey it. I will forestall their repair hither, and say you are not fit.

Ham. Not a whit, we defy augury: there's a special providence in the fall of a sparrow. If it be now, 't is not to come; if it be not to come, it will be now; if it be not now; yet it will come: the readiness is all: since no man has aught of what he leaves, what is 't to leave betimes?   198

Enter King, Queen, Laertes, and Lords, with other Attendants with foils and gauntlets. A table and flagons of wine on it.

King. Come, Hamlet, come, and take this hand from me.
                    [*The King puts Laertes' hand into Hamlet's.*]
Ham. Give me your pardon, sir: I 've done you wrong;   200
But pardon 't, as you are a gentleman.
This presence knows,
And you must needs have heard, how I am punish'd
With sore distraction. What I have done,
That might your nature, honour, and exception   205
Roughly awake, I here proclaim was madness.
Was 't Hamlet wrong'd Laertes? Never Hamlet:
If Hamlet from himself be ta'en away,
And when he 's not himself does wrong Laertes,
Then Hamlet does it not, Hamlet denies it.   210
Who does it, then? His madness: if 't be so,
Hamlet is of the faction that is wrong'd;
His madness is poor Hamlet's enemy.
Sir, in this audience,
Let my disclaiming from a purpos'd evil   215
Free me so far in your most generous thoughts,
That I have shot mine arrow o'er the house,
And hurt my brother.
Laer.   I am satisfied in nature,
Whose motive, in this case, should stir me most
To my revenge: but in my terms of honour   220
I stand aloof; and will no reconcilement,
Till by some elder masters, of known honour,
I have a voice and precedent of peace,
To keep my name ungor'd. But till that time,
I do receive your offer'd love like love,   225
And will not wrong it.
Ham.   I do embrace it freely;
And will this brother's wager frankly play.
Give us the foils. Come on.
Laer.   Come, one for me.
Ham. I 'll be your foil, Laertes: in mine ignorance

Your skill shall, like a star i' the darkest night,   230
Stick fiery off indeed.
Laer.   You mock me, sir.
Ham. No, by this hand.
King. Give them the foils, young Osric. Cousin Hamlet,
You know the wager?
Ham.   Very well, my lord;
Your grace hath laid the odds o' the weaker side.   235
King. I do not fear it; I have seen you both:
But since he is better'd, we have therefore odds.
Laer. This is too heavy, let me see another.
Ham. This likes me well. These foils have all a length?
[Prepare to Play.]
                                                                   240
Osr. Ay, my good lord.
King. Set me the stoups of wine upon that table.
If Hamlet give the first or second hit,
Or quit in answer of the third exchange,
Let all the battlements their ordnance fire;
The king shall drink to Hamlet's better breath;   245
And in the cup an union shall he throw,
Richer than that which four successive kings
In Denmark's crown have worn. Give me the cups;
And let the kettle to the trumpet speak,
The trumpet to the cannoneer without,   250
The cannons to the heavens, the heaven to earth,
"Now the king drinks to Hamlet." Come, begin:
And you, the judges, bear a wary eye.
Ham. Come on, sir.
Laer.   Come, my lord.   [They play.]
Ham.   One.
Laer.   No.
Ham.   Judgement.
Osr. A hit, a very palpable hit.
Laer.   Well; again.   255
King. Stay; give me drink. Hamlet, this pearl is thine;
Here's to thy health.
                [Trumpets sound, and shot goes off.]
                Give him the cup.
Ham. I 'll play this bout first; set it by awhile.
Come. [They play.] Another hit; what say you?
Laer. A touch, a touch, I do confess.   260
King. Our son shall win.
Queen.   He's fat, and scant of breath.
Here, Hamlet, take my napkin, rub thy brows:
The queen carouses to thy fortune, Hamlet.

Ham.   Good madam!
King.   Gertrude, do not drink.
Queen.   I will, my lord; I pray you, pardon me.   265
King.   [*Aside*] It is the poison'd cup: it is too late.
Ham.   I dare not drink yet, madam; by and by.
Queen.   Come, let me wipe thy face.
Laer.   My lord, I 'll hit him now.
King.   I do not think 't.
Laer.   [*Aside*] And yet 't is almost 'gainst my conscience.   270
Ham.   Come, for the third, Laertes: you but dally;
  I pray you, pass with your best violence;
  I am afeard you make a wanton of me.
Laer.   Say you so? come on.   [*Play.*]
Osr.   Nothing, neither way.   275
Laer.   Have at you now!
                    [*Laertes wounds Hamlet. In scuffling, they change
                        rapiers and Hamlet wounds Laertes.*]
King.   Part them; they are incens'd.
Ham.   Nay, come, again.   [*The Queen falls.*]
Osr.   Look to the queen there, ho!
Hor.   They bleed on both sides. How is 't, my lord?
Osr.   How is 't, Laertes?
Laer.   Why, as a woodcock to mine own springe, Osric;   280
  I am justly kill'd with mine own treachery.
Ham.   How does the queen?
King.   She swounds to see them bleed.
Queen.   No, no, the drink, the drink,—O my dear Hamlet,—
  The drink, the drink! I am poison'd.   [*Dies.*]
Ham.   O villainy!
  Ho! let the door be lock'd. Treachery! Seek it out.
Laer.   It is here, Hamlet: Hamlet, thou art slain;
  No medicine in the world can do thee good.
  In thee there is not half an hour of life;
  The treacherous instrument is in thy hand,
  Unabated and envenom'd: the foul practice
  Hath turn'd itself on me; lo, here I lie,
  Never to rise again: thy mother's poison'd:
  I can no more: the king, the king's to blame.
Ham.   The point envenom'd too!
  Then, venom, to thy work.   [*Hurts the King.*] 295
All.   Treason! treason!
King.   O, yet defend me, friends; I am but hurt.
Ham.   Here, thou incestuous, murderous, damned Dane.
  Drink off this potion. Is thy union here?
  Follow my mother.   [*King dies.*]

Laer.   He is justly serv'd;   300
  It is a poison temper'd by himself.
  Exchange forgiveness with me, noble Hamlet:
  Mine and my father's death come not upon thee,
  Nor thine on me!   [*Dies.*]
Ham. Heaven make thee free of it! I follow thee.   305
  I am dead, Horatio. Wretched queen, adieu!
  You that look pale and tremble at this chance,
  That are but mutes or audience to this act,
  Had I but time—as this fell sergeant, death,
  Is strict in his arrest—O, I could tell you—   310
  But let it be. Horatio, I am dead;
  Thou livest; report me and my cause aright
  To the unsatisfied.
Hor.   Never believe it:
  I am more an antique Roman than a Dane:
  Here's yet some liquor left.
Ham.   As th' art a man,   315
  Give me the cup; let go; by heaven, I'll have 't.
  O good Horatio, what a wounded name,
  Things standing thus unknown, shall live behind me!
  If thou didst ever hold me in thy heart,
  Absent thee from felicity awhile,   320
  And in this harsh world draw thy breath in pain,
  To tell my story.

                    [*March afar off, and shot within.*]
                What warlike noise is this?
Osr. Young Fortinbras, with conquest come from Poland,
  To the ambassadors of England gives
  This warlike volley.
Ham.   O, I die, Horatio;   325
  The potent poison quite o'er-crows my spirit:
  I cannot live to hear the news from England;
  But I do prophesy th' election lights
  On Fortinbras: he has my dying voice;
  So tell him, with the occurrents, more or less,   330
  Which have solicited. The rest is silence.   [*Dies.*]
Hor. Now cracks a noble heart. Good night, sweet prince;
  And flights of angels sing thee to thy rest!
  Why does the drum come hither?

Enter Fortinbras and English Ambassador, with drums, colours, and attendants.

  Fort. Where is this sight?
  Hor.   What is it ye would see?   335
  If aught of woe or wonder, cease your search.

Fort. This quarry cries on havoc. O proud death,
What feast is toward in thine eternal cell,
That thou so many princes at a shot
So bloodily hast struck?

Amb.   The sight is dismal;   34·
And our affairs from England come too late:
The ears are senseless that should give us hearing,
To tell him his commandment is fulfill'd,
That Rosencrantz and Guildenstern are dead.
Where should we have our thanks?

Hor.   Not from his mouth,   34ξ
Had it the ability of life to thank you:
He never gave commandment for their death.
But since, so jump upon this bloody question,
You from the Polack wars, and you from England,
Are here arriv'd, give order that these bodies   350
High on a stage be placed to the view;
And let me speak to the yet unknowing world
How these things came about: so shall you hear
Of carnal, bloody, and unnatural acts,
Of accidental judgements, casual slaughters,   355
Of deaths put on by cunning and forc'd cause,
And, in this upshot, purposes mistook
Fall'n on the inventors' heads: all this can I
Truly deliver.

Fort.   Let us haste to hear it,
And call the noblest to the audience.   360
For me, with sorrow I embrace my fortune:
I have some rights of memory in this kingdom,
Which now to claim my vantage doth invite me.

Hor. Of that I shall have also cause to speak,
And from his mouth whose voice will draw no more: 365
But let this same be presently perform'd,
Even while men's minds are wild; lest more mischance,
On plots and errors, happen.

Fort.   Let four captains
Bear Hamlet, like a soldier, to the stage;
For he was likely, had he been put on,   37ᴄ
To have prov'd most royally: and, for his passage,
The soldiers' music and the rites of war
Speak loudly for him.
Take up the body: such a sight as this
Becomes the field, but here shows much amiss.   375
Go, bid the soldiers shoot.

                *[Exeunt, marching; after which a peal of ordnance
                              is shot off.]*

FINIS.

NOTES AND QUESTIONS ON "HAMLET"

IN GENERAL

1. Read the play rapidly to get the story as a whole.
2. The setting of the play:
   (a) The time:
   > Since in Act III, Sc. 1, lines 165–166 the king says, "He shall with speed to England for the demand of our neglected tribute," and there is further reference to Denmark's power over England in Act IV, Sc. 3, lines 58–65, it is inferred that the scene of the story is laid at a time just after the Danish Conquest of England in the ninth century. The time element is blurred, however, by the reference to sixteenth century dramatic conditions.
   (b) The place:
   > Elsinore, Denmark, and vicinity.
   (c) Background circumstances:
   > (1) When the play opens, Claudius is king of Denmark, having recently become such by secretly murdering his brother, King Hamlet, and two months later marrying his brother's widow, who was the legal heiress to the throne. According to the law at that time, a married woman conferred upon her husband all of her rights of ownership.

   > (2) Hamlet, the young prince, who had been at school in Wittenberg, was called home to Denmark by his father's death. At the beginning of the play he is in deep distress not only because of the loss of his father, but because of his mother's hasty marriage.

   > (3) In the opening scene of the play we find Denmark making preparations for war because of the threatened attack upon it by the young prince Fortinbras, who wanted to regain by force of arms the kingdom which his father, now dead, had gambled away to the king of Denmark.

3. The theme of the play is revenge as a moral, a sacred duty. (There was no law that could handle such a case as presented itself.)

4. The tragedy of the play comes because young Hamlet, upon whom the duty is laid, neglects to do, in time, what he has promised, and therefore becomes personally responsible for the deaths which result through his irresolution. His sin is not of commission, as in the case of Macbeth, but of omission. Hamlet's whole life, thus far, has made him peculiarly unfit for such a task. The terrible duty is too great for him to perform, and he dies as a result. Someone has likened Hamlet to a beautiful vase, intended for flowers, but in which an acorn is planted. When the plant expands, the vase is necessarily shattered.

5. The supernatural element.—In Shakespeare's time all the people were

superstitious. Whether Shakespeare believed in ghosts or not, we cannot say, but, since he wrote for an audience that did, he would seize the opportunity to make use of such things for dramatic material.

6. Note the *incitement*, the *climax*, the *concluding crisis*, the *retarding point*, and the *catastrophe* of this play.

7. "Hamlet" is called Shakespeare's masterpiece.

In Particular

Act I.—Scene I.[1]

(1) What is the setting of this scene?

(2) What is the general condition of affairs in Denmark at the opening of the play?

(3) What is the state of mind of the soldiers? What indications of nervousness?

(4) Why has Horatio come? What is his attitude at first toward the story which the soldiers tell him? Why?

(5) What is meant by line 42?

(6) What effect does the appearance of the ghost have on Horatio?

(7) What is his explanation for its coming? On what based?

(8) How does his opinion compare with those held by the soldiers?

(9) What is the reason for the preparation for war?

(10) What was indicated by the repeated visits of the ghost? Why was it silent?

(11) What was Horatio's plan for getting the ghost to speak?

(12) Sum up what has been accomplished by this scene. How, from it, are you sure the play will be a tragedy? What influence will pervade the play? Who is to be the leading character? What provision is made here for the final ending of the play?

Scene 2.

(1) What is the setting? What costumes would be appropriate? How is Hamlet dressed?

(2) What is the main dramatic purpose of this scene?

(3) What is the present occasion for the meeting of Claudius with his court?

(4) What are the chief characteristics of the king shown? Are any of them kingly qualities? Why is he especially careful to say what he does in lines 14–16? Is he a man of action? Prove.

(5) What is your first impression of Laertes? Polonius? The Queen?

(6) Why is Laertes in Denmark? What is his request of the king?

[1] Things especially to look for in the *first* scene of a Shakespearian play: (1) It always indicates the comic, or tragic, or serious trend of the play; (2) it always introduces the leading character (usually indirectly); it always strikes the keynote of the play, thus giving a hint as to what will influence the action throughout.

(7) What is your first impression of Hamlet? What is signified by the fact that his *first speech* is an *aside?* What did he mean by it? What is Hamlet's state of mind as shown by the five speeches he makes before he is left alone? What is the nature of each speech? What is his attitude toward the king? Why? Toward the queen? Why?

(8) What three requests does the queen make of Hamlet? Why in each case?

(9) Does he grant any or all of them?

(10) Why is the king anxious to have Hamlet remain in Denmark? Is his reason the same as the queen's?

(11) What is the importance of a soliloquy in a Shakespeare play?

(12) What information does this soliloquy of Hamlet give? What is Hamlet's wish?

(13) What is the force of Hamlet's comparison, "That was to this, Hyperion to a satyr"?

(14) What do you learn here regarding Hamlet's father? His mother?

(15) Explain "Like Niobe, all tears."

(16) What idea of Hamlet himself in lines "No more like my father than I to Hercules"?

(17) What is Hamlet's state of mind in the closing line of the soliloquy? Has he any thought of revenge?

(18) What difference in rank between Horatio, Marcellus, and Bernardo? How does Hamlet show this? Whom does he address in "Good even, sir"?

(19) What is the reason why Horatio is in Denmark?

(20) Explain lines 179–181. What is Hamlet's spirit here?

(21) Memorize Hamlet's tribute to his father, lines 187–188.

(22) Meaning of "cap-a-pie," line 200, and "beaver," line 230?

(23) What was the effect on Hamlet of Horatio's news? Why does he insist upon silence?

(24) What is Hamlet's interpretation of the coming of the ghost? Does it agree with Horatio's?

Scene 3.

(1) What is the setting of this scene? What new character is introduced?

(2) Explain lines 2–4.

(3) What is the nature of Laertes' advice to his sister?

(4) What is the effect on Ophelia? What is your impression of her?

(5) Is Polonius sincere in his advice to Laertes? Does he *feel* what he says? Do you think he has a deep, wise, thoughtful nature, or do his sentiments sound like something memorized?

(6) Point out passages that would show Polonius to be garrulous; inquisitive; conceited. What other characteristics can you find?

(7) Are Laertes and Ophelia like their father in any way? If so, how?

(8) Does Ophelia have a deep love for Hamlet? Prove.

(9) What purpose does this scene serve?

Scene 4.

(1) What is the time and place of this scene?

(2) What Danish custom "more honored in the breach than the observance" is being discussed at the beginning of this scene?

(3) Is Horatio used to court life? Where had Hamlet known him? What proof that he is a Dane?

(4) What does Hamlet mean by "questionable shape," line 43?

(5) What is the reason why Horatio and Marcellus try to prevent Hamlet's following the ghost?

(6) Account for Hamlet's attitude toward life (line 65)?

(7) What does Hamlet mean by "I'll make a ghost of him that lets me"?

Scene 5.

(1) How does this ghost compare with the ghost of Banquo in "Macbeth"? What is signified by the fact that others see this ghost before Hamlet does?

(2) What information does Hamlet get from the ghost?

(3) What had been the supposed cause of the death of his father?

(4) Where is the starting point of the action of the play? What name is given to this point?

(5) What is indicated by line 40?

(6) Had the queen been a party to the crime?

(7) What indicates that she was ignorant of the cause of her husband's death?

(8) Why does the ghost caution Hamlet not to harm the queen?

(9) What is indicated regarding Hamlet's character in line 107?

(10) Would writing down a resolution strengthen it?

(11) What does Hamlet do instead of drawing his sword?

(12) What is Hamlet's state of mind when Horatio and Marcellus find him?

(13) What effect does Horatio's saying, "These are wild and whirling words, my lord," have upon Hamlet?

(14) What oath does he want the men to take? Why?

(15) What is signified by swearing on the sword?

(16) What effect on Hamlet of hearing the ghost speak again from below?

(17) What made Hamlet think of putting on the "antic disposition"?

(18) What is his real purpose for assuming madness? Is it to conceal his plan for revenge, or to cover his uncontrollable excite-

ment which might betray to the king that he knows his secret?
What use does he later make of it?

(19) What is Hamlet's state of mind in lines 189–190? What is indicated as to his character here?

(20) Why does Marcellus drop out of the play here? Why was he introduced?

(21) With what important thing does Act I end? (Always notice that each act of a Shakespearian play ends with an important thing.)

Act II. Scene 1.

(1) What is the ostensible reason why Polonius sends Reynaldo to Paris? What is the real reason? What other characteristics does Polonius show here? Does Polonius himself practice the lofty sentiments that he gave his son in parting?

(2) What was the full plan of Polonius for spying on Laertes? Notice each step that Reynoldo is expected to take.

(3) What does Polonius mean by, "It is a fetch of warrant"?

(4) What purposes did Shakespeare have in creating Polonius?

(5) What humor do you find?

(6) What is Ophelia's state of mind when she enters?

(7) Explain Hamlet's treatment of Ophelia in this scene. (It is not "antic disposition.")

(8) Why has he been going about the court for some days in untidy dress?

(9) How had Ophelia been treating Hamlet recently? Why?

(10) What had been his real feeling toward her? What is his need now? What is the reason he does as he does here?

(11) What was the effect of his visit on Ophelia?

(12) What was the effect of her report upon Polonius?

(13) What was the only reason why Polonius had told Ophelia to repel Hamlet's advances?

(14) How does this scene affect your feeling for Hamlet? Is it to be wondered at that he should give the estimate, "Frailty, thy name is woman" (Act I, Sc. 2, line 146), when the only two women he had known well were the queen and Ophelia?

Scene 2.

(1) Who are Rosencrantz and Guildenstern? Why have they come? Can you distinguish between them? What is their general character?

(2) What is the king's theory as to Hamlet's madness? What is the queen's theory? What is that of Polonius?

(3) Why is reference so often made to Fortinbras? Notice that he was mentioned in the first scene of the play. Is he necessary to the

action? What is the dramatic reason for the request sent by old Norway?

(4) What characteristics, noted before, does Polonius show in this scene? Do you find any humorous passages? What are they?

(5) Why does Ophelia consent so readily to betray Hamlet's confidences? Are any excuses to be made for her?

(6) What explanation can you find for the peculiarities shown in the letter which Hamlet sends to Ophelia?

(7) What purpose did he have in sending it? Is there genuine affection shown? Is he trying to reach her soul?

(8) Why does he throw in the odd expressions? If she cannot understand the truth, does he want the letter to mystify any one who may read it?

(9) Is there any indication that Hamlet may have been afraid that he had misjudged Ophelia when he saw her in her room? Why does he give her another chance to understand him? What would her ability to understand mean to him?

(10) What effect does the letter have on Ophelia? On Polonius?

(11) Is the king as sure as Polonius that Hamlet is mad on account of love?

(12) What does the queen think about it?

(13) What plan does Polonius suggest to prove his point?

(14) Is the king interested in the experiment? Why?

(15) Have we seen any examples thus far of Hamlet's "antic disposition"?

(16) When does he always make use of it?

(17) What did Hamlet mean by calling Polonius a "fish-monger"? Was it the truth? How?

(18) How did Polonius regard this speech?

(19) Do Hamlet's speeches here sound like insanity? What "method in his madness" do you find?

(20) Why has the author withdrawn our sympathy so completely from Polonius? Why are we amused instead of shocked to hear the old man made fun of?

(21) Do we agree with Hamlet in calling Polonius a "tedious old fool"?

(22) Was Polonius able to "board" Hamlet as he had boasted in line 169? What did he accomplish?

(23) What change in Hamlet when he sees Rosencrantz and Guildenstern?

(24) What is his attitude toward them at first? Does he put on the "antic disposition" here?

(25) When does Hamlet first show suspicions regarding the two young men? Why?

(26) How do they manage the case?

(27) Why does Hamlet tell them why they were sent for?

(28) What news does he get from them?

(29) Why have the players come to Elsinore?

(30) Was Hamlet unwise in telling Rosencrantz and Guildenstern that he was "but mad north-north-west"? Did they understand him?

(31) Explain his treatment of Polonius when he comes to announce the actors. Is there still "method in his madness"?

(32) Why does he say what he does about Polonius' daughter? Does he know anything about Polonius' theory regarding his madness, or does he blame Polonius for coming between him and Ophelia?

(33) Explain lines 389–394.

(34) Why does Hamlet ask for a "taste of their quality"?

(35) What plan does Hamlet form? Why?

(36) What is Hamlet's mood after he is left alone at the end of Act II?

(37) What proof that he understands himself? Why has n't he carried out the command of the ghost? What excuse does he make?

(38) What is the important thing with which Act II ends?

(39) What has been accomplished in the play by Act II?

(40) What is vitally interesting the king? What two things does he do in his attempts to find out?

(41) What is vitally interesting Hamlet? What does he do in order to find out?

Act III.—Scene 1.

(1) What is the setting of this scene?

(2) Would the king and queen oppose the marriage of Hamlet and Ophelia if it is proved that she is the cause of his madness?

(3) Why is Ophelia willing to let herself be used as a trap for her lover?

(4) What is Hamlet's state of mind before he notices Ophelia in the attitude of prayer?

(5) What is the question he is trying to decide?

(6) What decision does he reach? Why?

(7) What is the first effect upon him of the sight of Ophelia here?

(8) What does he mean by lines 89–90?

(9) How does Ophelia bungle her part?

(10) What is the effect on Hamlet? Does he for the moment believe she is worse than she is?

(11) Explain Hamlet's treatment of Ophelia here. Is it "antic disposition," violent anger, or real insanity? Prove.

(12) What speech did Hamlet give for the benefit of Polonius? For the king's benefit?

(13) Is he sure they are listening?

(14) What is the effect of all this on Ophelia? Do you feel sorry for her?

(15) What is the effect upon the king? Does he believe longer in the theory of Polonius?

(16) Is Polonius convinced? What is his new plan?

Scene 2.

(1) What is the reason for Hamlet's careful directions to the players? Would this advice be good to follow to-day?

(2) How does Hamlet contrive to be left alone with Horatio before the beginning of the play? Why?

(3) What is Hamlet's attitude toward Horatio? Why is Horatio introduced in the play?

(4) What request does Hamlet make of Horatio?

(5) What does he mean by "I must be idle"?

(6) Plan out the setting of this scene.

(7) Why does Hamlet put on the "antic disposition" here?

(8) Why does he insist on sitting with Ophelia?

(9) What is the effect of this on Polonius?

(10) What is the result of Hamlet's experiment?

(11) Up to this point has Hamlet really been justified in not obeying the command of the ghost? Why?

(12) Has he now any reason for delay?

(13) What is his state of mind after the king and court have rushed from the room? Of what other occasion are you reminded here?

(14) Why does Hamlet call for music?

(15) How does Hamlet succeed in turning the tables on Rosencrantz and Guildenstern? Why does he insist on Guildenstern playing the recorder? How does he at last make himself understood? Could a madman do this?

(16) Explain the word "fret" in line 344.

(17) How does Hamlet further show energy in this scene?

(18) Why does n't he do the thing he promised when he feels "now could I drink hot blood"? What excuse does he make?

(19) Explain lines 363–366.

Scene 3.

(1) What contrast between the king and Hamlet as regards ability to act?

(2) What is the king's plan regarding Hamlet? What two reasons does he have for wanting to send him out of Denmark?

(3) What is the climax of the play? Just when does Hamlet lose control of the situation?

(4) Why does n't he kill the king when he has such a good chance?

(5) What results because he does not kill the king here?

Scene 4.

(1) Is the king any longer interested in Polonius' plan of testing Hamlet further? Why?

(2) What is Hamlet's true feeling in this scene with his mother? Does he put on the "antic disposition" here?

(3) What causes the death of Polonius? Why can Hamlet act promptly here?

(4) What is the importance of this point in the play? What is it called? What effect does it have on the development of the plot?

(5) Why is Hamlet so indifferent to what he has done?

(6) What is the reason why the ghost comes?

(7) What is the effect on Hamlet?

(8) Why is the ghost not visible to the queen? What proof that Shakespeare does not represent this as a vision of Hamlet's mind? How does the queen regard it?

(9) Why does the queen here make promises she later does not keep?

(10) What is the reason why Hamlet is affected by Polonius' death in the last of this scene when he was indifferent at the moment?

(11) Explain Hamlet's last speech in Act III. Has he any plans? What is meant by "two crafts" in line 210?

(12) With what important thing does Act III end?

Act IV.—Scene 1.

(1) What is the effect on the king of the news of Polonius' death?

(2) What action does he immediately take?

(3) What is the king's reason for "calling our wisest friends"?

Scene 2.

(1) Does Hamlet show insanity in this scene; is he putting on the "antic disposition" or is he simply mocking? Prove.

(2) Is there any meaning in his calling Rosencrantz a *sponge?*

(3) In saying "The body is with the king, but the king is not with the body"? Could any one explain the meaning of a *madman's* utterances?

Scene 3.

(1) What reason could Hamlet possibly have in hiding the body of Polonius?

(2) What threats does Hamlet give the king here?

(3) How does this scene show the king to be a man of action?

(4) What new plan has the king formed as shown in his soliloquy at end of scene? In his earlier plan for sending Hamlet to England had he intended his death? Why is he sure England will do as he says?

Scene 4.

(1) What is the dramatic purpose of mentioning Fortinbras again? What connection has this scene with the last scene where Fortinbras is mentioned?

(2) What contrasts can you make between Hamlet and Fortinbras?

(3) What is Hamlet's chief defect of character? Is he conscious of this defect? Prove.

(4) Of what other scene does this remind you?

(5) Has Hamlet mental energy? Does that in any way affect his physical energy? If so, how?

Scene 5.

(1) Plan out this scene for the stage.

(2) What is the new result of Hamlet's deed?

(3) What are the causes which have led to Ophelia's insanity? Is it her father's death alone?

(4) Why does the queen refuse at first to see Ophelia?

(5) Why does she later consent?

(6) Why did Shakespeare introduce these mad scenes of Ophelia?

(7) Does Hamlet's "antic disposition" bear any resemblance to them?

(8) Many people seriously argue that Shakespeare intended Hamlet to be really insane. What arguments on the subject might be based on this scene? Are they for, or against, such a theory?

(9) Why is Ophelia able to sing whole stanzas of songs and repeat old sayings? Is there any coherence in the way she makes use of these?

(10) What have you noticed about Hamlet's speeches in this respect?

(11) Enumerate the "sorrows" that the king says have come in battalions.

(12) What is indicated by the king's having Switzers instead of native Danes in his body guard?

(13) What is the reason for the shout of the Danish people?

(14) Are they disloyal to Hamlet?

(15) What characteristics of Laertes are shown here?

(16) What reason did he have for his attitude toward the king?

(17) Would most young courtiers do as Laertes does here under the same circumstances?

(18) What is the attitude of the king here? What does he accomplish because of it?

(19) Was the king really guiltless of Polonius' death, as he says?

(20) Account for the effect that Ophelia's madness has on Laertes. Had he been kept in ignorance of this?

(21) How does the king quiet Laertes?

Scene 6.

(1) What information is given in the letter which Horatio receives?

(2) Did the pirate ship come by accident or by appointment? Which seems likely considering what Hamlet said in the last speech of Act III? What light is thrown on this in Act V, Scene 2, lines 1–55?

(3) What is meant by "They knew what they did"?

Scene 7.

(1) What explanations did the king give Laertes?

(2) Are there indications that the king really loved the queen?

(3) Was it a wise thing, under the circumstances, for Hamlet to let the king know he had returned? Why did he do it?

(4) Is the king at any time guilty of irresolution? What plan does he set forth? How was it likely to succeed?

(5) What motive did the king have in telling Laertes to "keep close within your chamber"? Was it for the safety of Laertes or himself? How?

(6) Why does Shakespeare make us lose sympathy for Laertes?

(7) What part of the plot against Hamlet was Laertes' suggestion?

(8) What was the full plan?

(9) What is the dramatic effect of the news of Ophelia's death before the encounter between Hamlet and Laertes?

(10) Sum up, thus far, the results of Hamlet's irresolution.

(11) With what important thing does Act IV end?

Act V.—Scene 1.

(1) Why does Shakespeare give us the grave-digger scene?

(2) To what scene in "Macbeth" is this comparable?

(3) What characteristics of Hamlet are shown here?

(4) What do you learn regarding Hamlet's age? Does it seem consistent with the picture you had formed of him?

(5) In what manner does Hamlet first learn of Ophelia's death? What is the effect on him?

(6) Show that it is in keeping with Laertes' other acts for him to jump into Ophelia's grave.

(7) Why does Hamlet do so, too? Was this "antic disposition"?

(8) What does the king mean by the last two lines of Scene 1?

Scene 2.

(1) What is the story Hamlet tells Horatio? What explanation does this give to the coming of the pirate ship?

(2) If Hamlet had known that the ship was coming, would he have sent Rosencrantz and Guildenstern on to their death? If he had planned for it, would he have told Horatio so?

(3) Do Rosencrantz and Guildenstern deserve their death? Are they tragic characters or victims?

(4) Where did Hamlet place the responsibility for their death? For the death of Polonius?

(5) What does Hamlet imply in "The interim is mine"? Has he any definite plans?

(6) Why has Osric come? Whose place in the play does he seem to be taking?

(7) Why does Hamlet treat him as he does? Why use such big words?

(8) What is the importance to the play as a whole of Hamlet's saying, "How if I answer 'No'," to the invitation to fence with Laertes? What would have happened if he had said "No"? What name is given to this point in the play?

(9) Why does the second lord come so soon?

(10) What message does the queen send? Why?

(11) What feeling does Hamlet have here? Why doesn't he yield to it?

(12) Why does the king want Hamlet to shake hands with Laertes before they fence?

(13) What characteristic of Hamlet is shown here?

(14) Does Hamlet's saying he was insane make him so?

(15) Is he sincere in denying a "purposed evil" against Laertes?

(16) What feeling do you have for Laertes here? Why?

(17) Why does the king drink?

(18) What is the feeling of the king when the queen reaches for the poisoned cup? Why does he not prevent her from drinking the wine?

(19) Which character dies first? Why? Prove that the queen is a tragic character and not a victim. What is the degree of her guilt?

(20) When does Hamlet first understand the plot against him?

(21) When does Laertes first really understand the situation?

(22) Was Laertes a tragic character or a victim? Prove.

(23) What was his attitude toward Hamlet at the last? Why?

(24) What is the dramatic reason for the king's dying before Hamlet and Laertes?

(25) Why should Laertes die before Hamlet? How can you account for Hamlet's dying last when he was wounded even before the queen died? What is the dramatic reason for this? How has Shakespeare made it seem plausible?

(26) Prove that Hamlet is a tragic character.

(27) What did Horatio mean by, "I am more an antique Roman than a Dane"?

(28) How does Hamlet insure that Horatio will not take his own life?

(29) Why was Horatio introduced into the play?

(30) How does the arrival of Fortinbras seem plausible? What is Shakespeare's purpose in bringing him at this moment?

(31) What purpose does Fortinbras serve in the play?

(32) What is Hamlet's last message?

(33) What news came from England at the end of this scene?

(34) Why should Fortinbras have the last speech of the play?

(35) Are we satisfied with the ending? Was it inevitable?

(36) What indications that Fortinbras would make a stronger king than Hamlet?

(37) How differently would the play have ended if Laertes and Hamlet had not both been wounded before the queen said she was poisoned? Why did Shakespeare arrange it as he did?

Some General Questions:

(1) To what extent does humor enter into this play? How does it compare with "Macbeth" in that respect? What other comparisons can you make between it and "Macbeth"?

(2) Bring all the arguments you can find throughout the play to support the opinion that Shakespeare did not intend Hamlet to be insane at any time. What proof do you find that Horatio did not believe him to be mad? What proof that the king did not believe him mad?

(3) Notice familiar quotations. See how many you can find. No other play of Shakespeare, perhaps, has so many widely quoted passages.

(4) Show that this play embodies the characteristics of the older drama, pointed out earlier. Show that it is true to the laws of tragedy as Shakespeare handled it.

The Drama from Shakespeare to the Nineteenth Century.— Shakespeare so far outdistanced all of the other playwrights, that it is not surprising that the drama rapidly declined after his death. Ben Jonson was the greatest of his immediate successors, but Jonson's interest was in the classical instead of the romantic drama as handled by Shakespeare. Although he strove hard to keep the stage free from moral corruption, he was not great enough to prevent the drama from a downward course. The other playwrights of the time endeavored to please the polluted taste of a frivolous, corrupt court, and gave such sensational and immoral plays that, at

SHAKESPEARE'S GRAVE IN STRATFORD CHURCH CHANCEL

last, the theaters were closed by act of Parliament, twenty-six years after Shakespeare's death.

For nearly two hundred and seventy-five years there were no plays of any real worth produced in England with the exception of the prose comedies of Goldsmith and Sheridan, which were brought out during the years from 1768 to 1777. Goldsmith's "She Stoops to Conquer" (1773), founded on an actual experience of his own youth, is the best of these plays. It has retained its popularity up to the present time, and has never met with failure, it is said, although often performed by amateurs as well as by professionals. Goldsmith's other comedy, "The Good-Natured Man," was first acted in 1768. It has many good scenes, but the play, as a whole, has not had the success which attended "She Stoops to Conquer." Sheridan's "The Rivals" (1775) and "The School for Scandal" (1777) are still popular. These four eighteenth century comedies are rapid of action and the scenes are full of genuine humor.

For Optional Readings on the Earlier Drama:

> Any tragedy by Shakespeare.
> Any comedy by Shakespeare.
> Any dramatic history by Shakespeare.
> "She Stoops to Conquer," by Goldsmith.
> "The Good-Natured Man," by Goldsmith.
> "The Rivals," by Sheridan.
> "The School for Scandal," by Sheridan.

SUGGESTIONS TO STUDENTS

The following outline will aid you in writing your reports on any of these older plays:

(1) Give name of play and author.

(2) Give its classification.

(3) What is the chief conflict set forth? What is its effect on the reader?

(4) What is the setting of this play? (Time, place, attendant circumstances.)

(5) Who is the hero? The heroine? What do you think of them?

(6) Name two important incidents in which the hero figures. Does the heroine appear in either or both of these?

(7) Who are the chief complicating characters? (Those who cause the trouble.)

(8) Who are the chief resolving characters? (Those who clear away the difficulties.)

(9) How are the difficulties removed?

(10) What is the main plot? What characters are grouped around it?
(11) What sub-plots did you find?
(12) Where did you find examples of foreshadowing? Suspense? Surprise?
(13) Where is the incitement? The climax? The catastrophe?
(14) Did you find the play interesting?

The Mask [1] as a Dramatic Form.[2]—The mask is a form of dramatic poetry, but it is really more nearly related to the opera than the drama. It is also closely akin to the pageants of modern times. The main interest of a mask is usually in the splendid setting, elaborate costumes, music, dancing, and tableaux, rather than in the words. With the exception of Milton, the writers of masks did not attempt to give the words a true literary value. They were content to have the interest centered in the elaborate spectacle. For that reason the masks of Ben Jonson, the most famous writer of this type, have little hold upon us to-day when the pomp and scenic effects which attended them in the past no longer exist. Milton, on the contrary, gave us in "Comus" a dramatic poem that has a permanent place in literature, irrespective of its setting, because its appeal is not only to the ear and the eye but to the emotions and intellect as well.

As the name implies, the mask has disguise or hidden identity as its chief feature and the characters are allegorical. The supernatural also plays an important part. No attempt is made to present life as it really is. Unlike the regular plays, which were given with little scenery, at the public theaters, by professional players and were attended by all ranks and conditions of men, the masks were private, social entertainments. They were always presented by amateurs, usually of some noble house, and were given in honor of a great occasion such as a visit from royalty, an installation into a high office, a birthday, or a marriage. The expense attending the production of a mask made it impossible for them to be enjoyed by any but the wealthy. "The Triumph of Peace," a mask given in 1634, the same year as "Comus," cost £21,000. Since this expenditure was for but one performance, it can be seen why the mask was never a popular dramatic form.

Closely connected with Ben Jonson and Milton, who were the greatest writers of masks, were Henry Lawes, private musician to

[1] Also spelled *masque*.
[2] Since the mask and the dramatic monologue are usually in the poetic form, they will be treated here before the modern drama, which is chiefly in prose.

James I, who composed the musical numbers, and Inigo Jones, the famous architect, who prepared the scenery for the chief masks of the time. When these men died, the mask practically disappeared until its revival in the pageants and spectacles of the twentieth century. Of recent years these masks have attained a high degree of popularity in connection with the celebrations marking the historical events of various cities, especially in the United States. These modern masks differ from those of earlier times, for the most part, in being given as public, rather than as private, entertainments. They are still presented largely by amateurs, although this is not necessarily so. They are also put on with very much less expense than in the past.

COMUS

John Milton

THE PERSONS

The Attendant Spirit, afterwards in the habit of Thyrsis.
Comus, with his crew.
The Lady.
First Brother.
Second Brother.
Sabrina, the Nymph.

The chief persons who presented this mask were
The Lord Brackly.
Mr. Thomas Egerton, his brother.
The Lady Alice Egerton.

The First Scene Discovers a Wild Wood

The Attendant Spirit descends or enters.

Before the starry threshold of Jove's court
My mansion is, where those immortal shapes
Of bright aerial spirits live insphered
In regions mild of calm and serene air,
Above the smoke and stir of this dim spot,   5
Which men call Earth, and, with low-thoughted care,
Confined and pestered in this pinfold here,
Strive to keep up a frail and feverish being,
Unmindful of the crown that Virtue gives,
After this mortal change, to her true servants,   10
Amongst the enthronèd gods on sainted seats.

Yet some there be that by due steps aspire
To lay their just hands on that golden key
That opes the palace of eternity.
To such my errand is; and, but for such,   15
I would not soil these pure ambrosial weeds
With the rank vapours of this sin-worn mould.
  But to my task. Neptune, besides the sway
Of every salt flood, and each ebbing stream,
Took in by lot, 'twixt high and nether Jove,   20
Imperial rule of all the sea-girt isles,
That, like to rich and various gems, inlay
The unadornèd bosom of the deep;
Which he, to grace his tributary gods,
By course commits to several government,   25
And gives them leave to wear their sapphire crowns,
And wield their little tridents. But this Isle,
The greatest and the best of all the main,
He quarters to his blue-haired deities;
And all this tract that fronts the falling sun   30
A noble Peer of mickle trust and power
Has in his charge, with tempered awe to guide
An old and haughty nation, proud in arms:
Where his fair offspring, nursed in princely lore,
Are coming to attend their father's state,   35
And new-intrusted sceptre. But their way
Lies through the perplexed paths of this drear wood,
The nodding horror of whose shady brows
Threats the forlorn and wandering passenger;
And here their tender age might suffer peril,   40
But that, by quick command from Sovran Jove,
I was dispatched for their defence, and guard.
And listen why; for I will tell you now
What never yet was heard in tale or song,
From old or modern bard, in hall or bower.   .   45
Bacchus, that first from out the purple grape
Crushed the sweet poison of misusèd wine,
After the Tuscan mariners transformed
Coasting the Tyrrhene shore, as the winds listed,
On Circe's island fell. (Who knows not Circe,   50
The daughter of the Sun, whose charmèd cup
Whoever tasted, lost his upright shape,
And downward fell into a grovelling swine?)
This Nymph, that gazed upon his clustering locks,
With ivy berries wreathed, and his blithe youth,   55
Had by him, ere he parted thence, a son

Much like his father, but his mother more,
Whom therefore she brought up, and Comus named:
Who, ripe and frolic of his full-grown age,
Roving the Celtic and Iberian fields, 60
At last betakes him to this ominous wood,
And, in thick shelter of black shades imbowered,
Excels his mother at her mighty art;
Offering to every weary traveller
His orient liquor in a crystal glass, 65
To quench the drouth of Phœbus; which as they taste
(For most do taste through fond intemperate thirst),
Soon as the potion works, their human count'nance,
The express resemblance of the gods, is changed
Into some brutish form of wolf or bear, 70
Or ounce or tiger, hog or bearded goat,
All other parts remaining as they were.
And they, so perfect is their misery,
Not once perceive their foul disfigurement,
But boast themselves more comely than before, 75
And all their friends and native home forget,
To roll with pleasure in a sensual sty.
Therefore, when any favoured of high Jove
Chances to pass through this adventurous glade,
Swift as the sparkle of a glancing star 80
I shoot from heaven, to give him safe convoy,
As now I do. But first I must put off
These my sky robes, spun out of Iris' woof,
And take the weeds and likeness of a swain,
That to the service of this house belongs, 85
Who, with his soft pipe and smooth-dittied song,
Well knows to still the wild winds when they roar,
And hush the waving woods; nor of less faith,
And in this office of his mountain watch,
Likeliest, and nearest to the present aid 90
Of this occasion. But I hear the tread
Of hateful steps; I must be viewless now.

*Comus enters, with a charming-rod in one hand, his glass in the other;
with him a rout of monsters, headed like sundry sorts of wild beasts,
but otherwise like men and women, their apparel glistering; they
come in making a riotous and unruly noise, with torches in their
hands.*

Comus. The Star that bids the shepherd fold,
Now the top of heaven doth hold;
And the gilded car of day 95

His glowing axle doth allay
In the steep Atlantic stream;
And the slope sun his upward beam
Shoots against the dusky pole,
Pacing toward the other goal   100
Of his chamber in the east.
Meanwhile, welcome joy and feast,
Midnight shout and revelry,
Tipsy dance and jollity.
Braid your locks with rosy twine,   105
Dropping odours, dropping wine,
Rigor now is gone to bed,
And Advice with scrupulous head,
Strict Age, and sour Severity,
With their grave saws, in slumber lie.   110
We that are of purer fire
Imitate the starry quire,
Who, in their nightly watchful spheres,
Lead in swift round the months and years.
The sounds and seas, with all their finny drove,   115
Now to the moon in wavering morrice move;
And on the tawny sands and shelves
Trip the pert fairies and the dapper elves;
By dimpled brook and fountain-brim
The wood-nymphs, decked with daisies trim,   120
Their merry wakes and pastimes keep:
What hath night to do with sleep?
Night hath better sweets to prove;
Venus now wakes, and wakens Love.
Come, let us our rites begin;   125
'T is only daylight that makes sin,
Which these dun shades will ne'er report.
Hail, goddess of nocturnal sport,
Dark-veiled Cotytto, to whom the secret flame
Of midnight torches burns! mysterious dame,   130
That ne'er art called, but when the dragon womb
Of Stygian darkness spets her thickest gloom,
And makes one blot of all the air!
Stay thy cloudy ebon chair,
Wherein thou ridest with Hecat', and befriend   135
Us thy vowed priests, till utmost end
Of all thy dues be done, and none left out;
Ere the babbling eastern scout,
The nice morn on the Indian steep,
From her cabined loophole peep,   140

And to the tell-tale Sun descry
Our concealed solemnity.
Come, knit hands, and beat the ground,
In a light fantastic round.

THE MEASURE.

Break off, break off! I feel the different pace   145
Of some chaste footing near about this ground.
Run to your shrouds, within these brakes and trees;
Our number may affright. Some virgin sure
(For so I can distinguish by mine art)
Benighted in these woods! Now to my charms,   150
And to my wily trains; I shall ere long
Be well stocked with as fair a herd as grazed
About my mother Circe. Thus I hurl
My dazzling spells into the spongy air,
Of power to cheat the eye with blear illusion,   155
And give it false presentments, lest the place
And my quaint habits breed astonishment,
And put the damsel to suspicious flight;
Which must not be, for that 's against my course.
I, under fair pretence of friendly ends,   160
And well-placed words of glozing courtesy,
Baited with reasons not unplausible,
Wind me into the easy-hearted man,
And hug him into snares. When once her eye
Hath met the virtue of this magic dust,   165
I shall appear some harmless villager,
Whom thrift keeps up about his country gear.
But here she comes; I fairly step aside
And hearken, if I may her business hear.

The Lady enters.

Lady.   This way the noise was, if mine ear be true,   170
My best guide now; methought it was the sound
Of riot and ill-managed merriment,
Such as the jocund flute or gamesome pipe
Stirs up among the loose unlettered hinds,
When, for their teeming flocks and granges full,   175
In wanton dance they praise the bounteous Pan,
And thank the gods amiss. I should be loath
To meet the rudeness and swilled insolence
Of such late wassailers; yet, oh! where else
Shall I inform my unacquainted feet   180
In the blind mazes of this tangled wood?

My brothers, when they saw me wearied out
With this long way, resolving here to lodge
Under the spreading favour of these pines,
Stepped, as they said, to the next thicket-side 185
To bring me berries, or such cooling fruit
As the kind hospitable woods provide.
They left me then, when the gray-hooded Even,
Like a sad votarist in palmer's weed,
Rose from the hindmost wheels of Phœbus' wain. 190
But where they are, and why they came not back,
Is now the labour of my thoughts. 'T is likeliest
They had ingaged their wandering steps too far;
And envious darkness, ere they could return,
Had stole them from me: else, O thievish Night, 195
Why shouldst thou, but for some felonious end,
In thy dark lantern thus close up the stars
That Nature hung in heaven, and filled their lamps
With everlasting oil, to give due light
To the misled and lonely traveller? 200
This is the place, as well as I may guess,
Whence even now the tumult of loud mirth
Was rife, and perfect in my listening ear;
Yet nought but single darkness do I find.
What might this be? A thousand fantasies 205
Begin to throng into my memory,
Of calling shapes, and beckoning shadows dire,
And airy tongues, that syllable men's names
On sands, and shores, and desert wildernesses.
These thoughts may startle well, but not astound 210
The virtuous mind, that ever walks attended
By a strong-siding champion, Conscience.
Oh, welcome, pure-eyed Faith, white-handed Hope,
Thou hovering angel, girt with golden wings,
And thou, unblemished form of Chastity! 215
I see ye visibly, and now believe
That He, the Supreme Good, to whom all things ill
Are but as slavish officers of vengeance,
Would send a glistering guardian, if need were,
To keep my life and honour unassailed. 220
Was I deceived, or did a sable cloud
Turn forth her silver lining on the night?
I did not err: there does a sable cloud
Turn forth her silver lining on the night,
And casts a gleam over this tufted grove 225
I can not hallo to my brothers, but

Such noise as I can make to be heard farthest
I'll venture; for my new-enlivened spirits
Prompt me, and they perhaps are not far off.

Song.

Sweet Echo, sweetest nymph, that liv'st unseen   230
    Within thy airy shell
By slow Meander's margent green,
And in the violet-embroidered vale
    Where the lovelorn nightingale
Nightly to thee her sad song mourneth well: 235
Canst thou not tell me of a gentle pair
    That likest thy Narcissus are?
    Oh, if thou have
Hid them in some flowery cave,
    Tell me but where,   240
Sweet Queen of Parley, Daughter of the Sphere!
So may'st thou be translated to the skies,
And give resounding grace to all heaven's harmonies.

Enter Comus.

Comus. Can any mortal mixture of earth's mould
Breathe such divine enchanting ravishment?   245
Sure something holy lodges in that breast,
And with these raptures moves the vocal air
To testify his hidden residence.
How sweetly did they float upon the wings
Of silence, through the empty-vaulted night,   250
At every fall smoothing the Raven down
Of darkness till it smiled! I have oft heard
My mother Circe with the Sirens three,
Amidst the flowery-kirtled Naiades,
Culling their potent herbs, and baleful drugs,   255
Who, as they sung, would take the prisoned soul,
And lap it in Elysium: Scylla wept,
And chid her barking waves into attention,
And fell Charybdis murmured soft applause.
Yet they in pleasing slumber lulled the sense,   260
And in sweet madness robbed it of itself;
But such a sacred and home-felt delight,
Such sober certainty of waking bliss
I never heard till now. I'll speak to her,
And she shall be my queen.—Hail, foreign wonder!   265
Whom certain these rough shades did never breed,
Unless the goddess that in rural shrine

Dwellest here with Pan or Sylvan, by blest song
Forbidding every bleak unkindly fog
To touch the prosperous growth of this tall wood.   270
Lady. Nay, gentle shepherd, ill is lost that praise
That is addressed to unattending ears.
Not any boast of skill, but extreme shift
How to regain my severed company,
Compelled me to awake the courteous Echo   275
To give me answer from her mossy couch.
Comus. What chance, good lady, hath bereft you thus?
Lady. Dim darkness, and this leavy labyrinth.
Comus. Could that divide you from near-ushering guides?
Lady. They left me weary on a grassy turf.   280
Comus. By falsehood, or discourtesy, or why?
Lady. To seek i' th' valley some cool friendly spring.
Comus. And left your fair side all unguarded, Lady?
Lady. They were but twain, and purposed quick return.
Comus. Perhaps forestalling night prevented them.   285
Lady. How easy my misfortune is to hit!
Comus. Imports their loss, beside the present need?
Lady. No less than if I should my brothers lose.
Comus. Were they of manly prime, or youthful bloom?
Lady. As smooth as Hebe's their unrazored lips.   290
Comus. Two such I saw, what time the laboured ox
In his loose traces from the furrow came,
And the swinked hedger at his supper sat.
I saw them under a green mantling vine,
That crawls along the side of yon small hill,   295
Plucking ripe clusters from the tender shoots:
Their port was more than human, as they stood.
I took it for a faery vision
Of some gay creatures of the element,
That in the colours of the rainbow live,   300
And play i' the plighted clouds. I was awe-strook,
And, as I passed, I worshiped. If those you seek,
It were a journey like the path to Heaven
To help you find them.
Lady.   Gentle villager,
What readiest way would bring me to that place?   305
Comus. Due west it rises from this shrubby point.
Lady. To find that out, good shepherd, I suppose,
In such a scant allowance of star-light,
Would overtask the best land-pilot's art,
Without the sure guess of well-practised feet.   310
Comus. I know each lane, and every alley green,

Dingle, or bushy dell, of this wild wood,
And every bosky bourn from side to side,
My daily walks and ancient neighbourhood;
And if your stray attendants be yet lodged,   315
Or shroud within these limits, I shall know
Ere morrow wake, or the low-roosted lark
From her thatched pallet rouse: if otherwise,
I can conduct you, Lady, to a low
But loyal cottage, where you may be safe   320
Till further quest.

Lady.   Shepherd, I take thy word,
And trust thy honest-offered courtesy,
Which oft is sooner found in lowly sheds.
With smoky rafters, than in tapestry halls
And courts of princes, where it first was named,   325
And yet is most pretended. In a place
Less warranted than this, or less secure,
I cannot be, that I should fear to change it.
Eye me, blest Providence, and square my trial
To my proportioned strength! Shepherd, lead on.   330

Enter the Two Brothers.

Elder Brother. Unmuffle, ye faint stars, and thou, fair moon,
That wont'st to love the traveller's benison,
Stoop thy pale visage through an amber cloud,
And disinherit Chaos, that reigns here
In double night of darkness and of shades;   335
Or if your influence be quite dammed up
With black usurping mists, some gentle taper,
Though a rush-candle from the wicker hole
Of some clay habitation, visit us
With thy long levelled rule of streaming light;   340
And thou shalt be our Star of Arcady,
Or Tyrian Cynosure.

Second Brother.   Or, if our eyes
Be barred that happiness, might we but hear
The folded flocks, penned in their wattled cotes,
Or sound of pastoral reed with oaten stops,   345
Or whistle from the lodge, or village cock
Count the night watches to his feathery dames,
'T would be some solace yet, some little cheering
In this close dungeon of innumerous boughs.
But, oh, that hapless virgin, our lost sister!   350
Where may she wander now, whether betake her
From the chill dew, amongst rude burs and thistles?

Perhaps some cold bank is her bolster now,
Or 'gainst the rugged bark of some broad elm
Leans her unpillowed head, fraught with sad fears. 355
What if in wild amazement and affright,
Or while we speak within the direful grasp
Of savage hunger, or of savage heat!
Elder Brother. Peace, brother; be not over-exquisite
To cast the fashion of uncertain evils; 360
For, grant they be so, while they rest unknown,
What need a man forestall his date of grief,
And run to meet what he would most avoid?
Or, if they be but false alarms of fear,
How bitter is such self-delusion! 365
I do not think my sister so to seek,
Or so unprincipled in virtue's book,
And the sweet peace that goodness bosoms ever,
As that the single want of light and noise
(Not being in danger, as I trust she is not) 370
Could stir the constant mood of her calm thoughts,
And put them into misbecoming plight.
Virtue could see to do what Virtue would
By her own radiant light, though sun and moon
Were in the flat sea sunk. And Wisdom's self 375
Oft seeks to sweet retired solitude,
Where, with her best nurse, Contemplation,
She plumes her feathers, and lets grow her wings,
That, in the various bustle of resort,
Were all to-ruffled, and sometimes impaired. 380
He that has light within his own clear breast,
May sit i' the center, and enjoy bright day;
But he that hides a dark soul and foul thoughts,
Benighted walks under the midday sun;
Himself is his own dungeon.
Second Brother. 'T is most true 385
That musing meditation most affects
The pensive secrecy of desert cell,
Far from the cheerful haunt of men and herds,
And sits as safe as in a senate-house;
For who would rob a hermit of his weeds, 390
His few books, or his beads, or maple dish,
Or do his gray hairs any violence?
But beauty, like the fair Hesperian tree
Laden with blooming gold, had need the guard
Of dragon-watch with unenchanted eye 395
To save her blossoms, and defend her fruit

From the rash hand of bold Incontinence.
You may as well spread out the unsunned heaps
Of miser's treasure by an outlaw's den,
And tell me it is safe, as bid me hope   400
Danger will wink on opportunity,
And let a single helpless maiden pass
Uninjured in this wild surrounding waste.
Of night, or loneliness, it recks me not;
I fear the dread events that dog them both,   405
Lest some ill-greeting touch attempt the person
Of our unownèd sister.
Elder Brother.   I do not, brother,
Infer, as if I thought my sister's state
Secure without all doubt or controversy;
Yet where an equal poise of hope and fear   410
Does arbitrate the event, my nature is
That I incline to hope, rather than fear,
And gladly banish squint suspicion.
My sister is not so defenceless left
As you imagine; she has a hidden strength   415
Which you remember not.
Second Brother.   What hidden strength,
Unless the strength of Heaven, if you mean that?
Elder Brother. I mean that too, but yet a hidden strength,
Which, if Heaven gave it, may be termed her own.
'T is chastity, my brother, chastity: 420
She that has that, is clad in complete steel,
And, like a quivered nymph with arrows keen,
May trace huge forests, and unharboured heaths,
Infamous hills, and sandy perilous wilds;
Where, through the sacred rays of chastity,   425
No savage fierce, bandite, or mountaineer,
Will dare to soil her virgin purity.
Yea, there where very desolation dwells,
By grots and caverns shagged with horrid shades,
She may pass on with unblenched majesty,   430
Be it not done in pride, or in presumption.
Some say no evil thing that walks by night,
In fog, or fire, by lake or moorish fen,
Blue meager hag, or stubborn unlaid ghost,
That breaks his magic chains at curfew time,   435
No goblin, or swart faery of the mine,
Hath hurtful power o'er true virginity.
Do ye believe me yet, or shall I call
Antiquity from the old schools of Greece

To testify the arms of chastity? 440
Hence had the huntress Dian her dread bow,
Fair silver-shafted queen for ever chaste,
Wherewith she tamed the brinded lioness
And spotted mountain-pard, but set at nought
The frivolous bolt of Cupid; gods and men 445
Feared her stern frown, and she was queen o' the woods.
What was that snaky-headed Gorgon shield
That wise Minerva wore, unconquered virgin,
Wherewith she freezed her foes to congealed stone,
But rigid looks of chaste austerity, 450
And noble grace that dashed brute violence
With sudden adoration and blank awe?
So dear to Heaven is saintly chastity
That, when a soul is found sincerely so,
A thousand liveried angels lackey her, 455
Driving far off each thing of sin and guilt,
And in clear dream and solemn vision,
Tell her of things that no gross ear can hear;
Till oft converse with heavenly habitants
Begins to cast a beam on the outward shape, 460
The unpolluted temple of the mind,
And turns it by degrees to the soul's essence,
Till all be made immortal. But, when lust,
By unchaste looks, loose gestures, and foul talk,
But most by lewd and lavish act of sin, 465
Lets in defilement to the inward parts,
The soul grows clotted by contagion,
Imbodies, and imbrutes, till she quite lose
The divine property of her first being.
Such are those thick and gloomy shadows damp 470
Oft seen in charnel vaults, and sepulchres,
Lingering and sitting by a new-made grave,
As loth to leave the body that it loved,
And linked itself by carnal sensuality
To a degenerate and degraded state. 475
Second Brother. How charming is divine philosophy!
Not harsh and crabbed, as dull fools suppose,
But musical as is Apollo's lute,
And a perpetual feast of nectared sweets,
Where no crude surfeit reigns.
Elder Brother. List! list! I hear 480
Some far-off hallo break the silent air.
Second Brother. Methought so too; what should it be?
Elder Brother. For certain,

Either some one, like us night-foundered here,
Or else some neighbour woodman, or, at worst,
Some roving robber calling to his fellows.　　　　485
Second Brother. Heaven keep my sister! Again, again, and near!
Best draw, and stand upon our guard.
Elder Brother.　　　　　　　　　　I 'll hallo.
If he be friendly, he come well; if not,
Defence is a good cause, and Heaven be for us!

Enter the Attendant Spirit, habited like a shepherd.

That hallo I should know. What are you? Speak.　　　490
Come not too near; you fall on iron stakes else.
Spirit. What voice is that, my young Lord? speak aga
Second Brother. O brother, 't is my father's shepherd, sure.
Elder Brother. Thyrsis? Whose artful strains have oft delayed
The huddling brook to hear his madrigal,　　　495
And sweetened every musk-rose of the dale.
How camest thou here, good swain? hath any ram
Slipped from the fold, or young kid lost his dam,
Or straggling wether the pent flock forsook?
How couldst thou find this dark sequestered nook?　　　500
Spirit. O my loved master's heir, and his next joy,
I came not here on such a trivial toy
As a strayed ewe, or to pursue the stealth
Of pilfering wolf; not all the fleecy wealth
That doth enrich these downs is worth a thought　　　505
To this my errand, and the care it brought.
But, oh! my virgin Lady, where is she?
How chance she is not in your company?
Elder Brother. To tell thee sadly, Shepherd, without blame
Or our neglect, we lost her as we came.　　　510
Spirit. Ay me unhappy! then my fears are true.
Elder Brother. What fears, good Thyrsis? Prithee briefly shew.
Spirit. I 'll tell ye. 'T is not vain or fabulous
(Though so esteemed by shallow ignorance),
What the sage poets, taught by the heavenly Muse,　　　515
Storied of old in high immortal verse
Of dire Chimeras and enchanted isles,
And rifted rocks whose entrance leads to Hell;
For such there be, but unbelief is blind.
Within the navel of this hideous wood,　　　520
Immured in cypress shades, a sorcerer dwells,
Of Bacchus and of Circe born, great Comus,
Deep skilled in all his mother's witcheries;
And here to every thirsty wanderer

By sly enticement gives his baneful cup,   525
With many murmurs mixed, whose pleasing poison
The visage quite transforms of him that drinks,
And the inglorious likeness of a beast
Fixes instead, unmoulding reason's mintage
Charactered in the face. This I have learnt   530
Tending my flocks hard by i' the hilly crofts
That brow this bottom glade; whence night by night
He and his monstrous rout are heard to howl
Like stabled wolves, or tigers at their prey,
Doing abhorrèd rites to Hecate   535
In their obscurèd haunts of inmost bowers.
Yet have they many baits and guileful spells
To inveigle and invite the unwary sense
Of them that pass unweeting by the way.
This evening late, by then the chewing flocks   540
Had ta'en their supper on the savoury herb
Of knot-grass dew-besprent, and were in fold,
I sate me down to watch upon a bank
With ivy canopied, and interwove
With flaunting honeysuckle, and began,   545
Wrapt in a pleasing fit of melancholy,
To meditate my rural minstrelsy,
Till fancy had her fill; but ere a close,
The wonted roar was up amidst the woods,
And filled the air with barbarous dissonance;   550
At which I ceased, and listened them a while,
Till an unusual stop of sudden silence
Gave respite to the drowsy-flighted steeds
That draw the litter of close-curtained Sleep.
At last a soft and solemn-breathing sound   555
Rose like a steam of rich distilled perfumes,
And stole upon the air, that even Silence
Was took ere she was ware, and wished she might
Deny her nature, and be never more,
Still to be so displaced. I was all ear,   560
And took in strains that might create a soul
Under the ribs of death. But, oh! ere long
Too well did I perceive it was the voice
Of my most honoured Lady, your dear sister.
Amazed I stood, harrowed with grief and fear;   565
And "O poor hapless nightingale," thought I,
"How sweet thou sing'st, how near the deadly snare!"
Then down the lawns I ran with headlong haste,
Through paths and turnings often trod by day,

Till, guided by mine ear, I found the place 570
Where that damned wizard, hid in sly disguise
(For so by certain signs I knew), had met
Already, ere my best speed could prevent,
The aidless innocent Lady, his wished prey;
Who gently asked if he had seen such two, 575
Supposing him some neighbour villager.
Longer I durst not stay, but soon I guessed
Ye were the two she meant; with that I sprung
Into swift flight, till I had found you here;
But further know I not.

Second Brother.   O night and shades, 580
How are ye joined with Hell in triple knot,
Against the unarmed weakness of one virgin,
Alone and helpless! Is this the confidence
You gave me, brother?

Elder Brother.   Yes, and keep it still;
Lean on it safely; not a period 585
Shall be unsaid for me. Against the threats
Of malice or of sorcery, or that power
Which erring men call Chance, this I hold firm:
Virtue may be assailed, but never hurt,
Surprised by unjust force, but not enthralled; 590
Yea, even that which mischief meant most harm,
Shall, in the happy trial, prove most glory.
But evil on itself shall back recoil,
And mix no more with goodness, when at last,
Gathered like scum, and settled to itself, 595
It shall be in eternal restless change
Self-fed and self-consumed. If this fail,
The pillared firmament is rottenness,
And earth's base built on stubble. But come, let's on!
Against the opposing will and arm of Heaven 600
May never this just sword he lifted up;
But for that damned magician, let him be girt
With all the grisly legions that troop
Under the sooty flag of Acheron,
Harpies and Hydras, or all the monstrous forms 605
'Twixt Africa and Ind, I'll find him out,
And force him to return his purchase back,
Or drag him by the curls to a foul death,
Cursed as his life.

Spirit.   Alas! good venturous youth,
I love thy courage yet, and bold emprise; 610
But here thy sword can do thee little stead.

Far other arms and other weapons must
Be those that quell the might of hellish charms;
He with his bare wand can unthread thy joints,
And crumble all thy sinews.
Elder Brother.   Why, prithee, Shepherd,   615
How durst thou then thyself approach so near
As to make this relation?
Spirit.   Care and utmost shifts
How to secure the Lady from surprisal,
Brought to my mind a certain shepherd lad,
Of small regard to see to, yet well skilled   620
In every virtuous plant and healing herb
That spreads her verdant leaf to the morning ray.
He loved me well, and oft would beg me sing;
Which, when I did, he on the tender grass
Would sit, and hearken even to ecstasy,   625
And in requital ope his leathern scrip,
And shew me simples of a thousand names,
Telling their strange and vigorous faculties.
Amongst the rest a small unsightly root,
But of divine effect, he culled me out: 630
The leaf was darkish, and had prickles on it,
But in another country, as he said,
Bore a bright golden flower, but not in this soil:
Unknown, and like esteemed, and the dull swain
Treads on it daily with his clouted shoon;   635
And yet more med'cinal is it than that Moly
That Hermes once to wise Ulysses gave.
He called it Hæmony, and gave it me,
And bade me keep it as of sovran use
'Gainst all enchantments, mildew blast, or damp,   640
Or ghastly Furies' apparition.
I pursed it up, but little reckoning made,
Till now that this extremity compelled.
But now I find it true; for by this means
I knew the foul enchanter, though disguised,   645
Entered the very lime-twigs of his spells,
And yet came off. If you have this about you
(As I will give you when we go), you may
Boldly assault the necromancer's hall;
Where if he be, with dauntless hardihood,   650
And brandished blade rush on him, break his glass,
And shed the luscious liquor on the ground;
But seize his wand. Though he and his curst crew
Fierce sign of battle make, and menace high,

Or, like the sons of Vulcan, vomit smoke,   655
Yet will they soon retire, if he but shrink.
Elder Brother.   Thyrsis, lead on apace; I'll follow thee;
And some good angel bear a shield before us!

*The Scene changes to a stately palace, set out with all manner of delicious-
ness; soft music, tables spread with all dainties. Comus appears with
his rabble, and the Lady set in an enchanted chair, to whom he offers
his glass, which she puts by, and goes about to rise.*

Comus.   Nay, Lady, sit; if I but wave this wand,
Your nerves are all chained up in alabaster,   660
And you a statue; or as Daphne was,
Root-bound, that fled Apollo.
Lady.   Fool, do not boast;
Thou canst not touch the freedom of my mind
With all thy charms, although this corporal rind
Thou hast immanacled, while Heaven sees good.   665
Comus.   Why are you vexed, Lady? why do you frown?
Here dwell no frowns, nor anger; from these gates
Sorrow flies far. See, here be all the pleasures
That fancy can beget on youthful thoughts,
When the fresh blood grows lively, and returns   670
Brisk as the April buds in primrose season.
And first behold this cordial julep here,
That flames and dances in his crystal bounds,
With spirits of balm and fragrant syrups mixed.
Not that Nepenthes, which the wife of Thone   675
In Egypt gave to Jove-born Helena
Is of such power to stir up joy as this,
To life so friendly, or so cool to thirst.
Why should you be so cruel to yourself,
And to those dainty limbs, which Nature lent   680
For gentle usage and soft delicacy?
But you invert the covenants of her trust,
And harshly deal, like an ill borrower,
With that which you received on other terms;
Scorning the unexempt condition   685
By which all mortal frailty must subsist,
Refreshment after toil, ease after pain,
That have been tired all day without repast,
And timely rest have wanted. But, fair Virgin,
This will restore all soon.
Lady.   'T will not, false traitor!   690
'T will not restore the truth and honesty
That thou hast banished from thy tongue with lies.

Was this the cottage and the safe abode
Thou told'st me of? What grim aspects are these,
These ugly-headed Monsters? Mercy guard me!   695
Hence with thy brewed enchantments, foul deceiver!
Hast thou betrayed my credulous innocence
With vizored falsehood and base forgery?
And would'st thou seek again to trap me here
With liquorish baits, fit to ensnare a brute?   700
Were it a draught for Juno when she banquets,
I would not taste thy treasonous offer. None
But such as are good men can give good things;
And that which is not good, is not delicious
To a well-governed and wise appetite.   705
Comus. O foolishness of men! that lend their ears
To those budge doctors of the Stoic fur,
And fetch their precepts from the Cynic tub,
Praising the lean and sallow Abstinence!
Wherefore did Nature pour her bounties forth   710
With such a full and unwithdrawing hand,
Covering the earth with odours, fruits, and flocks,
Thronging the seas with spawn innumerable,
But all to please and sate the curious taste?
And set to work millions of spinning worms,   715
That in their green shops weave the smooth-haired silk
To deck her sons; and, that no corner might
Be vacant of her plenty, in her own loins
She hutched the all-worshipped ore and precious gems,
To store her children with. If all the world   720
Should, in a pet of temperance, feed on pulse,
Drink the clear stream, and nothing wear but frieze,
The All-giver would be unthanked, would be unpraised,
Not half his riches known, and yet despised;
And we should serve him as a grudging master,   725
As a penurious niggard of his wealth;
And live like Nature's bastards, not her sons,
Who would be quite surcharged with her own weight,
And strangled with her waste fertility:
The earth cumbered, and the winged air darked with plumes,   730
The herds would over-multitude their lords;
The sea o'erfraught would swell, and the unsought ·diamonds
Would so emblaze the forehead of the deep,
And so bestud with stars, that they below
Would grow inured to light, and come at last   735
To gaze upon the sun with shameless brows.
List, Lady; be not coy, and be not cozened

With that same vaunted name, Virginity.
Beauty is Nature's coin; must not be hoarded,
But must be current; and the good thereof   740
Consists in mutual and partaken bliss,
Unsavoury in the enjoyment of itself.
If you let slip time, like a neglected rose
It withers on the stalk with languished head.
Beauty is Nature's brag, and must be shown   745
In courts, at feasts, and high solemnities,
Where most may wonder at the workmanship.
It is for homely features to keep home;
They had their name thence: coarse complexions
And cheeks of sorry grain will serve to ply   750
The sampler, and to tease the huswife's wool.
What need a vermeil-tinctured lip for that,
Love-darting eyes, or tresses like the morn?
There was another meaning in these gifts;
Think what, and be advised; you are but young yet.   755
Lady. I had not thought to have unlocked my lips
In this unhallowed air, but that this juggler
Would think to charm my judgment, as mine eyes,
Obtruding false rules pranced in reason's garb.
I hate when vice can bolt her arguments,   760
And virtue has no tongue to check her pride.
Impostor! do not charge most innocent Nature,
As if she would her children should be riotous
With her abundance: she, good cateress,
Means her provision only to the good,   765
That live according to her sober laws,
And holy dictate of spare temperance.
If every just man that now pines with want
Had but a moderate and beseeming share
Of that which lewdly-pampered luxury   770
Now heaps upon some few with vast excess,
Nature's full blessings would be well dispensed
In unsuperfluous even proportion,
And she no whit encumbered with her store;
And then the Giver would be better thanked,   775
His praise due paid; for swinish gluttony
Ne'er looks to Heaven amidst his gorgeous feast,
But with besotted base ingratitude
Crams, and blasphemes his Feeder. Shall I go on?
Or have I said enough? To him that dares   780
Arm his profane tongue with contemptuous words
Against the sun-clad power of Chastity,

Fain would I something say,—yet to what end?
Thou hast not ear, nor soul, to apprehend
The sublime notion and high mystery,   785
That must be uttered to unfold the sage
And serious doctrine of Virginity.
And thou art worthy that thou shouldst not know
More happiness than this thy present lot.
Enjoy your dear wit, and gay rhetoric,   790
That hath so well been taught her dazzling fence;
Thou art not fit to hear thyself convinced.
Yet, should I try, the uncontrollèd worth
Of this pure cause would kindle my rapt spirits
To such a flame of sacred vehemence,   795
That dumb things would be moved to sympathize,
And the brute earth would lend her nerves, and shake,
Till all thy magic structures, reared so high,
Were shattered into heaps o'er thy false head.
Comus. She fables not; I feel that I do fear   800
Her words set off by some superior power;
And, though not mortal, yet a cold shuddering dew
Dips me all o'er, as when the wrath of Jove
Speaks thunder, and the chains of Erebus
To some of Saturn's crew. I must dissemble,   805
And try her yet more strongly. Come, no more!
This is mere moral babble, and direct
Against the canon laws of our foundation;
I must not suffer this, yet 't is but the lees
And settlings of a melancholy blood.   810
But this will cure all straight; one sip of this
Will bathe the drooping spirits in delight,
Beyond the bliss of dreams. Be wise, and taste.

*The Brothers rush in with swords drawn, wrest his glass out of his hand
and break it against the ground; his rout make sign of resistance,
but are all driven in. The Attendant Spirit comes in.*

Spirit. What! have you let the false enchanter 'scape?
O ye mistook; ye should have snatched his wand,   815
And bound him fast: without his rod reversed,
And backward mutters of dissevering power,
We cannot free the Lady that sits here,
In stony fetters fixed and motionless.
Yet stay, be not disturbed; now I bethink me,   820
Some other means I have which may be used,
Which once of Melibœus old I learnt,
The soothest shepherd that e'er piped on plains.

There is a gentle nymph not far from hence,
That with moist curb sways the smooth Severn stream; 825
Sabrina is her name, a Virgin pure;
Whilom she was the daughter of Locrine,
That had the sceptre from his father Brute.
She, guiltless damsel, flying the mad pursuit
Of her enragèd stepdame, Guendolen, 830
Commended her fair innocence to the flood,
That stayed her flight with his cross-flowing course.
The water nymphs that in the bottom played,
Held up their pearlèd wrists, and took her in,
Bearing her straight to aged Nereus' hall; 835
Who, piteous of her woes, reared her lank head,
And gave her to his daughters to imbathe
In nectared lavers strewed with asphodel,
And through the porch and inlet of each sense
Dropt in ambrosial oils, till she revived, 840
And underwent a quick immortal change,
Made Goddess of the river. Still she retains
Her maiden gentleness, and oft at eve
Visits the herds along the twilight meadows,
Helping all urchin blasts, and ill-luck signs 845
That the shrewd meddling Elf delights to make,
Which she with precious vialed liquors heals;
For which the shepherds at their festivals
Carol her goodness loud in rustic lays,
And throw sweet garland wreaths into her stream 850
Of pansies, pinks, and gaudy daffodils.
And, as the old swain said, she can unlock
The clasping charm, and thaw the numbing spell,
If she be right invoked in warbled song;
For maidenhood she loves, and will be swift 855
To aid a virgin, such as was her self,
In hard-besetting need. This will I try,
And add the power of some adjuring verse.

Song.

Sabrina fair,
    Listen where thou art sitting 860
Under the glassy, cool, translucent wave,
    In twisted braids of lilies knitting
The loose train of thy amber-dropping hair;
    Listen for dear honour's sake,
    Goddess of the silver lake, 865
        Listen and save.

Listen, and appear to us
In name of great Oceanus,
By the earth-shaking Neptune's mace,
And Tethys' grave, majestic pace;   870
By hoary Nereus' wrinkled look,
And the Carpathian wizard's hook;
By scaly Triton's winding shell,
And old sooth-saying Glaucus' spell;
By Leucothea's lovely hands,   875
And her son that rules the strands;
By Thetis' tinsel-slippered feet,
And the songs of Sirens sweet;
By dead Parthenope's dear tomb,
And fair Ligea's golden comb,   880
Wherewith she sits on diamond rocks
Sleeking her soft alluring locks;
By all the nymphs that nightly dance
Upon thy streams with wily glance;
Rise, rise, and heave thy rosy head   885
From thy coral-paven bed,
And bridle in thy headlong wave,
Till thou our summons answered have.

                Listen and save!

Sabrina rises, attended by water nymphs, and sings.

By the rushy-fringèd bank,   890
Where grows the willow and the osier dank,
   My sliding chariot stays,
Thick set with agate, and the azure sheen
Of turkis blue, and emerald green,
   That in the channel strays;   895
Whilst from off the waters fleet,
Thus I set my printless feet
O'er the cowslip's velvet head,
That bends not as I tread.
Gentle swain, at thy request   900
I am here.
Spirit. Goddess dear,
We implore thy powerful hand
To undo the charmèd band
Of true virgin here distressed   905
Through the force and through the wile
Of unblest enchanter vile.
Sabrina. Shepherd, 't is my office best
  To help ensnarèd chastity;

Brightest Lady, look on me.　　　　　　　910
Thus I sprinkle on thy breast
Drops that from my fountain pure
I have kept of precious cure;
Thrice upon thy finger's tip,
Thrice upon thy rubied lip;　　　　　　915
Next this marble venomed seat,
Smeared with gums of glutinous heat,
I touch with chaste palms moist and cold—
Now the spell hath lost his hold;
And I must haste ere morning hour　　　920
To wait in Amphitrite's bower.

Sabrina descends, and the Lady rises out of her seat.

Spirit. Virgin, daughter of Locrine,
　　Sprung of old Anchises' line,
　　May thy brimmèd waves for this
　　Their full tribute never miss　　　　925
　　From a thousand petty rills,
　　That tumble down the snowy hills:
　　Summer drought, or singèd air
　　Never scorch thy tresses fair,
　　Nor wet October's torrent flood　　　930
　　Thy molten crystal fill with mud;
　　May thy billows roll ashore
　　The beryl and the golden ore;
　　May thy lofty head be crowned
　　With many a tower and terrace round,　　935
　　And here and there thy banks upon
　　With groves of myrrh and cinnamon.
　　Come, Lady, while Heaven lends us grace,
　　Let us fly this cursèd place,
　　Lest the Sorcerer us entice　　　　940
　　With some other new device.
　　Not a waste, or needless sound,
　　Till we come to holier ground.
　　I shall be your faithful guide
　　Through this gloomy covert wide;　　　945
　　And not many furlongs thence
　　Is your Father's residence,
　　Where this night are met in state
　　Many a friend to gratulate
　　His wished presence, and beside　　　950
　　All the swains that there abide,
　　With jigs and rural dance resort.

We shall catch them at their sport,
And our sudden coming there
Will double all their mirth and cheer.   955
Come, let us haste; the stars grow high,
But Night sits monarch yet in the mid sky.

*The Scene changes, presenting Ludlow Town and the President's Castle;
then come in country dancers, after them the Attendant Spirit with
the two Brothers and the Lady.*

Song.

Spirit.   Back, shepherds, back! enough your play
            Till next sunshine holiday.
            Here be, without duck or nod,   960
            Other trippings to be trod
            Of lighter toes, and such court guise
            As Mercury did first devise
            With the mincing Dryades
            On the lawns and on the leas.   965

This second Song presents them to their Father and Mother.

            Noble Lord and Lady bright,
            I have brought ye new delight;
            Here behold so goodly grown
            Three fair branches of your own.
            Heaven hath timely tried their youth,   970
            Their faith, their patience, and their truth,
            And sent them here through hard assays
            With a crown of deathless praise,
            To triumph in victorious dance
            O'er sensual folly and intemperance.   975

            The dances ended, the Spirit epilogizes.

Spirit.   To the ocean now I fly,
            And those happy climes that lie
            Where day never shuts his eye,
            Up in the broad fields of the sky.
            There I suck in the liquid air   980
            All amidst the gardens fair
            Of Hesperus, and his daughters three
            That sing about the golden tree.
            Along the crispèd shades and bowers
            Revels the spruce and jocund Spring;   985
            The Graces, and the rosy-bosomed Hours
            Thither all their bounties bring;

There eternal Summer dwells,
And West-winds, with musky wing,
About the cedarn alleys fling   990
Nard and cassia's balmy smells.
Iris there with humid bow
Waters the odorous banks, that blow
Flowers of more mingled hew
Then her purfl'd scarf can shew,   995
And drenches with Elysian dew
(List, mortals, if your ears be true)
Beds of hyacinth and roses,
Where young Adonis oft reposes,
Waxing well of his deep wound   1000
In slumber soft, and on the ground
Sadly sits th' Assyrian queen;
But far above in spangled sheen
Celestial Cupid, her fam'd son, advanc't,
Holds his dear Psyche sweet intranc't,   1005
After her wandering labours long.
Till free consent the gods among
Make her his eternal bride,
And from her fair unspotted side
Two blissful twins are to be born,   1010
Youth and Joy; so Jove hath sworn.
    But now my task is smoothly done:
I can fly, or I can run
Quickly to the green earth's end,
Where the bowed welkin slow doth bend,   1015
And from thence can soar as soon
To the corners of the Moon.
    Mortals, that would follow me,
Love Virtue, she alone is free;
She can teach you how to clime   1020
Higher than the spheary chime:
Or, if Virtue feeble were,
Heaven itself would stoop to her.

NOTES AND QUESTIONS ON "COMUS"

1. The title. Milton himself gave to this mask the simple title
"A Masque presented at Ludlow Castle." In old Greek *Comus*
meant *merry-making,* or *merry-makers.* In later mythology it was
the name given to the god of merry-making. Milton, by representing him as the son of Bacchus, the god of wine, and Circe, the
sorceress, ascribes to him a new power unknown to him in older
stories.

2. **The occasion for this mask.**—The mask was written at the request of Henry Lawes, the musical composer, who arranged the music and setting for it. It was given at the estate of the Earl of Bridgewater, to celebrate his inauguration as Lord President of Wales.

3. The actors.—The actors were all amateurs, among them being the two sons and the daughter of the Earl of Bridgewater—who took the parts of the Two Brothers and the Lady—and Henry Lawes, who represented the Attendant Spirit.

4. The theme.—The theme is the triumph of purity,—the incorruptibility of true virtue.

5. The lesson taught.—This mask teaches that a person who is truly good and pure can go through the perils of earth unharmed.

6. The setting:—
   (a) Places:
       (1) The wood.
       (2) The palace of Comus.
       (3) The castle of the Earl of Bridgewater.
   (b) Time: 1634, on the day the Earl of Bridgewater was inaugurated.
   (c) The attendant circumstances:
       The three children of the Earl are on their way to their father's inauguration when they are represented as having the adventures described.

7. The atmosphere. The atmosphere is classical rather than English. Notice the large number of classical allusions.

8. Some questions based on this mask:—
   (a) What are the three natural divisions of this mask? What changes of scenes are necessitated? Are these simple, or otherwise? Why has the author given a classical atmosphere to the mask? Is anything gained by it? Judging from "Comus," how does a mask compare with a regular play as regards dramatic appeal—action, characters, conversation? Where does the main interest of a mask lie?
   (b) The characters:
       (1) *The Attendant Spirit.*
           Who is he? Why has he come? What means does he take to accomplish his task? Why didn't he rescue the Lady himself? What part does he have in her rescue? Why did he take the form of a well-known person when talking to the two Brothers? Why is he given the *first* and the *last* speeches of the mask? What is his allegorical significance? (He stands for Divinity—the Guardian Spirit who works through human agency. "Heaven helps those who try to help

themselves." God prompts us to help ourselves and others.)

(2) *Comus.*

Who is he? Parentage? Power? How is this power greater than Circe's? Why is he here? Why does he banish his crew when he hears the Lady? What were Comus's methods of work as shown by the way he approaches the Lady?

(a') Why does he use the magic dust? Its effect? Does Evil usually seek to cast a glamour over its victim? Why?

(b') What pretense does Comus make?

(c') What is his apparent attitude toward the Lady?

(d') What is the nature of the story he tells her? What is meant by Comus's glass? His wand? Why is Comus's palace made so beautiful?

(3) *Comus's Crew.*

Who are they? How has Comus gained them? Why have they human bodies but heads of beasts? Why are they not aware of their own condition?

(4) *The Lady.*

Why is she alone? Her character? Her faith? Why does she sing? What is the effect on Comus? How does Comus deceive the Lady? Why does she accept his offer? How does she find out that Comus is evil? Why does Comus succeed in gaining even a small power over the Lady? What does she stand for in the allegory? What is the cause of her strength? What is meant by her being bound to the chair?

(5) *The Two Brothers.*

What do they stand for in the allegory? From what two different standpoints do they view life? Which one is the sister most like? What do you think of their conversation from a dramatic standpoint? What help did they get from the Attendant Spirit? (Notice that, although the Elder Brother has *faith,* he also combines with it *works.* "Faith without works is dead.") Why do the Brothers succeed in breaking the glass of Comus but not in getting his wand? Why does the author allow Comus to escape?

(6) *Sabrina.*

Who is she? Could the Attendant Spirit have done this work as well? Why is she introduced? What does she use to loosen the bonds of the Lady? What is signified by the fact that neither the Lady nor the Brothers are able to win the full victory alone?

(7) Why are these children allowed to have this experience? What is tested by it? How does this story pay a compliment to the Earl of Bridgewater?

(8) Learn the memory gems scattered through the poem, especially those in lines 373–375; 453–456; 589; 593; 1018–1023.

(9) Milton himself said "Wherever I go, the sentiment of the last two lines of my 'Comus' is always my fixed belief."

"Caliban by the Yellow Sands," a Modern Mask.—In connection with its celebration of the Shakespeare Tercentenary, New York City produced the most elaborate mask of modern times, "Caliban by the Yellow Sands," in the Stadium of the College of the City of New York, May 23–27, 1916. Percy MacKaye was the author of this mask; Miss Mary Porter Beegle was the organizing chairman who originated the idea, and Josef Urban, the Viennese artist, designed the settings and arranged the elaborate system of lighting. The acting, music, dancing, costumes, and other features were in the hands of competent artists in each line.

In this mask the poor half-formed monster, Caliban, of Shakespeare's "Tempest," was put under the spell of the magician Prospero, and, in the presence of Miranda and the sprite Ariel, was shown a large number of scenes from Shakespeare, together with a series of interludes representing life in many different nations and periods of time. The great center ring of the Stadium was covered with yellow canvas to represent the sands, and here, around a large hour-glass, were presented dances and pageants representing dramatic art in Egypt, Greece, Rome, France, Germany, Spain, and Elizabethan England.

The following brief outline of the plot of "Caliban by the Yellow Sands" appeared in one of the New York papers:

The story of the mask begins with *Ariel*, a winged spirit typifying light and truth, imprisoned in the jaws of the idol of *Setebos*, god of primeval force and father of *Caliban*, the brutish primeval man. *Caliban* taunts *Ariel*. *Lust*, *War*, and *Death*, the priests of *Setebos*, perform a weird ritual before the idol. *Miranda*, a spirit, enters with her father, *Prospero*, who typifies the art of the theater. *Prospero* releases *Ariel*, commanding him to educate *Caliban* instead of seeking revenge.

Prospero, to help, reveals the pageant of the theater in three great

JOHN DREW AS SHAKESPEARE
In "Caliban by the Yellow Sands"

ages—Egyptian, Greek, and Roman. On the inner stage scenes from various Shakespeare plays are shown.

The second interlude is a merry festival of Elizabethan England, given to revive the drooping *Miranda*. *Caliban* woos *Miranda,* and calls upon *War* to dethrone *Prospero*. *Prospero* summons the spirit of *Time* to his aid, and *Time* calls his artists. The theaters of the world group themselves about him. The spirit of Shakespeare enters and speaks the lines from "The Tempest":

"We are such stuff as dreams are made on, and our little life is rounded with a sleep."

Caliban is profoundly imprest, and, kneeling with the assembled thousands around him, he pays homage to Shakespeare, symbolizing the regenerated man awakened to his higher destiny.

The Dramatic Monologue.—The greatest master of the dramatic monologue was Robert Browning, who did his best work in the last half of the nineteenth century. This type, as the name indicates, has but one speaker and is not adapted for regular stage presentation. It is, however, sometimes used for declamatory purposes.

Browning's monologues are all soul-studies. In each one of them he chooses a particular crisis in the life of the speaker, makes him lay bare the depths of his soul and unconsciously reveal all the hidden springs and motives for action. Thus from the one moment we can really understand the whole life—what it has been, as well as the direction toward which it is tending. Among the best of Browning's monologues are "My Last Duchess," "The Patriot," "Saul," "Andrea del Sarto," "Cleon," "Mulèykeh," and "Abt Vogler." Most of these are rather difficult reading, but "My Last Duchess" is easy to understand and will best illustrate this type.

The scene of this monologue is laid in Italy during the Italian Renaissance. The speaker is a haughty duke, who, although he loves culture and works of art to a high degree, is hard and cruel. The duke has been making arrangements for his marriage with the daughter of a count. He and the count's agent are just about to descend the grand staircase in the ducal palace, when he stops and draws the curtain hanging over the picture of his last duchess. He wishes to signify to the agent certain characteristics that he does not want to find in the new duchess, but he in reality reveals his own selfish, sordid nature.

MY LAST DUCHESS [1]

Robert Browning

That's my last Duchess painted on the wall,
Looking as if she were alive. I call
That piece a wonder, now: Fra Pandolf's hands
Worked busily a day, and there she stands.
Will it please you sit and look at her? I said   5
"Fra Pandolf" by design, for never read
Strangers like you that pictured countenance,
The depth and passion of its earnest glance,
But to myself they turned (since none puts by
The curtain I have drawn for you, but I)   10
And seemed as they would ask me, if they durst,
How such a glance came there; so, not the first
Are you to turn and ask thus. Sir, 't was not
Her husband's presence only, called that spot
Of joy into the Duchess' cheek: perhaps   15
Fra Pandolf chanced to say, "Her mantle laps
Over my lady's wrist too much," or "Paint
Must never hope to reproduce the faint
Half-flush that dies along her throat": such stuff
Was courtesy, she thought, and cause enough   20
For calling up that spot of joy. She had
A heart—how shall I say?—too soon made glad,
Too easily impressed: she liked whate'er
She looked on, and her looks went everywhere.
Sir, 't was all one! My favour at her breast,   25
The dropping of the daylight in the West,
The bough of cherries some officious fool
Broke in the orchard for her, the white mule
She rode with round the terrace—all and each
Would draw from her alike the approving speech,   30
Or blush, at least. She thanked men,—good! but thanked
Somehow—I know not how—as if she ranked
My gift of a nine-hundred-years-old name
With anybody's gift. Who'd stoop to blame
This sort of trifling? Even had you skill   35
In speech—(which I have not)—to make your will
Quite clear to such an one, and say, "Just this
Or that in you disgusts me; here you miss,
Or there exceed, the mark"—and if she let
Herself be lessoned so, nor plainly set   40

[1] By permission of the Macmillan Company.

ROBERT BROWNING
The Greatest Writer of Dramatic Monologues

Her wits to yours, forsooth, and made excuse,
—E'en then would be some stooping; and I choose
Never to stoop. Oh sir, she smiled, no doubt,
Whence'er I passed her; but who passed without
Much the same smile? This grew; I gave commands; 45
Then all smiles stopped together. There she stands
As if alive. Will 't please you rise? We 'll meet
The company below, then. I repeat,
The Count your master's known munificence
Is ample warrant that no just pretence 50
Of mine for dowry will be disallowed;
Though his fair daughter's self, as I avowed
At starting, is my object. Nay, we 'll go
Together down, sir. Notice Neptune, though,
Taming a sea-horse, thought a rarity, 55
Which Claus of Innsbruck cast in bronze for me!

The Beginning of the Modern Drama.[1]—From the time of Goldsmith and Sheridan to the closing years of the nineteenth century, there were no plays written that were worthy of note. Although Byron, Shelley, Tennyson, and Browning wrote some poems that they called dramas, these lacked certain essentials which prevented their success on the stage. It was not until about 1890, therefore, that the regular drama in England was revived under the inspiration and leadership of the great Norwegian writer, Ibsen. Since then there have been many successful plays written both in England and America.

Some Characteristics and Tendencies of the Modern Drama.— The modern drama, in general, seems to fall into three more or less distinct types which, in turn, are sub-divided into a number of other classes. The three main types include the romantic, the realistic, and the symbolic plays. These, however, sometimes shade into each other so that one may exhibit characteristics of the other forms.

The romantic plays, which try to make us forget, rather than remember, the realities of life and to draw us away from our own stern, or prosaic, work-a-day world into one of imagination and

The Romantic Plays

dreams, is divided, according to subject-matter, into several classes ranging from those whose aim is to arouse pleasurable emotions, to those which depict the most terrible of tragic scenes. In every case the situations and characters are felt to be imagi-

[1] It will be noted that much that is given under the modern drama applies to prose as well as poetry. The transition from poetry to prose in this book is made through the drama, which is divided between the two forms.

nary rather than real, although there may be some matter-of-fact details. Among the many varieties of romantic plays may be mentioned, especially, those filled with love, adventure, and, usually, humor, where interesting or thrilling circumstances are presented just for themselves, though, occasionally, for the sake of some background idea as well. Here may be classed such British plays as "The Amazons," by Arthur Wing Pinero; "What Every Woman Knows," "The Admirable Crichton," and "A Kiss for Cinderella," by James M. Barrie; the French plays, "Cyrano de Bergerac," "The Romancers," and "Princess Far-Away," by Edmond Rostand; and most of the American plays by Clyde Fitch and Augustus Thomas. These plays are all full of spirit and swift action.

In the realistic plays, the dramatists do not attempt to amuse, to teach a lesson, or prove a point; but to set forth life exactly as it is, stripped of all glamour, and to strive to understand its problems.

The Realistic Plays
Here they are not interested in the deeds or action but in the reasons why men strive and suffer. There can, therefore, be no artificial plan of arrangement into introduction, rising and falling action, and solution of difficulties, but the course of life is followed just as it is lived. The situations are simple; the number of characters is usually very small—four or five at the most. The main interest is in the conversation. It is in the realistic plays that we find the truly modern idea of tragedy. A tragic character of such a play is not one who, in the old Shakespearian sense, defies some moral law and meets a just punishment, but one who is forced to suffer and succumb to certain things in this complex life, over which he has little, or no, control. The moment chosen as the center of such a play is that of some crisis in a person's life which comes from the very nature of things and not from what he has done. Thus environment—outward social, industrial, political, or racial circumstances—and heredity are the prime causes. The tragedy comes because a person cannot find peace since he cannot adjust himself to the conditions of his life. The end of such a play is, therefore, not a state of peace, but, instead, is abrupt and incomplete.

The plays of John Galsworthy are among the very best examples of this type. In his "Justice" he gives an illustration of the unjust condemnation of a man because the criminal courts fail to understand his individual case and how to deal with it. In "The Silver Box" he shows the inequalities in the administration of justice where, for a similar offense, the rich man goes free while the poor man is dragged off to prison. In "Strife" he centers the interest in the conflict between labor and capital. The eminent dramatic critic, Professor Lewisohn, has said, "Galsworthy's dialogue is the best dramatic dialogue in the language. Its illusion of reality is complete. . . . He above all other men now in view seems called and chosen as the great modern dramatist of the English tongue."

Among the other classes of realistic plays may be mentioned Granville Barker's "The Voysey Inheritance," which shows how the business or financial world may affect family life, and "The Melting Pot" by Israel Zangwill, which deals with the problem of race antagonisms. Other problems handled in plays of this type are those dealing with tenement regulations, sanitation, factory legislation, political corruption, and various evils in our social, industrial, political, and personal life.

The symbolic plays make an especial appeal to the imagination and emotions and open the door into the world of spirit, mysticism, and allegory. These plays vary from those of almost pure fancy touched with allegory, through those where the alle-
The Symbolic Plays gory is strongly marked, to others which, though romantic or realistic in the main, have allegorical threads or characters running through them. Here, then, may be classed "The Land of Heart's Desire," "The Countess Cathleen," "The Hour Glass," and "Cathleen ni Houlihan" by William Butler Yeats; "The Blue Bird" by Maeterlinck; "Peter Pan" by James M. Barrie; "Chantecler" by Edmond Rostand; "The Piper" by Josephine Preston Peabody; "The Servant in the House" by Charles Rann Kennedy; "The Passing of the Third Floor Back" by Jerome K. Jerome; and "The Travelling Man" by Lady Gregory. In each of the last three plays mentioned, there is found among the other characters one in human form who symbolizes the spirit of Christ.

Aside from the three main types, given above, into which the modern drama may be divided, other classifications are sometimes made, but the different plays in such groups would also be included under the romantic, the realistic, or the symbolic types. The most important of these classes are the one-act plays, the poetic plays, and the Irish or Celtic plays.

Among the one-act plays may be mentioned Synge's "Riders to the Sea," Gibson's seventeen little plays in "Daily Bread,"

Lady Gregory's "The Rising of the Moon," "Spreading the
News," and "McDonough's Wife," Yeats's "A
One-Act Pot of Broth" and "The Hour Glass," Zona Gale's
Plays "Neighbors," Stuart Walker's "Trimplet," Bar-
rie's "Rosalind," and Dunsany's "A Night at the
Inn."

Besides Rostand's "Cyrano de Bergerac," "Chantecler," and
"Princess Far-Away," which are in the poetic form although known
chiefly to Americans through prose translations, there are few act-
able modern poetic plays. Stephen Phillips has
Poetic Plays done the best work in England, probably, in this
particular line, but his plays have never reached
the highest success, although the poetry is good and
there are many powerful scenes and beautiful, spectacular settings.
Some other poetic plays that have been written are Alfred Noyes's
"Sherwood"; most of Yeats's plays; Peabody's "The Piper,"
"Marlowe," and "The Wolf of Gubbio"; Percy MacKaye's
"Jeanne d'Arc" and "The Canterbury Pilgrims," and Van Dyke's
"The House of Rimmon." The chief trouble with the poetic plays
thus far is that they are not both dramatic and poetic at the same
time, with the emphasis on the dramatic.

The last type of plays produced in modern times that we will
mention here is the one developed by the Irish school of dramatists—Synge, Lady Gregory, and Yeats. These playwrights have
all been mentioned in connection with the different
types described above, but it is in their plays deal-
The Irish ing especially with Irish folk-lore, Irish history, and
Plays Irish peasant life that they are distinct from the
others. Imbued with the spirit of patriotism, these
writers have worked to set forth the stories and legends and the
real peasant life of their native land.

Some Ways in Which the Modern Drama [1] **Differs from the
Older Drama.—**

1. It centers the tragedy not in what people do, but in what they
   suffer and endure.
2. The chief interest is often in the thoughts expressed rather
   than in the action.
3. The modern play often begins just before what would be the

[1] In this discussion of the modern drama only those types and characteristics that are of most interest to young people are mentioned. It must be remembered that there are others.

catastrophe of an older play. The time of action is thus shortened and the necessity for changes of scenes is eliminated. The play is then concerned with the results of something that happened long before the first scene opens.

4. The ending of a modern play does not always find the difficulties smoothed away. In Galsworthy's "Silver Box," for instance, the play does not end with the bettering of conditions for the poor Jones family whose miseries have aroused our sympathies. It ends with the despair of the poor wife as her husband is dragged away to prison. Life does not stop with the fall of the curtain, and we are left to wonder what will happen next to these people whose fortunes we have been following.

5. Every device that tends to remind us of the author is a fault in a play, because this spoils the illusion of reality. For this reason the soliloquy and aside remarks are falling into disuse. In the older plays these were regarded as indispensable. To-day the dramatists follow life in making us know people by giving us one impression after another of them. We learn to understand them by noticing how they are regarded by every other character in the play as well as by watching their actions and words to others. When the soliloquy is not meant to address the audience, but seems the natural expression of a tortured soul, it may be justified, but even then it should never be more than a brief ejaculation.

6. In the modern plays the action is very direct and simple, there being little or no striving after spectacular effects.

7. There is seldom more than one scene to an act, on the modern stage, and the number of acts varies from one to four.

8. Most of the modern plays are written in prose.

9. The modern plays, to a very large degree, reflect the social and industrial conditions of modern life.

10. Speeches are natural instead of rhetorical.

11. There are no romantic heroes, heroines, or villains, but the themes and characters are commonplace.

12. Artificial devices like disguises, lost wills and letters, and information gained through eavesdropping, are no longer used in the best plays.

13. There is also a tendency in the modern play to present important episodes rather than a real plot. Plays like "Little Women" and "Milestones" are examples. There seems to

be a development of character rather than of plot. The causes of character growth, from one time to another, form, thus, the real action of the play. Such a play is really a character study in dramatic form.

Some Examples of Modern Plays.—

THE FAMILY'S PRIDE [1]

A PLAY IN ONE ACT BY WILFRID WILSON GIBSON (1914)

Persons: MARTHA IRWIN, *a widow.*
　　　　KATHERINE IRWIN, *her daughter.*
　　　　AGNES IRWIN, *her daughter-in-law.*
　　　　EMMA PRUDDAH, *a neighbor.*

Scene: MARTHA IRWIN'S *cottage at dawn.*

Katherine. She has not stirred,
　Nor spoken all the night,
　Though I have never left her.
Emma. I could not sleep for thinking of her face.
　My man still slumbers soundly;　　　　　　　　　5
　And it's so many nights
　Since he has stretched his body on a bed,
　I would not wake him.
　There's little rest for men at sea,
　Cramped in a narrow bunk,　　　　　　　　　　10
　Betwixt the watches,
　For an hour or so.
　And he has slept
　All night long,
　As soundly as a boat becalmed.　　　　　　　　15
　And it was good to see him
　Sleeping there,
　As I recalled the wakeful nights
　I'd been alone.
　It's weary waiting for your man's return;　　　　20
　But, when he comes again . . .
Katherine. She has not stirred,
　Nor spoken once,
　Nor lifted up her eyes
　The livelong night;　　　　　　　　　　　　　25
　Nor can I rouse her now.
　And she has taken neither bite nor sup.

[1] Used by permission and special arrangement with the owners of the copyright, the Macmillan Company.

Agnes, John's wife,
And Michael's lass have been,
Though they, poor wenches, 30
Were distraught themselves.
But nothing rouses her;
And she has scarcely breathed,
Since first I broke the news to her,
And told her that her sons were drowned. 35
She stayed at home,
While I went down
To meet the Boats,
Saying that wives and maids
Should be the first to welcome 40
The men on their return.

Emma. 'T was well she did not go.

Katherine. When first I heard the tidings,
I was stunned,
And stood awhile, dumfounded. 45
Then I remembered . . .
And I shook myself,
And ran straight home to her,
Lest she should hear of her sons' death
From any stranger's lips. 50
She stood upon the threshold.
'Waiting them,
A smile of welcome on her face.
But when she saw me come, alone,
She caught her breath, 55
And looked into my eyes,
And spake to me,
Ere I could utter aught:
"And has the sea kept all?"
And I . . . 60
I could but answer, "All!"
She asked no more,
But turned upon her heel,
And went indoors,
And sat down by the hearth. 65
She has not stirred
Nor spoken since to me;
Though once I heard her
Murmur to herself
Her dead sons' names, 70
Slowly, as though she feared
Lest they should slip her memory.

"John, William, Michael, Mark, and little Pete,"
She murmured to herself;
And neither stirred nor spake again.   75
Emma.   It's well that you are left her.
Katherine.   My name she did not breathe.
I'm naught to her;
She never called for me.
Her sons were all-in-all to her.   80
I grudged them not her whole heart's love. . . .
My brothers! . . .
Now I've none but her,
And she has no one left
To keep life in her heart.   85
Emma.   Nay, do not say so;
You're her daughter, lass.
Katherine.   Her sons were all-in-all,
And they are dead.
'T was strange she never asked me how they died;   90
She must have seen them drowning
In my eyes.
And I have told her nothing more,
For she has asked nothing.
And yet, what should she ask?   95
What was there left to tell her heart?
Her mother's heart knew all,
Ere aught was told.
Emma.   Lass, 't was a cruel storm.
My husband scarce escaped.   100
"The Family's Pride" . . .
Katherine.   Nay, spare me, neighbor, now.
I cannot listen to that tale again—
I who have looked upon that face all night,
And harkened for a word from those dumb lips.   105
Had she but wept,
Or spoken once to me,
I might have helped her somewhat,
Even I.
Oh, how I long to lay that aching brow   110
In slumber on my breast.
And yet,
I dare not lay my hand on her
Lest she turn round on me,
And realize   115
That only I am left her.
Emma.   [*Going to the door*] Agnes comes.

And brings her babe with her.
Perhaps the boy will rouse your mother.

[*To* Agnes, *as she enters.*]

Lass, lay him in her lap.   120
He'll rouse the spark of life in her,
And wake her from her brooding on the dead.

[Agnes *goes forward without speaking, and lays the child in its grandmother's lap.* Martha Irwin *gazes at it, then takes it to her breast,
looking up at* Agnes.]

Martha.   Yes, I will tend the boy,
While you go down . . .
To meet your husband, Agnes.   125
Lass, away!
The Boats will soon be in,
And you will be the first to greet . . .
My son . . . your husband . . .
For he's yours . . .   130
As well as mine . . .
And I must share with you.
The Boats will soon be in,
And soon my eyes shall look upon my sons—
My bonnie sons. . . .   135
John, William, Michael, Mark,
And little Pete . . .
Though even Peter is not little now;
He's a grown man,
Though he's my youngest son.   140
And still . . .
It seems but such a little while
Since I held John,
My eldest,
In my arms,   145
As now . . .
I hold his son.
But . . . lass . . . away!
To greet . . . your husband . . .
And . . . my son . . .   150
Agnes.   O God, have pity!
Emma.   She does not know what she is saying;
Her grief has been too much for her.
Martha.   Away . . . away . . .
You'll be too late . . .   155
But, Katherine,

Stay with me . . .
I think . . .
I 've suddenly grown old,
And I would have you with me . . .   160
Till . . . they come.
Emma. Look to the child!
She does n't know . . .
'T will fall!
Agnes. Nay, but I have it safe.   165
Emma. The end is not far off.
Katherine. Come, mother,
Lay your head upon my bosom.
Martha. Ah, daughter, is that you?
Yes, I am weary . . .   170
And would rest awhile. . . .
I hope they 'll come
Before it 's cold. . . .
And you have set five plates?
And not forgotten Peter's knife?   175
The Boats will soon be in . . .
And I shall look upon my sons,
Once more, before I die . . .
For I am nigh death, Katherine. . . .
Hark . . . they come . . .   180
Their feet are on the threshold. . . .
Katherine, quick . . .
Fling the door wide . . .
That I . . . may look . . .
On them . . .   185
My sons . . .
Oh!
Katherine. Death has pitied her.

THE TRAITOR [1]

A Play in One Act by Percival Wilde

CHARACTERS

Colonel Sir Robert Anstruther, K. C. M. G.
Major MacLaurin, V. C.
Captain Grantham.
Captain Bates.
Captain Parker.
Captain Willoughby.
Lieutenant Edwards.
Other officers of the Fusiliers; an Orderly.

the scene—Colonel Anstruther's *Tent.*

the place—*South Africa.*

the time—*The Boer War.*

As the curtain rises Colonel Anstruther *and* Major MacLaurin *are discovered, seated on camp chairs, near a plain deal table. At intervals an orderly is seen passing the door of the tent. It is after nightfall, and a flickering light is cast by a few lamps. There is a long pause.*

MacLaurin (vehemently). It's hell, Colonel, that's what it is! It's hell.

Anstruther (after a silence). You have n't a suspicion?

MacLaurin. No. . . . He's clever—too clever! Damn him!

Anstruther. There's never been anything like it in the history of the regiment.

MacLaurin. I would n't believe it if you told me. I would n't believe it unless I knew it at first hand. That an Englishman—an Englishman——

Anstruther. A traitor.

MacLaurin (nodding bitterly). Yes.

Anstruther. There have been traitors before.

MacLaurin. But not in the Fusiliers!

Anstruther. Thank God, no.

MacLaurin. The first thing that made me suspect was a month ago: at Spiesfontein: when the Boers shelled us.

Anstruther. It was queer, was n't it?

MacLaurin. It was much worse than queer! They knew our position! They knew our strength! There was not a wasted shot!

Anstruther (*gravely*). It cost us thirty-eight men.

MacLaurin (*with a nasty contraction of his under lip*). Yes. And more the next day, and the day after. Then they drove us here: bottled us up. And the shooting! Have you ever *seen* such shooting? Somebody has given them maps.

Anstruther. Yes; that's pretty clear.

MacLaurin. It was one of our own officers: that's pretty clear also.

Anstruther. I'm afraid so.

MacLaurin. Who was it?

Anstruther (*after a pause*). I will tell you that in fifteen minutes.

MacLaurin. You mean it?

Anstruther (*nodding slowly*). Yes.

MacLaurin. How I'd love to get my hands around his throat!

Anstruther. You'll have your chance, Cecil.

MacLaurin. Do you know the man?

Anstruther. I think so.

MacLaurin. What's his name?

Anstruther (*quietly*). Wait! Wait! . . . I have sent for the officers.

MacLaurin (*dejectedly*). Then you *don't* know.

Anstruther. I'm almost sure, Cecil.

Orderly (*appearing at the entrance of the tent*). Colonel!

Anstruther. Yes?

Orderly. The officers, sir.

Anstruther. Ask them to come in, orderly.

(*The* Orderly *salutes and exits.*)

MacLaurin. One of our own officers! What a horrible——

Anstruther (*interrupting*). Sh! (*The officers enter, saluting as they do so.*) Is Lieutenant Edwards there?

Grantham. He's coming, sir.

Anstruther. Will you sit down, gentlemen? (*He turns to* Captain Willoughby.) Everything quiet, Captain?

Willoughby (*nodding*). Just been the rounds, sir.

(Lieutenant Edwards *appears. His uniform is torn and soiled, his face haggard, his general appearance that of a man near the end of his strength.*)

Anstruther. Ah, here you are. Come in, Lieutenant.

Edwards. I'm sorry if I'm late, sir.

Anstruther. It's all right. Sit down. (*There is a pause. Then he addresses the assembled officers in a low voice.*) Gentlemen, I have asked you here to lay a matter before you. The Articles of War prescribe certain rules for our conduct. Those rules are supposed to be followed absolutely. But I am violating no secret if I say that under certain circumstances it becomes permissible to—to overlook some of them. Whether we do so or not depends upon your judgment. . . . Lieutenant Edwards, as you know, was captured by the enemy four days ago.

(*There is a general murmur of assent.*)

Anstruther. Lieutenant Edwards escaped to-day. Lieutenant Edwards told me to-day what took place in the interim. It appears that the Boers wanted information as to the disposition of our forces—as to our strength —as to our plans—information which Lieutenant Edwards could give them.

Parker (*to* Edwards). You did n't tell them, did you?

Anstruther. He refused to speak, Captain Parker. Then . . . Edwards, tell them what followed.

Edwards. They could n't get anything out of me, so—so they put me to the torture.

A Lieutenant. Good God!

Edwards. They held my feet to the fire—they tied a cord around my forehead——

Anstruther (*interrupting coldly*). The details are of no consequence, sir.

Edwards. No, sir.

Anstruther. They tortured you to make you tell. Did you tell?

Bates. You did n't, man!

Grantham. Of course he did n't!

Anstruther. Did you tell, sir?

Edwards. They tortured me, sir, they were killing me——

Anstruther (*insistently*). Did you tell?

Edwards (*after a tense pause*). Yes, sir.

MacLaurin (*rushing at him*). You—you traitor!

Anstruther (*arresting him*). Stop! (*To the others, who have risen.*) Sit down, gentlemen!

Edwards (*sobbing*). I could n't help it! I swear I could n't help it! I stood it for ten hours—for ten livelong hours—I fainted twice, and they waited till I came to, each time and then——

MacLaurin. You told!

Edwards. I could n't stand the pain. It was killing me.

MacLaurin. You coward!

Edwards (*springing up*). Major!

Anstruther (*sternly*). Sit down, sir! (*There is a pause.*) Gentlemen, I have asked you here to judge this man.

Parker. Why, there 's nothing to do but——

Anstruther (*interrupting*). Just a minute, Captain. The Articles of War prescribe death. (*There is an affirmatory murmur.*) Lieutenant Edwards has betrayed military secrets. But whether one man dies or does not die is of no great consequence. This is not a court-martial: no report of what takes place here will ever reach the outside world. Lieutenant

Edwards was compelled to do what he did: it was not a voluntary act. He claims—well, it is not necessary for me to repeat what he said: you can imagine what it was. It is for you to decide what is to be done: it is for you to punish—or not to punish. Gentlemen, the matter is in your hands.

(*He walks to the door of the tent. The officers rise, and form a group.*)

Edwards (*seizing* Grantham's *sleeve as he passes*). Billy!

(Grantham *shakes him off in silence.*)

A Lieutenant. What a thing to happen to the regiment!

Edwards (*turning to him eagerly*). Gerald, if you knew——

The Lieutenant (*cutting him short*). I don't want to.

(*He turns his back.*)

MacLaurin. Gentlemen, as senior officer present I put the question to you——

Edwards. But hear me first——

MacLaurin. There is nothing you can say, sir. (*He turns to the others.*) The Articles of War prescribe death for the officer who forgets his oath of allegiance to his Sovereign. I so vote. Gentlemen?

(*A chorus of "Ayes"; a single "Nay."*)

MacLaurin. Again, gentlemen?

(*There is still one "Nay."*)

MacLaurin (*frowning*). The "ayes" have it.

(*He crosses silently to* Anstruther.)

Edwards (*hysterically*). You're not going to see me killed, are you? Why, I couldn't do anything else——

A Lieutenant. Edwards, you were an officer and a gentleman once. Try to remember it.

Anstruther (*returning*). I believe you have voted, gentlemen?

MacLaurin. There is only one against, sir.

Anstruther (*addressing the officers*). And you are still of the same opinion?

(*A general murmur of assent.*)

Anstruther. Major MacLaurin.

MacLaurin. Yes, sir.

Anstruther. Some time to-morrow you will go for a walk with Lieuten-ant Edwards.

MacLaurin. Yes, sir.

Anstruther. You will go some distance from camp—not less than a mile, I should say.

MacLaurin. Yes, sir.

Anstruther. On this walk there will be an accident. What kind of an accident does not matter. Revolvers have been known to explode while being cleaned. Or, if you prefer, there is a dangerous cliff towards the south. At any rate, there *will* be an accident.

MacLaurin. Yes, sir.

Anstruther. From this accident Lieutenant Edwards will not recover. And you will make it your business to see that there *is* such an accident.

MacLaurin. Yes, sir.

Anstruther (*to* Edwards). You may write what letters you please to-night—under Major MacLaurin's supervision. There is to be nothing which would lead persons to suspect the truth. They will be ordinary letters—such as you might write any time—no farewells. You understand, sir? (Edwards *does not answer. He repeats the question.*) You understand, sir?

Edwards (*saluting with an effort*). Yes, sir.

Anstruther. That is all.

Edwards (*offering his hand*). Good-by, sir.

Anstruther (*turning his back*). I said that was all, sir.

Captain Willoughby. No, sir, that is not all!

Anstruther (*wheeling in surprise*). Sir?

Willoughby. It is hellish, what you are doing! It's not right; it's not fair that you should send this poor boy to his death like this! *You* would have done the same thing if you had been in his place! He told, that is true, but you would have told, too! Just look at him: see the mark of the cord around his forehead: imagine what he went through! He did what he had to, and you, you sanctimonius beggars, you would have done no better!

                        (Edwards *bursts into an hysterical laugh.*)

Willoughby (*continuing excitedly*). *I* was the one who voted against death! You would n't hear him, no, you would n't listen to a word in his defense. And it's murder that you're doing! Murder! (*He pauses as he notices the peculiar expression on* Anstruther's *face. He finishes weakly*): You must let him go, sir! You must let him go!

Anstruther (*after a pause, in a grim tone*). Yes.

MacLaurin (*voicing a general protest*). What are you doing, Colonel?

Anstruther (*silences him with a gesture*).

Willoughby. You will do what is right, Colonel!

Anstruther (*emphatically*). Yes. (*He detains the officers as they start to leave the tent.*) Wait a minute, gentlemen. (*He pauses; then, quietly*): Gentlemen, there has been a traitor amongst you for a long time. I was unable to find out who it was; so Lieutenant Edwards and I put together this story. Lieutenant Edwards was never captured by the enemy: he was never tortured: he never told. But it was sure that one man would be merciful to a traitor: the man who himself might be discovered any day. (*He pauses; then, suddenly*): Captain Willoughby, at dawn a firing squad will escort you out of camp—and shoot you!

CURTAIN

OPTIONAL READINGS IN THE MODERN DRAMA

Note.—Report on as many plays as you have time for. Give for each the name of play and author; classify according to main class of plays represented, giving reasons for classification; classify, where possible, as to sub-class. What points of difference did you note between this and an older play? How did it compare in interest? Give in a sentence or two what the play is about.

"The Doll's House"........................Henrik Ibsen
"Strife" ....John Galsworthy
"Justice" ....John Galsworthy
"The Silver Box" ....John Galsworthy
"The Pigeon" ....John Galsworthy
"On the Road," from "Daily Bread".........Wilfrid W. Gibson
"The Night Shift," from "Daily Bread"......Wilfrid W. Gibson
"The First Born," from "Daily Bread"......Wilfrid W. Gibson
"The Shirt," from "Daily Bread"...........Wilfrid W. Gibson
"The Furnace," from "Daily Bread"........Wilfrid W. Gibson
"Riders to the Sea" ....John Millington Synge
"The Travelling Man"....................Lady Augusta Gregory
"The White Cockade" ....Lady Augusta Gregory
"The Gaol Gate"........................Lady Augusta Gregory
"The Rising of the Moon" ....Lady Augusta Gregory
"McDonough's Wife" ....Lady Augusta Gregory
"The Work-House Ward"..................Lady Augusta Gregory
"Spreading the News"....................Lady Augusta Gregory
"The Land of Heart's Desire".............William Butler Yeats
"The Hour Glass" ....William Butler Yeats
"On Baile's Strand".....................William Butler Yeats
"Cathleen ni Houlihan"..................William Butler Yeats
"The Countess Cathleen"..................William Butler Yeats
"A Pot of Broth" ....William Butler Yeats
"Sherwood" ....Alfred Noyes
"Herod" ....Stephen Phillips
"Ulysses" ....Stephen Phillips
"The Bluebird" ....Maurice Maeterlinck
"The Piper"............................Josephine Preston Peabody
"Marlowe" ....Josephine Preston Peabody
"The Wolf of Gubbio"....................Josephine Preston Peabody
"The Servant in the House"...............Charles Rann Kennedy
"The Passing of the Third Floor Back"... ..Jerome K. Jerome
"Fanny and the Servant Problem"...........Jerome K. Jerome
"The Amazons"..........................Arthur Wing Pinero
"Sweet Lavender" ....Arthur Wing Pinero
"The Manœuvres of Jane".................H. A. Jones

REVIEW [1]

1. Before turning to Book Two, sum up what you have gained from a study of poetry. How do you think the three main classes of poetry compare in interest? Can you distinguish one kind from another instantly? Can you easily distinguish the main types under each general class? Can you take a poem and prove its classification by pointing out its characteristics? Do you feel that you know some of the best writers of each type? Have you enjoyed the work?

2. For your theme work try dramatizing a short-story by O. Henry or some other author who has given a good deal of dialogue. Be sure to notice whether it would be *actable*. Look over examples of modern plays to see just what methods are used as to general arrangement, and the indication of speakers and of stage directions.

[1] This usually marks the end of the first semester's work.

BOOK TWO

TYPES OF PROSE

Prose literature is divided into the following important classes: (1) the prose drama,[1] (2) the essay, (3) prose fiction, (4) the oration, (5) miscellaneous prose forms.

[1] Treated in connection with dramatic poetry.

CHAPTER I

THE ESSAY

Characteristics of the Essay.—The essay is that type of literature in which the author gives, in prose, his own thoughts on life
or any of its phases. It is, therefore, the prose form which most
nearly corresponds to lyric poetry. It may treat any subject from
the light, humorous, trivial things to the deepest thoughts that the
soul can fathom. There is no definite form which essays must take.
They are as varied as the writers themselves, and show, through and
through, each author's personality. They may deal with subjects
drawn from biography, history, personal life, travel, nature, art,
or criticism. They may be written to entertain, to inform the
mind, or to teach moral or religious truths. There are but three
characteristics that will aid us in defining this type. These are:
(1) in every essay the author himself is prominent, since we are
made to see through his eyes the things which have interested him;
(2) the essay is in prose; and (3) it is always artistic. If practical
things are discussed, they are always put in an artistic form and
appeal to the imagination and emotions. This especially distinguishes the true essay from other short prose types that are written
only to inform or teach.

Although there are no definite forms, there are several general
classes into which essays may be roughly grouped. These very
frequently overlap. They may be historical, biographical, personal, imaginative, narrative, didactic, critical, reflective, philosophical, or religious. They must, however, all be interesting and
worth while.

The essay never gives an exhaustive treatment of any subject,
but, as its name implies, is an *attempt* to set forth only those phases
or things that the author may choose to express. It is suggestive
and rambling rather than complete and direct. It may vary in
length from one page to a hundred or more. It usually is divided
into three main parts: (1) the introduction; (2) the body, consisting of a series of paragraphs, more or less closely related, in which
the subject is developed; and (3) the conclusion. This is not al-

ways the case. Bacon, especially, grouped his thoughts around a central idea without any effort at an orderly, logical paragraph development.

Usually the author of an essay is especially particular about his literary style. This, of course, is important; and yet the thought, the mood, experience, or observations are more so. Essay writers are usually people who have plenty of time for reflection.

In reading an essay one should notice what is revealed of the author's own experiences and personality, as well as the important thoughts which he wished to impart. The central thought of an essay can usually be summed up in a single sentence. The essay occasionally resembles fiction by its use of the character sketch [1] and the drama by the dialogue [2] that it sometimes uses.

The Great Essayists.—Although there is essay material to be found in the older literature of the world, it was the French writer, Montaigne, who in 1571 first applied to his prose pieces the term *essais* which has designated the type in modern times. We thus think of Montaigne as our first real essayist. Twenty-seven years later Francis Bacon used the name for the first time in English when he applied it to ten short prose pieces that he had written. This number of his essays was increased to fifty-eight in 1625. From that time almost nothing was done toward developing the essay until the time of Addison and Steele in the first part of the eighteenth century. Their essays, written for the *Tatler* and *Spectator*, were bright, usually humorous, and chatty, and had a much greater influence on later writers than did Bacon's deep, philosophical truths, jotted down in memorandum style. Several other eighteenth century writers tried to write essays, but without much success. It was not until the time of Lamb, Hazlitt, and De Quincey, in the first part of the nineteenth century, that the great period of essay writing began. Since then there have been many essayists. Macaulay, Carlyle, Ruskin, Thackeray, Arnold, Stevenson, Irving, Emerson, Lowell, and Holmes wrote during the last part of the nineteenth century; while Benson, Chesterton, Van Dyke, Crothers, Briggs, Mabie [1] and Miss Repplier are among the best known writers who are handling this type today.

[1] "The De Coverley Papers" are essays of this kind.
[2] "The Autocrat of the Breakfast Table" is full of dialogue.
[3] Hamilton Mabie died on December 31, 1916.

SUGGESTIONS TO STUDENTS

1. Read the essay, in each case, through in order to get the author's viewpoint and thought.

2. Just as in the lyric poems, some of these essays will need to be carefully studied to get the thought. Others, that are easier to understand, may be talked over informally and enjoyed. Imagine that the author is sitting in your midst. Note his personality and get acquainted with him. Do you think you would like to have him for a friend? What have you learned about him from this essay? 3. What seemed to be the author's purpose in writing this essay? What is its central thought? 4. Was the essay light, humorous, chatty, fanciful, or full of deep thought? 5. Was the subject drawn from biography, history, personal life, travel, nature, or did it seem to have some other source? 6. Did it have the three important characteristics of an essay?

7. Did it have a regular, logical paragraph development, or were the thoughts arranged in a sort of cluster? 8. Can you classify this essay? 9. Did you enjoy it?

Some Examples of Essays.—

FRANCIS BACON (1561–1626)

OF REVENGE

Revenge is a kind of wild justice, which the more man's nature runs to, the more ought law to weed it out. For, as for the first wrong, it doth but offend the law; but the revenge of that wrong putteth the law out of office. Certainly, in taking revenge a man is but even with his enemy; but in passing it over, he is superior: for it is a prince's part to pardon. And Solomon, I am sure, saith, "It is the glory of a man to pass by an offence." That which is past is gone and irrevocable, and wise men have enough to do with things present and to come: therefore they do but trifle with themselves that labor in past matters. There is no man doth a wrong for the wrong's sake; but thereby to purchase himself profit, or pleasure, or honor, or the like. Therefore why should I be angry with a man for loving himself better than me? And if any man should do wrong, merely out of ill-nature, why, yet it is but like the thorn or briar, which prick and scratch, because they can do no other. The most tolerable sort of revenge is for those wrongs which there is no law to remedy: but then let a man take heed the revenge be such as there is no law to punish; else a man's enemy is still beforehand, and it is two for one. Some, when they take revenge, are desirous the party should know whence it cometh: this is the more generous. For the delight seemeth to be not so much in doing the hurt, as in making the party repent: but base and crafty cowards are like the arrow that flieth in the dark. Cosmus, Duke of

Florence,[1] had a desperate [2] saying against perfidious or neglecting friends, as if those wrongs were unpardonable. "You shall read," saith he, "that we are commanded to forgive our enemies; but you never read, that we are commanded to forgive our friends." But yet the spirit of Job was in a better tune: "Shall we," saith he, "take good at God's hands, and not be content to take evil also?" And so of friends in a proportion. This is certain, that a man that studieth revenge, keeps his own wounds green,[3] which otherwise would heal and do well. Public revenges are for the most part fortunate: as that for the death of Cæsar; [4] for the death of Pertinax; [5] for the death of Henry the Third of France; [6] and many more. But in private revenges it is not so; nay, rather, vindictive persons live the life of witches; [7] who as they are mischievous, so end they unfortunate.

OF RICHES

I cannot call riches better than the baggage of virtue. The Roman word is better, "impedimenta." [1] For as the baggage is to an army, so is riches to virtue. It cannot be spared, nor left behind, but it hindereth the march; yea, and the care of it sometimes loseth or disturbeth the victory. Of great riches there is no real use, except it be in the distribution; the rest is but conceit.[2] So saith Solomon, "Where much is, there are many to consume it; and what hath the owner, but the sight of it with his eyes?" [3] The personal fruition [4] in any man cannot reach to feel great riches: there is a custody of them; or a power of dole and donative of them; or a fame of them; but no solid use to the owner. Do you not see what feigned prices are set upon little stones and rarities? And what works of ostentation are undertaken, because there might seem to be some use of great riches? But then you will say, they may be of use to buy men out of dangers or troubles. As Solomon saith, "Riches are as a strong hold in the imagination of the rich man." [5] But this is excellently expressed, that it is in imagination, and not always in fact. For certainly great riches have sold more men than they have bought out.

Seek not proud riches, but such as thou mayest get justly, use soberly, distribute cheerfully, and leave contentedly. Yet have no abstract nor friarly contempt of them: but distinguish, as Cicero saith well of Rabirius Posthumus; [6] "in studio rei amplificandæ apparebat, non avaritiæ prædam, sed instrumentum bonitati quæri." [7] Hearken also to Solomon and beware of hasty gathering of riches: "Qui festinat ad divitias, non erit insons." [8] The poets feign, that when Plutus,[9] which is riches, is sent from Jupiter,[10] he limps, and goes slowly; but when he is sent from Pluto,[11] he runs, and is swift of foot: meaning, that riches gotten by good means and just labor, pace slowly; but when they come by the death of others, as by the course of inheritance, testaments, and the like, they come tumbling upon a man. But it might be applied likewise to Pluto, taking him for the devil. For when riches come from the devil, as by fraud, and oppression, and unjust means, they come upon speed. The ways to enrich are many, and most of them foul. Parsimony is one of the best, and yet is not innocent: for it withholdeth men from works of liberality and charity. The improvement of the ground is the most natural obtaining of riches; for it is our great mother's blessing, the earth's; but it is slow. And yet, where men of great wealth do stoop to husbandry, it multiplieth riches exceedingly. I knew a nobleman in England that had the greatest audits [12] of any man in my time: a great grazier, a great sheep-master, a great timber-man, a great collier, a great corn-master, a great lead-man; and so of iron, and a number of the like points of husbandry: so as the earth seemed a sea to him, in respect of the perpetual importation. It was truly observed by one, that himself came very hardly to a little riches, and very easily to great riches. For when a man's stock is come to that, that he can expect [13] the prime of markets, and overcome [14] those bargains which for their greatness are few men's money, and be partner in the industries of younger men, he cannot but increase mainly. The gains of ordinary trades and vocations are honest, and furthered by two things, chiefly by diligence, and by a good name for good and fair dealing. But the gains of bargains are of a more doubtful nature; when men shall wait upon others' necessity, broke [15] by servants and instruments to draw them on, put off others cunningly that would be better chapmen,[16] and the like practices, which are crafty and naught. As for the chopping of bargains,[17] when a man buys, not to hold, but to sell over again, that commonly grindeth double, both upon the seller and upon the buyer. Sharings [18] do greatly enrich, if the hands be well chosen that are trusted. Usury [19] is the certainest means of gain, though one of the worst, as that whereby a man doth eat his bread "in sudore vultus alieni;" [20] and besides, doth plough upon Sundays.[21] But yet certain though it be, it hath flaws; for that the scriveners [22] and brokers [23] do value unsound men,[24] to serve their own turn. The fortune in being the first in an invention or in a privilege, doth cause sometimes a wonderful overgrowth in riches; as it was with the first sugar-man in the Canaries. Therefore, if a man can play the true logician,[25] to have as well judgment as invention, he may do great matters, especially if the times be fit. He that resteth upon gains certain, shall hardly grow to great riches. And he that puts all upon adventures doth oftentimes break, and come to poverty: it is good therefore to guard adventures with certainties that may uphold losses. Monopolies, and co-emption of wares [26] for resale, where they are not restrained, are great means to enrich; especially if the party have intelligence what things are like to come into request, and so store himself beforehand. Riches gotten by service,[27] though it be of the best rise, yet when they are gotten by flattery, feeding humors, and other servile conditions, they may be placed amongst the worst. As for fishing for testaments and executorships, as Tacitus saith of Seneca, "Testamenta et orbos tanquam indagine capi," [28] it is yet worse; by how much men submit themselves to meaner persons than in service. Believe not much them that seem to despise riches; for they despise them that despair of them: and none worse when they come to them. Be not penny-wise; riches have wings, and sometimes they fly away of themselves, sometimes they must be set flying to bring in more. Men leave their riches either to their kindred, or to the public: and moderate portions prosper best in both. A great state left to an heir, is as a lure to all the birds of prey round about to seize on him, if he be not the better stablished in years and judgment. Likewise glorious gifts and foundations are like sacrifices without salt; and but the painted sepulchres of alms, which soon will putrefy and corrupt inwardly. Therefore measure not thine advancements by quantity, but frame them by measure: and defer not charities till death: for certainly, if a man weigh it rightly, he that doth so, is rather liberal of another man's than of his own.

OF STUDIES

Studies serve for delight, for ornament, and for ability. Their chief use for delight, is in privateness [1] and retiring; for ornament, is in discourse; and for ability, is in the judgment and disposition of business. For expert [2] men can execute, and perhaps judge of particulars, one by one; but the general counsels, and the plots and marshalling of affairs, come best from those that are learned. To spend too much time in studies, is sloth: to use them too much for ornament, is affectation; to make judgment wholly by their rules, is the humor of a scholar. They perfect nature, and are perfected by experience: for natural abilities are like natural plants, that need pruning by study; and studies themselves do give forth directions too much at large, except they be bounded in by experience. Crafty men contemn studies; simple men admire them; and wise men use them: for they teach not their own use: but that is a wisdom without[3] them, and above them, won by observation. Read not to contradict and confute; nor to believe and take for granted; nor to find talk and discourse; but to weigh and consider. Some books are to be tasted, others to be swallowed, and some few to be chewed and digested; that is, some books are to be read only in parts; others to be read but not curiously; [4] and some few to be read wholly, and with diligence and attention. Some books also may be read by deputy, and extracts made of them by others; but that would be only in the less important arguments, and the meaner sort of books: else distilled [5] books are like common distilled waters, flashy [6] things. Reading maketh a full man; conference [7] a ready man; and writing an exact man. And therefore if a man write little, he had need have a great memory; if he confer little, he had need have a present wit; [8] and if he read little, he had need have much cunning, to seem to know that he doth not. Histories make men wise; poets, witty; the mathematics, subtile; natural philosophy, deep; moral, grave; logic and rhetoric, able to contend. "Abeunt studia in mores." [9] Nay, there is no stond [10] or impediment in the wit, but may be wrought out by fit studies; like as diseases of the body may have appropriate exercises: bowling is good for the stone and reins; [11] shooting for the lungs and breast; gentle walking for the stomach; riding for the head; and the like. So if a man's wit be wandering, let him study the mathematics; for in demonstrations, if his wit be called away never so little, he must begin again: if his wit be not apt to distinguish or find differences, let him study the Schoolmen; [12] for they are *cymini sectores:* [13] if he be not apt to beat over matters, and to call up one thing to prove and illustrate another, let him study the lawyers' cases: so every defect of the mind may have a special receipt.

OF GREAT PLACE

Men in Great Place are thrice servants; servants of the Sovereign or State, servants of fame, and servants of business. So as they have no freedom, neither in their persons, nor in their actions, nor in their times. It is a strange desire to seek power and to lose liberty: or to seek power over others and to lose power over a man's self. The rising unto place is laborious; and by pains men come to greater pains: and it is sometimes base; and by indignities men come to dignities. The standing is slippery, and the regress is either a downfall or at least an eclipse, which is a melancholy thing. *Cum non sis qui fueris, non esse cur velis vivere.*[1] Nay, retire men cannot when they would, neither will they when it were reason, but are impatient of privateness, even in age and sickness, which require the shadow; like old townsmen, that will be still sitting at their street door, though thereby they offer age to scorn. Certainly great persons had need to borrow other men's opinions to think themselves happy. For if they judge by their own feeling, they cannot find it; but if they think with themselves what other men think of them, and that other men would fain be as they are, then they are happy as it were by report, when, perhaps, they find the contrary within. For they are the first that find their own griefs, though they be the last that find their own faults. Certainly, men in great fortunes are strangers to themselves, and while they are in the puzzle of business, they have no time to tend their health, either of body or mind. *Illi mors gravis incubat, qui notus nimis omnibus, ignotus moritur sibi.*[2]

In place there is license to do good and evil, whereof the latter is a curse; for in evil, the best condition is not to will, the second not to can.[3] But power to do good is the true and lawful end of aspiring. For good thoughts, though God accept them, yet towards men are little better than good dreams, except they be put in act; and that cannot be without power and place, as the vantage and commanding ground. Merit and good works is the end of man's motion, and conscience of the same is the accomplishment of man's rest. For if a man can be a partaker of God's theatre,[4] he shall likewise be partaker of God's rest. *Et conversus Deus, ut aspiceret opera, quæ fecerunt manus suæ vidii quod omnia essent bona nimis;*[5] and then the Sabbath.

In the discharge of thy place set before thee the best examples; for imitation is a globe of precepts. And after a time set before thee thine own example, and examine thyself strictly whether thou didst not best at first. Neglect not also the examples of those that have carried themselves ill in the same place; not to set off thyself by taxing their memory, but to direct thyself what to avoid. Reform, therefore, without bravery,[6] or scandal of former times and persons: but yet set it down to thyself, as well to create good precedents as to follow them. Reduce things to the first institution, and observe wherein and how they have degenerated: but yet ask counsel of both times; of the ancient time, what is best; and of the latter time, what is fittest. Seek to make thy course regular, that men may know beforehand what they may expect; but be not too positive and peremptory, and express thyself well when thou digressest from thy rule. Preserve the right of thy place, but stir not questions of jurisdiction; and rather assume thy right in silence, and *de facto*,[7] than voice it with claims and challenges. Preserve likewise the rights of inferior places, and think it more honor to direct in chief than to be busy in all. Embrace and invite helps and advices touching the execution of thy place; and do not drive away such as bring thee information, as meddlers, but accept of them in good part.

The vices of authority are chiefly four: delays, corruption, roughness, and facility. For delays: give easy access; keep times appointed; go through with that which is in hand, and interlace not business but of necessity. For corruption: do not only bind thine own hands or thy servants' hands from taking, but bind the hands of suitors also from offering. For integrity used doth the one; but integrity professed, and with a manifest detestation of bribery, doth the other. And avoid not only the fault but the suspicion. Whosoever is found variable and changeth manifestly without manifest cause, giveth suspicion of corruption. Therefore always when thou changest thine opinion or course, profess it plainly, and declare it, together with the reasons that move thee to change, and do not think to steal[8] it. A servant or a favorite, if he be inward, and no other apparent cause of esteem, is commonly thought but a by-way to close corruption. For roughness; it is a needless cause of discontent: severity breedeth fear, but roughness breedeth hate. Even reproofs from authority ought to be grave, and not taunting. As for facility,[9] it is worse than bribery. For bribes come but now and then; but if importunity or idle respects lead a man, he shall never be without. As Solomon saith, *To respect persons it is not good, for such a man will transgress for a piece of bread.*[10]

It is most true that was anciently spoken, *A place showeth the man.* And it showeth some to the better, and some to the worse. *Omnium consensu, capax imperii, nisi imperasset,*[11] said Tacitus of Galba,[12] but of

Vespasian [13] he saith, *Solus imperantium, Vespasianus mutatus in melius.*[14] Though the one was meant of sufficiency, the other of manners and affection. It is an assured sign of a worthy and generous spirit, whom honor amends. For honor is, or should be, the place of virtue: and as in nature things move violently to their place and calmly in their place, so virtue in ambition is violent, in authority settled and calm.

All rising to great place is by a winding stair; and if there be factions, it is good to side a man's self whilst he is in the rising, and to balance himself when he is placed.

Use the memory of thy predecessor fairly and tenderly; for if thou dost not, it is a debt will surely be paid when thou art gone. If thou have colleagues, respect them; and rather call them when they look not for it, than exclude them when they have reason to look to be called. Be not too sensible or too remembering of thy place in conversation and private answers to suitors; but let it rather be said, *When he sits in place he is another man.*

OF FRIENDSHIP

It had been hard for him [1] that spake it, to have put more truth and untruth together in few words, than in that speech, *Whosoever is delighted in solitude, is either a wild beast or a god.* For it is most true, that a natural and secret hatred and aversation towards society, in any man, hath somewhat of the savage beast; but it is most untrue, that it should have any character at all of the divine nature, except it proceed, not out of a pleasure in solitude, but out of a love and desire to sequester a man's self for a higher conversation; such as is found to have been falsely and feignedly in some of the heathen, as Epimenides [2] the Candian, Numa [3] the Roman, Empedocles [4] the Sicilian, and Apollonius [5] of Tyana, and truly and really in divers of the ancient hermits and holy fathers of the Church. But little do men perceive what solitude is, and how far it extendeth. For a crowd is not company, and faces are but a gallery of pictures, and talk but a tinkling cymbal,[6] where there is no love. The Latin adage meeteth with it a little: *Magna civitas, magna solitudo,*[7] because in a great town friends are scattered; so that there is not that fellowship, for the most part, which is in less neighborhoods. But we may go further, and affirm most truly, that it is a mere and miserable solitude to want true friends, without which the world is but a wilderness. And, even in this sense also of solitude, whosoever in the frame of his nature and affections is unfit for friendship, he taketh it of the beast, and not from humanity.

A principal fruit of friendship is the ease and discharge of the fulness and swellings of the heart, which passions of all kinds do cause and induce. We know diseases of stoppings and suffocations are the most dangerous in the body; and it is not much otherwise in the mind. You may take sarza to open the liver, steel to open the spleen, flower of sulphur for the lungs, castoreum for the brain; but no receipt openeth the heart but a true friend; to whom you may impart griefs, joys, fears, hopes, suspicions, counsels, and whatsoever lieth upon the heart to oppress it, in a kind of civil shrift or confession.

It is a strange thing to observe how high a rate great kings and monarchs do set upon this fruit of friendship whereof we speak, so great as they purchase it many times at the hazard of their own safety and greatness. For princes, in regard of the distance of their fortune from that of their subjects and servants, cannot gather this fruit, except (to make themselves capable thereof) they raise some persons to be as it were companions, and almost equals to themselves, which many times sorteth to [8] inconvenience. The modern languages give unto such persons the name of favorites, or privadoes; as if it were matter of grace or conversation. But the Roman name attaineth the true use and cause thereof, naming them *Participes curarum;* [9] for it is that which tieth the knot. And we see plainly that this hath been done, not by weak and passionate princes only, but by the wisest and most politic that ever reigned: who have oftentimes joined to themselves some of their servants, whom both themselves have called friends, and allowed others likewise to call them in the same manner, using the word which is received between private men.

L. Sylla,[10] when he commanded Rome, raised Pompey, after surnamed the Great, to that height that Pompey vaunted himself for Sylla's overmatch. For when he had carried the consulship for a friend of his, against the pursuit of Sylla, and that Sylla did a little resent thereat, and began to speak great, Pompey turned upon him again, and in effect bade him be quiet; *for that more men adored the sun rising than the sun setting.* With Julius Cæsar, Decimus Brutus had obtained that interest, as he set him down in his testament for heir in remainder after his nephew. And this was the man that had power with him to draw him forth to his death. For when Cæsar would have discharged the senate, in regard of some ill presages, and especially a dream of Calphurnia, this man lifted him gently by the arm out of his chair, telling him he hoped he would not dismiss the senate till his wife had dreamed a better dream. And it seemeth his favor was so great, as Antonius, in a letter, which is recited verbatim in one of Cicero's Philippics, called him *venefica, witch,* as if he had enchanted Cæsar. Augustus raised Agrippa,[11] though of mean birth, to that height, as, when he consulted with Mæcenas [12] about the marriage of his daughter Julia, Mæcenas took the liberty to tell him, that *he must either marry his daughter to Agrippa, or take away his life: there was no third way, he had made him so great.* With Tiberius Cæsar, Sejanus [13] had ascended to that height, as they two were termed and reckoned as a pair of friends. Tiberius, in a letter to him, saith, *Hæc pro amicitia nostra non occultavi;* [14] and the whole senate dedicated an altar to Friendship, as to a goddess, in respect of the great dearness of friendship between them two. The like, or more, was between Septimius Severus [15] and Plautianus. For he forced his eldest son to marry the daughter of Plautianus, and would often maintain Plautianus in doing affronts to his son; and did write also, in a letter to the senate, by these words: *I love the man so well, as I wish he may over-live me.* Now, if these princes had been as a Trajan, or a Marcus Aurelius,[16] a man might have thought that this had proceeded of an abundant goodness of nature; but being men so wise, of such strength and severity of mind, and so extreme lovers of themselves, as all these were, it proveth, most plainly, that they found their own felicity, though as great as ever happened to mortal men, but as a half piece, except they might have a friend to make it entire. And yet, which is more, they were princes that had wives, sons, nephews; and yet all these could not supply the comfort of friendship.

It is not to be forgotten what Comineus [17] observeth of his first master, Duke Charles the Hardy, namely, that he would communicate his secrets with none; and, least of all, those secrets which troubled him most. Whereupon he goeth on, and saith that towards his later time *that closeness did impair and a little perish his understanding.* Surely Comineus mought have made the same judgment also, if it had pleased him, of his second master, Louis XI., whose closeness was indeed his tormentor. The parable of Pythagoras [18] is dark, but true, *Cor ne edito:* Eat not the heart. Certainly, if a man would give it a hard phrase, those that want friends to open themselves unto are cannibals of their own hearts. But one thing is most admirable (wherewith I will conclude this first fruit of friendship), which is, that this communicating of a man's self to his friend, works two contrary effects: for it redoubleth joys, and cutteth griefs in halfs. For there is no man that imparteth his joys to his friend, but he joyeth the more; and no man that imparteth his griefs to his friend, but he grieveth the less. So that it is, in truth, of operation upon a man's mind of like virtue as the alchemists use to attribute to their stone for man's body, that it worketh all contrary effects, but still to the good and benefit of nature; but yet, without praying in aid of alchemists, there is a manifest image of this in the ordinary course of nature. For in bodies, union strengtheneth and cherisheth any natural action, and, on the other side, weakenth and dulleth any violent impression: and even so is it of minds.

The second fruit of friendship is healthful and sovereign for the understanding, as the first is for the affections. For friendship maketh indeed a fair day in the affections from storm and tempests; but it maketh daylight in the understanding, out of darkness and confusion of thoughts; neither is this to be understood only of faithful counsel, which a man receiveth from his friend; but before you come to that, certain it is, that whosoever hath his mind fraught with many thoughts, his wits and understanding do clarify and break up, in the communicating and discoursing with another: he tosseth his thoughts more easily; he marshalleth them more orderly; he seeth how they look when they are turned into words; finally, he waxeth wiser than himself: and that more by an hour's discourse than by a day's meditation. It was well said by Themistocles [19] to the king of Persia, that *speech was like cloth of Arras*,[20] *opened and put abroad, whereby the imagery doth appear in figure; whereas in thoughts they lie but as in packs*. Neither is this second fruit of friendship, in opening the understanding, restrained only to such friends as are able to give a man counsel. They indeed are best; but, even without that, a man learneth of himself, and bringeth his own thoughts to light, and whetteth his wits as against a stone, which itself cuts not. In a word, a man were better relate himself to a statua or picture, than to suffer his thoughts to pass in smother.

Add now, to make this second fruit of friendship complete, that other point which lieth more open, and falleth within vulgar observation; which is faithful counsel from a friend. Heraclitus [21] saith well, in one of his enigmas. *Dry light is ever the best*. And certain it is, that the light a man receiveth by counsel from another is drier and purer than that which cometh from his own understanding and judgment; which is ever infused and drenched in his affections and customs. So as there is as much difference between the counsel that a friend giveth, and that a man giveth himself, as there is between the counsel of a friend and of a flatterer; for there is no such flatterer as is a man's self, and there is no such remedy against flattery of a man's self as the liberty of a friend. Counsel is of two sorts; the one concerning manners, the other concerning business. For the first, the best preservative to keep the mind in health is the faithful admonition of a friend. The calling of a man's self to a strict account is a medicine sometimes too piercing and corrosive. Reading good books of morality is a little flat and dead; observing our faults in others is sometimes unproper for our case; but the best receipt (best, I say, to work, and best to take) is the admonition of a friend.

It is a strange thing to behold what gross errors and extreme absurdities many (especially of the greater sort) do commit, for want of a friend to tell them of them; to the great damage both of their fame and fortune. For, as St. James saith, they are as men, *that look sometimes into a glass, and presently forget their own shape and favor*.[22] As for business, a man may think if he will, that two eyes see no more than one; or that a gamester seeth always more than a looker-on; or that a man in anger is as wise as he that hath said over the four and-twenty letters; or that a musket may be shot off as well upon the arm as upon a rest; and such other fond and high imaginations, to think himself all in all. But when all is done, the help of good counsel is that which setteth business straight. And if any man think that he will take counsel, but it shall be by pieces; asking counsel in one business of one man, and in another business of another man; it is well (that is to say, better, perhaps, than if he asked none at all), but he runneth two dangers. One, that he shall not be faithfully counselled: for it is a rare thing, except it be from a perfect and entire friend, to have counsel given, but such as shall be bowed and crooked to some ends which he hath that giveth it. The other, that he shall have counsel given, hurtful and unsafe (though with good meaning), and mixed partly of mischief and partly of remedy. Even as if you would call a physician, that is thought good for the cure of the disease you complain of but is unacquainted with your body, and therefore, may put you in a way for present cure, but overthroweth your health in some other kind, and so cure the disease, and kill the patient. But a friend, that is wholly acquainted with a man's estate, will beware, by furthering any present business, how he dasheth upon other inconvenience. And, therefore, rest not upon scattered counsels, for they will rather distract and mislead than settle and direct.

After these two noble fruits of friendship (peace in the affections, and support of the judgment), followeth the last fruit, which is, like the pomegranate, full of many kernels: I mean, aid and bearing a part in all actions and occasions. Here, the best way to represent to life the manifold use of friendship, is to cast and see how many things there are which a man cannot do himself; and then it will appear that it was a sparing speech of the ancients, to say, that *a friend is another himself;* for that a friend is far more than himself. Men have their time, and die many times in desire of some things which they principally take to heart; the bestowing [23] of a child, the finishing of a work, or the like. If a man have a true friend, he may rest almost secure that the care of those things will continue after him. So that a man hath, as it were, two lives in his desires. A man hath a body, and that body is confined to a place; but where friendship is, all offices of life are, as it were, granted to him and his deputy. For he may exercise them by his friend. How many things are there which a man cannot, with any face or comeliness, say or do himself! A man can scarce allege his own merits with modesty, much less extol them; a man cannot sometimes stoop to supplicate or beg; and a number of the like; but all these things are graceful in a friend's mouth, which are blushing in a man's own. So, again, a man's person hath many proper relations which he cannot put off. A man cannot speak to his son but as a father; to his wife but as a husband; to his enemy but upon terms: whereas a friend may speak as the case requires, and not as it sorteth with the person. But to enumerate these things were endless: I have given the rule: where a man cannot fitly play his own part, if he have not a friend, he may quit the stage.

"OF REVENGE"

1 Cosmo de Medici (1519–1574), famed as a patron of literature and art.
2 Desperate—extremely severe.
3 Green—fresh, open.
4 The conspirators who assassinated Cæsar, B. C. 44, all met violent deaths.
5 Pertinax, a Roman emperor, was put to death by the prætorian guards. The legions on the frontiers heard of it, marched to Rome, and put their leader,

Septimius Severus, on the throne. The prætorians were disbanded and banished from Rome.

6 The assassin of Henry III was killed at once by the royal guards.

7 Witches were supposed to come wholly under the power of Satan when they died.

"OF RICHES"

1 Hindrances or impediments. The baggage of an army.

2 Imagination.

3 *Ecclesiastes* v. 11.

4 Enjoyment.

5 *Proverbs* x. 15.

6 Rabirius Posthumus, a Roman knight whom the senate accused of having lent large amounts of money to the King of Egypt. Cicero defended him and he was acquitted.

7 "In studio rei," etc. "In his desire to increase his riches, it was evident that he sought not the gratification of avarice but the means of doing good."

8 *Proverbs* xxviii. 20. "He that maketh haste to be rich, shall not be innocent."

9 Plutus, the god of riches.

10 Jupiter, the king of gods and men.

11 Pluto, the god of the lower world.

12 Audits, rent rolls.

13 Expect, wait for.

14 Overcome, take advantage of.

15 Broke by, make use of an agent to draw a man on.

16 Chapmen, merchants, buyers.

17 Buying up large quantities of a commodity in order to raise the price, a "corner."

18 Sharings, partnerships.

19 Usury, interest.

20 "In sudore," etc. "In the sweat of another's brow."

21 Plow on Sundays.—Receiving interest money on Sundays as well as week days.

22 Scrivener, one who draws up business papers.

23 Brokers, agents.

24 Unsound financially.

25 Skilled in logic; one who exercises judgment.

26 Co-emption of wares, the purchase of the whole quantity of a commodity.

27 Public service.

28 "Wills and childless parents, taken as with a net."

"OF STUDIES"

This is called Bacon's best essay.

1 In privacy, solitude.

2 Expert, experienced.

3 Outside of them.

4 Not carefully.

5 Distilled—book reviews or reports.

6 Insipid.

7 Conversation.

8 Quick wit.

9 "Abeunt studia," etc. "Studies pass into habits."

10 Stond—stoppage, obstacle.

11 Kidneys.

12 The Schoolmen, philosophers of the Middle Ages.

13 "Cymini sectores," splitters of cummin seed; splitters of hairs.

"OF GREAT PLACE"

1 "Cum non sis," etc. "Since you are not what you were, there is no reason why you should wish to live."

2 "Illi mors gravis," etc. "Death presses heavily upon him who, too well known to all others, dies unknown to himself."

3 To be able.

4 God's work.

5 "Et conversus Deus," etc. "And God turned to behold the works that his hands had made, and saw that all was very good."—Gen. I. 31.

6 Bravado, boasting.

7 De facto, as though unchallenged, in fact, actually.

8 To hide the fact.

9 Facility—yielding easily, pliabilty.

10 *Proverbs* xxviii. 21.

11 "Omnium consensu," etc. "Had he never been emperor, universal opinion would have held him fit to rule."

12 Galba's career before becoming emperor of Rome was of such a nature that he would always have been thought fit to be an emperor, if he had never reigned. He gave himself up to be ruled by favorites, and was deposed and killed by the prætorians.

13 Vespasian, the only Roman emperor who was made better by the office.

14 "Solus imperantium," etc. "Alone of all the emperors, Vespasian was changed for the better."

"OF FRIENDSHIP"

1 Him—Aristotle in his "Politica."

2 Epimenides, a poet of Crete. According to the story, he fell asleep in a cave and slept for fifty-seven years.

3 Numa, the second king of Rome. He is said to have been helped by the nymph Egeria to devise wise laws for Rome.

4 Empedocles, a Sicilian philosopher who is said to have thrown himself into the crater of Mt. Etna so that he would so completely disappear from the earth that he would be regarded as a god. An eruption of the volcano, however, threw up one of his sandals and so his disappearance was explained.

5 Apollonius was a magician. He pretended to perform miracles.

6 See *I Corinthians* XIII. 1.

7 "Magna civitas," etc. "A great city is a great solitude."

8 Sorteth to,—results in.

9 "Participes curarum,"—sharers of cares.

10 L. Sylla—Sulla, dictator of Rome, B. C. 82–79.

11 Agrippa, a Roman general under Augustus.

12 Mæcenas, the chief favorite of Augustus. He was a friend and patron of Virgil.

13 Sejanus, chief minister of Tiberius and commander of the prætorian guard. He became so infamous and disloyal that Tiberius finally had him put to death.

14 "Haec pro amicitia," etc. "These things, because of our friendship, I have not kept secret from you."

15 Septimius Severus, a Roman emperor (A. D. 193–211).

16 Trajan and Marcus Aurelius were known as good emperors of Rome.

17 Comineus—Philip de Comines, a French historian under Charles the

Bold of Burgundy, and, later, Louis XI of France. Charles and Louis were bitter enemies.

[18] Pythagoras, a Greek philosopher (B. C. 540–510).

[19] Themistocles, the Greek statesman who created the naval greatness of Athens. In the last part of his life he was ostracized and took refuge in Persia. Here the Persian king Artaxerxes made him governor of Magnesia in Asia Minor.

[20] The great tapestry industry at Arras, France, was not built up until during the Middle Ages. Themistocles, who died about 460 B. C., could have known nothing about it. What he said was, "A man's discourse is like a rich Persian carpet."

[21] Heraclitus, a Greek philosopher. His outlook on life was so severe and gloomy that he was called the weeping philosopher.

[22] *James* i. 23.

[23] Bestowing—providing for.

JOSEPH ADDISON (1672–1719)

REFLECTIONS IN WESTMINSTER ABBEY

When I am in a serious humor, I very often walk by myself in Westminster Abbey; where the gloominess of the place and the use to which it is applied, with the solemnity of the building and the condition of the people who lie in it, are apt to fill the mind with a kind of melancholy, or rather thoughtfulness, that is not disagreeable. I yesterday passed a whole afternoon in the churchyard, the cloisters, and the church, amusing myself with the tombstones and inscriptions that I met with in those several regions of the dead. Most of them recorded nothing else of the buried person but that he was born upon one day and died upon another; the whole history of his life being comprehended in those two circumstances that are common to all mankind. I could not but look upon these registers of existence, whether of brass or marble, as a kind of satire upon the departed persons who had left no other memorial of them but that they were born and that they died. They put me in mind of several persons mentioned in the battles of heroic poems, who have sounding names given them for no other reason but that they may be killed, and are celebrated for nothing but being knocked on the head. The life of these men is finely described in Holy Writ by "the Path of an Arrow," which is immediately closed up and lost.

Upon my going into the church, I entertained myself with the digging of a grave; and saw in every shovelful of it that was thrown up the fragment of a bone or skull intermixed with a kind of fresh mouldering earth that some time or other had a place in the composition of a human body. Upon this, I began to consider with myself what innumerable multitudes of people lay confused together under the pavement of that ancient cathedral; how men and women, friends and enemies, priests and soldiers, monks and prebendaries,[1] were crumbled amongst one another and blended together in the same common mass; how beauty,

POETS' CORNER, WESTMINSTER ABBEY

strength, and youth, with old age, weakness, and deformity, lay undistinguished in the same promiscuous heap of matter.

After having thus surveyed this great magazine of mortality, as it were, in the lump, I examined it more particularly by the accounts which I found on several of the monuments which are raised in every quarter of that ancient fabric. Some of them were covered with such extravagant epitaphs that, if it were possible for the dead person to be acquainted with them, he would blush at the praises which his friends have bestowed upon him. There are others so excessively modest, that they deliver the character of the person departed in Greek or Hebrew, and by that means are not understood once in a twelvemonth. In the poetical quarter, I found there were poets who had no monuments, and monuments which had no poets. I observed indeed that the present war [2] had filled the church with many of these uninhabited monuments, which had been erected to the memory of persons whose bodies were perhaps buried in the plains of Blenheim,[3] or in the bosom of the ocean.

I could not but be very much delighted with several modern epitaphs, which are written with great elegance of expression and justness of thought, and therefore do honor to the living as well as to the dead. As a foreigner is very apt to conceive an idea of the ignorance or politeness of a nation from the turn of their public monuments and inscriptions, they should be submitted to the perusal of men of learning and genius before they are put in execution. Sir Cloudesley Shovel's [4] monument has very often given me great offence. Instead of the brave rough English admiral, which was the distinguishing character of that plain gallant man, he is represented on his tomb by the figure of a beau, dressed in a long periwig,[5] and reposing himself upon velvet cushions under a canopy of state. The inscription is answerable to the monument; for instead of celebrating the many remarkable actions he had performed in the service of his country, it acquaints us only with the manner of his death, in which it was impossible for him to reap any honor. The Dutch, whom we are apt to despise for want of genius, show an infinitely greater taste of antiquity and politeness in their buildings and works of this nature, than what we meet with in those of our own country. The monuments of their admirals, which have been erected at the public expense, represent them like themselves; and are adorned with rostral crowns and naval ornaments, with beautiful festoons of sea weed, shells, and coral.

But to return to our subject. I have left the repository of our English kings for the contemplation of another day, when I shall find my mind disposed for so serious an amusement. I know that entertainments of this nature are apt to raise dark and dismal thoughts in timorous minds and gloomy imaginations; but for my own part, though I am always serious, I do not know what it is to be melancholy, and can therefore take a view of nature in her deep and solemn scenes, with the same pleasure as in her most gay and delightful ones. By this means I can improve myself with those objects which others consider with terror. When I look upon the tombs of the great, every emotion of envy dies in me; when I read the epitaphs of the beautiful, every inordinate desire goes out; when I meet with the grief of parents upon a tombstone, my heart melts with compassion; when I see the tomb of the parents themselves, I consider the vanity of grieving for those whom we must quickly follow. When I see kings lying by those who deposed them, when I consider rival wits placed side by side, or the holy men that divided the world with their contests and disputes, I reflect with sorrow and astonishment on the little competitions, factions, and debates of mankind. When I read the several dates of the tombs, of some that died yesterday, and some six hundred years ago, I consider that great day when we shall all of us be contemporaries, and make our appearance together.

"REFLECTIONS ON WESTMINSTER ABBEY"

1 Prebendaries. Clergymen who received regular pay in consideration of their officiating at stated times in a collegiate or cathedral church. Prebend —a regular allowance.

2 The present war was the War of the Spanish Succession.

3 Blenheim. A village in Bavaria where the great English general, Marlborough, and his ally, Prince Eugene of Savoy, won a victory over the French, 1704.

4 Sir Cloudsley Shovel. An English admiral, drowned in 1707 when his fleet was wrecked off the Scilly Islands.

5 Periwig. A headdress of false hair; a long wig.

CHARLES LAMB (1775–1834)

DREAM CHILDREN

Children love to listen to stories about their elders, when *they* were children; to stretch their imagination to the conception of a traditionary great-uncle or grandame, whom they never saw. It was in this spirit that my little ones crept about me the other evening to hear about their great-grandmother Field, who lived in a great house in Norfolk (a hundred times bigger than that in which they and papa lived) which had been the scene—so at least it was generally believed in that part of the country —of the tragic incidents which they had lately become familiar with from the ballad of the Children in the Wood. Certain it is that the whole story of the children and their cruel uncle was to be seen fairly carved out in wood upon the chimney-piece of the great hall, the whole story down to the Robin Redbreasts, till a foolish rich person pulled it down to set up a marble one of modern invention in its stead, with no story upon it. Here Alice put out one of her dear mother's looks, too tender to be called upbraiding. Then I went on to say, how religious and how good their great-grandmother Field was, how beloved and respected by everybody, though she was not indeed the mistress of this great house, but had only the charge of it (and yet in some respects she might be said to be the mistress of it too) committed to her by the owner, who preferred living in a newer and more fashionable mansion which he had purchased somewhere in the adjoining county, but still she lived in it in a manner as if it had been her own, and kept up the dignity of the great house in a sort while she lived; which afterwards came to decay, and was nearly pulled down, and all its old ornaments stripped and carried away to the owner's other house, where they were set up, and looked as awkward as if someone were to carry away the old tombs they had seen lately at the Abbey, and stick them up in Lady C's tawdry gilt drawing-room. Here John smiled, as much as to say, "that would be foolish indeed." And then I told how, when she came to die, her funeral was attended by a concourse of all the poor, and some of the gentry too, of the neighborhood for many miles round, to show their respect for her memory, because she had been such a good and religious woman; so good indeed that she knew all the Psaltery by heart, ay, and a great part of the Testament besides. Here little Alice spread her hands. Then I told what a tall, upright, graceful person their great-grandmother Field once was; and how in her youth she was esteemed the best dancer—here Alice's little right foot played an involuntary movement, till upon my looking grave, it desisted—the best dancer, I was saying, in the county, till a cruel disease, called a cancer, came, and bowed her down with pain; but it could never bend her good spirits, or make them stoop, but they were still upright, because she was so good and religious. Then I told how she was used to sleep by herself in a lone chamber of the great lone house; and how she believed that an apparition of two infants was to be seen at midnight gliding up and down the great staircase near where she slept, but she said "those innocents would do her no harm," and how frightened I used to be, though in those days I had my maid to sleep with me, because I was never half so good or religious as she— and yet I never saw the infants. Here John expanded all his eyebrows and tried to look courageous. Then I told how good she was to all her grand-children, having us to the great house in the holydays, where I in particular used to spend many hours by myself, in gazing upon the old busts of the Twelve Cæsars, that had been Emperors of Rome, till the old marble heads would seem to live again, or I to be turned into marble with them; how I never could be tired with roaming about that huge mansion, with its vast empty rooms, with their worn-out hangings, fluttering tapestry, and carved oaken panels, with the gilding almost rubbed out—sometimes in the spacious old-fashioned gardens, which I had almost to myself, unless when now and then a solitary gardening man would cross me—and how the nectarines and peaches hung upon the walls, without my ever offering to pluck them, because they were forbidden fruit, unless now and then—and because I had more pleasure in strolling about among the old melancholy-looking yew trees, or the firs, and picking up the red berries, and the fir apples, which were good for nothing but to look at—or in lying about upon the fresh grass, with all the fine garden smells around me—or basking in the orangery, till I could almost fancy myself ripening too along with the oranges and the limes in that grateful warmth—or in watching the dace that darted to and fro in the fishpond, at the bottom of the garden, and here and there a great sulky pike hanging midway down the water in silent state, as if it mocked at their impertinent friskings—I had more pleasure in these busy-idle diversions than in all the sweet flavors of peaches, nectarines, oranges, and such like common baits of children. Here John slily deposited back upon the plate a bunch of grapes, which, not unobserved by Alice, he had meditated dividing with her, and both seemed willing to relinquish them for the present as irrelevant. Then, in somewhat a more heightened tone, I told how, though their great-grandmother Field loved all her grand-children, yet in an especial manner she might be said to love their uncle John L——, because he was so handsome and spirited a youth, and a king to the rest of us; and, instead of moping about in solitary corners, like some of us, he would mount the most mettlesome horse he could get, when but an imp no bigger than themselves, and make it carry him half over the county in a morning, and join the hunters when there were any out—and yet he loved the old great house and gardens too, but had too much spirit to be always pent up within their boundaries—and how their uncle grew up to man's estate as brave as he was handsome, to the admiration of everybody, but of their great-grandmother Field most especially; and how he used to carry me upon his back when I was a lame-footed boy—for he was a good bit older than me—many a mile when I could not walk for pain; and how in after life he became lame-footed too, and I did not always (I fear) make allowances enough for him when he was impatient, and in pain, nor remember sufficiently how considerate he had been to me when I was lame-footed; and how when he died, though he had not been dead an hour, it seemed as if he had died a great while ago, such a distance there is betwixt life and death; and how I bore his death as I thought pretty well at first, but afterward it haunted and haunted me; and though I did not cry or take it to heart as some do, and as I think he would have done if I had died, yet I missed him all day long, and knew not till then how much I had loved him. I missed his kindness, and I missed his crossness, and wished him to be alive again, to be quarreling with him (for we quarreled sometimes), rather than not have him again, and was as uneasy without him, as he their poor uncle must have been when the doctor took off his limb. Here the children fell a-crying, and asked if their little mourning which they had on was not for uncle John, and they looked up, and prayed me not to go on about their uncle, but to tell them some stories about their pretty dead mother. Then I told how for seven long years, in hope sometimes, sometimes in despair, yet persisting ever, I courted the fair Alice W——n; and, as much as children could understand, I explained to them what coyness, and difficulty, and denial meant in maidens—when suddenly, turning to Alice, the soul of the first Alice looked out at her eyes with such a reality of re-presentment, that I became in doubt which of them stood there before me, or whose that bright hair was; and while I stood gazing, both the children gradually grew fainter to my view, receding, and still receding till nothing at last but two mournful features were seen in the uttermost distance, which, without speech, strangely impressed upon me the effects of speech: "We are not of Alice, nor of thee, nor are we children at all. The children of Alice call Bertrum father. We are nothing; less than nothing, and dreams. We are only what might have been, and must wait upon the tedious shores of Lethe millions of ages before we have existence, and a name," and immediately awaking, I found myself quietly seated in my bachelor armchair, where I had fallen asleep, with the faithful Bridget unchanged by my side—but John L. (or James Elia) was gone forever.

"DREAM CHILDREN"

1. This is called the most pathetic of Lamb's essays. It was written only a few weeks after the death of his brother John. John Lamb is called "Cousin James Elia," and Mary, "Cousin Bridget," in the essays.

2. Lamb never married because of the terrible malady in his family. He had loved a girl, Ann Simmons, who later married William Bertrum; and so "the children of Alice [his name for Ann] call Bertrum father." Some things in this essay are imaginary, but a large part of it is based on memory. In "Mackery End in Hertfordshire" the same great house is described where Mary Field, Lamb's grandmother, lived.

3. Notice that Lamb did not paragraph this essay.

JOHN RUSKIN (1819–1900)

PART III OF QUEENS' GARDENS

Thus far, then, of the nature, thus far of the teaching, of woman, and thus of her household office, and queenliness. We come now to our last, our widest question,—What is her queenly office with respect to the state?

Generally, we are under an impression that a man's duties are public, and a woman's private. But this is not altogether so. A man has a personal work or duty, relating to his own home, and a public work or duty, which is the expansion of the other, relating to the state. So a woman has a personal work or duty, relating to her own home, and a public work or duty, which is also the expansion of that.

Now, the man's work for his own home is, as has been said,[1] to secure its maintenance, progress, and defence; the woman's to secure its order, comfort, and loveliness.

Expand both these functions. The man's duty, as a member of a commonwealth, is to assist in the maintenance, in the advance, in the defence of the state. The woman's duty, as a member of the commonwealth, is to assist in the ordering, in the comforting, and in the beautiful adornment of the state.

What the man is at his own gate, defending it, if need be, against insult and spoil, that also, not in a less, but in a more devoted measure, he is to be at the gate of his country, leaving his home, if need be, even to the spoiler, to do his more incumbent work there.

And, in like manner, what the woman is to be within her gates, as the centre of order, the balm of distress, and the mirror of beauty: that she is also to be without her gates, where order is more difficult, distress more imminent, loveliness more rare.

And as within the human heart there is always set an instinct for all real duties,—an instinct which you cannot quench, but only warp and corrupt if you withdraw it from its true purpose:—as there is the intense instinct of love, which, rightly disciplined, maintains all the sanctities of life, and, misdirected, undermines them, and *must* do either the one or the other;—so there is in the human heart an inextinguishable instinct, the love of power, which, rightly directed, maintains all the majesty of law and life, and, misdirected, wrecks them.

Deep rooted in the innermost life of the heart of man, and of the heart of woman, God set it there, and God keeps it there. Vainly, as falsely, you blame or rebuke the desire of power!—For Heaven's sake, and for Man's sake, desire it all you can. But *what* power? That is all the question. Power to destroy? the lion's limb, and the dragon's breath? Not so. Power to heal, to redeem, to guide, and to guard. Power of the sceptre and shield; the power of the royal hand that heals in touching,—that binds the fiend, and looses the captive; the throne that is founded on the rock of Justice, and descended from only by steps of Mercy. Will you not covet such power as this, and seek such throne as this, and be no more housewives, but queens?

It is now long since the women of England arrogated, universally, a title which once belonged to nobility only; and having once been in the habit of accepting the simple title of gentlewoman, as correspondent to that of gentleman, insisted on the privilege of assuming the title of "Lady," * which properly corresponds only to the title of "Lord."

* I wish there were a true order of chivalry instituted for our English youth of certain ranks, in which both boy and girl should receive, at a given age, their knighthood and ladyhood by true title; attainable only by certain probation and trial both of character and accomplishment; and to be forfeited, on conviction, by their peers, of any dishonorable act. Such an institution would be entirely, and with all noble results, possible, in a nation which loved honor. That it would not be possible among us, is not to the discredit of the scheme.—*Ruskin.*

I do not blame them for this; but only for their narrow motive in this. I would have them desire and claim the title of Lady, provided they claim, not merely the title, but the office and duty signified by it. Lady means "bread-giver" or "loaf-giver," and Lord means "maintainer of laws," and both titles have reference, not to the law which is maintained in the house, nor to the bread which is given to the household; but to law maintained for the multitude, and to bread broken among the multitude. So that a Lord has legal claim only to his title in so far as he is the maintainer of the justice of the Lord of Lords; and a Lady has legal claim to her title, only so far as she communicates that help to the poor representatives of her Master, which women once, ministering to Him of their substance, were permitted to extend to that Master Himself,[2] and when she is known, as He Himself once was, in breaking of bread.[3]

And this beneficent and legal dominion, this power of the Dominus, or House-Lord, and of the Domina, or House-Lady, is great and venerable, not in the number of those through whom it has lineally descended, but in the number of those whom it grasps within its sway; it is always regarded with reverent worship wherever its dynasty is founded on its duty, and its ambition correlative with its beneficence. Your fancy is pleased with the thought of being noble ladies, with a train of vassals? Be it so; you cannot be too noble, and your train cannot be too great; but see to it that your train is of vassals whom you serve and feed, not merely of slaves who serve and feed *you;* and that the multitude which obeys you is of those whom you have comforted, not oppressed,—whom you have redeemed, not led into captivity.

And this, which is true of the lower or household dominion, is equally true of the queenly dominion;—that highest dignity is open to you, if you will also accept that highest duty. Rex et Regina—Roi et Reine— *"Right*-doers"; they differ from the Lady and Lord, in that their power is supreme over the mind as over the person—that they not only feed and clothe, but direct and teach. And whether consciously or not, you must be, in many a heart, enthroned: there is no putting by that crown; queens you must always be; queens to your lovers; queens to your husbands and your sons; queens of higher mystery to the world beyond, which bows itself, and will forever bow, before the myrtle crown and the stainless sceptre of womanhood. But, alas! you are too often idle and careless queens, grasping at majesty in the least things, while you abdicate it in the greatest; and leaving misrule and violence to work their will among men, in defiance of the power which, holding straight in gift from the Prince of all Peace,[4] the wicked among you betray, and the good forget.

"Prince of Peace." Note that name. When kings rule in that name, and nobles, and the judges of the earth, they also, in their narrow place, and mortal measure, receive the power of it. There are no other rulers than they: other rule than theirs is but *mis*rule; they who govern verily "Dei gratiâ"[5] are all princes, yes, or princesses, of Peace. There is not a war in the world, no, nor an injustice, but you women are answerable for it; not in that you have provoked, but in that you have not hindered. Men, by their nature, are prone to fight; they will fight for any cause, or for none. It is for you to choose their cause for them, and to forbid them when there is no cause. There is no suffering, no injustice, no misery in the earth, but the guilt of it lies with you. Men can bear the sight of it, but you should not be able to bear it. Men may tread it down without sympathy in their own struggle; but men are feeble in sympathy, and contracted in hope; it is you only who can feel the depths of pain, and conceive the way of its healing. Instead of trying to do this, you turn away from it; you, shut yourselves within your park walls and garden gates; and you are content to know that there is beyond them a whole world in wilderness—a world of secrets which you dare not penetrate, and of suffering which you dare not conceive.

I tell you that this is to me quite the most amazing among the phenomena of humanity. I am surprised at no depths to which, when once warped from its honor, that humanity can be degraded. I do not wonder at the miser's death, with his hands, as they relax, dropping gold. I do not wonder at the sensualist's life, with the shroud wrapped about his feet. I do not wonder at the single-handed murder of a single victim, done by the assassin in the darkness of the railway, or reed-shadow of the marsh. I do not even wonder at the myriad-handed murder of multitudes, done boastfully in the daylight, by the frenzy of nations, and the immeasurable, unimaginable guilt, heaped up from hell to heaven, of their priests and kings. But this is wonderful to me—oh, how wonderful!—to see the tender and delicate woman among you, with her child at her breast, and a power, if she would wield it, over it, and over its father, purer than the air of heaven, and stronger than the seas of earth—nay, a magnitude of blessing which her husband would not part with for all that earth itself, though it were made of one entire and perfect chrysolite,[6]—to see her abdicate this majesty to play at precedence with her next-door neighbor! This is wonderful—oh, wonderful!—to see her, with every innocent feeling fresh within her, go out in the morning into her garden to play with the fringes of its guarded flowers, and lift their heads when they are drooping, with her happy smile upon her face, and no cloud upon her brow, because there is a little wall around her place of peace; and yet she knows, in her heart, if she would only look for its knowledge, that, outside of that little rose-covered wall, the wild-grass, to the horizon, is torn up by the agony of men, and beat level by the drift of their life-blood.

Have you ever considered what a deep under-meaning there lies, or at least may be read, if we choose, in our custom of strewing flowers before those whom we think most happy? Do you suppose it is merely to deceive them into the hope that happiness is always to fall thus in showers at their feet?—that wherever they pass they will tread on herbs of sweet scent, and that the rough ground will be made smooth for them by depth of roses! So surely as they believe that, they will have, instead, to walk on bitter herbs and thorns; and the only softness to their feet will be of snow. But it is not thus intended they should believe; there is a better meaning in that old custom. The path of a good woman is indeed strewn with flowers; but they rise behind her steps, not before them. "Her feet have touched the meadows, and left the daisies rosy."

You think that only a lover's fancy;—false and vain? How if it could be true? You think this also, perhaps, only a poet's fancy—

> "Even the light harebell raised its head
> Elastic from her airy tread."

But it is little to say of a woman, that she only does not destroy where she passes. She should revive; the harebells should bloom, not stoop, as she passes. You think I am rushing into wild hyperbole? Pardon me, not a whit—I mean what I say in calm English, spoken in resolute truth. You have heard it said—(and I believe there is more than fancy even in that saying, but let it pass for a fanciful one)—that flowers only flourish rightly in the garden of some one who loves them. I know you would like that to be true; you would think it a pleasant magic if you could flush your flowers into brighter bloom by a kind look upon them: nay, more, if your look had the power, not only to cheer, but to guard; —if you could bid the black blight turn away, and the knotted caterpillar spare—if you could bid the dew fall upon them in the drought, and say to the south wind, in frost—"Come, thou south, and breathe upon my garden, that the spices of it may flow out." [7] This you would think a great thing? And do you think it not a greater thing, that all this (and how much more than this!) you *can* do, for fairer flowers than these— flowers that could bless you for having blessed them, and will love you for having loved them;—flowers that have thoughts like yours, and lives like yours; and which, once saved, you save forever? Is this only a little power? Far among the moorlands and the rocks,—far in the darkness of the terrible streets,—these feeble florets are lying, with all their fresh leaves torn, and their stems broken—will you never go down to them, nor set them in order in their little fragrant beds, nor fence them, in their trembling, from the fierce wind? Shall morning follow morning, for you, but not for them; and the dawn rise to watch, far away, those frantic Dances of Death; [8] but no dawn rise to breathe upon these living banks of wild violet, and woodbine, and rose; nor call to you, through your casement,—call (not giving you the name of the English poet's lady, [9] but the name of Dante's great Matilda, who on the edge of happy Lethe, [10] stood, wreathing flowers with flowers), saying,—

> "Come into the garden, Maud.
> For the black bat, night, has flown,
> And the woodbine spices are wafted abroad,
> And the musk of the roses blown"? [11]

Will you not go down among them?—among those sweet living things, whose new courage, sprung from the earth with the deep color of heaven upon it, is starting up in strength of goodly spire; and whose purity, washed from the dust, is opening, bud by bud, into the flower of promise; —and still they turn to you and for you, "The Larkspur listens—I hear, I hear! And the Lily whispers—I wait."

Did you notice that I missed two lines when I read you that first stanza; and think that I had forgotten them? Hear them now:—

> "Come into the garden, Maud,
> For the black bat, night, has flown,
> Come into the garden, Maud,
> I am here at the gate alone."

Who is it, think you, who stands at the gate of this sweeter garden, alone, waiting for you? Did you ever hear, not of a Maud, but of a Madeleine, who went down to her garden in the dawn, and found One waiting at the gate, whom she supposed to be the gardener? Have you not sought Him often; sought Him in vain, all through the night; sought Him in vain at the gate of that old garden where the fiery sword is set? He is never there; but at the gate of *this* garden He is waiting always— waiting to take your hand—ready to go down to see the fruits of the valley, to see whether the vine has flourished, and the pomegranate budded. There you shall see with Him the little tendrils of the vines that His hand is guiding—there you shall see the pomegranate springing where His hand cast the sanguine seed;—more: you shall see the troops of the angel keepers that, with their wings, wave away the hungry birds from the pathsides where He has sown, and call to each other between the vine-yard rows, "Take us the foxes, the little foxes that spoil the vines, for our vines have tender grapes." Oh—you queens—you queens! among the hills and happy greenwood of this land of yours, shall the foxes have holes and the birds of the air have nests; and in your cities shall the stones cry out against you, that they are the only pillows where the Son of Man can lay His head?

PART III "OF QUEENS' GARDENS"

From "Sesame and Lilies." This general title is given to two lectures by Ruskin. The first, "Sesame," has as its sub-title, "Of Kings' Treasuries"; the second, "Lilies," has as its sub-title, "Of Queens' Gardens." Parts I and II of "Queens' Gardens" discuss respectively the education of woman and her household office. The part given here treats of woman's office in respect to the state.

This lecture was delivered orally, but when written or printed it belongs to the essay type.

[1] "As has been said"—given in Part II, par. 68.
[2] See *Matthew* xxv. 40.
[3] See *Luke* viii. 2. 3.

4 See *Isaiah* ix. 6.

5 "Dei gratiâ"—by the grace of God. These words appear in the title given to the King of England.

6 "Of one entire and perfect chrysolite." Ruskin is here quoting from Shakespeare's *Othello,* Act. V. Sc. 2, line 145.

7 See *Song of Solomon,* iv. 16.

8 Holbein, the famous Dutch painter, gave the name "Dance of Death" to a series of pictures showing how Death lurks near in all the activities of life.

9 Tennyson's *Maud.* "Matilda" is an equivalent for "Maud."

10 Lethe,—the river of forgetfulness in the lower world.

11 From Tennyson's *Maud.*

ROBERT LOUIS STEVENSON (1850–1894)

ON THE ENJOYMENT OF UNPLEASANT PLACES

It is a difficult matter to make the most of any given place, and we have much in our own power. Things looked at patiently from one side after another generally end by showing a side that is beautiful. A few months ago some words were said in the *Portfolio* as to an "austere regimen in scenery"; and such a discipline was then recommended as "healthful and strengthening to the taste." That is the text, so to speak, of the present essay. This discipline in scenery, it must be understood, is something more than a mere walk before breakfast to whet the appetite. For when we are put down in some unsightly neighborhood, and especially if we have come to be more or less dependent on what we see, we must set ourselves to hunt out beautiful things with all the ardour and patience of a botanist after a rare plant. Day by day we perfect ourselves in the art of seeing nature more favourably. We learn to live with her, as people learn to live with fretful or violent spouses: to dwell lovingly on what is good, and shut our eyes against all that is bleak or inharmonious. We learn, also, to come to each place in the right spirit. The traveller, as Brantôme [1] quaintly tells us, *"fait des discours en soi pour se soutenir en chemin";* [2] and into these discourses he weaves something out of all that he sees and suffers by the way; they take their tone greatly from the varying character of the scene; a sharp ascent brings different thoughts from a level road; and the man's fancies grow lighter as he comes out of the wood into a clearing. Nor does the scenery any more affect the thoughts than the thoughts affect the scenery. We see places through our humours as through differently colored glasses. We are ourselves a term in the equation, a note of the chord, and make discord or harmony almost at will. There is no fear for the result, if we can but surrender ourselves sufficiently to the country that surrounds and follows us, so that we are ever thinking suitable thoughts or telling ourselves some suitable sort of story as we go. We become thus, in some sense, a centre of beauty; we are provocative of beauty, much as a gentle and sincere character is provocative of sincerity and gentleness in others. And even where there is no harmony to be elicited by the quickest and most obedient of spirits, we may still embellish a place with some attraction of romance. We may learn to go far afield for associations, and handle them lightly when we have found them. Sometimes an old print comes to our aid; I have seen many a spot lit up at once with picturesque imaginations, by a reminiscence of Callot,[3] or Sadeler,[4] or Paul Brill.[5] Dick Turpin [6] has been my lay figure for many an English lane. And I suppose the Trossachs [7] would hardly be the Trossachs for most tourists if a man of admirable romantic instinct had not peopled it for them with harmonious figures, and brought them thither their minds rightly prepared for the impression. There is half the battle in this preparation. For instance: I have rarely been able to visit, in the proper spirit, the wild and inhospitable places of our own Highlands. I am happier where it is tame and fertile, and not readily pleased without trees. I understand that there are some phases of mental trouble that harmonise well with such surroundings, and that some persons, by the dispensing power of the imagination, can go back several centuries in spirit, and put themselves into sympathy with the hunted, houseless, unsociable way of life that was in its place upon these savage hills. Now, when I am sad, I like nature to charm me out of my sadness, like David before Saul,[8] and the thought of these past ages strikes nothing in me but an unpleasant pity; so that I can never hit on the right humour for this sort of landscape, and lose much pleasure in consequence. Still, even here, if I were only let alone, and time enough were given, I should have all manner of pleasure, and take many clear and beautiful images away with me when I left. When we cannot think ourselves into sympathy with the great features of a country, we learn to ignore them, and put our head among the grass for flowers, or pore, for long times together, over the changeful current of a stream. We come down to the sermon in stone,[9] when we are shut out from any poem in the spread landscape. We begin to peep and botanise, we take an interest in birds and insects, we find many things beautiful in miniature. The reader will recollect the little summer scene in *Wuthering Heights* [10]—the one warm scene, perhaps, in all that powerful, miserable novel—and the great feature that is made therein by grasses and flowers and a little sunshine: this is in the spirit of which I now speak. And, lastly, we can go indoors; interiors are sometimes as beautiful, often more picturesque, than the shows of the open air, and they have that quality of shelter of which I shall presently have more to say.

With all this in mind, I have often been tempted to put forth the paradox that any place is good enough to live a life in, while it is only in a few, and those highly favoured, that we can pass a few hours agreeably. For, if we only stay long enough, we become at home in the neighbourhood. Reminiscences spring up, like flowers, about uninteresting corners. We forget to some degree the superior loveliness of other places, and fall

into a tolerant and sympathetic spirit which is its own reward and jus-
tification. Looking back the other day on some recollections of my own,
I was astonished to find how much I owed to such a residence; six weeks
in one unpleasant country-side had done more, it seemed, to quicken
and educate my sensibilities than many years in places that jumped more
nearly with my inclination.

The country to which I refer was a level and treeless plateau, over
which the winds cut like a whip. For miles on miles it was the same. A
river, indeed, fell into the sea near the town where I resided; but the
valley of the river was shallow and bald, for as far up as ever I had the
heart to follow it. There were roads, certainly, but roads that had no
beauty or interest; for, as there was no timber, and but little irregularity
of surface, you saw your whole walk exposed to you from the beginning:
there was nothing left to fancy, nothing to expect, nothing to see by the
wayside, save here and there an unhomely-looking homestead, and here
and there a solitary, spectacled stone-breaker; and you were only accompanied, as you went doggedly forward, by the gaunt telegraph-posts and
the hum of the resonant wires in the keen sea-wind. To one who has
learned to know their song in warm pleasant places by the Mediterranean,
it seemed to taunt the country, and make it still bleaker by suggested contrast. Even the waste places by the side of the road were not, as
Hawthorne liked to put it, "taken back to Nature" by any decent
covering of vegetation. Wherever the land had the chance, it seemed
to lie fallow. There is a certain tawny nudity of the South, bare
sunburnt plains, coloured like a lion, and hills clothed only in the blue
transparent air; but this was of another description—this was the naked-
ness of the North; the earth seemed to know that it was naked, and was
ashamed and cold.

It seemed to be always blowing on that coast. Indeed, this had passed
into the speech of the inhabitants, and they saluted each other when they
met with "Breezy, breezy," instead of the customary "Fine day" of
farther south. These continual winds were not like the harvest breeze, that
just keeps an equable pressure against your face as you walk, and serves
to set all the trees talking over your head, or bring round you the smell of
the wet surface of the country after a shower. They were of the bitter,
hard, persistent sort, that interferes with sight and respiration, and makes
the eyes sore. Even such winds as these have their own merit in proper
time and place. It is pleasant to see them brandish great masses of
shadow. And what a power they have over the colour of the world!
How they ruffle the solid woodlands in their passage, and make them
shudder and whiten like a single willow! There is nothing more vertigin-
ous than a wind like this among the woods, with all its sight and noises;
and the effect gets between some painters and their sober eyesight, so
that, even when the rest of their picture is calm, the foliage is coloured
like foliage in a gale. There was nothing, however, of this sort to be

noticed in a country where there were no trees and hardly any shadows, save the passive shadows of clouds or those of rigid houses and walls. But the wind was nevertheless an occasion of pleasure; for nowhere could you taste more fully the pleasure of a sudden lull, or a place of opportune shelter. The reader knows what I mean; he must remember how, when he has sat himself down behind a dyke on a hill-side, he delighted to hear the wind hiss vainly through the crannies at his back; how his body tingled all over with warmth, and it began to dawn upon him, with a sort of slow surprise, that the country was beautiful, the heather purple, and the faraway hills all marbled with sun and shadow. Wordsworth, in a beautiful passage of the "Prelude," has used this as a figure for the feeling struck in us by the quiet by-streets of London after the uproar of the great thoroughfares; and the comparison may be turned the other way with as good effect:

> "Meanwhile the roar continues, till at length,
> Escaped as from an enemy we turn,
> Abruptly into some sequester'd nook,
> Still as a shelter'd place when winds blow loud!"

I remember meeting a man once, in a train, who told me of what must have been quite the most perfect instance of this pleasure of escape. He had gone up, one sunny, windy morning, to the top of a great cathedral somewhere abroad; I think it was Cologne Cathedral, the great unfinished marvel [11] by the Rhine; and after a long while in dark stairways, he issued at last into the sunshine, on a platform high above the town. At that elevation [12] it was quite still and warm; the gale was only in the lower strata of the air, and he had forgotten it in the quiet interior of the church and during his long ascent; and so you may judge of his surprise when, resting his arms on the sunlit balustrade and looking over into the *Place* far below him, he saw the good people holding on their hats and leaning hard against the wind as they walked. There is something, to my fancy, quite perfect in this little experience of my fellow-traveller's. The ways of men seem always very trivial to us when we find ourselves alone on a church-top, with the blue sky and a few tall pinnacles, and see far below us the steep roofs and foreshortened buttresses, and the silent activity of the city streets; but how much more must they not have seemed so to him as he stood, not only above other men's business, but above other men's climate, in a golden zone like Apollo's! [13]

This was the sort of pleasure I found in the country of which I write. The pleasure was to be out of the wind, and to keep it in memory all the time, and hug oneself upon the shelter. And it was only by the sea that any such sheltered places were to be found. Between the black worm-eaten headlands there are little bights and havens, well screened from the wind and the commotion of the external sea, where the sand and weeds look up into the gazer's face from a depth of tranquil water, and the sea-birds, screaming and flickering from the ruined crags, alone disturb the silence and the sunshine. One such place has impressed itself on my memory beyond all others. On a rock by the water's edge, old fighting men of the Norse breed had planted a double castle; the two stood wall to wall like semi-detached villas; and yet feud had run so high between their owners, that one, from out of a window, shot the other as he stood in his own doorway. There is something in the juxtaposition of these two enemies full of tragic irony. It is grim to think of bearded men and bitter women taking hateful counsel together about the two hall-fires at night, when the sea boomed against the foundations and the wild winter wind was loose over the battlements. And in the study we may reconstruct for ourselves some pale figure of what life then was. Not so when we are there; when we are there such thoughts come to us only to intensify a contrary impression, and association is turned against itself. I remember walking thither three afternoons in succession, my eyes weary with being set against the wind, and how, dropping suddenly over the edge of the down, I found myself in a new world of warmth and shelter. The wind, from which I had escaped, "as from an enemy," was seemingly quite local. It carried no clouds with it, and came from such a quarter that it did not trouble the sea within view. The two castles, black and ruinous as the rocks about them, were still distinguishable from these by something more insecure and fantastic in the outline, something that the last storm had left imminent and the next would demolish entirely. It would be difficult to render in words the sense of peace that took possession of me on these three afternoons. It was helped out, as I have said, by the contrast. The shore was battered and bemauled by previous tempests; I had the memory at heart of the insane strife of the pigmies who had erected these two castles and lived in them in mutual distrust and enmity, and knew I had only to put my head out of this little cup of shelter to find the hard wind blowing in my eyes; and yet there were the two great tracts of motionless blue air and peaceful sea looking on, unconcerned and apart, at the turmoil of the present moment and the memorials of the precarious past. There is ever something transitory and fretful in the impression of a high wind under a cloudless sky; it seems to have no root in the constitution of things; it must speedily begin to faint and wither away like a cut flower. And on those days the thought of the wind and the thought of human life came very near together in my mind. Our noisy years did indeed seem moments in the being of the eternal silence; [14] and the wind, in the face of that great field of stationary blue, was as the wind of a butterfly's wing. The placidity of the sea was a thing likewise to be remembered. Shelley speaks of the sea as "hungering for calm," and in this place one learned to understand the phrase. Looking down into these green waters from the broken edge of the rock, or swimming leisurely in the sunshine, it seemed to me that they were enjoying their own tranquillity; and when now and again it was disturbed by a wind ripple on the surface, or the quick black passage of a fish far below, they settled back again (one could fancy) with relief.

On shore, too, in the little nook of shelter, everything was so subdued and still that the least particular struck in me a pleasurable surprise. The desultory crackling of the whin-pods [15] in the afternoon sun usurped the ear. The hot, sweet breath of the bank, that had been saturated all day long with sunshine, and now exhaled it into my face, was like the breath of a fellow-creature. I remember that I was haunted by two lines of French verse; in some dumb way they seemed to fit my surroundings and give expression to the contentment that was in me, and I kept repeating to myself,—

> "Mon cœur est un luth suspendu,
> Sitôt qu'on le touche, il résonne."

I can give no reason why these lines came to me at this time; and for that very cause I repeat them here. For all I know, they may serve to complete the impression in the mind of the reader, as they were certainly a part of it for me.

And this happened to me in the place of all others where I liked least to stay. When I think of it I grow ashamed of my own ingratitude. "Out of the strong came forth sweetness." There, in the bleak and gusty North, I received, perhaps, my strongest impression of peace. I saw the sea to be great and calm; and the earth, in that little corner, was all alive and friendly to me. So, wherever a man is, he will find something to please and pacify him: in the town he will meet pleasant faces of men and women, and see beautiful flowers at a window, or hear a cage-bird singing at the corner of the gloomiest street; and for the country, there is no country without some amenity—let him only look for it in the right spirit, and he will surely find.

"ON THE ENJOYMENT OF UNPLEASANT PLACES"

Stevenson was twenty-three years old when he wrote this essay. What is its central thought? Has Stevenson given any things in this essay that are applicable to everyday life? What of the author's personality, character, and experiences are revealed?

1 Brantôme (1534–1614), a French ecclesiast who was a great traveller.
2 "Fait des discours en soi pour se soutenir en chemin." The traveller talks to himself to keep up his courage on the road.
3 Jacques Callot (1592–1635), a French artist.
4 Gilles Sadeler (1570–1629), a Dutch artist and engraver.
5 Paul Brill (1555–1626), a Dutch painter.
6 Dick Turpin, an English highwayman, hanged 1739.
7 The Trossachs, a beautiful, rugged region in Scotland made famous by Sir Walter Scott in "The Lady of the Lake."
8 David before Saul, I Samuel xvi. 14–23.
9 Sermon in stone. See Shakespeare's "As You Like It," Act II. Sc. 1.
10 "Wuthering Heights," a novel by Emily Brontë.

11 Unfinished marvel. Cologne Cathedral was six hundred thirty-two years being built, it not being completed until 1880. This essay was written in 1873.
12 At that elevation. The towers of the Cathedral of Cologne are at least 500 feet high.
13 Like Apollo's. Apollo was the Greek god of the sun.
14 Our noisy years. See Wordsworth's "Intimations of Immortality."
15 Whin-pods. The seed-pods of the gorse.

ARTHUR CHRISTOPHER BENSON (1862-　　)

From THE UPTON LETTERS [1]

Upton, August 4, 1904.

My dear Herbert,—I have just been over to Woodcote; I have had a few days here alone at the end of the half, and was feeling so stupid and lazy this morning that I put a few sandwiches in my pocket and went off on a bicycle for the day. It is only fifteen miles from here, so that I had two or three hours to spend there. You know I was born at Woodcote and lived there till I was ten years old. I don't know the present owner of the Lodge, where we lived; but if I had written and asked to go and see the house, they would have invited me to luncheon, and all my sense of freedom would have gone.

It is thirty years since we left, and I have not been there, near as it is, for twenty years. I did not know how deeply rooted the whole scene was in my heart and memory, but the first sight of the familiar places gave me a very curious thrill, a sort of delicious pain, a yearning for the old days—I can't describe it or analyse it. It seemed somehow as if the old life must be going on there behind the pine woods, if I could only find it; as if I could have peeped over the palings and seen myself going gravely about some childish business in the shrubberies. I find that my memory is curiously accurate in some respects, and curiously at fault in others. The scale is all wrong. What appears to me in memory to be an immense distance, from Woodcote to Dewhurst, for instance, is now reduced to almost nothing; and places which I can see quite accurately in my mind's eye are now so different that I can hardly believe that they were ever like what I recollect of them. Of course the trees have grown immensely; young plantations have become woods, and woods have disappeared. I spent my time in wandering about, retracing the childish walks we used to take, looking at the church, the old houses, the village green, and the mill-pool. One thing came home to me very much. When I was born, my father had only been settled at Woodcote for two years; but, as I grew up, it seemed to me we must have lived there for all eternity; now I see that he was only one in a long procession of human visitants who have inhabited and loved the place. Another thing that has gone is the mystery of it all. Then, every road was a little ribbon of familiar ground stretching out to the unknown; all the fields and woods

1 Used by permission of G. P. Putnam's Sons, publishers.

which lay between the roads and paths were wonderful secret places, not to be visited. I find I had no idea of the lie of the ground, and, what is more remarkable, I don't seem ever to have seen the views of the distance with which the place now abounds. I suppose that when one is a small creature, palings and hedges are lofty obstacles; and I suppose also that the little busy eyes are always searching the nearer scene for things to *find*, and do not concern themselves with what is far. The sight of the Lodge itself, with its long white front, among the shrubberies and across the pastures was almost too much for me; the years seemed all obliterated in a flash, and I felt as if it was all there unchanged.

I suppose I had a very happy childhood; but I certainly was not in the least conscious of it at the time. I was a very quiet, busy child, with all sorts of small secret pursuits of my own to attend to, to which lessons and social engagements were sad interruptions; but now it seems to be like a golden, unruffled time full of nothing but pleasure. Curiously enough, I can't remember anything but the summer days there; I have no remembrance of rain or cold or winter or leafless trees— except days of snow when the ponds were frozen and there was the wild excitement of skating. My recollections are all of flowers, and roses, and trees in leaf, and hours spent in the garden. In the very hot summer weather, my father and mother used to dine out in the garden, and it seems now to me as if they must have done so all the year round; I can remember going to bed, with my window open onto the lawn, and hearing the talk, and the silence, and then the soft clink of the things being removed as I sank into sleep. It is a great mystery, that faculty of the mind for forgetting all the shadows and remembering nothing but the sunlight; [1] it is so deeply rooted in humanity that it is hard not to believe that it means something; one dares to hope that if our individual life continues after death, this instinct—if memory remains—will triumph over the past, even in the case of lives of sordid misery and hopeless pain.

Then, too, one wonders what the strong instinct of permanence means, in creatures that inhabit the world for so short and troubled a space; why instinct should so contradict experience; why human beings have not acquired in the course of centuries a sense of the fleetingness of things. All our instincts seem to speak of permanence; all our experience points to swift and ceaseless change. I cannot fathom it.

As I wandered about Woodcote, my thoughts took a sombre tinge, and the *lacrimæ rerum*,[2] the happy days gone, the pleasant groups broken up to meet no more, the old faces departed, the voices that are silent— all these things began to weigh on my mind with a sad bewilderment. One feels so independent, so much the master of one's fate; and yet, when one returns to an old home, one begins to wonder whether one has any power of choice at all. There is this strange fence of self and identity drawn for me round one tiny body; all that is outside of it has no existence for me apart from consciousness. These are fruitless thoughts, but one cannot always resist them; and why one is here, what these vivid feelings mean, what one's heart-hunger for the sweet world and for beloved people means—all this is dark and secret; and the strong tide bears us on, out of the little harbor of childhood into unknown seas.

Dear Woodcote, dear remembered days, beloved faces and voices of the past, old trees and fields! I cannot tell what you mean and what you are; but I can hardly believe that, if I have a life beyond, it will not somehow comprise you all; for indeed you are my own for ever; you are myself, whatever that self may be.—Ever yours,

T. B.

THE UPTON LETTERS

Although the "Upton Letters" are in the letter form, they are essays.

Mr. Benson is the son of an Archbishop of Canterbury. He was a master at Eton for a number of years and is now a Fellow of Magdalene College, Cambridge.

The "Upton Letters" were first published anonymously in 1905. Herbert, the man addressed, is an imaginary person, but the places are real.

---

[1] Mr. Benson has in another place expressed this thought thus: "Time has a wonderful and tender way of obliterating all that is harsh and dark and sad, and leaving only the pure gold of memory."

[2] "Lachrimæ rerum," the tears of things, Virgil's *Æneid*, I, 462.

ESSAYS FOR OPTIONAL READINGS

Give name of essay and author in each case. What is the general classification? What did you learn regarding the author's personality, character, or experience? Did you add anything to your own store of information? Were there any helpful ideas that you could apply in your own life? Was there any humor or pathos shown? Was the author's thought easy or hard to follow? Was this essay long or short? Did you, or did you not, enjoy reading it? Give reasons.

"Against Idleness" .... Michel Montaigne
"Of Adversity" .... Francis Bacon
"Of Goodness, and Goodness of Nature"...... Francis Bacon
"Of Suspicion" .... Francis Bacon
"Of Discourse" .... Francis Bacon
"The Head-Dress" .... Joseph Addison
"The Burden of Mankind" .... Joseph Addison
"The Spectator" from "Sir Roger de Coverley
    Papers" .... Joseph Addison
"A Sunday with Sir Roger" .... Joseph Addison
"Sir Roger in Westminster Abbey"........... Joseph Addison

Any essays by............................Henry Van Dyke
"Among Friends" ....Samuel McChord Crothers
"The Evolution of the Gentleman"..........Samuel McChord Crothers
"The Gentle Reader".......................Samuel McChord Crothers
Any essay by.............................Arthur C. Benson
Any essay in "School, College, and Character".LeBaron R. Briggs
Any essay in "On the Choice of Books"......Frederic Harrison
Any essay by.............................Gilbert K. Chesterton
Any essay by.............................Agnes Repplier
Any essay by.............................David Starr Jordan
Any essay in "Essays Every Child Should
    Know" ....Hamilton Mabie
Any essay in "Essays and Essay Writing"
    (Atlantic Essays), edited by ....William Tanner
Any essay by.............................Hamilton Mabie
Any essay in the collection, "Selected Essays,"
    edited by.............................Claude Fuess
"The Course of American History" from "Mere
    Literature" ....Woodrow Wilson
"A Student in Arms".......................Donald W. A. Hankey
"Concerning Breakfast" ....E. V. Lucas
"Adventures in Contentment"................David Grayson
"Adventures in Friendship" ....David Grayson
"A Message to Garcia" ....Elbert Hubbard

REVIEW

1. Review what you have learned about essays and essay writers.

2. For your theme work try writing an essay in imitation of Bacon, or take one of Bacon's subjects and write an essay giving the twentieth century viewpoint and method of handling material.

CHAPTER II

PROSE FICTION

Classes of Prose Fiction.—Prose fiction includes all prose narratives (except the drama) in which the story told is not real, but a product of the imagination. Although closely related to the drama, it is distinct from it since it contains descriptive material which could not be used for stage presentation. The types of prose fiction are:—the prose allegory, prose romance, tale of adventure or experience, novel, novelette, and short-story.

The Prose Allegory.—The prose allegory is a prose form in which there is a long, implied comparison between unlike things. It is therefore a metaphor expanded to a considerable length. The greatest prose allegory in the literature of the world [1] is Bunyan's "Pilgrim's Progress" published in 1678. The characters in this work are depicted vividly and the experiences seem very real. A child enjoys the story as such, but an older person is interested in the allegory which lies beneath. "Pilgrim's Progress," because of its realism, as well as its strong appeal to the imagination, had a great influence on the development of the modern novel, although the latter did not appear until the following century. Another prose allegory which is especially popular with children because of its wealth of imagination is "Gulliver's Travels" by Jonathan Swift, published in 1726. Most of the prose allegories are classed under other types as well. Thus "The Vision of Mirza" and "Burden of Mankind" by Addison are not only allegories but essays. Many of our dramas, novels, and short-stories are also allegories.

The Prose Romance.—The early prose romance had the same general characteristics that we noted in the metrical romance, excepting that it was in the prose form. The author gave full reign to his imagination, no attempt being made to bound it in by facts or probabilities. Many of the circumstances were not only highly improbable but really impossible. These romances, both in the prose and metrical forms, were very popular in the Middle Ages.

---

[1] The other great allegories of world literature, "The Faerie Queene" and "The Divine Comedy," are in poetic form.

They are also a delight to the children of to-day, for in childhood imagination is at its height. Many of the Arthur stories, which appeared in such numbers in the twelfth and thirteenth centuries, were metrical romances, but there were prose ones among them. In 1470 "The Morte d'Arthur" by Sir Thomas Malory was completed. This was not only the greatest English literary work of the fifteenth century, but it is our greatest treasure-house in prose of the legends and stories of King Arthur and the Knights of the Round Table. All later writers who have made use of Arthurian material have obtained it from Malory.

Some other well-known prose romances of the past are the so-called "Travels of Sir John Mandeville" in the fourteenth century, and More's "Utopia," Sidney's "Arcadia," Lyly's "Euphues," Lodge's "Rosalind," [1] and Greene's "Pandosto" [1] of the sixteenth century.

In the later romances the events shown are usually more probable than in those of the past, but still there is an unnatural glamour over life in general, and the adventures and incidents are of more importance than anything else.

The Tale of Adventure or Experience.—In the romance the imagination has full swing, but in the tale of adventure or experience the reason keeps the imagination from absurdities and unrealities. Though there are often many exciting adventures and hair-breadth escapes, they must be within the limits of probability. The tale is not a novel, because it has no plot development. It is made up of one thrilling or interesting experience after another, but any of these could be omitted or new ones added without harm to the story as a whole. This, of course, would be impossible in a novel. As the romance is most popular in childhood, the tale of adventure or experience is the type of greatest interest in early youth. Probably the best known tale that we have is "Robinson Crusoe" by Defoe (1719). Besides this, "Captain Singleton" by Defoe (1720), Cooper's "Leather-Stocking Tales" (1823–1841), Mark Twain's "The Adventures of Tom Sawyer" (1876) and "Huckleberry Finn," Stevenson's "Treasure Island" (1883), Quiller-Couch's "The Splendid Spur" (1889), Kipling's "Kim" (1901), and Jack London's "Call of the Wild" and "White Fang" are some of the best examples of these tales.

The Beginning of the Modern Novel.—The tale was nearer the novel-type than the romance, yet it lacked the important novel-

[1] Shakespeare's "As You Like It" was founded on Lodge's "Rosalind," and his "Winter's Tale" on Greene's "Pandosto."

element, plot. The true modern novel, therefore, did not make its appearance until 1740. Samuel Richardson, a London printer, was asked to write a set of letters to be used as models by those who found letter-writing difficult. He happened to think of the plan of having the letters tell a story, and the first modern novel, "Pamela, or Virtue Rewarded," was the result. This was published in four volumes and was so popular that the author wrote "Clarissa Harlowe" in eight volumes, and later "Sir Charles Grandison" in seven volumes. These were all in the form of letters, and their purpose, Richardson said, was "to inculcate virtue and good manners." His purpose was so obvious that, as some one expressed it, he "inflicted morality" upon people.

A lawyer and literary man of the time, Henry Fielding, one who had a wider experience of life than Richardson, was disgusted with the sentimental preaching of "Pamela." He accordingly began a burlesque upon it, in which he made Joseph Andrews, Pamela's brother, the chief character. He had not gone far in the story, however, before he became so interested in it that he forgot all about the satire and wrote a truly great novel, "Joseph Andrews" (1742). Later he wrote three other novels, the greatest of all being "Tom Jones" (1749). Other novel writers of the eighteenth century were Smollett, Sterne, Oliver Goldsmith, and Miss Fanny Burney. Of these Goldsmith is especially noted as the author of "The Vicar of Wakefield."

Other Novelists of the Eighteenth Century

The best English novelists in the early part of the nineteenth century were Sir Walter Scott (1771–1832) and Jane Austen (1775–1817).

Scott created the historical novel, and, beginning with "Waverley" in 1814, he wrote seventeen of these novels in which he made real to his readers life in a past age. Some of his scenes were laid in the Holy Land in the time of the Crusades; others in Norman England; in Elizabethan England; in the time of Cromwell and the Stuart kings; in Scotland in the days of the Covenanters, and of the Jacobites; and in France and Burgundy in the time of Louis XI and Charles the Bold. Besides these historical novels, Scott wrote twelve others on Scottish life and manners. Among them, "The Heart of Midlothian" and "Guy Mannering" are called his very best works. Scott's novels are filled with the romantic spirit, but they are somewhat removed from the true romance type by reason of their well-constructed

Novelists of the Early Nineteenth Century

plots and probable incidents. They show life as seen through the imagination rather than through observation, and emphasize the story, rather than character and life. They are therefore romantic novels.

Jane Austen was the greatest of our early realists. Her field of observation was a very small one, being confined to her own village and its surroundings, but she portrayed life as she found it with such sympathy, humor, and accuracy that she, to-day, is being regarded more and more as one of our greatest novelists. Her best works are "Pride and Prejudice," "Sense and Sensibility" and "Emma."

First in the works of Dickens, Thackeray, George Eliot, and Hawthorne, and later in those of Stevenson, Meredith, Hardy, and W. D. Howells, we find the best English and American novels of the last part of the nineteenth century. Of these writers, Thackeray, George Eliot, Meredith, Hardy, and Howells are realists[1] in the way they handle their materials; Hawthorne and Stevenson are romanticists; while Dickens mingles together both romantic and realistic elements.

Later Nineteenth Century Novelists

Among the great number of English novelists that have appeared during the opening years of the twentieth century, the foremost are generally regarded by critics to be John Galsworthy, Joseph Conrad, Arnold Bennett, Herbert George Wells, Eden Phillpotts, Maurice Hewlett, William Frend De Morgan William John Locke, James M. Barrie, and Mrs. Humphry Ward.

Novelists of the Twentieth Century

Galsworthy has satirized the aristocratic classes in modern English society in "The Man of Property" (1906), "The Country House" (1907), "Fraternity" (1909), and "The Patrician (1911). Joseph Conrad gained the materials for his "Lord Jim" (1900), "Typhoon" (1903), "Chance" (1912), and other sea stories during seventeen years spent in the English merchant marine service. Arnold Bennett's best works, "The Old Wives' Tale" (1908) and "Clayhanger" (1910) are from his Five Town Series dealing with life in the Staffordshire pottery district. H. G. Wells's best novels show his deep interest in science and sociology. "The Time Machine" (1895) "Kipps" (1905), "Bealby" (1915), and "Mr.

[1] "Realism," said William Dean Howells, "is nothing more and nothing less than the truthful treatment of material," while Scott said it was "the exquisite touch which renders commonplace things and characters interesting for the truth of the description and the sentiment."

Britling Sees It Through'' are representatives of his work. Eden Phillpotts has laid his scenes among the peasants on the moors and farms of Devonshire. Some of the most interesting of these are "The Children of the Mist" (1898) and "Demeter's Daughter" (1911). Maurice Hewlett is a romanticist, as is shown in two of his best known novels, "The Life and Death of Richard Yea-and-Nay" (1900) and "The Stooping Lady" (1907). William Frend De Morgan did not know that he had the ability to write novels until he was sixty-seven years of age. Then, while convalescing from an illness, he discovered his power in this field, and found a secure place in the hearts of his readers. "Joseph Vance" (1906), "Alice-for-Short" (1907), and "Somehow Good" (1908) are well worth reading. The experiences of Charles Heath in "Alice-for-Short" are chiefly De Morgan's own. Locke's "The Beloved Vagabond" (1906), Barrie's "The Little Minister" (1897), Mrs. Humphry Ward's "Marcella," and "The Garden of Allah" by Robert S. Hichens are some of the other well received novels of the present century.

A novel representing American life in its entirety has never been produced, nor has any whole section of the country found expression in any one work. We have had some good novels which portrayed different parts of the South, or the West, or the New England States, for instance, but each writer dealt with only his own distinct part. The great American novel has not only not appeared, but it never will come, it is thought. The late critic, James Gibbons Huneker, said in this connection, "The Great American novel will be in the plural; thousands perhaps. America is a chord of many nations, and to find the keynote we must play much and varied music."

Some of the best present-century novels by American authors are to be found in the works of Winston Churchill, Booth Tarkington, William Allen White, Stewart Edward White, Mary Johnston, Edna Ferber, F. Hopkinson Smith, Henry Sydnor Harrison,[1] Mrs. Mary Stansbury Watts, Henry James, and Ellen Glasgow.

Some Characteristics of the Modern Novel.—Every novel must have at least three elements: a setting, a plot, and one or more characters. In some novels the setting is emphasized, while in others stress is laid on either the plot or the portrayal of character. Frequently all three have nearly an equal prominence.

The setting of a novel includes the time, the place and the background or enveloping circumstances of the story. Sometimes it

[1] Especially "Queed."

emphasizes a certain locality, like the mountain regions of Kentucky and Tennessee, or the wilds of Wyoming; sometimes it sets forth a definite historical period, or it may center the attention upon some great industry or occupation, like that of lumbering, in Stewart Edward White's "Blazed Trail." In any case the setting should be in keeping with the story that is told. This has not always been the case in the novels of the past, but in modern fiction the setting is so closely welded with the action that it is often the cause of what happens; and, should it be changed, the characters and what they do must necessarily change also.

The plot is the skeleton or framework which gives shape and proportion to the novel. It is essential, though often faintly drawn. It usually consists of a main thread and one or two others woven together. Each of these threads is made up of a series of related events so arranged that the first either directly or indirectly causes the one that follows. Occasionally a plot runs in an inverse order, beginning with results and from these going back to causes. Though this series of events is at intervals interrupted or blocked for a time, it ultimately reaches a definite culmination. In arranging a plot the author chooses just how much he will set forth; and decides whether he will tell his story in detail, making it cover a long period of time and involve many characters, or organize the material so compactly that it will include but few characters and cover a short time. He must have his plot complete before he writes the story, so that nothing will creep in to break the unity.

The characters of a great novel may be many or few, but they must be true to life and worth knowing. They can never be puppets which the author manipulates to suit his own whims. If he once places his characters in certain circumstances and situations of life, they must act in accordance with the laws of those circumstances and situations, whether the author wishes it or not. The incidents which take place, then, have to happen. The author may have no choice in the matter. The characters thus determine the plot, and not the plot the characters.

The general structure of a novel is very similar to that of an older play, there being in both an introduction of characters and situations, an incitement, an ascending action, climax, descending action, and catastrophe or *dénouement*. The novel also makes use of incidents and situations to reveal or determine character; and of surprise and suspense to sustain interest. The novel, however, has a much greater freedom in many particulars than the drama. The climax, for instance, is seldom so carefully placed. Often there is only a series of smaller climaxes instead, and sometimes the climax seems to coincide with the conclusion. There is somewhere, though, the great knot which ties the threads of the plot together; and, at the last, this knot is untied and the difficulties are resolved, in whole or in part. But the author of a great novel always leaves his reader with the feeling that the story told is but a chapter from the larger book of life.

The Study of a Novel.—At this point in the course the study of a particular novel should be made. For this work read ''A Tale of Two Cities,'' using a text from any of the series of classics.

NOTES, COMMENTS, AND QUESTIONS OF "A TALE OF TWO CITIES"

Long before Dickens began to plan out the characters and plot for "A Tale of Two Cities," he was filled with a desire to write a novel with the French Revolution as a setting. He, accordingly, began to read everything he could find on the history of that time; and, when he finally did arrange his characters and incidents, they were especially vivid, and true to the background. The work was finished in 1859.

The story is more direct and the threads of the plot are more closely woven together in "A Tale of Two Cities" than in any other of Dickens's works. Although the plot and setting are more prominent than the characters, Dickens has here made one advancement in character delineation over his other novels. Instead of having his people unchanged by their experiences, he has in this novel shown real character development in at least two persons, Sydney Carton and Jerry Cruncher.

The Time Element.

The events of Book I are represented as happening in 1775; those of Book II from 1780 to 1792; and those of Book III from the autumn of 1792 to 1794. The background events which connect the lives of Dr. Manette, Charles Darnay, and the Defarges occurred eighteen years before the story proper begins.

The General Structure of this Novel.

    (1) The introduction:
        Book I, and the first three chapters of Book II, give the introduction of characters, and the underlying situations.
    (2) The beginning of the action:
        Charles Darnay's trial for treason, Book II, Chapters 2 and 3, is the beginning of the action. Here the threads of Darnay, Lucie Manette, and Sydney Carton become entangled.

After the portrait by Daniel Maclise.

CHARLES DICKENS

(3) The climax or turning point:

In the chapter entitled "Drawn to the Loadstone Rock," Charles Darnay gets the letter from Gabelle which takes him to France. This is the turning point.

(4) The concluding crisis:

The point which follows closely the climax and changes suddenly the course of the story, is the arrest of Darnay upon entering France.

(5) The retarding point:

The point where another ending to the story is suggested is in the first part of the chapter, "The Knock at the Door." After this point there is no possible release for Charles except through the great sacrifice.

(6) The catastrophe:

The death of Sydney Carton.

It will be noticed that the plot is very dramatic, following almost exactly the structure of a play. Dickens was undecided for a time whether to handle his material as a novel, or to throw it into the dramatic form.

Book the First. "Recalled to Life"

Book I is taken up with (1) the general condition of affairs in England and France in 1775; (2) the introduction of several characters who are to be prominent in the story; and (3) certain background circumstances that are necessary for the understanding of the main action. The characters introduced are Dr. Manette and his daughter, Lucie; the latter's old nurse, Miss Pross; Mr. Jarvis Lorry, the representative of Tellson's Banking House of London; Jerry Cruncher, the odd-job-man connected with Tellson's; and the group of people in the Paris wine-shop—Monsieur and Madame Defarge, Gaspard, and the three Jacques.

Chapter I. "The Period."

(1) How does this chapter strike the key-note of the story?

(2) Who were the "king with a large jaw and queen with a plain face, on the throne of England" (1775)?

(3) Who were the "king with a large jaw and queen with a fair face, on the throne of France"?

(4) Look up the story of the famous Cock-lane ghost. See "Reader's Hand Book."

(5) Mrs. Southcott was a woman who claimed to have prophetic power. Why does the author mention Mrs. Southcott and the Cock-lane ghost here?

Chapter II. "The Mail."

    (1) What conditions referred to in Chapter I are illustrated in this chapter?

    (2) What characters prominent in the story are introduced here? How many passengers are on the coach?

    (3) How is the reader's interest aroused?

    (4) Notice the plot points of this chapter:

        (a) Mr. Lorry's getting the note brought by Jerry, "Wait in Dover for Mam'selle."

        (b) The reply sent back, "Recalled to life."

        (c) Effect of this reply, "Recalled to life," on Jerry: "That's a blazing strange message. . . . You'd be in a blazing bad way, if recalling to life was to come into fashion, Jerry!"

Chapter III. "The Night Shadows."

    (1) What two purposes does this chapter serve?

    (2) What are the mysterious things about Jerry? Notice the use of suspense.

    (3) What were the dreams of Mr. Lorry that night on the mail coach? Can you discover any causes for them?

    (4) What plot points do you find here?

Chapter IV. "The Preparation."

    (1) Why does the author not describe Mr. Lorry until this chapter? What is your first impression of him? How old a man?

    (2) What is the real purpose of this chapter?

    (3) What new characters are introduced? Impression of them?

    (4) What mystery is cleared up in this chapter?

    (5) What was a *lettre-de-cachet?* What reference to one here?

Chapter V. "The Wine-Shop."

    (1) What special purpose does this chapter serve?

    (2) How does the author foreshadow later events in the episode of the wine-cask? What other examples of foreshadowing in this chapter?

    (3) Why does the author describe with such detail the Saint Antoine district?

    (4) What feeling is aroused in the reader here?

    (5) What new characters are introduced in this chapter?

    (6) Why does the author describe Monsieur and Madame Defarge so carefully? What impression do you get of their characters?

    (7) What is the most characteristic description of Madame?

    (8) What is the purpose of the signals and signs used by Madame Defarge?

(9) What is indicated by the fact that each of the three men in the wine-shop was called Jacques?

(10) Why are the three Jacques allowed to go up to the fifth story room?

(11) Why have Mr. Lorry and Miss Manette come to the wine-shop?

(12) The effect of their visit on the Defarges?

(13) Why does Defarge make the noise at the door of that fifth-story room?

(14) Why is the room so dark?

Chapter VI. "The Shoemaker."

(1) Is "Recalled to Life" an appropriate name for Book I?

(2) What is gathered here regarding Dr. Manette's past history?

(3) Why was the street so deserted when they finally came down to the carriage?

(4) What "catch-phrase" does Dickens use in his references to Madame Defarge?

(5) What was Dr. Manette's request as they were leaving?

(6) What is indicated by the interest shown in Dr. Manette by the officer at the Barrier?

(7) Why has Dickens divided his story into *Books?*

(8) What is the relation of Book I to the rest of the story?

(9) What is its central thought?

BOOK THE SECOND. "THE GOLDEN THREAD"

Chapter I. "Five Years After"

(1) Why is Tellson's Bank described at length?

(2) Why is so much said here regarding Temple Bar and the laws for the punishment of criminals?

(3) What new characters are introduced in this chapter?

(4) How is the mystery concerning Jerry Cruncher intensified?

(5) What is the description of Jerry's personal appearance?

(6) How is Young Jerry a "chip of the old block"?

(7) What purpose does this chapter serve?

(8) Where is the humor?

Chapter II. "A Sight."

(1) Points in this chapter which emphasize the Jerry mystery?

(2) Condition of the jails and court rooms in 1780?

(3) What was the particular case on trial at the Old Bailey?

(4) Why was there so much interest in it?

(5) What new character is introduced here?

(6) What is your first impression of him?

(7) What description did the author give of Jerry that you are reminded of every time you see him?

(8) Who were the two witnesses against the prisoner, mentioned here?

Chapter III. "A Disappointment."

The following arrangement for a mock trial scene is based on Chapter III and the last two pages and a half of Chapter II. It is suggestive only.

THE TRIAL OF CHARLES DARNAY [1]

Dramatis Personæ

THE LORD CHIEF JUSTICE.
MR. ATTORNEY-GENERAL.
MR. SOLICITOR-GENERAL.
MR. STRYVER—*Counsel for Prisoner.*
MR. CARTON (*the "wigged gentleman"*).
MR. CHARLES DARNAY, *the prisoner at the bar.*

WITNESSES:

MR. JARVIS LORRY.
DR. MANETTE.
MISS LUCIE MANETTE.
JOHN BARSAD.
ROGER CLY.
JOHN DOE (*name given to witness unnamed in book*).

The CLERK *of the Court,* BAILIFF, *and other officers.*
The JURYMEN.

SCENE:—*The Old Bailey Court Room. Court of the King's Bench.*

Bailiff. O hear yez! O hear yez! The Court of King's Bench of His Majesty, King George the Third, is now in session! Silence in the Court!

My Lord. We will hear the reading of the Journal of the Court.

Clerk of Court. In the case of Rex versus Charles Darnay begun in his Majesty's Court of King's Bench on yesterday, March the ninth, of the year of Our Lord One thousand seven hundred and eighty, the said defendant, Charles Darnay, pleaded *Not Guilty* to an indictment denouncing him as a traitor to our serene, illustrious, and excellent prince, our Lord, the King, by reason of his having, on divers occasions and by

[1] This arrangement was worked out in class, a large part being done by the pupils themselves.

divers means and ways, assisted Louis the XVI, King of France, in his wars against our said serene, illustrious, and excellent King; that is to say, by coming and going, between the dominions of our said serene, illustrious and excellent Lord, the King, and those of the said Louis, King of France, and wickedly falsely, and traitorously revealing to the said Louis, King of France, what forces our said serene, illustrious, and excellent King had in preparation to send to Canada and North America.

Therefore, the aforesaid Charles Darnay stands here before you on trial for his life, on this second day of the trial, March the tenth, in the year of Our Lord Seventeen hundred and eighty. The jury has been duly sworn and Mr. Attorney-General will now proceed with the case on behalf of the state and our illustrious, serene, and excellent monarch, King George the Third.

Mr. Attorney-Gen. My Lord and Gentlemen of the Jury, I have to inform you that the prisoner before you, though young in years, is old in treasonable practices which claim the forfeit of his life. This correspondence with the public enemy is not a correspondence of to-day, or of yesterday, or even of last year or the year before It is certain that the prisoner has for longer than that been in the habit of passing and re-passing between France and England on secret business of which he can give no honest account.

If it were in the nature of traitorous ways to thrive (which happily it never is) the real wickedness and guilt of his business might have remained undiscovered. Providence, however, has put it into the heart of a person who is beyond fear and beyond reproach, to ferret out the nature of the prisoner's schemes and, struck with horror, to disclose them to his Majesty's Chief Secretary of State and most honorable Privy Council. This patriot will be produced before you. His position and attitude are, on the whole, sublime. He has been the prisoner's friend, but, at once in an auspicious and an evil hour, detecting his infamy, he has resolved to immolate the traitor he can no longer cherish in his bosom on the sacred altar of his country. If statues were erected in Britain, as in ancient Greece and Rome, to public benefactors, this shining citizen would assuredly have one. As they are not so decreed, he probably will not have one.

Virtue, as has been observed by the poets (in many passages which I well know the jury will have, word for word, at the tips of their tongues), is, in a manner, contagious; more especially the bright virtue known as patriotism, or love of country. The lofty example of this immaculate and unimpeachable witness for the Crown—to refer to whom however unworthily is an honor—has communicated itself to the prisoner's servant and has engendered in him a holy determination to examine his master's table-drawers and pockets, and secrete his papers. I am prepared to hear some disparagement attempted of this admirable servant, but, in a general way, I prefer him to my own brothers and sisters, and honor him more than my father and mother. I call with confidence on the jury to come and do likewise. The evidence of these two witnesses, coupled with the documents of their discovery that will be produced, will show the prisoner to have been furnished with lists of his Majesty's forces, and of their disposition and preparation both by sea and land, and will prove no doubt that he has habitually conveyed such information to a hostile power.

These lists cannot be proved to be in the prisoner's handwriting; but it is all the same, indeed, it is rather the better for the prosecution, as showing the prisoner to be artful in his precautions. The proof will go back four years, and will show the prisoner to be already engaged in these pernicious missions within a few weeks before the date of the very first action fought between the British troops and the Americans.

For these reasons, the Jury, being a loyal jury (as you know you are), must positively find the prisoner *Guilty* and make an end of him. whether you like it or not. You never can lay your heads upon your pillows; you never can tolerate the idea of your wives laying their heads upon their pillows; you never can endure the notion of your children laying their heads upon their pillows; in short, there never more can be, for you or yours, any laying of heads upon pillows at all, unless the prisoner's head is taken off. That head, I demand of you, and on the faith of my solemn asseveration that I already consider the prisoner as good as dead and gone.

Mr. Solicitor-Gen. (*calls* John Barsad *to witness-box*). Is your name John Barsad?

Barsad. It is.

Mr. Solicitor-Gen. What is your occupation?

Barsad. I am a gentleman.

Mr. Solicitor-Gen. Do you know the prisoner?

Barsad. I do. He was once my friend.

Mr. Solicitor-Gen. Why do you renounce your friendship for him?

Barsad. In an auspicious and evil hour I detected his infamy. Struck with horror, I resolved at once to immolate the traitor I could no longer cherish in my bosom, on the sacred altar of my country. I thereupon ferreted out the nature of the prisoner's schemes and disclosed them to his Majesty's Chief Secretary of State and most honorable Privy Council.

Mr. Solicitor-Gen. Very well, that will do.

Mr. Carton. (*A colleague of the prisoner's Counsel. He sits looking at the ceiling of the Court. He has papers before him.*) I beg leave to ask the witness a few questions. Is your name John Barsad?

Barsad. It is.

Mr. Carton. Have you ever been a spy yourself?

Barsad. No. I scorn the base insinuation.

Mr. Carton. What do you live upon?

Barsad. My property.

Mr. Carton. Where is your property?

Barsad. I don't precisely remember where it is.

Mr. Carton. What is it?

Barsad. No business of anybody's.

Mr. Carton. Did you inherit it?

Barsad. Yes, I did.

Mr. Carton. From whom?

Barsad. A distant relation.

Mr. Carton. Very distant?

Barsad. Rather.

Mr. Carton. Ever been in prison?

Barsad. Certainly not!

Mr. Carton. Never in a debtors' prison?

Barsad. I don't see what that has to do with it.

Mr. Carton. Never in a debtors' prison?—Come, once again. Never?

Barsad. Yes.

Mr. Carton. How many times?

Barsad. Two or three times.

Mr. Carton. Not five or six?

Barsad. Perhaps.

Mr. Carton. Of what profession?

Barsad. Gentleman.

Mr. Carton. Ever been kicked?

Barsad. Might have been.

Mr. Carton. Frequently?

Barsad. No.

Mr. Carton. Ever kicked down stairs?

Barsad. Decidedly not; I once received a kick on the top of a staircase and fell down stairs of my own accord.

Mr. Carton. Were you kicked on that occasion for cheating at dice?

Barsad. Something to that effect was said by the intoxicated liar who committed the assault, but it was not true.

Mr. Carton. Do you swear it was not true?

Barsad. Positively.

Mr. Carton. Did you ever live by cheating at play?

Barsad. Never.

Mr. Carton. Did you ever live by play?

Barsad. Not more than other gentlemen do.

Mr. Carton. Did you ever borrow money of the prisoner?

Barsad. Yes.

Mr. Carton. Ever pay him?

Barsad. No.

Mr. Carton. Was not this intimacy with the prisoner in reality a very slight one, forced upon the prisoner in coaches, inns, and packets?

Barsad. No.

Mr. Carton. Sure you saw the prisoner with these lists?

Barsad. Certain.

Mr. Carton. You knew no more about the lists?

Barsad. No.

Mr. Carton. Expect to get anything by this evidence?

Barsad. No.

Mr. Carton. Not in regular government pay and employment to lay traps?

Barsad. Oh dear no!

Mr. Carton. Or to do anything?

Barsad. Oh dear no!

Mr. Carton. Swear that?

Barsad. Over and over again.

Mr. Carton. No motives but sheer patriotism?

Barsad. None whatever.

Mr. Carton. That is sufficient.

(Barsad *leaves witness-box.*)

Mr. Stryver (calls Roger Cly). Is your name Roger Cly?

Cly. It is.

Mr. Stryver. Do you know the prisoner?

Cly. I do.

Mr. Stryver. When did you first become acquainted with him?

Cly. Four years ago.

Mr. Stryver. Under what circumstances?

Cly. I was his servant.

Mr. Stryver. How did you become his servant?

Cly. I asked the prisoner on board the Calais packet if he wanted a handy fellow, and the prisoner engaged me.

Mr. Stryver. You didn't ask the prisoner to take you as an act of charity?

Cly. Never thought of such a thing.

Mr. Stryver. When did you first have suspicions of the prisoner?

Cly. Soon after I entered his service.

Mr. Stryver. Did you see similar lists to these then?

Cly. Yes, over and over again.

Mr. Stryver. Where?

Cly. In arranging the prisoner's clothes while traveling.

Mr. Stryver. Where did you get these lists?

Cly. I took them from the drawer of the prisoner's desk.

Mr. Stryver. You had not put them there first?

Cly. Indeed not.

Mr. Stryver. Did you ever see the prisoner make use of them?

Cly. I saw him show these identical lists to French gentlemen.

Mr. Stryver. Where?

Cly. Both in Calais and Boulogne.

Mr. Stryver. Why did you inform upon him?

Cly. I loved my country and I could not bear it.

Mr. Stryver. You have never been suspected of stealing a silver tea-pot?

Cly. I was so maligned respecting a mustard-pot, but it turned out to be a plated one.

Mr. Stryver. How long have you known the last witness?

Cly. Seven or eight years.

Mr. Stryver. How did that happen?

Cly. Only a coincidence.

Mr. Stryver. Isn't it a curious coincidence?

Cly. Not particularly so; most coincidences are curious.

Mr. Stryver. Isn't it a curious coincidence, that true patriotism was *his* only motive, too?

Cly. No. He is a true Briton and I hope there are many like him.

Mr. Stryver. That is sufficient.

(Mr. Attorney-General *calls* Mr. Jarvis Lorry *to witness-stand.*)

(As the examination of Mr. Lorry, Miss Manette, and Dr. Manette is given by direct questions and answers in the chapter "A Disappointment," that dialogue can be taken directly from the book at this point.)

(*After examining* Mr. Lorry, Miss Manette, *and* Dr. Manette. Mr. Attorney-General *sits down.*)

Mr. Stryver. (*Calls* John Doe *to identify prisoner.*) Is your name John Doe?

Doe. It is.

Mr. Stryver. Look on the prisoner. Have you ever seen him before?

Doe. I have.

Mr. Stryver. Where?

Doe. In the coffee-room of a hotel in the garrison and dockyard town of Brighton.

Mr. Stryver. When was this?

Doe. On a Friday night in November, 1775.

Mr. Stryver. Have you ever seen him on any other occasion?

Doe. No.

Mr. Stryver. Are you sure that the man you saw at the inn was the prisoner?

Doe. I am very sure.

(*The Wigged Gentleman, who has been looking at the ceiling, writes a word or two on a piece of paper, screws it up, and tosses it to* Mr. Stryver.)

Mr. Stryver. (*Reads paper and looks with great attention and curiosity at the prisoner.*) You say again you are quite sure that it was the prisoner that you saw?

Doe. I am quite sure.

Mr. Stryver. Did you ever see any one very like the prisoner?

Doe. Not so like that I could be mistaken.

Mr. Stryver. Look well upon that gentleman, my learned friend there, and then look well upon the prisoner. How say you? Are they very like each other?

Doe. (*Astonished and hesitating.*) Very like! Very like!

Mr. Stryver. (*To* My Lord.) My Lord, I pray you bid my learned friend lay aside his wig.

My Lord. (*Ungraciously.*) Shall we next try Mr. Carton for treason?

Mr. Stryver. No, My Lord, but I would ask the witness to tell me whether what happened once, might happen twice; whether he would have been so confident if he had seen this illustration of his rashness sooner; whether he would be so confident, having seen it. That is sufficient.

Mr. Stryver. (*Makes his appeal to the Jury.*) My Lord, and Gentlemen of the Jury: I think we can prove conclusively that the so-called patriot, John Barsad, is a hired spy and traitor, an unblushing trafficker in blood, and one of the greatest scoundrels upon the earth since accursed Judas. That the so-called virtuous servant, Roger Cly, is his friend and partner and is worthy to be. That the watchful eyes of these forgers and false swearers have rested on the prisoner as a victim, because some family affairs in France—he being of French extraction—have necessitated his making those passages across the Channel. What those affairs are, a consideration for others near and dear to him forbid him even for his life to disclose.

That the evidence that has been warped and wrested from the young lady whose anguish in giving it you have witnessed, comes to nothing, involving only the mere little gallantries and politenesses likely to pass between any young gentleman and young lady so thrown together; with the exception of that reference to George Washington which is altogether too extravagant and impossible to be regarded in any other light than as a monstrous joke. It would be a weakness in the government to break down in this attempt to practice for popularity on the lowest national antipathies and fears; and, therefore, Mr. Attorney-General has made the most of it. Nevertheless, it rests upon nothing save that vile and infamous character of evidence too often disfiguring such cases, and of which the state trials of this country are full.

My Lord. (*Breaking in.*) I cannot sit upon this Bench and suffer those allusions.

Mr. Attorney-General. (*Makes his appeal to the Jury.*) My Lord, and Gentlemen of the Jury: You have just heard the base insinuations that have been made by the prisoner's counsel. You must take them for what they are worth. You surely cannot believe that these two noble gentlemen have been so wicked as to enter into a plot to defame an innocent man. Consider their testimony; their evident unwillingness to bring accusations against a friend, their attempts to smother their suspicions. All these bespeak the innate fineness of their friendships, and yet the great and abiding love which they bore their country, their patriotism, rising to sublime heights, brought them at last to sacrifice friendship on the sacred altar of Country. "Not that I loved Cæsar less, but that I loved Rome more," was as true of them as it was of Brutus of old. Can you for one moment suspect them of the charges which have been brought against them? Do their faces look the part? No, a thousand times, No! Why cannot the prisoner give his reasons for making the numerous trips between France and England? He cannot because they would incriminate him! The two noble patriots, Mr. Barsad and Mr. Cly, are a hundred times better than I thought them to be and the prisoner is a hundred times worse. Surely his statement regarding the infamous rebel, George Washington, cannot be thus lightly thrust aside. That statement alone proves his treason.

Think of the magnitude of your decision. Shall traitors defy our laws? Shall our enemies escape the dire justice which they deserve? Think of all this and, when you decide, let the verdict be, *Guilty*.

My Lord. (*Gives charge to Jury*.) Gentlemen of the Jury, you have now heard the testimony presented on both sides in this case against the prisoner, Charles Darnay. It is now your solemn duty to deliberate upon this question and render your verdict according to the merits of the case and with due regard for the majesty of the law. You may now retire. Officer, accompany the Jury to the Jury room. A recess in the court is declared.

(1) What turned the scale in favor of Charles Darnay?
(2) Why is this chapter called "A Disappointment"?
(3) What is meant by the "baffled blue-flies"?

Chapter IV. "Congratulatory."

(1) What explanation is found in this chapter for the title, "The Golden Thread," which Dickens has given to Book II?
(2) What impression of Mr. Stryver is obtained here? How does it compare with the first impression of him?
(3) Where in this chapter has the author aroused curiosity? Notice his frequent use of suspense.
(4) Trace Mr. Carton through this chapter. How does your impression of him here compare with the one gained in the court room?
(5) What reasons had he for disliking Charles Darnay?
(6) What was the highest point of his insolence here?
(7) What was the reason why Carton flung his glass against the wall?
(8) What was the characterization which Carton gave of himself?

Chapter V. "The Jackal."
 (1) Explain the title of this chapter. How is it appropriate?
 (2) What were Stryver's ambitions?
 (3) Where had Stryver found his jackal? What of their past history gained here?
 (4) Why was it that the Stryver clerk never assisted at these conferences?
 (5) Why does Carton call Miss Manette "a golden-haired doll"?
 (6) What effect do the last two paragraphs of this chapter have on the reader's opinion of Carton?
 (7) Why was the pillow "wet with wasted tears"?
 (8) Memorize the last paragraph of this chapter.
 (9) What is the fatal defect in Sydney Carton?

Chapter VI. "Hundreds of People."
 (1) What is the time of this chapter with reference to the last?
 (2) What was the peculiar feature about the location of Dr. Manette's residence?
 (3) On what occasion was the reader first introduced to Miss Pross? What are her dominant traits of character?
 (4) What information is gained here regarding her brother Solomon?
 (5) What is gathered in this chapter regarding Dr. Manette's life since his restoration?
 (6) What two possible reasons did Dickens have for naming this chapter "Hundreds of People"?
 (7) Notice later in the story how many times you are reminded of this chapter.
 (8) What hints can you find in Chapters III, IV, and V that Sydney Carton is especially interested in Miss Manette?
 (9) How does the author stimulate curiosity regarding Dr. Manette?

Chapter VII. "Monseigneur in Town."
 (1) Look up the causes of the French Revolution as given in the histories.
 (2) What causes of the French Revolution are here depicted concretely?
 (3) What are the real purposes of this chapter?
 (4) Show how "the leprosy of unreality disfigured every human creature in attendance upon Monseigneur."
 (5) What use of foreshadowing here?
 (6) What new character is introduced in this chapter?
 (7) How is our curiosity aroused regarding this man? What is his attitude toward Monseigneur?
 (8) What two distinct purposes are served by the incident at the Saint Antoine fountain?
 (9) Where before in the story did we see Gaspard?

(10) What others of these people have we met before? What indications of their power?

(11) Notice in this chapter the beginning of a second plot.

Chapter VIII. "Monseigneur in the Country."

(1) What foreshadowing in the second, third, and fourth paragraphs of this chapter?

(2) Why might the carriage have been lighter? (Two reasons.)

(3) What other causes of the French Revolution are given concretely in this chapter?

(4) Why were there no dogs to be seen in the village?

(5) What were the Furies in Greek mythology?

(6) In what way did Monsieur the Marquis seem to be attended by the Furies?

(7) Notice the three significant references to the Furies in this chapter.

(8) What is the purpose in introducing the poor woman with her petition?

(In Chapters VII and VIII Dickens sometimes refers to Monseigneur as a class and again as an individual.)

Chapter IX. "The Gorgon's Head."

(1) What was the Gorgon's head in Greek mythology?

(2) What is the significance of the title of this chapter?

(3) Who is Monsieur the Marquis? What is the character of the man?

(4) What is the feeling between him and Charles Darnay?

(5) What of Charles Darnay's past history is revealed here?

(6) For what purpose had the Marquis gone to Paris? Why had he attended the reception the day before? What indication at that time as to his success?

(7) What mysteries are cleared up in this chapter?

(8) Why had Charles Darnay gone back and forth between France and England, as was brought out in Chapter VI?

(9) Had the Marquis anything to do with Charles's imprisonment for treason?

(10) What indication that Charles has been closely watched?

(11) Is Charles in any danger on this present occasion? Why is he here?

(12) How has the author made use of foreshadowing here?

(13) Why does Dickens make the Marquis review the day's events before going to bed?

(14) Where is the first hint given that the Marquis is to be murdered? Trace the series of hints to the full revelation of the deed.

(15) What is signified by the actions of the mender of roads and the villagers?

(16) Why does Dickens liken Gabelle and his servant to "a *new version* of the German ballad of Leonora"?

(17) What is meant by the statement that the stone face added to the Château that night was the one "for which it had waited through about two hundred years"?

(18) What hints as to the identity of the murderer? Why was the note signed "Jacques"?

(19) What hints as to when the deed was done?

Chapter X. "Two Promises."

(1) What is the time of this chapter with reference to the last one?

(2) Does Darnay have any knowledge regarding the causes of Dr. Manette's past trouble? What is the reason why he hesitates to ask the doctor's consent?

(3) In what figurative language did Dickens tell us that Darnay was a tutor at Cambridge a part of the time?

(4) What were the two promises?

(5) What was the cause of Dr. Manette's relapse that night?

Chapter XI. "A Companion Picture."

(1) Explain the meaning of this title. To what is this picture a companion?

(2) What is the chief interest of this chapter?

(3) Of what importance is it to the story as a whole?

(4) Does it further the plot in any way?

(5) What is your feeling for Carton here?

Chapter XII. "A Fellow of Delicacy."

(1) What is the chief purpose of this chapter?

(2) Why is Stryver so sure of success in his love-making?

(3) What is the reason for this title?

(4) How does Stryver turn the tables on Mr. Lorry? Why does he do it?

Chapter XIII. "The Fellow of No Delicacy."

(1) What is the meaning of the title of this chapter?

(2) How does this chapter affect our feeling toward Carton?

(3) Why is Carton so sure there can be no chance for himself?

(4) Why does he tell Miss Manette of his love when he knows there is no hope?

Chapter XIV. "The Honest Tradesman."

(1) Why does Dickens introduce this chapter just here?

(2) What is the nature of the chapters preceding and following it?

(3) Does this chapter affect the plot any? Its purpose?

(4) Notice the things in this chapter which arouse curiosity:

    (a) "Funerals had at all times a remarkable attraction for Mr. Cruncher."

    (b) Jerry "modestly concealed his spiky head from the observation of Tellson's, in the further corner of the mourning coach."

    (c) "Mr. Cruncher remained behind in the churchyard, to confer and condole with the undertakers."

    (d) He made a short call on ———— on his way back.

    (e) Jerry's going fishing.

    (f) Young Jerry's remark that his father's fishing-rods get rusty. Compare with this the speech of Young Jerry in the last paragraph of Chapter I of this book.

    (g) Jerry's objection to Mrs. Cruncher's "floppings."

    (h) Jerry's fishing tackle.

(5) Whose funeral procession was this? Why so treated?

(6) Why was Jerry's companion in the night's adventure called "a disciple of Izaak Walton"?

(7) Why was there no "fish" for breakfast?

(8) What was the effect on Jerry when he learned of his young son's ambition? Why is Young Jerry introduced into the story?

Chapter XV. "Knitting."

(1) Where is this scene laid?

(2) Account for the subdued excitement in Saint Antoine.

(3) Why has Defarge brought the mender of roads to Paris?

(4) What signal was given to the three Jacques? Compare with that given to the same three men in Chapter V of Book I.

(5) Why are the people of Saint Antoine so much interested in the story told by the mender of roads?

(6) Why was the fountain chosen for the place of Gaspard's execution?

(7) What is the full significance of the decision made by the four Jacques regarding the "Château and all the race"?

(8) What is meant by the title of this chapter?

(9) Why is the mender of roads taken to Versailles?

(10) Why is Madame Defarge so busy knitting on this trip?

(11) What is her own explanation of her work?

(12) What kind of a man is the mender of roads?

Chapter XVI. "Still Knitting."

(1) Notice throughout the story the constant use of significant details, showing that the author always has in mind the effects he wants to produce. For instance, in this chapter notice how we are constantly reminded of the condition of the people:

    (a) "The few village scarecrows—in quest of herbs to eat and fragments of sticks to burn."

    (b) "Their starved fancy."

    (c) "A rumor just lived in the village—had a faint and bare existence there, as its people had."

    (d) "A skinny finger," etc.

(2) What is indicated by the fact that one of the *police* gave the Defarges information regarding the spy?

(3) Which is the more important character, Monsieur or Madame Defarge?

(4) Which one has the stronger personality? In what ways?

(5) What use of surprise in this chapter?

(6) Is it natural to find the Englishman, Barsad, as a spy on the French people? How has Dickens arranged for the plausibility of this circumstance?

(7) Notice carefully the signals given in the wine-shop. What were they for?

(8) What was the result of the spy's efforts *to pick up* or *make* crumbs?

(9) What was Madame knitting?

(10) What was the one evident "hit" that the spy made on this visit?

(11) Compare Monsieur and Madame at this moment.

(12) Why should this news have such an effect?

(13) What indicates the power the Defarges have in Saint Antoine?

(14) What was Defarge's characterization of his wife in next to the last paragraph of this chapter? Do you agree with him?

Chapter XVII. "One Night."

(1) What was the time of this chapter?

(2) Why does Dr. Manette refer to his old life here?

Chapter XVIII. "Nine Days."

(1) What caused the relapse of Dr. Manette?

(2) Is Dr. Manette's mental state as bad as when you saw him in Paris? Why?

(3) Why was the plan of action arranged by Mr. Lorry and Miss Pross a wise one?

Chapter XIX. "An Opinion."

(1) What is the importance of this chapter in the story as a whole?

(2) What was Dr. Manette's opinion regarding another attack?

Chapter XX. "A Plea."

(1) What was Carton's request? In what way does this chapter tie a knot in the plot?

Chapter XXI. "Echoing Footsteps."

(1) What is the approximate date of this chapter?

(2) What place has Carton in the family life of the Darnays?

(3) How are we reminded in this chapter of the general title of the second book? Of that Sunday night under the plane trees, nine years before?

(4) How many years have gone by since the beginning of the story? How old is Mr. Lorry now? Dr. Manette?

(5) Why in the one chapter has the author presented a scene in Soho and one in Saint Antoine?

(6) What changes have the years brought to each? How many years did Monsieur and Madame Defarge have to wait, after that talk in the wine-shop, before the "lightning" was made and stored and the "earthquake" prepared?

(7) Where was the storehouse of weapons? ("Thrown up from the *depth below.*")

(8) Compare the account given in the histories of the storming of the Bastille with the one given here. Notice especially Carlyle's "History of the French Revolution," Part I, Book V, Chapter 6.

(9) Why was Defarge so interested in 105 North Tower?

(10) What was the result of his search?

(11) What foreshadowing is given in this chapter?

Chapter XXII. "The Sea Still Rises."

(1) Changes in Saint Antoine after the storming of the Bastille?

(2) Explain: "The image had been hammering into this for hundreds of years, and the last finishing blows had told mightily on the expression."

(3) What is the author's purpose in introducing the Foulon story?

(4) Notice the descriptions in the closing paragraphs of this chapter.

Chapter XXIII. "Fire Rises."

(1) What is the central thought of this chapter?

(2) How is the plot advanced?

(3) How is Dickens true to history in this chapter?

(4) What changes do you note in the mender of roads? Gabelle?

(5) If Gabelle had pitched himself head foremost over the parapet, as he at one time contemplated, what effect would it have had on the story?

Chapter XXIV. "Drawn to the Loadstone Rock."

(1) What is the time of this chapter with reference to the last one in which we saw the Darnays? How old is little Lucie?

(2) What historical happenings are hinted at in this chapter? Follow closely the historical account of:

    (a) The Emigration of Nobles.

    (b) The "Joyous Entry" from Versailles.

    (c) The Flight of the King.

    (d) Massacre of the Swiss Guards.

(3) Explain the third paragraph of this chapter.

(4) Why was Tellson's bank an important place at this time?

(5) What was the chain of circumstances which led Charles Darnay to the "Loadstone Rock"?

(6) Explain the meaning of the title of chapter.

(7) What were Charles's motives for going to France? Why did he not see his danger?

(8) How has Dickens made it seem natural for Mr. Lorry to go to France? Jerry Cruncher?

(9) What is the importance of this chapter to the story as a whole?

BOOK THE THIRD. "THE TRACK OF A STORM"

Chapter I. "In Secret."

(1) How does the author make it clear to us that conditions have changed in France?

(2) What help did Gabelle's letter give Charles in getting to Paris?

(3) What was the effect upon Defarge when he learned who Charles was? Why?

(4) Why was Charles placed "in secret"? What advantage did this prove to him?

(5) Was this advantage intended when he was so placed?

(6) Why were the company of ladies and gentlemen that Charles sees in the prison described as ghosts?

Chapter II. "The Grindstone."

(1) What were the headquarters of Tellson's Bank in Paris?

(2) What advantages were gained from its location?

(3) Look up the account, given in the histories, of the "Jail Delivery."

(4) Why did Dr. Manette and Lucie come to Paris?

(5) Why should they bring the child and Miss Pross? Was this necessary? Show that these events are consistent with what you know of these characters.

(6) Why was Doctor Manette's influence so great?

Chapter III. "The Shadow."

(1) What is the significance of this title?

(2) Why did Madame Defarge go to see Lucie? Why was she still knitting?

(3) Did she know before that there was a child?

(4) Why did they allow Charles to write a note home but would not allow a reply to it?

(5) What foreshadowing is used here?

Chapter IV. "Calm in Storm."

(1) What was the check which prevented Charles's release?

(2) Why was the Doctor so strong and calm during the terrible time?

(3) Why were Charles's letters never sent by the Doctor's hand?

(4) Explain what is meant by the "deluge of the Year One of Liberty —the deluge rising from below, not falling from above, and with the windows of Heaven shut, not opened."

(5) What prevented Charles from being brought to trial?

(6) Follow the account of events given in history here. Is Dickens accurate in historical details?

(7) Explain: "The name of the strong man of Old Scripture had descended to the chief functionary who worked it [La Guillotine], but so armed, he was stronger than his namesake, and blinder, and tore away the gates of God's own Temple every day."

(Dickens has here made a mistake in the name. It was not "Samson" but "Sanson.")

Chapter V. "The Wood-Sawyer."

(1) What is the time of this chapter with reference to Charles's imprisonment?

(2) What example of Lucie's faithfulness here?

(3) What was the reason why Lucie did not dare to make a sign toward the prison?

(4) Why was Charles able to climb up to the window at *three* in the afternoon but not at other times?

(5) Who is the wood-sawyer? Why in Paris?

(6) Why did he keep saying, "But it's not my business"?

(7) What was the carmagnole?

(8) What was the popular Revolution song of 1792?

(9) What was the significance of Madame Defarge's appearance just at the moment that Lucie was weeping and kissing her hand toward the prison?

(10) What use of suspense in the last paragraph of this chapter?

Chapter VI. "Triumph."

(1) What was the average number of minutes given to each of the fifteen prisoners who were tried before Charles?

(2) How did it happen that so much more time was given to Charles's case?

(3) By what means does Dickens keep us in doubt as to the results of this trial?

(4) Why had Charles never seen Defarge during this year and a half?

(5) How did this trial compare with Charles's trial in England? What were the conditions regarding lawyers, judge, and jury?

(6) What was the accusation this time?

(7) Why did the Defarges allow him to be acquitted? Did they foresee this result? Why did n't they prevent it? Was there any danger that Charles would escape them?

(8) Why did they avoid looking at Charles? Why did they disappear so soon?

(9) Why did the populace carry Charles home?

(10) What is the application of the title of this chapter?

Chapter VII. "A Knock at the Door."

(1) What example of foreshadowing in the beginning of this chapter?

(2) What purposes have Miss Pross and Jerry Cruncher served thus far in the story? Have they done anything to further the plot?

(3) Why could Charles not leave Paris at once?

(4) What use of suspense in this chapter?

Chapter VIII. "A Hand at Cards."

(1) Why does Dickens arrange it so that Miss Pross and Jerry are the ones to come upon Solomon?

(2) Does Solomon fulfill your expectations, judging by what Miss Pross had said of him earlier in the story?

(3) Why did Dickens bring Jerry Cruncher to Paris?

(4) What was the chain of circumstances which brought Sydney Carton up at the moment when Jerry was struggling to remember Barsad's name?

(5) Where did Dickens prepare us for Carton's familiarity with the French language and the city of Paris? (See Chapter V of Book II.)

(6) What was a "Sheep of the Prisons"?

(7) In what capacity was Barsad found when we saw him first in Paris?

(8) Why is Barsad willing to go to the bank with Carton?

(9) Why does Carton ask Jerry to go too?

(10) Why do the Darnays not know that Carton is in Paris?

(11) What is the significance of the title of this chapter?

(12) Enumerate the ways in which Carton had the advantage over Barsad. What is he trying to gain?

(13) Of what importance is Jerry's knowledge of Barsad and Cly?

(14) Why did Sydney pour out that last glass of brandy upon the hearth?

(15) Why does Dickens end the chapter in mystery?

Chapter IX. "The Game Made."

(1) What three purposes are served by the conversation between Mr. Lorry and Jerry while Carton and the spy are in the next room?

(2) How has Jerry changed since he left London?

(3) Why did Carton not take Mr. Lorry into his confidence here?

(4) What did he tell him he had accomplished in his talk with Barsad?

(5) Why does Carton want Lucie kept in ignorance regarding this arrangement?

(6) Why does Carton want his presence in the city kept from Lucie?

(7) Why is there mention here of Mr. Lorry's Leave to Pass?

(8) What is the author's reason for giving this conversation between Carton and Mr. Lorry?

(9) Trace Sydney Carton from his leaving Mr. Lorry at the Darnay gate to his appearance at Charles Darnay's second trial.

(10) What is signified by the wood-sawyer's remark: "Aha, a perfect Frenchman. Good-night, Englishman"?

(11) Why does Carton carry the little child across the street?

(12) What use of surprise in the trial of Charles?

(13) Did you understand that Defarge found anything when he examined the cell, No. 105 North Tower, at the time of the storming of the Bastille? How does Dickens skillfully throw his reader off the track there? Go back and notice the details given in Chapter XXI of Book II.

Chapter X. "The Substance of the Shadow."

(1) Why this title? Connect with the chapter entitled "The Shadow."

(2) When was this diary written? How long after it was written was it read in court? How long before the trial did the things related happen?

(3) Why had Dickens given us so little information regarding Dr. Manette's imprisonment?

(4) Does this paper change our attitude toward Madame Defarge?

(5) What was the effect upon the jury and people assembled?

(6) What reference to Madame Defarge in the paper?

(7) What reference to Charles Darnay and his mother?

(8) How has Dickens made this paper seem like a real one?

(9) What dramatic touches in it?

(10) What mysteries are cleared up by it?

Chapter XI. "Dusk."

(1) Why does Dickens make us think there is no chance for the escape of Charles? What is Carton's part here?

(2) What did little Lucie hear Carton say as he bent to kiss her mother? When had he made a similar remark? (See the closing paragraph of Chapter XIII, Book II.)

(3) Why does Carton urge Dr. Manette to make every effort to save Charles? Find two reasons.

(4) Did he expect him to succeed?

(5) What double meanings in the closing words of this chapter?

Chapter XII. "Darkness."

(1) What caused Carton to go to the wine-shop in Saint Antoine?

(2) Why did he re-arrange his hair and dress before entering the wine-shop?

(3) Why did he speak in "indifferent French"?

(4) What was the effect of his appearance there upon Madame Defarge?

(5) Why did Defarge himself bring him the wine?

(6) What information did he get at the wine-shop? How?

(7) Why were the Defarges off their guard?

(8) What use of surprise is made here?

(9) Why did Carton ask to be directed towards the National Palace?

(10) Is Dr. Manette's relapse natural under the circumstances?

(11) What were Carton's directions to Mr. Lorry?

(12) How does he make sure that they will be carried out to the letter?

(13) Why does n't Carton take Mr. Lorry into his confidence?

(14) How do he and Mr. Lorry get Dr. Manette to go home?

(15) Why did Carton plan for the carriage to start before the execution?

Chapter XIII. "Fifty-two."

(1) What effect does Charles's forgetting all about Carton in writing his farewell letters have upon us?

(2) Why has Darnay not seen Barsad?

(3) How does Carton succeed in getting Darnay to do as he wants?

(4) Why does he dictate the letter to Darnay? To whom addressed?

(5) What was Darnay's last conscious thought? Why the reproachful look?

(6) Why does Dickens introduce the little seamstress here, so late in the story?

(7) Why does the author stop to tell us of the departure of the Darnay family before finishing Carton's story?

(8) How does he lead us to know that they got out of France safely?

(9) What hint was also given to that effect in mentioning little Lucie in the middle of Chapter XI, Book III?

Chapter XIV. "The Knitting Done."

(1) Why does Madame Defarge have her conference with the Vengeance and Jacques Three at the wood-sawyer's shed instead of at the wine-shop?

(2) What time was set for denouncing Dr. Manette, Lucie, and her child? What was to be the charge?

(3) What hint that Defarge himself was in danger?

(4) Why did Madame Defarge decide to go to Lucie's home before the hour for the execution?

(5) Why were Miss Pross and Jerry Cruncher left behind the rest of the family? What would have happened if they had gone with the others?

(6) What were Jerry's vows taken at this time?

(7) Notice how Dickens mingles comic and pathetic elements together.

(8) What use of surprise?

(9) What were the fears of Miss Pross while waiting for Jerry in front of the Cathedral?

Chapter XV. "The Footsteps Die Out Forever."

(1) What is the force of this title?

(2) Explain paragraphs 1 and 2.

(3) Why were the people so interested in Evrémonde?

(4) In how many ways did John Barsad show that he was trying to help Carton and his friends?

(5) What sign of softening in him? What has caused it?

(6) How has the author reduced the horror at the end?

(7) What method does Dickens use to wind up the threads of his story?

(8) Is this epilogue necessary? Is it artistic? Are there things here that we could have inferred from our knowledge of French history? Are there things given that are not essential? For instance, are we sure without being told that Carton's name would be revered? That Mr. Lorry would leave his property to the Darnays? Where is the *logical* end of the story?

General Questions.

(1) Select from the book as a whole six incidents which reveal character.

(2) Name an incident in the story which determines the action of a person.

(3) Name a character that was developed by adverse circumstances.

(4) Name a character that was developed by the influence upon it of another person.

(5) Where in the story has the author contrasted characters?

(6) Name a person of the story who complicates the plot. Show how.

(7) Name a person who helps to unravel the plot. Show how.

(8) Are there any persons who do not further the plot? Why introduced? What do you consider to be the main thread of this story?

(9) Are there any sub-plots?

(10) Point out examples of mystification, foreshadowing, suspense, surprise.

(11) How is the plot influenced by the setting? What situations are determined by the setting?

(12) Where are the chief scenes of the story located?

(13) Try to determine the reason the author had for the introduction of each character in the story. For instance, what use is made of Stryver, Mr. Lorry, Jerry, Miss Pross, etc.?

(14) Who is the central figure of this story? How are the other characters connected with this character?

(15) In how many chapters can you recall the contents just by the title?

(16) What do you think of Dickens's choice of titles?

(17) Of the three essential elements of a novel, do you find one emphasized more than the others, or are all three of nearly equal prominence?

(18) How is the setting in keeping with the story told?

(19) Could any of the events depicted be omitted without loss?

(20) What indications that Dickens made his plot before he began to write?

(21) What important changes in the ending of this novel would be necessitated if the following circumstances were changed:

   (a) If Defarge had not succeeded in his search on the day of the storming of the Bastille?

   (b) If Gaspard had not been captured after his year of hiding?

   (c) If Gabelle had been killed on the night that he hid on his house-top?

   (d) If Jerry Cruncher had not gone to Paris?

   (e) If there had been room for Miss Pross and Jerry in the carriage with the family?

   (f) If Madame Defarge had waited until after the execution before going to the Darnay apartment?

(22) Do the characters seem to do things of their own will, or do you feel that the author is moving them to suit himself?

(23) How does Dickens get his characters from England to France so that their going, in each case, seems perfectly natural?

(24) Would you, or would you not, like to read other novels by Dickens, judging from this one?

The Novelette.—The novelette is simply a short novel. It usually has a simpler plot than a novel and not so many characters and incidents, but in general structure and method of arrangement it is the same. It is often as short as a short-story, but it differs greatly from the latter in form. Thackeray's "Dennis Haggerty's Wife," George Eliot's "Amos Barton," and Kipling's "The Light that Failed" are neither novels nor short-stories, since they are too short for the former classification and not compressed enough for the latter.

SUGGESTIONS TO STUDENTS

For your theme work here it would be interesting to write novelettes. The class should be divided into groups made up of five or six students, each student writing a chapter. The one in each group who writes the last chapter must give the name to the story. Each student should try to leave his chapter at an interesting place for the next one to take up. Clues thrown out in other chapters should be followed out, and the one writing the last chapter in each case should see that all threads of the story are satisfactorily completed. Remember what Carlyle said in his "Essay on Burns" regarding "the duty of staying at home." In other words, be sure to write about things with which you are familiar. A good deal of rivalry might be aroused among the groups in striving to produce the most interesting novelette. It would take five or six weeks, probably, for the completion of this work. This would not interfere with the regular theme work, excepting that students writing chapters would be excused from the theme of their particular week.

SOME GOOD NOVELS FOR OPTIONAL READING

Note.—Write a report of the novel, or novels, read, making use of the following suggestions: Give name of book and author. Is the title an appropriate one? What seems to be the main purpose of this novel? What is the main plot? What sub-plots do you find? How are the sub-plots connected with the main plot? Which is made most prominent in the novel—plot, setting, or character study—or are they of equal interest? To how great a degree are the events dependent on the setting? Are the characters few or many? Are they true to life? Who is the hero? The heroine? Where is the highest point of interest? Point out examples of foreshadowing, surprise, and suspense. Is the book interesting? Would you call this a realistic or a romantic novel? Do you think you would like to read other novels by the same author?

Memorize something worth while from each novel if possible.

Any novel by Scott   not read before
Any novel by Jane Austen   not read before
Any novel by Dickens   not read before
Any novel by Thackeray   not read before
Any novel by George Eliot   not read before
Any novel by Stevenson   not read before
Any novel by Hawthorne   not read before

"The Vicar of Wakefield" ....Oliver Goldsmith
"Jane Eyre".................................. Charlotte Brontë
"Scottish Chiefs" ....Jane Porter
"The Last Days of Pompeii"...................Bulwer Lytton

"The Blazed Trail" ....Stewart Edward White
"The Crisis" ....Churchill
"Richard Carvel" ....Churchill
"The Crossing" ....Churchill
"Coniston" ....   Churchill
"Mr. Crewe's Career" ....Churchill
"The Sky Pilot" ....Connor
"The Man from Glengarry" ....Connor
"The Virginian" ....Wister
"Queed" ....Harrison
"The Conquest of Canaan" ....Tarkington
"The Gentleman from Indiana" ....Tarkington
"Monsieur Beaucaire" ....Tarkington
"The Turmoil" ....Tarkington
"The Fortunes of Oliver Horn" ....F. Hopkinson Smith
"Caleb West, Master Diver"..................F. Hopkinson Smith
"Peter" ....F. Hopkinson Smith
"Lord Jim" ....Conrad
"The Typhoon" ....Conrad
"Christine" ....Alice Cholmondeley
"Les Misérables" (French novel)............Victor Hugo
"Toilers of the Sea" (French novel)............Victor Hugo

The Short-Story.—The short-story differs from the novel and novelette in general structure. A true example of this type shows the following characteristics:

(1) There is no character introduced that is not absolutely necessary for the most artistic results.

(2) The action is given in the shortest possible time without sacrificing the highest effect.

(3) There is little or no change of scene.

(4) There is but one impression, or strong emotion, produced in the course of the story.

(5) Not one word is used that can be omitted, or that does not have a direct bearing on the story.

(6) There is but a single experience selected for treatment instead of the varied experiences of a life.

(7) The plot is never complicated.

(8) The short-story may usually be read in a very short time, and thus a strong effect is gained.

(9) The opening paragraph—even the first sentence, is of especial importance. It arouses and holds the attention.

(10) The story closes just as soon as its purpose is accomplished.

(11) The end of a short-story is in keeping with its beginning. It is enfolded in the beginning as a rose is in the bud.

(12) The short-story usually follows the same unities that are emphasized in the classic drama—those of time, place, and action. Thus the compression is very great—a single time, a single place, and a single action.

(13) A perfect short-story cannot be added to without serious injury, nor can a part be taken away from it without harm.

(14) The story is told rapidly, but the interest is never sacrificed to brevity.

(15) Although every short-story has all three elements, setting, characters, and action, only one is emphasized in each story.

(16) Because of the swiftness of the movement of a short-story, the opening paragraph informs the reader whether setting, characters, or action will play the greatest part.

(17) In a story of character, the attention is focused on some odd, unusual personality. Although setting and action are also given, they are subordinated to the character delineation. In a story of setting, the place is so prominent that the characters and action are but slightly drawn, while in a story of incident, the action overshadows everything else.

Mr. Clayton Hamilton in his "Materials and Methods of Fiction," in commenting on Edgar Allan Poe's artistic work in the short-story, said, "He began a story of setting with description; a story of character with a remark made by, or made about, the leading actor; and a story of action with a sentence pregnant with potential incident. Furthermore, he conveyed in his very first sentence a subtle sense of the emotional tone of the entire narrative." As regards the close of these stories, Mr. Hamilton further pointed out, "Poe shows his artistry in stopping at the very moment when he has attained completely his pre-established design."

The Standardization of the Short-Story.—Although the short-story is a very old form, some true ones being found in the Bible, it was not really distinguished as a special literary type until Edgar Allan Poe laid down the principles for it. Since then writers of short-stories have deliberately worked along the lines pointed out by Poe, and all work is judged now by these standards. Professor Brander Matthews was the one who suggested the use of the hyphen to distinguish the modern, more exact type of "short-story" from the old, indefinite form.

The Greatest Writers of the Short-Story.—The best work in

the short-story has been done in America and France, although the
type is found in the literature of most of the European nations.
In America the leaders in this form are Poe, Hawthorne, Bret
Harte, "O. Henry," [1] and Henry James. Besides these, there have
been excellent stories written by Stockton, Aldrich, Hale, Bunner,
Freeman, Alice Brown, Josephine Daskam Bacon, Garland, "Octave Thanet," [2] and many others. In France the best short-story
writers are De Maupassant, Coppée, Balzac, Daudet, Mérimée, and
Anatole France. In England, Kipling and Stevenson have done
the best work. Among other nations the most noteworthy stories
have been produced by Turgenieff and Tolstoi in Russia, and
by Björnson in Norway.

Some Examples of the Short-Story.—

THE BIRTHMARK [3] (1843)

NATHANIEL HAWTHORNE (1804–1864)

In the latter part of the last century there lived a man of science,
eminently proficient in every branch of natural philosophy, who not long
before our story opens had made experience of a spiritual affinity more
attractive than any chemical one. He had left his laboratory to the care
of an assistant, cleared his fine countenance from the furnace smoke,
washed the stain of acids from his fingers, and persuaded a beautiful
woman to become his wife. In those days when the comparatively recent
discovery of electricity and other kindred mysteries of Nature seemed to
open paths into the region of miracle, it was not unusual for the love
of science to rival the love of woman in its depth and absorbing energy.
The higher intellect, the imagination, the spirit, and even the heart
might all find their congenial aliment in pursuits which, as some of their
ardent votaries believed, would ascend from one step of powerful intelligence to another, until the philosopher should lay his hand on the secret
of creative force and perhaps make new worlds for himself. We know
not whether Aylmer possessed this degree of faith in man's ultimate control over Nature. He had devoted himself, however, too unreservedly to
scientific studies ever to be weaned from them by any second passion.
His love for his young wife might prove the stronger of the two; but it
could only be by intertwining itself with his love of science, and uniting
the strength of the latter to his own.

Such a union accordingly took place, and was attended with truly remarkable consequences and a deeply impressive moral. One day, very

---

[1] The pen name for William Sidney Porter.
[2] The pen name for Miss Alice French.
[3] Used by permission of Houghton Mifflin Company.

soon after their marriage, Aylmer sat gazing at his wife with a trouble in his countenance that grew stronger until he spoke.

"Georgiana," said he, "has it never occurred to you that the mark upon your cheek might be removed?"

"No, indeed," said she, smiling; but perceiving the seriousness of his manner, she blushed deeply. "To tell you the truth, it has been so often called a charm that I was simple enough to imagine it might be so."

"Ah, upon another face perhaps it might," replied her husband; "but never on yours. No, dearest Georgiana, you came so nearly perfect from the hand of Nature that this slightest possible defect, which we hesitate whether to term a defect or a beauty, shocks me, as being the visible mark of earthly imperfection."

"Shocks you, my husband!" cried Georgiana, deeply hurt; at first reddening with momentary anger, but then bursting into tears. "Then why did you take me from my mother's side? You cannot love what shocks you!"

To explain this conversation it must be mentioned that in the centre of Georgiana's left cheek there was a singular mark, deeply interwoven, as it were, with the texture and substance of her face. In the usual state of her complexion—a healthy though delicate bloom—the mark wore a tint of deeper crimson, which imperfectly defined its shape amid the surrounding rosiness. When she blushed it gradually became more indistinct, and finally vanished amid the triumphant rush of blood that bathed the whole cheek with its brilliant glow. But if any shifting motion caused her to turn pale there was the mark again, a crimson stain upon the snow, in what Aylmer sometimes deemed an almost fearful distinctness. Its shape bore not a little similarity to the human hand, though of the smallest pygmy size. Georgiana's lovers were wont to say that some fairy at her birth hour had laid her tiny hand upon the infant's cheek, and left this impress there in token of the magic endowments that were to give her such sway over all hearts. Many a desperate swain would have risked life for the privilege of pressing his lips to the mysterious hand. It must not be concealed, however, that the impression wrought by this fairy sign manual varied exceedingly, according to the difference of temperament in the beholders. Some fastidious persons—but they were exclusively of her own sex—affirmed that the bloody hand, as they chose to call it, quite destroyed the effect of Georgiana's beauty, and rendered her countenance even hideous. But it would be as reasonable to say that one of those small blue stains which sometimes occur in the purest statuary marble would convert the Eve of Powers to a monster. Masculine observers, if the birthmark did not heighten their admiration, contented themselves with wishing it away, that the world might possess one living specimen of ideal loveliness without the semblance of a flaw. After his marriage,—for he thought little or nothing of the matter before,—Aylmer discovered that this was the case with himself.

Had she been less beautiful,—if Envy's self could have found aught else to sneer at,—he might have felt his affection heightened by the prettiness of this mimic hand, now vaguely portrayed, now lost, now stealing forth again and glimmering to and fro with every pulse of emotion that throbbed within her heart; but seeing her otherwise so perfect, he found this one defect grow more and more intolerable with every moment of their united lives. It was the fatal flaw of humanity which Nature, in one shape or another, stamps ineffaceably on all her productions, either to imply that they are temporary and finite, or that their perfection must be wrought by toil and pain. The crimson hand expressed the ineludible gripe in which mortality clutches the highest and purest of earthly mould, degrading them into kindred with the lowest, and even with the very brutes, like whom their visible frames return to dust. In this manner, selecting it as the symbol of his wife's liability to sin, sorrow, decay, and death, Aylmer's sombre imagination was not long in rendering the birthmark a frightful object, causing him more trouble and horror than ever Georgiana's beauty, whether of soul or sense, had given him delight.

At all the seasons which should have been their happiest, he invariably and without intending it, nay, in spite of a purpose to the contrary, reverted to this one disastrous topic. Trifling as it at first appeared, it so connected itself with innumerable trains of thought and modes of feeling that it became the central point of all. With the morning twilight Aylmer opened his eyes upon his wife's face and recognized the symbol of imperfection; and when they sat together at the evening hearth his eyes wandered stealthily to her cheek, and beheld, flickering with the blaze of the wood fire, the spectral hand that wrote mortality where he would fain have worshipped. Georgiana soon learned to shudder at his gaze. It needed but a glance with the peculiar expression that his face often wore to change the roses of her cheek into a deathlike paleness, amid which the crimson hand was brought strongly out, like a bas-relief of ruby on the whitest marble.

Late one night when the lights were growing dim, so as hardly to betray the stain on the poor wife's cheek, she herself, for the first time, voluntarily took up the subject.

"Do you remember, my dear Aylmer," said she, with a feeble attempt at a smile, "have you any recollection of a dream last night about this odious hand?"

"None! none whatever!" replied Aylmer, starting; but then he added, in a dry, cold tone, affected for the sake of concealing the real depth of his emotion, "I might well dream of it; for before I fell asleep it had taken a pretty firm hold of my fancy."

"And you did dream of it?" continued Georgiana, hastily; for she dreaded lest a gush of tears should interrupt what she had to say. "A terrible dream! I wonder that you can forget it. Is it possible to forget this one expression?—'It is in her heart now; we must have it out!' Reflect, my husband; for by all means I would have you recall that dream."

The mind is in a sad state when Sleep, the all-involving, cannot confine her spectres within the dim region of her sway, but suffers them to break forth, affrighting this actual life with secrets that perchance belong to a deeper one. Aylmer now remembered his dream. He had fancied himself with his servant Aminadab, attempting an operation for the removal of the birthmark; but the deeper went the knife, the deeper sank the hand, until at length its tiny grasp appeared to have caught hold of Georgiana's heart; whence, however, her husband was inexorably resolved to cut or wrench it away.

When the dream had shaped itself perfectly in his memory, Aylmer sat in his wife's presence with a guilty feeling. Truth often finds its way to the mind close muffled in robes of sleep, and then speaks with uncompromising directness of matters in regard to which we practise an unconscious self-deception during our waking moments. Until now he had not been aware of the tyrannizing influence acquired by one idea over his mind, and of the lengths which he might find it in his heart to go for the sake of giving himself peace.

"Aylmer," resumed Georgiana, solemnly. "I know not what may be the cost to both of us to rid me of this fatal birthmark. Perhaps its removal may cause cureless deformity; or it may be the stain goes as deep as life itself. Again: do we know that there is a possibility, on any terms, of unclasping the firm gripe of this little hand which was laid upon me before I came into the world?"

"Dearest Georgiana, I have spent much thought upon the subject," hastily interrupted Aylmer. "I am convinced of the perfect practicability of its removal."

"If there be the remotest possibility of it," continued Georgiana, "let the attempt be made at whatever risk. Danger is nothing to me; for life, while this hateful mark makes me the object of your horror and disgust,—life is a burden which I would fling down with joy. Either remove this dreadful hand, or take my wretched life! You have deep science. All the world bears witness of it. You have achieved great wonders. Cannot you remove this little, little mark, which I cover with the tips of two small fingers? Is this beyond your power, for the sake of your own peace, and to save your poor wife from madness?"

"Noblest, dearest, tenderest wife," cried Aylmer, rapturously, "doubt not my power. I have already given this matter the deepest thought—thought which might almost have enlightened me to create a being less perfect than yourself. Georgiana, you have led me deeper than ever into the heart of science. I feel myself fully competent to render this dear cheek as faultless as its fellow; and then, most beloved, what will be my triumph when I shall have corrected what Nature left imperfect in her fairest work! Even Pygmalion, when his sculptured woman assumed life, felt not greater ecstasy than mine will be."

"It is resolved, then," said Georgiana, faintly smiling. "And, Aylmer, spare me not, though you should find the birthmark take refuge in my heart at last."

Her husband tenderly kissed her cheek—her right cheek—not that which bore the impress of the crimson hand.

The next day Aylmer apprised his wife of a plan that he had formed whereby he might have opportunity for the intense thought and constant watchfulness which the proposed operation would require; while Georgiana, likewise, would enjoy the perfect repose essential to its success. They were to seclude themselves in the extensive apartments occupied by Aylmer as a laboratory, and where, during his toilsome youth, he had made discoveries in the elemental powers of Nature that had roused the admiration of all the learned societies in Europe. Seated calmly in this laboratory, the pale philosopher had investigated the secrets of the highest cloud region and of the profoundest mines; he had satisfied himself of the causes that kindled and kept alive the fires of the volcano; and had explained the mystery of fountains, and how it is that they gush forth, some so bright and pure, and others with such rich medicinal virtues, from the dark bosom of the earth. Here, too, at an earlier period, he had studied the wonders of the human frame, and attempted to fathom the very process by which Nature assimilates all her precious influences from earth and air, and from the spiritual world, to create and foster man, her masterpiece. The latter pursuit, however, Aylmer had long laid aside in unwilling recognition of the truth—against which all seekers sooner or later stumble—that our great creative Mother, while she amuses us with apparently working in the broadest sunshine, is yet severely careful to keep her own secrets, and, in spite of her pretended openness, shows us nothing but results. She permits us, indeed, to mar, but seldom to mend, and, like a jealous patentee, on no account to make. Now, however, Aylmer resumed these half-forgotten investigations; not, of course, with such hopes or wishes as first suggested them; but because they involved much physiological truth and lay in the path of his proposed scheme for the treatment of Georgiana.

As he led her over the threshold of the laboratory, Georgiana was cold and tremulous. Aylmer looked cheerfully into her face, with intent to reassure her, but was so startled with the intense glow of the birthmark upon the whiteness of her cheek that he could not restrain a strong convulsive shudder. His wife fainted.

"Aminadab! Aminadab!" shouted Aylmer, stamping violently on the floor.

Forthwith there issued from an inner apartment a man of low stature, but bulky frame, with shaggy hair hanging about his visage, which was grimed with the vapors of the furnace. This personage had been Aylmer's underworker during his whole scientific career, and was admirably fitted for that office by his great mechanical readiness, and the skill with which, while incapable of comprehending a single principle, he executed all the details of his master's experiments. With his vast strength, his shaggy hair, his smoky aspect, and the indescribable earthiness that incrusted him, he seemed to represent man's physical nature; while Aylmer's slender figure, and pale, intellectual face, were no less apt a type of the spiritual element.

"Throw open the door of the boudoir, Aminadab," said Aylmer, "and burn a pastil."

"Yes, master," answered Aminadab, looking intently at the lifeless form of Georgiana; and then he muttered to himself, "If she were my wife, I'd never part with that birthmark."

When Georgiana recovered consciousness she found herself breathing an atmosphere of penetrating fragrance, the gentle potency of which had recalled her from her deathlike faintness. The scene around her looked like enchantment. Aylmer had converted those smoky, dingy, sombre rooms, where he had spent his brightest years in recondite pursuits, into a series of beautiful apartments not unfit to be the secluded abode of a lovely woman. The walls were hung with gorgeous curtains, which imparted the combination of grandeur and grace that no other species of adornment can achieve; and as they fell from the ceiling to the floor, their rich and ponderous folds, concealing all angles and straight lines, appeared to shut in the scene from infinite space. For aught Georgiana knew, it might be a pavilion among the clouds. And Aylmer, excluding the sunshine, which would have interfered with his chemical processes, had supplied its place with perfumed lamps, emitting flames of various hue, but all uniting in a soft, impurpled radiance. He now knelt by his wife's side, watching her earnestly, but without alarm; for he was confident in his science, and felt that he could draw a magic circle round her within which no evil might intrude.

"Where am I? Ah, I remember," said Georgiana, faintly; and she placed her hand over her cheek to hide the terrible mark from her husband's eyes.

"Fear not, dearest!" exclaimed he. "Do not shrink from me! Believe me, Georgiana, I even rejoice in this single imperfection, since it will be such a rapture to remove it."

"Oh, spare me!" sadly replied his wife. "Pray do not look at it again. I never can forget that convulsive shudder."

In order to soothe Georgiana, and, as it were, to release her mind from the burden of actual things, Aylmer now put in practice some of the light and playful secrets which science had taught him among its profounder lore. Airy figures, absolutely bodiless ideas, and forms of unsubstantial beauty came and danced before her, imprinting their momentary footsteps on beams of light. Though she had some indistinct idea of the method of these optical phenomena, still the illusion was almost perfect enough to warrant the belief that her husband possessed sway over the spiritual world. Then again, when she felt a wish to look forth from her seclusion, immediately, as if her thoughts were answered, the possession of external existence flitted across a screen. The scenery and the figures of actual life were perfectly represented, but with that bewitching yet indescribable difference which always makes a picture, an image, or a shadow so much more attractive than the original. When wearied of this, Aylmer bade her cast her eyes upon a vessel containing a quantity of earth. She did so, with little interest at first; but was soon startled to perceive the germ of a plant shooting upward from the soil. Then came the slender stalk; the leaves gradually unfolded themselves; and amid them was a perfect and lovely flower.

"It is magical!" cried Georgiana. "I dare not touch it."

"Nay, pluck it," answered Aylmer,—"pluck it, and inhale its brief perfume while you may. The flower will wither in a few moments and leave nothing save its brown seed vessels; but thence may be perpetuated a race as ephemeral as itself."

But Georgiana had no sooner touched the flower than the whole plant suffered a blight, its leaves turning coal-black as if by the agency of fire.

"There was too powerful a stimulus," said Aylmer, thoughtfully.

To make up for this abortive experiment, he proposed to take her portrait by a scientific process of his own invention. It was to be effected by rays of light striking upon a polished plate of metal. Georgiana assented; but, on looking at the result, was affrighted to find the features of the portrait blurred and indefinable; while the minute figure of a hand appeared where the cheek should have been. Aylmer snatched the metallic plate and threw it into a jar of corrosive acid.

Soon, however, he forgot these mortifying failures. In the intervals of study and chemical experiment he came to her flushed and exhausted, but seemed invigorated by her presence, and spoke in glowing language of the resources of his art. He gave a history of the long dynasty of the alchemists, who spent so many ages in quest of the universal solvent by which the golden principle might be elicited from all things vile and base. Aylmer appeared to believe that, by the plainest scientific logic, it was altogether within the limits of possibility to discover this long-sought medium; "but," he added, "a philosopher who should go deep enough to acquire the power would attain too lofty a wisdom to stoop to the exercise of it." Not less singular were his opinions in regard to the elixir vitæ. He more than intimated that it was at his option to concoct a liquid that should prolong life for years, perhaps interminably; but that it would produce a discord in Nature which all the world, and chiefly the quaffer of the immortal nostrum, would find cause to curse.

"Aylmer, are you in earnest?" asked Georgiana, looking at him with amazement and fear. "It is terrible to possess such power, or even to dream of possessing it."

"Oh, do not tremble, my love," said her husband. "I would not wrong either you or myself by working such inharmonious effects upon our lives; but I would have you consider how trifling, in comparison, is the skill requisite to remove this little hand."

At the mention of the birthmark, Georgiana, as usual, shrank as if a red-hot iron had touched her cheek.

Again Aylmer applied himself to his labors. She could hear his voice in the distant furnace room giving directions to Aminadab, whose harsh, uncouth, misshapen tones were audible in response, more like the grunt or growl of a brute than human speech. After hours of absence, Aylmer reappeared and proposed that she should now examine his cabinet of chemical products and natural treasures of the earth. Among the former he showed her a small vial, in which, he remarked, was contained a gentle yet most powerful fragrance, capable of impregnating all the breezes that blow across the kingdom. They were of inestimable value, the contents of that little vial; and, as he said so, he threw some of the perfume into the air and filled the room with piercing and invigorating delight.

"And what is this?" asked Georgiana, pointing to a small crystal globe containing a gold-colored liquid. "It is so beautiful to the eye that I could imagine it the elixir of life."

"In one sense it is," replied Aylmer; "or, rather, the elixir of immortality. It is the most precious poison that ever was concocted in this world. By its aid I could apportion the lifetime of any mortal at whom you might point your finger. The strength of the dose would determine whether he were to linger out years, or drop dead in the midst of a breath. No king on his guarded throne could keep his life if I, in my private station, should deem that the welfare of millions justified me in depriving him of it."

"Why do you keep such a terrific drug?" inquired Georgiana in horror.

"Do not mistrust me, dearest," said her husband, smiling; "its virtuous potency is yet greater than its harmful one. But see! here is a powerful cosmetic. With a few drops of this in a vase of water, freckles may be washed away as easily as the hands are cleansed. A stronger infusion would take the blood out of the cheek, and leave the rosiest beauty a pale ghost."

"Is it with this lotion that you intend to bathe my cheek?" asked Georgiana, anxiously.

"Oh, no," hastily replied her husband; "this is merely superficial. Your case demands a remedy that shall go deeper."

In his interviews with Georgiana, Aylmer generally made minute inquiries as to her sensations and whether the confinement of the rooms and the temperature of the atmosphere agreed with her. The questions had such a particular drift that Georgiana began to conjecture that she was already subjected to certain physical influences, either breathed in with the fragrant air or taken with her food. She fancied likewise, but it might be altogether fancy, that there was a stirring up of her system—a strange, indefinite sensation creeping through her veins, and tingling, half painfully, half pleasurably, at her heart. Still, whenever she dared to look into the mirror, there she beheld herself pale as a white rose and with the crimson birthmark stamped upon her cheek. Not even Aylmer now hated it so much as she.

To dispel the tedium of the hours which her husband found it necessary to devote to the process of combination and analysis, Georgiana turned over the volumes of his scientific library. In many dark old tomes she met with chapters full of romance and poetry. They were the works of philosophers of the middle ages, such as Albertus Magnus, Cornelius Agrippa, Paracelsus, and the famous friar who created the prophetic Brazen Head. All these antique naturalists stood in advance of their centuries, yet were imbued with some of their credulity, and therefore were believed, and perhaps imagined themselves to have acquired from the investigation of Nature a power above Nature, and from physics a sway over the spiritual world. Hardly less curious and imaginative were the early volumes of the Transactions of the Royal Society, in which the members, knowing little of the limits of natural possibility, were continually recording wonders or proposing methods whereby wonders might be wrought.

But to Georgiana the most engrossing volume was a large folio from her husband's own hand, in which he had recorded every experiment of his scientific career, its original aim, the methods adopted for its development, and its final success or failure, with the circumstances to which either event was attributable. The book, in truth, was both the history and emblem of his ardent, ambitious, imaginative, yet practical and laborious life. He handled physical details as if there were nothing beyond them; yet spiritualized them all, and redeemed himself from materialism by his strong and eager aspiration towards the infinite. In his grasp the veriest clod of earth assumed a soul. Georgiana, as she read, reverenced Aylmer and loved him more profoundly than ever, but with a less entire dependence on his judgment than heretofore. Much as he had accomplished, she could not but observe that his most splendid successes were almost invariably failures, if compared with the ideal at which he aimed. His brightest diamonds were the merest pebbles, and felt to be so by himself, in comparison with the inestimable gems which lay hidden beyond his reach. The volume, rich with achievements that had won renown for its author, was yet as melancholy a record as ever mortal hand had penned. It was the sad confession and continual exemplification of the shortcomings of the composite man, the spirit burdened with clay and working in matter, and of the despair that assails the higher nature at finding itself so miserably thwarted by the earthly part. Perhaps every man of genius, in whatever sphere, might recognize the image of his own experience in Aylmer's journal.

So deeply did these reflections affect Georgiana that she laid her face upon the open volume and burst into tears. In this situation she was found by her husband.

"It is dangerous to read in a sorcerer's books," said he with a smile, though his countenance was uneasy and displeased. "Georgiana, there are pages in that volume which I can scarcely glance over and keep my senses. Take heed lest it prove as detrimental to you."

"It has made me worship you more than ever," said she.

"Ah, wait for this one success," rejoined he, "then worship me if you will. I shall deem myself hardly unworthy of it. But come, I have sought you for the luxury of your voice. Sing to me, dearest."

So she poured out the liquid music of her voice to quench the thirst of his spirit. He then took his leave with a boyish exuberance of gayety, assuring her that her seclusion would endure but a little longer, and that the result was already certain. Scarcely had he departed when Georgiana felt irresistibly impelled to follow him. She had forgotten to inform Aylmer of a symptom which for two or three hours past had begun to excite her attention. It was a sensation in the fatal birthmark, not painful, but which induced a restlessness throughout her system. Hastening after her husband, she intruded for the first time into the laboratory.

The first thing that struck her eye was the furnace, that hot and feverish worker, with the intense glow of its fire, which by the quantities of soot clustered above it seemed to have been burning for ages. There was a distilling apparatus in full operation. Around the room were retorts, tubes, cylinders, crucibles, and other apparatus of chemical research. An electrical machine stood ready for immediate use. The atmosphere felt oppressively close, and was tainted with gaseous odors which had been tormented forth by the processes of science. The severe and homely simplicity of the apartment, with its naked walls and brick pavement, looked strange, accustomed as Georgiana had become to the fantastic elegance of her boudoir. But what chiefly, indeed almost solely, drew her attention, was the aspect of Aylmer himself.

He was pale as death, anxious and absorbed, and hung over the furnace as if it depended upon his utmost watchfulness whether the liquid which it was distilling should be the draught of immortal happiness or misery. How different from the sanguine and joyous mien that he had assumed for Georgiana's encouragement!

"Carefully now, Aminadab; carefully, thou human machine; carefully, thou man of clay!" muttered Aylmer, more to himself than his assistant. "Now, if there be a thought too much or too little, it is all over."

"Ho! ho!" mumbled Aminadab. "Look, master! look!"

Aylmer raised his eyes hastily, and at first reddened, then grew paler than ever, on beholding Georgiana. He rushed towards her and seized her arm with a gripe that left the print of his fingers upon it.

"Why do you come hither? Have you no trust in your husband?" cried he, impetuously. "Would you throw the blight of that fatal birth-mark over my labors? It is not well done. Go, prying woman, go!"

"Nay, Aylmer," said Georgiana with the firmness of which she possessed no stinted endowment, "it is not you that have a right to complain. You mistrust your wife; you have concealed the anxiety with which you watch the development of this experiment. Think not so unworthily of me, my husband. Tell me all the risk we run, and fear not that I shall shrink; for my share in it is far less than your own."

"No, no, Georgiana!" said Aylmer, impatiently; "it must not be."

"I submit," replied she calmly. "And, Aylmer, I shall quaff whatever draught you bring me; but it will be on the same principle that would induce me to take a dose of poison if offered by your hand."

"My noble wife," said Aylmer, deeply moved, "I knew not the height and depth of your nature until now. Nothing shall be concealed. Know, then, that this crimson hand, superficial as it seems, has clutched its grasp into your being with a strength of which I had no previous conception. I have already administered agents powerful enough to do aught except to change your entire physical system. Only one thing remains to be tried. If that fail us we are ruined."

"Why did you hesitate to tell me this?" asked she.

"Because, Georgiana," said Aylmer, in a low voice, "there is danger."

"Danger? There is but one danger—that this horrible stigma shall be left upon my cheek!" cried Georgiana. "Remove it, remove it, whatever be the cost, or we shall both go mad!"

"Heaven knows your words are too true," said Aylmer, sadly. "And now, dearest, return to your boudoir. In a little while all will be tested."

He conducted her back and took leave of her with a solemn tenderness which spoke far more than his words how much was now at stake. After his departure Georgiana became rapt in musings. She considered the character of Aylmer, and did it completer justice than at any previous moment. Her heart exulted, while it trembled, at his honorable love— so pure and lofty that it would accept nothing less than perfection nor miserably make itself contented with an earthlier nature than he had dreamed of. She felt how much more precious was such a sentiment than that meaner kind which would have borne with the imperfection for her sake, and have been guilty of treason to holy love by degrading its perfect ideal to the level of the actual; and with her whole spirit she prayed that for a single moment, she might satisfy his highest and deepest conception. Longer than one moment she well knew it could not be; for his spirit was ever on the march, ever ascending, and each instant required something that was beyond the scope of the instant before.

The sound of her husband's footsteps aroused her. He bore a crystal goblet containing a liquor colorless as water, but bright enough to be the draught of immortality. Aylmer was pale; but it seemed rather the consequence of a highly-wrought state of mind and tension of spirit than of fear or doubt.

"The concoction of the draught has been perfect," said he, in answer to Georgiana's look. "Unless all my science have deceived me, it cannot fail."

"Save on your account, my dearest Aylmer," observed his wife, "I might wish to put off this birthmark of mortality by relinquishing mortality itself in preference to any other mode. Life is but a sad possession to those who have attained precisely the degree of moral advancement at which I stand. Were I weaker and blinder it might be happiness. Were I stronger, it might be endured hopefully. But, being what I find myself, methinks I am of all mortals the most fit to die."

"You are fit for heaven without tasting death!" replied her husband. "But why do we speak of dying? The draught cannot fail. Behold its effect upon this plant."

On the window seat there stood a geranium diseased with yellow blotches, which had overspread all its leaves. Aylmer poured a small quantity of the liquid upon the soil in which it grew. In a little time, when the roots of the plant had taken up the moisture, the unsightly blotches began to be extinguished in a living verdure.

"There needed no proof," said Georgiana, quietly. "Give me the goblet. I joyfully stake all upon your word."

"Drink, then, thou lofty creature!" exclaimed Aylmer, with fervid admiration. "There is no taint of imperfection on thy spirit. Thy sensible frame, too, shall soon be all perfect."

She quaffed the liquid and returned the goblet to his hand.

"It is grateful," said she with a placid smile. "Methinks it is like water from a heavenly fountain; for it contains I know not what of unobtrusive fragrance and deliciousness. It allays a feverish thirst that had parched me for many days. Now, dearest, let me sleep. My earthly senses are closing over my spirit like the leaves around the heart of a rose at sunset."

She spoke the last words with a gentle reluctance, as if it required almost more energy than she could command to pronounce the faint and lingering syllables. Scarcely had they loitered through her lips ere she was lost in slumber. Aylmer sat by her side, watching her aspect with the emotions proper to a man the whole value of whose existence was involved in the process now to be tested. Mingled with this mood, however, was the philosophic investigation characteristic of the man of science. Not the minutest symptom escaped him. A heightened flush of the cheek, a slight irregularity of breath, a quiver of the eyelid, a hardly perceptible tremor through the frame,—such were the details which, as the moments passed, he wrote down in his folio volume. Intense thought had set its stamp upon every previous page of that volume, but the thoughts of years were all concentrated upon the last.

While thus employed, he failed not to gaze often at the fatal hand, and not without a shudder. Yet once, by a strange and unaccountable impulse, he pressed it with his lips. His spirit recoiled, however, in the very act; and Georgiana, out of the midst of her deep sleep, moved uneasily and murmured as if in remonstrance. Again Aylmer resumed his watch. Nor was it without avail. The crimson hand, which at first had been strongly visible upon the marble paleness of Georgiana's cheek, now grew more faintly outlined. She remained not less pale than ever; but the birthmark, with every breath that came and went, lost somewhat of its former distinctness. Its presence had been awful; its departure was more awful still. Watch the stain of the rainbow fading out of the sky, and you will know how that mysterious symbol passed away.

"By Heaven! it is well-nigh gone!" said Aylmer to himself, in almost irrepressible ecstasy. "I can scarcely trace it now. Success! success! And now it is like the faintest rose color. The lightest flush of blood across her cheek would overcome it. But she is so pale!"

He drew aside the window curtain and suffered the light of natural day to fall into the room and rest upon her cheek. At the same time he heard a gross, hoarse chuckle, which he had long known as his servant Aminadab's expression of delight.

"Ah, clod! ah, earthly mass!" cried Aylmer, laughing in a sort of frenzy, "you have served me well! Matter and spirit—earth and heaven—have both done their part in this! Laugh, thing of the senses! You have earned the right to laugh."

These exclamations broke Georgiana's sleep. She slowly unclosed her eyes and gazed into the mirror which her husband had arranged for that purpose. A faint smile flitted over her lips when she recognized how barely perceptible was now that crimson hand which had once blazed forth with such disastrous brilliancy as to scare away all their happiness. But then her eyes sought Aylmer's face with a trouble and anxiety that he could by no means account for.

"My poor Aylmer!" murmured she.

"Poor? Nay, richest, happiest, most favored!" exclaimed he. "My peerless bride, it is successful! You are perfect!"

"My poor Aylmer," she repeated, with a more than human tenderness, "you have aimed loftily; you have done nobly. Do not repent that, with so high and pure a feeling, you have rejected the best the earth could offer. Aylmer, dearest Aylmer, I am dying!"

Alas! it was too true! The fatal hand had grappled with the mystery of life, and was the bond by which an angelic spirit kept itself in union with a mortal frame. As the last crimson tint of the birthmark—that sole token of human imperfection—faded from her cheek, the parting breath of the now perfect woman passed into the atmosphere, and her soul, lingering a moment near her husband, took its heavenward flight. Then a hoarse, chuckling laugh was heard again! Thus ever does the gross fatality of earth exult in its invariable triumph over the immortal essence which, in this dim sphere of half development, demands the completeness of a higher state. Yet, had Aylmer reached a profounder wisdom, he need not thus have flung away the happiness which would have woven his mortal life of the selfsame texture with the celestial. The momentary circumstance was too strong for him; he failed to look beyond the shadowy scope of time, and, living once for all in eternity, to find the perfect future in the present.

"THE BIRTHMARK"

It was Hawthorne's custom to keep a note-book in which he placed suggestions that might be used for his stories. The following note is evidently his basis for "The Birthmark": "A person to be the death of his beloved in trying to raise her to more than mortal perfection."

Notice how many of the characteristics of a perfect short-story are to be found in "The Birthmark."

THE PIT AND THE PENDULUM (1843)

EDGAR ALLAN POE (1809–1849)

.   .   .   .

I was sick—sick unto death with that long agony; and when they at length unbound me, and I was permitted to sit, I felt that my senses were leaving me. The sentence—the dread sentence of death—was the last of distinct accentuation which reached my ears. After that, the sound of the inquisitorial voices seemed merged in one dreamy indeterminate hum. It conveyed to my soul the idea of *revolution*, perhaps from its association in fancy with the burr of a mill-wheel. This only for a brief period; for presently I heard no more. Yet, for a while, I saw; but with how terrible an exaggeration! I saw the lips of the black-robed judges. They appeared to me white, whiter than the sheet upon which I trace these words, and thin even to grotesqueness; thin with the intensity of their expression of firmness,—of immovable resolution, of stern contempt of human torture. I saw that the decrees of what to me was Fate were still issuing from those lips. I saw them writhe with a deadly locution. I saw them fashion the syllables of my name; and I shuddered because no sound succeeded. I saw, too, for a few moments of delirious horror, the soft and nearly imperceptible waving of the sable draperies which enwrapped the walls of the apartment. And then my vision fell upon the seven tall candles upon the table. At first they wore the aspect of charity, and seemed white slender angels who would save me; but then, all at once,

From an old daguerreotype.

EDGAR ALLAN POE
One of the World's Greatest Short-Story Writers

there came a most deadly nausea over my spirit, and I felt every fibre in my frame thrill as if I had touched the wire of a galvanic battery, while the angel forms became meaningless spectres, with heads of flame, and I saw that from them there would be no help. And then there stole into my fancy, like a rich musical note, the thought of what sweet rest there must be in the grave. The thought came gently and stealthily, and it seemed long before it attained full appreciation; but just as my spirit came at length properly to feel and entertain it, the figures of the judges vanished, as if magically, from before me; the tall candles sank into nothingness; their flames went out utterly; the blackness of darkness supervened; all sensations appeared swallowed up in a mad rushing descent as of the soul into Hades. Then silence, and stillness, and night were the universe.

I had swooned; but still will not say that all of consciousness was lost. What of it there remained I will not attempt to define, or even to describe; yet all was not lost. In the deepest slumber—no! In delirium —no! In a swoon—no! In death—no! even in the grave all is not lost. Else there is no immortality for man. Arousing from the most profound of slumbers, we break the gossamer web of *some* dream. Yet in a second afterward (so frail may that web have been) we remember not that we have dreamed. In the return to life from the swoon there are two stages: first, that of the sense of mental or spiritual, secondly, that of the sense of physical, existence. It seems probable that if, upon reaching the second stage, we could recall the impressions of the first, we should find these impressions eloquent in memories of the gulf beyond. And that gulf is—what? How at least shall we distinguish its shadows from those of the tomb? But if the impressions of what I have termed the first stage are not at will recalled, yet, after a long interval, do they not come unbidden, while we marvel whence they come? He who has never swooned is not he who finds strange palaces and wildly familiar faces in coals that glow; is not he who beholds floating in mid-air the sad visions that the many may not view; is not he who ponders over the perfume of some novel flower; is not he whose brain grows bewildered with the meaning of some musical cadence which has never before arrested his attention.

Amid frequent and thoughtful endeavors to remember, amid earnest struggles to regather some token of the state of seeming nothingness into which my soul had lapsed, there have been moments when I have dreamed of success; there have been brief, very brief periods when I have conjured up remembrances which the lucid reason of a later epoch assures me could have had reference only to that condition of seeming unconsciousness. These shadows of memory tell, instinctively, of tall figures that lifted and bore me in silence down—down—still down—till a hideous dizziness oppressed me at the mere idea of the interminableness of the descent. They tell also of a vague horror at my heart, on account of that heart's un-

natural stillness. Then comes a sense of sudden motionlessness throughout all things; as if those who bore me (a ghastly train!) had outrun
in their descent the limits of the limitless, and paused from the wearisome-
ness of their toil. After this I call to mind flatness and dampness; and
then all is *madness*—the madness of a memory which busies itself among
forbidden things.

Very suddenly there came back to my soul motion and sound—the
tumultuous motion of the heart, and, in my ears, the sound of its beating. Then a pause in which all is blank. Then again sound, and motion, and touch—a tingling sensation pervading my frame. Then the mere
consciousness of existence, without thought—a condition which lasted
long. Then, very suddenly, *thought,* and shuddering terror, and earnest
endeavor to comprehend my true state. Then a strong desire to lapse into
insensibility. Then a rushing revival of soul and a successful effort to
move. And now a full memory of the trial, of the judges, of the sable
draperies, of the sentence, of the sickness, of the swoon. Then entire forgetfulness of all that followed; of all that a later day and much earnestness
of endeavor have enabled me vaguely to recall.

So far, I had not opened my eyes. I felt that I lay upon my back, unbound. I reached out my hand, and it fell heavily upon something
damp and hard. There I suffered it to remain for many minutes, while I
strove to imagine where and *what* I could be. I longed yet dared not to
employ my vision. I dreaded the first glance at objects around me. It
was not that I feared to look upon things horrible, but that I grew aghast
lest there should be *nothing* to see. At length, with a wild desperation
at heart, I quickly unclosed my eyes. My worst thoughts, then, were confirmed. The blackness of eternal night encompassed me. I struggled for
breath. The intensity of the darkness seemed to oppress and stifle me.
The atmosphere was intolerably close. I still lay quietly, and made effort
to exercise my reason. I brought to mind the inquisitorial proceedings,
and attempted from that point to deduce my real condition. The sentence
had passed; and it appeared to me that a very long interval of time had
since elapsed. Yet not for a moment did I suppose myself actually dead.
Such a supposition, notwithstanding what we read in fiction, is altogether
inconsistent with real existence;—but where and in what state was I? The
condemned to death, I knew, perished usually at the *autos-da-fé,*[1] and one
of these had been held on the very night of the day of my trial. Had
I been remanded to my dungeon to await the next sacrifice, which would
not take place for many months? This I at once saw could not be.
Victims had been in immediate demand. Moreover, my dungeon, as well
as all the condemned cells at Toledo, had stone floors, and light was not
altogether excluded.

A fearful idea now suddenly drove the blood in torrents upon my heart,
and for a brief period I once more relapsed into insensibility. Upon
recovering, I at once started to my feet, trembling convulsively in every

fibre. I thrust my arms wildly above and around me in all directions.
I felt nothing; yet dreaded to move a step, lest I should be impeded by
the walls of a *tomb*. Perspiration burst from every pore, and stood in
cold, big beads upon my forehead. The agony of suspense grew at length
intolerable, and I cautiously moved forward, with my arms extended, and
my eyes straining from their sockets, in the hope of catching some faint
ray of light. I proceeded for many paces; but still all was blackness and
vacancy. I breathed more freely. It seemed evident that mine was not,
at least, the most hideous of fates.

And, now, as I still continued to step cautiously onward, there came
thronging upon my recollection a thousand vague rumors of the horrors of
Toledo. Of the dungeons there had been strange things narrated—fables
I had always deemed them—but yet strange, and too ghastly to repeat,
save in a whisper. Was I left to perish of starvation in this subterranean
world of darkness; or what fate, perhaps even more fearful, awaited me?
That the result would be death, and a death of more than customary bitter-
ness, I knew too well the character of my judges to doubt. The mode
and the hour were all that occupied or distracted me.

My outstretched hands at length encountered some solid obstruction.
It was a wall, seemingly of stone masonry—very smooth, slimy, and cold.
I followed it up; stepping with all the careful distrust with which certain antique narratives had inspired me. This process, however, afforded
me no means of ascertaining the dimensions of my dungeon; as I might
make its circuit, and return to the point whence I set out, without being
aware of the fact, so perfectly uniform seemed the wall. I therefore
sought the knife which had been in my pocket when led into the inquisitorial chamber; but it was gone; my clothes had been exchanged for a
wrapper of coarse serge. I had thought of forcing the blade in some
minute crevice of the masonry, so as to identify my point of departure.
The difficulty, nevertheless, was but trivial; although, in the disorder of
my fancy, it seemed at first insuperable. I tore a part of the hem from
the robe and placed the fragment at full length, and at right angles to
the wall. In groping my way around the prison I could not fail to
encounter this rag upon completing the circuit. So, at least, I thought;
but I had not counted upon the extent of the dungeon, or upon my own
weakness. The ground was moist and slippery. I staggered onward for
some time, when I stumbled and fell. My excessive fatigue induced me
to remain prostrate; and sleep soon overtook me as I lay.

Upon awaking, and stretching forth an arm, I found beside me a loaf
and a pitcher with water. I was too much exhausted to reflect upon
this circumstance, but ate and drank with avidity. Shortly afterward,
I resumed my tour around the prison, and with much toil came at last
upon the fragment of the serge. Up to the period when I fell, I had
counted fifty-two paces, and upon resuming my walk, I had counted
forty-eight more—when I arrived at the rag. There were in all, then,

a hundred paces; and, admitting two paces to the yard, I presumed the dungeon to be fifty yards in circuit. I had met, however, with many angles in the wall, and thus I could form no guess at the shape of the vault; for vault I could not help supposing it to be.

I had little object—certainly no hope—in these researches; but a vague curiosity prompted me to continue them. Quitting the wall, I resolved to cross the area of the enclosure. At first, I proceeded with extreme caution, for the floor, although seemingly of solid material, was treacherous with slime. At length, however, I took courage, and did not hesitate to step firmly—endeavoring to cross in as direct a line as possible. I had advanced some ten or twelve paces in this manner, when the remnant of the torn hem of my robe became entangled between my legs. I stepped on it and fell violently on my face.

In the confusion attending my fall, I did not immediately apprehend a somewhat startling circumstance, which yet, in a few seconds afterward, and while I still lay prostrate, arrested my attention. It was this: my chin rested upon the floor of the prison, but my lips and the upper portion of my head, although seemingly at a less elevation than the chin, touched nothing. At the same time, my forehead seemed bathed in a clammy vapor, and the peculiar smell of decayed fungus arose to my nostrils. I put forward my arm, and shuddered to find that I had fallen at the very brink of a circular pit, whose extent, of course, I had no means of ascertaining at the moment. Groping about the masonry just below the margin, I succeeded in dislodging a small fragment, and let it fall into the abyss. For many seconds I hearkened to its reverberations as it dashed against the sides of the chasm in its descent; at length there was a sullen plunge into water, succeeded by loud echoes. At the same moment there came a sound resembling the quick opening and as rapid closing of a door overhead, while a faint gleam of light flashed suddenly through the gloom, and as suddenly faded away.

I saw clearly the doom which had been prepared for me, and congratulated myself upon the timely accident by which I had escaped. Another step before my fall, and the world had seen me no more. And the death just avoided was of that very character which I had regarded as fabulous and frivolous in the tales respecting the Inquisition. To the victims of its tyranny there was the choice of death with its direst physical agonies, or death with its most hideous moral horrors. I had been reserved for the latter. By long suffering my nerves had been unstrung, until I trembled at the sound of my own voice, and had become in every respect a fitting subject for the species of torture which awaited me.

Shaking in every limb, I groped my way back to the wall—resolving there to perish rather than risk the terrors of the wells, of which my imagination now pictured many in various positions about the dungeon. In other conditions of mind, I might have had courage to end my misery at once, by a plunge into one of these abysses; but now I was the veriest of cowards. Neither could I forget what I had read of these pits—that the *sudden* extinction of life formed no part of their most horrible plan.

Agitation of spirit kept me awake for many long hours; but at length I again slumbered. Upon arousing, I found by my side, as before, a loaf and a pitcher of water. A burning thirst consumed me, and I emptied the vessel at a draught. It must have been drugged—for scarcely had I drunk, before I became irresistibly drowsy. A deep sleep fell upon me—a sleep like that of death. How long it lasted, of course I know not; but, when once again I unclosed my eyes, the objects around me were visible. By a wild, sulphurous lustre, the origin of which I could not at first determine, I was enabled to see the extent and aspect of the prison.

In its size I had been greatly mistaken. The whole circuit of its walls did not exceed twenty-five yards. For some minutes this fact occasioned me a world of vain trouble; vain indeed—for what could be of less importance, under the terrible circumstances which environed me, than the mere dimensions of my dungeon? But my soul took a wild interest in trifles, and I busied myself in endeavors to account for the error I had committed in my measurement. The truth at length flashed upon me. In my first attempt at exploration I had counted fifty-two paces, up to the period when I fell: I must then have been within a pace or two of the fragment of serge; in fact, I had nearly performed the circuit of the vault. I then slept—and, upon awaking, I must have returned upon my steps, thus supposing the circuit nearly double what it actually was. My confusion of mind prevented me from observing that I began my tour with the wall to the left, and ended it with the wall to the right.

I had been deceived, too, in respect to the shape of the enclosure. In feeling my way, I had found many angles, and thus deduced an idea of great irregularity; so potent is the effect of total darkness upon one arousing from lethargy or sleep! The angles were simply those of a few slight depressions, or niches, at odd intervals. The general shape of the prison was square. What I had taken for masonry, seemed now to be iron, or some other metal, in huge plates, whose sutures or joints occasioned the depression. The entire surface of this metallic enclosure was rudely daubed in all the hideous and repulsive devices to which the charnel superstition of the monks has given rise. The figures of fiends in aspects of menace, with skeleton forms, and other more really fearful images, overspread and disfigured the walls. I observed that the outlines of these monstrosities were sufficiently distinct, but that the colors seemed faded and blurred, as if from the effects of a damp atmosphere. I now noticed the floor, too, which was of stone. In the centre yawned the circular pit from whose jaws I had escaped; but it was the only one in the dungeon.

All this I saw distinctly and by much effort, for my personal condition had been greatly changed during slumber. I now lay upon my back, and at full length, on a species of low framework of wood. To this I was securely bound by a long strap resembling a surcingle. It passed in many convolutions about my limbs and body, leaving at liberty only my head, and my left arm to such extent that I could, by dint of much exertion, supply myself with food from an earthen dish which lay by my side on the floor. I saw, to my horror, that the pitcher had been removed. I say, to my horror—for I was consumed with intolerable thirst. This thirst it appeared to be the design of my persecutors to stimulate, for the food in the dish was meat pungently seasoned.

Looking upward, I surveyed the ceiling of my prison. It was some thirty or forty feet overhead, and constructed much as the side walls. In one of its panels a very singular figure riveted my whole attention. It was the painted figure of Time as he is commonly represented, save that, in lieu of a scythe, he held what, at a casual glance, I supposed to be the pictured image of a huge pendulum, such as we see on antique clocks. There was something, however, in the appearance of this machine which caused me to regard it more attentively. While I gazed directly upward at it (for its position was immediately over my own), I fancied that I saw it in motion. In an instant afterward the fancy was confirmed. Its sweep was brief, and of course slow. I watched it for some minutes, somewhat in fear, but more in wonder. Wearied at length with observing its dull movement, I turned my eyes upon the other objects in the cell.

A slight noise attracted my notice, and, looking to the floor, I saw several enormous rats traversing it. They had issued from the well, which lay just within view to my right. Even then, while I gazed, they came up in troops, hurriedly, with ravenous eyes, allured by the scent of the meat. From this it required much effort and attention to scare them away.

It might have been half an hour, perhaps even an hour (for I could take but imperfect note of time) before I again cast my eyes upward. What I then saw, confounded and amazed me. The sweep of the pendulum had increased in extent by nearly a yard. As a natural consequence, its velocity was also much greater. But what mainly disturbed me, was the idea that it had perceptibly *descended*. I now observed—with what horror it is needless to say—that its nether extremity was formed of a crescent of glittering steel, about a foot in length from horn to horn; the horns upward, and the under edge evidently as keen as that of a razor. Like a razor also, it seemed massy and heavy, tapering from the edge into a solid and broad structure above. It was appended to a weighty rod of brass, and the whole *hissed* as it swung through the air.

I could no longer doubt the doom prepared for me by monkish ingenuity in torture. My cognizance of the pit had become known to the inquisitorial agents—*the pit*, whose horrors had been destined for so bold a recusant as myself—*the pit*, typical of hell, and regarded by rumor as the Ultima Thule [2] of all their punishments. The plunge into this pit I had avoided by the merest of accidents, and I knew that surprise, or entrapment into torment, formed an important portion of all the grotesquerie of these dungeon deaths. Having failed to fall, it was no part of the demon plan to hurl me into the abyss; and thus (there being no alternative), a different and milder destruction awaited me. Milder! I half smiled in my agony as I thought of such application of such a term.

What boots it to tell of the long, long hours of horror more than mortal, during which I counted the rushing oscillations of the steel! Inch by inch —line by line—with a descent only appreciable at intervals that seemed ages—down and still down it came! Days passed—it might have been that many days passed—ere it swept so closely over me as to fan me with its acrid breath. The odor of the sharp steel forced itself into my nostrils. I prayed—I wearied heaven with my prayer for its more speedy descent. I grew frantically mad, and struggled to force myself upward against the sweep of the fearful cimeter. And then I fell suddenly calm, and lay smiling at the glittering death, as a child at some rare bauble.

There was another interval of utter insensibility; it was brief; for, upon again lapsing into life, there had been no perceptible descent in the pendulum. But it might have been long; for I knew there were demons who took note of my swoon, and who could have arrested the vibration at pleasure. Upon my recovery, too, I felt very—oh, inexpressibly— sick and weak, as if through long inanition. Even amid the agonies of that period the human nature craved food. With painful effort, I outstretched my left arm as far as my bonds permitted, and took possession of the small remnant which had been spared me by the rats. As I put a portion of it within my lips, there rushed to my mind a half-formed thought of joy—of hope. Yet what business had *I* with hope? It was, as I say, a half-formed thought: man has many such, which are never completed. I felt that it was of joy—of hope; but I felt also that it had perished in its formation. In vain I struggled to perfect—to regain it. Long suffering had nearly annihilated all my ordinary powers of mind. I was an imbecile—an idiot.

The vibration of the pendulum was at right angles to my length. I saw that the crescent was designed to cross the region of the heart. It would fray the serge of my robe—it would return and repeat its operations —again—and again. Notwithstanding its terrifically wide sweep (some thirty feet or more), and the hissing vigor of its descent, sufficient to sunder these very walls of iron, still the fraying of my robe would be all that, for several minutes, it would accomplish. And at this thought I paused. I dared not go farther than this reflection. I dwelt upon it with a pertinacity of attention—as if, in so dwelling, I could arrest *here* the descent of the steel. I forced myself to ponder upon the sound of the crescent as it should pass across the garment—upon the peculiar thrilling sensation which the friction of cloth produces on the nerves. I pondered upon all this frivolity until my teeth were on edge.

Down—steadily down it crept. I took a frenzied pleasure in contrasting its downward with its lateral velocity. To the right—to the left—far and wide—with the shriek of a damned spirit! to my heart, with the stealthy pace of the tiger! I alternately laughed and howled, as the one or the other idea grew predominant.

Down—certainly, relentlessly down! It vibrated within three inches of my bosom! I struggled violently—furiously—to free my left arm. This was free only from the elbow to the hand. I could reach the latter from the platter beside me to my mouth, with great effort, but no farther. Could I have broken the fastenings above the elbow, I would have seized and attempted to arrest the pendulum. I might as well have attempted to arrest an avalanche!

Down—still unceasingly—still inevitably down! I gasped and struggled at each vibration. I shrank convulsively at its every sweep. My eyes followed its outward or upward whirls with the eagerness of the most unmeaning despair; they closed themselves spasmodically at the descent, although death would have been a relief, oh, how unspeakable! Still I quivered in every nerve to think how slight a sinking of the machinery would precipitate that keen, glistening axe upon my bosom. It was *hope* that prompted the nerve to quiver—the frame to shrink. It was *hope*—the hope that triumphs on the rack—that whispers to the death-condemned even in the dungeons of the Inquisition.

I saw that some ten or twelve vibrations would bring the steel in actual contact with my robe; and with this observation there suddenly came over my spirit all the keen, collected calmness of despair. For the first time during many hours—or perhaps days—I *thought*. It now occurred to me, that the bandage, or surcingle, which enveloped me, was unique. I was tied by no separate cord. The first stroke of the razor-like crescent athwart any portion of the band would so detach it that it might be unwound from my person by means of my left hand. But how fearful, in that case, the proximity of the steel! The result of the slightest struggle, how deadly! Was it likely, moreover, that the minions of the torturer had not foreseen and provided for this possibility? Was it probable that the bandage crossed my bosom in the track of the pendulum? Dreading to find my faint, and, as it seemed, my last hope frustrated, I so far elevated my head as to obtain a distinct view of my breast. The surcingle enveloped my limbs and body close in all directions—*save in the path of the destroying crescent.*

Scarcely had I dropped my head back into its original position, when there flashed upon my mind what I cannot better describe than as the unformed half of that idea of deliverance to which I have previously alluded, and of which a moiety [3] only floated indeterminately through my brain when I raised food to my burning lips. The whole thought was now present—feeble, scarcely sane, scarcely definite—but still entire. I proceeded at once, with the nervous energy of despair, to attempt its execution.

For many hours the immediate vicinity of the low framework upon which I lay had been literally swarming with rats. They were wild, bold, ravenous—their red eyes glaring upon me as if they waited but for motionlessness on my part to make me their prey. "To what food," I thought, "have they been accustomed in the well?"

They had devoured, in spite of all my efforts to prevent them, all but a small remnant of the contents of the dish. I had fallen into an habitual see-saw, or wave of the hand about the platter; and, at length, the unconscious uniformity of the movement deprived it of effect. In their voracity the vermin frequently fastened their sharp fangs in my fingers. With the particles of the oily and spicy viand which now remained I thoroughly rubbed the bandage wherever I could reach it; then, raising my hand from the floor, I lay breathlessly still.

At first, the ravenous animals were startled and terrified at the change —the cessation of movement. They shrank alarmedly back; many sought the well. But this was only for a moment. I had not counted in vain upon their voracity. Observing that I remained without motion, one or two of the boldest leaped upon the framework, and smelt at the surcingle. This seemed the signal for a general rush. Forth from the well they hurried in fresh troops. They clung to the wood—they overran it, and leaped in hundreds upon my person. The measured movement of the pendulum disturbed them not at all. Avoiding its strokes, they busied themselves with the anointed bandage. They pressed—they swarmed upon me in ever-accumulating heaps. They writhed upon my throat; their cold lips sought my own; I was half stifled by their thronging pressure; disgust, for which the world has no name, swelled my bosom, and chilled, with a heavy clamminess, my heart. Yet one minute, and I felt that the struggle would be over. Plainly I perceived the loosening of the bandage. I knew that in more than one place it must be already severed. With a more than human resolution I lay *still*.

Nor had I erred in my calculations—nor had I endured in vain. I at length felt that I was *free*. The surcingle hung in ribbons from my body. But the stroke of the pendulum already pressed upon my bosom. It had divided the serge of the robe. It had cut through the linen beneath. Twice again it swung, and a sharp sense of pain shot through every nerve. But the moment of escape had arrived. At a wave of my hand my deliverers hurried tumultuously away. With a steady movement— cautious, sidelong, shrinking, and slow—I slid from the embrace of the bandage and beyond the reach of the scimeter. For the moment, at least, *I was free.*

Free!—and in the grasp of the Inquisition! I had scarcely stepped from my wooden bed of horror upon the stone floor of the prison, when the motion of the hellish machine ceased, and I beheld it drawn up, by some invisible force, through the ceiling. This was a lesson which I took desperately to heart. My every motion was undoubtedly watched. Free! —I had but escaped death in one form of agony to be delivered unto worse than death in some other. With that thought I rolled my eyes nervously around on the barriers of iron that hemmed me in. Something unusual —some change which, at first, I could not appreciate distinctly—it was obvious, had taken place in the apartment. For many minutes of a dreamy and trembling abstraction I busied myself in vain, unconnected conjecture. During this period, I became aware, for the first time, of the origin of the sulphurous •light which illumined the cell. It proceeded from a fissure, about half an inch in width, extending entirely around the prison at the base of the walls, which thus appeared and were completely separated from the floor. I endeavored, but of course in vain, to look through the aperture.

As I arose from the attempt, the mystery of the alteration in the chamber broke at once upon my understanding. I have observed that, although the outlines of the figures upon the walls were sufficiently distinct, yet the colors seemed blurred and indefinite. These colors had now assumed, and were momentarily assuming, a startling and most intense brilliancy, that gave to the spectral and fiendish portraitures an aspect that might have thrilled even firmer nerves than my own. Demon eyes, of a wild and ghastly vivacity, glared upon me in a thousand directions, where none had been visible before, and gleamed with the lurid lustre of a fire that I could not force my imagination to regard as unreal.

Unreal!—Even while I breathed there came to my nostrils the breath of the vapor of heated iron! A suffocating odor pervaded the prison. A deeper glow settled each moment in the eyes that glared at my agonies! A richer tint of crimson diffused itself over the pictured horrors of blood. I panted! I gasped for breath! There could be no doubt of the design of my tormentors—oh, most unrelenting! oh, most demoniac of men! I shrank from the glowing metal to the centre of the cell. Amid the thought of the fiery destruction that impended, the idea of the coolness of the well came over my soul like balm. I rushed to its deadly brink. I threw my straining vision below. The glare from the enkindled roof illumined its inmost recesses. Yet, for a wild moment, did my spirit refuse to comprehend the meaning of what I saw. At length it forced— it wrestled its way into my soul—it burned itself in upon my shuddering reason. Oh, for a voice to speak!—oh, horror!—oh, any horror but this! With a shriek, I rushed from the margin, and buried my face in my hands—weeping bitterly.

The heat rapidly increased, and once again I looked up, shuddering as with a fit of the ague. There had been a second change in the cell— and now the change was obviously in the *form*. As before, it was in vain that I at first endeavored to appreciate or understand what was taking place. But not long was I left in doubt. The inquisitorial vengeance had been hurried by my twofold escape, and there was to be no more dallying with the King of Terrors. The room had been square. I saw that two of its iron angles were now acute—two, consequently, obtuse. The fearful difference quickly increased with a low rumbling or moaning sound. In an instant the apartment had shifted its form into that of a lozenge. But the alteration stopped not here—I neither hoped nor desired it to stop. I could have clasped the red walls to my bosom as a garment of eternal peace. "Death," I said, "any death but that of the pit!" Fool! might I not have known that *into the pit* it was the object of the burning iron to urge me? Could I resist its glow? or if even that, could I withstand its pressure? And now, flatter and flatter grew the lozenge, with a rapidity that left me no time for contemplation. Its centre, and, of course, its greatest width, came just over the yawning gulf. I shrank back—but the closing walls pressed me resistlessly onward. At length for my seared and writhing body there was no longer an inch of foothold on the firm floor of the prison. I struggled no more, but the agony of my soul found vent in one loud, long and final scream of despair. I felt that I tottered upon the brink—I averted my eyes—

There was a discordant hum of human voices! There was a loud blast as of many trumpets! There was a harsh grating as of a thousand thunders! The fiery walls rushed back! An outstretched arm caught my own as I fell, fainting, into the abyss. It was that of General Lasalle. The French army had entered Toledo. The Inquisition was in the hands of its enemies.

"THE PIT AND THE PENDULUM"

[1] Autos-da-fé—a special session of the court of the Spanish Inquisition at which the formal declaration of the death sentence was made.
[2] Ultima Thule—the last extremity—the utmost limit.
[3] Moiety—a half, a small part.

What is the single effect aimed at in this story?
Is this a story of setting, character, or action?
How many of the characteristics of the perfect short-story are to be found here?

THE MASQUE OF THE RED DEATH

EDGAR ALLAN POE

The "Red Death" had long devastated the country. No pestilence had ever been so fatal, or so hideous. Blood was its avatar and its seal—the redness and the horror of blood. There were sharp pains, and sudden dizziness, and then profuse bleeding at the pores, with dissolution. The scarlet stains upon the body, and especially upon the face, of the victim were the pest ban which shut him out from the aid and from the sympathy of his fellow-men. And the whole seizure, progress, and termination of the disease were the incidents of half an hour.

But the Prince Prospero was happy and dauntless and sagacious. When his dominions were half depopulated, he summoned to his presence a thousand hale and light-hearted friends from among the knights and dames of his court, and with these retired to the deep seclusion of one of his castellated abbeys. This was an extensive and magnificent structure, the creation of the Prince's own eccentric yet august taste. A strong and lofty wall girdled it in. This wall had gates of iron. The courtiers, having entered, brought furnaces and massy hammers, and welded the bolts. They resolved to leave means neither of ingress or egress to the sudden impulses of despair or of frenzy from within. The abbey was amply provisioned. With such precautions the courtiers might bid defiance to contagion. The external world could take care of itself. In the meantime it was folly to grieve, or to think. The Prince had provided all the appliances of pleasure. There were buffoons, there were improvisatori, there were ballet dancers, there were musicians, there was Beauty, there was wine. All these and security were within. Without was the "Red Death."

It was toward the close of the fifth or sixth month of his seclusion, and while the pestilence raged most furiously abroad, that the Prince Prospero entertained his thousand friends at a masked ball of the most unusual magnificence.

It was a voluptuous scene, that masquerade. But first let me tell of the rooms in which it was held. There were seven—an imperial suite. In many palaces, however, such suites form a long and straight vista, while the folding-doors slide back nearly to the walls on either hand, so that the view of the whole extent is scarcely impeded. Here the case was very different, as might have been expected from the Prince's love of the bizarre. The apartments were so irregularly disposed that the vision embraced but little more than one at a time. There was a sharp turn at every twenty or thirty yards, and at each turn a novel effect. To the right and left, in the middle of each wall, a tall and narrow Gothic window looked out upon a closed corridor which pursued the windings of the suite. These windows were of stained glass, whose color varied in accordance with the prevailing hue of the decorations of the chamber into which it opened. That at the eastern extremity was hung, for example, in blue—and vividly blue were its windows. The second chamber was purple in its ornaments and tapestries, and here the panes were purple. The third was green throughout, and so were the casements. The fourth was furnished and lighted with orange, the fifth with white, the sixth with violet. The seventh apartment was closely shrouded in black velvet tapestries that hung all over the ceiling and down the walls, falling in heavy folds upon a carpet of the same material and hue. But, in this chamber only, the color of the windows failed to correspond with the decorations.

The panes here were scarlet—a deep blood-color. Now in no one of the seven apartments was there any lamp or candelabrum, amid the profusion of golden ornaments that lay scattered to and fro or depended from the roof. There was no light of any kind emanating from lamp or candle within the suite of chambers. But in the corridors that followed the suite there stood, opposite to each window, a heavy tripod, bearing a brazier of fire, that projected its rays through the tinted glass and so glaringly illumined the room. And thus were produced a multitude of gaudy and fantastic appearances. But in the western or black chamber the effect of the firelight that streamed upon the dark hangings through the blood-tinted panes was ghastly in the extreme, and produced so wild a look upon the countenances of those who entered that there were few of the company bold enough to set foot within its precincts at all.

It was in this apartment, also, that there stood against the western wall a gigantic clock of ebony. Its pendulum swung to and fro with a dull, heavy, monotonous clang; and when the minute-hand made the circuit of the face, and the hour was to be stricken, there came from the brazen lungs of the clock a sound which was clear and loud and deep and exceedingly musical, but of so peculiar a note and emphasis that, at each lapse of an hour, the musicians of the orchestra were constrained to pause, momentarily, in their performance, to harken to the sound; and thus the waltzers perforce ceased their revolutions; and there was a brief disconcert of the whole gay company; and, while the chimes of the clock yet rang, it was observed that the giddiest grew pale and the more aged and sedate passed their hands over their brows as if in confused revery or meditation. But when the echoes had fully ceased, a light laughter at once pervaded the assembly; the musicians looked at each other and smiled as if at their own nervousness and folly, and made whispering vows, each to the other, that the next chiming of the clock should produce in them no similar emotion; and then, after the lapse of sixty minutes (which embrace three thousand and six hundred seconds of the Time that flies) there came yet another chiming of the clock, and then were the same disconcert and tremulousness and meditation as before.

But, in spite of these things, it was a gay and magnificent revel. The tastes of the Prince were peculiar. He had a fine eye for colors and effects. He disregarded the *decora* of mere fashion. His plans were bold and fiery, and his conceptions glowed with barbaric lustre. There are some who would have thought him mad. His followers felt that he was not. It was necessary to hear and see and touch him to be *sure* that he was not.

He had directed, in great part, the movable embellishments of the seven chambers, upon occasion of this great *fête;* and it was his own guiding taste which had given character to the masqueraders. Be sure they were grotesque. There were much glare and glitter and piquancy and phantasm—much of what has been since seen in *Hernani*. There were arabesque figures with unsuited limbs and appointments. There were delirious fancies such as the madman fashions. There was much of the beautiful, much of the wanton, much of the bizarre, something of the terrible, and not a little of that which might have excited disgust. To and fro in the seven chambers there stalked, in fact, a multitude of dreams. And these—the dreams—writhed in and about, taking hue from the rooms, and causing the wild music of the orchestra to seem as the echo of their steps. And, anon, there strikes the ebony clock which stands in the hall of velvet. And then, for a moment, all is still, and all is silent save the voice of the clock. The dreams are stiff-frozen as they stand. But the echoes of the chime die away—they have endured but an instant—and a light, half-subdued laughter floats after them as they depart. And now again the music swells, and the dreams live, and writhe to and fro more merrily than ever, taking hue from the many-tinted windows through which stream the rays from the tripods. But to the chamber which lies most westwardly of the seven, there are now none of the maskers who venture; for the night is waning away, and there flows a ruddier light through the blood-colored panes; and the blackness of the sable drapery appals; and to him whose foot falls upon the sable carpet, there comes from the near clock of ebony a muffled peal more solemnly emphatic than any which reaches *their* ears who indulge in the more remote gayeties of the other apartments.

But these other apartments were densely crowded, and in them beat feverishly the heart of life. And the revel went whirlingly on, until at length there commenced the sounding of midnight upon the clock. And then the music ceased, as I have told; and the evolutions of the waltzers were quieted; and there was an uneasy cessation of all things as before. But now there were twelve strokes to be sounded by the bell of the clock; and thus it happened, perhaps, that more of thought crept, with more of time, into the meditations of the thoughtful among those who revelled. And thus, too, it happened, perhaps, that before the last echoes of the last chime had utterly sunk into silence, there were many individuals in the crowd who had found leisure to become aware of the presence of a masked figure which had arrested the attention of no single individual before. And the rumor of this new presence having spread itself whisperingly around, there arose at length from the whole company a buzz, or murmur, expressive of disapprobation and surprise—then, finally, of terror, of horror, and of disgust.

In an assembly of phantasms such as I have painted, it may well be supposed that no ordinary appearance could have excited such sensation. In truth the masquerade license of the night was nearly unlimited; but the figure in question had out-Heroded Herod, and gone beyond the bounds of even the Prince's indefinite decorum. There are chords in the hearts of the most reckless which cannot be touched without emotion. Even with the utterly lost, to whom life and death are equally jests, there are matters of which no jests can be made. The whole company, indeed, seemed now deeply to feel that in the costume and bearing of the stranger neither wit nor propriety existed. The figure was tall and gaunt, and shrouded from head to foot in the habiliments of the grave. The mask which concealed the visage was made so nearly to resemble the countenance of a stiffened corpse that the closest scrutiny must have had difficulty in detecting the cheat. And yet all this might have been endured, if not approved, by the mad revellers around. But the mummer had gone so far as to assume the type of the Red Death. His vesture was dabbled in *blood* —and his broad brow, with all the features of the face, was besprinkled with the scarlet horror.

When the eyes of Prince Prospero fell upon this spectral image (which with a slow and solemn movement, as if more fully to sustain its *rôle,* stalked to and fro among the waltzers) he was seen to be convulsed, in the first moment, with a strong shudder either of terror or distaste; but, in the next, his brow reddened with rage.

"Who dares?" he demanded hoarsely of the courtiers who stood near him—"who dares insult us with this blasphemous mockery? Seize him and unmask him—that we may know whom we have to hang at sunrise, from the battlements!"

It was in the eastern or blue chamber in which stood the Prince Prospero as he uttered these words. They rang throughout the seven rooms loudly and clearly—for the Prince was a bold and robust man, and the music had become hushed at the waving of his hand.

It was in the blue room where stood the Prince, with a group of pale courtiers by his side. At first, as he spoke, there was a slight rushing movement of this group in the direction of the intruder, who at the moment was also near at hand, and now, with deliberate and stately step, made closer approach to the speaker. But from a certain nameless awe with which the mad assumptions of the mummer had inspired the whole party, there were found none who put forth hand to seize him; so that, unimpeded, he passed within a yard of the Prince's person; and while the vast assembly, as if with one impulse, shrank from the centres of the rooms to the walls, he made his way uninterruptedly, but with the same solemn and measured step which had distinguished him from the first, through the blue chamber to the purple—through the purple to the green— through the green to the orange—through this again to the white—and even thence to the violet, ere a decided movement had been made to arrest him. It was then, however, that the Prince Prospero, maddening with rage and the shame of his own momentary cowardice, rushed hurriedly through the six chambers, while none followed him on account of a deadly terror that had seized upon all. He bore aloft a drawn dagger, and had approached, in rapid impetuosity, to within three or four feet of the retreating figure, when the latter, having attained the extremity of the velvet apartment, turned suddenly and confronted his pursuer. There was a sharp cry—and the dagger dropped gleaming upon the sable carpet, upon which, instantly afterwards, fell prostrate in death the Prince Prospero. Then, summoning the wild courage of despair, a throng of the revellers at once threw themselves into the black apartment, and, seizing the mummer, whose tall figure stood erect and motionless within the shadow of the ebony clock, gasped in unutterable horror at finding the grave cerements and corpse-like mask, which they handled with so violent a rudeness, untenanted by any tangible form.

And now was acknowledged the presence of the Red Death. He had come like a thief in the night. And one by one dropped the revellers in the blood-bedewed halls of their revel, and died each in the despairing posture of his fall. And the life of the ebony clock went out with that of the last of the gay. And the flame of the tripods expired. And Darkness and Decay and the Red Death held illimitable dominion over all.

"THE MASQUE OF THE RED DEATH"

Point out similarities and contrasts between this story and "The Pit and the Pendulum" as regards the author's method of work.

What part is played by the ebony clock in this story?

See dictionary for avatar, improvisatori, bizarre, decora, Hernani, arabesque, mummer.

For the use of the expression, "out-Heroded Herod," see Hamlet's directions to the players in "Hamlet." Herod, a character in the old Miracle and Mystery plays, was wont to speak in a loud, extravagant fashion, fairly rending the air with his ravings, much to the amusement of the crowd.

MARKHEIM [1] (1884)

ROBERT LOUIS STEVENSON (1850-1894)

"Yes," said the dealer, "our windfalls are of various kinds. Some customers are ignorant, and then I touch a dividend on my superior knowledge. Some are dishonest," and here he held up the candle, so that the light fell strongly on his visitor, "and in that case," he continued, "I profit by my virtue."

Markheim had but just entered from the daylight streets, and his eyes had not yet grown familiar with the mingled shine and darkness in the shop. At these pointed words, and before the near presence of the flame, he blinked painfully and looked aside.

The dealer chuckled. "You come to me on Christmas Day," he resumed, "when you know that I am alone in my house, put up my shutters, and make a point of refusing business. Well, you will have to pay for that; you will have to pay for my loss of time, when I should be balancing my books; you will have to pay, besides, for a kind of manner

[1] Used by permission and special arrangement with Charles Scribner's Sons.

that I remark in you to-day very strongly. I am the essence of discretion, and ask no awkward questions; but when a customer cannot look me in the eye, he has to pay for it." The dealer once more chuckled; and then, changing to his usual business voice, though still with a note of irony, "You can give, as usual, a clear account of how you came into the possession of the object?" he continued. "Still your uncle's cabinet? A remarkable collector, sir!"

And the little pale, round-shouldered dealer stood almost on tiptoe, looking over the top of his gold spectacles, and nodding his head with every mark of disbelief. Markheim returned his gaze with one of infinite pity, and a touch of horror.

"This time," said he, "you are in error. I have not come to sell, but to buy. I have no curios to dispose of; my uncle's cabinet is bare to the wainscot; even were it still intact, I have done well on the Stock Exchange, and should more likely add to it than otherwise, and my errand to-day is simplicity itself. I seek a Christmas present for a lady," he continued, waxing more fluent as he struck into the speech he had prepared; "and certainly I owe you every excuse for thus disturbing you upon so small a matter. But the thing was neglected yesterday; I must produce my little compliment at dinner; and, as you very well know, a rich marriage is not a thing to be neglected."

There followed a pause, during which the dealer seemed to weigh this statement incredulously. The ticking of many clocks among the curious lumber of the shop, and the faint rushing of the cabs in a near thoroughfare, filled up the interval of silence.

"Well, sir," said the dealer, "be it so. You are an old customer after all; and if, as you say, you have the chance of a good marriage, far be it from me to be an obstacle. Here is a nice thing for a lady, now," he went on, "this hand glass—fifteenth century, warranted; comes from a good collection, too; but I reserve the name, in the interests of my customer, who was just like yourself, my dear sir, the nephew and sole heir of a remarkable collector."

The dealer, while he thus ran on in his dry and biting voice, had stooped to take the object from its place; and, as he had done so, a shock had passed through Markheim, a start both of hand and foot, a sudden leap of many tumultuous passions to the face. It passed swiftly as it came, and left no trace beyond a certain trembling of the hand that now received the glass.

"A glass," he said hoarsely, and then paused, and repeated it more clearly. "A glass? For Christmas! Surely not."

"And why not?" cried the dealer. "Why not a glass?"

Markheim was looking upon him with an indefinable expression. "You ask me why not?" he said. "Why, look here—look in it—look at yourself! Do you like to see it? No! nor I—nor any man."

The little man had jumped back when Markheim so suddenly confronted him with the mirror; but now, perceiving there was nothing worse on hand, he chuckled. "Your future lady, sir, must be pretty hard favored," said he.

"I ask you," said Markheim, "for a Christmas present, and you give me this—this damned reminder of years and sins and follies—this hand-conscience! Did you mean it? Had you a thought in your mind? Tell me. It will be better for you if you do. Come, tell me about yourself. I hazard a guess now, that you are in secret a very charitable man?"

The dealer looked closely at his companion. It was very odd, Markheim did not appear to be laughing; there was something in his face like an eager sparkle of hope, but nothing of mirth.

"What are you driving at?" the dealer asked.

"Not charitable?" returned the other, gloomily. "Not charitable; not pious; not scrupulous; unloving; unbeloved; a hand to get money, a safe to keep it. Is that all? Dear God, man, is that all?"

"I will tell you what it is," began the dealer, with some sharpness, and then broke off again into a chuckle. "But I see this is a love match of yours, and you have been drinking the lady's health."

"Ah!" cried Markheim, with a strange curiosity. "Ah, have you been in love? Tell me about that."

"I!" cried the dealer. "I in love! I never had the time, nor have I the time to-day for all this nonsense. Will you take the glass?"

"Where is the hurry?" returned Markheim. "It is very pleasant to stand here talking; and life is so short and insecure that I would not hurry away from any pleasure—no, not even from so mild a one as this. We should rather cling, cling to what little we can get, like a man at a cliff's edge. Every second is a cliff, if you think upon it—a cliff a mile high —high enough, if we fall, to dash us out of every feature of humanity. Hence it is best to talk pleasantly. Let us talk of each other; why should we wear this mask? Let us be confidential. Who knows, we might become friends?"

"I have just one word to say to you," said the dealer. "Either make your purchase, or walk out of my shop."

"True, true," said Markheim. "Enough fooling. To business. Show me something else."

The dealer stooped once more, this time to replace the glass upon the shelf, his thin blond hair falling over his eyes as he did so. Markheim moved a litle nearer, with one hand in the pocket of his greatcoat; he drew himself up and filled his lungs; at the same time many different emotions were depicted together on his face—terror, horror, and resolve, fascination, and a physical repulsion; and through a haggard lift of his upper lip, his teeth looked out.

"This, perhaps, may suit," observed the dealer; and then, as he began to re-arise, Markheim bounded from behind upon his victim. The long skewer-like dagger flashed and fell. The dealer struggled like a hen, striking his temple on the shelf, and then tumbled on the floor in a heap.

Time had some score of small voices in that shop, some stately and slow as was becoming to their great age, others garrulous and hurried. All these told out the seconds in an intricate chorus of tickings. Then the passage of a lad's feet, heavily running on the pavement, broke in upon these smaller voices and startled Markheim into the consciousness of his surroundings. He looked about him awfully. The candle stood on the counter, its flame solemnly wagging in a draught; and by that inconsiderable movement, the whole room was filled with noiseless bustle and kept heaving like a sea: the tall shadows nodding, the gross blots of darkness swelling and dwindling as with respiration, the faces of the portraits and the china gods changing and wavering like images in water. The inner door stood ajar, and peered into that leaguer of shadows with a long slit of daylight like a pointing finger.

From these fear-stricken rovings, Markheim's eyes returned to the body of his victim, where it lay both humped and sprawling, incredibly small and strangely meaner than in life. In these poor, miserly clothes, in that ungainly attitude, the dealer lay like so much sawdust. Markheim had feared to see it, and, lo! it was nothing. And yet, as he gazed, this bundle of old clothes and pool of blood began to find eloquent voices. There it must lie; there was none to work the cunning hinges or direct the miracle of locomotion—there it must lie till it was found. Found! aye, and then? Then would this dead flesh lift up a cry that would ring over England, and fill the world with the echoes of pursuit. Ay, dead or not, this was still the enemy. "Time was that when the brains were out," he thought; and the first word struck into his mind. Time, now that the deed was accomplished—time, which had closed for the victim, had become instant and momentous for the slayer.

The thought was yet in his mind, when, first one and then another, with every variety of pace and voice—one deep as the bell from a cathedral turret, another ringing on its treble notes the prelude of a waltz—the clocks began to strike the hour of three in the afternoon.

The sudden outbreak of so many tongues in that dumb chamber staggered him. He began to bestir himself, going to and fro with the candle, beleaguered by moving shadows, and startled to the soul by chance reflections. In many rich mirrors, some of home designs, some from Venice or Amsterdam, he saw his face repeated and repeated, as it were an army of spies; his own eyes met and detected him; and the sound of his own steps, lightly as they fell, vexed the surrounding quiet. And still, as he continued to fill his pockets, his mind accused him, with a sickening iteration, of the thousand faults of his design. He should have chosen a more quiet hour; he should have prepared an alibi; he should not have used a knife; he should have been more cautious, and only bound and gagged the dealer, and not killed him; he should have been more bold, and killed the servant also; he should have done all things otherwise; poignant regrets, weary, incessant toiling of the mind to change what was unchangeable, to plan what was now useless, to be the architect of the irrevocable past. Meanwhile, and behind all this activity, brute terrors, like the scurrying of rats in a deserted attic, filled the more remote chambers of his brain with riot; the hand of the constable would fall heavy on his shoulder, and his nerves would jerk like a hooked fish; or he beheld, in galloping defile, the dock, the prison, the gallows, and the black coffin. Terror of the people in the street sat down before his mind like a besieging army. It was impossible, he thought, but that some rumor of the struggle must have reached their ears and set on edge their curiosity; and now, in all the neighboring houses, he divined them sitting motionless and with uplifted ear—solitary people, condemned to spend Christmas dwelling alone on memories of the past, and now startlingly recalled from that tender exercise; happy family parties, struck into silence round the table, the mother still with raised finger: every degree and age and humor, but all, by their own hearths, prying and hearkening and weaving the rope that was to hang him. Sometimes it seemed to him he could not move too softly; the clink of the tall Bohemian goblets rang out loudly like a bell; and alarmed by the bigness of the ticking, he was tempted to stop the clocks. And then, again, with a swift transition of his terrors, the very silence of the place appeared a source of peril, and a thing to strike and freeze the passer-by; and he would step more boldly, and bustle aloud among the contents of the shop, and imitate, with elaborate bravado, the movements of a busy man at ease in his own house.

But he was now so pulled about by different alarms that, while one portion of his mind was still alert and cunning, another trembled on the brink of lunacy. One hallucination in particular took a strong hold on his credulity. The neighbor hearkening with white face beside his window, the passer-by arrested by a horrible surmise on the pavement—these could at worst suspect, they could not know; through the brick walls and shuttered windows only sounds could penetrate. But here, within the house, was he alone? He knew he was; he had watched the servant set forth sweethearting, in her poor best, "out for the day" written in every ribbon and smile. Yes, he was alone, of course; and yet, in the bulk of empty house about him, he could surely hear a stir of delicate footing —he was surely conscious, inexplicably conscious, of some presence. Ay, surely; to every room and corner of the house his imagination followed it; and now it was a faceless thing, and yet had eyes to see with; and again it was a shadow of himself; and yet again behold the image of the dead dealer, reinspired with cunning and hatred.

At times, with a strong effort, he would glance at the open door which still seemed to repel his eyes. The house was tall, the skylight small and dirty, the day blind with fog; and the light that filtered down to the ground story was exceedingly faint, and showed dimly on the threshold of the shop. And yet, in that strip of doubtful brightness, did there not hang wavering a shadow?

Suddenly, from the street outside, a very jovial gentleman began to beat with a staff on the shop door, accompanying his blows with shouts and railleries in which the dealer was continually called upon by name: Markheim, smitten into ice, glanced at the dead man. But no! he lay quite still; he was fled away far beyond earshot of these blows and shoutings; he was sunk beneath seas of silence; and his name, which would once have caught his notice above the howling of a storm, had become an empty sound. And presently the jovial gentleman desisted from his knocking and departed.

Here was a broad hint to hurry what remained to be done, to get forth from this accusing neighborhood, to plunge into a bath of London multitudes, and to reach, on the other side of day, that haven of safety and apparent innocence—his bed. One visitor had come: at any moment another might follow and be more obstinate. To have done the deed, and yet not to reap the profit, would be too abhorrent a failure. The money, that was now Markheim's concern; and as a means to that, the keys.

He glanced over his shoulder at the open door, where the shadow was still lingering and shivering; and with no conscious repugnance of the mind, yet with a tremor of the belly, he drew near the body of his victim. The human character had quite departed. Like a suit half-stuffed with bran, the limbs lay scattered, the trunk doubled, on the floor; and yet the thing repelled him. Although so dingy and inconsiderable to the eye, he feared it might have more significance to the touch. He took the body by the shoulders, and turned it on its back. It was strangely light and supple, and the limbs, as if they had been broken, fell into the oddest postures. The face was robbed of all expression; but it was as pale as wax, and shockingly smeared with blood about one temple. That was, for Markheim, the one displeasing circumstance. It carried him back, upon the instant, to a certain fair-day in a fishers' village; a gay day, a piping wind, a crowd upon the street, the blare of brasses, the booming of drums, the nasal voice of a ballad singer; and a boy going to and fro, buried over head in the crowd and divided between interest and fear, until, coming out upon the chief place of concourse, he beheld a booth and a great screen with pictures, dismally designed, garishly colored: Brownrigg with her apprentice; the Mannings with their murdered guest; Weare in the death grip of Thurtell; and a score besides of famous crimes. The thing was as clear as an illusion; he was once again that little boy; he was looking once again, and with the same sense of physical revolt, at these vile pictures; he was still stunned by the thumping of the drums. A bar of that day's music returned upon his memory; and at that, for the first time, a qualm came over him, a breath of nausea, a sudden weakness of the joints, which he must instantly resist and conquer.

He judged it more prudent to confront than to flee from these considerations; looking the more hardily in the dead face, bending his mind to realize the nature and greatness of his crime. So little a while ago that face had moved with every change of sentiment, that pale mouth had spoken, that body had been all on fire with governable energies; and now, and by his act, that peace of life had been arrested, as the horologist,[1] with interjected finger, arrests the beating of the clock. So he reasoned in vain; he could rise to no more remorseful consciousness; the same heart which had shuddered before the painted effigies of crime, looked on its reality unmoved. A best, he felt a gleam of pity for one who had been endowed in vain with all those faculties that can make the world a garden of enchantment, one who had never lived and who was now dead. But of penitence, no, not a tremor.

With that, shaking himself clear of these considerations, he found the keys and advanced toward the open door of the shop. Outside, it had begun to rain smartly; and the sound of the shower upon the roof had banished silence. Like some dripping cavern, the chambers of the house were haunted by an incessant echoing, which filled the ear and mingled with the ticking of the clocks. And, as Markheim approached the door, he seemed to hear, in answer to his own cautious tread, the steps of another foot withdrawing up the stair. The shadow still palpitated loosely on the threshold. He threw a ton's weight of resolve upon his muscles, and drew back the door.

The faint, foggy daylight glimmered dimly on the bare floor and stairs; on the bright suit of armor posted, halbert in hand, upon the landing; and on the dark wood-carvings and framed pictures that hung against the yellow panels of the wainscot. So loud was the beating of the rain through all the house that, in Markheim's ears, it began to be distinguished into many different sounds. Footsteps and sighs, the tread of regiments marching in the distance, the chink of money in the counting, and the creaking of doors held stealthily ajar, appeared to mingle with the patter of the drops upon the cupola and the gushing of the water in the pipes. The sense that he was not alone grew upon him to the verge of madness. On every side he was haunted and begirt by presences. He heard them moving in the upper chambers; from the shop, he heard the dead man getting to his legs; and as he began with a great effort to mount the stairs, feet fled quietly before him and followed stealthily behind. If he were but deaf, he thought, how tranquilly he would possess his soul! And then again, and hearkening with ever fresh attention, he blessed himself for that unresting sense which held the outposts and stood a trusty sentinel upon his life. His head turned continually on his neck; his eyes, which seemed starting from their orbits, scouted on every side, and on every side were half rewarded as with the tail of something nameless vanishing. The four-and-twenty steps to the first floor were four-and-twenty agonies.

On that first story the doors stood ajar, three of them like three ambushes, shaking his nerves like the throats of cannon. He could never again, he felt, be sufficiently immured and fortified from men's observing eyes; he longed to be home, girt in by walls, buried among bedclothes, and invisible to all but God. And at that thought he wondered a little, recollecting tales of other murderers and the fear they were said to entertain of heavenly avengers. It was not so, at least, with him. He feared the laws of nature, lest, in their callous and immutable procedure, they should preserve some damning evidence of his crime. He feared tenfold more, with a slavish, superstitious terror, some scission in the continuity of man's experience, some wilful illegality of nature. He played a game of skill, depending on the rules, calculating consequence from cause; and what if nature, as the defeated tyrant overthrew the chessboard, should break the mould of their succession? The like had befallen Napoleon (so writers said) when the winter changed the time of its appearance. The like might befall Markheim: the solid walls might become transparent and reveal his doings like those of bees in a glass hive; the stout planks might yield under his foot like quicksands and detain him in their clutch; aye, and there were soberer accidents that might destroy him: if, for instance, the house should fall and imprison him beside the body of his victim; or the house next door should fly on fire, and the firemen invade him from all sides. These things he feared; and, in a sense, these things might be called the hands of God reached forth against sin. But about God himself he was at ease; his act was doubtless exceptional, but so were his excuses, which God knew; it was there, and not among men, that he felt sure of justice.

When he got safe into the drawing-room, and shut the door behind him, he was aware of a respite from alarms. The room was quite dismantled, uncarpeted besides, and strewn with packing cases and incongruous furniture; several great pier glasses, in which he beheld himself at various angles, like an actor on a stage; many pictures, framed and unframed, standing, with their faces to the wall; a fine Sheraton sideboard, a cabinet of marquetry, and a great old bed, with tapestry hangings. The windows opened to the floor; but by great good fortune the lower part of the shutters had been closed, and this concealed him from the neighbors. Here, then, Markheim drew in a packing case before the cabinet, and began to search among the keys. It was a long business, for there were many; and it was irksome, besides; for, after all, there might be nothing in the cabinet, and time was on the wing. But the closeness of the occupation sobered him. With the tail of his eye he saw the door—even glanced at it from time to time directly, like a besieged commander pleased to verify the good estate of his defences. But in truth he was at peace. The rain falling in the street sounded natural and pleasant. Presently, on the other side, the notes of a piano were wakened to the music of a hymn, and the voices of many children took up the air and words. How stately, how comfortable was the melody! How fresh the youthful voices! Markheim gave ear to it smilingly, as he sorted out the keys; and his mind was thronged with answerable ideas and images; church-going children and the pealing of the high organ; children afield, bathers by the brookside, ramblers on the brambly common; kite-flyers in the windy and cloud-navigated sky; and then, at another cadence of the hymn, back again to church, and the somnolence of summer Sundays, and the high, genteel voice of the parson (which he smiled a little to recall), and the painted Jacobean tombs, and the dim lettering of the Ten Commandments in the chancel.

And as he sat thus, at once busy and absent, he was startled to his feet. A flash of ice, a flash of fire, a bursting gush of blood, went over him, and then he stood transfixed and thrilling. A step mounted the stair slowly and steadily, and presently a hand was laid upon the knob, and the lock clicked, and the door opened.

Fear held Markheim in a vice. What to expect he knew not, whether the dead man walking, or the official ministers of human justice, or some chance witness blindly stumbling in to consign him to the gallows. But when a face was thrust into the aperture, glanced round the room, looked at him, nodded and smiled as if in friendly recognition, and then withdrew again, and the door closed behind it, his fear broke loose from his control in a hoarse cry. At the sound of this the visitant returned.

"Did you call me?" he asked pleasantly, and with that he entered the room and closed the door behind him.

Markheim stood and gazed at him with all his eyes. Perhaps there was a film upon his sight, but the outlines of the newcomer seemed to change and waver like those of the idols in the wavering candlelight of the shop: and at times he thought he knew him; and at times he thought he bore a likeness to himself; and always, like a lump of living terror, there lay in his bosom the conviction that this thing was not of the earth and not of God.

And yet the creature had a strange air of the commonplace, as he stood looking on Markheim with a smile; and when he added: "You are looking for the money, I believe?" it was in the tones of everyday politeness.

Markheim made no answer.

"I should warn you," resumed the other, "that the maid has left her sweetheart earlier than usual and will soon be here. If Mr. Markheim be found in this house, I need not describe to him the consequences."

"You know me?" cried the murderer.

The visitor smiled. "You have long been a favorite of mine," he said; "and I have long observed and often sought to help you."

"What are you?" cried Markheim: "the devil?"

"What I may be," returned the other, "cannot affect the service I propose to render you."

"It can," cried Markheim; "it does! Be helped by you? No, never; not by you! You do not know me yet; thank God, you do not know me!"

"I know you," replied the visitant, with a sort of kind severity or rather firmness. "I know you to the soul."

"Know me!" cried Markheim. "Who can do so? My life is but a travesty and slander on myself. I have lived to belie my nature. All men do; all men are better than this disguise that grows about and stifles them. You see each dragged away by life, like one whom bravos have seized and muffled in a cloak. If they had their own control—if you could see their faces, they would be altogether different, they would shine out for heroes and saints! I am worse than most; myself is more overlaid; my excuse is known to me and God. But, had I the time, I could disclose myself."

"To me?" inquired the visitant.

"To you before all," returned the murderer. "I supposed you were intelligent. I thought—since you exist—you would prove a reader of the heart. And yet you would propose to judge me by my acts! Think of it; my acts! I was born and I have lived in a land of giants; giants have dragged me by the wrists since I was born out of my mother— the giants of circumstance. And you would judge me by my acts! But can you not look within? Can you not understand that evil is hateful to me? Can you not see within me the clear writing of conscience, never blurred by any wilful sophistry although too often disregarded? Can you not read me for a thing that surely must be common as humanity— the unwilling sinner?"

"All this is very feelingly expressed," was the reply, "but it regards me not. These points of consistency are beyond my province, and I care not in the least by what compulsion you may have been dragged away, so as you are but carried in the right direction. But time flies; the servant delays, looking in the faces of the crowd and at the pictures on the hoard-ings, but still she keeps moving nearer; and remember, it is as if the gallows itself were striding toward you through the Christmas streets! Shall I help you—I, who know all? Shall I tell you where to find the money?"

"For what price?" asked Markheim.

"I offer you the service for a Christmas gift," returned the other.

Markheim could not refrain from smiling with a kind of bitter triumph. "No," said he, "I will take nothing at your hands; if I were dying of thirst, and it was your hand that put the pitcher to my lips, I should find the courage to refuse. It may be credulous, but I will do nothing to com-mit myself to evil."

"I have no objection to a death-bed repentance," observed the visitant.

"Because you disbelieve their efficacy!" Markheim cried.

"I do not say so," returned the other; "but I look on these things from a different side, and when the life is done my interest falls. The man has lived to serve me, to spread black looks under color of religion, or to sow tares in the wheat field, as you do, in a course of weak compliance with desire. Now that he draws so near to his deliverance, he can add but one act of service—to repent, to die smiling, and thus to build up in confidence and hope the more timorous of my surviving followers. I am not so hard a master. Try me. Accept my help. Please yourself in life as you have done hitherto; please yourself more amply, spread your elbows at the board; and when the night begins to fall and the curtains to be drawn, I tell you, for your greater comfort, that you will find it even easy to compound your quarrel with your conscience, and to make a truckling peace with God. I came but now from such a death-bed, and the room was full of sincere mourners, listening to the man's last words; and when I looked into that face, which had been set as a flint against mercy, I found it smiling with hope."

"And do you, then, suppose me such a creature?" asked Markheim. "Do you think I have no more generous aspirations than to sin, and sin, and sin, and, at last, sneak into heaven? My heart rises at the thought. Is this, then, your experience of mankind? or is it because you find me with red hands that you presume such baseness? and is this crime of murder indeed so impious as to dry up the very springs of good?"

"Murder is to me no special category," replied the other. "All sins are murder, even as all life is war. I behold your race, like starving mariners on a raft, plucking crusts out of the hands of famine and feeding on each other's lives. I follow sins beyond the moment of their acting; I find in all that the last consequence is death; and to my eyes, the pretty maid who thwarts her mother with such taking graces on a question of a ball, drips no less visibly with human gore than such a murderer as yourself. Do I say that I follow sins? I follow virtues also; they differ not by the thickness of a nail, they are both scythes for the reaping angel of Death. Evil, for which I live, consists not in action but in character. The bad man is dear to me; not the bad act, whose fruits, if we could follow them far enough down the hurtling cataract of the ages, might yet be found more blessed than those of the rarest virtues. And it is not because you have killed a dealer, but because you are Markheim, that I offered to forward your escape."

"I will lay my heart open to you," answered Markheim. "This crime on which you find me is my last. On my way to it I have learned many lessons; itself is a lesson, a momentous lesson. Hitherto I have been driven with revolt to what I would not; I was a bond-slave to poverty, driven and scourged. There are robust virtues that can stand in these temptations; mine was not so: I had a thirst of pleasure. But to-day, and out of this deed, I pluck both warning and riches—both the power and a fresh resolve to be myself. I become in all things a free actor in the world; I begin to see myself all changed, these hands the agents of good, this heart at peace. Something comes over me out of the past; something of what I have dreamed on Sabbath evenings to the sound of the church organ, of what I forecast when I shed tears over noble books, or talked, an innocent child, with my mother. There lies my life; I have wandered a few years, but now I see once more my city of destination."

"You are to use this money on the Stock Exchange, I think?" remarked the visitor; "and there, if I mistake not, you have already lost some thousands?"

"Ah," said Markheim, "but this time I have a sure thing."

"This time, again, you will lose," replied the visitor, quietly.

"Ah, but I keep back the half!" cried Markheim.

"That also you will lose," said the other.

The sweat started upon Markheim's brow. "Well, then, what matter?" he exclaimed. "Say it be lost, say I am plunged again in poverty, shall one part of me, and that the worse, continue until the end to override the better? Evil and good run strong in me, hailing me both ways. I do not love the one thing, I love all. I can conceive great deeds, renunciations, martyrdoms; and though I be fallen to such a crime as murder, pity is no stranger to my thoughts. I pity the poor; who knows their trials better than myself? I pity and help them; I prize love, I love honest laughter; there is no good thing nor true thing on earth but I love it from my heart. And are my vices only to direct my life, and my virtues to lie without effect, like some passive lumber of the mind? Not so; good, also, is a spring of acts."

But the visitant raised his finger. "For six-and-thirty years that you have been in this world," said he, "through many changes of fortune and varieties of humor, I have watched you steadily fall. Fifteen years ago you would have started at a theft. Three years back you would have blenched at the name of murder. Is there any crime, is there any cruelty or meanness, from which you still recoil?—five years from now I shall detect you in the fact! Downward, downward lies your way; nor can anything but death avail to stop you."

"It is true," Markheim said huskily, "I have in some degree complied with evil. But it is so with all: the very saints, in the mere exercise of living, grow less dainty, and take on the tone of their surroundings."

"I will propound to you one simple question," said the other; "and as you answer, I shall read to you your moral horoscope.[2] You have grown in many things more lax; possibly you do right to be so; and at any account, it is the same with all men. But granting that, are you in any one particular, however trifling, more difficult to please with your own conduct, or do you go in all things with a looser rein?"

"In any one?" repeated Markheim, with an anguish of consideration. "No," he added, with despair, "in none! I have gone down in all."

"Then," said the visitor, "content yourself with what you are, for you will never change; and the words of your part on this stage are irrevocably written down."

Markheim stood for a long while silent, and indeed it was the visitor who first broke the silence. "That being so," he said, "shall I show you the money?"

"And grace?" cried Markheim.

"Have you not tried it?" returned the other. "Two or three years ago, did I not see you on the platform of revival meetings, and was not your voice the loudest in the hymn?"

"It is true," said Markheim; "and I see clearly what remains for me by way of duty. I thank you for these lessons from my soul; my eyes are opened, and I behold myself at last for what I am."

At this moment, the sharp note of the door-bell rang through the house; and the visitant, as though this were some concerted signal for which he had been waiting, changed at once in his demeanor.

"The maid!" he cried. "She has returned, as I forewarned you, and there is now before you one more difficult passage. Her master, you must say, is ill; you must let her in, with an assured but rather serious countenance—no smiles, no overacting, and I promise you success! Once the girl is within, and the door closed, the same dexterity that has already rid you of the dealer will relieve you of this last danger in your path. Thenceforward you have the whole evening—the whole night, if needful—to ransack the treasures of the house and to make good your safety. This is help that comes to you with the mask of danger. Up!" he cried: "up, friend; your life hangs trembling in the scales: up, and act!"

Markheim steadily regarded his counsellor. "If I be condemned to evil acts," he said, "there is still one door of freedom open—I can cease from action. If my life be an ill thing, I can lay it down. Though I be, as you say truly, at the beck of every small temptation, I can yet, by one decisive gesture, place myself beyond the reach of all. My love of good is damned to barrenness; it may, and let it be! But I have still my hatred of evil; and from that, to your galling disappointment, you shall see that I can draw both energy and courage."

The features of the visitor began to undergo a wonderful and lovely change: they brightened and softened with a tender triumph; and, even as they brightened, faded and dislimned. But Markheim did not pause to watch or understand the transformation. He opened the door and went downstairs very slowly, thinking to himself. His past went soberly before him; he beheld it as it was, ugly and strenuous like a dream, random as chance-medley—a scene of defeat. Life, as he thus reviewed it, tempted him no longer; but on the farther side he perceived a quiet haven for his bark. He paused in the passage, and looked into the shop, where the candle still burned by the dead body. It was strangely silent. Thoughts of the dealer swarmed into his mind, as he stood gazing. And then the bell once more broke out into impatient clamor.

He confronted the maid upon the threshold with something like a smile.

"You had better go for the police," said he: "I have killed your master."

"MARKHEIM"

Markheim has just committed his first great crime. This is a psychological story. Its chief interest is in watching the workings of a man's mind under such circumstances. This is really the struggle between Markheim and his better self. He tries to justify his act to his conscience, but at last gives up and faces the consequences of his deed.

What use is made in the story of the clocks, the mirrors, the rain on the roof, the hymn sung by childish voices?

1 Horologist—one skilled in the science of time-pieces.
2 Horoscope—a forecasting of the future. The horoscope of a person's life was originally drawn up from the appearance of the planets at the time of his birth.

THE PIECE OF STRING [1] (1884)

GUY DE MAUPASSANT (1850–1893)

On all the roads about Goderville the peasants and their wives were coming toward the town, for it was market day. The men walked at an easy gait, the whole body thrown forward with every movement of their long, crooked legs, misshapen by hard work, by the bearing down on the plough which at the same time causes the left shoulder to rise and the figure to slant; by the mowing of the grain, which makes one hold his knees apart in order to obtain a firm footing; by all the slow and laborious tasks of the fields. Their starched blue blouses, glossy as if varnished, adorned at the neck and wrists with a bit of white stitchwork, puffed out about their bony chests like balloons on the point of taking flight, from which protrude a head, two arms, and two feet.

Some of them led a cow or a calf at the end of a rope. And their wives, walking behind the beast, lashed it with a branch still covered with leaves, to hasten its pace. They carried on their arms great baskets, from which heads of chickens or of ducks were thrust forth. And they walked with a shorter and quicker step than their men, their stiff, lean figures wrapped in scanty shawls pinned over their flat breasts, their heads enveloped in a white linen cloth close to the hair, with a cap over all.

Then a *char-à-bancs*[1] passed, drawn by a jerky-paced nag, with two men seated side by side shaking like jelly, and a woman behind, who clung to the side of the vehicle to lessen the rough jolting.

On the square at Goderville there was a crowd, a medley of men and beasts. The horns of the cattle, the high hats, with a long, hairy nap, of the wealthy peasants, and the head-dresses of the peasant women, appeared on the surface of the throng. And the sharp, shrill, high-pitched

1 Used by permission of and special arrangement with G. P. Putnam's Sons. Reprinted from "Little French Masterpieces."

voices formed an incessant, uncivilized uproar, over which soared at times a roar of laughter from the powerful chest of a sturdy yokel,[2] or the prolonged bellow of a cow fastened to the wall of a house.

There was an all-pervading smell of the stable, of milk, of the dunghill, of hay, and of perspiration—that acrid, disgusting odor of man and beast peculiar to country people.

Master Hauchecorne, of Bréauté, had just arrived at Goderville, and was walking toward the square, when he saw a bit of string on the ground. Master Hauchecorne, economical like every true Norman, thought that it was well to pick up everything that might be of use; and he stooped painfully, for he suffered with rheumatism. He took the piece of slender cord from the ground, and was about to roll it up carefully, when he saw Master Malandain, the harness-maker, standing in his doorway and looking at him. They had formerly had trouble on the subject of a halter, and had remained at odds, being both inclined to bear malice. Master Hauchecorne felt a sort of shame at being seen thus by his enemy, fumbling in the mud for a bit of string. He hurriedly concealed his treasure in his blouse, then in his breeches pocket; then he pretended to look on the ground for something else, which he did not find; and finally he went on toward the market, his head thrust forward, bent double by his pains.

He lost himself at once in the slow-moving, shouting crowd, kept in a state of excitement by the interminable bargaining. The peasants felt of the cows, went away, returned, sorely perplexed, always afraid of being cheated, never daring to make up their minds, watching the vendor's eye, striving incessantly to detect the tricks of the man and the defect in the beast.

The women, having placed their great baskets at their feet, took out their fowls, which lay on the ground, their legs tied together, with frightened eyes and scarlet combs.

They listened to offers, adhered to their prices, short of speech and impassive of face; or else, suddenly deciding to accept the lower price offered, they would call out to the customer as he walked slowly away:—

"All right, Mast' Anthime. You can have it."

Then, little by little, the square became empty, and when the Angelus struck midday those who lived too far away to go home betook themselves to the various inns.

At Jourdain's the common room was full of customers, as the great yard was full of vehicles of every sort—carts, cabriolets,[3] *chars-à-bancs,* tilburys,[4] unnamable carriages, shapeless, patched, with their shafts reaching heavenward like arms, or with their noses in the ground and their tails in the air.

The vast fireplace, full of clear flame, cast an intense heat against the backs of the row on the right of the table. Three spits were revolving, laden with chickens, pigeons, and legs of mutton; and a delectable odor of roast meat, and of gravy dripping from the browned skin, came forth from the hearth, stirred the guests to merriment, and made their mouths water.

All the aristocracy of the plough ate there, at Mast' Jourdain's, the innkeeper and horse-trader—a shrewd rascal who had money.

The dishes passed and were soon emptied, like the jugs of yellow cider. Every one told of his affairs, his sales and his purchases. They inquired about the crops. The weather was good for green stuffs, but a little wet for wheat.

Suddenly a drum rolled in the yard, in front of the house. In an instant everybody was on his feet, save a few indifferent ones; and they all ran to the door and windows, with their mouths still full and napkins in hand.

Having finished his long tattoo, the public crier shouted in a jerky voice, making his pauses in the wrong places:

"The people of Goderville, and all those present at the market are informed that between—nine and ten o'clock this morning on the Beuzeville—road, a black leather wallet was lost, containing five hundred—francs, and business papers. The finder is requested to carry it to—the mayor's at once, or to Master Fortuné Houlbrèque of Manneville. A reward of twenty francs will be paid."

Then he went away. They heard once more in the distance the muffled roll of the drum and the indistinct voice of the crier.

Then they began to talk about the incident, reckoning Master Houlbrèque's chance of finding or not finding his wallet.

And the meal went on.

They were finishing their coffee when the corporal of gendarmes appeared in the doorway.

He inquired:

"Is Master Hauchecorne of Bréauté here?"

Master Hauchecorne, who was seated at the farther end of the table, answered:—

"Here I am."

And the corporal added:

"Master Hauchecorne, will you be kind enough to go to the mayor's office with me? Monsieur the mayor would like to speak to you."

The peasant, surprised and disturbed, drank his *petit verre* [5] at one swallow, rose, and, even more bent than in the morning, for the first steps after each rest were particularly painful, he started off, repeating:

"Here I am, here I am."

And he followed the brigadier.

The mayor was waiting for him, seated in his arm-chair. He was the local notary, a stout, solemn-faced man, given to pompous speeches.

"Master Hauchecorne," he said, "you were seen this morning, on the Beuzeville road, to pick up the wallet lost by Master Houlbrèque of Manneville."

The rustic, dumfounded, stared at the mayor, already alarmed by this suspicion which had fallen upon him, although he failed to understand it.

"I, I—I picked up that wallet?"

"Yes, you."

"On my word of honor, I didn't even so much as see it."

"You were seen."

"They saw me, me? Who was it saw me?"

"Monsieur Malandain, the harness-maker."

Thereupon the old man remembered and understood; and flushing with anger, he cried:

"Ah! he saw me, did he, that sneak? He saw me pick up this string, look, m'sieu' mayor."

And fumbling in the depths of his pocket, he produced the little piece of cord.

But the mayor was incredulous and shook his head.

"You won't make me believe, Master Hauchecorne, that Monsieur Malandain, who is a man deserving of credit, mistook this string for a wallet."

The peasant, in a rage, raised his hand, spit to one side to pledge his honor, and said:

"It's God's own truth, the sacred truth, all the same, m'sieu' mayor. I say it again, by my soul and my salvation."

"After picking it up," rejoined the mayor, "you hunted a long while in the mud, to see if some piece of money had n't fallen out."

The good man was suffocated with wrath and fear.

"If any one can tell—if any one can tell lies like that to ruin an honest man! If any one can say—"

To no purpose did he protest; he was not believed.

He was confronted with Monsieur Malandain, who repeated and maintained his declaration. They insulted each other for a whole hour. At his own request, Master Hauchecorne was searched. They found nothing on him. At last the mayor, being sorely perplexed, discharged him, but warned him that he proposed to inform the prosecuting attorney's office and to ask for orders.

The news had spread. On leaving the mayor's office, the old man was surrounded and questioned with serious or bantering curiosity, in which, however, there was no trace of indignation. And he began to tell the story of the string. They did not believe him. They laughed.

He went his way, stopping his acquaintances, repeating again and again his story and his protestations, showing his pockets turned inside out, to prove that he had nothing.

They said to him:

"You old rogue, va!"

And he lost his temper, lashing himself into a rage, feverish with excitement, desperate because he was not believed, at a loss what to do, and still telling his story.

Night came. He must needs go home. He started with three neigh,
bors, to whom he pointed out the place where he had picked up the
bit of string: and all the way he talked of his misadventure.

During the evening he made a circuit of the village of Bréauté, in order
to tell everybody about it. He found none but incredulous listeners.

He was ill over it all night.

The next afternoon, about one o'clock, Marius Paumelle, a farmhand
employed by Master Breton, a farmer of Ymauville, restored the wallet
and its contents to Master Houlbrèque of Manneville.

The man claimed that he had found it on the road; but, being unable
to read, had carried it home and given it to his employer.

The news soon became known in the neighborhood; Master Hauchecorne
was informed of it. He started out again at once, and began to tell his
story, now made complete by the dénouement. He was triumphant.

"What made me feel bad," he said, "was n't so much the thing itself,
you understand, but the lying. There's nothing hurts you so much as
being blamed for lying."

All day long he talked of his adventure; he told it on the roads to
people who passed; at the wine-shop to people who were drinking; and
after church on the following Sunday. He even stopped strangers to
tell them about it. His mind was at rest now, and yet something em-
barrassed him, although he could not say just what it was. People
seemed to laugh while they listened to him. They did not seem convinced.
He felt as if remarks were made behind his back.

On Tuesday of the next week, he went to market at Goderville, impelled
solely by the longing to tell his story.

Malandain, standing in his doorway, began to laugh when he saw
him coming. Why?

He accosted a farmer from Criquetot, who did not let him finish, but
poked him in the pit of his stomach, and shouted in his face: "Go on,
you old fox!" Then he turned on his heel.

Master Hauchecorne was speechless, and more and more disturbed.
Why did he call him "old fox"?

When he was seated at the table, in Jourdain's inn, he set about explaining the affair once more.

A horse-trader from Montvilliers called out to him:

"Nonsense, nonsense, you old dodger! I know all about your string!"

"But they've found the wallet!" faltered Hauchecorne.

"None of that, old boy; there's one who finds it, and there's one who
carries it back. I don't know just how you did it, but I understand
you."

The peasant was fairly stunned. He understood at last. He was accused of having sent the wallet back by a confederate, an accomplice.

He tried to protest. The whole table began to laugh.

He could not finish his dinner, but left the inn amid a chorus of jeers.

He returned home, shamefaced and indignant, suffocated by wrath, by confusion, and all the more cast down because, with his Norman cunning, he was quite capable of doing the thing with which he was charged, and even of boasting of it as a shrewd trick. He had a confused idea that his innocence was impossible to establish, his craftiness being so well known. And he was cut to the heart by the injustice of the suspicion.

Thereupon he began once more to tell of the adventure, making the story longer each day, adding each time new arguments, more forcible protestations, more solemn oaths, which he devised and prepared in his hours of solitude, his mind being wholly engrossed by the story of the string. The more complicated his defence and the more subtle his reasoning, the less he was believed.

"Those are a liar's reasons," people said behind his back.

He realized it; he gnawed his nails, and exhausted himself in vain efforts.

He grew perceptibly thinner.

Now the jokers asked him to tell the story of "The Piece of String" for their amusement, as a soldier who has seen service is asked to tell about his battles. His mind, attacked at its source, grew feebler.

Late in December he took to his bed.

In the first days of January he died, and in his delirium of the death agony, he protested his innocence, repeating:

"A little piece of string—a little piece of string—see, here it is, m'sieu' mayor."

"THE PIECE OF STRING"

How does this story compare in interest with the others read?

What characteristics of the artistic short-story are to be found?

Prove that the story makes a single impression although the events are spread over several months.

1 Char-à-bancs (shä'-rä--bän')—a long, light, open vehicle.
2 Yokel—rustic.
3 Cabriolets—cabs.
4 Tilbury—a gig, or two-wheeled open carriage drawn by one horse.
5 Petit verre—little glass.

A CHAPARRAL CHRISTMAS GIFT [1] (1910)

O. HENRY [2] (1865–1910)

The original cause of the trouble was about twenty years in growing. At the end of the time it was worth it.

1 Used by permission of and special arrangement with Doubleday, Page & Company, owners of the copyright.
2 Nom-de-plume of William Sidney Porter.

Had you lived anywhere within fifty miles of Sundown Ranch you would have heard of it. It possessed a quantity of jet-black hair, a pair of extremely frank, deep-brown eyes and a laugh that rippled across the prairie like the sound of a hidden brook. The name of it was Rosita McMullen; and she was the daughter of old man McMullen of the Sundown Sheep Ranch.

There came riding on red roan steeds—or, to be more explicit, on a painted and a flea-bitten sorrel—two wooers. One was Madison Lane, and the other was the Frio Kid. But at that time they did not call him the Frio Kid, for he had not earned the honors of special nomenclature. His name was simply Johnny McRoy.

It must not be supposed that these two were the sum of the agreeable Rosita's admirers. The bronchos of a dozen others champed their bits at the long hitching rack of the Sundown Ranch. Many were the sheeps'-eyes that were cast in those savannas that did not belong to the flocks of Dan McMullen. But of all the cavaliers, Madison Lane and Johnny McRoy galloped far ahead, wherefore they are to be chronicled.

Madison Lane, a young cattleman from the Nueces country, won the race. He and Rosita were married one Christmas day. Armed, hilarious, vociferous, magnanimous, the cowmen and the sheepmen, laying aside their hereditary hatred, joined forces to celebrate the occasion.

Sundown Ranch was sonorous with the cracking of jokes and six-shooters, the shine of buckles and bright eyes, the outspoken congratulations of the herders of kine.

But while the wedding feast was at its liveliest there descended upon it Johnny McRoy, bitten by jealousy, like one possessed.

"I'll give you a Christmas present," he yelled, shrilly, at the door, with his .45 in his hand. Even then he had some reputation as an offhand shot.

His first bullet cut a neat underbit in Madison Lane's right ear. The barrel of his gun moved an inch. The next shot would have been the bride's had not Carson, a sheepman, possessed a mind with triggers somewhat well oiled and in repair. The guns of the wedding party had been hung, in their belts, upon nails in the wall when they sat at table, as a concession to good taste. But Carson, with great promptness, hurled his plate of roast venison and frijoles at McRoy, spoiling his aim. The second bullet, then, only shattered the white petals of a Spanish dagger flower suspended two feet above Rosita's head.

The guests spurned their chairs and jumped for their weapons. It was considered an improper act to shoot the bride and groom at a wedding. In about six seconds there were twenty or so bullets due to be whizzing in the direction of Mr. McRoy.

"I'll shoot better next time," yelled Johnny; "and there'll be a next time." He backed rapidly out the door.

Carson, the sheepman, spurred on to attempt further exploits by the success of his plate-throwing, was first to reach the door. McRoy's bullet from the darkness laid him low.

The cattlemen then swept out upon him, calling for vengeance, for, while the slaughter of a sheepman has not always lacked condonement, it was a decided misdemeanor in this instance. Carson was innocent; he was no accomplice at the matrimonial proceedings; nor had any one heard him quote the line "Christmas comes but once a year" to the guests.

But the sortie failed in its vengeance. McRoy was on his horse and away, shouting back curses and threats as he galloped into the concealing chaparral.

That night was the birthnight of the Frio Kid. He became the "bad man" of that portion of the state. The rejection of his suit by Miss McMullen turned him to a dangerous man. When officers went after him for the shooting of Carson, he killed two of them, and entered upon the life of an outlaw. He became a marvellous shot with either hand. He would turn up in towns and settlements, raise a quarrel at the slightest opportunity, pick off his man and laugh at the officers of the law. He was so cool, so deadly, so rapid, so inhumanly bloodthirsty that none but faint attempts were ever made to capture him. When he was at last shot and killed by a little one-armed Mexican, who was nearly dead himself from fright, the Frio Kid had the deaths of eighteen men on his head. About half of these were killed in fair duels depending upon the quickness of the draw. The other half were men whom he assassinated from absolute wantonness and cruelty.

Many tales are told along the border of his impudent courage and daring. But he was not one of the breed of desperadoes who have seasons of generosity and even of softness. They say he never had mercy on the object of his anger. Yet at this and every Christmastide it is well to give each one credit, if it can be done, for whatever speck of good he may have possessed. If the Frio Kid ever did a kindly act or felt a throb of generosity in his heart it was once at such a time and season, and this is the way it happened.

One who has been crossed in love should never breathe the odor from the blossoms of the ratama tree. It stirs the memory to a dangerous degree.

One December in the Frio country there was a ratama tree in full bloom, for the winter had been as warm as springtime. That way rode the Frio Kid and his satellite and co-murderer, Mexican Frank. The Kid reined in his mustang, and sat in his saddle, thoughtful and grim, with dangerously narrowing eyes. The rich, sweet scent touched him somewhere beneath his ice and iron.

"I don't know what I 've been thinking about, Mex," he remarked in his usual mild drawl, "to have forgot all about a Christmas present I got to give. I 'm going to ride over to-morrow night and shoot Madison

Lane in his own house. He got my girl—Rosita would have had me if he had n't cut into the game. I wonder why I happened to overlook it up to now?"

"Ah, shucks, Kid," said Mexican, "don't talk foolishness. You know you can't get within a mile of Mad Lane's house to-morrow night. I see old man Allen day before yesterday, and he says Mad is going to have Christmas doings at his house. You remember how you shot up the festivities when Mad was married, and about the threats you made? Don't you suppose Mad Lane 'll kind of keep his eye open for a certain Mr. Kid? You plumb make me tired, Kid, with such remarks."

"I 'm going," repeated the Frio Kid, without heat, "to go to Madison Lane's Christmas doings, and kill him. I ought to have done it a long time ago. Why, Mex, just two weeks ago I dreamed me and Rosita was married instead of her and him; and we was living in a house, and I could see her smiling at me, and—oh! h—l, Mex, he got her; and I 'll get him—yes, sir, on Christmas Eve he got her, and then 's when I 'll get him."

"There 's other ways of committing suicide," advised Mexican. "Why don't you go and surrender to the sheriff?"

"I 'll get him," said the Kid.

Christmas Eve fell as balmy as April. Perhaps there was a hint of far-away frostiness in the air, but it tingled like seltzer, perfumed faintly with late prairie blossoms and the mesquite grass.

When night came the five or six rooms of the ranch-house were brightly lit. In one room was a Christmas tree, for the Lanes had a boy of three, and a dozen or more guests were expected from the nearer ranches.

At nightfall Madison Lane called aside Jim Belcher and three other cowboys employed on his ranch.

"Now, boys," said Lane, "keep your eyes open. Walk around the house and watch the road well. All of you know the Frio Kid, as they call him now, and if you see him, open fire on him without asking any questions. I 'm not afraid of his coming around, but Rosita is. She 's been afraid he 'd come in on us every Christmas since we were married."

The guests had arrived in buckboards and on horseback, and were making themselves comfortable inside.

The evening went along pleasantly. The guests enjoyed and praised Rosita's excellent supper, and afterward the men scattered in groups about the rooms or on the broad gallery, smoking and chatting.

The Christmas tree, of course, delighted the youngsters, and above all were they pleased when Santa Claus himself in magnificent white beard and furs appeared and began to distribute the toys.

"It 's my papa," announced Billy Sampson, aged six. "I 've seen him wear 'em before."

Berkly, a sheepman, an old friend of Lane, stopped Rosita as she was passing by him on the gallery, where he was sitting smoking.

"Well, Mrs. Lane," said he, "I suppose by this Christmas you've gotten over being afraid of that fellow McRoy, have n't you? Madison and,
I have talked about it, you know."

"Very nearly," said Rosita, smiling, "but I am still nervous sometimes.
I shall never forget that awful time when he came so near to killing us."

"He's the most cold-hearted villain in the world," said Berkly. "The
citizens all along the border ought to turn out and hunt him down like a
wolf."

"He has committed awful crimes," said Rosita, "but—I—don't—know.
I think there is a spot of good somewhere in everybody. He was not always bad—that I know."

Rosita turned into the hallway between the rooms. Santa Claus, in
muffling whiskers and furs, was just coming through.

"I heard what you said through the window, Mrs. Lane," he said. "I
was just going down in my pocket for a Christmas present for your
husband. But I've left one for you instead. It's in the room to your
right."

"Oh, thank you, kind Santa Claus," said Rosita, brightly.

Rosita went into the room, while Santa Claus stepped into the cooler
air of the yard.

She found no one in the room but Madison.

"Where is my present that Santa said he left for me in here?" she
asked.

"Haven't seen anything in the way of a present," said her husband,
laughing, "unless he could have meant me."

The next day Gabriel Radd, the foreman of the X. O. Ranch, dropped
into the post-office at Loma Alta.

"Well, the Frio Kid's got his dose of lead at last," he remarked to the
postmaster.

"That so? How'd it happen?"

"One of old Sanchez's Mexican sheep herders did it!—think of it!
the Frio Kid killed by a sheep herder! The Greaser saw him riding along
past his camp about twelve o'clock last night, and was so skeered that he
up with a Winchester and let him have it. Funniest part of it was that
the Kid was dressed all up with white Angora-skin whiskers and a regular
Santy Claus rig-out from head to foot. Think of the Frio Kid playing
Santy!"

"A CHAPARRAL CHRISTMAS GIFT"

The scene of this story is laid in southern Texas near the border.
Notice the use of surprise. This is characteristic in O. Henry's work.

SOME SHORT-STORIES FOR OPTIONAL READING

Read as many of these short-stories as you have time for, using the following suggestions in writing your reports:

Give author and author's nationality. Which predominates in the story —setting, characters, or plot? Comment on the time, place, and movement of events. Do you find any characters that are not absolutely necessary? Does the story produce a single effect? How has the author handled his opening paragraph? The close of the story? What, in a sentence or two, is the main point of the story? Point out any instances of humor or pathos. Was the story interesting? Did the interest lie in the subject matter, or the way the story was told, or in both? Does this story in general conform, or not, to the usual characteristics of a short-story? How?

"The Fall of the House of Usher"............Poe
"The Gold Bug" ....Poe
"The Cask of Amontillado"..................Poe
"The Tell-Tale Heart" ....Poe
"The Purloined Letter" ....Poe
"A Descent into the Maelstrom"............ Poe
"Ligeia" ....Poe
"Drowne's Wooden Image" ....Hawthorne
"The Ambitious Guest".....................Hawthorne
"Dr. Heidegger's Experiment"...............Hawthorne
"Ethan Brand" ....Hawthorne
"Wakefield" ....Hawthorne
"Feathertop" ....Hawthorne
"The Minister's Black Veil".................Hawthorne
"Baa, Baa, Black Sheep" ....Kipling
"Moti Guj—Mutineer" ....Kipling
"Wee Willie Winkie" ....Kipling
"The Man Who Would Be King" ....Kipling
"The Strange Ride of Morrowbie Jukes"........Kipling
"Namgay Doola" ....Kipling
"Without Benefit of Clergy" ....Kipling
"They" ....Kipling
"The Man Who Was" ....Kipling
"The Pavilion on the Links" ....Stevenson
"The Merry Men" ....Stevenson
"The Story of the Young Man with the Cream
    Tarts" ....Stevenson
"The Bottle Imp" ....Stevenson
"The House with the Green Blinds".........Stevenson
"The Adventure of the Hansom Cab" ....Stevenson

Any story from any of the various collections published for school use.

REVIEW

1. Before going on to the next type, review what you have learned about the different kinds of prose fiction. How are they distinguished? Why are they all classed as fiction? Which of these kinds did you enjoy most? Why? What writers have done the best work in each type?

2. For your theme work try one of the following subjects:

> (1) Write a new *Arthur* story, creating a new knight of the Round Table and giving his adventures.

> (2) Write a prose romance, using the old setting but treating some modern theme allegorically. For instance, draw material from the World War, letting the lady to be rescued be Civilization, or Liberty, or Belgium.

> (3) Write a short-story, trying to make it conform as far as possible to the characteristics of the type. Confine yourself to one event, one place, and one time.

CHAPTER III

THE ORATION

Changing Ideals Regarding Public Speaking.—Oratory in the old sense, an elaborate appeal to the emotions spoken in public assemblies, is dying out. Public speaking of a simpler kind, appealing to the will through the intellect, is, however, a form in constant use. Instead of the few gifted orators of the past, we have come to a time when the multifarious demands of our complex life have made good public speakers of the many.

Characteristics of Modern Oratory.—Modern speeches are much more direct and to the point than those of the past. An effective speech is always simple in structure, earnest and sincere in spirit, true in its statements, progressive, even rapid, in its course, forceful and keenly alive to the significance of the occasion which calls it out; it shows a thorough understanding of the questions involved, and it usually makes no attempt to appeal directly to the emotions.

Occasions for Speeches.—The speech must be adapted to the audience and the occasion. It may be made for the purpose of giving information, of defending a cause, of persuading to a course of action, of eulogizing some person or thing, of commemorating, of welcoming, of bidding farewell, or of dedicating to a particular service, and it may be of a political, social, educational, or religious nature.

Speeches may usually be divided into the following classes, according to their underlying purposes: (1) those for special occasions, being very varied in nature; (2) political speeches; (3) popular lectures and addresses; and (4) sermons.

A good speech has an orderly plan which is easy to follow. It usually divides naturally into three parts—the introduction, the main discussion, and the conclusion. In the introduction the speaker tries to win the attention and interest of his hearers. He simply and briefly states his standpoint and gives any information necessary to the understanding of the question under discussion. Sometimes a more abrupt beginning is good, but in any case the introduction must bear a close relation to what follows. In the main body of the speech, if there are many phases of a question, these are arranged in logical order and clearly treated. Definitions, illustrations, concrete examples—anything that will make the points more forceful are given. In the conclusion there is usually a summary made, and sometimes here an emotional appeal is justified. The conclusion is brief and to the point and is closely unified with all that has gone before.

Great Public Speakers.—The greatest orators of the past were Demosthenes in Greece, Cicero in Rome, Burke in England, and Daniel Webster in America. Besides these there have been many others whom their countrymen have delighted to honor. Among these may be mentioned Æschines, Cato, Pitt, Fox, Sheridan, Macaulay, Disraeli, Gladstone, Patrick Henry, Hamilton, Jefferson, Clay, Calhoun, Edward Everett, Lincoln, Wendell Phillips, Carl Schurz, Henry Ward Beecher, Phillips Brooks, Henry W. Grady, John Hay, Elihu Root, William Jennings Bryan, Theodore Roosevelt, Arthur James Balfour, David Lloyd-George, and Woodrow Wilson.

The greatest orator of Europe to-day is said to be René Viviani, of France.

Some Examples of the Modern Speech.—

SECOND INAUGURAL ADDRESS

ABRAHAM LINCOLN [1] (1809–1865)

MARCH 4, 1865

FELLOW-COUNTRYMEN: At this second appearing to take the oath of the Presidential office, there is less occasion for an extended address than there was at the first. Then a statement somewhat in detail of a course to be pursued seemed very fitting and proper. Now, at the expiration of four years, during which public declarations have been constantly called forth on every point and phase of the great contest which still absorbs the attention and engrosses the energies of the nation, little that is new could be presented.

The progress of our arms, upon which all else chiefly depends, is as well known to the public as to myself, and it is, I trust, reasonably satisfactory and encouraging to all. With high hope for the future, no prediction in regard to it is ventured.

On the occasion corresponding to this four years ago, all thoughts were anxiously directed to an impending civil war. All dreaded it, all sought

[1] Notice the simplicity of all of Lincoln's speeches.

to avoid it. While the inaugural address was being delivered from this place, devoted altogether to saving the Union without war, insurgent agents were in the city, seeking to destroy it with war—seeking to dissolve the Union and divide the effects by negotiation. Both parties deprecated war, but one of them would make war rather than let the nation survive, and the other would accept war rather than let it perish, and the war came. One-eighth of the whole population were colored slaves, not distributed generally over the Union, but localized in the southern part of it. These slaves constituted a peculiar and powerful interest. All knew that this interest was somehow the cause of the war. To strengthen, perpetuate, and extend this interest was the object for which the insurgents would rend the Union by war, while the Government claimed no right to do more than to restrict the territorial enlargement of it.

Neither party expected for the war the magnitude or the duration which it has already attained. Neither anticipated that the cause of the conflict might cease, even before the conflict itself should cease. Each looked for an easier triumph, and a result less fundamental and astounding.

Both read the same Bible and pray to the same God, and each invokes His aid against the other. It may seem strange that any men should dare to ask a just God's assistance in wringing their bread from the sweat of other men's faces, but let us judge not, that we be not judged. The prayer of both could not be answered. That of neither has been answered fully. The Almighty has His own purposes. Woe unto the world because of offences, for it must needs be that offences come, but woe to that man by whom the offence cometh. If we shall suppose that American slavery is one of those offences which, in the providence of God, must needs come, but which having continued through His appointed time, He now wills to remove, and that He gives to both North and South this terrible war as the woe due to those by whom the offence came, shall we discern there any departure from those Divine attributes which the believers in a living God always ascribe to Him? Fondly do we hope, fervently do we pray, that this mighty scourge of war may speedily pass away. Yet if God wills that it continue until all the wealth piled by the bondsman's two hundred and fifty years of unrequited toil shall be sunk, and until every drop of blood drawn with the lash shall be paid by another drawn with the sword, as was said three thousand years ago, so still it must be said, that the judgments of the Lord are true and righteous altogether.

With malice towards none, with charity for all, with firmness in the right as God gives us to see the right, let us strive on to finish the work we are in, to bind up the nation's wounds, to care for him who shall have borne the battle, and for his widow and his orphans, to do all which may achieve and cherish a just and a lasting peace among ourselves and with all nations.

OUR NATIONAL RESPONSIBILITIES

THEODORE ROOSEVELT (1858–1919)

[Inaugural Address Delivered at Washington, March 4, 1905]

No people on earth have more cause to be thankful than ours, and this is said reverently, in no spirit of boastfulness in our own strength, but with gratitude to the Giver of Good, who has blessed us with the conditions which have enabled us to achieve so large a measure of well-being and of happiness. To us as a people it has been granted to lay the foundations of our national life in a new continent. We are the heirs of the ages, and yet we have had to pay few of the penalties which in old countries are exacted by the dead hand of a bygone civilization. We have not been obliged to fight for our existence against any alien race; and yet our life has called for the vigor and effort without which the manlier and hardier virtues wither away. Under such conditions it would be our own fault if we failed; and the success which we have had in the past, the success which we confidently believe the future will bring, should cause in us no feeling of vainglory, but rather a deep and abiding realization of all which life has offered us; a full acknowledgment of the responsibility which is ours; and a fixed determination to show that under a free government a mighty people can thrive best, alike as regards the things of the body and the things of the soul.

Much has been given to us, and much will rightfully be expected from us. We have duties to others and duties to ourselves; and we can shirk neither. We have become a great nation, forced by the fact of its greatness into relations with the other nations of the earth; and we must behave as beseems a people with such responsibilities. Toward all other nations, large and small, our attitude must be one of cordial and sincere friendship. We must show not only in our words but in our deeds that we are earnestly desirous of securing their good will by acting toward them in a spirit of just and generous recognition of all their rights. But justice and generosity in a nation, as in an individual, count most when shown not by the weak but by the strong. While ever careful to refrain from wronging others, we must be no less insistent that we are not wronged ourselves. We wish peace; but we wish the peace of justice, the peace of righteousness. We wish it because we think it is right and not because we are afraid. No weak nation that acts manfully and justly should ever have cause to fear us, and no strong power should ever be able to single us out as a subject for insolent aggression.

Our relations with the other Powers of the world are important; but still more important are our relations among ourselves. Such growth in wealth, in population, and in power as this nation has seen during the century and a quarter of its national life is inevitably accompanied by a like growth in the problems which are ever before every nation that rises to greatness. Power invariably means both responsibility and danger. Our forefathers faced certain perils which we have outgrown. We now face other perils, the very existence of which it was impossible that they should foresee. Modern life is both complex and intense, and the tremendous changes wrought by the extraordinary industrial development of the last half century are felt in every fiber of our social and political being. Never before have men tried so vast and formidable an experiment as that of administering the affairs of a continent under the form of a democratic republic. The conditions which have told for our marvelous material well-being, which have developed to a very high degree our energy, self-reliance, and individual initiative, have also brought the care and anxiety inseparable from the accumulation of great wealth in industrial centers. Upon the success of our experiment much depends; not only as regards our own welfare, but as regards the welfare of mankind. If we fail, the cause of free self-government throughout the world will rock to its foundations; and therefore our responsibility is heavy, to ourselves, to the world as it is to-day, and to the generations yet unborn. There is no good reason why we should fear the future, but there is every reason why we should face it seriously, neither hiding from ourselves the gravity of the problems before us nor fearing to approach these problems with the unbending, unflinching purpose to solve them aright.

Yet, after all, though the problems are new, though the tasks set before us differ from the tasks set before our fathers who founded and preserved this Republic, the spirit in which these tasks must be undertaken and these problems faced, if our duty is to be well done, remains essentially unchanged. We know that self-government is difficult. We know that no people needs such high traits of character as that people which seeks to govern its affairs aright through the freely expressed will of the freemen who compose it. But we have faith that we shall not prove false to the memories of the men of the mighty past. They did their work; they left us the splendid heritage we now enjoy. We in our turn have an assured confidence that we shall be able to leave this heritage unwasted and enlarged to our children and our children's children. To do so we must show, not merely in great crises, but in the everyday affairs of life, the qualities of practical intelligence, of courage, of hardihood and endurance, and above all the power of devotion to a lofty ideal, which made great the men who founded this Republic in the days of Washington, which made great the men who preserved this Republic in the days of Abraham Lincoln.

Notes.—Compare this inaugural address with that of Lincoln in 1865. What changes do you find in the view-point? Are these due to the time, the man, or to other causes?

How are we "heirs of the ages"? Point out some specific things that we have inherited. How do we compare with other nations in this respect?

Compare some of the perils which our forefathers faced with those to which Roosevelt refers; to those of the present time. What does the speaker especially point out as our responsibilities as a nation? What national characteristics does he say we must have for the highest success? Memorize something from his speech.

THE WAR MESSAGE

WOODROW WILSON (1856–   )

Address of the President of the United States, Delivered at a Joint Session of the Two Houses of Congress, April 2, 1917

GENTLEMEN OF THE CONGRESS:

I have called the Congress into extraordinary session because there are serious, very serious, choices of policy to be made, and made immediately, which it was neither right nor constitutionally permissible that I should assume the responsibility of making.

On the third of February last I officially laid before you the extraordinary announcement of the Imperial German Government that on and after the first day of February it was its purpose to put aside all restraints of law or of humanity and use its submarines to sink every vessel that sought to approach either the ports of Great Britain and Ireland or the western coasts of Europe or any of the ports controlled by the enemies of Germany within the Mediterranean. That had seemed to be the object of the German submarine warfare earlier in the war, but since April of last year the Imperial Government had somewhat restrained the commanders of its undersea craft in conformity with its promise then given to us that passenger boats should not be sunk and that due warning would be given to all other vessels which its submarines might seek to destroy, when no resistance was offered or escape attempted, and care taken that their crews were given at least a fair chance to save their lives in their open boats. The precautions taken were meager and haphazard enough, as was proved in distressing instance after instance in the progress of the cruel and unmanly business, but a certain degree of restraint was observed. The new policy has swept every restriction aside. Vessels of every kind, whatever their flag, their character, their cargo, their destination, their errand, have been ruthlessly sent to the bottom without warning and without thought of help or mercy for those on board, the vessels of friendly neutrals along with those of belligerents. Even hospital ships and ships carrying relief to the sorely bereaved and stricken people of Belgium, though the latter were provided with safe conduct through the proscribed areas by the German Government itself and were distinguished by unmistakable marks of identity, have been sunk with the same reckless lack of compassion or of principle.

I was for a little while unable to believe that such things would in fact be done by any government that had hitherto subscribed to the humane practice of civilized nations. International law had its origin in the attempt to set up some law which would be respected and observed upon the seas, where no nation had right of dominion and where lay the free highways of the world. By painful stage after stage has that law been built up, with meager enough results, indeed, after all was accomplished that could be accomplished, but always with a clear view, at least, of what the heart and conscience of mankind demanded. This minimum of right the German Government has swept aside under the plea of retaliation and necessity and because it had no weapons which it could use at sea except these which it is impossible to employ as it is employing them without throwing to the winds all scruples of humanity or of respect for the understandings that were supposed to underlie the intercourse of the world. I am not now thinking of the loss of property involved, immense and serious as that is, but only of the wanton and wholesale destruction of the lives of noncombatants, men, women, and children, engaged in pursuits which have always, even in the darkest periods of modern history, been deemed innocent and legitimate. Property can be paid for; the lives of peaceful and innocent people can not be. The present German submarine warfare against commerce is a warfare against mankind.

It is a war against all nations. American ships have been sunk, American lives taken, in ways which it has stirred us very deeply to learn of, but the ships and people of other neutral and friendly nations have been sunk and overwhelmed in the waters in the same way. There has been no discrimination. The challenge is to all mankind. Each nation must decide for itself how it will meet it. The choice we make for ourselves must be made with a moderation of counsel and a temperateness of judgment befitting our character and our motives as a nation. We must put excited feeling away. Our motive will not be revenge or the victorious assertion of the physical might of the nation, but only the vindication of right, of human right, of which we are only a single champion.

When I addressed the Congress on the twenty-sixth of February last I thought that it would suffice to assert our neutral rights with arms, our right to use the seas against unlawful interference, our right to keep our people safe against unlawful violence. But armed neutrality, it now appears, is impracticable. Because submarines are in effect outlaws when used as the German submarines have been used against merchant shipping, it is impossible to defend ships against their attacks as the law of nations has assumed that merchantmen would defend themselves against privateers or cruisers, visible craft giving chase upon the open sea. It is common prudence in such circumstances, grim necessity indeed, to endeavor to destroy them before they have shown their own intention. They must be dealt with upon sight, if dealt with at all. The

German Government denies the right of neutrals to use arms at all within the areas of the sea which it has proscribed, even in the defense of rights which no modern publicist has ever before questioned their right to defend. The intimation is conveyed that the armed guards which we have placed on our merchant ships will be treated as beyond the pale of law and subject to be dealt with as pirates would be. Armed neutrality is ineffectual enough at best; in such circumstances and in the face of such pretensions it is worse than ineffectual: it is likely only to produce what it was meant to prevent; it is practically certain to draw us into the war without either the rights or the effectiveness of belligerents. There is one choice we can not make, we are incapable of making: we will not choose the path of submission and suffer the most sacred rights of our nation and our people to be ignored or violated. The wrongs against which we now array ourselves are no common wrongs; they cut to the very roots of human life.

With a profound sense of the solemn and even tragical character of the step I am taking and of the grave responsibilities which it involves, but in unhesitating obedience to what I deem my constitutional duty, I advise that the Congress declare the recent course of the Imperial German Government to be in fact nothing less than war against the government and people of the United States; that it formally accept the status of belligerent which has thus been thrust upon it; and that it take immediate steps not only to put the country in a more thorough state of defense, but also to exert all its power and employ all its resources to bring the Government of the German Empire to terms and end the war.

What this will involve is clear. It will involve the utmost practicable cooperation in counsel and action with the governments now at war with Germany, and, as incident to that, the extension to those governments of the most liberal financial credits, in order that our resources may so far as possible be added to theirs. It will involve the organization and mobilization of all the material resources of the country to supply the materials of war and serve the incidental needs of the nation in the most abundant and yet the most economical and efficient way possible. It will involve the immediate full equipment of the navy in all respects, but particularly in supplying it with the best means of dealing with the enemy's submarines. It will involve the immediate addition to the armed forces of the United States already provided for by law in case of war at least five hundred thousand men, who should, in my opinion, be chosen upon the principle of universal liability to service, and also the authorization of subsequent additional increments of equal force so soon as they may be needed and can be handled in training. It will involve also, of course, the granting of adequate credits to the Government, sustained, I hope, so far as they can equitably be sustained by the present generation, by well conceived taxation.

I say sustained so far as may be equitable by taxation because it seems to me that it would be most unwise to base the credits which will now be necessary entirely on money borrowed. It is our duty, I most respectfully urge, to protect our people so far as we may against the very serious hardships and evils which would be likely to arise out of the inflation which would be produced by vast loans.

In carrying out the measures by which these things are to be accomplished, we should keep constantly in mind the wisdom of interfering as little as possible in our own preparation and in the equipment of our own military forces with the duty—for it will be a very practical duty —of supplying the nations already at war with Germany with the materials which they can obtain only from us or by our assistance. They are in the field, and we should help them in every way to be effective there.

I shall take the liberty of suggesting, through the several executive departments of the Government, for the consideration of your committees, measures for the accomplishment of the several objects I have mentioned. I hope that it will be your pleasure to deal with them as having been framed after very careful thought by the branch of the Government upon which the responsibility of conducting the war and safeguarding the nation will most directly fall.

While we do these things, these deeply momentous things, let us be very clear, and make very clear to all the world what our motives and our objects are. My own thought has not been driven from its habitual and normal course by the unhappy events of the last two months, and I do not believe that the thought of the nation has been altered or clouded by them. I have exactly the same things in mind now that I had in mind when I addressed the Senate on the twenty-second of January last; the same that I had in mind when I addressed the Congress on the third of February and on the twenty-sixth of February. Our object now, as then, is to vindicate the principles of peace and justice in the life of the world as against selfish and autocratic power, and to set up amongst the really free and self-governed peoples of the world such a concert of purpose and of action as will henceforth ensure the observance of those principles. Neutrality is no longer feasible or desirable where the peace of the world is involved and the freedom of its peoples, and the menace to that peace and freedom lies in the existence of autocratic governments backed by organized force which is controlled wholly by their will, not by the will of the people. We have seen the last of neutrality in such circumstances. We are at the beginning of an age in which it will be insisted that the same standards of conduct and of responsibility for wrong done shall be observed among nations and their governments that are observed among the individual citizens of civilized states.

We have no quarrel with the German people. We have no feeling towards them but one of sympathy and friendship. It was not upon their impulse that their government acted in entering this war. It was not with their previous knowledge or approval. It was a war determined upon as wars used to be determined upon in the old, unhappy days when peoples were nowhere consulted by their rulers and wars were provoked and waged in the interest of dynasties or of little groups of ambitious men who were accustomed to use their fellow men as pawns and tools. Self-governed nations do not fill their neighbor states with spies or set the course of intrigue to bring about some critical posture of affairs which will give them an opportunity to strike and make conquest. Such designs can be successfully worked out only under cover and where no one has the right to ask questions. Cunningly contrived plans of deception or aggression, carried, it may be, from generation to generation, can be worked out and kept from the light only within the privacy of courts or behind the carefully guarded confidences of a narrow and privileged class. They are happily impossible where public opinion commands and insists upon full information concerning all the nation's affairs.

A steadfast concert for peace can never be maintained except by a partnership of democratic nations. No autocratic government could be trusted to keep faith within it or observe its covenants. It must be a league of honor, a partnership of opinion. Intrigue would eat its vitals away; the plottings of inner circles who could plan what they would and render account to no one would be a corruption seated at its very heart. Only free peoples can hold their purpose and their honor steady to a common end and prefer the interests of mankind to any narrow interest of their own.

Does not every American feel that assurance has been added to our hope for the future peace of the world by the wonderful and heartening things that have been happening within the last few weeks in Russia? Russia was known by those who knew it best to have been always in fact democratic at heart, in all the vital habits of her thoughts, in all the intimate relationships of her people that spoke their natural instinct, their habitual attitude towards life. The autocracy that crowned the summit of her political structure, long as it had stood and terrible as was the reality of its power, was not in fact Russian in origin, character, or purpose; and now it has been shaken off and the great, generous Russian people have been added in all their native majesty and might to the forces that are fighting for freedom in the world, for justice, and for peace. Here is a fit partner for a League of Honor.

One of the things that have served to convince us that the Prussian autocracy was not and could never be our friend is that from the very outset of the present war it has filled our unsuspecting communities and even our offices of government with spies, and set criminal intrigues everywhere afoot against our national unity of counsel, our peace within and without, our industries and our commerce. Indeed, it is now evident that its spies were here even before the war began; and it is unhappily not a matter of conjecture but a fact proved in our courts of justice that the intrigues which have more than once come perilously near to disturbing the peace and dislocating the industries of the country have been carried on at the instigation, with the support, and even under the personal direction of official agents of the Imperial Government accredited to the Government of the United States. Even in checking these things and trying to extirpate them we have sought to put the most generous interpretation possible upon them because we knew that their source lay, not in any hostile feeling or purpose of the German people towards us (who were, no doubt, as ignorant of them as we ourselves were), but only in the selfish designs of a government that did what it pleased and told its people nothing. But they have played their part in serving to convince us at last that that government entertains no real friendship for us and means to act against our peace and security at its convenience. That it means to stir up enemies against us at our very doors the intercepted note to the German Minister at Mexico City is eloquent evidence.

We are accepting this challenge of hostile purpose because we know that in such a government, following such methods, we can never have a friend; and that in the presence of its organized power, always lying in wait to accomplish we know not what purpose, there can be no assured security for the democratic governments of the world. We are now about to accept gauge of battle with this natural foe to liberty, and shall, if necessary, spend the whole force of the nation to check and nullify its pretensions and its power. We are glad, now that we see the facts with no veil of false pretense about them, to fight thus for the ultimate peace of the world and for the liberation of its peoples, the German peoples included: for the rights of nations great and small and the privilege of men everywhere to choose their way of life and of obedience. The world must be made safe for democracy. Its peace must be planted upon the tested foundations of political liberty. We have no selfish ends to serve. We desire no conquest, no dominion. We seek no indemnities for ourselves, no material compensation for the sacrifices we shall freely make. We are but one of the champions of the rights of mankind. We shall be satisfied when those rights have been made as secure as the faith and the freedom of nations can make them.

Just because we fight without rancor and without selfish object, seeking nothing for ourselves but what we shall wish to share with all free peoples, we shall, I feel confident, conduct our operations as belligerents without passion, and ourselves observe with proud punctilio the principles of right and of fair play we profess to be fighting for.

I have said nothing of the governments allied with the Imperial Government of Germany because they have not made war upon us or challenged us to defend our right and our honor. The Austro-Hungarian Government has, indeed, avowed its unqualified endorsement and acceptance of the reckless and lawless submarine warfare adopted now without disguise by the Imperial German Government, and it has therefore not been possible for this Government to receive Count Tarnowski, the Ambassador recently accredited to this Government by the Imperial and Royal Government of Austria-Hungary; but that Government has not actually engaged in warfare against citizens of the United States on the seas, and I take the liberty, for the present at least, of postponing a discussion of our relations with the authorities at Vienna. We enter this war only where we are clearly forced into it because there are no other means of defending our rights.

It will be all the easier for us to conduct ourselves as belligerents in a high spirit of right and fairness because we act without animus, not in enmity towards a people or with the desire to bring any injury or disadvantage upon them, but only in armed opposition to an irresponsible government which has thrown aside all considerations of humanity and of right and is running amuck. We are, let me say again, the sincere friends of the German people, and shall desire nothing so much as the early reestablishment of intimate relations of mutual advantage between us,—however hard it may be for them, for the time being, to believe that this is spoken from our hearts. We have borne with their present government through all these bitter months because of that friendship,—exercising a patience and forbearance which would otherwise have been impossible. We shall, happily, still have an opportunity to prove that friendship in our daily attitude and actions towards the millions of men and women of German birth and native sympathy who live amongst us and share our life, and we shall be proud to prove it towards all who are in fact loyal to their neighbors and to the government in the hour of test. They are, most of them, as true and loyal Americans as if they had never known any other fealty or allegiance. They will be prompt to stand with us in rebuking and restraining the few who may be of a different mind and purpose. If there should be disloyalty, it will be dealt with with a firm hand of stern repression; but, if it lifts its head at all, it will lift it only here and there and without countenance except from a lawless and malignant few.

It is a distressing and oppressive duty, Gentlemen of the Congress, which I have performed in thus addressing you. There are, it may be, many months of fiery trial and sacrifice ahead of us. It is a fearful thing to lead this great peaceful people into war, into the most terrible and disastrous of all wars, civilization itself seeming to be in the balance. But the right is more precious than peace, and we shall fight for the things which we have always carried nearest our hearts,—for democracy, for the right of those who submit to authority to have a voice in their own governments, for the rights and liberties of small nations, for a universal dominion of right by such a concert of free peoples as shall bring peace and safety to all nations and make the world itself at last free. To such a task we can dedicate our lives and our fortunes, everything that we are and everything that we have, with the pride of those who know that the day has come when America is privileged to spend her blood and her might for the principles that gave her birth and happiness and the peace which she has treasured. God helping her, she can do no other.

Note.—As the immediate result of this speech the Senate voted for war 82 to 6, and the House of Representatives, 373 to 50. The officially annotated text of this message may be found in bulletin No. 1 of the War Information Series, published June, 1917, by the Committee on Public Information, Washington, D. C., and also in "Democracy To-Day" by Christian Gauss, published by the Scott, Foresman Company.

The text of this address was ordered by the Minister of Public Instruction to be read to the pupils of all the schools in France.

AMERICA'S ENTRANCE INTO THE WAR

DAVID LLOYD-GEORGE (1863–   )

[Speech Before the American Luncheon Club, London, April 12, 1917]

I am in the happy position of being, I think, the first British Minister of the Crown who, speaking on behalf of the people of this country, can salute the Ame ican nation as comrades in arms. I am glad; I am proud. I am glad not merely because of the stupendous resources which this great nation will bring to the succor of the alliance, but I rejoice as a democrat that the advent of the United States into this war gives the final stamp and seal to the character of the conflict as a struggle against military autocracy throughout the world.

That was the note that ran through the great deliverance of President Wilson. It was echoed, sir, in your resounding words to-day. The United States of America have the noble tradition, never broken, of having never engaged in war except for liberty. And this is the greatest struggle for liberty that they have ever embarked upon. I am not at all surprised, when one recalls the wars of the past, that America took its time to make up its mind about the character of this struggle. In Europe most of the great wars of the past were waged for dynastic aggrandizement and conquest. No wonder when this great war started that there were some elements of suspicion still lurking in the minds of the people of the United States of America. There were those who thought perhaps

that kings were at their old tricks—and although they saw the gallant
Republic of France fighting, they some of them perhaps regarded it as
the poor victim of a conspiracy of monarchial swashbucklers. The fact
that the United States of America has made up its mind finally makes it
abundantly clear to the world that this is no struggle of that character,
but a great fight for human liberty.

They naturally did not know at first what we had endured in Europe
for years from this military caste in Prussia. It never has reached the
United States of America. Prussia was not a democracy. The Kaiser
promises that it will be a democracy after the war. I think he is right.
But Prussia not merely was not a democracy. Prussia was not a State;
Prussia was an army. It had great industries that had been highly
developed; a great educational system; it had its universities; it had developed its science.

All these were subordinate to the one great predominant purpose, the
purpose of all—a conquering army which was to intimidate the world.
The army was the spear-point of Prussia; the rest was merely the haft.
That was what we had to deal with in these old countries. It got on the
nerves of Europe. They knew what it all meant. It was an army that
in recent times had waged three wars,[1] all of conquest, and the unceasing
tramp of its legions through the streets of Prussia, on the parade grounds
of Prussia, had got into the Prussian head. The Kaiser, when he witnessed on a grand scale his reviews, got drunk with the sound of it.
He delivered the law to the world as if Potsdam was another Sinai, and
he was uttering the law from the thunder clouds.

But make no mistake. Europe was uneasy. Europe was half intimi-
dated. Europe was anxious. Europe was apprehensive. We knew the
whole time what it meant. What we did not know was the moment it
would come.

This is the menace, this is the apprehension from which Europe has
suffered for over fifty years. It paralyzed the beneficent activity of all
States, which ought to be devoted to concentrating on the well-being of
their peoples. They had to think about this menace, which was there
constantly as a cloud ready to burst over the land. No one can tell except
Frenchmen what they endured from this tyranny, patiently, gallantly,
with dignity, till the hour of deliverance came. The best energies of
domestic science had been devoted to defending itself against the impending blow. France was like a nation which put up its right arm to
ward off a blow, and could not give the whole of her strength to the
great things which she was capable of. That great, bold, imaginative,
fertile mind, which would otherwise have been clearing new paths for
progress, was paralyzed.

That is the state of things we had to encounter. The most characteristic
of Prussian institutions is the Hindenburg line. What is the Hindenburg line? The Hindenburg line is a line drawn in the territories of

other people, with a warning that the inhabitants of those territories shall not cross it at the peril of their lives. That line has been drawn in Europe for fifty years.

You recollect what happened some years ago in France, when the French Foreign Minister [2] was practically driven out of office by Prussian interference. Why? What had he done? He had done nothing which a Minister of an independent State had not the most absolute right to do. He had crossed the imaginary line drawn in French territory by Prussian despotism, and he had to leave. Europe, after enduring this for generations, made up its mind at last that the Hindenburg line must be drawn along the legitimate frontiers of Germany herself. There could be no other attitude than that for the emancipation of Europe and the world.

It was hard at first for the people of America quite to appreciate that Germany had not interfered to the same extent with their freedom, if at all. But at last they endured the same experience as Europe had been subjected to. Americans were told that they were not to be allowed to cross and recross the Atlantic except at their peril. American ships were sunk without warning. American citizens were drowned, hardly with an apology—in fact, as a matter of German right. At first America could hardly believe it. They could not think it possible that any sane people should behave in that manner. And they tolerated it once,[3] and they tolerated it twice,[4] until it became clear that the Germans really meant it. Then America acted, and acted promptly.

The Hindenburg line was drawn along the shores of America, and the Americans were told they must not cross it. America said, "What is this?" Germany said, "This is our line, beyond which you must not go," and America said, "The place for that line is not the Atlantic, but on the Rhine—and we mean to help you roll it up."

There are two great facts which clinch the argument that this is a great struggle for freedom. The first is the fact that America has come in. She would not have come in otherwise. The second is the Russian revolution. When France in the eighteenth century sent her soldiers to America to fight for the freedom and independence of that land, France also was an autocracy in those days. But Frenchmen in America, once they were there—their aim was freedom, their atmosphere was freedom, their inspiration was freedom. They acquired a taste for freedom, and they took it home, and France became free. That is the story of Russia. Russia engaged in this great war for the freedom of Serbia, of Montenegro, of Bulgaria, and has fought for the freedom of Europe. They wanted to make their own country free, and they have done it. The Russian revolution is not merely the outcome of the struggle for freedom. It is a proof of the character of the struggle for liberty, and if the Russian people realize, as there is every evidence they are doing, that national discipline is not incompatible with national freedom—nay, that national discipline is essential to the security of national freedom—they will, indeed, become a free people.

I have been asking myself the question, Why did Germany, deliberately, in the third year of the war, provoke America to this declaration and to this action—deliberately, resolutely? It has been suggested that the reason was that there were certain elements in American life, and they were under the impression that they would make it impossible for the United States to declare war. That I can hardly believe. But the answer has been afforded by Marshal von Hindenburg himself, in the very remarkable interview which appeared in the press, I think, only this morning.

He depended clearly on one of two things. First, that the submarine campaign would have destroyed international shipping to such an extent that England would have been put out of business before America was ready. According to his computation, America cannot be ready for twelve months. He does not know America. In the alternative, that when America is ready, at the end of twelve months, with her army, she will have no ships to transport that army to the field of battle. In von Hindenburg's words, "America carries no weight," I suppose he means she has no ships to carry weight. On that, undoubtedly, they are reckoning.

Well, it is not wise always to assume that even when the German General Staff, which has miscalculated so often, makes a calculation it has no ground for it. It therefore behooves the whole of the Allies, Great Britain and America in particular, to see that that reckoning of von Hindenburg is as false as the one he made about his famous line, which we have broken already.

The road to victory, the guarantee of victory, the absolute assurance of victory, is to be found in one word—ships; and a second word—ships; and a third word—ships. And with that quickness of apprehension which characterizes your nation, Mr. Chairman, I see that they fully realize that, and to-day I observe that they have already made arrangements to build one thousand 3000-tonners for the Atlantic. I think that the German military advisers must already begin to realize that this is another of the tragic miscalculations which are going to lead them to disaster and to ruin. But you will pardon me for emphasizing that. We are a slow people in these islands—slow and blundering—but we get there. You get there sooner, and that is why I am glad to see you in.

But may I say that we have been in this business for three years? We have, as we generally do, tried every blunder. In golfing phraseology, we have got into every bunker.[5] But we have got a good niblick.[5] We are right out on the course.[5] But may I respectfully suggest that it is worth America's while to study our blunders, so as to begin just where we are now and not where we were three years ago? That is an advantage. In war, time has as tragic a significance as it has in sickness. A step, which, taken to-day, may lead to assured victory, taken to-morrow may barely avert disaster. All the Allies have discovered that. It was a new country for us all. It was trackless, mapless. We had to go by instinct. But we found the way, and I am so glad that you are sending your great naval and military experts here, just to exchange experience with men who have been through all the dreary, anxious crises of the last three years.

America has helped us even to win the battle of Arras. Do you know that these guns which destroyed the German trenches, shattered the barbed wire—I remember, with some friends of mine whom I see here, arranging to order the machines to make those guns from America. Not all of them—you got your share, but only a share, a glorious share. So that America has also had her training. She has been making guns, making ammunition, giving us machinery to prepare both; she has supplied us with steel, and she has got all that organization and she has got that wonderful facility, adaptability, and resourcefulness of the great people which inhabits that great continent. Ah! It was a bad day for military autocracy in Prussia when it challenged the great Republic of the West. We know what America can do, and we also know that now she is in it she will do it. She will wage an effective and successful war.

There is something more important. She will insure a beneficent peace. I attach great importance—and I am the last man in the world, knowing for three years what our difficulties have been, what our anxieties have been, and what our fears have been—I am the last man to say that the succor which is given to us from America is not something in itself to rejoice in, and to rejoice in greatly. But I don't mind saying that I rejoice even more in the knowledge that America is going to win the right to be at the conference table when the terms of peace are being discussed. That conference will settle the destiny of nations—the course of human life—for God knows how many ages. It would have been tragic for mankind if America had not been there, and there with all the influence, all the power, and the right which she has now won by flinging herself into this great struggle.

I can see peace coming now—not a peace which will be the beginning of war; not a peace which will be an endless preparation for strife and bloodshed; but a real peace. The world is an old world. It has never had peace. It has been rocking and swaying like an ocean, and Europe —poor Europe!—has always lived under the menace of the sword. When this war began, two-thirds of Europe were under autocratic rule. It is the other way about now, and democracy means peace. The democracy of France did not want war; the democracy of Italy hesitated long before they entered the war; the democracy of this country shrank from it— shrank and shuddered—and never would have entered the caldron had it not been for the invasion of Belgium. The democracies sought peace; strove for peace. If Prussia had been a democracy there would have been no war.   Strange things have happened in this war.   There are stranger things to come, and they are coming rapidly.

There are times in history when this world spins so leisurely along its destined course that it seems for centuries to be at a standstill; but there are also times when it rushes along at a giddy pace, covering the track of centuries in a year.   Those are the times we are living in now.   Six weeks ago Russia was an autocracy; she now is one of the most advanced democracies in the world.   To-day we are waging the most devastating war that the world has ever seen; to-morrow—perhaps not a distant to-morrow—war may be abolished forever from the category of human crimes. This may be something like the fierce outburst of winter which we are now witnessing before the complete triumph of the sun.   It is written of those gallant men who won that victory on Monday—men from Canada, from Australia, and from this old country, which has proved that in spite of its age it is not decrepit—it is written of those gallant men that they attacked with the dawn—fit work for the dawn!—to drive out of forty miles of French soil those miscreants who had defiled it for three years. "They attacked with the dawn." [6]   Significant phrase!

The breaking up of the dark rule of the Turk, which for centuries has clouded the sunniest land in the world, the freeing of Russia from an op-pression which has covered it like a shroud for so long, the great declara-tion of President Wilson, coming with the might of the great nation which he represents into the struggle for liberty, are heralds of the dawn. "They attacked with the dawn," and these men are marching forward in the full radiance of that dawn, and soon Frenchmen and Americans, British, Italians, Russians, yea, and Serbians, Belgians, Montenegrins, will march into the full light of a perfect day.

Notes on America's Entrance Into the War

[1] The three wars which Prussia waged for conquest before the World War were: (1) The Danish War (1864), in which, through the aid of Austria, Schleswig and Holstein were wrested from Denmark.   (2) The "Six Weeks' War" with Austria (1866), which grew out of dividing the spoils of the former war.   As a result Prussia increased her territory one-half.   (3) The Franco-Prussian War (1870–1871), by means of which she gained Alsace-Lorraine.

[2] The French Foreign Minister was Delcassé.   The event referred to was in connection with the First Morocco crisis of 1905–1906.   The German ambas-sador to France in demanding the dismissal of M. Delcassé said, "His policy is a menace to Germany, and you may rest assured we shall not wait for it to be realized."

[3] The sinking of the *Lusitania*, May 7, 1915.

[4] The sinking of the *Sussex*, March 24, 1916.

[5] How do these golfing terms apply?

[6] "They attacked with the dawn." The reference is to the battle of Vimy Ridge.

SPEECH GIVEN IN THE UNITED STATES SENATE

Introducing Baron Moncheur, the Head of the Belgian Commission, June 22, 1917

THOMAS R. MARSHALL (1854–   )

Senators, since that far-off, unrecorded hour when our ancestors began their slow westward movement, unnumbered and unremembered, thousands have died upon the field of battle for love, for hate, for liberty, for conquest, as freemen or as slaves. Every note in the gamut of human passion has been written in the anvil chorus of war. Many have struck the redeeming blow for their own country, but few have unsheathed their swords without the hope of self-aggrandizement. It remained for little Belgium to write in the blood of her martyred sons and daughters a new page in the annals of diplomacy, to inscribe thereon that the dishonor of a people is the aggregate of the selfishness of its citizens; that the honor of a people is the aggregate of the self-sacrifice of its citizens; that treaties are made to be kept, not broken; that a people may dare to walk through "the valley of the shadow of death," touching elbows with their convictions, but they dare not climb to the mountain tops of safety if thereby they walk over the dead bodies of their high ideals; that a people may safely die if thereby they can compel an unwilling world to toss upon their new-made graves the white lily of a blameless life.

Here, Senators, ends all I know, and here begins what I believe: Belgium shall arise. The long night of her weeping shall end; the morning of a day of joy shall break over her desolated homes, her devastated fields, and her profaned altars. When it breaks, humanity will learn that when mankind gambles with truth and honor and humanity, the dice of the gods are always loaded.

To me, in all profane history, there is no sadder, sweeter, sublimer character than Sidney Carton. Dreamer of dreams, he walked his lonely, only way. In all the history of nations there is no sadder, sweeter, sublimer story than the story of Belgium. Doer of deeds, she, too, has walked her lonely, only way—the via dolorosa that leads to duty, death, and glory. Out of the depths and across the deeps the representatives of the remnant of her people and the guardians of her honor have come to us this day.

I present to you the chairman of that mission, Baron Moncheur.

SOME SPEECHES FOR OPTIONAL READINGS

Note.—Give name of speech, the speaker, the occasion for its deliverance and a brief summary of the main points brought out.

"Farewell Address" (September 19, 1796)..George Washington
"Speech on a Resolution to Put Virginia into
    a State of Defense" (1775)...........Patrick Henry
"On Conciliation with America" (1775).....Edmund Burke
"The Bunker Hill Monument" (1825).....Daniel Webster
"The Character of Washington" (1832)....Daniel Webster
"The Second Bunker Hill Oration" (1843)..Daniel Webster
"Speech on Copyright" (1841)...........Thomas B. Macaulay
"True Americanism" (1858)..............Carl Schurz
"International Arbitration"................Carl Schurz
Speech at Cooper Institute (1860)........Abraham Lincoln
The First Inaugural Address (1861).......Abraham Lincoln
The Last Public Address (April 11, 1865)..Abraham Lincoln
"Toussaint L'Ouverture" (1861).........Wendell Phillips
"The New South" (1886).................Henry W. Grady
"Address at a Meeting in Behalf of the Chil-
    dren's Aid Society" (1892)............Phillips Brooks
"America's Love of Peace"................John Hay
"The Pan-American Spirit" ....Elihu Root
"The Puritan Spirit" ....Albert J. Beveridge
"Americanism" ....Theodore Roosevelt
"Public Duty of Educated Men"...........George William Curtis
"Salt" ....Henry Van Dyke
"Equipment for Service" ....Woodrow Wilson
"Abraham Lincoln" ....Woodrow Wilson
"A World League for Peace" (January 22,
    1917) ....Woodrow Wilson
"Flag Day Address" (June 14, 1917)......Woodrow Wilson
Any other speeches by.................. Woodrow Wilson
Any of the speeches in the collection "The
    Forum of Democracy," ed. by..........Watkins & Williams
Any of the speeches in "Democracy To-day,"
    ed. by ....Christian Gauss
Any of the speeches in "Addresses of Wood-
    row Wilson," ed. by.................. George McLean Harper
Speech on the Dedication of Mount Theodore
    Roosevelt (July 4, 1919)............Major-General Leonard Wood
"Apostrophe to the American Flag"......Maria Sanford

Miscellaneous Prose Forms.—It was stated in the introductory chapter of this book that not everything that has been written or printed is to be regarded as real literature. Only that which is artistic and appeals to our love for the beautiful, the true, and the good things of life and of the spirit can be called literature in its truest sense. Literature in this narrower meaning would thus exclude many useful writings that have as their only purpose the setting forth of facts as such. There are some works of a practical nature like histories, biographies, books of travel, autobiographies, letters, journals, memoirs, or even scientific and philosophical works, that may be regarded as true literature although written for an entirely different purpose. It is, however, only when such writings are expressed in beautiful and fitting language and appeal to the imagination and emotions, as well as to the understanding, that they may be so regarded.

An Example of Miscellaneous Literature.—

EXTRACT FROM THE PASTORAL LETTER OF CARDINAL MERCIER, DECEMBER 25, 1914

My dearest brethren, I desire to utter, in your name and my own, the gratitude of those whose age, vocation, and social conditions cause them to benefit by the heroism of others, without bearing in it any active part.

If any man had rescued you from shipwreck or from fire, you would assuredly hold yourselves bound to him by a debt of everlasting thankfulness. But it is not one man, it is two hundred and fifty thousand men, who fought, who suffered, who fell for you, so that Belgium might keep her independence, her dynasty, her patriotic unity; so that after the vicissitudes of battle she might rise nobler, purer, more erect, and more glorious than before.

In your name I sent them the greeting of our fraternal sympathy and our assurance that not only do we pray for the success of their arms and for the eternal welfare of their souls, but that we also accept for their sake all the distress, whether physical or moral, that falls to our own share in the oppression that hourly besets us, and all that the future may have in store for us, in humiliation for a time, in anxiety, and in sorrow. In the day of final victory we shall be in honor; it is just that to-day we should all be in grief.

Oh, all too easily do I understand how natural instinct rebels against the evils that have fallen upon Belgium; the spontaneous thought of mankind is ever that virtue should have its instantaneous crown, and injustice its immediate retribution. But the ways of God are not our ways. Providence gives free way, for a time measured by divine wisdom, to human passions and the conflict of desires. God, being eternal, is patient. The last word is the word of mercy, and it belongs to those who believe in love.

Better than any other man, perhaps, do I know what our country has undergone. These four last months have seemed to me age-long. By thousands have our brave ones been mown down; wives, mothers, are weeping for those they shall never see again; hearths are desolate; dire poverty spreads; anguish increases. I have traversed the greater part of the districts most terribly devastated in my diocese, and the ruins I beheld were more dreadful than I, prepared by the saddest of forebodings, could have imagined. Churches, schools, asylums, hospitals, convents, in great numbers, are in ruins. Entire villages have all but disappeared.

In the dear city of Louvain, perpetually in my thoughts, the magnificent church of St. Peter will never recover its former splendor. The ancient college of St. Ives, the art schools, the consular and commercial schools of the University, the old markets, our rich library with its collections, its unique and unpublished manuscripts, its archives, its galleries—all this accumulation of intellectual, of historic, of artistic riches, the fruits of the labor of five centuries—all is in the dust.

Many a parish has lost its pastor. In my diocese alone I know that thirteen priests were put to death. Thousands of Belgian citizens have been deported to the prisons of Germany. Hundreds of innocent men have been shot or burned. We can neither number our dead nor complete the measure of our ruins.

And there where lives were not taken, and there where the stones of buildings were not thrown down, what anguish unrevealed! Families, hitherto living at ease, now in bitter want; all commerce at an end; all careers ruined; industry at a standstill; thousands upon thousands of workingmen without employment; workingwomen, shop girls, humble servant girls, without the means of earning their bread; and poor souls forlorn on the bed of sickness and fever, crying, "O Lord, how long, how long?" There is nothing to reply. The reply remains the secret of God.

Yes, dearest brethren, it is the secret of God. He is the master of events and the sovereign director of the human multitude. As for us, my brethren, we will adore Him in the integrity of our souls. Not yet do we see, in all its magnificence, the revelation of His wisdom, but our faith trusts Him with it all. Before His justice we are humble, and in His mercy hopeful.

God will save Belgium, my brethren, you cannot doubt it. Nay, rather, He is saving her. Across the smoke of conflagration, across the stream of blood, have you not glimpses, do you not perceive, signs of His love for us? Is there a patriot among us who does not know that Belgium has grown great? Nay, which of us would have the heart to cancel this last page in the national history? Which of us does not exult in the brightness of the glory of this shattered nation? When a mighty foreign power, confident in its own strength and defiant of the faith of treaties, dared to threaten us in our independence, then did all Belgians rise as one man.

Belgium gave her word of honor to defend her independence. She

PRESIDENT WILSON AND CARDINAL MERCIER
In front of the Cardinal's residence in Malines

kept her word. The other Powers had agreed to protect and to respect Belgian neutrality. Germany has broken her word; England has been faithful to it. These are the facts. We should have acted unworthily had we evaded our obligation. And now we would not rescind our first resolution; we exult in it. Being called upon to write a most solemn page in the history of our country, we resolved that it should be also a sincere, also a glorious page. And as long as we are compelled to give proof of endurance, so long we shall endure.

Truce then, my brethren, to all murmurs of complaint. Not only to the Redeemer's example shall you look, but also to that of the thirty thousand, perhaps forty thousand, men who have already shed their life blood for their country. In comparison with them what have you endured who are deprived of the daily comforts of your lives? Let the patriotism of our army, the heroism of our King and our beloved Queen, serve to stimulate us and support us. Let us bemoan ourselves no more. Let us deserve the coming deliverance. Let us hasten it by our prayers. Courage, brethren. Suffering passes away; the crown of life for our souls, the crown of glory for our nation, shall not pass.

SOME EXAMPLES OF MISCELLANEOUS PROSE

The Bible. King James's version (1611) The Bible contains many types of Literature.

"The Complete Angler" (1653) .... Walton
"Diary" (1660–1669) .... Samuel Pepys
"Journal to Stella" (1710–1713) .... Jonathan Swift
"Life of Johnson" (1784–1791) .... James Boswell
"Decline and Fall of the Roman Empire" (1776) ... Edward Gibbon
"Letters and Journal" .... Thomas Gray
"Autobiography" .... Benjamin Franklin
"Life of Goldsmith" .... Washington Irving
"Sketches of my Literary Life and Opinions"
  ("Biographia Literaria") .... S. T. Coleridge
"Lectures on Shakespeare" ....
"Confessions of an English Opium Eater" .... Thomas De Quincey
"Life of Nelson" .... Robert Southey
"Imaginary Conversations" .... Walter S. Landor
"History of England" ....
"Sartor Resartus" .... Thomas Carlyle
"The French Revolution" .... Thomas Carlyle
"Modern Painters" ....
"Stones of Venice" .... John Ruskin
"Seven Lamps of Architecture" .... John Ruskin
"Præterita" .... John Ruskin
"Autobiography" .... Thomas Huxley
"Letters" .... Robert and Elizabeth
                                               Browning
"The Oregon Trail" .... Francis Parkman
"How I Found Livingstone" .... Henry M. Stanley
"The Winning of the West" .... Theodore Roosevelt

SOME FAMOUS CHARACTERS FROM LITERATURE

In what work found?   By whom written?

1. Puck
2. Gurth,
3. Portia
4. Gama
5. Joseph Andrews,
6. The Red Cross Knight
7. Dobbin
8. Friar Tuck,
9. Bassanio
10. Olivia Primrose
11. Caliban
12. Sabrina
13. Babbie
14. Dunstan Cass
15. Uriah Heep
16. Dame Quickly,
17. Miranda
18. Una,
19. Pompilia
20. Lorna Doone
21. Antonio
22. Beelzebub
23. Charles Darnay
24. Virginius
25. Pamela
26. Mr. Hardcastle
27. Nancy Lammeter
28. Tiny Tim
29. Hector
30. Micawber
31. Banquo
32. Gareth
33. Claudius
34. Lady Teazle
35. Lady Macbeth
36. Lady Castlewood
37. Lady Dedlock

38. Lady Margaret
39. Lady Clare
40. Lady Rowena
41. Sir Gawain
42. Sir Roger De Coverley
43. Sir Toby Belch
44. Sir Andrew Aguecheek
45. Sir Bors
46. Sir Patrick Spens
47. Sir Peter Teazle
48. The Black Knight
49. The Green Knight
50. Hrothgar
51. Achilles
52. Polonius
53. Galahad
54. Roderick Dhu
55. Theseus
56. Æneas
57. Dr. Primrose
58. Dr. Manette
59. Doctor Faustus
60. Paris
61. Little John
62. Sohrab
63. The Attendant Spirit
64. Tam o'Shanter
65. Friday
66. Brutus
67. Hermia
68. Henry Esmond
69. Dolly Winthrop
70. Childe Harold
71. Arcite
72. Dido
73. Giant Despair,
74. Gloriana

75. Markheim
76. Pistol
77. Little Emily
78. Annie Lee
79. John Gilpin
80. Aurora Leigh
81. Helen
82. Cousin Bridget
83. Scrooge
84. Jacques
85. Diomedes
86. Nancy Sykes
87. Lilia
88. Evangeline
89. Michael
90. Dinah Morris
91. Iago
92. Lydia Languish
93. Mercutio
94. Ophelia
95. John Silver
96. Jeanie Deans
97. John Ridd
98. Merlin
99. Priam
100. Touchstone
101. Little Nell
102. Wamba
103. Cassius
104. Godfrey Cass
105. Oberon
106. Regan
107. Guinevere
108. Prospero
109. Gulliver
110. Belial
111. Mazeppa
112. William Legrand
113. Sidney Carton
114. Falstaff
115. Pippa
116. Timotheus
117. Thomas à Becket
118. Mark Antony
119. Agamemnon
120. Modred
121. Colonel Newcome
122. Meg Merrilies
123. Rebecca
124. Becky Sharp
125. Romeo
126. Hecuba
127. Adam Bede
128. Desdemona
129. Robin Hood
130. Ellen Douglas
131. Blanche de Maletroit
132. Prince Hal
133. Cordelia
134. Madame Defarge
135. Madame Eglantyne
136. Mr. Macey
137. Menelaus
138. The Spectator
139. Rip
140. David Balfour
141. Horatio
142. Bottom
143. Locksley
144. Andromache.
145. Scyld
146. Florian
147. Lorenzo
148. Brunhild
149. Rosencrantz
150. Jerry Cruncher.
151. Priscilla
152. Philip Nolan
153. Mephistopheles
154. Mr. Worldly-Wiseman
155. Guy Mannering
156. Laertes
157. Amy Robsart
158. Juliet
159. Ferrex and Porrex
160. Tito Melema
161. Joseph Surface.
162. Sherlock Holmes
163. Amelia Sedley
164. Hepzibah

165. Duessa
166. Constance de Beverley
167. Jane Eyre
168. Shylock
169. Ariel
170. Emelye
171. The Wedding Guest
172. Rosalind
173. Mr. Burchell
174. Tom Tulliver
175. Mr. Marlow
176. Tom Jones
177. Tom Sawyer
178. Adam Winthrop
179. De Wilton
180. Miss Pross
181. Nydia
182. Arac
183. Maid Marian
184. Horatius
185. Belinda
186. Othello
187. Bill Sykes
188. Lycidas
189. Titania
190. Malcolm Graeme
191. Maurya
192. Tony Lumpkin
193. Goneril
194. Silas Lapham
195. Hippolyta
196. Sairy Gamp
197. Captain Absolute

198. Chaos
199. Paul Dombey
200. Mrs. Malaprop
201. Orlando
202. Sancho Panza
203. Ichabod Crane
204. "Bess, the landlord's daughter"
205. Romola
206. Denis de Beaulieu
207. Maggie Tulliver
208. Walter Vivian
209. Fagin
210. Fluellen,
211. Palamon
212. Peggotty
213. Eppie
214. Christian
215. Mammon
216. Miss Hardcastle
217. Mr. Pickwick
218. Maud
219. Front-de-Bœuf
220. Mr. Bennett
221. Harry Baillie
222. Hester Prynne
223. Rustum
224. Lear
225. Judge Pyncheon
226. John Alden
227. Natty Bumpo
228. Defarge

SOME WELL KNOWN TITLES OF PIECES OF LITERATURE

Name author, when known, and the type represented.

(These titles are all given in this book.)

1. "Drake"
2. "The Fall of the House of Usher"
3. "Rosabelle"
4. "Sir Gawain and the Green Knight"
5. "Hind Horn"
6. "Beowulf"
7. "Sohrab and Rustum"
8. "The Comedy of Errors"
9. "On First Looking into Chapman's Homer"
10. "To the West Wind"
11. "Markheim"
12. "My Last Duchess"
13. "Comus"
14. "The Island of Skyros"
15. "Il Penseroso"
16. "In Memoriam"
17. "Alexander's Feast"
18. "Caliban by the Yellow Sands"
19. "Macbeth"
20. "Intimations of Immortality"
21. "Ralph Royster Doyster"
22. "The Sire de Malétroit's Door"
23. "On the Enjoyment of Unpleasant Places"
24. "Doctor Faustus"
26. "Julius Cæsar"
25. "Tale of Two Cities"
27. "Of Friendship"
28. "The Chaparral Christmas Gift"
29. "On His Having Arrived at the Age of Twenty-Three"

30. "On a Grecian Urn"
31. "Adonaïs"
32. "The Traitor"
33. "The Highwayman"
34. "Tent on the Beach"
35. "Lycidas"
36. "The Masque of the Red Death"
37. "Dream Children"
38. "The Patrician"
39. "Of Studies"
40. "The Silver Box"
41. "Complaint to his Empty Purse"
42. "Upton Letters"
43. "The Land of Heart's Desire"
44. "L'Allegro"
45. "The Harp that Once through Tara's Halls"
46. "The Well of St. Keyne"
47. "Suspiria"
48. "The Pit and the Pendulum"
49. "Our National Responsibilities"
50. "The Brothers"
51. "The Faerie Queene"
52. "The Birthmark"
53. "The Family's Pride"
54. "Scots Wha Ha Wi Wallace Bled"
55. "Paradise Lost"
56. "Sir Patrick Spens"
57. "Canterbury Tales"
58. "Cymbeline"
59. "A Mile with Me"
60. "Sesame and Lilies"

493

61. "Pride and Prejudice"
62. "Wee Willie Winkie."
63. "Joseph Vance."
64. "Peter Pan."
65. "A Piece of String"
66. "Reflections in Westminster Abbey"
67. "The Heart of Midlothian"

68. "The Servant in the House"
69. "The Man Who Was"
70. "Hamlet"
71. "The Twa Sisters"
72. "Paradise Regained"
73. "To the Fire-Bringer"
74. "America"
75. "Guy Mannering"

APPENDIX

SUGGESTED MINIMUM REFERENCE LIBRARY LIST[1]

Homer's *Iliad*, tr. Bryant, W. C. (Houghton, 1904)................$1.00
Homer's *Odyssey*, tr. Palmer, G. H. (Houghton, 1913)............ 1.00
Virgil's *Æneid*, tr. Conington, J. (Scott, 1916)................. .40
Nibelungenlied, tr. Shumway (Houghton, 1909)................. 2.00
One Hundred Narrative Poems, Comp. Teter, G. (Scott, 1918)..... .46
Spenser's *Faery Queene*, Book I, ed. Winstanley, L. (Putnam, 1915).. .65
English Popular Ballads, ed. Hart, W. M. (Scott, 1916).......... .40
The Ballad Book, ed. Bates, K. L. (Sibley, 1913)................ .60
Palgrave's *Golden Treasury of Songs and Lyrics* (Macmillan)...... .25
Manly's *English Prose and Poetry* (1137–1892) (Ginn, 1916)...... 2.00
Pancoast's English Prose and Verse (Holt, 1915)................. 1.75
Newcomer and Andrews's *Twelve Centuries of English Poetry and
    Prose*, (Scott, 1910).. 2.40
Longfellow's *Complete Poetical Works* (Houghton, 1908)......... 1.00
Whittier's *Complete Poetical Works* (Houghton, 1904)........... 1.00
Tennyson's *Complete Poetical Works* (Houghton, 1914)........... 1.50
Shakespeare's *Complete Works*, ed. Neilson, W. A. Cambridge ed.
    (Houghton, 1906)... 3.00
Scott's *Complete Poetical Works* (Houghton, 1916)............. 1.00
The Little Book of Modern Verse, ed. Rittenhouse, Jessie B. (Hough-
    ton, 1917)... .55
A Treasury of War Poetry, ed. Clarke, G. H. (Houghton, 1917).... .52
Collected Poems, 2 Vols., Alfred Noyes (Stokes, 1913)........... 3.50
Fires, Gibson, W. W. (Macmillan, 1912)....................... 1.25
The Van Dyke Book, Van Dyke, Henry (Scribner, 1905).......... .50
The Piper, Peabody, Josephine Preston (Houghton, 1909, 1919).... .52
Riders to the Sea, Synge, J. M. (Luce, 1911)................... .50
The Servant in the House, Kennedy, Charles Rann (Harper, 1908).. 1.25
The Melting Pot, Zangwill, Israel (Macmillan, 1914).............. 1.25
Ulysses, Phillips, Stephen (Macmillan, 1908)...................
Plays, Galsworthy, John ("Silver Box," "Strife," etc.) (Scribner,
    1909) 1.50
Seven Short Plays, Gregory, Lady Augusta (G. P. Putnam's Sons,
    1915) 1.50

[1] It will be noted that many of the books listed here will be useful in earlier high school years as well.

Short-Stories for High Schools, ed. Mikels, Rosa M. R. (Scribner, 1915) .... .90
Types of the Short-Story, ed. Haydrick, B. A. (Scott, 1913)...... .44
Modern Short Stories, Law (Century, 1918)...................... 1.25
Selected Essays, ed. Fuess, C. M. (Houghton, 1914).............. .40
Essays, English and American, ed. Alden, R. M. (Scott, 1918)...... .52
Selections from the Best English Essays, ed. Cody, Sherman (McClurg, 1903).. 1.25
Century Readings in English Literature, Cunliffe, Pyre & Young, (Century, 1910)... 3.50
Century Readings in American Literature, Pattee (Century, 1919) 3.50
Facts and Backgrounds of Literature, Reynolds & Greever (Century 1920).. 1.50
The Forum of Democracy, ed. Watkins & Williams (Allyn, 1917)... 1.00
Democracy To-day, Gauss, Christian (Scott, 1918)................ .48
English Literature, Long, William J. (Ginn, 1909)............... 1.35
History of English Literature, Hinchman (Century, 1915)......... 2.00
New English Literature, Halleck, R. P. (Am. Book, 1913).......... 1.30
English Literature, Miller, Edwin L. (Lippincott, 1917) 1.38
Any standard novels.

The publishers referred to above are:

1 Houghton Mifflin Co., Boston.
2 Scott, Foresman & Co., Chicago.
3 Sibley & Co., Boston.
4 Macmillan Co., N. Y.
5 Ginn & Co., Boston.
6 Frederick A. Stokes Co., N. Y.
7 Charles Scribner's Sons, N. Y.
8 Harper & Bros., N. Y.
9 American Book Co., N. Y.
10 G. P. Putnam's Sons, N. Y. and London.
11 A. C. McClurg & Co., Chicago.
12 Allyn & Bacon, Boston.
13 John W. Luce & Co., Boston.
14 Henry Holt & Co., New York.
15 The Century Co., New York.
16 J. B. Lippincott Co., Philadelphia and London

TABLE OF FOREIGN AUTHORS

NATIONALITY	AUTHOR	WITH WHAT TYPE MENTIONED
Hebrew	David (1040–993 B. C.)	Lyric poetry
Greek	Homer (c. 9th Cent. B. C.)	Great epic
"	Æschylus (525-456 B. C.)	Drama
"	Pindar (522-448 (?) B. C.)	Lyric poetry—the ode
"	Sophocles (496–406 B. C.)	Drama
"	Euripides (480–406 B. C.)	"
"	Æschines (389-314 B. C.)	Oration
"	Demosthenes (384(?)–322 B. C.)	"
Roman	Plautus (254(?)–184 B. C.)	Drama
"	Cato (234–149 B. C.)	Oration
"	Terence (190(?)–159(?) B. C.)	Drama
"	Cicero (106–43 B. C.)	Oration
"	Virgil (70–19 B. C.)	Great epic
"	Seneca (4(?) B. C.–65 A. D.)	Drama
Persian	"Firdausi" (Abul Kasim Mansur) 940 (?)–1020(?) A. D.)	Great epic
Italian	Dante (1265–1321 A. D.)	" "
Portuguese	Camoëns (1524–1580 A. D.)	" "
French	Montaigne (1533–1592 A. D.)	Essay
Italian	Tasso (1544–1595 A. D.)	Great epic
German	Goethe (1749–1832 A. D.)	Drama
French	Balzac (1799–1850 A. D.)	Short-story
Finnish	Lönnrot (1802–1884 A. D.)	Great epic
French	Hugo (1802–1885 A. D.)	Novel
German Jew.	Auerbach (1812–1882 A. D.)	"
Russian	Turgenieff (1818–1883 A. D.)	Short-story
Norwegian	Ibsen (1828–1906 A. D.)	Drama
Russian	Tolstoi (1829–1910 A. D.)	Short-story
Norwegian	Björnson (1832–1910 A. D.)	" "
French	Daudet (1840–1897 A. D.)	" "
"	Coppée (1842–1908 A. D.)	" "
"	"France" (J. Anatole Thibault) (1844– A. D.)	" "
"	Maupassant (1850–1893 A. D.)	" "
Belgian	Maeterlinck (1862– A. D.)	Drama
French	Rostand (1868– A. D.)	"
"	Viviani (——)	Oration
Belgian	Mercier (——)	Miscellaneous Prose

WORKS OF BRITISH AND AMERICAN AUTHORS ACCORDING TO LITERARY PERIODS

THE ANGLO-SAXON PERIOD (450–1050)

NATIONALITY	AUTHOR	WORK	TYPE
	Unknown	"Beowulf"	Great epic

THE ANGLO-NORMAN PERIOD (1066–1350)

NATIONALITY	AUTHOR	WORK	TYPE
	Unknown	"Sir Gawain and the Green Knight"	Metrical romance
	Unknown	Ballads—especially the "Robin Hood Ballads"	Ballad
		Miracle and mystery plays from 1110 to about 1400	Drama

THE AGE OF CHAUCER (1350–1400)

NATIONALITY	AUTHOR	WORK	TYPE
British	Geoffrey Chaucer 1340(?)–1400	"The Canterbury Tales," especially "The Knight's Tale,"	Metrical tale
British	Geoffrey Chaucer	"Complaint to His Empty Purse"	Simple lyric
British	Unknown	Ballads (continued)	Ballad
British	Unknown	"Travels of Sir John Mandeville" (1356)	Prose romance (?)
British	Unknown	Miracle and mystery plays (continued)	Drama
British	Unknown	Beginning of Moralities	Drama

THE REVIVAL OF LEARNING PERIOD (1400–1550)

NATIONALITY	AUTHOR	WORK	TYPE
British	Sir Thomas Malory	"Morte d'Arthur" (1470, pub. by Caxton 1485)	Prose romance
British	Sir Thomas More	"Utopia" (1516)	Prose romance
British	Wyatt and Surrey	Sonnets (c. 1557)	Sonnet
British	Unknown	Ballads (continued)	Ballad
British	Unknown	Morality plays—"Everyman" and others.	Drama
British	John Heywood	Interludes—"The Four P's" and others	Drama

THE ELIZABETHAN AGE (1550–1620)

British	...Nicholas Udall	"Ralph Royster Doyster" (the first real comedy in England)	Drama
British	...William Stevenson	"Gammer Gurton's Needle"	Drama
British	...Sackville and Norton	"Gorboduc" (the first tragedy in England)	Drama
British	...	The plays of Greene, Lyly, Peele, Nash, Kyd, Lodge, etc.	Drama
British	...Edmund Spenser (1552–1599)	"Faerie Queene," and sonnets	Metrical romance / Sonnet
British	...Sir Philip Sidney (1554–1586)	"Arcadia," and sonnets	Prose romance / Sonnet
British	...John Lyly (1554 (?)–1606)	"Euphues"	Prose romance
British	...Thomas Lodge (1558–1625)	"Rosalind"	Prose romance
British	...Robert Greene (1560–1592)	"Pandosto"	Prose romance
British	...Francis Bacon (1561–1626)	Essays	Essays
British	...Michael Drayton (1563–1631)	"Ballad of Agincourt"	Imitation ballad
British	...Christopher Marlowe (1564–1593)	"Doctor Faustus," "Edward the Second," and other plays	Drama
British	...William Shakespeare (1564–1616)	"Hamlet" and other plays, sonnets, and songs	Drama, sonnets and song
British	...Ben Jonson (1573(?)–1637)	"Song to Celia," masks, and comedies	Song, mask and drama

THE PURITAN AGE (1620–1660)

British	...Izaak Walton (1593–1683)	"The Complete Angler"	Miscellaneous lit.
		The King James Version of "The Bible" (1611)	Miscellaneous lit.
British	...John Milton (1608–1674)	"On the Morning of Christ's Nativity"	Ode
British	...John Milton	Sonnets	Sonnet
British	...John Milton	"L'Allegro"	Simple lyric
British	...John Milton	"Il Penseroso"	Simple lyric
British	...John Milton	"Comus"	Mask
British	...John Milton	"Lycidas"	Elegy and pastoral

WORKS OF BRITISH AND AMERICAN AUTHORS ACCORDING TO LITERARY PERIODS—*Continued*

NATIONALITY	AUTHOR	WORK	TYPE
British	John Milton (1608–1674)	"Paradise Lost" (1667) [1]	Great epic
British	John Milton	"Paradise Regained" (1671)	Great epic
British	John Bunyan (1628–1688)	"Pilgrim's Progress"	Prose allegory

THE RESTORATION PERIOD (1660–1700)

British	John Dryden (1631–1700)	"Ode to St. Cecelia's Day"	Ode
British	John Dryden	"Alexander's Feast"	Ode
British	Samuel Pepys (1633–1703)	Diary (1660–1669)	Miscellaneous lit.

THE EIGHTEENTH CENTURY (1700–1800)

British	Nahum Tate (1652–1715)	"While Shepherds Watched Their Flocks by Night" (1702)	Sacred song
British	Daniel Defoe (1661(?)–1731)	"Robinson Crusoe" and "Captain Singleton"	Tale of adventure
British	Jonathan Swift (1667–1745)	"Gulliver's Travels," "Journal to Stella"	Prose allegory / Miscellaneous lit.
British	Joseph Addison (1672–1719)	"Spectator" and "Tatler" papers, especially the "De Coverley Papers," "Reflections in Westminster Abbey," "Vision of Mirza," "Head-Dress"	Essay
British	Richard Steele (1672–1729)	"Spectator" and "Tatler" papers, especially "Recollections of Childhood" and "A Visit to a Friend"	Essay
British	Isaac Watts (1674–1748)	"Praise God from Whom All Blessings Flow" (1719)	Sacred song
British	Alexander Pope (1688–1744)	"Rape of the Lock"	Mock-epic
British	Alexander Pope	"Essay on Criticism"	Didactic poetry
British	Alexander Pope	"Essay on Man"	Didactic poetry

[1] "Paradise Lost" and "Paradise Regained" are placed here with the rest of Milton's works, but they really belong to the next period.

Nationality	Author	Work	Type
British	Alexander Pope (1688-1744)	"The Dunciad"	Satiric poetry
British	Samuel Richardson (1689-1761)	"Pamela" (the first real novel) (1740)	Novel
British	Samuel Richardson	"Clarissa Harlowe"	Novel
British	Samuel Richardson	"Sir Charles Grandison"	Novel
American	Benjamin Franklin (1706-1790)	"Autobiography"	Miscellaneous lit.
British	Charles Wesley (1707-1788)	"Hark, the Herald Angels Sing" (1739)	Sacred song
British	Charles Wesley	"Jesus, Lover of My Soul" (1740)	Sacred song
British	Henry Fielding (1707-1754)	"Joseph Andrews"	Novel
British	Henry Fielding	"Tom Jones"	Novel
British		Novels by Sterne and Smollett	Novel
British	Thomas Gray (1716-1771)	"Elegy Written in a Country Church-yard"	Elegy
British	Thomas Gray	Letters and Journal	Miscellaneous lit.
British	Thomas Gray	"Ode to Spring"	Ode
British	Thomas Gray	"The Bard"	Ode
British	Thomas Gray	"On a Distant Prospect of Eton College"	Ode
British	William Collins (1721-1759)	"Ode to Evening"	Ode
British	William Collins	"The Passions: An Ode to Music"	Ode
British	Oliver Goldsmith (1728-1774)	"The Vicar of Wakefield"	Novel
British	Oliver Goldsmith	"She Stoops to Conquer"	Drama
British	Oliver Goldsmith	"The Good-Natured Man"	Drama
British	Oliver Goldsmith	"The Deserted Village"	Descriptive poetry
British	Edmund Burke (1729-1797)	"On Conciliation with America"	Oration
British	William Cowper (1731-1800)	"On Receipt of My Mother's Picture"	Simple lyric
British	William Cowper	"The Loss of the Royal George"	Elegy
British	William Cowper	"To Mary"	Simple lyric
British	William Cowper	"John Gilpin's Ride"	Imitation ballad
British	William Cowper	"O for a Closer Walk with God"	Sacred song
British	Augustus Toplady	"Rock of Ages" (1776)	Sacred song
American	George Washington (1732-1799)	Farewell Address	Oration
American	Patrick Henry (1736-1799)	Speeches	Oration
American	Francis Hopkinson (1737-1791)	"The Battle of the Kegs"	Imitation ballad
British	Edward Gibbon (1737-1794)	"Decline and Fall of the Roman Empire" (1776)	Miscellaneous lit.
British	James Boswell (1740-1795)	"Life of Johnson"	Miscellaneous lit.
American	Thomas Jefferson (1743-1826)	Speeches	Oration
British	Sir William Jones (1746-1794)	"What Constitutes a State"	Ode

WORKS OF BRITISH AND AMERICAN AUTHORS ACCORDING TO LITERARY PERIODS—*Continued*

NATION-ALITY	AUTHOR	WORK	TYPE
British	Charles Fox (1749–1806)	Speeches	Oration
British	Richard Sheridan (1751–1816)	"The Rivals" (1775)	Drama
British	Richard Sheridan	"The School for Scandal" (1777)	Drama
British	Fanny Burney (1752–1840)	"Evelina"	Novel
British	Thomas Chatterton (1752–1770)	"The Bristowe Tragedy"	Imitation ballad
British	Thomas Chatterton	"A True Ballad of Charitie"	Imitation ballad
British	William Blake (1757–1827)	"To an Evening Star"	Simple lyric
British	William Blake	"To the Muses"	Simple lyric
American	Alexander Hamilton (1757–1801)	Speeches	Oration
British	Robert Burns (1759–1796)	Songs (many of them)	Song
British	Robert Burns	"Cotter's Saturday Night"	Descriptive poetry (pastoral)
British	Robert Burns	"A Bard's Epitaph"	Elegy
British	Robert Burns	"Lament for Culloden"	Elegy
British	Robert Burns	"Tam o' Shanter"	Metrical tale
British	Robert Burns	"Highland Mary"	Elegy
British	Robert Burns	"The De'il's awa wi' the Excise Man"	Imitation ballad
British	Robert Burns	"A Man's a Man for a' That"	Simple lyric
British	Robert Burns	"To a Mouse"	Simple lyric
British	Robert Burns	"To a Mountain Daisy"	Simple lyric
British	William Pitt (1759–1806)	Speeches	Oration

THE NINETEENTH CENTURY—AGE OF ROMANTICISM (1800–1850)

British	Lady Caroline Nairne (1766–1845)	"The Land o' the Leal"	Song
American	Joseph Hopkinson (1770–1842)	"Hail, Columbia"	Patriotic song
British	William Wordsworth (1770–1850)	"Intimations of Immortality"	Ode
British	William Wordsworth	Sonnets	Sonnet
British	William Wordsworth	"Michael"	Metrical tale
British	William Wordsworth	"Ode to Duty"	Ode
British	William Wordsworth	"The Daffodils"	Simple lyric
British	William Wordsworth	"To the Daisy"	Simple lyric

British	William Wordsworth (1770-1850)	"We Are Seven"	Simple lyric
British	William Wordsworth	"The Reverie of Poor Susan"	Simple lyric
British	William Wordsworth	"She Was a Phantom of Delight"	Simple lyric
British	William Wordsworth	"She Dwelt Among the Untrodden Ways"	Elegy
British	Sir Walter Scott (1771-1832)	"Lady of the Lake"	Metrical romance
British	Sir Walter Scott	"Marmion"	Metrical romance
British	Sir Walter Scott	"Lay of the Last Minstrel"	Metrical romance
British	Sir Walter Scott	"Waverley" and other novels	Novel
British	Sir Walter Scott	"Jock o' Hazeldean"	Imitation ballad
British	Sir Walter Scott	"Lochinvar"	Imitation ballad
British	Sir Walter Scott	"Rosabelle"	Imitation ballad
British	Sir Walter Scott	"Hail to the Chief"	Song
British	Sir Walter Scott	"Ave Maria,"	Song
British	Sir Walter Scott	"The Coronach"	Elegy
British	Samuel T. Coleridge (1772-1834)	"The Rime of the Ancient Mariner"	Imitation ballad
British	Samuel T. Coleridge	"Lectures on Shakespeare"	Miscellaneous lit.
British	Samuel T. Coleridge	"Sketches of My Literary Life and Opinions"	Miscellaneous lit.
British	Robert Southey (1774-1843)	"The Battle of Blenheim"	Imitation ballad
British	Robert Southey	"The Well of St. Keyne"	Imitation ballad
British	Robert Southey	"The Life of Nelson"	Miscellaneous lit.
British	Jane Austen (1775-1817)	"Pride and Prejudice"	Novel
British	Jane Austen	"Sense and Sensibility"	Novel
British	Jane Austen	"Emma"	Novel
British	Charles Lamb (1775-1834)	"Essays of Elia,"—especially "Dream Children"	Essay
British	Charles Lamb	"Dissertation on Roast Pig," "Mackery End," and "Christ's Hospital Five and Thirty Years Ago"	Essay
British	Walter S. Landor (1775-1864)	"Imaginary Conversations"	Miscellaneous lit.
British	Jane Porter (1776-1850)	"Scottish Chiefs"	Novel
British	Thomas Campbell (1777-1844)	"The Soldier's Dream"	Simple lyric
British	Thomas Campbell	"Lord Ullin's Daughter"	Metrical tale
British	Thomas Campbell	"Ye Mariners of England"	Ode
American	Henry Clay (1777-1852)	Speeches	Oration
British	William Hazlitt (1778-1830)	"On Going a Journey"	Essay
British	William Hazlitt	"On a Sun Dial"	Essay

WORKS OF BRITISH AND AMERICAN AUTHORS ACCORDING TO LITERARY PERIODS—*Continued*

NATIONALITY	AUTHOR	WORK	TYPE
British	William Hazlitt (1778–1830)	"On the Feeling of Immortality in Youth"	Essay
British	Thomas Moore (1779–1852)	"The Journey Onward"	Simple lyric
British	Thomas Moore	"Lalla Rookh"	Metrical romance
British	Thomas Moore	"The Harp that Once through Tara's Halls"	Song
British	Thomas Moore	"Oft in the Stilly Night"	Song
British	Thomas Moore	"The Last Rose of Summer"	Song
British	Thomas Moore	"Believe Me If All Those Endearing Young Charms"	Song
American	Francis S. Key (1779–1843)	The Star-Spangled Banner (1814)	Patriotic song
American	John C. Calhoun (1782–1850)	Speeches	Oration
American	Daniel Webster (1782–1852)	"Bunker Hill", and other speeches	Oration
American	Washington Irving (1783–1859)	"Sketch Book"	Essays
American	Samuel Woodworth (1785–1842)	"The Old Oaken Bucket" (1826)	Song
British	Thomas De Quincey (1785–1859)	"Confessions of an English Opium Eater"	Miscellaneous lit.
British	Thomas De Quincey	"Meeting with Coleridge"	Essay
British	Thomas De Quincey	"Levana and Our Ladies of Sorrow"	Essay
British	Thomas De Quincey	"Joan of Arc" and "The English Mail Coach"	Essay
British	George Gordon, Lord Byron (1788–1824)	"Mazeppa"	Metrical tale
British	George Gordon, Lord Byron	"The Prisoner of Chillon"	Metrical tale
British	George Gordon, Lord Byron	"Sonnet on Chillon"	Sonnet
British	George Gordon, Lord Byron	"Apostrophe to the Ocean" (from "Childe Harold's Pilgrimage")	Ode
British	George Gordon, Lord Byron	Ode: "Oh Venice! Venice!"	Ode
British	George Gordon, Lord Byron	"Elegy on Thyrza"	Elegy
British	George Gordon, Lord Byron	"Elegy"	Elegy
British	George Gordon, Lord Byron	"She Walks in Beauty"	Simple lyric
British	George Gordon, Lord Byron	"When We Two Parted"	Simple lyric
American	James Fenimore Cooper (1789–1851)	"The Leather-Stocking Tales"	Tales of adventure
British	Charles Wolfe (1791–1823)	"The Burial of Sir John Moore"	Elegy
British	Percy B. Shelley (1792–1822)	"Adonais"	Elegy
British	Percy B. Shelley	"Ode to Liberty"	Ode

British	Percy B. Shelley (1792–1822)	"Ode to a Cloud"	Ode
British	Percy B. Shelley	"Ode to a Skylark"	Ode
British	Percy B. Shelley	"Ode to Night"	Ode
British	Percy B. Shelley	"Ode to the West Wind"	Ode
British	Percy B. Shelley	"Ozymandias"	Sonnet
British	Percy B. Shelley	"The Recollection"	Simple lyric
British	Percy B. Shelley	"Lines Written Among the Euganean Hills"	Simple lyric
American	John Howard Payne (1792–1852)	"Home, Sweet Home" (1823)	Song
British	Mrs. Felicia Hemans (1793–1835)	"Casabianca"	Imitation ballad
American	Edward Everett (1794–1865)	Speeches	Oration
British	John Keats (1795–1821)	"Ode to a Nightingale"	Ode
British	John Keats	"Ode on a Grecian Urn"	Ode
British	John Keats	"To Autumn"	Ode
British	John Keats	Ode: "Bards of Passion and of Mirth"	Ode
British	John Keats	"Lines on the Mermaid Tavern"	Simple lyric
British	John Keats	"Eve of St. Agnes"	Metrical tale
British	John Keats	"On First Looking into Chapman's Homer"	Sonnet
British	John Keats	"The Grasshopper and Cricket"	Sonnet
British	John Keats	"To Sleep"	Sonnet
British	John Keats	"Bright Star"	Sonnet
British	Thomas Hood (1799–1845)	"Ruth"	Simple lyric
British	Thomas Hood	"The Song of the Shirt"	Simple lyric
British	Thomas Hood	"Past and Present"	Simple lyric
British	Cardinal Newman (1801–1890)	"Lead, Kindly Light" (1833)	Sacred song
British	Benjamin Disraeli (1804–1881)	Speeches	Oration
American	Edgar Allan Poe (1809–1849)	"Annabel Lee"	Elegy
American	Edgar Allan Poe	"The Raven"	Metrical tale
American	Edgar Allan Poe	"The Pit and the Pendulum," "The Gold Bug," "The Tell-Tale Heart," and other short-stories	Short-story
American	Frances Osgood (1811–1850)	"Driving Home the Cows"	Imitation ballad
British	Charlotte Brontë (1816–1855)	"Jane Eyre" (1847)	Novel
American	Henry F. Lyte (1793–1847)	"Abide With Me" (1847)	Sacred song

WORKS OF BRITISH AND AMERICAN AUTHORS ACCORDING TO LITERARY PERIODS—*Continued*

THE NINETEENTH CENTURY—VICTORIAN AGE (1850–1900)

Nationality	Author	Work	Type
American	W. C. Bryant (1794–1878)	"Thanatopsis"	Elegy
American	W. C. Bryant	"Sella"	Metrical tale
American	W. C. Bryant	"The Flood of Years"	Ode
American	W. C. Bryant	"Antiquity of Freedom"	Ode
American	W. C. Bryant	"To a Waterfowl"	Simple lyric
American	W. C. Bryant	"Robert o' Lincoln"	Simple lyric
British	Thomas Carlyle (1795–1881)	"Essay on Burns"	Essay
British	Thomas Carlyle	"Sartor Resartus"	Miscellaneous lit.
British	Thomas Carlyle	"Heroes and Hero-Worship"	Essays
British	Thomas B. Macaulay (1800–1859)	"French Revolution"	Miscellaneous lit.
British	Thomas B. Macaulay	"History of England"	Miscellaneous lit.
British	Thomas B. Macaulay	"Speech on Copyright"	Oration
British	Thomas B. Macaulay	"Essay on Milton"	Essay
British	Thomas B. Macaulay	"Essay on Warren Hastings"	Essay
British	Thomas B. Macaulay	"Essay on Clive"	Essay
British	Thomas B. Macaulay	"Horatius at the Bridge" from "Lays of Ancient Rome"	Imitation ballad
American	Ralph Waldo Emerson (1803–1882)	Essays	Essay
American	Ralph Waldo Emerson	"Each and All"	Simple lyric
American	Ralph Waldo Emerson	"Rhodora"	Simple lyric
British	Bulwer-Lytton (1803–1873)	"Last Days of Pompeii"	Novel
American	Nathaniel Hawthorne (1804–1864)	"The Birthmark"	Short-story
American	Nathaniel Hawthorne	"The Ambitious Guest"	Short-story
American	Nathaniel Hawthorne	"Drowne's Wooden Image"	Short-story
American	Nathaniel Hawthorne	"Dr. Heidegger's Experiment"	Short-story
American	Nathaniel Hawthorne	"Ethan Brand"	Short-story
American	Nathaniel Hawthorne	"Wakefield"	Short-story
American	Nathaniel Hawthorne	"Feathertop"	Short-story
American	Nathaniel Hawthorne	"The Minister's Black Veil"	Short-story
American	Nathaniel Hawthorne	"House of Seven Gables" and other novels	Novel

	Author	Title	Type
British	Mrs. Elizabeth Browning (1806–1861)	"The Cry of the Children"	Simple lyric
British	Mrs. Elizabeth Browning	"Aurora Leigh"	Metrical romance
British	Mrs. Elizabeth Browning	"On Cowper's Grave"	Simple lyric
British	Mrs. Elizabeth Browning	"A Musical Instrument"	Imitation ballad
British	Mrs. Elizabeth Browning	"Sonnets from the Portuguese"	Sonnet
American	Henry W. Longfellow (1807–1882)	"The Arrow and Song"	Song
American	Henry W. Longfellow	"The Day is Done"	Song
American	Henry W. Longfellow	"The Bridge"	Song
American	Henry W. Longfellow	"The Wreck of the Hesperus"	Imitation ballad
American	Henry W. Longfellow	"The Skeleton in Armor"	Imitation ballad
American	Henry W. Longfellow	"The Psalm of Life"	Simple lyric
American	Henry W. Longfellow	"The Builders"	Simple lyric
American	Henry W. Longfellow	"Footsteps of Angels"	Elegy
American	Henry W. Longfellow	"Resignation"	Elegy
American	Henry W. Longfellow	"The Curfew"	Elegy
American	Henry W. Longfellow	"Nature"	Song
American	Henry W. Longfellow	"Suspiria"	Sonnet
American	Henry W. Longfellow	"Courtship of Miles Standish"	Elegy
American	Henry W. Longfellow	"Evangeline"	Metrical tale
American	Henry W. Longfellow	"Tales of a Wayside Inn"	Metrical tale
American	Henry W. Longfellow	"Skipper Ireson's Ride"	Metrical tale
American	J. G. Whittier (1807–1892)	"Maud Muller"	Imitation ballad
American	J. G. Whittier	"Pipes of Lucknow"	Imitation ballad
American	J. G. Whittier	"Eternal Goodness"	Simple lyric
American	J. G. Whittier	"The Tent on the Beach"	Simple lyric
American	J. G. Whittier	"Barbara Frietchie"	Metrical tale
American	J. G. Whittier	"Mabel Martin"	Metrical tale
American	J. G. Whittier	"The Barefoot Boy"	Metrical tale
American	Samuel F. Smith (1808–1895)	"America"	Simple lyric
British	Alfred Tennyson (1809–1892)	"In Memoriam"	Patriotic song
British	Alfred Tennyson	"Break, Break, Break"	Elegy
British	Alfred Tennyson	"The Princess"	Elegy
British	Alfred Tennyson	"Merlin and the Gleam"	Metrical romance
British	Alfred Tennyson	"Enoch Arden"	Simple lyric
British	Alfred Tennyson	"The Victim"	Metrical tale
British	Alfred Tennyson	"Dora"	Metrical tale

WORKS OF BRITISH AND AMERICAN AUTHORS ACCORDING TO LITERARY PERIODS—*Continued*

NATION-ALITY	AUTHOR	WORK	TYPE
British	Alfred Tennyson (1809–1892)	"The Gardener's Daughter"	Metrical tale
British	Alfred Tennyson	"The Defense of Lucknow"	Metrical tale
British	Alfred Tennyson	"The Lord of Burleigh"	Metrical tale
British	Alfred Tennyson	"Rizpah"	Metrical tale
British	Alfred Tennyson	"Lady Clare"	Metrical tale
British	Alfred Tennyson	"The May Queen"	Metrical tale
British	Alfred Tennyson	"In the Children's Hospital"	Metrical tale
British	Alfred Tennyson	"The Revenge"	Imitation ballad
British	Alfred Tennyson	"Come into the Garden, Maud"	Song
British	Alfred Tennyson	"Blow, Bugle, Blow"	Song
British	Alfred Tennyson	"Sweet and Low"	Song
British	Alfred Tennyson	"Tears, Idle Tears"	Song
British	Alfred Tennyson	"Ring Out, Wild Bells"	Song
British	Alfred Tennyson	"Ode on the Death of the Duke of Wellington"	Ode and elegy
British	Alfred Tennyson	"Crossing the Bar"	Simple lyric
American	William E. Gladstone (1809–1898)	Speeches	Oration
American	Abraham Lincoln (1809–1865)	Gettysburg Address	Oration
American	Abraham Lincoln	First Inaugural Address (1861)	Oration
American	Abraham Lincoln	Second Inaugural Address	Oration
American	Abraham Lincoln	Speech at Cooper Institute (1860)	Oration
American	Abraham Lincoln	Last Public Address	Oration
American	Oliver Wendell Holmes (1809–1894)	"Under the Violets"	Elegy
American	Oliver Wendell Holmes	"The One-Hoss Shay"	Imitation ballad
American	Oliver Wendell Holmes	"Ballad of the Oysterman"	Imitation ballad
American	Oliver Wendell Holmes	"How the Old Horse Won the Bet"	Metrical tale
American	Oliver Wendell Holmes	"Grandmother's Story of Bunker Hill Battle"	Metrical tale
American	Oliver Wendell Holmes	"The Chambered Nautilus"	Simple lyric
American	Oliver Wendell Holmes	"Autocrat of the Breakfast Table"	Essays
British	Mrs. Elizabeth C. Gaskell (1810–1865)	"Cranford"	Novel
American	Wendell Phillips (1811–1884)	"Toussaint L'Ouverture" (1861)	Oration

British	W. M. Thackeray (1811–1863)	"Nil Nisi Bonum"	Essay
British	W. M. Thackeray	"De Finibus"	Essay
British	W. M. Thackeray	"Henry Esmond" and other novels	Novel
British	Charles Dickens (1812–1870)	"The Tale of Two Cities" and other novels	Novel
British	Charles Dickens	"The Ivy Green"	Song
British	Robert Browning (1812–1889)	"Hervé Riel"	Imitation ballad
British	Robert Browning	"How They Brought the Good News"	Imitation ballad
British	Robert Browning	"The Pied Piper"	Metrical tale
British	Robert Browning	"Prospice"	Elegy
British	Robert Browning	Song from "Pippa Passes"	Song
British	Robert Browning	"Cavalier Tunes"	Song
British	Robert Browning	"Home Thoughts from Abroad"	Simple lyric
British	Robert Browning	"Home Thoughts from the Sea"	Simple lyric
British	Robert Browning	"My Last Duchess"	Dramatic monologue
British	Robert Browning	"Cleon"	Dramatic monologue
British	Robert Browning	"Abt Vogler"	Dramatic monologue
British	Robert Browning	"Muléykeh"	Dramatic monologue
British	Robert Browning	"Andrea del Sarto"	Dramatic monologue
British	Robert Browning	The Browning Letters (Mr. and Mrs. Browning)	Miscellaneous lit.
American	Henry Ward Beecher (1813–1887)	Sermons	Oration
British	Charles Reade (1814–1884)	"The Cloister and the Hearth"	Novel
British	Charles Mackay (1814–1889)	"The Miller of the Dee"	Imitation ballad
British	"George Eliot" (1819–1880)	"Adam Bede" and other novels	Novel
British	John Ruskin (1819–1900)	"Praeterita"	Miscellaneous lit.
British	John Ruskin	"Sesame and Lilies"	Essay
British	John Ruskin	"Ethics of the Dust"	Essay
British	John Ruskin	"Crown of Wild Olives"	Essay
British	John Ruskin	"Modern Painters"	Miscellaneous lit.
British	John Ruskin	"Stones of Venice"	Miscellaneous lit.
British	John Ruskin	"Seven Lamps of Architecture"	Miscellaneous lit.
British	Charles Kingsley (1819–1875)	"Westward Ho!"	Novel
American	Julia Ward Howe (1819–1910)	"Battle Hymn of the Republic"	Patriotic song
American	James Russell Lowell (1819–1891)	"The Vision of Sir Launfal"	Metrical tale
American	James Russell Lowell	"The Courtin'"	Imitation ballad
American	James Russell Lowell	"The Commemoration Ode"	Ode

WORKS OF BRITISH AND AMERICAN AUTHORS ACCORDING TO LITERARY PERIODS—*Continued*

NATIONALITY	AUTHOR	WORK	TYPE
American	James Russell Lowell (1819–1891)	"Books and Libraries"	Essay
American	Walt Whitman (1819–1892)	"O Captain, My Captain!"	Elegy
American	Walt Whitman (1819–1892)	"When Lilacs Last in the Door-yard Bloom'd"	Elegy
American	Edward Everett Hale (1822–1909)	"The Man Without a Country"	Short-story
American	T. B. Read (1822–1872)	"Sheridan's Ride"	Metrical tale
British	Matthew Arnold (1822–1888)	"Sohrab and Rustum"	An episode from a great epic
British	Matthew Arnold	"Thyrsis"	Elegy
British	Matthew Arnold	"The Forsaken Merman"	Imitation ballad
American	George W. Curtis (1824–1892)	"The Public Duty of Educated Men"	Oration
American	Francis Parkman (1825–1893)	"The Oregon Trail"	Miscellaneous lit.
British	R. D. Blackmore (1825–1900)	"Lorna Doone"	Novel
British	Thomas Huxley (1825–1895)	"Autobiography"	Miscellaneous lit.
British	Thomas Huxley	"A Piece of Chalk"	Essay
British	Adelaide Procter (1825–1864)	"The Lost Chord"	Song
American	Stephen Foster (1826–1864)	"The Old Folks at Home" ("Suanee River") and "My Old Kentucky Home"	Song
British	Dinah M. Craik (1826–1887)	"John Halifax"	Novel
American	J. T. Trowbridge (1827–1917)	"Darius Green and His Flying Machine"	Imitation ballad
American	Lew Wallace (1827–1905)	"Ben Hur"	Novel
British	Dante Rossetti (1828–1882)	"The Sonnet"	Sonnet
British	George Meredith (1828–1909)	"The Ordeal of Richard Feverel"	Novel
American	Carl Schurz (1829–1906)	"True Americanism" (1858)	Oration
American	Charles Dudley Warner (1829–1900)	"A-Hunting the Deer"	Essay
American	Charles Dudley Warner	"Lost in the Woods"	Essay
American	Charles Dudley Warner	"Camping Out"	Essay
American	Charles Dudley Warner	"What Some People Call Pleasure"	Essay
American	S. Weir Mitchell (1829–1914)	"Hugh Wynne"	Novel
American	Frank R. Stockton (1834–)	"Now the Day Is Over"	Short-story
British	S. Baring-Gould (1834–)	"The Lady or the Tiger?"	Sacred song
American	Phillips Brooks (1835–1893)	"Address at a Meeting in Behalf of the Children's Aid Society"	Oration

American	S. L. Clemens "Mark Twain" (1835–1910)	"Adventures of Tom Sawyer"	Tale of adventure
American	S. L. Clemens "Mark Twain"	"Huckleberry Finn"	Tale of adventure
American	S. L. Clemens "Mark Twain"	"The $1,000,000 Bank Note"	Short-story
American	S. L. Clemens "Mark Twain"	"A Double-Barreled Detective Story"	Short-story
American	Henry Grady	"The New South" (1886)	Oration
American	Mrs. Mary A. Lathbury	"Day Is Dying in the West" (1877)	Song
American	Bret Harte (1836–1902)	"Luck of Roaring Camp"	Short-story
American	Bret Harte	"Outcasts of Poker Flat"	Short-story
American	Bret Harte	"Tennessee's Partner"	Short-story
American	T. B. Aldrich (1836–1907)	"Marjorie Daw"	Short-story
American	John Burroughs (1837–)	"Waiting"	Simple lyric
American	W. D. Howells (1837–1920)	"The Rise of Silas Lapham"	Novel
American	W. D. Howells	"The Sleeping-Car", and Other Farces	Drama
American	W. D. Howells	"The Mouse Trap"	Drama
British	Algernon Swinburne (1837–1909)	"Etude Réaliste"	Simple lyric
British	Algernon Swinburne	"The Salt of the Earth"	Simple lyric
British	Thomas Hardy (1840–)	"Far from the Madding Crowd"	Novel
British	Thomas Hardy	"Then and Now" (1914)	Simple lyric
British	Thomas Hardy	"Men Who March Away" (1914)	Song
American	Edward Roland Sill (1841–1887)	"The Fool's Prayer"	Metrical tale
American	Sidney Lanier (1842–1881)	"Ballad of Trees and the Master"	Imitation ballad
American	Sidney Lanier	"Tampa Robins"	Simple lyric
American	Sidney Lanier	"Marshes of Glynn"	Simple lyric
American	Sidney Lanier	"The Power of Prayer, or the First Steamboat on the Alabama"	Metrical tale
British	Henry M. Stanley (1841–1904)	"How I Found Livingstone"	Miscellaneous lit.
American	George Herbert Palmer (1842–)	"Life of Alice Freeman Palmer"	Miscellaneous lit.
British	Robert L. Stevenson (1850–1894)	"In Memoriam F. A. S."	Elegy
British	Robert L. Stevenson	"Requiem"	Elegy
British	Robert L. Stevenson	"Lost Youth"	Simple lyric
British	Robert L. Stevenson	"The Celestial Surgeon"	Simple lyric
British	Robert L. Stevenson	"The Song of the Road"	Simple lyric
British	Robert L. Stevenson	"Markheim"	Short-story
British	Robert L. Stevenson	"The Sire de Malétroit's Door"	Short-story
British	Robert L. Stevenson	"The Story of the Young Man with the Cream Tarts"	Short-story

WORKS OF BRITISH AND AMERICAN AUTHORS ACCORDING TO LITERARY PERIODS—*Continued*

NATIONALITY	AUTHOR	WORK	TYPE
British	Robert L. Stevenson (1850–1894)	"The Pavilion on the Links"	Short-story
British	Robert L. Stevenson	"The Merry Men"	Short-story
British	Robert L. Stevenson	"The Bottle Imp"	Short-story
British	Robert L. Stevenson	"The House with the Green Blinds"	Short-story
British	Robert L. Stevenson	"The Adventures of the Hansom Cab"	Short-story
British	Robert L. Stevenson	"El Dorado"	Essay
British	Robert L. Stevenson	"Æs Triplex"	Essay
British	Robert L. Stevenson	"Lantern Bearers"	Essay
British	Robert L. Stevenson	"Walking Tours"	Essay
British	Robert L. Stevenson	"An Inland Voyage"	Essay
British	Robert L. Stevenson	"Travels with a Donkey"	Essay
British	Robert L. Stevenson	"A Christmas Sermon"	Essay
British	Robert L. Stevenson	"On the Enjoyment of Unpleasant Places"	Essay
British	Robert L. Stevenson	"Treasure Island"	Tale of adventure
British	Robert L. Stevenson	"The Master of Ballantrae" and other novels	
American	Eugene Field (1850–1895)	"The Grandsire"	Novel
American	Eugene Field	"Little Blue Pigeon"	Elegy
American	Eugene Field	"Little Boy Blue"	Song
American	Eugene Field	"Wynken, Blynken, and Nod"	Song
American	Eugene Field	"Hush-a-by, Sweet, My Own"	Song
American	David Starr Jordan (1851–)	"Life's Enthusiasms"	Song
American	David Starr Jordan	"The Strength of Being Clean"	Essay
American	David Starr Jordan	"The Call of the Twentieth Century"	Essay
American	J. Whitcomb Riley (1853–1916)	"The Call of the Nation"	Essay
American	H. C. Bunner (1855–1896)	"Knee-Deep in June"	Simple lyric
American	H. C. Bunner	"The Way to Aready"	Simple lyric
American	H. C. Bunner	"The Nice People"	Short-story
American	H. C. Bunner	"The Tenor"	Short-story
American	H. C. Bunner	"The Love Letters of Smith"	Short-story
American	Hamlin Garland (1860–)	"Zenobia's Infidelity"	Short-story
American		Short-stories	Short-story

American	Mary E. Wilkins-Freeman (1862–)	"The New England Nun"	Short-story
American	Mary E. Wilkins-Freeman	"A Village Singer"	Short-story
American	Mary E. Wilkins-Freeman	"A Kitchen Colonel"	Short-story
American	Mary E. Wilkins-Freeman	"The Revolt of Mother"	Short-story
British	Sir Arthur Quiller-Couch (1863–)	"The Splendid Spur"	Tale of adventure
American	Richard Hovey (1864–1900)	"The Call of the Bugles"	Simple lyric
American	Richard Hovey	"At the End of the Day"	Ode
American	Richard Harding Davis (1864–1916)	"Soldiers of Fortune"	Novel
British	Rudyard Kipling (1865)	"The Widow's Party"	Imitation ballad
British	Rudyard Kipling	"Danny Deever"	Imitation ballad
British	Rudyard Kipling	"Fuzzy Wuzzy"	Imitation ballad
British	Rudyard Kipling	"Ballad of East and West"	Imitation ballad
British	Rudyard Kipling	"Mandalay"	Imitation ballad
British	Rudyard Kipling	"The Last Suttee"	Imitation ballad
British	Rudyard Kipling	"Gift of the Sea"	Imitation ballad
British	Rudyard Kipling	"Soldier, Soldier"	Imitation ballad
British	Rudyard Kipling	"Tommy"	Imitation ballad
British	Rudyard Kipling	"If"	Simple lyric
British	Rudyard Kipling	"L'Envoi"	Simple lyric
British	Rudyard Kipling	"The Recessional"	Sacred song
British	Rudyard Kipling	"Avenge, O Lord, Thy Slaughtered Saints"	Ode
British	Rudyard Kipling	"The Light that Failed"	Novelette
British	Rudyard Kipling	"Baa, Baa, Black Sheep"	Short-story
British	Rudyard Kipling	"Wee Willie Winkie"	Short-story
British	Rudyard Kipling	"The Man Who Would Be King"	Short-story
British	Rudyard Kipling	"The Man Who Was"	Short-story
British	Rudyard Kipling	"They"	Short-story
British	Rudyard Kipling	"Without Benefit of Clergy"	Short-story
British	Rudyard Kipling	"Namgay Doola"	Short-story
British	Rudyard Kipling	"Moti-Guj-Mutineer"	Short-story
British	Rudyard Kipling	"The Strange Ride of Morrowbie Jukes"	Short-story

THE TWENTIETH CENTURY (1900-   )[1]

POETS

Benét, William Rose
Binyon, Laurence
Bridges, Robert
Brooke, Rupert
Brown, Abbie F.
Burr, Amelia
Burton, Richard
Bynner, Witter
Carman, Bliss
De la Mare, Walter
Garrison, Theodosia
Gibson, Wilfred W.
Gilder, R. W.
Hagedorn, Hermann
Helston, John
Henley, William E.

Kipling, Rudyard
Le Gallienne, Richard
Lindsay, Vachel
Lowell, Amy
MacKaye, Percy
Markham, Edwin
Masefield, John
Masters, Edgar Lee
McCrae, John
Meynell, Alice
Moody, William V.
Neihardt, John
Noyes, Alfred
Peabody, Josephine P.
Phillips, Stephen
Rice, Cale Young

Rittenhouse, Jessie
Russell, George ("A. E.")
Scollard, Clinton
Scott, Frederick George
Seeger, Alan
Teasdale, Sara
Thomas, Edith
Untermeyer, Louis
Van Dyke, Henry
Vernéde, Robert
Wattles, Willard
Widdemer, Margaret
Woodberry, George
Wyatt, Edith
Yeats, William Butler

DRAMATISTS

Barker, Granville
Barrie, James M.
Belasco, David
Dunsany, Lord
Fitch, Clyde
Galsworthy, John
Gale, Zona
Gibson, Wilfrid W.
Gregory, Lady Augusta
Housman, Laurance

Jerome, Jerome K.
Jones, Henry Arthur
Kennedy, Charles R.
Knoblauch, Edward
MacKaye, Percy
Maeterlinck, M.
Murray, T. C.
Peabody, Josephine P.
Phillips, Stephen
Pinero, Arthur W.

Robertson, F. W.
Rostand, Edmond
Synge, John M.
Thomas, Augustus
Van Dyke, Henry
Walker, Stuart
Wilde, Percival
Yeats, William B.
Zangwill, Israel

ESSAYISTS

Benson, Arthur C.
Briggs, Le Baron R.
Chesterton, G. K.
Crothers, Samuel M.
Grayson, David

Hankey, Donald
Harrison, Frederic
Hubbard, Elbert
Lucas, E. V.

Mabie, Hamilton W.
Repplier, Agnes
Van Dyke, Henry
Wilson, Woodrow

NOVELISTS

Barrie, James M.
Bennett, Arnold
Cholmondeley, Alice
Churchill, Winston
Connor, Ralph
Conrad, Joseph
Crawford, F. Marion
Deland, Margaret
De Morgan, W. F.
Ferber, Edna

Galsworthy, John
Glasgow, Ellen
Harrison, W. S.
Hewlett, Maurice
Johnston, Mary
Locke, W. J.
Norris, Frank
Page, Thomas N.
Parker, Sir Gilbert

Phillpotts, Eden
Smith, F. Hopkinson
Tarkington, Booth
Ward, Mrs. Humphry
Watts, Mrs. Mary S.
Wells, H. G.
White, Stewart E.
White, William A.
Wister, Owen

[1] Only the authors mentioned in this book are named here.

SHORT-STORY WRITERS

Brown, Alice
Ferber, Edna
Freeman, Mary E.
  Wilkins

"O. Henry" (W. S. Porter)
James, Henry
Kipling, Rudyard
Smith, F. Hopkinson

Stimson, T. J.
"Thanet, Octave" (Alice French)
White, Stewart E.

SPEECH-MAKERS

Balfour, Arthur James
Beveridge, Albert
Bryan, W. J.
George, David Lloyd-

Hay, John
Marshall, Thomas R.
Roosevelt, Theodore
Root, Elihu

Van Dyke, Henry
Viviani, René
Wilson, Woodrow

MISCELLANEOUS WRITERS

Addams, Jane
Aldrich, Mildred
Antin, Mary
Dawson, Coningsby
Hagedorn, Hermann

Hay, Ian
Huard, Frances Wilson
Keller, Helen
Mercier, Cardinal
Palmer, George H.

Riis, Jacob
Roosevelt, Theodore
Steiner, E. A.
Turczynowicz, Laura
Washington, Booker

INDEX OF SELECTIONS

INDEX OF AUTHORS

GENERAL INDEX

525